PERSONNEL

D0075441

Third Edition

PERSONNEL
Human Resource Management

Michael R. Carrell
Dean, School of Business and Public Administration
California State University, Bakersfield

Frank E. Kuzmits
Professor of Management
University of Louisville

Norbert F. Elbert
Brown & Williamson Professor of Management
Bellarmine College

HF
5549
.C295
1989

Merrill Publishing Company
A Bell & Howell Information Company
Columbus   Toronto   London   Melbourne

INDIANA-
PURDUE
LIBRARY

FORT WAYNE

WITHDRAWN

Cover Art: ICOM, Inc.

Published by Merrill Publishing Company
A Bell & Howell Information Company
Columbus, Ohio 43216

FTW
AGM8893

This book was set in Meridien and Univers.

Administrative Editor: John Stout
Developmental Editor: Dwayne Martin
Production Coordinator: Carol S. Sykes
Art Coordinator: Vincent A. Smith
Cover Designer: Cathy Watterson
Photo Editor: Gail Meese

Photo credits: All photos copyrighted by individuals or companies listed.
Archives of Labor & Urban Affairs, Wayne State University, pp. 2, 258, 370,
514, 562; Jean Greenwald/Merrill, pp. 40, 216; courtesy Western Electric,
p. 66; Larry Hamill/Merrill, pp. 106, 146; Lloyd Lemmerman/Merrill, p. 294;
courtesy Honda of America, p. 328; Jo Hall/Merrill, p. 428; Peter Kresan,
p. 466; Kevin Fitzsimons/Merrill, p. 608; Doug Martin/Merrill, p. 644; Gail
Meese/Merrill, p. 670; and courtesy Xerox Corp., p. 696.

Copyright © 1989, 1986, 1982 by Merrill Publishing Company. All rights reserved. No part of this book may be reproduced in any form, electronic or
mechanical, including photocopy, recording, or any information storage
and retrieval system, without permission in writing from the publisher.
''Merrill Publishing Company'' and ''Merrill'' are registered trademarks of
Merrill Publishing Company.

Library of Congress Catalog Card Number: 89–60094
International Standard Book Number: 0–675–20670–7
Printed in the United States of America
1 2 3 4 5 6 7 8 9—92 91 90 89

Dedicated to

Colleen, for giving me the courage I needed;
Shari, my intelligent and beautiful daughter,
    in hopes that she finds a career she likes;
Amber, the cutest baby in the world;
And my parents, *Archie and Myrtle Carrell,*
    whose support, love, and understanding are never-ending.

My loving sisters, *Pat, Linda,* and *Lisa.*

The memory of my parents, *Mary and Andrew Elbert,*
    who taught me that anything is possible.

Preface

Regardless of size or type of business, people are the most important asset of any organization. Successful performance of the human resource management (HRM) function can greatly enhance an organization's bottom line. Personnel practitioners, however, are challenged more today than at any time in our history by a changing and more demanding labor force, with high expectations about the work place. At the same time, rapidly advancing technologies and outside influences are changing the nature of the work itself. Thus, it is becoming increasingly critical (and difficult) to create and maintain a work environment that motivates and satisfies human resources.

This book focuses on the policies, methods, and techniques that professional personnel and human resource managers create and implement to achieve successful human resource programs. We stress, however, that *all* managers are managers of personnel; therefore, we have written this book for all business students—not just those who intend to pursue a career in the personnel field. Much of the material (for example, about employee selection, job design, performance appraisal, training and development, career management, safety and health, labor relations, and personnel problem solving) is as important to the operating manager as it is to the personnel

manager. For this reason, we not only describe effective human resource programs but also show how to apply and manage them. Throughout the book, we include many practical illustrations and examples to help students understand the personnel manager's role, responsibilities, and relationships with other managers and administrators.

FEATURES NEW TO THIS EDITION

In this edition we welcome a new coauthor, Norbert F. Elbert of Bellarmine College. Dr. Elbert's specific contributions include:

New Chapters on Small Business and Computers in HRM

New chapters in this edition are Chapter 16, "HRM for the Small Business," and Chapter 17, "Computers and the Human Resource Department." Since about 80 percent of all Americans work for small businesses, we feel that the unique characteristics, needs, and practices of the small-business enterprise will be of interest to our readers. In addition, the field of computers has dramatically changed many personnel practices in recent years; hence, a basic understanding of this technology is important to appreciate fully the personnel/HRM function.

International HRM

A new feature of this edition is the chapter-ending sections on international personnel/HRM activities. The globalization of the world economy has rapidly increased the need for U.S. managers to be aware of the business practices of other countries and cultures. Important international differences in the personnel/HRM field are presented in these sections. Additional new features to this edition include:

Experiential Exercises

For instructors who wish to reinforce personnel concepts and theories, we have provided experiential exercises at the end of each chapter. These exercises were selected from Frank Kuzmits's *Experiential Exercises in Personnel/Human Resource Management*, second edition, also published by Merrill Publishing Company. The experiential exercises are designed to help students apply their knowledge to real-life situations.

Review Cases

We have added an extended review case at the end of each part of the book. These cases are more comprehensive than the chapter-ending cases and provide an alternative method of applying the chapter material.

Chapter Objectives

Each chapter opens with a list of behavioral learning objectives that inform the reader of the key terms and concepts to be presented in the chapter. This feature is intended to help the student gain an overview of the chapter material.

A Glossary

To assist in learning, a glossary of all the important terms presented in the text has been added at the back of the book. If a concept is not clear when reading a chapter, the student can turn immediately to the Glossary for clarification before reading further.

Test Bank Diskette

The extensive test bank found in the instructor's manual is available on an IBM-compatible or MacIntosh diskette, a new feature of this edition.

Transparency Masters

An exciting new supplement is the comprehensive set of over 180 transparency masters. They are unique in that (1) we produced them using *The Print Shop* software program (Balsam and Kahn, Broderbund Software) to give us large type that can be read easily even from a considerable distance; (2) many contain graphic illustrations to add interest as well as to promote learning; (3) all were created specifically to be used as transparency masters—none are merely copies of material from the book; and (4) they provide broad coverage, drawing on content from the entire book.

ADDITIONAL TEXT FEATURES

In this new edition, we have retained the following successful features of earlier editions:

Personnel in the News

Each chapter contains brief articles about current personnel/human resource activities. The purpose of these articles is to report personnel activities that affect the day-to-day working lives of many supervisors and managers.

Conclusions and Applications

Each chapter concludes with several brief summary statements emphasizing the important points of the chapter and their relationship to the management of human resources.

Key Terms and Concepts

This section lists the important terms and concepts discussed in the chapter, including much of the vocabulary unique to the personnel management field. The reader should be able to recognize, define, and discuss the terms after completing the chapter.

Review Questions

After reading the chapter, the student should be able to answer these straightforward questions, which focus on the major areas covered. If the review questions present any difficulty, the student should reread the appropriate material.

Discussion Questions

The discussion questions are designed to stimulate and enhance classroom discussion of the chapter material; they can also be used for homework assignments.

Case Studies

A short case study at the end of each chapter relates to the material in the chapter. The case studies may be used in a variety of ways: for classroom or small-group discussion, for individual verbal or written presentation, or as homework assignments.

Instructor's Manual

A comprehensive Instructor's Manual to accompany this book is available from the publisher. The Manual includes a test bank of more than 1,000 multiple-choice and true/false items written and classroom tested by the authors, which is available on IBM-compatible or MacIntosh. Also included are answers to discussion questions, as well as discussions of the chapter-ending case studies and part-ending review cases.

We welcome your ideas and suggestions for making the next edition of this book as enjoyable, interesting, and informative as possible. To share your comments, please write to us at the Office of the Dean, School of Business and Public Administration, California State University, Bakersfield, 9001 Stockdale Highway, Bakersfield, California 93311–1099.

ACKNOWLEDGMENTS

Many people have contributed directly or indirectly to this project. First, we sincerely thank those who have influenced our careers: President Tomás A. Arciniega and Vice President Fred H. Dorer, California State University, Bakersfield; Dean William H. Peters, American University; Dean Lynn Spruill, Oregon State University; Marc J. Wallace, Jr., and James L. Gibson, University of Kentucky; Dean Robert Alexander, Marshall University; Robert Myers, Jerald Smith, Joe Grant, John Paul Nelson, Jay Vahaly, Lyle Sussman, and Richard Herden, University of Louisville; William Sharbrough, The Citadel; Dean John E. Dittrich, West Texas State University; Andrew Hailey, Millsaps College; Warren S. Blumenfeld, Georgia State University; Dean Richard Feltner and Richard Dolin, Bellarmine College; Dean Robert L. Taylor, University of Louisville; David Coffee, West Carolina University; and special thanks to Louisville Mayor, Jerry Abramson.

We also wish to thank the office staff who helped prepare the manuscript, especially Gary Van Den Heuvel, as well as Janice Pollard, Karen Barnett, Carol Huff, Barbara Elbert, and Laura Ahrens.

Several reviewers made very helpful suggestions for improving this book. Special thanks go to Sinclair E. Hugh (SPHR), Cal Poly-Pomona; Irvin A. Zaenglein, Northern

Michigan University; Robert Hatfield, University of Louisville; James E. McCulloch, Louisville Gas and Electric Company; and Craig Matta, Brown and Williamson Corporation. Finally, our thanks to those who reviewed the manuscript for Merrill Publishing Company: Donald Caruth, East Texas State University; Kermit R. Davis, Jr., Auburn University; Jack L. Dustman, Northern Arizona State University; Thomas C. Head, Clarkson University; Herff L. Moore, University of Central Arkansas; Herbert S. Parker, Kean College of New Jersey; Velma Pomrenke, The University of Akron; Abdullan Pooyan, University of North Dakota; George S. Roukis, Hofstra University; Charlotte Sutton, Auburn University; Alfred W. Travers, Indiana Vocational Technical College; and Michael J. Vest, Virginia Polytechnic Institute and State University.

Michael R. Carrell
Frank E. Kuzmits
Norbert F. Elbert

Brief Contents

Contents

PERSONNEL

Chapter One   **Introduction**

Chapter Outline

PERSONNEL: PAST AND PRESENT
Scientific Management
Human Relations
Human Resources

PERSONNEL FUNCTIONS
Job Analysis and Design
Recruitment and Selection
Appraisal, Training, and Development
Compensation and Health
Employee Relations

PERSONNEL DEPARTMENT ROLES
Policies
Critical Policy Issues
Personnel Policies Changing America
Communication
Advice
Services
Control

PERSONNEL DEPARTMENT ORGANIZATION
Jobs
Structure
Responsibilities

CURRENT PROBLEMS, ISSUES, AND TRENDS
Productivity Growth
Quality of Working Life
Safety and Health
Equal Employment Opportunity
Increased Use of Computers
Professionalism in Personnel

EXTERNAL INFLUENCES
Laws
Labor Unions
Labor Market
Society
Technology

CAREER OPPORTUNITIES
Salaries

INTERNATIONAL HUMAN RESOURCE MANAGEMENT

CONCLUSIONS AND APPLICATIONS

Chapter Objectives

1. To trace the history of the field of personnel/human resource management.
2. To describe the major functions and roles of the personnel/human resource department.
3. To understand the structure of the personnel/human resource department.
4. To identify the major problems and issues faced by human resource professionals today.

3

5. To recognize the external influences that shape the human resource function.
6. To understand the importance of the personnel/human resource department in affecting organizational communication.
7. To explain the career opportunities that exist within the personnel/human resource field.

NOT all top managers agree that personnel management is of primary importance, but the consensus among them is that the effectiveness of an organization's personnel and human resource program will have a direct bearing on its ability to prosper in a competitive environment.

What is a personnel management program? What does it include? Who is responsible for the management of personnel? What are "good" personnel management practices, and how are they implemented? Questions such as these are the focus of this book.

Both terms—*personnel* and *human resource department*—are used in organizations, and which is "correct" has received a great deal of discussion among personnel (or human resource) directors. The L. M. Berry Company, the *Yellow Pages* giant in Dayton, Ohio, changed from *personnel* to *human resource department* to better reflect management's employee philosophy. The newer term, *human resource*, is usually intended to signify that management realizes it is dealing with human beings.[1]

An American Society for Personnel Administration survey of over 1,200 organizations found the following choice of department names: *personnel*, 47 percent; *human resources*, 40 percent; *employee* or *industrial relations*, 10 percent. Larger organizations tend to use the term *human resource*.[2] This may be due to the shift that has occurred in recent years among various planning and policy functions in higher management.[3]

In practice, *personnel* and *human resource management* are synonymous and are defined as a set of programs, functions, and activities designed to maximize both personal and organizational goals.

PERSONNEL: PAST AND PRESENT

Modern personnel management is radically different from personnel management of decades ago. Since the turn of the century, the managerial philosophy that has defined the personnel function has undergone significant changes. In the last eighty years, both the scientific management approach and the human relations approach have appeared and declined; today what has popularly become known as the *human resource* approach has emerged.

Scientific Management

The technique of scientific management was the first radical change in what most owners and managers of the early 1900s generally considered the most effective means of managing employees—constant supervision and threats of the loss of their jobs (similar to that of Dickens's Ebenezer Scrooge). Before the advent of scientific management all employees were considered equally productive, and if their productivity did not measure up, they deserved to be quickly terminated. The founders of the scientific management movement believed differently. Instead of simply relying on the use of fear and intimidation, Frederick Taylor, Frank and Lillian Gilbreth, and Henry Gantt believed that managers should take a scientific and objective approach in studying

Human Resources

What makes an organization effective? Is it the land, buildings, capital, patents, and technology it owns? To be sure, an organization's tangible assets are important factors in its success. But more and more, managers today recognize that an organization's *people*—its *human resources*—are its most critical assets.

Consider the fast-food industry. Scores of companies have entered, and left the industry in bankruptcy. Any fast-food firm with enough capital can buy bricks and mortar, ovens, tables and chairs, buns and hamburgers, and advertising space in the local newspaper and on television. But success demands much more than the kinds of assets that show up on balance sheets. It takes a competent, dedicated, motivated group of human resources to make the organization work, and work effectively.

Why do firms like McDonald's and Kentucky Fried Chicken thrive in the face of mounting competition and fickle consumer tastes? Simply because they pay a great deal of attention to their *people*—they take very seriously the human resource functions of employee selection, training and development, compensation, quality of work life, employee/management relations, and a great many other important personnel activities.

Testimony to the growing influence of the human resources role is not hard to find. In their bestseller *In Search of Excellence,* Thomas Peters and Robert Waterman state:

> Although most top managements assert that their companies care for their people, the excellent companies are distinguished by the intensity and pervasiveness of this concern. . . . We are not talking about mollycoddling. We are talking about tough-minded respect for the individual and the willingness to train him, to set reasonable and clear expectations for him and to grant him practical autonomy to step out and contribute directly to his job.*

*T. Peters and R. Waterman, Jr., *In Search of Excellence* (New York: Harper & Row, 1982), p. 239.

how work can be most efficiently designed. Taylor, the "father of scientific management," and the others employed scientific data collection and analysis methods often found in research laboratories at that time. He emphasized the study of the motions required for each job, the tools utilized, and the time required for each task. Then, based on scientific data instead of a boss's subjective judgment, fair performance standards for each job could be determined. Workers who produced output above the standard would receive additional incentive pay. At the time, all employees were generally given the same daily or weekly wage, regardless of their individual efforts. The results of scientific management techniques received widespread praise in the newspapers and even in a series of congressional hearings on commerce held in 1914. Scientific management principles spread quickly, generally with success. However, the movement's treatment of the worker—someone motivated solely by money—led to problems.

Frederick Taylor declared that "one of the very first requirements for a man who is fit to handle pig iron as a regular occupation is that he shall be so stupid and so phlegmatic that he more nearly resembles in his mental makeup the ox than any other type."[4] Taylor's oft-quoted comment underscores a widespread managerial attitude of the early twentieth century: along with raw materials, capital, and machinery, the employee is simply another factor of production. As such, the scientific management approach resulted in work methods and techniques which showed great concern for employee output but little concern for employee satisfaction. So-called time and motion studies replaced "rule-of-thumb" work methods with the "one best way" to perform a task. Typically, the one best way to do the job was highly specialized and routine, involving little mental effort and few opportunities to make decisions or use judgment. Proponents of scientific management are quick to point out that the average turn-of-the-century worker had little formal education and few skills or abilities that could be applied to organizational problems.

The concept of the *economic man*, embraced by many managers and administrators during the early part of the century, held that a worker is motivated primarily by economic gain and that a worker's output can be maximized only through financial incentives. With that concept in mind, Taylor created the *differential piece-rate system*, whereby workers would receive a higher rate of pay per piece produced after the daily output standard had been achieved. Through the differential piece-rate system (together with other techniques of scientific management), workers were expected to produce at a maximum level in order to satisfy what was believed to be their only work-related need: money.

The personnel departments of large manufacturing companies during the early years of the century had the traditional responsibilities of recruiting, selection, training, and health and safety. But the main focus of their activities was the implementation of scientific-management techniques. For example, the personnel staff conducted time and motion studies and fatigue studies, performed job analyses, prepared job specifications, and created wage incentive programs.[5] During this period, many personnel departments also actively supported welfare programs that would enhance the well-being of their workers. Those programs, which addressed the physical, social, and educational needs of the worker, encompassed such matters as vacations, personal hygiene, job training, instruction in English for the purpose of naturalization (a great many factory workers were immigrants), lunchrooms, company housing, employee loans, insurance plans, and recreational programs. Many welfare programs were initially implemented to reduce the resentment caused by long hours, low wages, harsh working conditions, and exploitative supervision. Such welfare programs generally reflected the paternalistic attitude of management common at the time: "We know what is best for you. Do as we say, and everything will be all right." But paternalistic practices often failed to bring about the unquestioned acceptance of authority that management expected. Primarily for that reason, the popularity of employee welfare programs declined during the 1920s and 1930s.

Human Relations

During the 1930s and 1940s, with impetus provided by the classic Hawthorne studies, management's attention shifted from scientific management to human relations. The Hawthorne studies demonstrated that employee productivity was affected not only by the way the job was designed and the manner in which employees were rewarded economically but also by certain social and psychological factors.[6] Hawthorne researchers Elton Mayo and F. J. Roethlisberger discovered that employees' feelings, emotions, and sentiments were strongly affected by such work conditions as group relationships, leadership styles, and support from management.[7] And those feelings could, in turn, have a significant impact on productivity. Thus, it was asserted, treating employees with dignity would both enhance employee satisfaction and enable the achievement of higher productivity. The Mayo-Roethlisberger research led to the widespread implementation of behavioral-science techniques in industry, including supervisory training programs that emphasized support and concern for workers, programs to strengthen lines of communication between labor and management, and counseling programs whereby employees were encouraged to discuss both work and personal problems with trained counselors. The personnel staff was primarily responsible for designing and implementing such programs.

The shift to human relations was also influenced by the growing strength of unions during the period. The rise of unionism was largely the result of passage of the Wagner Act of 1935, which gave workers the legal right to organize and to bargain collectively with employers in disputes about wages, job security, benefits, and many other work conditions. Although the Wagner Act did not legislate good human relations, it did compel many employers to improve their personnel programs (i.e., employee relations) in an effort to keep unions out. With unionization came formal grievance procedures, which provided employees with a measure of protection against arbitrary or despotic supervision. Although unionization led to an erosion of labor–management relations in some firms, in many other companies it resulted in greater acceptance of the principles of human relations.

The human relations approach was no doubt instrumental in improving the working environment of a great many workers, but it achieved only minimal success in increasing worker output and enhancing job satisfaction. The lackluster performance of the approach is attributable to the following:

- The approach was based on an oversimplified concept of human behavior in an organizational setting. The notion that "a happy worker is a hard worker"—generally presented to management as an untested hypothesis—is now recognized to be valid for only part of the work force.
- The approach failed to consider the concept of individual differences. Each worker is a unique and complex person with different wants, needs, and values. What motivates one worker may not motivate another; "being happy" or "feeling good" may have little or no impact on the productivity of certain employees.
- The approach failed to recognize the need both for job structure and for controls on employee behavior, and it largely neglected the importance of procedures, standards, and work rules in guiding employees toward the goals of the organization.

- The approach failed to recognize that good human relations are but one of many conditions necessary to sustain a high level of employee motivation. For instance, productivity may also be improved with performance-appraisal systems, career-development programs, job-enrichment programs, and selection-and-placement systems that successfully match the employee with the job.

The human relations approach fell out of favor with management during the 1950s and 1960s and is considered passé today. While good human relations is still an important organizational objective, the human relations approach is no longer the predominant one guiding leadership style within organizations. Good feelings are necessary but certainly not sufficient to ensure peak levels of employee satisfaction and productivity.

Human Resources

The emerging trend in personnel management is clearly toward the adoption of the human resource approach, through which organizations benefit in two significant ways: an increase in organizational effectiveness and the satisfaction of each employee's needs. Rather than addressing organizational goals and employee needs as separate and exclusive, the human resources approach holds that organizational goals and human needs are mutual and compatible: one set need not be gained at the expense of the other.

The human resource approach is relatively new in the management of people. The term became popular during the early 1970s as research in the behavioral sciences showed that managing people as resources rather than as factors of production or as human beings who act solely on the basis of feelings and emotions could result in real benefits to both the organization and the employee. As impor-

tant as the approach has become, the term *human resources*—like many other terms in the management literature—is hard to define with a great deal of clarity. Nonetheless, a number of principles provide the basis for a human resources approach:

- Employees are investments that will, if effectively managed and developed, provide long-term rewards to the organization in the form of greater productivity.
- Policies, programs and practices must be created that satisfy both the economic and emotional needs of employees.
- A working environment must be created in which employees are encouraged to develop and utilize their skills to the maximum extent.
- Personnel programs and practices must be implemented with the goal of balancing the needs and requirements of both the organization and the employee.

PERSONNEL FUNCTIONS

The personnel management program of each organization is unique, and personnel activities will vary somewhat from firm to firm. Yet trends clearly indicate that the scope of personnel responsibilities is increasing in organizations of all sizes. Personnel functions described in this book include:

- Job analysis and design
- Recruitment and selection
- Appraisal, training, and development
- Compensation and health
- Employee relations

Job Analysis and Design

For an employee to perform satisfactorily, his or her skills, abilities, and motives to perform the job must match the job's requirements. A mismatch may lead to poor performance, absenteeism, turnover, and other problems. Through a process called *job analysis*, the skills and abilities to perform a specific job are determined. In chapter 2, we will present various job-analysis techniques and discuss how job-analysis data are used to create effective human resource programs.

When scientific management was popular, jobs were designed to be simple and routine so that unskilled workers could be quickly trained to do the work. A primary assumption of such job design was that the average worker had no need to gain satisfaction from work and had neither the skill nor the inclination to participate in work decisions. No doubt many assumptions about turn-of-the-century workers were valid. But though employee needs and motives have experienced many changes since the formative years of industrialization, job design in many organizations still resembles that of scientific management. Organizational research shows that employees are not only demanding more satisfying and rewarding work but also demonstrating that their involvement in decision making can enhance rather than impair organizational effectiveness. In chapter 3 we will explore job design as well as various strategies for scheduling the workweek and improving the quality of work life.

Recruitment and Selection

To a great degree, organizational effectiveness depends on the effectiveness of its employees. Without a high-quality labor force, an organization is destined to mediocre performance. For this reason, the recruitment of human resources is a critical personnel function. Recruiting and selecting a qualified labor force involves a variety of personnel activities, including analysis of the labor market, long-term planning, interviewing, and testing. Chapters 4 and 5 are the focus of these topics.

Appraisal, Training, and Development

Organizational growth is closely related to the development of its human resources. When employees fail to grow and develop in their work, a stagnant organization most likely will result. A strong employee development program does not guarantee organizational success, but such a program is generally found in successful, expanding organizations.

One important developmental function is the appraisal of employee performance. During an appraisal process, employees become aware of any performance deficiencies they may have and are informed of what they must do to improve their performance and thus become promotable. Various methods and techniques of performance appraisal, with their advantages and disadvantages, will be described in chapter 6.

For many organizations, the heart of the development process is composed of on-the-job and off-the-job activities that teach employees new skills and abilities. Because modern managers recognize the benefits derived from the training and developmental process, expenditures for employee education are at an all-time high. This rise in employee education has been accompanied by growing professionalism in the training field and a demand for competent, qualified trainers.

Training and development offers many rewards but also poses many problems for training personnel: Who should be trained and why? What training techniques should be used? Is training cost-effective? The training and development of both managerial and nonmanagerial personnel are the focus of chapters 7 and 8.

Chapter 9 deals with a relative newcomer to the personnel field: career management. Personnel managers are giving increasing attention to processes and activities that enhance career advancement and solve problems employees encounter along their career paths. While career management is difficult to implement, advances in recent years have brought about improvements in the decision-making processes that affect employees' careers.

Compensation and Health

The issue of compensation has long posed problems for the personnel manager: How should jobs be evaluated to determine their worth? Are wage and salary levels competitive? Are they fair? Is it possible to create an incentive compensation system tied to performance? Techniques for evaluating the financial worth of jobs and other issues pertaining to the design of pay systems are discussed in chapter 10.

An increasingly important part of compensation is employee benefits. Because the cost of benefits for many organizations is now averaging as much as 40 percent of total payroll costs, employers are trying to control benefit costs without seriously affecting the overall compensation program. The kinds of benefits that employers may offer and the considerations that should be given to planning a total benefits package are discussed in chapter 11.

An increasingly important concern to the employee today is health and safety. Each year accidents, injuries, and occupational diseases cost billions of dollars in medical expenses, medical insurance, equipment damage, and production problems. Although much is being done to improve the workplace environment, there is still considerable room for improvement. In chapter 12 we will explore important health and safety legislation and describe various strategies for strengthening an organization's health and safety program.

Employee Relations

Labor unions exert a powerful force upon employers and influence personnel policies and programs for union employees. Because union participation in personnel decision making may have great impact on the economic condition of the firm, managers must understand a union's philosophies and goals and explore ways in which a cooperative rather than an adversarial relationship may be achieved. Union goals, union organizational structure, the union-organizing drive, the collective bargaining process, and techniques for handling employee grievances are examined in chapters 13 and 14.

Chapter 15 focuses on a problem that has plagued managers for centuries: the unsatisfactory employee. The employee who fails to perform up to expectations not only can be costly to management but can also create stress, frustration, and tension within the work group. For these reasons, managers must recognize the causes of unsatisfactory performance and be able to bring about a permanent improvement in job behavior. In chapter 15, emphasis will be placed on the philosophies and techniques of discipline and counseling.

Small business owners often perform personnel activities in addition to many other duties. Their unique personnel needs and practices are discussed in chapter 16. Today organizations of all sizes have found many computer applications in the personnel field. These common computer techniques are outlined in chapter 17.

Many personnel problems—such as absenteeism, turnover, job dissatisfaction, and unfair employee treatment—are costly and slow an organization's productivity rate. Modern personnel administrators must create strategies to resolve these problems. To do so, they must possess a complete understanding of the research process: how to conduct research and develop research strategies, how to analyze research data, and how to apply research to strengthen the personnel program. In chapter 18, we will describe ways in which common problems may be researched and solved.

PERSONNEL DEPARTMENT ROLES

The primary task of the personnel department is to ensure that the organization's human resources are utilized and managed as effectively as possible. Personnel administrators help design and implement policies and programs that enhance human abilities and improve the organization's overall effectiveness. Top executives have learned—sometimes the hard way—that inattention to personnel relations and neglect of personnel programs are often causes of poor labor-management relations, excessive absenteeism and turnover, law suits charging discrimination, and substandard productivity. More and more, leaders of public and private organizations recognize that *people* are the organization's primary resource and acknowledge the personnel department's role in developing that resource.

To acquire and retain an organization's human resources, personnel administrators perform five critical roles: create and implement policy, maintain communication, offer advice, provide services, and control personnel programs and procedures. Let us more fully examine the multiple roles of the personnel staff.

Policies

Policies are guides to management's thinking, and they help management achieve the organization's personnel objectives. Policies also help define acceptable and unacceptable be-

havior and establish the organization's position on an issue. Top personnel officials—the vice-president of personnel or the personnel department heads—are generally responsible for policy making. In critical personnel matters, such as equal employment or management development, the policies may be drafted by a personnel committee for approval by the chief executive officer. Personnel committees generally include members from both line and staff departments. A *line function* is one that is directly related to the achievement of an organization's goals. In a typical manufacturing enterprise, line functions include production and sales. In a university, teaching is a line function and the faculty are line personnel. *Staff* generally refers to a department that provides specialized services for the entire organization. Staff departments normally include engineering, research and development, purchasing, quality control, legal, finance, and personnel. Line managers not only bring experience to the personnel committee but are also more likely to support the policies they help create.

To be maximally effective, personnel policies should be in writing and should be communicated to all employees. To ensure that employees are familiar with personnel policies, many organizations—particularly large firms and government agencies—publish a personnel policy manual. Each manager receives a copy of the manual with instructions to review it in detail with all new employees. Updates of the manual may be posted on bulletin boards, and supervisors may be required to discuss policy revisions with their employees. A well-written and well-used policy manual can be a valuable aid not only in orienting new employees to the work place but also in settling differences between supervisors and subordinates.

A survey was undertaken to determine the importance of human resource policies and the kinds of policies that characterize both effective and ineffective companies. The sample included 785 "opinion leaders" who were assumed to be well-informed on current human resource issues. Most respondents—92 percent—believed that human resource policies and practices were of "utmost importance" or were "very important" for business success.

The opinion leaders were also asked to state the characteristics of companies that manage their human resources effectively and those companies that do not. The following are characteristics of effective companies, listed in descending order of frequency mentioned:[8]

- Genuine concern for people; positive view of employees as assets
- Good training, development, and advancement opportunities
- Pay well; good compensation programs
- Able to retain employees; low turnover
- Good internal communication; open communication
- Top management committed to and supportive of human resources
- Encourage employee participation

The following are characteristics of ineffective companies, listed in descending order of frequency mentioned:[9]

- Do not view employees as important assets; show little concern for work force
- Manage in an autocratic or bureaucratic manner; rigid and inflexible
- Little or no employee development; an ineffective internal advancement process
- Poor internal communication
- Unclear or outdated policies; inconsistently administered
- High turnover

Critical Policy Issues

Most of the critical issues facing the management of human resources are included in four broad areas: employee influence, personnel flow, reward systems, and work systems. Each of these areas must be addressed regardless of the industry, size of the firm, or types of employees involved. By developing critical human resource policies with those four areas in mind, decision makers can create human resource programs in a unified and systematic manner rather than by accident or by gut reaction to problems and pressures. Such decisions involve choices, and choices are most effectively made through planned policies and practices.[10]

Employee Influence   With the increasing popularity of quality circles, cooperative labor-management relationships, and other forms of worker participation, more and more organizations are developing policies which define the scope and breadth of employee influence in managing the organization. Such policies specify the degree of authority and responsibility that are delegated to employees and employee groups, and the way in which those relationships (e.g., quality circles vs. self-managed work groups) may most effectively be institutionalized. Policies defining the degree of employee influence deal with such diverse matters as organizational goals, compensation, working conditions, career advancement, and job design.

Personnel Flow   Attention must be paid to the task of ensuring that *personnel flow*—the management of people into, through, and out of the organization—meets the organization's long-term requirements for the number and kinds of human resources. Decisions about selection, promotion, job security, career development and advancement, fair treatment, and termination must be made in light of profits, growth, and other critical organizational goals.

Reward Systems The objectives of reward systems include the attraction, motivation, and retention of employees at all organizational levels. The accomplishment of these objectives forces management to consider a number of critical policy issues: Should pay incentives reward individual or group behavior? Should profits or reductions in operating costs be shared by employees? If so, how? Should employees be involved in the design and administration of the pay system? What is the most effective mix of pay and nonpay rewards to motivate performance? Answers to these questions will define a critical aspect of the employee-employer relationship.

Work Systems Work systems are concerned with the design of work: how tasks, and technologies are defined and arranged, the quantity and kinds of decisions that people make, and the extent to which quality of work life is an important organizational goal. Policy decisions that affect work systems include the kinds of manufacturing and office technologies implemented, and the way in which labor is divided.

Personnel Policies Changing America

What are some examples of innovative policies that are increasing productivity, profits, and employee morale?[11]

- The Vulcan Materials Company in Birmingham, Alabama, reduced its costs through a gain-sharing program in which the company and employees equally share any cost savings.

- Burlington Industries, faced with a massive influx of imported textiles, directly involved all employees in quality circles to develop just-in-time product delivery and increase its competitiveness in the market.
- The Tandy Corporation, with over 80 percent of its employees in sales, developed a computerized selection interview process to determine a candidate's aptitude for qualifying customers, closing sales, and providing customer service.
- The First Interstate Bank, Ltd., of Los Angeles redesigned its compensation program to include base pay plus incentives based on financial results, with different measurements for different jobs.

Communication

A key to effective management is the development and maintenance of a good flow of communication to and from all employees. Employers should strive to keep employees informed about the company's policies, programs, and products. At the same time, employees should be encouraged to submit suggestions and report problems, which should be quickly and objectively investigated. The personnel department plays a central role in providing several avenues of communication. It is often the first contact an employee has with a new employer and is often the source employees turn to for answers to questions or for advice. Much important information must be communicated to all employees concerning the history, policies, and objectives of the employer; wage and benefits information; and general personnel policies concerning vacations, sick leave, insurance, and so on. Often the personnel department initially acquaints all employees with this information via an employee orientation program. Even more important is the ability of employees to find such information when they need it later in their careers. Therefore many personnel departments develop an employee handbook, which is a written reference source for employees covering all aspects of personnel policies and programs, including pay, benefits, performance appraisals, promotions, retirement, grievance handling, and so on. A well-written, up-to-date handbook saves supervisors and personnel employees countless hours spent answering employee questions. For those cases in which the handbook does not directly answer employees' questions, it should direct them to the right individual or office.

The personnel department also plays an important role in the design and operation of other avenues of management-employee communication, such as:

- *Bulletin boards.* Communications of a general nature including official notices of policy changes, personal employee news such as marriages or births, and government notices may be posted on an employee bulletin board. In addition, employees may be allowed to post their own items of interest.
- *Communication meetings.* Top management can hold open meetings with small groups of employees to answer questions and provide an opportunity for employees to raise topics of interest to them. These regular meetings may also be used to present special issues such as a new health insurance program. If such meetings are held regularly and employees develop a sense that management has a sincere interest in their concerns, they can provide an excellent source of upward communication.
- *Newsletters.* The widespread use of com-

puters and newsletter software programs has made the employee newsletter a popular communication technique. News of a general nature, such as the beginning of an employee assistance program, as well as announcements (e.g., employee of the month), social activities, and personnel changes, can be easily and effectively communicated in an informal style. Newsletters can be mailed to retirees, laid-off employees, and others who normally do not have access to bulletin boards. A newsletter is generally an efficient and effective method of downward employee communication.

- *Employee problems.* A critical communication need is to provide employees with a comfortable and effective means for bringing problems or complaints to management. Written grievance procedures for employees and management are followed by virtually all unionized and many nonunion employers. The first step is usually to present the problem to the immediate supervisor. If the problem concerns the supervisor or the employee is not satisfied with the first step, the second step is usually to approach the supervisor's supervisor. A third level available to the employee is often the personnel director or general manager. Union-negotiated grievance procedures almost always include an outside arbitrator as a fourth and final step, a practice receiving increased use by nonunion employers.
- *Open door.* An often-practiced communication technique is the open door policy. Usually at a specified time each week or month, a manager's door is open to any employee who has a suggestion, question, or complaint. If over time the manager makes employees feel comfortable

using this process and each action receives a follow-up investigation (often by the personnel office), this technique can effectively open lines of communication between employees and management.

Advice

Over the past several decades, management has become increasingly complex. A restrictive legal environment, sophisticated technologies, a restive labor force, and demands by various societal groups for more "socially responsible activities" are a few of the pressures felt by managers. To cope with complex issues, managers often turn to staff experts for advice and counsel. Some questions that personnel staff members may be asked to answer include:

- How do I deal with an employee who I suspect is on drugs?
- How do I meet my equal employment goals without raising cries of "reverse discrimination?"
- How do I tell a high-achieving employee that the budget will not allow a merit increase this year?
- How do I counsel a manager who is suffering a midcareer crisis?
- How do I deal with an employee who has been with the company for twenty-five years but can no longer perform effectively?
- How can I increase employee morale?

In theory, advice from the personnel staff may be accepted or rejected. Line managers who think the advice is not sound have the prerogative to disregard it. Of course, the rejection of staff advice will be inversely proportional to the confidence a manager has in staff experts. Thus, all staff members have an obligation to ensure that their advice is sound, objective, and fair and will contribute to the goals of the organization.

Services

The services provided by the personnel department generally are the permanent human resource programs and activities that aid line managers and administrators in performing their jobs. Separating services from other personnel responsibilities is difficult. On the one hand, the personnel department—like each staff unit—exists to serve other organizational units, and practically all personnel activities may be broadly labeled as some form of service. On the other hand, the following personnel functions are clearly services:

- Recruitment, selection, and placement programs
- Equal employment opportunity activities
- Administration of employee benefits programs
- Training and development programs
- Personnel research
- Company recreation programs
- Labor relations activities
- Employee counseling programs
- Employee suggestion programs

An important service of the personnel department is providing decision makers with innovative techniques that help solve human resource problems and result in better utilization of human resources. Studies in organizational behavior and industrial psychology have led to programs that have increased employee productivity, reduced absenteeism and turnover, eliminated blue-collar and white-collar boredom, enhanced the quality of working life, and increased organizational profits. Many such programs will be discussed in this textbook.

Control

Like the quality control department in practically every manufacturing concern, the personnel department performs important control functions for the management of human resources. For example, a written policy on equal employment opportunity is ineffectual unless executives are aware of the policy and adhere to it. Personnel administrators are responsible for monitoring personnel goals and guidelines to ensure their achievement. Common control activities include:

- Collection and analysis of hiring, selection, placement and promotion data to ensure that equal employment opportunity laws and policies are being observed.
- Analysis of performance-appraisal records to determine if appraisals are being conducted in an unbiased manner.
- Analysis of statistics on absenteeism, grievances, and accidents to determine where problems are most critical and what may be done to reduce them.

Because of the nature of these activities, personnel staff members generally possess the authority necessary to carry out control functions. In theory, line managers and other leaders must cooperate with those personnel officials, but the latter must ensure that decision makers fully understand all personnel policies, procedures, and standards so that resentment and conflict are not created when control activities are performed. Further, personnel administrators should be tactful when putting pressure on managers to conform to personnel guidelines. Harmonious relationships between the personnel department and other organizational units will ensure compliance with guidelines with a minimum of stress to the organization.

PERSONNEL DEPARTMENT ORGANIZATION

We shall use the common term *personnel department* throughout this book to refer to the organizational unit that assumes responsibility for human resource programs and activities. Other names for the same unit include the *industrial relations department*, the *employee relations department*, and the *human resource department*.

Jobs

The personnel department normally contains clerical (support), professional, and managerial jobs. Clerical employees include clerks, typists, receptionists, and lower-level administrative assistants. Professional employees are specialists in fields such as counseling, employee development, employee testing, or labor relations. They often possess college degrees in business administration and may have concentrated their studies in human resources. Lower-level employees are occasionally promoted to professional positions and are given both on- and off-the-job training for their new roles. The managers oversee the clerical and professional employees and coordinate the organization's personnel activities. Top personnel managers formulate personnel policies and create important personnel programs.

Structure

The personnel department in medium to large companies contains individual work groups organized by function. A personnel manager heads each group, providing leadership to the professional and clerical employees. The personnel department may be headed by a vice-president of personnel or human resources who reports to the president. An example of the personnel structure for a medium or large organization is shown in Figure 1–1.

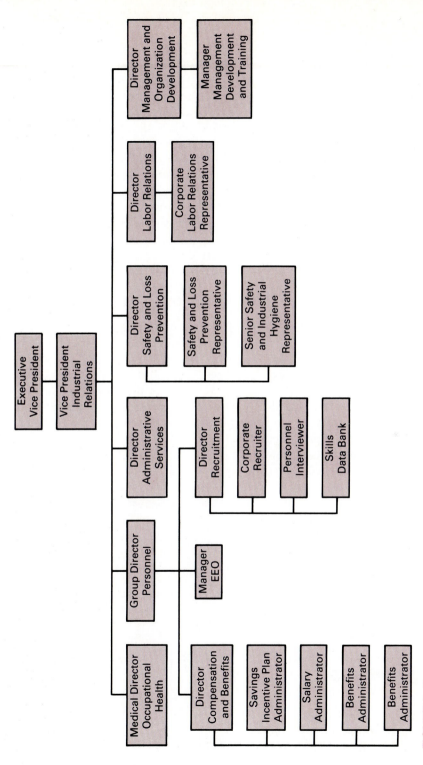

FIGURE 1–1

The structure of the personnel department in a medium to large company (Source: Allen R. Janger. *The Personnel Function: Changing Objectives and Organization, Report 712* [New York: The Conference Board, 1977]:71. Used with permission.)

Large corporations generally have divisions in many states and foreign countries. Each division is usually run independently as a decentralized profit center. Division managers have their own staff services, such as engineering, accounting, finance, legal, and personnel. The corporate personnel staff, however, generally creates major personnel policies and programs for recruiting, management development, equal employment opportunity, and wages and salaries. Divisional personnel managers put the policies into operation so that there is consistency across all divisions. Each personnel manager has some flexibility in his or her division's program.

Responsibilities

The responsibility for performing the personnel function does not reside only in the personnel department; all managers at all levels of the organization share in that responsibility. For example, the branch manager of a bank will normally interview job applicants, orient new employees, train and develop new and current employees, evaluate employee performance, and so on. In most organizations, particularly larger ones, the personnel staff designs personnel policies and procedures and the operating managers implement them. On occasion, line managers help design personnel policies and personnel staffers help implement them. But the primary responsibility for implementation of personnel policies and procedures rests with those who are responsible for day-to-day supervision of subordinates.

CURRENT PROBLEMS, ISSUES, AND TRENDS

To a large extent, the personnel department's newfound yet well-deserved prestige is the result of the enormous responsibilities undertaken by personnel managers today. Many problems and issues that have traditionally been the responsibility of the personnel department remain so. Examples are the recruitment, selection, orientation, and training of high-quality personnel; job analysis and job evaluation; labor relations; and employee appraisal systems. Modern problems and issues have created a new era of professionalism in personnel management. Some of these problems and issues are productivity improvement, the quality of working life, safety and health, equal employment opportunity, and the increased use of computers.

Productivity Growth

The United States leads the world in total output. The problem we face, however, is that our productivity growth per worker has lagged far behind that of many nations in recent years, as illustrated in Table 1–1. As a first step, many U.S. employers have closed plants, downsized operations, and reduced

TABLE 1–1

Growth in output per worker (1981–85 Average)[a]

Korea	6.0%
Japan	2.8%
Britain	2.5%
Norway	2.5%
Germany	2.2%
Sweden	2.2%
Belgium	1.7%
France	1.7%
Canada	1.6%
Netherlands	1.6%
Denmark	1.5%
United States	1.0%
Italy	0.7%

[a]Gross domestic product per employee.

Source: Bureau of Labor Statistics.

some pay and benefits. Continuing to confront the problem directly, many employers are now emphasizing getting "back to basics" in their personnel practices. The goal is to develop more sophisticated and efficient methods of managing our human resources. In particular, four major problems and potential solutions include:[12]

1. Problem: *Unclear accountability.* A significant number of employees are not aware of what aspects of the job are critical to the organization's success.
    Solution: *Specific performance goals.* Set such goals for employees at all levels. Written objectives should be clearly communicated to employees, with verbal follow-up discussions on an ongoing basis.
2. Problem: *Inflated performance appraisals.* Managers too often are not capable of or willing to evaluate honestly how well their employees are performing. Below-average performers are not even noticed.
    Solution: *Appraisals with teeth.* Honestly evaluate how well each employee is meeting the specific goals discussed. Give below-average performers a chance to improve, but don't be afraid to terminate lackluster performers who do not.
3. Problem: *Pay not tied to performance.* Many reward systems simply do not motivate employees. Even outstanding performers relax when they realize that hard work is not linked to their own economic gain. Average employees may be even less inspired.
    Solution: *Pay for performance.* Incentive programs may be companywide, such as profit sharing or gainsharing, or they may be designed to tie the individual's pay increase or bonus to work performance. Each employer needs to develop an individual or group incentive pay sys-

tem that directly links productivity to compensation.

4. Problem: *Lack of sufficient education and training.* Ambitious, hard-working employees cannot achieve their maximum productivity without a basic education and specific job skills. In the United States only 70 percent of students complete high school; in Japan, 98 percent finish. Also, says MIT's Lester C. Thurow, "their bottom half is beating our bottom half."
    Solution: *Focused employee training.* No-nonsense training programs should be designed to give employees specific job-related skills that enable them to perform more effectively.

Quality of Working Life

Sociologists have spoken of the quality of life. Behavioral scientists have also begun using a related term, *quality of working life (QWL).* The quality of working life refers to the extent to which employees' personal needs are met through their work. One's QWL improves as one's work meets more and more personal needs, such as security, responsibility, and self-esteem.[13] Many organizations consider that providing a good QWL to employees is both a social and an ethical responsibility. But there are strong indications that improvements in QWL favorably affect organizational performance. For example, the redesign of jobs at car and truck assembly plants involving the replacement of traditional assembly lines with work teams has led to lower turnover, less absenteeism, and improvements in product quality.[14]

Safety and Health

Creating a work environment that minimizes the likelihood of an accident or injury has long been a goal of both personnel specialists and operating managers. In the modern work place, a number of safety and health issues have proved difficult to resolve in both manufacturing and service industries. First, there is evidence that some work environments are responsible for cancer, infertility, lung disease, and other illnesses.[15] Unlike an accident or injury, occupational diseases are difficult to detect, and often they remain undetected until it is too late for a remedy. More and more, the work place is being labeled as hazardous to one's long-term health.

Second, job stress can be just as hazardous as an unsafe work place. Unlike accidents and injuries—which are of most concern in the construction, manufacturing, mining, and transportation industries—job stress can be a problem in any kind of firm in any job, whether it be blue-collar, clerical, managerial, or professional. Extreme stress can lead to ulcers, heart failure, nervous conditions, and other physiological or psychological impairments.[16] The potential impact of stress on job performance is obvious. Managers are now beginning to recognize potential personal and organizational job stress dangers and are seeking ways to recognize and reduce the problem.

Third, many employees suffer from some form of chemical dependency. About one in every ten employees suffers from a drinking problem that negatively affects performance. In the past, an alcoholic employee was either ignored or fired. But because such solutions failed to rehabilitate the sufferer, a growing number of firms have implemented employee assistance programs (EAP) whereby troubled employees (mostly alcoholic employees) are recognized, counseled, rehabilitated, and placed back on the job. Not every employee is successfully rehabilitated, but EAPs are said to enjoy up to a 70 percent success rate.[17] Most EAPs are administered within the personnel or human resource department. Such pro-grams will be discussed more extensively in chapter 12.

Equal Employment Opportunity

The U.S. Civil Rights Act of 1964 provided the legal framework for equal opportunity in all conditions of employment without regard to race, color, religion, sex, or national origin. With its passage, civil rights leaders envisioned a business environment devoid of discrimination and foresaw a day when minorities would enjoy the same economic status as the majority. But in the years since the passage of the act, that dream has not become a reality. Although gains were scored by women and minorities in the 1970s and 1980s, discriminatory practices still constitute an immoral and illegal part of personnel programs in many organizations.

Creating an environment in which equal employment opportunity is a reality rather than a popular slogan is no doubt one of the personnel manager's toughest jobs. Much like the plant foreman, who is often referred to as the "one in the middle" between labor and upper management, the personnel manager has the federal government pushing for compliance to the law while the operating manager presses for greater autonomy in making personnel decisions. The problem is greatly compounded by a national labor pool of qualified women and minorities not yet large enough to satisfy the equal employment goals that administrators strive to achieve. While equal opportunity legislation has been helpful for countless individual job seekers, it has also posed challenges that many personnel managers find difficult to meet.

A major problem involves the development and promotion of women into management. Women still face formidable barriers to management jobs, particularly for jobs above the first supervisory level. Among the many barriers are the notions that women can't handle "men's work" and that women lack the cool, rational temperament that decision makers must possess. Because of such reasoning, women are often excluded from training and development programs that would enable them to acquire management skills and abilities.

By designing programs and activities to strengthen opportunities for female employees, the personnel department can remove the barriers that keep many women out of the upper-level management. These programs include the scientific testing and assessment of managerial potential, the elimination of bias in performance appraisal programs, the implementation of training programs designed specifically for women, and the development of programs that illustrate the potential paths women may take to achieve management positions. Women have demanded their rights in the work place, and those demands will continue until equality is fully achieved.

Increased Use of Computers

Computers are not new to the personnel department, though in the past their use was primarily limited to payroll tasks and record keeping. Few organizations applied computer technology in a way that actually enhanced the personnel decision-making process. But with the advent of desktop microcomputers and an array of personnel-related software packages in the early 1980s, the use of computers in the personnel department has increased significantly.[18]

Three advantages of computerization are *speed, flexibility,* and *on-line capability.*[19] With the aid of desktop computers, a manager can quickly retrieve a vast amount of information about an employee's job status or a personnel activity. For example, an employee's work history, skills inventory, or attendance record can be obtained in a matter of seconds. Flexibility is achieved through the computer's ability to generate a wide variety of special reports and documents. Many personnel computer systems can automatically generate mandatory government statistics and reports. Further, many computer systems have the capacity to create special reports. For example, one firm's software package provides analysis of absenteeism in several ways, including which jobs and work sections show high rates of absence and which absence-related disciplinary actions have been most effective. *On-line capability* refers to the ability to retrieve stored information via a desktop computer terminal. On-line systems are easy to use and easy to update. They enable the user to build security into an information system that is not normally possible with conventional file systems.

Managers and personnel administrators are able to use desktop computers (when connected to a main computer) in a variety of functions and activities. Examples include multifunction payroll systems, salary and performance reviews, and skills inventory.[20] Computers may also be able to provide innovative methods of solving personnel problems, as suggested in the feature Can Computers Solve Personnel Problems? The following applications are discussed in chapter 17.

Multifunction Payroll Systems In addition to storing payroll information and printing paychecks and earnings, computerized payroll systems can prepare earnings histories and labor cost reports. For example, a system can compare labor cost projections to actual expenditures by project, product, or cost center. Such a system can also provide a variety of special control, audit, financial, and regulatory reports.

Personal Employee Data Personal information for every employee can be easily

Can Computers Solve Personnel Problems?

The secretary you hired a month ago is an excellent typist, well organized and never absent or late to work. She dresses right out of *Glamour* magazine. She also has a pleasing personality, makes friends easily, and is a joy to work with.

But there's one problem. She is constantly on the phone talking to friends—boyfriends, girl friends, and parents. She receives or makes about ten to twelve calls a day, and each call lasts about ten minutes. She wastes about ten to twelve hours a week on the phone.

What should be done about this employee? There are several approaches to solving this problem—some good and some not so good. Many supervisors and managers, particularly those with training and experience, would likely find a solution quickly and efficiently through effective counseling techniques.

But what about the new supervisor recently promoted from non-management ranks? For this person, correcting the performance problem without ruffling the secretary's feathers—and possibly harming her productivity—might be a tough job. Without guidance, some supervisors might not know where to begin.

Many new managers have a supportive boss or mentor to turn to for advice, but more and more bosses are plugging in their software disks to solve day-to day personnel problems. One such software package, called the *Management Edge*, provides managers with a detailed report about how to handle a variety of personnel problems.

To use the system, the boss enters information into the computer about both boss and employee. A report is then generated which includes a statement outlining how to motivate and discipline the problem employee. The report includes advice on communication, motivation, discipline, counseling, and other personnel issues.

Does the *Management Edge* work? Although research on that question is inconclusive, the company that developed and markets the system certainly thinks it does work. According to the firm's director of corporate communications, "The *Management Edge* software package is an expert system, which is essentially a practical application of artificial intelligence. While *Management Edge* costs $250, a consultant would cost close to a thousand dollars."*

*J. Mason, "Avoiding Personnel Fouls," *PC Week* (April 9, 1985): 50–52.

stored and retrieved with the aid of a computerized employee information profile. That profile may contain detailed family information, a chronological work history, performance rating and salary histories, school and training histories, and military data.

Salary and Performance Reviews Computerized salary and performance data include performance ratings and salary changes and may be displayed in a chronological format. An example of a salary and performance review is shown in Figure 1–2.

Skills Inventory A computerized skills inventory can aid personnel administrators and managers in making a variety of personnel decisions. Information often found on a skills inventory includes education, training, skills acquired, years of experience in various positions, and proficiency level for each skill acquired.

Benefits Systems With the aid of a computer, personnel administrators can closely monitor benefits programs. Information often found in benefits systems includes the kinds and types of coverage provided, coverage costs, and data for government-required reports on mandatory benefits such as social security. Many computerized benefits systems have the capability to print for each employee a comprehensive statement about such things as medical, sickness and disability, survivors, and retirement benefits.

Equal Employment Opportunity Federal employment legislation, in conjunction with positive attitudes about the hiring, training, and promotion of women and minorities, has led to a need for accurate information about the employment status of such employees. Computerized systems are used to monitor and analyze the hiring, training, and promotion of women and minorities. Computer systems may also be used to generate equal employment opportunity reports required by the government.

Absenteeism and Health and Safety A growing concern of many organizations is the high level of absenteeism and health-related problems that can reduce an organization's productivity. Information systems have been developed that can provide important absenteeism statistics, pinpoint chronically absent employees, and analyze absenteeism by department, supervisor, and section.

Labor Relations Computerized systems have been developed that greatly simplify the record-keeping and decision-making processes of labor relations. Computers help retain necessary seniority information about union employees, information about grievance hearings and settlements, and the results and status of disciplinary actions.

Professionalism in Personnel

Years ago, an important requirement for the personnel manager was that he or she "like people." Personnel activities were often conducted to keep people happy and satisfied, and personnel staff members were selected largely because they possessed an appropriate attitude or personality. Even today, many students opt for a career in personnel management because they "like people and want to help them."

Showing concern for the welfare of employees is an important trait for a member of the personnel staff, as well as for all managers and administrators. But "liking people" does little to describe the skills and abilities of the

SALARY AND PERFORMANCE　　　　　　　GATEWAY ENERGY LTD　　　　　　　　　　PAGE 14
REVIEWS***　　　　　　　　　　　　A DIVISION OF WORLDWIDE ENERGY　　　　　07/01/82

SALARY AND PERFORMANCE REVIEWS

L1　L1　　EMPL. NO.	***SALARY REVIEWS***					***PERFORMANCE REVIEWS***			
EMPLOYEE NAME	DATE	AMOUNT	PCT CHNG	REASON	JOB CODE	DATE	RATING	SUPERVISOR	JOB CODE
AF　03　　10375									
ANDERSON, ALFRED	06/01/82	$1,438.37	10.00	COST OF LIVING	MGR-036	06/01/82	41	J SMITH	MGR-036
	06/01/81	$1,307.61	10.00	COST OF LIVING	MGR-036	06/01/81	38	J SMITH	MGR-036
	06/01/80	$1,188.74	10.00	COST OF LIVING	MGR-036	05/01/80	38	J SMITH	MGR-036
	06/01/79	$1,080.67	10.00	COST OF LIVING	MGR-036	06/01/79	20	B GREENE	MGR-036
	06/01/78	$1,408.70	15.00	MERIT	MGR-036	06/01/78	20	B GREENE	MGR-036
	06/01/77	$　854.37	10.00	COST OF LIVING	SPV-138	06/01/77	20	D BUNTON	SPV-138
	06/01/76	$　705.44	9.00	COST OF LIVING	SPV-138	06/01/76	32	D BUNTON	SPV-138
	06/01/75	$　839.81	12.00	PROMOTION	SPV-138	06/01/75	32	D BUNTON	SPV-138
	06/01/74	$　518.40	8.00	COST OF LIVING	CLK-522	06/01/74	32	F FISHER	CLK-522
	06/01/73	$　480.00	8.00	COST OF LIVING	CLK-522	06/01/73	32	F FISHER	CLK-522
	NEXT SALARY REVIEW 06/01/83					NEXT PERFORMANCE REVIEW 06/01/83			
AF　03　　10445									
ANNISON, ALMA LOUISE	01/01/82	$　500.00	5.70	LONGEVITY	SEC-002	01/01/82	15	14411	SEC-002
	1/01/81	$　432.81	5.17	COST OF LIVING	SEC-002	1/01/81	15	14411	SEC-002
	1/01/80	$　423.50	5.34	PROMOTION	SEC-003	1/01/80	15	13900	SEC-003
	1/01/79	$　390.00	5.17	UNION CONTRACT	SEC-003	1/01/79	15	13900	SEC-003
	1/01/78	$　365.28	5.01	RECLASSIFICATION	SEC-003	1/01/78	15	13900	SEC-003
	1/01/77	$　350.00	5.12	MERIT	SEC-003	1/01/77	6	13900	SEC-003
	1/01/76	$　325.00	5.00	DEMOTION	SEC-004	1/01/76	6	63227	SEC-004
	1/01/75	$　300.00	4.83	COST OF LIVING	SEC-003	1/01/75	4	63227	SEC-003
	1/01/74	$　300.00	5.08	COST OF LIVING	SEC-Q04	1/01/74	4	63227	SEC-004
	1/01/73	$　300.00	5.35	COST OF LIVING	SEC-004	1/01/73	1	63227	SEC-004
	NEXT SALARY REVIEW 1/01/83					NEXT PERFORMANCE REVIEW 01/01/83			
AF　03　　10764									
BUNTON, DAVID B.	09/01/81	$5,000.00	25.00	UNION CONTRACT	MGR-023	09/01/81	17	98421	MGR-023
	09/01/80	$2,800.00	12.60	PROMOTION	MGR-023	09/01/80	17	98421	MGR-023
	09/01/79	$2,400.00	12.10	COST OF LIVING	MGR-023	09/01/79	16	98421	MGR-023
	09/01/78	$1,800.00	9.98	COST OF LIVING	MGR-023	09/01/78	16	98421	MGR-023
	NEXT SALARY REVIEW 09/01/82					NEXT PERFORMANCE REVIEW 09/01/82			
AF　03　　20032									
CARRINGTON, JOHN H.	03/01/82	$2,000.00	37.09	MERIT	FIN-001	02/26/82	11	74820	FIN-001
	03/01/81	$　500.00	10.22	COST OF LIVING	FIN-001				
	NEXT SALARY REVIEW 03-01-83					NEXT PERFORMANCE REVIEW 03-01-83			
AF　03　　34254									
HURD, HERBERT H.						09/01/81	44	14375	ACT-019
	NEXT SALARY REVIEW					NEXT PERFORMANCE REVIEW 09/01/82			

FIGURE 1–2

Computerized salary and performance report (Source: *The MSA Human Resource System* [Atlanta, GA: Management Science America, Inc., 1984]: 71. With permission.)

modern personnel administrator and even less to describe the personnel administrator of tomorrow. As the responsibilities of the personnel department continue to grow in importance and complexity, the capabilities of the personnel staff must also grow. In the 1980s and 1990s, personnel practitioners must become professionals who can effectively contribute to organizational goals by developing high-quality human resource programs.

The rising demand for professionalism in personnel has led to the creation of several educational programs designed specifically to prepare personnel decision makers for the challenges they will face. Several colleges and universities have created an undergraduate major in personnel administration/industrial relations (PAIR). A PAIR degree enables the student to concentrate in areas related to the personnel function.[21]

The American Society for Personnel Administration (ASPA) has developed two categories of personnel accreditation: the senior professional in human resources (SPHR) and the professional in human resources (PHR).

In addition to ASPA, other associations and societies that promote professionalism include the Academy of Management, the American Society of Training Directors (ASTD), the International Personnel Management Association (IPMA), the American Management Associations, and the Society for the Advancement of Management.

Those organizations meet regularly to discuss important topics and new developments in the field. Many personnel organizations also conduct educational seminars and publish journals; examples are the American Management Associations' *Personnel* and ASPA's *Personnel Administrator*. Such journals cover new developments in personnel, as well as methods and techniques for improving traditional functions.

EXTERNAL INFLUENCES

The discussion so far has provided ample proof that the personnel function is shaped and molded by forces outside of the organization, as Figure 1–3 illustrates. Because the personnel manager exerts little control over most of these forces, the external environment constrains and challenges the personnel staff. Personnel administrators must understand the nature and importance of the external environment and recognize its impact on current and future personnel activities.

Laws

The legal environment within which modern business organizations operate is a far cry from the laissez-faire environment Adam Smith advocated over 200 years ago in his classic work *The Wealth of Nations*. Personnel programs must not only satisfy the needs of both the organization and the employee, but must also satisfy innumerable legal requirements. Increasingly, legislative acts are helping to shape personnel programs, forcing personnel administrators to study the various

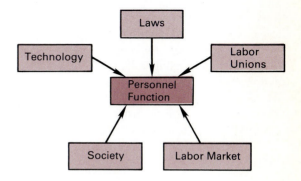

FIGURE 1–3

External forces that influence the personnel function

laws, to know how they are to be interpreted, and to understand how they affect the firm.

Labor Unions

Members of unions or employee associations make up about 18 percent of the labor force. The vast majority of rewards, rights, and working conditions of such employees are determined by collective bargaining agreements between management and the workers' representative—the union. In a unionized organization, the union constitutes the single most powerful force determining the way in which employees are managed and how personnel programs and activities are designed.

A union can have a profound impact on an organization's effectiveness; this impact may be viewed as positive or negative. A *Wall Street Journal*–George Gallup study found a wide divergence in attitudes toward unions among 782 top corporate executives. Although the executives often spoke of unions in positive terms, most thought unions were a detriment to organizational effectiveness. On the positive side, unions were praised for aiding labor-management communication, cooperating in attempts to increase productivity, helping to reduce labor costs, and cooperating with management against federal tariff reductions. On the negative side, unions were condemned for hurting productivity, creating inflexible work rules, making excessive wage demands, and causing inflation.[22] Regardless of the attitudes of managers, most agree that the influence of the union is felt in practically every personnel policy, program, and activity designed for the union employee.

Labor Market

A recurring problem for personnel managers is the recruitment and selection of qualified, motivated people at reasonable wages or salaries. Thus, labor market conditions, which are heavily influenced by the supply and demand for labor, determine if an organization can satisfy its objectives. Like the legal environment, the labor market is not influenced or controlled by any single force. Because labor market conditions are quite variable and sometimes unpredictable, the labor market often adds an element of frustration and uncertainty to a variety of personnel activities.

The federal government regularly publishes labor market information to assist the personnel specialist in the collection and analysis of labor market data. The U.S. Department of Labor's Bureau of Labor Statistics (BLS) is the primary collector and publisher of such information. State and local government agencies, employers' associations, and private groups also collect and publish data on labor market conditions.

The Plateaued Employee It may be hard to believe, but during the 1990s and beyond, there will be too many managers. When the Depression children went to work after World War II, they participated in the longest sustained economic boom America has ever had. Companies expanded their work force, thus creating many rapid promotional opportunities for a relatively small number of people. Moreover, as these conditions continued for about twenty-five years, a career of abnormally swift promotions became the rule rather than the exception. Now there are more people in the managerial pool than ever before, but fewer opportunities, thanks largely to a stagnant economy and the baby boom generation. Should the economy improve, the number of ambitious people who regard promotion as the only significant reward will still greatly outnumber the available management opportunities. Sooner or later, inevitably for almost everyone, the process of upward movement ends. When this happens, the employee has plateaued.

Managers are not the only ones experiencing the stress of plateauing. Professionals and employees who find themselves in jobs that offer limited mobility and few opportunities for the expansion of experience feel the same frustration and the stigma of failure. Symptoms include coming late, leaving early, absenteeism, and changes in personality such as irritability and hypersensitivity to criticism. Of course, these symptoms may reflect any number of problems, thus making it difficult for the superior to recognize and respond to the pain of the plateaued employee.

The personnel department is often expected to take the lead in addressing and resolving the plateaued employee's frustrations. This may mean encouraging managers at all levels to accept the reality that promotions do not go on forever. Or it may mean counseling or outplacement services for those who choose to leave. Increasing job mobility is another strategy as long as it is perceived as a positive change. Plateaued employees need to be encouraged to think about what work alternatives might exist for them, what they might prefer to do, and how those changes could be created. That is the challenge facing human resource managers today and well into the next century.

Society

America is changing, and our *work life* is changing too. Today a new social contract is being forged between employer and employee.[23] Employees are not being asked to give just "a fair day's work" but are being challenged to contribute quality, innovation, and excellence to their employers. The employers, in turn, are being challenged to give their employees greater participation in work place decisions, flexible hours, and a variety of new benefits such as child care, EAPs, and a healthy work environment.

The American economy is in a critical state. Trade deficits, the falling dollar, waning global influence, and the federal deficit are considered unmistakable signs of the decline. The effect on the U.S. work force has been substantial—unemployment for millions involved in layoffs or cutbacks, underemployment for millions more who take low-paying jobs to feed their families, and a lower standard of living for everyone. The challenge to the employer and the employee is the same: increase your productivity, develop competitive labor costs, and do not expect job security—earn it. The new emphasis in management is on the promotion of "innovation and entrepreneurship."[24]

Technology

An organization's *technology*—the methods and techniques used to produce goods and services—profoundly affects the skills and abilities that an organization's employees must possess. Consider the computer. As computers became common in the 1960s, many bookkeeping and clerical skills were no longer marketable; keypunching, programming, and systems analysis were in demand. But by the 1980s, data-entry technology such as the video display terminal (VDT) had all but eliminated the need for keypunching skills.

Robotics, the use of programmable robots to perform routine assembly operations was a high-growth industry in the early 1980s. By 1987, however, sales of robots had fallen sharply. Outside of the auto industry, the practical use of robots has not materialized. *Composites*, products consisting of graphite and epoxies, have changed the very materials machines work with—from steel and glass to plastics and synthetics. Thus the blue-collar machine operator may have been replaced with laser engineers and computer operators.

CAREER OPPORTUNITIES

The future holds numerous opportunities for students who seek careers in human resource management. The *Occupational Outlook Handbook* notes the following:[25]

> The number of personnel and labor relations specialists is expected to grow about as fast as the average for all occupations through the mid-1990s. Most growth will occur in the private sector as employers try to provide effective employee relations programs for an expanding and aging work force. Relatively little growth is anticipated in public personnel administration. As in virtually all occupations, most job openings will result from replacement needs.
>
> Demand for personnel and labor relations specialists is associated with employment conditions in the firms where they work. An expanding business may hire personnel specialists to handle additional paperwork, while a business that is reducing its operations will require fewer workers. During recessions, some industries may lay off or reduce the number of personnel and labor relations specialists.
>
> Other factors stimulate demand for personnel and labor relations specialists. Legislation setting standards in occupational safety and health, equal employment opportunity, and pensions has greatly increased record keeping and reporting requirements. Continued growth is foreseen as employers review and evaluate programs in these areas.
>
> Corporate recognition of the importance of human resource development will also spur demand. Greater investment in job-specific, employer-sponsored training and retraining is anticipated in the years ahead—a response to productivity concerns, the aging of the workforce, and technological advances that can suddenly leave large numbers of employees with obsolete skills.
>
> Although the number of jobs in this field is projected to increase through the mid-1990s, the job market is likely to remain competitive, particularly in labor relations.

Salaries

The increased responsibilities placed upon the personnel staff are resulting in more than new challenges and demands for innovative programs. The added expectations have also led to sizable increases in the amount of pay personnel professionals receive. In contrast to years past, personnel managers and administrators in many organizations receive compensation on par with jobs in marketing, manufacturing, accounting, and finance.

Typical entry-level jobs in personnel include job analyst, equal employment opportunity representative, benefits analyst, and training specialist. These positions generally require a bachelor's degree but no experience. Salaries vary widely, depending on the size and location of the firm as well as on the nature of its business.

INTERNATIONAL HUMAN RESOURCE MANAGEMENT

As recently as a decade ago, international human resource management (HRM) was more fiction than fact.[26] Global firms superimposed on their international subsidiaries the personnel practices of the corporate base. It was presumed that the organization's culture, management styles, and procedures for selection, appraisal, and reward systems that held true in the United States would work equally well anywhere else in the world. After all, aren't people really the same?

The assumption that national cultural differences do not matter that much because people have the same basic needs and values is risky. Evidence is fairly conclusive that national culture guides people's actions. In Italy, for example, a popular U.S. participative management strategy called management by objectives is unfavorably viewed as a Machiavellian power tactic.[27]

It is not only a question of different cultures. There are also differences in government policies and laws, as well as in labor-management relations. In Western Europe, for example, most workers have a legal right to participate in specific management decisions, such as profit sharing, plant expansion and closings, compensation, and work schedules.[28]

If the United States is to operate effectively at a global level, our global managers need to recognize that there are different ways of thinking, behaving, managing, and doing business. For that recognition to take place, the corporate headquarters must recognize that its ways of managing people reflect its own unique values, culture, management styles, and laws. And it must be prepared to reevaluate the way they see the world and the role of American management in that world.[29]

More and more, personnel practices are reflecting the particular conditions in each locality.[30] Global companies are developing global HRM strategies. Human resource policies are being reviewed in light of their applicability to specific cultures and laws. Today global managers are asking corporate officers plenty of tough questions: Which HRM policies should be global? Which ones should be local? How much expatriation (sending U.S. employees to other countries) should occur? In the developing countries, how does the global firm train local people in even the simplest technologies and management methods? How should the company screen for loyalty? How can it attract, retain, and motivate the local labor pool?

It is abundantly clear that a characteristic of successful global organizations is their sensitivity to the cultures they encounter. Suppose an Islamic employee of a U.S. firm located overseas needs medical insurance coverage for his family, which includes three wives. Is coverage provided? Does it sound far-fetched? Absurd as it sounds, polygamy is a perfectly legal and normal custom in most Moslem countries. Attempts to change local practices, much less religious ones, are always resisted. More often, corporate personnel practices have to be adapted to fit the prevailing national culture and laws if the company is to have any hope of operating effectively.

At the local level, not only should benefit packages be reviewed, but problem paths, grievance channels, and incentive pay plans as well. Individual bonuses, for example, may not have the positive impact on Japanese or Chinese nationals as they have on Americans. In fact, bonuses may lead to disastrous results in an Asian country. Recognition in the form of financial bonuses that singles out individual achievements can be humiliating to a worker in a society that prides itself on cooperation rather than competition.

The global company must be prepared to examine the unique needs of both natives and expatriates both at home and abroad. This certainly includes the need to be more consistent in the treatment of people working in the United States whose home country is elsewhere.[31] Suppose a multinational firm brings a British national to the United States on a nonimmigrant visa for a three-year assignment. Is it fair to deduct social security contributions when the employee won't be around to apply for benefits? What about "hardship" compensation for a Japanese executive working in Kentucky? After all, wouldn't U.S. citizens working abroad expect equal adjustments?

For human resource managers, the training and development implications are enormous. Today multinational firms, through their human resource departments, are training managers (and their families) for assignments abroad by giving them intense familiarization with other cultures. This wasn't always the case.

The Price of Cultural Misunderstanding

On a sea voyage, you are traveling with your wife, your child and your mother. The ship develops problems and starts to sink. Of your family, you are the only one who can swim and you can only save one other individual. Who would you save?

This question was posed to a group of men in Asia and the United States. In the United States, more than 60 percent of those responding said they would save the child, 40 percent would choose to save the wife, and none would have saved the mother. In the Eastern or Asian countries, 100 percent said they would save the mother. Their rationale? You can can always remarry and have more children—but you cannot have another mother. . . .

A U.S. design engineer working with his local affiliate office in Asia called for a general meeting of his professional staff. Wanting to be helpful and to give credit for the progress made on a project, he singled out for praise a particular individual. The person showed little if any emotion and did not seem pleased to be receiving the praise. The American later learned that this event caused considerable embarrassment to the individual since, in that country, collective effort is valued over individual effort and competition. . . .

When doing business overseas, Americans can't rely only on American values and behavior patterns. . . . What is good in one place ("Father is getting about the age where he would probably be happier in the senior citizens home in Arizona") is scandalous in another ("Look at how they treat older people in this country—it's awful"). . . .

Cross-cultural mistakes are expensive. Companies spend a minimum of $125,000 a year to have a U.S. manager working in an overseas position. Another less obvious factor is the human cost accrued when someone does poorly or comes home early from an overseas assignment. . . . In addition, there are three subtle results of business-related cross-cultural problems: missed opportunities, false efficiency and effectiveness, and cross-cultural mistakes.

Source: Adapted from James A. McCaffrey and Craig R. Hafner, "When Two Cultures Collide: Doing Business Overseas," *Training and Development Journal* (October 1985): 26. Copyright 1985, *Training and Development Journal,* American Society for Training and Development. Reprinted with permission. All rights reserved.

Horror stories abound about Americans who ventured into other countries with little or no predeparture training beyond which restaurants to visit. For example, there is the often told story about an American manager with a major defense contractor in Iran who got drunk and rode his motorcycle through the center of a mosque. Another story concerns a homesick California manager and his family who returned to the United States from Indonesia after less than two months on the job, causing the company to lose a great deal of money and face with local clients. In some parts of the world, loss of face can destroy any hope of building international business.

Until recently, American managers were considered innocents abroad. Fewer than one in ten could speak a foreign language, and only one in twenty had any international training.[32] Statistics such as these are improving—but only very slowly. The role of training is growing. There is new emphasis on preparing managers for attracting, retaining, and motivating employees in unfamiliar countries, and especially on transferring new technologies to developing countries.

The scope and activities of international human resource management practices are broader than U.S. human resource practices. The worldwide coordination of people is one of the most serious challenges confronting the multinational firm. It cannot be fully accomplished from the corporate home office alone. Operational personnel practices are increasingly being made at the local level. The corporate personnel staff must be able to balance long-term human resource strategies with these local practices.

It is a fact that American firms are expanding globally at a rate of 30 percent a year.[33] It is a fact the United States is also becoming an attractive haven to many European and Japanese companies. There is no longer a single marketplace—the United States—but a global marketplace. While the challenge for human resource managers remains the same, the rules are more complex. Instead of attracting, training, and motivating a homogeneous work force for a given culture, the scope has widened to include a truly heterogeneous work force representing a variety of cultures.

CONCLUSIONS AND APPLICATIONS

- The management of people has seen three distinct approaches since the turn of the century: scientific management, human relations, and human resources. The trend has been toward the human resources approach, whereby two complementary goals are sought: increased organizational effectiveness and the satisfaction of individual employee needs.
- A number of critical issues face personnel managers and administrators today. Improving worker productivity through human resource programs, policies, and techniques remains a challenge. Increasing the quality of working life (QWL) is a goal of many organizations, and programs such as the redesign of jobs have been implemented to enhance QWL.
- Safety and health issues have long been the concern of management, including the goal of minimizing industrial accidents and injuries. Health issues also include the detection and prevention of occupational disease, job stress, and chemical dependency. Concerns about equal employment opportunity focus not only on hiring women and minorities but also on creating opportunities within upper-level management.
- The use of computers in the management of human resources extends beyond processing the payroll and storing personal employee data. Computers are also used

in such activities as constructing employee profiles and collecting performance appraisal data.

- Because of modern demands and challenges, personnel decision makers must maintain the highest level of professionalism. To enhance the professional status of personnel officials, many colleges and universities have created degree programs in personnel administration/industrial relations (PAIR), and personnel associations have developed education and testing programs for certifying specialists and generalists.

- A variety of external forces and resources serve to influence and shape the personnel function: legislation, labor unions, labor market conditions, societal values and attitudes, and technological advancements. Personnel decision makers must recognize the power of these forces and examine how they affect the management of people within their own organizations.

- Although the personnel program of each organization will vary, the personnel departments of most large organizations have these common responsibilities: job design and analysis; recruitment and selection; appraisal, training, and development; compensation; and employee relations.

- Personnel managers and administrators perform a number of roles in achieving effective human resource management. These include creating personnel policies, offering advice to line managers, providing services (e.g., recruiting, training, and research), and controlling activities to ensure that personnel-related legislation and personnel policies are being followed.

- Jobs within the personnel department include clerical (support), professional, and managerial positions. The number of personnel and labor-relations employees is expected to grow as fast as the average for all occupations through the mid-1990s, with most growth occurring in the private sector.

- Multinational firms are increasing. The scope of personnel functions has broadened to include attracting, training, motivating a heterogeneous work force from a wide variety of cultures. Management styles, selection, appraisal, training, and reward systems need to be reevaluated in terms of the local culture if the company is to operate effectively. International personnel managers are faced with the challenge of balancing corporate long-term human resource policies and practices with the work force needs of their international subsidiaries.

CASE STUDY
Gripe Session at O'Malley's

O'Malley's Bar and Grill is a popular watering hole near one of Detroit's largest automobile plants. Assembly workers, supervisors, middle managers, administrators, and top-level executives are counted among the regulars. Why is O'Malley's so popular? Proprietor Tim O'Malley says, "People can come in here and unwind after a grueling day on the line or in the office. And in here everybody is the same—so you can see bigshot vice-presidents sitting next to sweaty assembly-line workers enjoying good conversation. And the fact that you can still get a glass of beer for fifty cents here doesn't hurt our business, either!"

This particular day found three engine-assembly supervisors tucked in a corner booth hotly discussing a common supervisory topic, employee motivation. Part of the conversation went like this:

Rafe Arnold: I tell you, man, sometimes I could just wring their necks. Out of thirty-four employees, I had twenty-two show up on time today! My section of the line was held up for an hour. And who catches hell for it? Me! All the yelling and screaming I do must go in one ear and out the other. Well, when I see somebody slough off from now on, I'm really going to crack down hard on them. I'll show no mercy! That'll shape them up!

Paul Ashbury: Rafe, old buddy, you've got it all wrong. Haven't you heard the old saw "you catch more flies with sugar than vinegar"? You've got to be nice to people. Treat them like human beings, not mindless robots. Say good morning to them. Send them a little card on their birthdays. Sit down and talk to them one-on-one every now and then. That's what employees really want—someone they can look up to and be real friends with. You've got to get out of the dark ages, Rafe. This is the twentieth century! Am I right, Leo?

Leo Avery: Well, I don't know. But I heard something very interesting the other day from our personnel manager. In Sweden, they make Volvos with small teams of workers instead of using assembly lines. The workers also make several decisions about their work, such as how the work should be planned and scheduled. And they take breaks whenever they want to. They're given a weekly quota and pretty much left alone to decide how to get the job done. Apparently, most workers are really satisfied with this arrangement. Absenteeism is low and quality is really high. I guess with that kind of work design, the employees take a lot more pride in their work than our workers do. Maybe we ought to look at the teamwork concept over here. We sure need something to help us compete with the imports.

Rafe: Ha Ha! Leo, you must have sniffed too much cleaning solvent today. You gotta be kidding. Are you going to let a twenty-year-old kid with a high school diploma decide how to build a $15,000 car? Come on! These guys and gals just want to come to work, do a simple job, get their paychecks, and leave at the end of the shift. I know—I've been around!

Questions

1. Analyze and discuss the differences in supervisory style among Rafe, Paul, and Leo. Whose management philosophy do you side with? Why?
2. The demographic makeup of the modern employee (primarily in terms of education) has changed drastically compared to that of the employee who toiled at the turn of the century. How have these changes affected the management of human resources?
3. Many management practitioners and authors think that all employees, including those at the lowest levels of the organization should be involved in the decision-making process. Do you agree or disagree? Why? What kinds of decisions should low-level employees such as assembly-line workers be involved in?

EXPERIENTIAL EXERCISE
Sources of Personnel Information

Purpose

To learn how to research a personnel/human resource topic and to gain practice in researching personnel-related issues in the library.

The Task

A number of topics related to the field of personnel/human resource management follow. Choose a topic of interest to you (or your instructor may assign a topic for you to research). After you have a chosen a topic, complete the following steps:

1. Find at least six recent references (or more, depending on your instructor's wishes) that pertain to your topic. Do not use a reference (e.g., *Personnel Journal*) more than once.
2. For each reference, indicate the title of the book, journal, and so on; the title of the journal article (if applicable); the author's name; the publisher and publication date. In addition, indicate how you located each reference (e.g., *Business Periodicals Index*).
3. Write a brief, one-paragraph abstract for each source (if your source is a book, review at least one important chapter and write the abstract for that chapter).

Personnel/Human Resource Topics
- Absenteeism: Causes and Cures
- Age Discrimination in Industry
- Assessment Centers: How Effective?
- Behaviorally Anchored Rating Scales (BARS): Advantages and Disadvantages
- Career Opportunities in Personnel/Human Resource Management
- Career Development
- Collective Bargaining Techniques
- Compensation: Problems and Issues
- Disciplinary Methods and Techniques
- Drug Usage Among Employees
- Employee Rehabilitation Programs
- Employee Stock Option Plans (ESOP): Current Controversies
- Executive Compensation Techniques
- Flextime: How Effective?
- Grievance Procedures
- Health Maintenance Organizations (HMO): Problems and Issues
- Incentive Compensation Systems
- Job Enrichment: Successes and Failures
- Labor Relations: Current Trends and Issues
- Management by Objectives (MBO)
- Occupational Safety and Health Act (OSHA): How Effective?

- Employee Orientation Programs
- Outplacement Programs for Managerial and Nonmanagerial Personnel
- Polygraph Usage
- Recruiting Problems and Issues
- Sexual Harassment: How to Prevent and Control
- Social Security: Why It's Failing
- Stress: What Causes It, How to Reduce It
- Test Validation Techniques
- Turnover: Causes and Cures
- Union-Management Relations: Current Trends and Issues
- Women and Work: Problems and Perspectives

KEY TERMS AND CONCEPTS

Computerization in personnel	Personnel roles
External environment	Plateaued employee
Human relations	Professionalism in personnel
Human resource management	Quality of working life (QWL)
PAIR	Robotics
Personnel management	Scientific management

REVIEW QUESTIONS

1. How do the scientific management, human relations, and human resource approaches to managing people differ? Why is the human resource approach considered by many to be better than the traditional ways of managing people?
2. What are the critical problems and issues facing personnel today?
3. What changes in society and within organizations have been instrumental in reshaping the personnel role?
4. Describe the forces that make up personnel's external environment.
5. What is the career outlook for those who wish to enter the field of personnel?
6. How were computers used by the personnel department in the past? What are some current applications of computers in human resource management? What are the advantages of using computers?
7. Describe the five roles carried out by personnel managers and administrators.
8. Do national cultural differences affect personnel actions?

DISCUSSION QUESTIONS

1. One often hears that the scientific management approach is still widely used in manufacturing and other forms of unskilled or semiskilled work. Why might this be so? Will scientific management principles still be used in the year 2000? Explain.

2. Why did the human relations approach decline in popularity? How important are good human relations? What else must a good manager do in addition to practicing good human relations?

3. The question of government interference in private enterprise has long been a hot topic for business practitioners. Have equal employment opportunity laws been, overall, good or bad for business? Good or bad for women and minorities? Do you feel that more equal employee opportunity legislation will be enacted in the coming years?

4. A great deal more professionalism is demanded from personnel officials today than in years past. Why might this be so?

ENDNOTES

1. J. T. Hoeg, " 'Human Resources' versus 'Personnel'," *Personnel* 64, no. 5 (May 1987): 72–73.

2. " 'Human Resources' Gains as Function," *Resource* (January 1986): 2–3.

3. Peter F. Drucker, "Good-Bye to the Old Personnel Department," *The Wall Street Journal* (May 22, 1986): 3.

4. Frederick W. Taylor, *Scientific Management* (New York: Harper & Brothers, 1947), pp. 45–46.

5. For a description of personnel functions and activities undertaken by large companies during the scientific management era, see Ordway Tead and Henry C. Metcalf, *Personnel Administration* (New York: McGraw-Hill, 1920).

6. For a detailed description of the Hawthorne studies, see F. J. Roethlisberger and W. J. Dickson, *Management and the Worker* (Cambridge, MA: Harvard University Press, 1939).

7. Not all researchers agree that changes in employee behavior were caused by changes in the work environment. For an alternative explanation, see H. M. Parsons, "What Happened at Hawthorne?" *Science* (March 8, 1974): 922–32.

8. S. W. Alper and R. E. Mandell, "What Policies and Practices Characterize the Most Effective HR Departments?" *Personnel Administrator* (November 1984): 120–124.

9. Ibid.

10. This discussion is taken from M. Beer, B. Spector, P. Lawrence, D. Mills, and R. Walton, "Managing Human Assets," *Personnel Administrator* (January 1985): 60–69.

11. Margaret Magnus, "Personnel Policies in Partnership with Profit," *Personnel Journal* (September 1987): 102–9.

12. Thomas Rollins and Jerrold R. Bratkovich, "Productivity's People Factor," *Personnel Administrator* 33, no. 2 (February 1988): 50–57. See also The Hay Group, "Compensation in the '90s: New Realities, New Rules, New Tools," *1987 Environmental Scans* (June 1987).

13. See J. R. Hackman and J. L. Suttle, *Improving Life at Work* (Santa Monica, CA: Goodyear, 1977).

14. R. B. Peterson, "Swedish Experiments in Job Reform," *Business Horizons* 19, no. 3 (June 1976): 16.

15. E. Price, "Occupational Diseases: The Scope," *Cleveland Plain Dealer* (September 3, 1979): E-2.

16. A. Brief, R. Schuler, and M. Van Sell, *Managing Job Stress* (Boston: Little, Brown, 1981).

17. "Summary of Third Report on Alcohol and Health," National Institute on Alcohol Abuse and Alcoholism (November 30, 1978), p. 6.

18. See A. J. Walker, "The Paperless Personnel Office," *Personnel Journal* (July 1980): 33.

19. Taken from *The MSA Human Resource System* (Atlanta, GA: Management Science America, Inc., 1984), p. 71.

20. Ibid.

21. For details concerning the basic PAIR course, see D. P. Rogers, "The Basic Course in Personnel Administration/Industrial Relations," *Collegiate News & Views* (Fall–Winter 1984): 5–7.

22. "Bosses Say Unions Do More Bad Than Good," *Wall Street Journal* (December 11, 1980): 28.

23. Jeffrey J. Hallett, "Worklife Visions," *Personnel Administrator* 32, no. 5 (May 1987): 56–65.

24. Ibid.

25. U.S. Department of Labor, *Occupational Outlook Handbook, 1984–85* ed. (Washinton, DC: U.S. Government Printing Office, 1984), p. 38.

26. The ideas presented here reflect those of Patrick V. Morgan, "International HRM: Fact or Fiction?" *Personnel Administrator* 31, no. 9 (September 1986): 42–47.

27. Geert Hofstede, "Motivation, Leadership, and Organization: Do American Theories Apply Abroad?" *Organizational Dynamics* (Summer 1980): 42–63.

28. Arvind V. Phatak, *International Dimensions of Management* (Kent Publishing Co., 1983), pp. 2–5.

29. Andre Laurent, "The Cross-Cultural Puzzle of International Human Resource Management" *Human Resource Management*, 25, no. 1 (Spring 1986): 91–102.

30. See Vladimir Pucik, "The International Management of Human Resources," in *Strategic Human Resource Management*, ed. C. Fombrun, N. Tichy, and M. Devanna (New York: John Wiley, 1984), p. 408.

31. See Morgan, "International HRM: Fact or Fiction?" p. 44.

32. For a detailed look at specific cultural characteristics, see Lennie Copeland and Lewis Griggs, *Going International* (New York: Random House, 1985) p. xxii.

33. Arant R. Negandhi, *International Management* (Boston: Allyn & Bacon, 1987) pp. 4–18.

Part One   Job Design and Selection

Chapter Two

Job Analysis

Chapter Outline

IMPORTANCE OF JOB ANALYSIS
PROGRAM IMPLEMENTATION
    Committee Review
    Information Collection
    Information Review
    Product Completion
    Future Use and Updating
JOB-ANALYSIS PROBLEMS
JOB DESCRIPTIONS
    Uses of Job Descriptions
    Legal Requirements
    Elements of the Job Description
CONCLUSIONS AND APPLICATIONS

Chapter Objectives

1. To understand the basic elements of a job analysis program.
2. To describe the end products of an analysis.
3. To identify the major methods of job analysis.
4. To discuss the future use and updating of analysis information.
5. To recognize the major elements of job descriptions.
6. To cite techniques useful in writing job descriptions.
7. To understand the uses of job descriptions.
8. To explain the legal requirements of job descriptions.

Just-in-Time Job Analysis

An innovative approach to job analysis has enabled the Great Falls Public Schools in Montana to hire severely disabled persons. Titled the *just-in-time (JIT)* approach to job analysis, JIT focuses on job tasks that require great amounts of time from professional and licensed staff members. By reviewing the specific skill requirements of these targeted tasks, possible barriers to employing the disabled, such as stress, speed, stamina, strength, transportation, and supervision, are analyzed. Where possible, routine tasks that have no barriers are isolated and new jobs created that can be filled by severely physically handicapped individuals. One example was found in school libraries: "There are many routine tasks such as shelving, stamping, and recovering books that do not require the skills of professionals. By making a few changes, we can create a job that a severely disabled person can do and at the same time give the library professionals more time to spend with the students."

The purpose of JIT, however, was not simply to consolidate lower-skilled tasks into a lower-paying job for a handicapped person. The purpose was, instead, to consolidate barrier-free tasks into a new position. Employees with disabilities were paid the same as other employees in similar positions. Once hired, disabled employees were evaluated according to the same performance standards as all other employees.

Source: Adapted from William H. Wagel, "Project Ace: New Opportunities for People with Disabilities," *Personnel* 65, no. 1 (January 1988): 9–13. Reprinted by permission of publisher. © 1988. American Management Association, New York. All rights reserved.

JOB analysis is the method by which management systematically investigates the tasks, duties, and responsibilities of an organization's jobs. The method includes investigating the level of decision making by employees within a job, the skills employees need to do a job adequately, the autonomy of the job in question, and the mental effort required to perform the job. Machines operated, reports completed, and specific financial or other responsibilities must be included in an analysis of jobs. Also examined in an analysis are the working conditions of the job, such as the levels of temperature, light, offensive fumes, and noise.

The process of job analysis is also known as *job review* or *job classification*. Whether one term or another is used by an organization is not important, because management will perform job analysis—whether indirectly through various techniques or in a direct, intentional job-analysis program.

Before discussing job analysis in more detail a number of related terms should be carefully defined:

Task   a distinct work activity that has an identifiable beginning and end (e.g., hand sorting a bag of mail into the appropriate boxes).

Duty   several tasks that are related by some sequence of events (e.g., pick up, sort, and deliver incoming mail).

Position   a collection of tasks and duties that are performed by one person (e.g., a mail-room clerk prepares outgoing mail, sorts incoming mail, and operates the addressing machine, postage machine, and related equipment).

Job   one or more positions within an organization (e.g., three mail clerks have the same job but different payroll positions).

Job Family   several jobs of a similar nature that may come into direct contact with one another or be spread throughout the organization (e.g., clerical jobs located in different departments).

Job Analysis   a systematic investigation into the tasks, duties, and responsibilities of a job.

Job Description   a written summary of the tasks, duties, and responsibilities of a job.

Job Specification   the minimum skills, education, and experience necessary for an individual to perform a job.

Job Evaluation   the determination of the worth of a job to an organization; job evaluation is usually a combination of a comparison of internal job levels and an analysis of the external job market.

Job Classification   the grouping or categorizing of jobs on some specified basis, such as by the nature of the work performed or by the level of pay; classification is often utilized as a simplified method of job analysis.

IMPORTANCE OF JOB ANALYSIS

Job analysis, an important personnel function, gathers information to be utilized in one or more other important functions, such as writing job descriptions, determining job specifications, or making job evaluations. The importance of a good job analysis is demonstrated by Figure 2–1. How the information is collected and used is of critical importance, because such information may directly affect employees, such as in pay or work assignments. Thus, job analysis may indirectly affect an employee's satisfaction and productivity.

The federal government, in particular the courts, have encouraged the use of job analysis and job descriptions so that organizations have specific objective methods of determining personnel decisions.

The 1978 *Uniform Guidelines* of the Equal Employment Opportunity Commission clearly require a systematic job analysis program to provide information for employee recruitment and selection.[1] The legal burden of proof is on the employer to provide evidence of proper job-related validation information, which is usually collected through job analysis.[2]

A job analysis is seldom the end product; instead, it provides the input to obtain end products systematically. A job analysis determines both the minimum and the desirable qualifications necessary to perform in a job. Such information is crucial in putting together a recruitment plan. In the selection process, an employee's relative abilities and skills must be evaluated. A job analysis indicates what tasks, duties, and responsibilities the job will

FIGURE 2–1
Job analysis

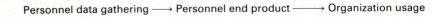

Personnel data gathering ⟶ Personnel end product ⟶ Organization usage

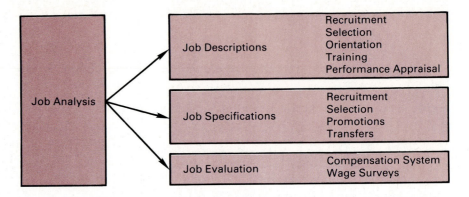

entail, how repetitive the job may be, or how much independence the job requires. By using that information during the interviewing procedure, the personnel interviewer can evaluate the qualifications of the person being considered for the job.

Once hired, the new employee needs to be oriented to the organization as quickly as possible. A job analysis yields what must be learned to complete the job successfully for the new employee. Often management will give new employees such information when hired. A complete job analysis will reveal if a new employee needs additional training in certain areas to complete the job successfully. This can usually be discerned by comparing the employee's past work history and training to the tasks specified in the job analysis.

Job analyses can also help management determine an equitable pay system. Almost all organizations desire to base a pay system on the relative value of each job to the organization. Difficult jobs, those that require specific abilities or those that are more hazardous, should receive more pay than less difficult jobs. Through job analysis, management can find out exactly what tasks are performed on each job and can compare individual tasks for similar jobs across the organization. Perfor-

mance appraisal—determining how well employees have performed their jobs in the past—as well as promotion decisions can be facilitated by a system that evaluates specific tasks that employees perform. Job analysis can be helpful in determining which duties and responsibilities should be considered in an evaluation.

A good job-analysis system is important to the personnel function, the primary focus of which is to maintain a high level of employee productivity and efficiency. Job analyses affect most areas of employment and therefore will indirectly affect performance appraisal, compensation, and training, which in turn affect employee performance and productivity.

PROGRAM IMPLEMENTATION

The creation and implementation of a job-analysis program will vary from firm to firm. Nonetheless, most organizations follow a standard format in conducting a job analysis. The steps that are generally included in most job-analysis procedures are committee review, information collection, information review, product completion, and future use and updating.

Committee Review

Experience indicates the best way to initiate an effective program is through a representative committee. The committee must make the critical decisions in choosing the appropriate job-analysis technique and the important job elements to be evaluated.[3] Working with the personnel department and the job analyst, the committee reviews information about each job within the organization and then makes difficult decisions comparing job factors, such as relative responsibility or working conditions.

Committee membership should include all the major departments to be studied in the job-analysis system. That is, if jobs to be analyzed are from six different departments, then each department should have representatives on the committee who understand the department's jobs and procedures. The committee should include personnel staff members who collect and evaluate job-analysis information on a firsthand basis. All of the people assigned to this committee should understand the standard operating procedures within the organization and be able to work well together.

The quality of the job analysis will depend upon the accuracy of the information gathered by the job analyst, the consistency and objectivity of the job analyst's evaluation of the information, and the ability of the committee members to make critical decisions when necessary. In this first step, the committee should decide the end products of the job analysis: Will the information be used to write job descriptions? Will the analysis be the basis for a system of job evaluation? Will it be used to determine minimum specifications for jobs in the organization? There may be more than one end product of job analysis.

The committee needs the cooperation of both employees and supervisors during information gathering. One reason for having each department represented is to allow committee members to report back to their departments about how the job analysis will proceed and to reassure fellow employees that the program is accurate and fair.

Information Collection

After the initial review, the committee must decide whether information should be collected by a method developed specifically for use in that organization or by a standardized method of job analysis. Standardized methods have the advantage of being previously tested and utilized, which increases their general validity. But one significant drawback of standardized methods is that they are not designed for use by a specific organization. Each method, whether standardized or not, has various strengths and weaknesses. Thus, a combination of methods may be used in an attempt to realize the strengths of each.[4]

U.S. Department of Labor The U.S. Department of Labor (DOL) has developed a standardized method for job analysis that uses four major categories:[5]

Worker Function what the worker does in relation to people, data, and things.

Work Fields the methods by which workers carry out the technological, sociological, or scientific requirements of the job.

Equipment Utilization the tools, machines, and equipment that must be utilized.

Products and Services the materials worked on, products produced, knowledge assembled, or services rendered.

One advantage of the DOL method is the utilization of the U.S. Employment Services' *Dictionary of Occupational Titles (DOT)*. The *DOT* classifies jobs by field of work, tasks performed, and the relationship of the job to data, people, and things. Each job title in the *DOT* system is given a six-digit code. The first digit indicates the general occupation, as shown in Table 2–1. The second and third digits provide a finer breakdown with respect to industry and function. The last three digits of the code are derived from the work function code, as illustrated in Table 2–2. A tax accounting job is given the code 160.162: "1" indicates professional; "60" indicates the accounting field; "1" indicates data coordinating; "6" indicates speaking or signaling (people contact); and "2" indicates operating or controlling.

The DOL method is primarily of use to smaller firms, where personnel specialists can quickly classify each of their jobs and use the *DOT* job descriptions. In other firms, specialists use the *DOT* as a starting point, modifying the standardized descriptions to fit their jobs. The *DOT's* greatest asset is its acceptance by federal employment agencies. According to the *Uniform Guidelines on Employee Selection Procedures,* "It is desirable to provide the user's job title(s) for the job(s) in question and the corresponding job title(s) and code(s) from U.S. Employment Services' *Dictionary of Occupational Titles.*"[6]

TABLE 2–1
General occupation code of the DOT

DOT 1st digit	Occupation
0, 1	Professional, technical, managerial
2	Clerical, sales
3	Service
4	Farming, fishery, forestry
5	Processing
6	Machine trades
7	Bench work
8	Structural work
9	Miscellaneous

Source: U.S. Department of Labor, *Dictionary of Occupational Titles,* 4th ed. (Washington, D.C.: U.S. Government Printing Office, 1977).

Position Analysis Questionnaire The *Position Analysis Questionnaire (PAQ)* is another standardized method of job analysis. The PAQ delineates 194 job elements, which fall into 27 job dimensions, which fall into 6 overall job divisions. The six divisions are:[7]

Information Input how information to do the job is received.

TABLE 2–2
Work function code of the *DOT*

Data (4th digit)	People (5th digit)	Things (6th digit)
0 Synthesizing	0 Mentoring	0 Setting Up
1 Coordinating	1 Negotiating	1 Precision Working
2 Analyzing	2 Instructing	2 Operating-Controlling
3 Compiling	3 Supervising	3 Driving-Operating
4 Computing	4 Diverting	4 Manipulating
5 Copying	5 Persuading	5 Tending
6 Comparing	6 Speaking-Signalling	6 Feeding-Offbearing
	7 Serving	7 Handling
	8 Taking Instructions–Helping	

Source: U.S. Department of Labor, *Dictionary of Occupational Titles,* 4th ed. (Washington, D.C.: U.S. Government Printing Office, 1977).

Mental Processes   the extent and type of decision making, planning, and organizing.

Work Output   tools, machines, and physical activity associated with the job.

Relationships   associations with co-workers, supervisors, customers, and so on.

Job Content   working conditions of the job, including hours and physical conditions.

Other Job Characteristics

The twenty-seven dimensions are the job families most common to organizations. Use of the PAQ requires that workers or supervisors be familiar enough with the job being analyzed to check which of the 194 job elements apply to the job in question. Figure 2–2 shows one page from the PAQ concerning information input.

The PAQ has the obvious advantage of being quantitative in nature. Having a quantitative system is helpful because the job analyst can easily differentiate between jobs by comparing the point totals of one job to those of another and, therefore, can assign jobs to different pay grades. The PAQ also has the advantage of being standardized: each job is looked at with the same criteria in mind. The PAQ has demonstrated a high degree of reliability even when the level of cooperation of employees is quite low or when attempts are made to manipulate the information provided.[8]

Functional Job Analysis   A modification of the DOL method was developed by Sidney A. Fine, at one time a member of the employment services division of DOL. Fine named his standardized system *Functional Job Analysis (FJA).*[9]

The FJA method is similar to the DOL method, with some improvements. For example, additional scales are used to measure (1) worker instructions, as shown in Figure

2–3; (2) educational development; (3) reasoning development; (4) mathematical development; and (5) language development. The DOL and FJA systems, like the PAQ system, have the advantage of being quantitative in nature. All three are organized and pretested, and each can be used systematically throughout an organization to complete a job analysis. But like all standardized methods, all three have the disadvantage of not being directly related to the specific behaviors required on jobs within any one organization.

Internal Methods   An alternative for management is to develop a job-analysis system specific to the organization. Such a system could include several different methods of collecting information. One method could be direct observation of all of the different jobs within an organization. If six or seven employees, for example, performed the same job, the analyst would only observe the two who performed that job most effectively. The analyst would try to note all the different tasks involved, the decisions made, and skills used, the interpersonal relationships utilized, and so on. One problem with direct observation is that it can only be used in repetitive, manual-labor jobs, and many modern jobs contain a large amount of mental activity. An analyst would not learn much from observing a bookkeeper who manipulates figures all day. Another problem is that some employees may resent being observed, while others may increase their normal work output when being observed. Such changes caused by observation are examples of the Hawthorne effect, first discovered in the early Hawthorne studies of human motivation. [10]

A more practical approach than direct observation is work sampling, in which a job analyst or manager randomly samples the content of a job instead of observing all of an employee's behavior. Work sampling is particularly useful for highly repetitive, mostly

1 INFORMATION INPUT

1.1 Sources of Job Information

Rate each of the following items in terms of the extent to which it is used by the worker as a source of information in performing the job.

NA	Does not apply
1	nominal/very infrequent
2	Occasional
3	Moderate
4	Considerable
5	Very substantial

1.1.1 Visual Sources of Job Information

1. __4__ Written materials (books, reports, office notes, articles, job instructions, signs, etc.)

2. __4__ Quantitative materials (such as graphs, accounts, specifications, tables of numbers, etc.)

3. __1__ Pictorial materials (picturelike materials used as sources of information, for example, drawings, blueprints, diagrams, maps, tracings, photographic films, X-ray films, TV pictures, etc.)

4. __NA__ Patterns/related devices (templates, stencils, patterns, etc., used as sources of information when observed during use; do not include here materials described in item 3 above)

5. __1__ Visual displays (dials, gauges, signal lights, radarscopes, speedometers, clocks, etc.)

6. __1__ Measuring devices (rulers, calipers, tire pressure gauges, scales, thickness gauges, pipettes, thermometers, protractors, etc., used to obtain visual information about physical measurements; do not include here devices described in item 5 above)

7. __NA__ Mechanical devices (tools, equipment, machinery, and other mechanical devices which are sources of information when observed during use or operation)

8. __NA__ Materials in process (parts, materials, objects, etc., which are sources of information when being modified, worked on, or otherwise processed, such as bread dough being mixed, workpiece being turned in a lathe, fabric being cut, shoe being resoled, etc.)

9. __NA__ Materials not in process (parts, materials, objects, etc., not in the process of being changed or modified, which are sources of information when being inspected, handled, packaged, distributed, or selected, etc., such as items or materials in inventory, storage, or distribution channels, items being inspected, etc.)

10. __NA__ Features of nature (landscapes, fields, geological samples, vegetation, cloud formations, and other features of nature which are observed or inspected to provide information)

11. __NA__ Features of environment created by people (structures, buildings, dams, highways, bridges, docks, railroads, and other altered aspects of the indoor or outdoor environment which are observed or inspected to provide job information; do not consider equipment, etc., that an individual uses during work, which are covered by item 7).

FIGURE 2–2

A page from the PAQ (Source: Adapted from the *Position Analysis Questionnaire:* Visual Sources of Job Information. PAQ Services, Inc. Logan, UT. Used with permission.)

The worker instructions scale defines *responsibility* in terms of the mix of specifications (that which is prescribed) and judgment (that which is specifically left to discretion) assigned to the worker. A worker's responsibilities may encompass several levels, depending on the activity(ies).

Level 1

Inputs, outputs, tools, equipment, and procedures are all specified. Almost everything the worker needs to know is contained in the assignment. The worker is to produce a specified amount of work or a standard number of units per day.

Level 2

Inputs, outputs, tools, and equipment are all specified, but the worker has some leeway in the procedures and methods used to get the job done. Almost all the information needed is provided in the daily assignment. Production is measured on a daily or weekly basis.

Level 3

Inputs and outputs are specified, but the worker has considerable freedom in procedures and timing, including the use of tools and equipment. The worker may have to refer to several standard sources for information (handbooks, catalogs, wall charts). Time to complete a particular product or service is specified, but this varies up to several hours.

Level 4

Output (product or service) is specified in the assignment, which may be in the form of a memorandum or of a schematic (sketch or blueprint). The worker must work out ways of getting the job done, including selection and use of tools and equipment, sequence of operations (tasks), and acquisition of important information (handbooks, etc.). The worker may either do work or set up standards and procedures for others.

Level 5

Same as Level 4, but in addition the worker is expected to know and employ theory—the whys and wherefores of the various options available for dealing with a problem—and can independently select from among them. Reading in the professional and/or trade literature may be required in order to gain this understanding.

Level 6

Various possible outputs are described that can meet stated technical or administrative needs. The worker must investigate the various possible outputs and evaluate them in regard to performance characteristics and input demands. This usually requires creative use of theory well beyond referring to standard sources. There is no specification of inputs, methods, sequences, sources, or the like.

Level 7

There is some question about what the need or problem really is or what directions should be pursued in dealing with it. In order to define it, to control and explore the behavior of the variables, and to formulate possible outputs and their performance characteristics, the worker must consult largely unspecified sources of information and devise investigations, surveys, or data-analysis studies.

Level 8

Information or direction comes to the worker in terms of needs (tactical, organizational, strategic, financial). The worker must call for staff reports and recommendations concerning methods of dealing with them. The worker coordinates both organizational and technical data in order to make decisions and determinations regarding courses of action (outputs) for major sections (divisions, groups) of the organization.

FIGURE 2–3

The worker instructions scale of the FJA (Source: Adapted from the scale developed by Sidney A. Fine, Ph.D. Advanced Research Resources Organization, Washington, D.C. Used with permission.)

PERSONNEL IN THE NEWS

The "We-They" Syndrome

At the Livonia, Michigan, Cadillac (GM) engine plant, so-called business teams restructured all jobs from 1980 to 1983. The primary goal was to destroy the old "we-they" management-labor thinking by reanalyzing jobs in the entire plant. Eventually 1,400 jobs were designed to belong to business teams of eight to fifteen employees. The teams were given control over scheduling and production decisions. An entire second level of GM managers was eliminated in the process. Several dozen job categories were replaced by a broader single job called *quality operator*. Each employee learns every job on at least two teams under a "pay for knowledge" program. The purpose was to eliminate specialized jobs in which employees did not learn, understand, or appreciate the job of their co-workers. Since the change, productivity is up over 100 percent and controllable costs are down 50 percent. Absenteeism has decreased by over 50 percent as employee morale has shot upward.

Source: Adapted from Bob Strammy, *Transforming the Workplace* (San Diego: Not Just Another Publishing Co., 1985). By permission.

mental jobs, as are often found in clerical and service concerns.[11]

Another alternative for job analysts is to perform all the different tasks necessary to complete a job so as to determine a job's requirements. This method is of limited usefulness because analysts can successfully perform only a few jobs in most organizations.

A common alternative is to interview either the employee or the immediate supervisor of each job, though the interviewer has a difficult time objectively collecting job information unless it has been possible to study the job ahead of time in order to ask the pertinent questions. If this method is used, the interviewer should keep the following in mind:

- Consult the supervisor of the job before deciding which persons to interview. If six or eight employees perform the same

job, ask the supervisor which two perform the job best and thus would interview accurately.

- Make sure that the interviewee understands the purpose of the job analysis. Many times employees fear that the interview will be used against them, such as increasing a job's expected output. Develop rapport with the employee as soon as possible, and express the stated goals of the job analysis program before the interview begins. Often it will be necessary to emphasize that there will be no increase in work load or reduction in pay as a result of the job analysis.

- Structure the interview as much as possible; decide what questions will be asked of all employees before any interviews begin. A structure assures standardization of format and comparability of information gathered. It also helps keep the interviews from deteriorating into bull sessions or complaint sessions.

■ Complete a rough draft of the interview and then go back to the employee to verify that your interpretation of the employee's statements is correct. After verification, contact the supervisor to check the accuracy of the information.

The primary disadvantage of the interview method is that the analyst must spend a great deal of time with each employee. Often employees will not respond to questions carefully because they feel on the spot during an interview. Also, comparison of information gathered from different interviews is difficult. Even structured interviews result in a lack of standardized information, especially if more than one analyst is conducting interviews.

Possibly the best method of developing an in-house system is by using the written questionnaire. A job-analysis questionnaire is faster and easier than an interview, and the use of the questionnaires almost always results in standardized, specific information about the jobs in an organization. Whenever information gathered through a questionnaire is insufficient, follow-up interviews can be scheduled with certain employees. Thus, the advantage of the interview—exploring specific topics the analyst is unclear about or gaining information not in the standardized questions—can often be achieved with a questionnaire. Very few standardized questionnaires require follow-up interviews.

Job-Analysis Questionnaires Figure 2–4 is a sample of a job-analysis questionnaire that has been used by both service and manufacturing organizations. When compiling a questionnaire, keep the following in mind:

Review questionnaires used by organizations, professional groups, or university researchers. Many items on other questionnaires may not have occurred to you. You can learn from other analysts' experiences.

Keep it short. Most people do not like completing questionnaires. Thus, the longer the questionnaire, the less attention will be paid to the items during its completion.

Have each questionnaire completed at work. Questionnaires completed at home often are not done earnestly. As important to the organization as job analysis is, it should be done on company time so that employees have adequate time to provide the information and do not look upon completion as an extra burden they must bear.

Categorize answers. Structure questions so that responses can be categorized as much as possible. Whenever possible, design closed-ended questions; have employees check one of several responses or indicate numbers or percentages for responses. Such a design avoids the gathering of information that is hard to compare or cannot be used by the analyst.

Test the questionnaire with several trusted employees. Many times the analyst will find that questions may be vague and misleading, or that important aspects of the jobs have been omitted.

Include one open-ended question. Always include at least one question that allows the employee to give any additional information that has not been transmitted in the rest of the written questionnaire. In that way, the analyst may discover important information about particular qualities of some jobs.

Information Review

Regardless of the method selected to collect information, the next step is to assemble and review that information with the employees and the job-analysis committee. After writing

1. Employee's Name: _____ Date Completed: _____

   Position Title: _____ Department: _____

   Title of Immediate Supervisor: _____

2. List the names and job titles of persons that you supervise, and the percentage of time spent in supervision.

Name	Title	Hrs. Per Day/Week Supervising
_____	_____	_____
_____	_____	_____

3. What is the lowest grade of grammar school, high school, or college that should have been completed by a person starting in your position?

   _____

4. What special type of training, skill, or experience should a person possess before starting in your position?

   _____

5. What training or experience have you received in your position, and how long would it take the average person to perform this work satisfactorily without close supervision?

   _____

   _____

6. What machines or equipment do you operate in your work and for what percentage of your time per day, week, or month?

Machine	%	Period
_____	_____	_____
_____	_____	_____

7. What do you consider to be the most important decisions that you alone make in the course of your work, and what percentage of your time is devoted to making such decisions?

   _____

   _____

8. What responsibility do you have for handling money, securities, inventory, or other valuables, and what is your estimate of their worth?

Responsibility	$ Worth per Week
_____	_____
_____	_____

FIGURE 2–4
A job-analysis questionnaire

9. What responsibility do you have in dealing with customers or other persons outside the company?

Person Contacted	Position	Nature of Contact	Frequency of Contact
_____	_____	_____	_____
_____	_____	_____	_____
_____	_____	_____	_____

10. What unusual aspects about your work and your work surroundings (working conditions, hours, out-of-town travel, physical requirements, etc.) should be included in a description of your job?

_____

_____

_____

11. What activities do you perform only at stated periods (weekly or monthly) or at irregular intervals?

Activity	Purpose	Interval
_____	_____	_____
_____	_____	_____
_____	_____	_____

12. List the specific duties you perform in the usual course of your daily work, and approximately what percentage of your workday is spent in each activity. (Please try to use active verbs such as type, file, interview, etc. On the following page you will find a sample list of duties that may be helpful in preparing your answer to this question).

_____

_____

_____

13. Discuss any considerations not covered in this questionnaire that you would consider important in writing a description of your job.

_____

_____

_____

THANK YOU FOR FILLING OUT THE QUESTIONNAIRE.

FIGURE 2–4
continued

a first draft of the standardized information collected, the analyst needs to make sure that the data are factually correct and complete and that a clear picture of the job is being presented. After checking with the employees and supervisors involved in gathering information, the analyst must take these first drafts to the job-analysis committee, which reviews each analysis to make sure that it is both objective and easily comparable with analyses of other jobs. The establishment of standardized categories of information about the jobs—such as work environment, decision making required, and supervision—makes comparisons among jobs easier. The more effort put into these first drafts, the easier it will be to determine the desired end products.

Product Completion

The fourth step involves the completion of whatever end products are desired by management. For example, job analysis data may be used to write job descriptions or job specifications, to conduct a job evaluation for wage and salary purposes, to determine training and development needs, and to create tests for employee selection.

Future Use and Updating

The last step in the job-analysis procedure will be to determine how the information will be stored for future use. The personnel department should have access to this information in case additional end products are desired. Also, the job-analysis committee will need to determine how to update the information periodically, because information gathered in the job-analysis process has a tendency to become obsolete over time. Changes will occur as supervisors train employees to accept more responsibility, as additional tasks are developed, or as organizational changes are made.

Updating the information in the job-analysis program maintains its accuracy and guarantees its usefulness in the future.

JOB-ANALYSIS PROBLEMS

Any job analysis will run into certain problems regardless of the size of the organization, the status of employee relations, or the abilities of those performing the analysis. One of the most common problems is employee fear. Often employees see a job analysis as a threat to their current jobs or pay levels or both. In the past, job analysis has been used as a means of expanding jobs while reducing the total number of employees. Job analysis has also been used to increase production rates and, therefore, decrease employees' pay. Organizations must overcome employee fears so that employees and their supervisors will give accurate information.

One of the most successful methods of reducing employee fear is to involve employees or their representatives in as many aspects of the job-analysis procedure as possible. Before the procedure begins, employees should be told why it has to be instituted, who will initiate it, how the employees will be affected, and why their input is critical. Management may want to make a written commitment that the organization will not terminate any employee, lower the pay of any employee, or decrease the total number of jobs because of the results of the job analysis. Such measures may enable the job analysts to obtain complete information from employees. It is unfortunate for job analysts that in past years job analysis has sometimes been used improperly.

A second problem of job analysis is the need to update the information. While any job analysis is being completed, jobs will be changing as the organization changes. As employees expand in their jobs, as work is reassigned within a department, as supervisors develop, the description of their jobs will necessarily have to change. The problem, then, becomes how to keep the information current. One method is the annual review of the job-analysis information, in which the personnel department sends the information to supervisors, asking them to note any changes that have occurred during the past year. A second method is to have managers submit proposed changes in jobs or reclassifications. This method is especially important when the reclassification may result in a change in pay.

Both methods have their problems. The annual review is quite time-consuming because every job must be reanalyzed each year. Also, when jobs are reviewed annually, employees sometimes expect that their jobs will always be reclassified—with accompanying pay increases. Another problem with an annual review is that whenever the content of a job is substantially increased only a week or two after the initial job analysis, employees in that job may be underpaid for the next forty or fifty weeks. Finally, the annual review looks at all jobs, even those which have not changed. Possibly 90 percent of the jobs do not need to be reexamined; only the 10 percent that have changed during the year need to be reviewed.

Constant updating by managers implies that only those jobs which need to be changed will be looked at. Also, this method results in more current data and ensures that employees will not have to wait months to have their jobs reclassified, with a possible change in salary or other benefits. A primary disadvantage of this method is that management may forget to keep up with changes. Thus, employees get frustrated, feel underpaid, or don't realize what must be done to have their jobs reclassified.

The two methods may be combined in some form, such as having biennial reviews with constant updates by managers who want to reclassify jobs. Yet combination systems contain the advantages as well as the disadvantages of the two methods, and therefore using such systems is less common than using one method or the other.

Another problem with job analysis occurs when a job is held by only one or two employees. In such a case, the analysis is often of the person's performance and not of the job itself. The analyst must look at what the job should entail and not at how well or how poorly one employee is performing the job.

One problem commonly occurs when job analyses form the basis for job descriptions handed out to new employees. Employees often feel that the description is a contract describing what they should and should not do on the job. When asked occasionally to do extra work or an unusual task, employees may respond, ''It's not in my description''—and by that reasoning resist performing the task. Management can change job descriptions by assigning added tasks to employees; but if a task is done only rarely or is never to be repeated, changing the job description for a single situation is unnecessary. Many organizations use *elastic clauses* in job descriptions, such as ''performs other duties as assigned.'' An elastic clause allows supervisors to assign employees duties different from those normally performed without changing the job descriptions.

JOB DESCRIPTIONS

The most common end product of a job analysis is a written job description. One of the oldest personnel tools, job descriptions have received renewed interest in recent years, primarily because of governmental regulatory guidelines. Job descriptions have no exact format and are often used for many different purposes.

Job Analysis Japanese Style

In Japan, job duties are generally broader, more ambiguous job responsibilities than those customarily found in the United States. It is assumed that those who are good enough to be hired can develop the necessary skills and versatility to perform in a variety of positions, much like players on a volleyball team.

Work is organized around groups of people instead of around individual skills. Employees work in teams, so that each shares a common point of view and learns all the duties of the unit. This means that workers use slack times to do other jobs, and if business falls off, they are able to fill in elsewhere as needed. There are, then, no clearcut job specifications and duties; the Japanese sense of collectivity precludes a strong identification with occupational expertise. Once employees grasp the company's philosophy, it is believed that they can deduce for themselves the necessary role as work situations arise; there is, therefore, little need for detailed instruction manuals and predetermined job rules. . . .

The difference in classification systems between a Japanese affiliate and an American-owned operation is aptly illustrated by an official in a Japanese motorcycle company. "Our hourly work force is almost exactly the size of theirs (the U.S. firm's), yet we have only 20 different job descriptions versus 150 for them." By following relatively nonspecialized career paths, employees become experts in the organization rather than experts in one functional specialty. This person-centered (as opposed to position-centered) system places a high premium on adaptability, a critical requirement in rapidly changing technologies that require integration of the whole company. . . .

Source: Adapted from James S. Bowman, "The Rising Sun in America (Part One)," *Personnel Administrator* 31, no. 9 (September 1986): 67, 114. Copyright 1986, The American Society for Personnel Administration, Alexandria, VA.

Uses of Job Descriptions

Over 100 major uses of job descriptions in the personnel function have been identified. Most employers, however, typically use them for five or six functions.[12] Job descriptions serve a variety of purposes for the personnel department. Several employment and compensation activities depend on job information normally included in the organization's job descriptions. In addition, the basic job information needed for such legal requirements as equal employment opportunity, affirmative action, overtime qualifications, and employee safety can be included in job descriptions. Collective bargaining agreements may also specify which duties are to be performed by each union employee covered by the agreement.

Recruitment   Job descriptions may be used to develop recruitment advertisements and to provide applicants with additional information about the job openings.

Interviewing   Job descriptions are often used when they include job specifications as a means of providing the interviewer with concise, accurate information about the job. The interviewer can then better match the applicant to the job opening and make sure that the minimum qualifications of the job are met by the applicant.

Orientation   New employees may be given job descriptions to spell out job requirements and areas to be evaluated.

Training   Organizations use job descriptions to specify both the training an employee requires for effective performance and the type of training current employees may need to become promotable.

Job Evaluation   Job descriptions often specify comparable factors in the job-evaluation process so that a job evaluator can compare the various jobs and make pay decisions. Personnel practice and federal laws require that such comparisons be based on job-required skill, effort, responsibility, and working conditions. The required documentation of such information is usually found in job descriptions. Thus, there is an inevitable link between pay and job descriptions. That link sometimes tempts managers to use fancy language and elaborate generalities to describe job duties in order to justify higher pay levels. The personnel managers are then forced to act as police officers to guard against such problems. The growth of computerized personnel

systems has greatly assisted the personnel manager in maintaining descriptions and evaluations which accurately match the job content within an organization.[13]

Wage Compensation Survey   Job descriptions give the personnel administrator the opportunity to estimate whether the wages being paid for a job are equitable in comparison with wages for similar jobs in other organizations in the community or throughout the country. Thus, job descriptions provide information for both internal comparisons (through job evaluation) and external comparisons (through survey analysis).

Performance Appraisal   Job descriptions may specify the basis on which an employee will be judged during performance appraisal. If employees are told which areas and duties they are responsible for performing, they are forewarned about what will eventually be evaluated.

Outplacement   Job descriptions may also play an important role in the career change process. Organizations that lay off workers temporarily or downsize permanently often want to assist affected employees. The personnel staff can use an employee's job description to help prepare a resume that gives detailed information. The personnel staff may also refer to the description when providing reference information to prospective employers.[14]

Legal Requirements

Job descriptions can be a great help to an organization as it attempts to comply with a number of important federal laws.

Fair Labor Standards Act of 1938   This act, which was amended in 1974, created the initial demand for job descriptions and made them popular in the 1940s. The act specifies, among other things, that employees must be paid a minimum wage. It also sets a forty-hour workweek by dividing employees into two categories—exempt and nonexempt. *Nonexempt* employees must be paid time and a half when they work more than forty hours per week. *Exempt* employees do not have to be paid overtime wages. Thus, an organization must determine whether each job is exempt or nonexempt through job analysis or by analyzing job descriptions. Basically, exempt positions are managerial, supervisory, technical, professional, and certain sales positions. Statutes similar to the federal Fair Labor Standards Act have been enacted in most states.

Equal Pay Act of 1963   This act requires that organizations give "equal pay for substantially equal work requiring equal skill, effort, responsibility, and working conditions." Job descriptions may be an organization's defense against charges of discrimination filed under the Equal Pay Act. Descriptions can be used to show that jobs are not substantially equal in terms of skill, effort, responsibility, or working conditions and, therefore, can be paid at different rates.

Title VII of the 1964 Civil Rights Act
Title VII prohibits discrimination in employment based on race, sex, age, creed, religion, or national origin. Job descriptions provide documentation that employees are hired and paid according to necessary job requirements.

Occupational Safety and Health Act of 1970   Job descriptions are required by this act to specify "elements of the job that endanger health, or are considered unsatisfactory or distasteful to the majority of the population." Providing a job description to employees as an advance notice is a good defense against possible legal actions by employees.

Collective Bargaining Demands   A longstanding union demand is "equal pay for equal work." Thus, job descriptions specifying work to be performed often stipulate certain pay for specific duties. Such pay considerations have been a critical area in labor negotiations for many years.

Elements of the Job Description

Although there is no universal format for job descriptions, most have certain common elements. A list of job duties is one element found in all job descriptions. Most will contain some identification and a brief job summary. They often contain job specifications, though it is also common practice to list specifications on separate forms.

Job Identification   The first part of a job description, the identification section, usually includes the title of the job, the location of the job (e.g., plant, department, or division), the title of the immediate supervisor, the job status (exempt or nonexempt), and the pay grade or pay range. This information is needed for general administrative and record-keeping functions. Job titles can be used to identify a particular job within an organization, but generally they cannot legally be used to compare jobs for pay purposes. The content of the job is described in the duties and responsibilities section. The content must be evaluated for pay considerations because job titles can be misleading; an administrative assistant in one organization may be quite different from one in another organization. A statement of location is required by the 1978 *Uniform Guidelines* when the job description is used to provide evidence of legality in an organization's selection procedures.[15]

Other useful elements sometimes included in the identification section are the name of the job analyst who approved the description, the name of the employee who provided the basic information, the date the description was approved, and, if applicable, the standard code number published in the *DOT*, the equal employment and affirmative action (EEO-1/ AAP) reporting category, and the point total in a point system of job evaluation.

Figure 2–5 is a sample job description. That description of a chief quality control engineer contains a particularly good example of job identification. The identification includes not only the usual information—such as job title, department, and title of the immediate supervisor—but also the job code, or the *DOT* job number. The exempt status of the job indicates a salaried position that does not pay overtime wages. The inclusion of a date on which the description was approved and the name of the person who approved it eliminates future questions or conflicts concerning accuracy or completeness. A pay grade is given so that employees or applicants can estimate the pay range for a job and its level within the organization. The "751" points refers to evaluation points; if the point total is close to the next highest pay grade, future reclassifications may move it up to the next highest pay grade.

Job Summary A job summary is a one-to three-line description of the essence of the job. Job summaries usually start with a verb, such as "supervises," "coordinates," or "directs." Job summaries should emphasize either the most common function, the primary output, or the objective of the job.

Job Duties and Responsibilities Job duties and responsibilities are the heart of the job description. There are two common formats for the duties section. One is a paragraph describing the job. The problem with this format is that a reader may find it difficult to recognize immediately which functions are impor-

tant. A more popular format is grouping the tasks of a job and listing them separately, as for example in Figure 2–5. The tasks might be grouped by functional categories, such as "supervision given," "organization of work," "physical demands," and "financial accountability." As with job summaries, each duty or responsibility should begin with a verb, such as "supervises" or "performs." The intention of the duties section is to give the reader a complete and concise account of what is being performed on the job—though it is not intended to be a training instrument to teach a novice how to perform the job. The estimated time spent on each duty often appears in parentheses after each duty is explained.

Job Specifications Job specifications, or minimum qualifications, state the qualifications job applicants must possess to be considered for the job. These qualifications are often grouped into three categories: skills, knowledge, and abilities (SKAs). *Knowledge* constitutes the body of information in a particular subject area that is required by a new employee to perform the job satisfactorily. *Skill* factors include observable capabilities performed on the job. *Ability* refers to any mental or physical activities required of a new employee. For example, a section supervisor might be required to know the safety regulations that affect the plant, to have the skill to operate a quality-control laser machine, and to have the ability to write daily work assignments. SKAs are most useful in personnel decision-making situations, such as selection, training, and performance evaluation.[16]

Job specifications may also include required education, experience, and training, as well as any specific certification required for the job. As a job specification, *effort* might encompass specific physical tasks the job holder must be able to perform or some necessary experience in a supervisory position. *Responsibil-*

Chief Quality Control Engineer
Job Title

156.132
Job Code

Manager of Quality Control
Title of Immediate Supervisor

Quality Control
Department

7
Bldg.

Louisville
Plant

Exempt
Status

August 12, 1986
Date

Robert Myers
Approved by

Kathy Johnson
written by

16
Grade

751
Points

1/2
EEO/AAP

SUMMARY

Supervises six salaried quality control personnel; plans, organizes, coordinates, and administers manufacturing activities.

JOB DUTIES

1. Establishes and maintains supplier contacts to assist in solving quality problems by evaluating contacts' quality capabilities, facilities, and quality systems. (10%)
2. Establishes and reviews goals, budgets, and work plans in the areas of quality, cost schedule attainment, and operator/equipment utilization. (10%)
3. Reviews product and process designs, identifying problems which might result in customer dissatisfaction or failure to meet established goals or allocated costs. (20%)
4. Specifies quality control methods and processes to support quality planning. Provides cost estimates and procures necessary tools and equipment to support overall project schedule. (10%)
5. Supplies input to manufacturing engineers on producibility and other quality matters. (20%)
6. Provides feedback on quality levels and costs during test runs and during production to measure system effectiveness. (10%)
7. Supervises six to eight salaried personnel assigned to the quality control engineering area. Trains new personnel in proper procedures and policy. Completes performance appraisals of subordinates. (20%)

FIGURE 2–5
A sample job description

ity might encompass reporting responsibility, supervisory responsibility for inventory maintenance, or financial responsibility such as making up shortages in a cash drawer. Job specifications might also include working conditions, such as the hours the employee must be available, as well as other unusual conditions, such as high levels of noise or fumes.

Figure 2–6, a description of a word processing secretary's job, contains job specifications that would allow an interviewer to decide easily and objectively if an applicant meets the qualifications. Although a specification may not always be quantitative in nature, it should be whenever possible. The first three specifications for the job are examples of

---

Job Title: *Word Processing Secretary*
Department: *Branch Administration*
Position of Immediate Supervisor: *Branch Administrative Manager*

I. GENERAL SUMMARY OF RESPONSIBILITIES:
    Types, edits, and distributes various correspondence to clients and internal staff. Transmits and proofs various essential status reports for day to day operations.

II. SPECIFIC JOB RESPONSIBILITIES:
    Types daily correspondence and sales orders from nine representatives from machine dictation and hard copy.   (40%)

    Proofreads and prepares final copies for distribution.   (10%)

    Receives handwritten copies and maintains priority file of reports and correspondence.   (5%)

    Types special projects, such as proposals, quotations, systems, analyses, and office surveys for marketing department.   (20%)

    Transmits computer programs via magnetic card typewriter and other telecommunication equipment.   (10%)

    Logs and maintains records of completed staff and client work.   (4%)

    Receives and assigns priority to special client and staff requests and special projects.   (5%)

    Serves as backup for receptionist.   (5%)

    Performs other duties as assigned.   (1%)

III. JOB SPECIFICATION:
    High school diploma required, with one or two years of college preferred.

    Training or one year's experience on magnetic card typewriter. Type 50 wpm.

    Able to file ten documents per minute without error.

    Must be able to consistently produce accurate, professional quality documents.

    Ability to work well with people in developing proposals is essential.

FIGURE 2–6
A sample job description

measurable or *verifiable* qualifications; the interviewer can verify that a person has a high school degree or college experience and can measure an applicant's typing and filing ability with standardized tests. The fourth and fifth specifications are important but are more vague and subjective—and thus subject to interviewer bias. Notice that the sample job description shown in Figure 2–5 does not contain a section on job specifications.

CONCLUSIONS AND APPLICATIONS

- A sound job-analysis program produces many benefits for an organization. Information critical to employment and compensation is collected on a systematic basis. Job descriptions, job specifications, and job evaluations can easily be produced from the job-analysis data. Thus critical personnel practices such as hiring, wage determination, and administrative record keeping are assisted by job analysis.

- The methods of information collection are twofold: standardized and internal. Internal written questionnaires are often faster and easier and can be tailored to the needs of the organization. Interviews with employees and supervisors can also be used to ensure complete and accurate information.

- The federal government and the courts have increased the pressure on personnel managers to utilize job analysis as a means of producing job-related job descriptions, hiring criteria, and compensation systems.

- Job descriptions generally should contain a complete identification of the job and its location within the organization. The section on duties and responsibilities should group all tasks into major functional categories, and each entry should begin with verbs. Job specifications should include all SKAs needed to perform the job, as well as other minimum qualifications.

CASE STUDY
Sacramento Frame Company

In 1955 Colleen and Maureen Wilson, two sisters who had moved west from Indiana, started a small frame shop. Their parents had operated a small but successful picture-frame business in Indiana, and the Wilsons decided to open their own business in California after visiting relatives in Sacramento. Their timing was excellent, and the business rapidly grew with the region. After a few years, they began producing frame parts and unassembled frames for sale to West Coast frame shops. In a relatively short time, the frame-production part of their business grew to over 200 employees. A new building had to be constructed in 1966.

The Wilsons decided that the new and larger facility demanded that they add several professional employees to their staff—including David Bridgers as personnel director. Bridgers had ten years' experience in personnel and had served as assistant director in a Davis, California, manufacturing firm. Given a free hand to institute a new professional personnel system, Bridgers developed a system of job analysis that included job descriptions for over sixty different jobs and a wage and salary system. Standard operating procedures and routine supervisory performance appraisals were also implemented. Personnel policies of promotion from within, substantial profit sharing, and a written grievance system were widely applauded by the firm's employees, and in return, productivity and morale were consistently high for a number of years.

By 1986, however, increased foreign competition and new production technologies had forced substantial changes at Sacramento Frame. Automated equipment forced the company to lay off over fifty employees whose jobs were no longer needed. New computer equipment replaced the old manually kept inventory, sales, and personnel records. About ten new employees were hired to maintain the new records system. These recent changes caused several occurrences of employee friction, such as this one in the cafeteria:

Barry: I love my new job—this is a great place to work.

John: You should! You computer jocks come in here and make more money than some of us who have been here for ten years. We built this business and you reap the big bucks!

Barry: Hey, I went to college at U. C. Davis for six years and have five more years experience at IBM. I paid my dues.

John: Not here you haven't. Several of my best friends were laid off because of the new robots we bought. Then you all get hired into new, high-paying jobs. I just spent nine months in night training to learn how to operate this new equipment—where were you?

Bridgers and the Wilsons are well aware of these morale problems and their effect on production. They have decided to implement a new job-analysis program as a means of addressing some of their problems.

Questions

1. What employee problems with the new program might be anticipated? How could they be minimized?
2. Did the Wilsons err in bringing in the computerized records systems?
3. What specific problems might be analyzed with a job-analysis program? What end products should it produce?
4. Suggest how the program might be structured to be successful.

EXPERIENTIAL EXERCISE
Writing Job Descriptions

Purpose

To conduct a brief job analysis and to create a job description.

Procedure

Break the class into small groups of four or five each. Each group must include at least one student who is currently employed or has recently been employed.

The Task

Using the information in this chapter, group members will perform a perfunctory job analysis with the student concerning his or her job. Once the job analysis has been performed, write a job description for that job. Be sure that your job description conforms to the characteristics of good job descriptions discussed in this chapter. Once the assignment has been finished, your instructor will lead a discussion concerning each group's job analysis and job description.

KEY TERMS AND CONCEPTS

Dictionary of Occupational Titles (DOT)

Elastic clause

Functional job analysis (FJA)

Job analysis

Job classification

Job descriptions

Job evaluation

Job specifications

Position Analysis Questionnaire (PAQ)

Skills, knowledge, ability (SKAs)

Verifiable specifications

REVIEW QUESTIONS

1. Define the practical relationship among job analysis, job descriptions, and job specifications.
2. What information is necessary to develop job descriptions? What are some of the qualities of a well-constructed job description?
3. How can a firm benefit from having a complete and accurate system of job descriptions and job specifications?
4. Outline the advantages and disadvantages of the various methods of job analysis.
5. How do governmental influences affect the process of job analysis?
6. If an organization has no formal system of job analysis, how might the objectives of job analysis be obtained?

DISCUSSION QUESTIONS

1. If you were a personnel specialist in a company that was introducing job analysis, how would you reassure employees who felt threatened?
2. When faced with the problem of updating job analysis information, would you favor an annual review or reclassification? Explain why.
3. Describe the methods you would use to gather job information in a bank, a small manufacturing firm, or a newspaper.
4. Discuss how job analysis could or could not resolve the following problems: (a) an employee who produces less than others doing the same job; (b) an employee who complains about a dirty work environment; (c) an employee who feels passed over when promotions are announced.

5. As a personnel manager, you must describe job analysis to employees. Which ideas would you stress for blue-collar workers? For white-collar workers?

ENDNOTES

1. "Uniform Guidelines on Employee Selection Procedures," *Federal Register* (August 25, 1978): 38302, 38306.
2. T. M. Stutzman, "Within Classification Job Differences," *Personnel Psychology* 36 (1983): 503–16.
3. Edward C. Brett and Charles M. Canning, "Job Evaluation and Your Organization: An Ideal Relationship?" *Personnel Administrator* 29, no. 4 (April 1984): 115–24.
4. E. L. Levine et al., "Evaluation of Job Analysis Methods by Experienced Job Analysts," *Academy of Management Journal* 26 (1983): 339–48.
5. U.S. Department of Labor, Manpower Administration, *Handbook for Analyzing Jobs* (Washington, D.C.: U.S. Government Printing Office, 1972), pp. 340–51.
6. *Uniform Guidelines,* pp. 38304, 38306.
7. Ernest J. McCormick, Paul J. Jeanneret, and Robert C. Mecham, "A Study of Job Characteristics and Job Dimensions as Based on the Position Analysis Questionnaire (PAQ)," *Journal of Applied Psychology* (August 1972): 347–68.
8. R. D. Arvey et al., "Narrative Job Descriptions as Potential Sources of Job Analysis Ratings," *Personnel Psychology* 35 (1982): 618–29.
9. Sidney A. Fine and Wretha Wiley, *An Introduction to Functional Job Analysis: A Scaling of Selected Tasks from the Social Welfare Field,* Methods for Manpower Analysis no. 4 (Kalamazoo, MI: Upjohn Institute for Employment Research, 1979), pp. 3–20.
10. Alex Carey, "The Hawthorne Studies: A Radical Criticism," *American Sociological Review* 32, no. 3 (1967): 403–16.
11. W. H. Weiss, "How to Work-Sample Your People," *Administrative Management* (June 14, 1982): 37–38, 49–50.
12. Philip Grant, "What Use Is a Job Description?" *Personnel Journal* 67, no. 2 (February 1988): 45–53.
13. E. James Brennan, "Job Descriptions and Pay: The Inevitable Link," *Personnel Journal* 63, no. 7 (July 1984): 18.
14. Grant, "What Use Is a Job description?" 48–49.
15. Mark A. Jones, "Job Descriptions Made Easy," *Personnel Journal* 63, no. 5 (May 1984): 31–34.
16. Ibid.

Chapter Three

Job Design

Chapter Objectives

1. To recognize how the design of a job affects employee motivation and ability.
2. To explain the concept of job specialization.
3. To cite various methods of designing motivating jobs.
4. To explain the role of ergonomics in job design.
5. To understand the need for quality-of-working-life (QWL) programs.
6. To describe alternatives to the forty-hour workweek.
7. To discuss why flextime programs are growing in popularity.
8. To outline the Volvo work group experience.

PERSONNEL
IN THE NEWS

Commuting by Computer

Honeywell, Inc., in 1985 asked 700 of its employees in high-technology jobs if, given the choice, they would prefer to (a) go to the office every day, (b) work primarily out of their home, (c) spend half their time at home and half at the office, (d) don't know.

Honeywell was surprised when 56 percent chose to go to the office every day, 36 percent chose to spend half their time there, and only 7 percent said they would prefer to work primarily at home. Honeywell's vice president of small computers and office systems group, Eugene Manno, noted that the biggest reason given for wanting to work in the office was "the need to be around other people and share ideas and camaraderie." Manno also noted several differences among groups of respondents. In general, the higher the job in the organization, the greater the desire to work at the office. Older workers preferred to work at the office more than their younger counterparts, and men preferred office work more than women. Among job categories, marketing professionals showed the greatest interest in working at home, whereas lawyers showed the greatest interest in working at the office.

Before the survey, Honeywell's top management thought that only technical problems had prevented telecommuting (working at home) from becoming popular with employees. But Manno concluded that the survey results made it clear that the needs of people—not technology—will determine the future trends in telecommuting. He predicts that workers will desire to split their time between the home and the office but that no more than 10 percent will choose to work primarily out of their home.

Source: Adapted from Mike Lewis, "Why Managers Feel at Home in the Office." Reprinted by permission from *Nation's Business* (March 1985). Copyright 1985, U.S. Chamber of Commerce.

WHAT employees actually do on the job—tasks performed, decisions made, equipment used—greatly affects job satisfaction, productivity, and several other factors. Highly paid employees have been known to quit and take lower-paying positions simply because they hated their work. Since the 1950s many changes have taken place in job-design theory and practice, resulting in the expansion of many jobs to include a wider range of activities and decision-making responsibilities. Individually or in groups, employees are being given greater responsibility for the design and control of their work, as well as more autonomy in deciding work methods. Many of those activities were previously part of the first-line supervisor's job and were recast as part of the subordinate's responsibilities. Modern job holders are often required to have greater decision-making responsibilities and control over their work. And the content of that work is less repetitive and more challenging than in years past.[1]

DESIGNING JOBS

Two of the most important concerns of personnel managers are employee productivity and job satisfaction. Personnel officers realize that a critical factor affecting these areas is the type of work performed by the employee. Job design determines how work is performed and, therefore, greatly affects how an employee feels about a job, how much authority an employee has over the work, how much decision making the employee has on the job, and how many tasks the employee should complete. Managers realize that job design determines both their working relationship with their employees and the relationship among the employees themselves. Job design determines the nature of social relationships that exist on the job, as well as the relationship between the employee and the work.

Job design is the manipulation of the content, functions, and relationships of jobs in a way that both accomplishes organizational purposes and satisfies the personal needs of individual job holders.[2] The content of a job encompasses the variety of tasks performed, the autonomy of the job holder, the routineness of tasks performed, the difficulty level of the tasks performed, and the identity of the job holder, or the extent to which the whole job is performed by the person involved.[3] The functions of a job encompass the work methods utilized as well as the coordination of the work, responsibility, information flow, and authority of the job. The relationships of a job encompass the work activities shared by the job holder and other individuals in the organization.[4]

Figure 3–1 shows how job design is of importance to both the worker and the organization. The design determines the way and the extent to which tasks are accomplished by

FIGURE 3–1

A framework for job design (From *Organizational Behavior and Performance,* 2nd ed., by Andrew D. Szilagyi and Marc J. Wallace [p. 149] Copyright ©1980 by Goodyear Publishing Company. Reprinted by permission)

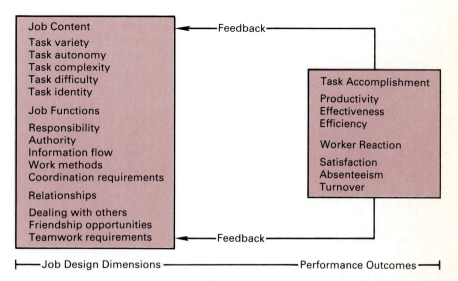

a job holder. At stake is a worker's satisfaction with the job situation—that is, the work itself. A worker's favorable reaction to job design means greater accomplishment, greater job satisfaction, less absenteeism, fewer grievances, and less turnover.

How should jobs be designed? This topic has been discussed widely since the Industrial Revolution. Traditional approaches to job design have been seriously questioned in recent years. Some job-design problems in the last twenty-five years have been caused by workers, who are increasingly dissatisfied with jobs designed for robots or mindless machines. Henry Ford described his assembly line as "a haven for those who haven't got the brains to do anything else." Ford's assembly line is an excellent example of the job-design method known as *job specialization*.

Job Specialization

Job specialization is characterized by jobs with very few tasks, and those tasks are repeated often during the workday and require few skills and little mental ability. Job specialization was the primary component of the scientific management developed by Frederick Taylor, who described management's role in job design as the three-step process.[5]

1. The manager determines the "one best way of performing the job."
2. The manager hires individuals according to their abilities, which match the needs of the job design. For example, a strong person is hired to carry heavy loads, a diligent person is hired to file records, and so on.
3. Management trains workers in the one best way the job should be performed. All planning, organizing, and control of the job are done by the manager.

Scientific management, which for many years was quite popular in the United States, has many advantages. First, management can hire unskilled labor for almost all operative jobs in the organization. Since highly specialized jobs are designed for people with very few skills or experience, most members of the work force can perform most of the lower-level jobs in a company. Second, unskilled workers are among the lowest-paid members of the work force. This was particularly true in the early 1900s, when unskilled workers were moving from agricultural areas to industrial centers and few unions protected them. Third, workers tend to make very few errors when performing simple, routine jobs. There are very few chances for mental errors, since managers organize the work flow so that the employee makes few decisions. Fourth, the average cost per unit decreases as jobs become highly specialized. As Henry Ford discovered, it is far more cost efficient to build cars on an assembly line where workers are trained to perform one or two routine tasks than to hire engineers or mechanics to assemble a complete automobile. This principle of reduced average cost per labor-dollar spent has long motivated industrial engineers to design highly specialized jobs.

Job Dimensions   The degree to which a job is highly specialized can be determined by measuring two dimensions of the job. The first dimension is the *scope*—how long it takes a worker to complete the total task. For example, an assembly-line worker in an early Ford plant might have taken five minutes to add a wiring harness to an automobile as it moved down the assembly line. After the wiring harness was added to one automobile the worker had five minutes to add a harness to the next car. Thus, the scope of the job, or the job cycle, was five minutes.

The second dimension measured to determine the degree of specialization is the *depth* of the job. This dimension is more difficult to determine because it cannot be measured in easily identifiable terms. Depth refers to how much planning, decision making, and controlling the worker does in the total job. For example: To what extent can a worker vary the methods utilized on the job? How many decisions can the worker make without supervisory approval? If various techniques and tools are determined solely by management, then the job is said to have very little depth. At the other end of the continuum, a job in which a worker performs independently contains great depth, or a great deal of autonomy.

Specialization Problems   Why is job specialization not the primary means of designing jobs today? Probably the most comprehensive answer to this question was given by Walker and Guest's 1950s study *The Man on the Assembly Line*. They found that the automobile industry was the epitome of job specialization in The United States. Walker and Guest heard several complaints from employees about their highly specialized jobs:[6]

Repetition   Employees performed only a few tasks, which had to be repeated many times a day. This quickly led to boredom. There was no challenge to learn anything new or to improve the job.

Mechanical Pacing   Employees were restricted by the assembly line, which made them maintain a certain regular pace of work. That is, employees could not take a break when needed or simply divert their attention to some other aspect of the job. Instead, their constant attention and effort had to be maintained at a certain speed—often too fast for some employees and too slow for others.

No End Product   Employees found that they were not producing any identifiable end product; consequently, they had little pride and enthusiasm in their work.

Little Social Interaction   Employees complained that because the assembly line required constant attention, there was little chance to interact on the casual basis with other employees. This made it difficult for employees to develop significant social bonds at work.

No Input   Employees complained that they had little chance to choose the methods by which they performed their jobs, the tools they used, or the work procedures. This lack of autonomy created a lack of interest in the job because there was nothing they could improve or change.

Walker and Guest found that employees had become disenchanted with highly specialized jobs following World War II, though they had been happy to perform those jobs in prior years. Several reasons could account for that change in attitude.

Before World War II, employees often were faced with a lean job market. They often thought that any job which allowed them to maintain a reasonable standard of living was a good job because jobs were scarce. After the war, employees found that there were often several jobs available. They no longer had to be satisfied with a boring, unchallenging job.

The general pay scales offered by firms increased substantially between the early 1900s and the 1950s, creating a true middle class. Employees could choose jobs for reasons other than income. The challenge, autonomy, nature, and working conditions of the job were also weighed when comparing jobs.

The educational level of employees rose quickly in the post–World War II period, and that level continued to rise thereafter. A much larger proportion of the total U.S. work force became educated beyond the elementary levels that were average for the industrial employee in the last century. A more highly educated employee often expects a challenging and rewarding career and is not happy with a boring job which requires little mental effort or ability.

The increase in service jobs also contributed to the disenchantment with specialized jobs. From the 1940s to the 1960s, more jobs became available in such service organizations as hospitals, educational institutions, hotels, restaurants, offices, and so on. While many service jobs were highly specialized, the proportion in service industries was usually less than the manufacturing industry. Also, the jobs which were not specialized increased during those years; employees could obtain nonspecialized jobs which were more interesting and challenging to them.

Walker and Guest's study outlined a problem of the 1950s and 1960s which still exists today. Industrial engineers developed a job-design approach that emphasized human engineering, often referred to as *ergonomics*, which treats the worker as part of the production function. The worker is trained to perform a specifically defined task, which requires no decision making.

Job Design and Motivation

The second major approach to job design emphasizes the human factors involved in jobs. This human relations approach recognizes the need to design jobs that are interesting and intrinsically rewarding. Unmotivated employees often have low levels of productivity, low interest in the quality of their products or services, and high levels of absenteeism and grievances. Such employees are apt to leave the organization whenever a better alternative is presented to them. Modern management has found that the increased cost of employee absenteeism and turnover, as well as the decreased productivity, may outweigh the advantages of highly specialized jobs. The problem is to balance the motivation and specialization aspects of each job. Table 3–1 shows the advantages of each of the two approaches to job design.

Thus, job performance is determined by the employee's motivation and relative ability to perform the job.[7] Employees' jobs must have high levels of both ability and motivation so that the employees can give high-level performances.[8]

Designing jobs interesting enough to motivate employees yet simple enough for most members of the work force to perform is quite a task. Personnel managers and industrial engineers attempt to design motivating jobs which have high levels of specialization. The usual result is that jobs which are specialized have motivation factors provided by other means. Often the other means must be created by the personnel office in the form of social functions, sports programs, or contests for employees. But such techniques do not replace the motivation employees lose when assigned to highly specialized jobs.

The need to design jobs that motivate employees is emphasized in basic management

TABLE 3–1	Specialization-intensive Jobs	Motivation-intensive Jobs
The advantages of the major approaches to design	High productivity of unskilled workers	High productivity of challenged workers
	Less training time required	Less absenteeism
	Easy to replace workers	Less turnover
	Few mental work errors	Higher product quality
	Greater manager control of operations	More employee ideas, suggestions
		Greater employee job satisfaction

theory. One of the early theories of job modification is Frederick Herzberg's *motivator-hygiene theory*, also known as the *two-factor theory*. Herzberg concluded from his studies that some job attributes are hygiene factors; they are important and cause employee dissatisfaction if not present at an acceptable level. Hygiene factors include such things as pay, supervision, working conditions, and work rules and policies. The presence of hygiene factors, according to Herzberg, will not motivate employees. Factors that do provide motivation include the work itself, recognition, achievement, responsibility, and opportunity for advancement.[9] These factors are basically the self-actualization needs found at the top of Maslow's hierarchy (see chapter 10). Herzberg's theory has received a great deal of discussion over the years, both pro and con. However, managers and job-design specialists generally agree that when designing jobs, opportunities for meaningful and challenging work, individual responsibility, achievement, and recognition should be maximized to provide motivating jobs.

Douglas McGregor's *theory X* and *theory Y* emphasized that employees' motivation and performance are strongly influenced by their beliefs. He concluded that theory X managers believe that:

- The average human being has an inherent dislike of work and will avoid it if possible.
- Because of this characteristic dislike of work, most people must be coerced, controlled, directed, and threatened with punishment to get them to put forth adequate effort toward the achievement of organizational objectives.
- The average human being prefers to be directed, wishes to avoid responsibility, has relatively little ambition, and wants security above all.[10]

Thus theory X managers will likely design jobs that are specialization intense and require constant, close supervision. Theory Y managers, however, believe that:

- The expenditure of physical and mental effort in work is as natural as play or rest. Depending upon controllable conditions, work may be a source of satisfaction (and will be voluntarily performed) or a source of punishment (and will be avoided if possible).
- External control and the threat of punishment are not the only means for bringing about effort toward achieving organizational objectives. Individuals will exercise self-direction and self-control in the service of objectives to which they are committed.
- Commitment to objectives is a function of the rewards associated with their achievement. The most significant of such rewards (e.g., the satisfaction of ego and self-actualization needs) can be direct products of the effort directed toward achieving organizational objectives.
- The average human being learns, under proper conditions, not only to accept but also to seek responsibility.
- The capacity to exercise a relatively high degree of imagination, ingenuity, and creativity in the solution of organizational problems is widely, not narrowly, distributed in the population.
- Under the conditions of modern organizational life, the intellectual potentialities of the average human beings are only partially used.[11]

Thus theory Y managers will likely design jobs that are motivation intense. McGregor believed that managers should adopt the theory Y approach if they want to maximize employee motivation and productivity. This approach emphasizes the need for employees to achieve personal satisfaction from their work.

A theory Z has been proposed by William Ouchi. This theory emphasizes that employees should have direct input into the design of their work and the improvement of efficiency through quality circles, a method of participative management. If employees are given the opportunity by management, they can work together (in quality circles) to identify and analyze work-related activities and problems and develop effective solutions.[12]

Design Solutions

Since Walker and Guest's study, organizations throughout the world have been grappling with the problem of job design. Although specialized jobs usually increase productivity on specific tasks, they usually result in dissatisfied workers. Employee productivity is what a firm usually considers most important when designing jobs. The advantages of jobs designed to be highly motivating are apparent, but it is often hard to measure the dollar value of lower absenteeism or higher quality.

Productivity is the ratio of some measurable unit of output to some unit of input.[13] To evaluate productivity, an organization must measure two variables: the output produced by an employee and the input given by the employee. Productivity is a measure of efficiency, or the amount of work employees accomplish during each workday. A familiar measure of productivity is miles per gallon; how many miles an automobile can be driven on each gallon of gasoline is a measure of that automobile's productivity.[14]

When measuring productivity, the denominator of the ratio is usually the number of hours worked. The numerator changes according to the work being accomplished. That is, the numerator is the unit by which employees' production is measured, such as the

units produced per hour, the customers served per day, or the clients contacted per week. In measuring plant output, labor-hour equivalents should be used in measuring productivity. Products should be expressed in terms of the hours required to produce them. This method is preferable to using dollar measures, which change quickly as costs and inflation change their values.[15]

Managers often rely on measures of productivity to gauge the efficiency of their departments. Supervisors interested in the direct productivity of employees may disregard other indices that increase the unit cost, such as absenteeism, turnover, or product quality. Thus, the advantages of highly specialized jobs are overemphasized when only the direct productivity of specialization is measured. Managers should also consider the indirect costs of job specialization in doing productivity estimates.

How much does turnover cost an organization? Administrators have only begun to measure the cost of turnover accurately. One cost estimate for a firm losing a college graduate who was on the job for two years is $2,000 or more.[16] The costs of absenteeism are measured more frequently because it is easier to measure those costs than to measure the costs of turnover, loyalty, or tenure. An example of how the costs of absenteeism are computed is illustrated in a later chapter.

During the 1960s, personnel managers began realizing that highly specialized jobs were greatly increasing total personnel costs.[17] Therefore, alternative solutions to the problems of job specialization were explored. Many of the first programs designed to ease the boredom of specialized jobs are still in existence. Some of the techniques considered highly effective by some organizations are considered ineffective by other organizations and partially effective by still others. There is no easy solution to the problem of motivating employees with highly specialized jobs. Nor is there an easy way to design jobs which will both motivate the employee and maintain maximum levels of productivity.

Pay Increases One of the most common techniques to solve the problem of lack of employee motivation is a round of pay increases. Managers and personnel officials have turned to the pay increase as a solution to many problems for decades. The pay increase gives an employee a greater sense of worth, more take-home pay, and more reason to stay with the organization in a job which my be boring or unchallenging.

How successful is the pay increase at solving motivational problems? The answer expressed by most personnel officers and managers is "not very." A good example of why pay increases do not solve employees' problems was demonstrated by the experience of a midwestern manufacturing firm. During a ten-year period, the firm's absentee level was close to 20 percent. Management decided that a major pay increase would make employees feel that their work was highly valued and consequently would decrease absenteeism, the organization's greatest problem. The level of absenteeism dropped during the first six months after the pay raise. However, one year later, absenteeism was higher than ever before. Why such a reaction? Possibly because once modern employees reach comfortable income levels, they value their leisure time much more than did their parents and grandparents. With a higher wage scale, employees can work fewer hours to maintain the same level of income. After a few months of working regularly for increased wages, employees realized that even though they held the same routine job, they could work fewer hours and still maintain the same standard of living. Therefore, the employee in a highly specialized, unchallenging job may not be motivated

by the additional income which can be earned by fewer absences.

Job Rotation Another technique designed to enhance employee motivation is job rotation, or periodically assigning employees to alternating jobs or tasks. For example, an employee may spend two weeks attaching bumpers to vehicles and the following two weeks making final checks of the chassis. During the next month the same employee may be assigned to two different jobs. Therefore, the employee would be rotated among four different jobs. The advantage of job rotation is that employees do not have the same routine job day after day.

Does job rotation solve the problem of boringly repetitive jobs? No. Job rotation only addresses the problem of assigning employees to jobs of limited scope; the depth of the job does not change. The job cycle of the actual daily work performed has not been lengthened or changed in any manner. Instead, employees are simply assigned to different jobs with different cycles.

Because job rotation does not change the basic nature of jobs, it is criticized as nothing more than having an employee perform several boring and monotonous jobs rather than being assigned to the same one.[18] Some employees dislike job rotation more than being assigned to one boring job because when they are assigned to one job they know exactly where to report and what work to expect each day. Workers quickly realize that job rotation does not increase their interest in their work.

Why then is job rotation still common practice? Although it seldom addresses the lack of employee motivation, it does give managers a means of coping with frequent absenteeism and high turnover. Thus, when absenteeism or turnover occurs in the work force, managers can quickly fill the vacated position because each employee can perform several jobs.

Job rotation is often effectively used as a training technique for the new, inexperienced employees. At higher organizational levels, rotation also helps develop managerial generalists because it exposes them to several different operations.[19]

Job Enlargement A third means of increasing employees' satisfaction with routine jobs is job enlargement, or increasing the number of tasks performed (i.e., increasing the scope of the job). Job enlargement, like job rotation, tries to eliminate short job cycles which create boredom. Unlike job rotation, job enlargement actually increases the job cycle. When a job is enlarged, either the tasks being performed are enlarged or several short tasks are given to one worker. Thus, the scope of the job is increased because there are many tasks to be performed by the same worker. Job-enlargement programs change many methods of operation—in contrast to job rotation, in which the same work procedures are used by workers who rotate through work stations. Although job enlargement actually changes the pace of the work and the operation by reallocating tasks and responsibilities, it does not increase the depth of a job.

The focus of designing work for job enlargement is the exact opposite of that for job specialization. Instead of designing jobs to be divided up into the fewest number of tasks per employee, a job is designed to have many tasks for the employee to perform. An enlarged job requires a longer training period because there are more tasks to be learned. Worker satisfaction should increase because boredom is reduced as the job scope is expanded.[20] However, job-enlargement programs are successful only if workers are more satisfied with jobs which have increased scope; such workers are less prone to resort to

absenteeism, grievances, slowdowns, and other means of displaying job dissatisfaction.

An early job-enlargement program at the Maytag Company is a good example of this approach. Maytag undertook fifteen job-enlargement projects during a three-year period. At the conclusion, Maytag managers observed the following:[21]

- Quality of production was improved.
- Production costs were lower.
- Employees reported higher job satisfaction. They especially preferred the slower work pace which resulted from an enlarged job that did not have a repetitive cycle and that required a greater variety of skills.
- Greater efficiency arose because of reduced materials handling and a stability of production standards being met.

Although job enlargement is still considered a valid means of addressing specialization problems, it has been augmented by a more sophisticated technique known as job enrichment. Most modern redesign projects involve job enrichment rather than job enlargement, although the two techniques have distinctly different applications.

Job Enrichment Job enrichment refers to a program designed to increase worker satisfaction derived from the work itself. Job enrichment changes the nature of the work to increase both the scope and the depth of a job. In a job-enrichment program the worker decides how the job is performed, planned, and controlled and makes decisions concerning the entire process. The job-enrichment approach to boring jobs is to give the individual employee more autonomy in performing that job. Employees decide how the job will be performed and receive less direct supervision on the job. As a result, the employee receives a greater sense of accomplishment as well as more authority and responsibility.

Job-enrichment programs are usually quite comprehensive; by their nature, they must involve large portions of the total work force in an organization. When one job is enriched, typically the functions of supervisors and other employees are altered to allow for the increased responsibility of the enriched job. Therefore, enrichment programs usually require a great deal of planning by top-level management, retraining of employees, and implementation by managers, who give up some of their authority and responsibility.

Job-enrichment programs often require a substantial change in a manager's leadership style and personal philosophy. Managers who have developed tight control over the operations within their areas must allow workers to make more decisions. A critical aspect of a successful job-enrichment program, therefore, is the ability of top-level managers to convince supervisors and lower managers that the program is in the best interest of the company and that their employees are able to take on increased responsibility and authority.[22]

Labor leaders have been skeptical of job-enrichment programs over the years. Typical responses range from mild skepticism to total opposition. Such negative feelings are not completely unjustified. In the past, managers introduced programs under the guise of "job enrichment" which increased output standards for employees or decreased the number of jobs by increasing the work each employee performed. Since most job-enrichment programs result in the employees' taking on additional responsibilities, determining whether a program will result in increased job autonomy or simply increase work loads is difficult. A well-known labor leader stated what many of his colleagues believe:[23]

Studies tend to prove that workers' dissatisfaction diminishes with age. That's because older workers have accrued more of the kinds of job enrichment that unions have fought for—better wages, shorter hours, vested pensions, a right to have a say in the working conditions, a right to be promoted on the basis of seniority, and all the rest. That's the kind of enrichment that unions believe in.

Job-enrichment programs can also be used successfully in service organizations. The First National Bank of Chicago, for example, redesigned the "paperwork assembly line" in a credit department. The 110 member department had been designed with highly specialized jobs. Tasks were fragmented for 80 percent of the employees; one person, for example, had only one task—feeding tape into a Telex machine. Over a six-month period, the employees and outside consultants totally redesigned all jobs by consolidating tasks to be performed by broadly trained workers. The employees then received training to upgrade their skills and were assigned to new, enriched jobs with 20 percent higher salaries. The result? The first year with the redesigned jobs produced:[24]

- Substantial increases in profits for the department ($2 million) and total volume sales.
- Higher employee job satisfaction and salaries.
- Improved customer relations due to shorter credit application approval time.

Autonomous Work Groups Job enrichment may involve autonomous work groups. Generally, when an autonomous work group is created, the group manages itself and controls the planning and decision making within the group. Members may elect their own leader or decide not to have a leader but to make decisions jointly. Typically, the group sets its own work quantity and even its quality output levels.[25]

Volvo Work Groups: Ten Years of Experience

Since Henry Ford designed his first automotive assembly line, all automobile plants around the world have been designed with one common principle—the machine-paced moving assembly line. The moving assembly line, by its very existence, required most jobs in an automotive plant to be designed with highly repetitive tasks. The line transports the car past a series of work stations where workers complete a small portion of the overall assembly required. The resentment against the machine pacing of the work, the repetition, and, above all, the boredom, have been confirmed by hundreds of thousands of workers, research studies, and many people who immediately think of the automobile assembly line when the subject of boring specialized jobs comes up—even though they have never even seen an automobile assembly plant!

Volvo, like all other auto producers, believed the specialized jobs caused high levels of absenteeism and turnover, lower product quality. Volvo also believed the specialized jobs were incompatible with the generally higher level of education in Sweden. Thus management sought a bold, innovative change in plant and job design for a newly planned facility. Volvo decided to build such a plant in Kalmar, Sweden. The new plant's design was founded in a new concept, according to Volvo President Pehr G. Gyllenhammar:

> The objective of Kalmar will be to arrange auto production in such a way that each employee will be able to find meaning and satisfaction in his work. That will be a factory which, without any sacrifice of efficiency or the company's financial objectives, will give employees opportunities to work in groups, to communicate freely among themselves, to switch from one job assignment to another, to vary their work pace, to identify with the product, to be conscious of a responsibility for quality, and to influence their own working environment.

The new Kalmar plant opened in 1974 and was considered . . . a breakthrough in auto manufacturing. The plant was, not just in theory but in reality, designed around the concept of the "assembly team." The teams of 15–20 people each have total autonomy over their work. Each team has its own materials inventory. The teams travel and work on metal transport carriers that are guided along magnetic tracks embedded in the floor. The carriers are constructed to allow workers to easily rotate car bodies 90 degrees to make all working positions comfortable. Workers can assemble the exhaust system while standing next to a rotated car on its side.

The first ten years' experience at Kalmar have produced mixed but generally very positive results. Designed for a production volume of 60,000 cars per year on two shifts, the plant, due to product sales, never exceeded 35,000 cars and in one year produced only 17,000. The planned second shift was not needed in the first ten years of Kalmar production, and therefore overhead costs have consistently been higher than planned. Absenteeism and turnover were higher than anticipated, possibly due to unexpected layoffs during low sales periods and a four-day work week experiment, which was abandoned.

The financial indicators of the Kalmar plant's first ten years were excellent. In comparison to other Volvo assembly plants:

- Kalmar reported the lowest total assembly costs/car of any plant.
- Direct labor hours/car were 25 percent lower than those of the closest plant.
- Overhead labor costs/car were lower than those of any other plant.

However,

- Kalmar had the highest depreciation costs and interest costs due to high initial investment.
- Electricity consumption was higher than that of other plants.
- The new employee training period is longer than that of other plants due to more complex job duties.

A random attitude survey combined with in-depth interviews concluded that most workers were very satisfied with the work group design. However, while they preferred the work group design, they did not like the job rotation used by many teams internally, and they generally believed that they had little control over their work methods or their work pace. These results were particularly surprising, since increased worker autonomy in these areas was a major goal of the team assembly design. Workers did report a high level of personal responsibility for avoiding job errors and a high level of personal interest in performing the job right the *first* time—a major quality control objective of the team design concept.

The wage system at Kalmar included a significant group incentive system based on production quantity and quality. Workers reported that they perceived the wage system as fair, and they believed that the incentive system stimulated them to achieve higher performance levels. Perhaps most important, a majority reported that they preferred no change in the wage system.

Volvo's management concluded that the first ten years of work teams at Kalmar were a success based on the "critical criteria of efficiency," which registered the following improvements:

- Total production time/car decreased by 40 percent
- Quality defects decreased by 39 percent

- Uptime (of production) increased from 96 to 99 percent
- Turnover of total inventories increased from 9 times/year to 21 times/year

Source: Adapted from Stefan Aguren et al., *Volvo Kalmar Revisited: Ten Years of Experience* (Stockholm: Volvo, 1985). Used by permission.

An early example of the autonomous work group involved the Sony Corporation of Japan, which first used work groups in the production of television sets. Rather than assembling the sets on the traditional assembly line, Sony tried autonomous work groups which selected their own leaders, set their own hours of work, and determined their own standards of efficiency and discipline. Each group was required to produce a certain number of completed units each week and was responsible for its error rate; the cost of deficient units was deducted from the group's paychecks. Sony's experiment was quite successful in increasing quality and productivity, as well as in reducing employee absenteeism and other common morale problems.

At the Xerox Corporation in the United States, a total redesign of jobs, workflow, and plant layout avoided a scheduled plant closing due to foreign competition. After only six months of study, a joint labor-management study team of other operations proposed the substantial changes as a means to cut costs and increase productivity. The heart of the change was a shift from individual job assignments to work groups. Each self-managed group was given productivity and quality goals and the authority to determine how to achieve them. New equipment and computers were also purchased. After only eight months, the total annual operating cost was reduced by $3.7 million. The redesign also produced a new collaborative spirit among all employees. Without reducing wages or benefits, they were competing effectively with foreign companies.[26]

Robotics Some experts believe that the technological revolution of the late twentieth century rivals the Industrial Revolution of the nineteenth century.[27] One of the most dramatic areas of development has been in robotics, or the use of robots to perform routine tasks. Industrial robots are often divided into two classes: *anthropomorphic* robots approximate the appearance and functions of humans; and *nonanthropomorphic* robots are machinelike and have limited functions.[28]

During the 1950s and 1960s, robots could not compete with human dexterity and human ability to make instant or complicated decisions. And though computerized automation was desirable, automated machinery could not easily be adapted to various production functions.

The development in the 1970s of the *microprocessor*, which automates production functions, and the *silicon chip*, a miniaturized system of integrated circuits, gave robots greater capabilities than were previously envisioned. The silicon chip can perform millions of calculations per second. Further, a calculation that cost 80 cents with 1950s computer technology was reduced to a cost of less than 1 cent with 1980s technology (with adjustment for inflation).[29]

The first generation of robots, which were built in the 1950s, performed simple jobs and had limited capabilities. The second generation of robots were built with the senses of vision and touch, making them more anthropomorphic in their complex capabilities and more adaptable to production needs. Carl Remick, a General Motors official, believes that second-generation robots also have decision-making capabilities, enabling them to react to their environment in a human like way.[30] Robots are particularly desirable for hazardous and dangerous jobs. In addition, a study conducted at Carnegie-Mellon University estimates that it will become technically feasible to replace *all* manufacturing operations in the automotive, electrical-equipment, machinery, and fabricated-metals industries with robots.[31]

The economics of robotics is quite simple. Robots, in comparison to human labor, can provide lower costs, higher reliability, and fewer errors. For example, the average labor cost in the United States has increased to about $15 per hour. Whereas the average cost of a robot is less than $5 per hour. Even more dramatic is that inflation will increase the cost of human labor, but additional technological advances will most likely decrease the cost of robotics.[32] General Motors, for example, recognizes that it can use robots at an average cost of $6 per hour for many functions previously performed by skilled workers at $20 per hour.[33]

At General Electric Company's Appliance Park in Louisville, Kentucky, refrigerator and dishwasher operations have been upgraded with $144 million in robots and other new assembly equipment. The new technology produced a 30 percent drop in field-service quality problems and a 20 percent drop in end-of-line repairs. The new robots perform most of the shaping, bending, and drilling work previously performed by workers. While employment was initially cut when the robots replaced workers, increased market share (already 10 percent for dishwashers) is actually expected to increase total employment over time.[34]

The increased use of robots is generally supported by both labor and management because of their concern for quality control and competitiveness in international markets.

Union leaders, anticipating the robotics revolution, bargained in the early 1980s for advance notice of the implementation of robots and for retraining rights so that members could develop new skills for long-term employment. William Winpisinger, president of the International Association of Machinists, argued that the replacement of human workers with robots will occur slowly and that unions should be concerned with a shortage of skilled workers to build and maintain the robots of the future.[35] In general, unions have not been opposed to robots if the affected workers are provided with the training necessary for the new jobs created by technological change. Although unions realize that robotics will reduce their membership, this is preferable to losing all jobs due to foreign competition.[36]

The Work Environment Designing and developing work spaces for employees is a critical and changing aspect of job design. The work environment—space, work surfaces, machines, light, and so on—affects employee morale, productivity, absenteeism, and turnover. The productivity considerations in the design of work spaces clearly take precedence over any status concerns. From the president's office to the mail room, the environment must be designed to maximize productivity. According to the facilities design manager at Sperry Univac in Blue Bell, Pennsylvania, work station design is "at the hub of solving the productivity demands" in the near future.[37]

A prevailing view among designers of work stations is that employees should participate in the design of their work environment and be allowed to personalize it with forms of self-expression. Other considerations of designers include adequate natural lighting, color to enliven the area, optimal layout of work space, and adequate rest areas (such as employee lounges). Over 50 percent of business offices designed in the 1980s have utilized *open-plan systems* to achieve these goals. Open-plan systems make use of panels to create modular work stations and work spaces without visible walls. Each employee's work area is nevertheless clearly defined. An advantage of such a system is that panels, tables, and desks can be easily moved as organizational needs evolve because of changes in size, equipment, or computer technology. Other advantages are relatively low costs, space savings, low maintenance, and great flexibility. Critics of these so-called erector-set environments complain about their lack of privacy (something managers may see as an advantage), high noise levels, and similarity of work spaces.[38]

Modern Job Design

In modern management the problem of designing jobs that are appealing to employees yet result in high productivity is a common one. When implementing a program designed to increase both the motivation and productivity of employees, management should consider the following issues:

- Is the problem one which can be addressed by enlarging the scope of most employees' jobs? Jobs traditionally designed to be routine and dull can often be improved by giving employees more and varied tasks to perform. Job rotation and job enlargement usually require minimal management, planning, and cost. More complete programs increase not only the scope of the job but, more importantly, its depth to make the job more motivating to employees. These programs are usually more expensive to develop and implement. Although job enrichment, autonomous work groups, and work simplification may involve greater

cost and time, they often reap greater returns.

- Any job design program should have two objectives: (1) to increase the general morale of employees in order to bring greater productivity and lower costs to the organization, and (2) to increase employee job satisfaction because jobs are more interesting and challenging. The objectives of both management and employees must be given equal weight because both must cooperate completely if such a program is to succeed.

- Different employees satisfy different needs in doing their jobs. Any job designer must consider that not all employees want either increased responsibility and authority or increased scope. A certain portion of the work force prefers specialized jobs so that they can easily learn their work, become proficient, and not worry about their job security. These employees often find personal achievement and growth outside the organization and do not seek high levels of autonomy and achievement through their jobs.

- Before considering a job-design program, an organization should carefully investigate the exact causes of employee problems. The design of the work may not be at the heart of those problems; they may be caused by poor supervision, lack of advancement, poor working conditions, or low pay.

- Finally, when embarking upon a job-design program, management should tap its greatest source of ideas and knowledge: its employees. This method was used to great advantage by Sony and Maytag.

American managers today face ever-increasing pressure to increase both the morale and the productivity of their employees, creating what has been called an "obsession with productivity improvement."[39] The causes of that pressure include growing international competition, a national decline in the rate of worker-productivity growth, and a rapidly changing work force.

The role of work in U.S. society has changed through the years. Work, defined as employment or productive activity, is an important part of every worker's life and a foundation of human society. Work shapes the country's economic wealth, the nature of friendships, individual self-worth, and individual values and world views. While job redesign efforts are important to the motivation and productivity of the work force, other factors such as employees' expectations, social norms, and concerns with nonwork parts of life are also critical factors.[40] Programs to increase productivity succeed only when they reflect the changing work values of employees.[41] At the heart of such programs is the need to meet the needs and expectations of the changing work force.

The change in the values and aspirations of modern employees has altered their attitude toward the work place. The post–World War II "baby boom" generation has matured and thus increased the average age of American workers, a trend which will continue past the year 2000.[42] The growing participation of women in the labor force has also helped change the needs and expectations of employees. The Bureau of Labor Statistics has estimated that between 1960 and 1985 the participation rate in the labor force for women rose from 37 to 54 percent while the rate for men declined from 82 to 77 percent.[43] The total labor force could be 60 percent female by 2000. Black and immigrant women began the trend; they were followed by young single women and mothers reentering the labor force after their children had grown. Finally, the trend included young mothers. Past social and cultural constraints, such as the stigma associating with working women, have all but disappeared. Although some women find work primarily to break away from the traditional household role, others work out of necessity. Only 25 percent of the female labor force is single; an additional 20 percent is divorced, separated, or widowed. The remaining 55 percent need the second income to keep pace with inflation or to supplement the income of their husbands. The educational level of the American work force has also changed. High school graduation has become a minimum norm for entry-level jobs, and the proportion of the U.S. labor force with a college degree rose from 14.7 percent in 1970 to 24.2 percent in 1987.[44]

Such changes in demographics brought a concomitant change in the "work ethic." The aspirations of the modern employee include greater emphasis on shared decision making, greater flexibility in the work environment, and greater balance between work and leisure[45]

Ergonomics Engineering the "human factor" in designing the employee's work station is often termed *ergonomics*. The relationship between the employees and their workstations is considered to include the machines used, lighting, noise, chairs, and so on. All of these factors can ultimately affect employee productivity. The IBM Corporation's *Ergonomics Handbook* (see Figure 3–2), stresses the need to design the job to fit the person in several respects, including:[46]

- *Posture.* Incorporate enough movement in the design of the job to prevent prolonged sitting or standing in the same position, which causes fatigue and discomfort.
- *The back.* About 80 percent of the U.S.

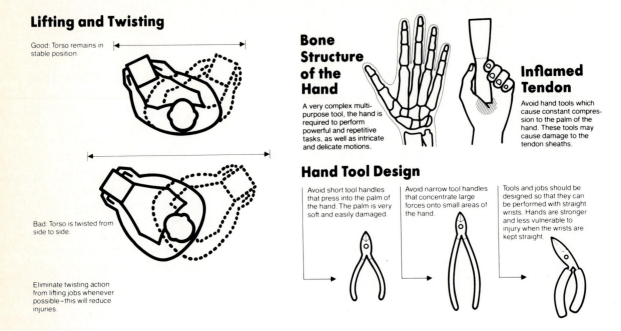

Lifting and Twisting

Good: Torso remains in stable position.

Bad: Torso is twisted from side to side.

Eliminate twisting action from lifting jobs whenever possible—this will reduce injuries.

Bone Structure of the Hand

A very complex multi-purpose tool, the hand is required to perform powerful and repetitive tasks, as well as intricate and delicate motions.

Inflamed Tendon

Avoid hand tools which cause constant compression to the palm of the hand. These tools may cause damage to the tendon sheaths.

Hand Tool Design

Avoid short tool handles that press into the palm of the hand. The palm is very soft and easily damaged.

Avoid narrow tool handles that concentrate large forces onto small areas of the hand.

Tools and jobs should be designed so that they can be performed with straight wrists. Hands are stronger and less vulnerable to injury when the wrists are kept straight.

FIGURE 3–2

Examples of ergonomics (Source: International Business Machines Corporation, *Ergonomic Handbook*. Used by permission.)

population suffers from back pain. The best way to reduce back injuries is to design lifting tasks carefully. Often a simple change in the layout of common lifting tasks can eliminate twisting of the torso when lifting, the most common cause of back injuries.

- *The Hand.* Excessive back-and-forth movement can cause inflammation of the hand. Women are three times more susceptible to repetitive-motion injury than men. An effective means of eliminating such injuries is to avoid the use of hand tools which cause constant compression of the palm of the hand.
- *The environment.* Noise can be distracting and harmful when it is higher than rou-

tine background noise. The use of sound-absorbing materials and machine covers can reduce many noises. Higher light levels are required for more intricate tasks such as detailed assembly or constant bookwork. Glare is one of the most frequent lighting problems. The position of the work in relation to the light source is critical. Windows and fixed ceiling lights can present difficult job design problems. The use of video display terminals (VDTs) presents significant design problems, since they require sitting for long periods of time and performing few eye, head, and hand movements. Eye strain and general fatigue can easily affect job performance. Thus, it is important to provide operators with ergonomically designed chairs for proper posture, adjustable terminal bases, and diffused lighting.

QWL Programs In the 1970s many different programs, often referred to as quality of working life or *QWL programs*, were designed and implemented to increase both satisfaction with the work environment and productivity. In such programs, the management, the union, and the employees determine together what actions, changes, and improvements can improve the QWL for all members of the organization and improve the effectiveness of both the company and the union. QWL programs attempt to establish cooperative relationships outside the traditional union-management relationship, that is, negotiations, grievance handling, and joint committees.[47]

QWL programs, some believe, hold the potential for significantly altering the conduct of labor relations. The national press and media have given a great deal of exposure to the so-called new industrial relations.[48] Unlike past efforts, QWL programs try to establish direct channels of communication between workers and their supervisors and give workers a greater voice in decision making.

One of the most widely heralded QWL programs was introduced by General Motors and the United Automobile Workers in the 1970s. This program, adopted by eighteen GM plants, was subjected to careful research and analysis. It was designed to enrich jobs by removing the most boring and repetitive tasks and by increasing employee autonomy. Plant-level data for a ten-year period showed that intensive QWL programs were associated with product quality and lower grievance and absentee rates. Analysts concluded that QWL efforts represent one possible strategy for breaking the traditional union-management cycle of high conflict and low trust.[49]

QWL programs offer hope by redirecting resources and energies from dealing with conflicts to concentrating on work problems, increasing worker motivation through greater participation in job-related decision making, and providing greater flexibility in human-resource management through less reliance on strict work rules and assignments.

Quality Circles One of the fastest-growing productivity improvement programs in the United States has been quality circles (QCs). The QC concept is generally one of people building rather than people using. Usually five to ten employees with common work interests meet voluntarily in groups once a week. The purpose of these meetings is to identify, analyze, and develop solutions to work problems. Solutions are presented to management for final approval. There is no reward for the circle members other than the recognition and satisfaction they receive from helping to increase efficiency. QC programs generally start with only two to three circles and then add circles as more employees become interested. Circles are independent; they are not part of the organization chart, members volunteer to participate, and they choose what problems to address and how to analyze them.

One characteristic that may affect the success of a QC is the level of self-confidence of its members. QCs whose members have high self-esteem generally are more skillful in "selling" their recommendations to top management. If the circle members do not initially possess self-esteem, they may develop increased confidence in their analytical and communication skills as the circle gains experience.[50]

QCs began in Japan in the early 1960s as part of a major effort to overcome its image as a producer of cheap, inferior goods. By the 1980s there was no question that Sony, Panasonic, Nissan, Toyota, and others had built a reputation for excellence. It is estimated that 80 percent of Japanese production workers participate in QCs.[51]

Lockheed Corporation, the first major American firm to try QCs, reported savings of $2.8 million and a 50 percent reduction in quality rejects—and they had just fifteen circles. Honeywell Corporation reported a six-to-one savings-to-costs ratio for its QC program, a ratio that appears to be the average for most QC programs.[52] QCs have experienced an unparalleled growth rate compared to other productivity enhancement programs in the private sector.[53] The growth rate is similar in the public sector.[54]

QCs are credited with producing quick, concrete, and impressive results when correctly implemented. Their advantages include:[55]

- The savings-to-costs ratios generally are higher than those achieved with other productivity improvement programs.
- Because the program is voluntary, employees and unions generally do not view them as another top-management cost-control effort.
- Employees enjoy the opportunity to be involved in management decisions, to develop new analytical and communication skills, and to improve the efficiency of the work place.
- Circle members who take advantage of the opportunity help their chances of promotion to supervisory positions.

The QC movement in the United States has entered a mature stage of development. The vast majority of programs have been successful, but there have been some failures. The most common causes of failure are poor training of circle leaders and members and, most often, a lack of genuine support from top

management. Such lack of support generally involves denial of circle proposals that QC members believe to be sound.[56] Thus, employee expectations of real involvement in decision making are raised at the start of the QC program and then lowered by top management's lack of trust and support. In such situations, QC programs may do more harm than good. Successful programs also face a problem: how to sustain positive results.

QCs may be a part of a broader change in American employee-management relations, one that emphasizes greater employee involvement and control in the work place. In cases of genuine commitment to increased participation in management, the next step may include *gain sharing,* in which employees share in any increase profits associated with the QCs.[57] Japanese QCs have operated with biannual bonuses to employees for many years. A more advanced form of the QC is *work-group autonomy,* which allows the QC teams to go beyond problem solving to daily self-management.

ALTERNATIVE WORK SCHEDULES

A relatively new approach to job boredom has been tried by a number of organizations. The nature of the work is not changed; instead, the worker is given an alternative work schedule. Forms of alternative work schedules include the compressed workweek, the discretionary workweek, and part-time work. Figure 3–3 shows the three main types of alternative work schedules and the various ways each is applied in organizations.

The Fair Labor Standards Act (FLSA) of 1938 established a standard workweek of forty hours for nonexempt employees by requiring overtime pay for hours over forty per week. The logical standard of a five-day workweek was quickly adopted by most employers

FIGURE 3–3
Alternative work
schedules (Source:
Adapted from J. W.
Newstrom and J. L.
Pierce, "Alternative
Work Schedules: The
State of the Art."
Reprinted with
permission from the
October 1979 issue of
the *Personnel
Administrator,*
Copyright 1979, The
American Society of
Personnel
Administration, 30
Park Drive, Berea,
OH, 44017.)

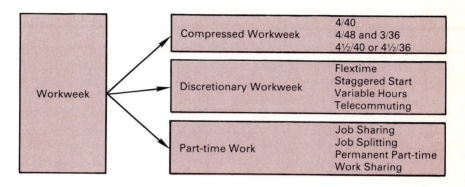

and became a social norm.[58] However, alternative work schedules began to gain in popularity when employers and employees began to realize significant advantages to altering the eight-hour, five-day norm that has existed for over fifty years.

Compressed Workweeks

Compressed workweeks are schedules with fewer than the traditional five workdays a week for forty hours, or 5/40. The hours worked per day are increased so that the hours worked per week still total forty. The most common compressed workweek is the *four-day workweek*. The four-day week is perhaps the oldest alternative work schedule, though there are a number of ways to devise compressed workweeks. Managers of large manufacturing organizations report substantial savings from compressed workweeks because of reduced start-up time and increased energy conservation. Savings typically are also gained from an increase in employee morale.

4/40 Workweek The usual four-day workweek consists of four ten-hour days, or 4/40. Sixty percent of all compressed workweeks fall into the 4/40 category. In practice, some of the forty-hour workweeks have actually become four nine-hour work periods as employees trade coffee breaks and clean-up time for extra hours off. With this scheme, managers believe that they are getting as much work accomplished in four nine-hour days as they might in a 5/40 workweek because they save start-up time as well as maintenance, which is often scheduled for the fifth day of work.[59]

With the 4/40 workweek, administrators primarily use one of two approaches. In the first approach, the company operates only four days a week; thus for three days each week there are no energy or start-up costs. In the second approach, employees work only four days per week but the organization actually operates seven days a week, using different shifts of employees.

The so-called eight-day week is similar to the 4/40 because employees work a four-day workweek; however, employees then have a four-day break during which the second-shift employees work ten hours a day for the four days. Thus, two shifts of workers alternate four-day cycles throughout the year. Under this four-day system, work is accomplished every day and total production is much higher than with other methods. The only disadvantage to the employee is that normal weekends and holidays must often be worked.[60]

4/48 and 3/36 Workweeks An alternative to the 4/40 compressed workweek is a week which rotates four-day and three-day shifts. In this arrangement, employees who work four twelve-hour days are off for three days. Then they work three twelve-hour days, followed by a four-day layoff. Thus, employees work forty-eight hours one week and thirty-six hours the next, or 4/48 and 3/36. For forty-eight-hour weeks they automatically receive eight hours of overtime pay. This system requires two crews of employees for each shift. One crew works from 9 P.M. to 9 A.M. as the night shift, while the other crew works from 9 A.M. to 9 P.M. as the day shift. In total then, four shifts of employees work twelve-hour days with three-day workweeks alternating with four-day workweeks throughout the year.[61]

One of the first organizations to alternate three- and four-day workweek schedules was the Monsanto Company. The program was designed by a committee of salaried and hourly employees. At the end of a six-month trial period, the four crews reported several positive results.[62]

1925

"A six day week, are you crazy? It will never happen!"

1965

"A four day week, are you crazy? It will never happen*"

2005

"A two day work week, are you crazy? It will never happen!"

FIGURE 3–4
The future workweek?

- Employee morale had improved. Ninety percent of the employees preferred the 4/48 and 3/36 to the old 4/40 workweek.
- Fewer shift changes resulted in increased productivity.
- Absenteeism decreased significantly and continued to decrease during the trial period.
- Turnover was reduced by almost 50 percent.
- There were no communication problems, since both supervisor and work crew rotated together. No fatigue problems were reported, and safety and quality records supported this observation. (Often this is not the case in four-day workweeks.)

The increased overtime cost was offset by the elimination of shift differentials which had previously been paid for rotating shifts. Thus, the organization benefited significantly, as did employees, without incurring many additional costs.[63]

4½/40 or 4½/36 Workweeks A third type of compressed workweek is the four and one-half day workweek. This workweek has been used with various total hours worked. Some administrators favor working for nine hours on Monday through Thursday and a half day on Friday, or a forty-hour week (4½/40). Their employees enjoy having scheduled time off for personal use. In other organizations, employees work eight-hour days on Monday through Thursday and work only a half day on Friday whenever scheduled production levels have been reached. Thus, employees are motivated to complete their work in thirty-six hours (4½/36). This incentive approach is particularly useful in organizations which produce individual orders and know which orders need to be finished by the end of the week or by a certain day.

A four and one-half day week has been successfully implemented in a small printing firm in a midwestern city. Previously, employees threatened to unionize because, among other grievances, they simply did not have enough free time to take care of personal business after work or on weekends. Management offered employees the incentive of leaving by noon on every Friday that all the work scheduled for the week was completed. By leaving at noon on Friday, the employees had time to shop and do other chores. After only a few months, morale increased significantly as absenteeism, grievances, and quality problems decreased. Employees were satisfied that they had the time necessary to complete their personal errands. This type of compressed workweek is very effective in manufacturing firms that cannot easily redesign their jobs to make them more rewarding to employees.

Discretionary Workweeks

Each of the three varieties of discretionary workweeks offers employees greater freedom in regulating their own lives. Retail stores, service agencies, and some manufacturers have met the demands of business with more satisfied, more productive employees working varied schedules.

Flextime A second type of alternative work schedule is flextime, (or flexitime), which provides a true alternative work schedule for employees, who may follow different schedules of work each day of the workweek. Flextime has been particularly beneficial to service organizations such as retail outlets, banks, savings and loan associations, and insurance companies.

Almost every survey shows companies reporting more advantages than disadvantages to flexible work schedules, regardless of type. Savings in employee turnover, absenteeism, and tardiness are reported so often and over such long periods of time that these advantages must be considered valid attributes of flexible schedules.

In a typical flextime system, the employer establishes a core time when all employees must work: for example, from 10:30 A.M. to 1:00 P.M. for a retail outlet where most customers come in during their lunch breaks. As Figure 3–5 demonstrates, the employer also establishes the total hours of operation during which the employee must work. Normally, the employee must work the core hours within the eight hours worked. If the core time is not worked, the employee does not get credit for the workday; usually an employee does not arrive at work at all if the core time cannot be worked. For service organizations, core time is a time during which most customers arrive, such as lunchtime for downtown retail organizations or five-to-nine for suburban shopping locations. The employee may choose a different starting and stopping time each day of the week, as long as the core time is worked and the total hours worked are within the hours the organization is open. The organization may alternate core times for dif-

ferent days of the week if this is necessary to meet customers' demands.

Most employees in the United States and elsewhere favor flextime operations. Employees particularly like the control flextime gives them over their personal lives. They can better schedule leisure activities and family responsibilities, and take care of personal business during normal work hours. Other flextime advantages for employees include reduced commuting time and faster shopping during slack times. Parents enjoy the advantages flextime gives them because they are often responsible for school-age children.

Organizations that have experimented with flextime report many advantages to the system: improved employee morale, increased productivity, and decreased absenteeism and turnover. Tardiness is practically eliminated since employees can start their total workday later and still work the same hours. Flextime also reduces timekeeping by supervisors. Employers report that employees usually arrive ready to begin working since personal needs can be taken care of before work. Another advantage is the reduction of overtime costs. By setting core hours during the busiest periods

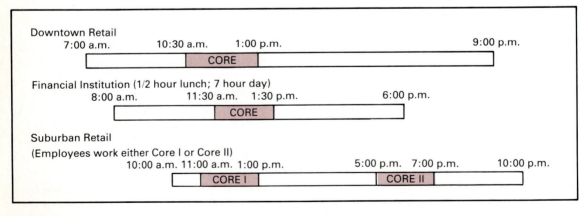

FIGURE 3–5
Flexible work schedules

of the day, manager's avoid scheduling overtime or hiring part-time employees for busy periods. Often retail and service organizations must overstaff to be sure that an adequate number of employees is available during a rush period. Overstaffing is less necessary in flextime.[64]

An American Management Association (AMA) survey of nongovernmental organizations with fifty or more employees found that almost 13 percent used some form of flextime. About one out of ten manufacturers and two out of ten finance and insurance companies use some form of flextime; other industries fall somewhere between those figures. Organizations responding to the AMA survey reported these advantages to their flextime systems:[65]

- Raised employee morale (almost always)
- Reduced tardiness (84 percent)
- Made employee commuting easier (75 percent)
- Reduced absenteeism (75 percent)
- Made recruiting easier (65 percent)
- Reduced turnover (50 percent)
- Increased productivity (50 percent)

Managers also reported that in many cases the quality of work during flextime was higher because employees concentrated on their tasks rather than on watching the clock. But administrators also found that supervision was far more difficult with the flextime system because of the staggered employee hours and fractured internal communications. Production managers had difficulty using flextime because interrelatedness of the work often required almost all employees to work together. In summary, the AMA's survey reported thirteen major successes with flextime for each failure.[66]

Flextime may be a key for employers who successfully attract and retain employees of diverse ethnic backgrounds. Arnold Manseth,

director of employee relations at the Pacific Northwest Bell Telephone Company, believes that trust between employer and employees is all that is required to implement flexible work hours. Manseth claims, "Today's employees are no longer content to follow their fathers' footsteps and put the job above everything else. Instead, they have learned to balance the job with other aspects of life, and are asking the employer to understand. For those [employers] who do, they'll find the quality of work will not drop. A happy employee is a productive one."[67]

Creating a flexible work force will also enable employers to retain older employees. By the 1990s, the United States will have the oldest work force in its history. Flextime allows older workers a great opportunity to ease their work demands while remaining productive.

Gus Tyler, assistant president of the International Ladies' Garment Workers Union, believes that flexible work hours will enhance U.S. competition in the international marketplace. If American companies were more willing to "loosen the boardroom grip" and encourage rather than disdain greater flexibility among their employees, they might find that they do not need to relocate to other countries. Instead, claims Tyler, we could regain paradise in America if companies were more flexible instead of cutting benefits and complaining about government overregulation.[68]

The Berol Corporation of Danbury, Connecticut, instituted a flextime program for its clerical and manufacturing employees, who may follow any work schedules as long as they are present for the core hours. The company required only that each department conduct its work flow as usual. For example, the customer service department had to be at least minimally staffed from 9 to 5 each working day; staffing arrangements were left up to the employees of the department. The Berol Corporation reduced absenteeism by 50 percent, eliminated tardiness, and decreased excused leave days by 80 percent. Berol reported that overall job performance improved and that flextime became a major reason for employees' job satisfaction and work performance.[69]

Staggered Start A second type of discretionary workweek system involves the staggered start, under which the employee chooses one of several alternative starting times and works a normal workday. Management determines how many employees will be needed at different hours during the day and defines different options from which employees may choose. Some managers prefer a group staggered start system, under which the entire work group that needs to work together to be productive works the same hours during the work day. The staggered start is not entirely new; it was first introduced in 1926 when New York City experimented with a similar system as a means of reducing rush-hour traffic congestion.[70]

A staggered start system does not have the many advantages of flextime. Employees do not control their workdays, as they do under flextime. The primary advantage for employees of a staggered start is that they may reduce their commuting time. Supervisors may allow employees to choose different starting times as an incentive in work performance.

The program initiated by the Colorado Springs division of Hewlett Packard is an example of flexible starting time. Under the Hewlett Packard system, day shift employees may come to work any time between 6:30 and 8:30 A.M. and night shift employees between 3:30 and 5:30 P.M. Eight and one-half hours after arriving, they leave. Very little data are available from firms which have experimented with flexible starting times, but Hewlett Packard reported that 97 percent of their employees favor the system.[71]

Variable Hours The variable hours system is similar to flextime in that employees have a wide latitude in defining their hours. Under a variable system, employees contract with their supervisors to work for a specified time each day, week, or month, with the possibility of varying schedules on a daily basis whenever agreeable to both parties. This system does not include the core-time component of the flextime system and avoids many of the communication problems flextime creates between employees and supervisors in organizing work on a daily basis.[72]

The variable hours system removes from the flextime system employees' ability to choose daily their starting and ending times. This control over personal and work hours is a major factor in the success of flextime systems. However, if a flextime system creates too many problems for supervisors, the variable hours system does give employees the latitude they need in scheduling their leisure time and family responsibilities. Under this system, the employee can still arrive at school on time to pick up children or attend continuing education classes at a nearby university.

Telecommuting New technological opportunities such as electronic mail and bulk-data transmission have created a new alternative in work scheduling called *telecommuting*. Telecommuting allows employees to complete some or all of their work at home. For example, computerized clerical work and computer programming can be accomplished at home because the job does not require constant supervision or contact with customers or co-workers. About 30,000 employees are working at home.[73] Estimates of the number of Americans who will use home offices by the year 2000 range as high as 22 percent of all jobs; the most common types of jobs will be computer data-entry tasks. IBM has over 2,000 employees with terminals at home.[74]

There are many potential benefits to telecommuting. Total labor costs may decline because employees work without direct supervision. Less office space is required, and employer utility costs are likely to drop. Employees enjoy flexibility in their work schedules, cost savings because of lunch at home and no commuting, and the opportunity to stay with their families.

But there are disadvantages to telecommuting. Employees miss the social contacts at work that are important for personal and professional needs. Also, they are not privy to the office grapevine or "old boy network."

Federal and state laws do not apply to telecommuters in many areas, such as safe working conditions, equipment, and employment status (full or part time).[75] In fact, the 1938 FLSA contains a "no homeworking" provision, which was upheld by a U.S. Appeals Court in 1984. The case involved the International Ladies Garment Workers' Union, which objected to retired women and housewives knitting at home because the union could not prevent "sweat-shop" conditions.[76] Unions in general are likely to be concerned about an increase in telecommuters, who are difficult to organize.

Telecommuting projects have produced an unexpected benefit in some cases—substantial productivity increases. Control Data conducted a program which resulted in productivity increases for individual employees of between 20 and 35 percent. New York Telephone reported increases of between 15 and 85 percent. The J. C. Penney telecommuting catalog-order program experienced not one paid sick day in its first two years.[77]

Part-time Work

Part-time work has become a very popular innovative scheduling alternative. The tremendous influx of women into the job market has increased the supply of part-time workers, as have family members looking for second incomes to keep pace with inflation. Managers have only begun to realize the benefits—higher enthusiasm and lack of boredom—which part-time employees may bring to specialized jobs.

Job Sharing In recent years, job sharing has evolved as an opportunity for career part-time employment. Job sharing generally refers to dividing full-time jobs into two or more part-time positions, often without particular regard for how the full-time job is divided. In personnel work, the term generally means that two employees hold a position together, whether as a team jointly reponsible for the position or as individuals responsible for only half of the position. So-called leisure sharing refers to a couple sharing a single position because they prefer the increased leisure time two household members gain by sharing a job. In this way, both of them can pursue careers.[78]

Job sharing as an alternative scheduling technique provides the organization with several possible advantages: increased productivity, a greater pool of qualified applicants, and reduced costs. The most common result is an influx of new energy and enthusiasm brought to the job by a second person. The company often gets more than twice the talent from having two workers perform the same job.[79] When job sharing was studied in the mass assembly department of a southeastern manufacturing firm, the scrap ratio was 12 percent lower and output was 7 percent higher for the shared-job positions. Workers found four hours to be far less tiring than eight and so were able to work at a faster pace. Also, fatigue-caused errors were greatly reduced.

The supervisor of a Wisconsin State telecommunications department stated that the primary advantage of job sharing is that employees working a few days a week or four hours a day are happier about their jobs than full-time workers. Many times the expenses of training, hiring of temporary workers, and overtime are reduced. Training costs are often reduced because one job-sharing employee can give on-the-job training to the other. Turnover costs are often reduced since job sharers with hours specifically tailored to their personal needs are less likely to leave the job for another one.

Job sharing has disadvantages. Communication problems may increase between job-sharing partners and between them and other members of the work force. Job sharing may make it difficult to assign responsibility to a particular individual. Benefit costs to the organization may increase, particularly if the Social Security (FICA) tax or state taxes for unemployment insurance cannot be prorated. Companies employing job sharers whose incomes exceed the FICA ceiling may pay additional FICA taxes. However, benefit costs usually decrease because the two part-time employees do not receive all the benefits of full-time employees. Perhaps the greatest obstacle to job sharing is that surveys show that job sharing is not positively viewed by managers. Generally they feel that job sharers do not take the shared job seriously enough or lack the commitment to a job that a full-time employee would have.

Steelcase, Inc., in Grand Rapids, Michigan, one of the nation's largest manufacturers of office furniture, first offered job sharing in 1983. After several years, Steelcase has concluded that job sharing lowers absenteeism and turnover by retaining employees who want part-time work. Equally important, it provides a resource for covering peak periods and offers a new option to older employees.[80]

Administrators considering job sharing should look carefully at several factors:

Eligibility Rules Management must determine the optimal number of job sharers in proportion to the total employees to minimize communication problems. Also, they must decide if job sharing will be available to current employees, outside applicants, or both. Management should also determine which jobs are to be included in the sharing program and how high up in the organization job sharers will be able to function effectively.

Job Descriptions Managers will need complete and accurate job descriptions to plan how two employees will perform the same task and which tasks are easily divisible between them.

Interview Process While interviewing, managers will want to be aware of the possibility of matching partners for job sharing so that fewer communication and personality problems will arise.

Fringe Benefits Management must determine equitable allocation of fringe benefits to job sharers. Most companies find that prorating benefits in proportion to salary is a good solution.

Performance Appraisals Administrators will need to consider whether normal performance-appraisal techniques are applicable for job sharers.

Promotion Management must determine if job sharers are eligible for promotion and to what extent their experience grants them the same amount of seniority as full-time employees.

Job Splitting A second method of scheduling part-time work is job splitting, in which the tasks of a single job are divided into two entirely separate part-time positions. The employees do not perform the same duties, as they do under job sharing; instead, the part-time employees may work the same days but on different tasks. Managers find that job splitting has most of the advantages of job sharing since employees are still performing in a part-time mode. Job splitting is sometimes referred to as job sharing since the latter term has wider usage and often includes situations where two or more employees work one full-time job.

Permanent Part-time Work Another method of scheduling part-time work is the time-tested permanent part-time. Retail and service organizations have found that permanent part-time positions have advantages. Permanent part-time employees can be hired at lower salaries and often do not have the morale problems of full-time employees. Further, employees performing permanent part-time work during peak demand hours are beneficial to organizations in a number of ways, as discussed in the feature "Peak-time Part-time Workers." Organizations catering to the general public find permanent part-time work schedules more beneficial than full-time schedules. Usually managers find that they need both types of schedules because technical or administrative positions cannot be adequately performed by part-time employees. Frequently, permanent part-time positions are restricted to entry-level positions such as clerks, tellers, clerical operatives, and sales representatives.

Work Sharing Strong economic growth and low unemployment in the post–World War II era generally resulted in few layoffs for employees. But severe recessions in the 1970s and 1980s brought long-term and in many cases permanent layoffs of thousands of U.S. workers. Economic recessions have become a way of life for many industries in the United States.

Work sharing reduces the number of employees who are laid off by asking all employees to work fewer hours. For example, Motorola, Inc., used work sharing by offering to keep employees scheduled for layoff if employees would work four days a week instead of five. Employees included in the plan would receive only 80 percent of their normal wages. Motorola had helped to pass an Arizona state law that allowed workers to collect unemployment compensation for the time not worked during work sharing. One employee, for example, received $12 in state unemployment due to a $40 cut in wages as a result of the work-sharing program. Only a few states, however, have enacted similar laws.[81] Many employees avoided economic hardship with this system. In addition, work sharing improved labor-management relations because everyone "pulled together" during hard times. Although Motorola continued to pay benefits to employees who would otherwise have been laid off, management believed that higher productivity from the thankful employees made up for the increased cost. Perhaps the greatest advantage of work sharing is that employees and their families are not subjected to the destructive psychological and financial stresses of a layoff, which sometimes leave lifelong scars.

An experiment in work sharing at the Van Nuys, California, General Motors plant produced mixed results. To avoid layoffs, GM and the United Auto Workers Union negotiated a plan whereby the reduction in hours was split between two shifts, each working for two weeks while the other was idle. The alternative was for the less senior half of the work force to be laid off indefinitely. The union members approved the plan by a 1,915 to 1,668 vote. When GM's management initiated the plan in 1988, the result was open hostility between the older workers who had given up their seniority rights (and their full-time

PERSONNEL IN THE NEWS

Peak-time Part-time Workers

The Provident Bank of Cincinnati, Ohio, has devised permanent part-time teller positions called *peak-time*. The peak-time system works the opposite of traditional pay systems because higher hourly rates are paid to employees who work fewer hours per day and fewer hours per week. The highest hourly rates are paid to those who report only two or three times per week and only work three or four hours per day. The innovative part-time, peak-time pay system was developed because efforts to recruit part-time employees at the hourly rate paid to full-time employees ($4.00/hr) had failed. Competent applicants were refusing to work for what they regarded as "counter help" rates, often about $2.50/hr after taxes and commuting costs. A peak-time ad in the local newspaper ($8.00/hr) attracted an abundance of attractive applicants, including some of the bank's full-time employees. The benefits realized by the bank from the peak-time teller program have included:

- An increase in minority applicants and hiring rates.
- Reduction of 90,000 man-hours as overstaffed full-time hours were reduced.
- Flexibility in scheduling, because of a large supply of tellers who could report on short notice.
- Reduced turnover and lower benefits costs (only full-time employees received full benefits).

Source: Stuart J. Mahlin, "Peak-time Pay: A Better Way to Attract and Keep Part-time Employees," *The Magazine of Bank Administration* (March 1984): 85–88. Used by permission.

---

hours) and the younger workers who had outvoted them. GM's management, however, was pleased with the work sharing plan because it allowed them to keep a mixture of older and younger employees.[82]

Disadvantages of Alternative Work Schedules

The alternatives just discussed are only the beginning of a trend toward new and varied work schedules. Managers, realizing that they cannot redesign all jobs to make them more challenging or interesting, use various scheduling techniques to give employees increased freedom to plan work or leisure time. The three major work scheduling alternatives—compressed workweek, discretionary workweek, and part-time work—have been successful for the most part. As Table 3–2 indicates, the advantage of alternative work schedules is a substantial gain in employees' satisfaction with their jobs and work environment. However, there are also disadvantages associated with alternative work schedules:

TABLE 3–2

A comparison of some alternative work schedules

	Four-day Workweek	Flextime	Job Sharing	Permanent Part-time
Employee Advantages				
Reduced commuting time	U	A	P	P
Less boredom on specialized jobs		P	U	U
Greater latitude in setting hours		A	P	P
Ease in completing personal business	A	A	A	A
Organization Advantages				
Decreased benefit costs			P	U
Increased energy conservation	U			
Less start-up time	U			
Decreased tardiness		A	U	U
Less absenteeism	P	U	U	U
Decreased wages		U	U	U
Disadvantages				
Fatigue	U			
Communication problems		P	P	P
Interrelated work problems		A	P	P
Poorer customer relations		P	P	P

(P = possibly, U = usually, A = always.)

Employee Resistance Employees often resist change of any type. Uncertain of what the new system will bring, and at least partially satisfied with the current system, many employees resist possible changes in their basic routine. When asked for their input about a possible change in work schedule, employees are concerned about the new schedule's effect on (1) their personal life, including their family; (2) organizational effectiveness, particularly work coordination; and (3) customer service. Their attitudes toward new work schedules tend to focus not only on personal and family effects, as might be expected, but also on the effects on the employer's cooperation and relations with customers. If such perceived problems materialize, managers will need to take action to alleviate the cause of the concern.[83]

Communication Problems Possibly the most common disadvantage encountered by any company using alternative work schedules is communication problems. Inconsistent work hours change common communication patterns; at times some employees may be inaccessible for group meetings or casual discussions. This problem can be minimized by proper management planning and correct implementation of the work schedule alternative which has been adopted.

Fatigue A major complaint of some employees about compressed workweek schedules is fatigue. Obviously, many compressed workweek schemes that involve longer days and mental and physical fatigue may become a real hardship. While many employees may not complain of fatigue directly, the later hours of the workday must be carefully monitored to make sure that fatigue is not becoming a major cause of increased injuries or decreased productivity during a compressed workweek schedule.

Interdependence of Jobs Real problems for flextime or part-time alternative work schedules are created by the interdependence of jobs. In fact, highly interdependent jobs such as assembly line operations probably make these scheduling procedures simply impractical. Flextime and other discretionary workweek programs have been utilized primarily by service or small manufacturing organizations which do not have highly interdependent jobs.

INTERNATIONAL HRM: MOTIVATION AND JOB DESIGN

A common stereotype that many Americans share is that people in underdeveloped countries do not have a strong work ethic. In fact, the economic failure of many Third World countries is often attributed to the easygoing temperament of the local population. Who hasn't seen a television commercial or advertisement depicting Caribbeans, Africans, Latins, or others as people who lie idle on a nearby beach?

National or ethnic "temperament," if it exists, is vastly overrated as an explanation for the failure to motivate people from underdeveloped countries. The problem boils down to not taking the time to learn why people work and how the job fits into their life.[84] Taking the time to learn the culture will usually pay off, especially in matching the right reward with the values of the culture.

In many cultures, monetary incentives in the form of higher wages and promotions for superior work will do wonders to motivate apparently lethargic people to become hardworking and ambitious. Jamaicans, for exam-

ple, who do not seem ambitious in their native country, work hard and do very well if they migrate to the United States. For many peoples, it is the opportunity to achieve, and not temperament, which is missing.

While the need to achieve would appear to be widely shared, there are cultures in which rigid class hierarchy restrains people from improving their social standing.[85] Western motivational strategies, such as incentive pay plans, often fail in Third World countries because the money cannot really improve their social standing. In the final analysis, the only way to know what will work is to know the national culture before designing jobs and identifying rewards.

CONCLUSIONS AND APPLICATIONS

- The tasks employees perform on the job and the variety, difficulty level, and autonomy of the job greatly affect job satisfaction and productivity.
- Modern employees, individually or in groups, are given greater responsibility for the design and control of their work. Simple, repetitive tasks are eliminated whenever possible, generally resulting in jobs that are more motivating and challenging. At the same time, some degree of job specialization is necessary so that new employees can learn their jobs quickly and make fewer errors.
- Programs such as job enrichment, job enlargement, work simplification, and autonomous work groups have resulted in redesigned jobs that were previously highly specialized and boring.
- QWL programs strive to change elements of the work place to meet the changing expectations of the modern work force. The younger, better-educated, and increasingly female labor force desires more challenging and interesting work, in-

creased decision-making roles (such as those offered through QCs), and a pleasant work environment.

- Alternative work schedules may provide employees with greater control over their hours, easier commuting, and greater ability to complete personal business during the week. Employers have also realized substantial benefits from such schedules, including reduced tardiness and absenteeism and increased employee morale, productivity, and quality. Discretionary workweeks, compressed workweeks, and part-time work offer different methods of scheduling, but they may not be equally beneficial to a specific organization.

- Volvo found assembly line boredom problems similar to those in U.S. plants. Their work group plant in Kalmar, Sweden, has proven to be an alternative worth consideration.

CASE STUDY
Design or Scheduling Problem?

Barsotti and Smith, Inc., a medium-sized manufacturing plant employing slightly over 300 persons, recently encountered turnover and absenteeism problems. The firm, located in a small midwestern town of about 20,000, produces tractor parts.

Only two years earlier, Barsotti and Smith had moved from Cleveland, Ohio, because of market considerations and union problems. Management believed that a midwestern location would greatly lower transportation costs since most customers were located further West. They also hoped that nonunion labor costs would be lower. About fifty employees decided to relocate in the Midwest. While the projected cost savings had materialized, the first two years brought unforeseen problems: absenteeism and turnover greatly disrupted production, and delivery dates were not being met.

President Jay Barsotti asked plant manager John Tong and personnel director Kate Merz to meet with him to discuss the situation.

Barsotti: "At first I thought these high levels of turnover and absenteeism were temporary problems of adjusting to a new location, but, my God, two years! What is causing this?"

Merz: "I'm getting good workers. Most are thankful to get jobs in this area so that they don't have to commute to a city or leave their families."

Tong: "I really don't understand it. Like she said, they're good workers. They don't loaf on the job or steal parts; they aren't even tardy! But after a few months they're absent a lot, and then they usually quit."

Merz: "We've had seventy percent turnover these first two years."

Barsotti: "Are they going somewhere else to work?"

Merz: "I don't think so. We are the largest employer in the county, and we pay better than anyone."

Barsotti: "Are they any different from the employees we had in Cleveland?"

Tong: "Yes, almost all of them are working wives and young men just out of high school. In Ohio we had almost all middle-aged or older men."

Barsotti: "Well, maybe the turkeys don't like the work."

Merz: "They seem to. . . . Most say they like working in small groups and electing their own supervisors."

Barsotti: "Well, maybe we should just wait and see."

Merz: "No, it's almost April, and the last two Aprils have been our worst turn-over months."

Barsotti: "Any suggestions?"

Tong: "Well, a couple workers have asked if they could work at night, but we don't need a second shift, and it would be too expensive to operate sixteen hours a day."

Barsotti: "We'd go broke fast."

Merz: "I've had a lot of women apply for part-time work, but we've always hired only full-time. Now that we're running out of applicants—"

Barsotti: "No! We tried part-time people five years ago; they don't have any loyalty."

Merz: "Well, we have had people who quit last year ask to be rehired; most had good records."

Barsotti: "I hate to bring back people who let us down once. We never did that in Ohio. Well, you two come up with something by Monday, when we meet again to decide what to do."

Questions

1. How can the organization determine what factors may be causing the high turnover and absenteeism?
2. What needs might the new work force have that are different from those of the Cleveland employees?
3. Describe some work-scheduling techniques that might be suggested to Barsotti.

EXPERIENTIAL EXERCISE
Can This Job Be Enriched?

Purpose

To explore the concept of job enrichment by determining whether a routine job has the potential for enrichment.

The basic steps to implement job enrichment include:

1. Select the job/jobs to be enriched. Criteria for selection include:
   a. Can changes be made without costly engineering modifications?
   b. Are job attitudes poor?
   c. Will motivation improve some area or areas of performance?
2. Thoroughly analyze the job, and develop a list of ways in which it may be enriched.
3. Screen out ideas that are considered "hygienic": for example, working conditions, pay, benefits, peer and supervisory relationships, and so on. Include

only motivators, such as job factors that enable the employee to make more decisions, and have greater responsibility for their work, as well as increased recognition.

The Task

For the following scenario, answer the following questions:

1. *Can* the job be enriched?
2. *Should* the job be enriched?
3. If you decide to enrich the job, *how* would you do so?
4. If you decide to enrich the job, what performance criteria would you use to determine whether your job-enrichment strategy was a success?

Bert Garner: Assembly-line Worker

Bert Garner works for General Electronics, Inc., a large manufacturer of home appliances. Garner is employed in a large plant that builds refrigerators. The refrigerators are built on an assembly line that snakes several hundred yards through the plant. He is responsible for attaching the freezer door to the refrigerator. As the refrigerator reaches his station, he picks up a door, several screws, and a screwdriver, and screws the door to the refrigerator. He does this more than 200 times a day.

Stacks of freezer doors are delivered to Garner's work station by another employee. Down the line, an inspector checks his work in addition to the work of other operators. Any item that needs to be reworked is removed from the refrigerator and set aside. The speed of the line—and thus the productivity rate—is determined by plant management. Any job changes are generally initiated by the industrial engineering staff.

When asked about his work, Garner responded, "It's a job. I'm not crazy about it, but it puts food on the table. Hell, who likes their job anyway? With the economy the way it is, I feel lucky just to have a job."

General Electronics' refrigerator assembly plant is about thirty-five years old. Capital improvements in the plant are seriously being considered by management to improve plant efficiency. Plans are to install more robot-type machines, particularly for jobs in which quality problems often exist. The labor-management climate is satisfactory, but the union's concern over management's plans for installing advanced technology has strained relations quite a bit.

KEY TERMS AND CONCEPTS

Compressed workweek	Job enlargement
Discretionary workweek	Job enrichment
Ergonomics	Job rotation
Flextime	Job scope and depth
Four-day workweek	Job sharing
Job design	Job splitting

Motivation intensive job

Open-plan systems

Permanent part-time work

Quality circles (QCs)

Quality of working life (QWL)

Robotics

Specialization intensive job

Staggered start

Telecommuting

Variable hours

Volvo work groups

Work groups

Work sharing

REVIEW QUESTIONS

1. In what types of organizations could flextime be most effective? Why?
2. Why are employees increasingly becoming dissatisfied with specialized jobs?
3. Why is it difficult to design highly motivating jobs that can be easily learned by most people?
4. What can be gained by using part-time workers instead of full-time workers?
5. Why might working spouses prefer a flextime schedule to a four-day work-week?

DISCUSSION QUESTIONS

1. Discuss the factors involved in redesigning jobs in an auto assembly plant or an insurance agency. Which company would find it easier to redesign jobs?
2. Would you prefer to work flextime, or a four-day, five-day, or eight-day week if you had an assembly line job? If you were a computer programmer? If you were a Fuller Brush salesperson?
3. If you managed a fast-food franchise, would you raise salaries or rotate, enlarge, or enrich jobs to decrease turnover and absenteeism? Explain your choice.
4. Can blue-collar employees on flextime be trusted to keep track of their own hours? Can white-collar workers? What factors would influence both groups?
5. How would you decide which work schedule would be most efficient in a car wash, an accounting firm, a gas station, or a veterinarian's office?
6. Could the Volvo work group design be successfully used in U.S. plants?

ENDNOTES

1. Toby Wall, "What's New in Job Design," *Personnel Management* (April 1984): 27–29.
2. John Ivancevich, Andrew Szilagyi, and Marc Wallace, Jr., *Organizational Behavior and Performance* (Santa Monica, CA: Goodyear, 1977), pp. 141–42.
3. Ibid., p. 141.
4. Ibid., p. 142.
5. F. W. Taylor, *The Principles of Scientific Management* (New York: Harper & Row, 1947).
6. C. R. Walker and R. H. Guest, *The Man on the Assembly Line* (Cambridge, MA: Harvard University Press, 1952).

7. Ernest J. McCormick, *Job Analysis: Methods and Applications* (New York: AMACOM, 1970), pp. 273–74.
8. James L. Gibson, John M. Ivancevich, and James H. Donnelly, Jr., *Organizations* (Dallas, TX: Business Publications, 1979), p. 282.
9. Frederick Herzberg et al., *The Motivation to Work* (New York: John Wiley, 1959): 59–83.
10. Douglas M. McGregor, *The Human Side of Enterprise* (New York: McGraw-Hill 1960): 33–35.
11. Ibid.
12. William G. Ouchi, *Theory Z* (Reading, MA: Addison-Wesley, 1981); pp. 1–7.
13. Mitchell S. Novit, *Essentials of Personnel Management* (Englewood Cliffs, NJ: Prentice-Hall, 1979), p. 178.
14. Ibid., pp. 178–79.
15. Leon Greenberg, *A Practical Guide to Productivity Measurement* (Washington, DC: Bureau of National Affairs, 1973).
16. Robert Sutermeister, *People and Productivity* (New York: McGraw-Hill, 1979), pp. 57–68.
17. Ibid.
18. Gibson, Ivancevich, Donnelly, *Organizations*, p. 285.
19. Paul Greenlaw and William Biggs, *Modern Personnel Management* (Philadelphia: Saunders, 1979), pp. 273–75.
20. Gibson, Ivancevich, Donnelly, *Organizations*, p. 285.
21. M. D. Kilbridge, "Reduced Costs through Enlargement: A Case," *Journal of Business* (October 1969): 357–62.
22. Novit, *Essentials of Personnel Management*, p. 183.
23. William W. Winpisinger, "Job Satisfaction," *AFL-CIO American Federationist* 80, no. 2 (1973): 9–10.
24. F. K. Plous, Jr., "Redesigning Work," *Personnel Administrator* 32, no. 5 (March 1987): 99.
25. Richard Woodman and John Serwood, "A Comprehensive Look at Job Design," *Personnel Journal* (August 1977): 384–86.
26. John G. Belcher, Jr., "The Role of Unions in Productivity Management," *Personnel* 65, no. 1 (January 1988): 54–58.
27. Sar A. Levitan and Clifford M. Johnson, "The Future of Work: Does It Belong to Us or to the Robots?" *Monthly Labor Review* 105, no. 9 (September 1982): 10.
28. George L. Whaley, "The Impact of Robotics Technology Upon Human Resource Management," *Personnel Administrator* 27, no. 9 (September 1982): 61.
29. Levitan and Johnson, "The Future of Work," p. 10.
30. Carl Remick, "Robots: New Faces on the Production Line," *Management Review* 68 (May 1979): 26.
31. Levitan and Johnson, "The Future of Work," pp. 11–12.
32. Whaley, "The Impact of Robotics," p. 61.
33. Levitan and Johnson, "The Future of Work," p. 12.
34. Rick Manning, "GE's Refrigerator Unit Warms Up to Change," *The Courier-Journal* (October 14, 1987): B1.
35. Levitan and Johnson, "The Future of Work," p. 13.

36. "Some Lessons Learned for the Decade Ahead," *U.S. News and World Report* *87*, no. 27 (December 31, 1979): 73–74.

37. Margaret Magnus, "Work Environment: Its Design and Implementation," *Personnel Journal* 60, no. 1 (January 1981): 27–31.

38. Ibid.

39. Edward J. O'Connor et al., "Work Constraints: Barriers to Productivity," *Personnel Administrator* 29, no. 5 (May 1984): 90–98.

40. Fred Best, "The Nature of Work in a Changing Society," *Personnel Journal* 64, no. 1 (January 1985): 37–42.

41. O'Connor et al., "Work Constraints," p. 90.

42. Best, "The Nature of Work in a Changing Society," p. 40–41.

43. U.S. Bureau of Labor Statistics, *Special Labor Force Reports* (Washington, DC: Government Printing Office, 1985) , pp. 18–26.

44. Sar A. Levitan, Garth L. Mangum, and Ray Marshall, *Human Resources and Labor Markets: Employment and Training in the American Economy*, 3rd ed. (New York: Harper & Row, 1981), pp. 275–77.

45. Best, "The Nature of Work in a Changing Society," pp. 40–41.

46. International Business Machines Corporation, "Ergonomics," *Personnel Journal* 65, no. 6 (June 1986): 95–102.

47. Less M. Oyley and Judith S. Ball, "Quality of Work Life: Initiating Success in Labor-Management Organizations," *Personnel Administrator* 27, no. 5 (May 1982): 27–29.

48. "The New Industrial Relations," *Business Week* (May 11, 1981): 85–98.

49. Harry C. Katz, Thomas A. Kochran, and Kenneth R. Gogeille, "Industrial Relations Performance and QWL Programs: An Interplant Analysis," *Industrial and Labor Relations Review* 37, no. 1 (October 1983): 3–17.

50. Joel Brockner and Ted Hess, "Self-Esteem and Task Performance in Quality Circles," *Academy of Management Journal* 29, no. 3 (September 1986): 617–23.

51. Michael R. Carrell and Christina Heavrin, *Collective Bargaining and Labor Relations* (Columbus, OH: Merrill, 1988), pp. 400–1.

52. R. Zemke, "Quality Circles—Can They Work in the United States?" *Journal of Applied Management* 56 (September/October 1980): 16–21.

53. H. N. Seelye and J. A. Sween, "Quality Circles in U.S. Industry: Survey Results," *Quality Circles Journal* 5 (November 1982): 26–29.

54. F. L. Crawford, *Quality Circles Results Measurement in the Federal Sector*, report no. 83-48OA (Maxwell AFB, Alabama, 1983).

55. C. Philip Alexander, "A Hidden Benefit of Quality Circles," *Personnel Journal* 63, no. 2 (February 1984): 54.

56. Robert P. Steel, "Factors Influencing the Success and Failure of Two Quality Circle Programs," *Journal of Management* 11, no. 1 (Spring 1985): 99–119.

57. Tomasz Mroczkowski, "Quality Circles, Fine—What Next?", *Personnel Administrator* 29, no. 6 (June 1984): 173–184.

58. Shirley J. Smith, "The Growing Diversity of Work Schedules," *Monthly Labor Review* 109, no. 11 (November 1986): 7–13.

59. "Flexible Work Schedules," *Small Business Report* (October 1978): 24–25.

60. Newstrom and Pierce, "Alternative Work Schedules," pp. 19–20.

61. "Flexible Work Schedules," pp. 24–25.

62. Ibid., pp. 25–26.

63. Ibid.

64. Keith Bernard, "Flextime's Potential for Management," *The Personnel Administrator* (October 1979): 51–54.

65. "Flexible Work Schedules," p. 24.

66. Ibid., p. 25.

67. James Fraze, "Preparing for a Different Future," *Resource* 7, no. 1 (January 1988): 1, 10.

68. Ibid.

69. "Flexible Work Schedules," *Small Business Report* (October 1978): 24–25.

70. Newstrom and Pierce, "Alternative Work Schedules," pp. 20–21.

71. Bernard, "Flextime's Potential for Management," pp. 51–53.

72. Newstrom and Pierce, "Alternative Work Schedules," pp. 20–21.

73. Richard Upton, "The 'Home Office' and the New Homeworkers," *Personnel Management* 21 (September 1984): 39–43.

74. Toby Kahn, "Vermont Home Knitters," *People Weekly* 21 (March 19, 1984): 64.

75. Marcia M. Kelley, "Exploring the Potentials of Decentralized Work Settings," *Personnel Administrator* 29, no. 2 (February 1984): 48–49.

76. Michael Lewis, "If You Worked Here You'd Be Home Now," *Nations Business* (April 1984): 38.

77. Upton, "The 'Home Office' and the New Homemakers," pp. 39–43.

78. Michael Frease and Robert A. Zawacki, "Job-Sharing: An Answer to Productivity Problems?" *The Personnel Administrator* (October 1979): 35–37.

79. Grett S. Meier, *Job Sharing* (Kalamazoo, MI: Upjohn Institute, 1978), pp. 1–3.

80. Kirkland Ropp, "The Solution: Steelcase Inc.," *Personnel Administrator* 32, no. 8 (August 1987): 79.

81. Heywood Klein, "Interest Grows in Worksharing, Which Lets Concerns Cut Workweeks to Avoid Layoffs," *Wall Street Journal* (April 7, 1983), p. 27.

82. Kenneth B. Noble, "Change in Seniority Rules Sparks War of Generations," *New York Times News Service* (March 15, 1988).

83. Randall B. Dunham and Jon L. Pierce, "Attitudes Toward Work Schedules: Construct Definition, Instrument Development, and Validation," *Academy of Management Journal* 29, no. 1 (March 1986): 170–82.

84. For an interesting discussion of specific motivation theories and their applicability to different cultures, see Geert Hofstede, "Motivation, Leadership, and Organization: Do American Theories Apply Abroad?" *Organizational Dynamics* (Summer 1980): 42–63.

85. For a discussion of how management styles vary across cultures, see Andre Laurent, "The Cross-Cultural Puzzle of International Human Management," *Human Resource Management,* 25, no. 1 (Spring 1986): 91–102.

Chapter Four
Personnel Recruitment

Chapter Outline

LABOR MARKET INFORMATION
    Operation of the Labor Market

HUMAN RESOURCES PLANNING
    Forecasts
    Entry-level Planning

RECRUITMENT SOURCES
    Internal Applicants
    External Applicants

METHODS OF RECRUITMENT
    Job Posting
    Direct Applications
    Employee Referrals
    Campus Recruiting
    Private Employment Agencies
    Advertising
    Hiring Alternatives
    Leasing Employees

COST-BENEFIT ANALYSIS OF RECRUITMENT

INTERNATIONAL HRM: STAFFING

CONCLUSIONS AND APPLICATIONS

Chapter Objectives

1. To explain how the labor market operates.
2. To understand the need for human resources planning (HRP).
3. To recognize the advantages of filling vacancies with internal job applicants.
4. To cite the keys to a successful job posting program.
5. To identify the advantages of filling vacancies with external job applicants.
6. To describe methods of recruiting qualified and available job applicants.
7. To develop alternatives to recruiting permanent new employees.

Resumania

Some time back, while excavating my desk top, I stumbled across an unopened press release of the variety which choke newsroom mailboxes and trash cans almost daily. However, I found this press release—from Robert Half, a New York employment specialist—well worth the reading. Half, who recruits financial executives, accountants, and data processors, has for many years been collecting inappropriate, unintentional, humorous, and self-defeating material that job candidates have included in their resumés. He calls it "resumania."

For example, a Salt Lake City bookkeeper wrote, "I am very conscientius and accurite." A Boston accountant stated, "My consideration will be given to relocation anywhere in the English-speaking world and/or Washington, D.C." A Cleveland computer programmer stipulated, "Will relocate anywhere—except Russia, Red China, Vietnam, or New York City."

Here's what some job hunters had to say when asked why they left their last job: "The sales manager was a dummy." "Responsibility makes me nervous." "The company made me a scapegoat—just like my three previous employers." "They insisted that all employees get to work by 8:45 every morning. Couldn't work under those conditions."

Under the heading of "I don't think they meant to say that," Half includes: "I am also a notary republic." "The firm currently employs 20 odd people."

Prospective employers are still trying to figure out the resumé of a San Jose, Calif., man who wrote, "Please call me after 5:30 P.M., because I am self-employed and my employer does not know I am looking for another job."

Resumania may be avoided, Half advised, by using logic and common sense and by making sure the completed resumé is written in a factual, business like, readable, and tactful manner. Examples of what not to do include the resumé of a Pittsburgh job seeker who described her ideal employer: "Perfect would be an organization beset with a variety of problems while simultaneously beginning to stir with the fever of acquisitions and diversification. As the nature of the job declines in the hierarchy of preferences, so obviously would come into play the decisiveness of compensating subordinating factors."

A New York credit manager (who should have pursued a career in law) wrote: "While I am open to the initial nature of an assignment, I am decidedly disposed that it be so oriented as to at least partially incorporate the experience enjoyed heretofore, and that it be configured so as to ultimately lead to the application of more rarefied facets of financial management as the major sphere of responsibility."

Finally, we are left to ponder the fate of an Omaha bank officer whose resumé read, "I can type, pitch hay, and shear sheep. I am also skilled at groundhog hunting and ballroom dancing." And what do you suppose ever happened to the Philadelphia computer operator who bragged, "I was proud to win the Gregg Typting Award"?

Source: Byron Crawford, "Resumania," *The Louisville Courier-Journal* (February 25, 1985): B–1. Reprinted by permission of the *Louisville Courier-Journal,* copyright 1985. All rights reserved.

EVERY organization regardless of its size, product, or service must recruit applicants to fill positions. Although there are few really new techniques in the recruitment field, recent emphasis on different recruitment methods and legal considerations have given personnel specialists a renewed interest in recruitment.

Recruitment is the process of acquiring applicants who are available and qualified to fill positions in the organization. Most often, personnel administrators will actively recruit only as positions become vacant. Through direct applications by individuals and by walk-in applicants, an organization can maintain a large pool of available and qualified applicants without much additional recruitment effort. But because of federal guidelines and the increasing need to hire the very best applicants, personnel administrators find it necessary to recruit even when they have a large number of available and qualified applicants.

The people most available for recruitment are the *unemployed,* who can be contacted through direct application, employment agencies, or by advertisements. Other sources often need to be considered when recruiting top candidates.

Part-time employees are good examples of recently developed recruitment sources. In past years some managers believed that part-time employees were not loyal to the organi-

zation and did not produce at the level of full-time employees. However, organizations have found that part-time employees are very productive and that there are qualified applicants who wish to work on a part-time basis. Due to a decrease in benefit costs and lower wages, part-time employees are often less expensive to the organization; if part-time employees can produce at the same level as full-time employees, they become an attractive alternative. Administrators have also found that part-time employees often have a greater enthusiasm for jobs that are traditionally boring and routine because they do not face constant repetition, day after day, for long periods of time.

Underemployed individuals are another group of applicants that can be successfully recruited. Due to a better-educated work force and a shortage of better-paying positions in many parts of the country and many occupations, some full-time employees feel they are underemployed because their jobs are unrelated to their interests and training. Many of these people are not actively looking for jobs, but they can be recruited by another organization because they would prefer jobs more in line with their training and skills.

Pirating takes place when search firms actively recruit employees from other organizations. Administrators may become aware of an able employee at a competitive firm or a firm in a related industry. They pirate an individual away from another employer by offering a more attractive salary, better working conditions, or other benefits. In some industries and for some large firms, pirating is preferred to hiring recent college graduates because trained, experienced persons can more quickly become productive and successful.

A rapidly growing labor market source is the *older worker*. Employers are increasingly turning to the recruitment of workers in the expanding forty-five to sixty-four age group (a 5 percent increase from 1985 to 1995) as the number of workers in the sixteen to twenty-four age group continues to decrease (a 20 percent decline). Several industries including fast-food, retailing, insurance, and temporary office help are actively recruiting the older worker.[1] Besides the change in demographics, Jim von Greup, director of public affairs for Walmart Department Stores, believes that there are other valid reasons to recruit older workers: "The older workers have good ethics and work habits. Generally, they have very good skills in dealing with the public, and in many cases they are good teachers for younger workers." Philip Johnson, human resources director of the Winn-Dixie supermarket chain adds, "They have the self-discipline to stick with a job and see it through."[2]

Bringing one's own retirees back to work has become common at the Travelers Insurance Company and many other firms. It has become usual, especially if there is a shortage of qualified labor, for employers to keep a pool of retirees on contract to perform various jobs if needed. An employer's own retirees can offer trained, low-cost, temporary or part-time help.[3]

LABOR MARKET INFORMATION

An organization's recruitment efforts must compare favorably with its competitors'. A firm's personnel department must realize that it is competing with other organizations in the local area for the same good job applicants. In most instances, some type of wage survey is used to maintain labor market information for the local area. Most professional organizations will conduct surveys not only for the local area but for regional and national areas as well. Professional positions require a greater regional and national emphasis because individuals seeking professional jobs are often more willing to relocate to take challenging jobs.

Within the local labor market, a firm can either compile its own survey of wages and positions or use published surveys for semi-skilled and unskilled jobs as well as clerical and other positions. Published surveys can be obtained from union groups, academic groups, and government sources. Local offices of the U.S. Employment Service are probably the most commonly used information source. The survey information available at these local offices is free and presented in a comprehensive, professional manner. The cost of personally compiling survey information for different jobs is quite prohibitive, even if it could be done completely and professionally. Because the U.S. Employment Service does the same surveying throughout the country and has comparative information for different localities, it is an attractive source of survey information.

One widely used statistic is the *unemployment rate*. Observing changes in the unemployment rate over a period of time can help a firm determine the labor market conditions of a local area. But the *labor force participation rate* for an area is also an important statistic which should be understood and utilized in the recruitment process. On several occasions the government has claimed that the total number of employees working had increased, while labor unions have indicated that the unemployment rate had increased.[4] Both statements can be true for the same period if many persons who are part of the *labor reserve* decide to join the labor force. Housewives, students, and retired individuals take jobs in hard times to supplement family incomes. The result is that more individuals are employed at the same time than the number of unemployed in an area increases due to layoffs and economic conditions. As a result, the unemployment rate increases even though more individuals are working in a labor market area.

Just as important as knowing the size of the labor market is knowing the going wage rates for the labor market. The recruiter must be able to make attractive, competitive offers to job applicants. As Table 4–1 illustrates, the U.S. Employment Service provides wage and salary information a recruiter can utilize to make the firm competitive in the local, regional, or national market.

The first step in the recruiting process is to determine the relevant labor market and its related information. The relevant labor market will determine which strategy and method of recruitment a firm will use. Recruiting methods are quite diverse in their expense and operation. Which one an organization chooses for its particular jobs is greatly affected by the survey information available.[5]

Operation of the Labor Market

Most economists claim that the labor market operates in a very predictable pattern: to get more individuals into the labor supply, a firm should offer higher wages as an incentive. This economic principle assumes that applicants are aware of the wages and benefits offered by different organizations. It also assumes that a wage and benefit comparison will be the basis of accepting or rejecting job offers. In reality, the labor market does not operate according to the simple economic model of wage levels and labor supply. Instead, most applicants who are looking for jobs or who consider themselves underemployed are not aware of the labor market in their area. Often they have only general notions, at best, of what the going wage rates are, unless they are in a heavily unionized or specialized field. Even if they do know the going wage rates for their jobs, they usually have a difficult time comparing the benefit plans of different organizations. Many do not even consider the benefit plans when comparing organizations. Faced with a lack of information, applicants often concentrate on the nature of the work, whether it is pleasant and desirable, the gross salary, and, perhaps, opportunities for promotion.

There is a tendency for hourly workers to seek jobs informally through newspapers and friends. Typically, hourly individuals do not know what the labor market wage rate is. If they quit one job before finding a new job, they feel compelled to accept the next offer they receive. Hourly workers also tend to stay in one labor market rather than look for jobs in other labor markets.

Professional workers generally know more about the market and have a better idea about the going wage rates. They tend to compare the benefits of various organizations to some degree. Usually professional workers have a broader geographic market, are willing to relocate, and will interview in other geographic areas. Membership in professional organizations that provide national and regional wage surveys helps professional personnel keep abreast of the job market. Typically, professional personnel will stay in their jobs until they find more desirable jobs; thus, they do not feel compelled to take the first new job that is offered to them.

HUMAN RESOURCES PLANNING

How many people will we need? What specific skills will be needed by employees three years from now that they do not currently

TABLE 4–1

Average weekly earnings of office, professional, and technical workers, by sex, in Louisville, Kentucky, for November, 1983

Sex, Occupation, and Industry Division	Number of Workers	Weekly Hours (standard)	Weekly earnings (in dollars)
Office Occupations—Men			
Messengers	35	39.0	198.50
Order clerks	186	40.0	339.00
Accounting clerks	86	39.0	346.50
Manufacturing	50	39.0	368.50
Accounting clerks III.	39	39.0	405.50
Office Occupations—Women			
Secretaries	1,207	39.0	329.50
Manufacturing	681	39.0	351.50
Nonmanufacturing	526	39.5	301.00
Transportation and utilities	102	39.0	373.50
Secretaries I	256	39.5	277.00
Manufacturing	102	39.0	308.50
Nonmanufacturing	154	39.5	256.00
Secretaries II	270	39.5	322.00
Manufacturing	158	39.0	354.50
Nonmanufacturing	112	38.5	276.00
Secretaries III	478	38.5	331.50
Manufacturing	287	39.0	342.00
Nonmanufacturing	191	39.0	316.00
Transportation and utilities	36	39.5	397.00
Secretaries IV	98	38.5	402.50
Nonmanufacturing	38	39.5	379.50
Secretaries V	105	39.5	400.00
Typists	227	38.0	211.50
Nonmanufacturing	209	38.0	209.00
Typists I	141	38.0	205.50
Nonmanufacturing	130	37.5	205.00
Typists II	82	38.5	217.50
Nonmanufacturing	66	38.5	192.50
File clerks	85	38.0	181.50
Nonmanufacturing	61	38.5	172.00
File clerks I	53	38.5	173.00
Nonmanufacturing	36	38.0	228.00
Receptionists	32	37.5	224.00
Switchboard operators	110	39.0	192.50
Nonmanufacturing	96	39.0	180.00
Switchboard operator-receptionists	219	39.5	228.50
Manufacturing	100	40.0	235.00
Nonmanufacturing	119	39.0	223.00
Order clerks	174	39.5	248.50
Accounting clerks	1,189	39.0	266.00
Manufacturing	352	39.5	308.50
Nonmanufacturing	837	38.5	248.00
Transportation and utilities	179	39.0	333.50

Sex, Occupation, and Industry Division	Number of Workers	Weekly Hours (standard)	Weekly Earnings (in dollars)
Accounting clerks I	124	29.0	207.50
Manufacturing	27	39.5	299.00
Nonmanufacturing	97	38.5	182.00
Accounting clerks II	604	39.0	233.50
Manufacturing	172	39.5	263.00
Nonmanufacturing	432	39.0	221.50
Transportation and utilities	67	40.0	280.00
Accounting clerks III	354	38.5	302.00
Manufacturing	85	40.0	322.00
Nonmanufacturing	269	38.0	296.00
Accounting clerks IV	107	39.0	400.00
Manufacturing	68	40.0	411.00
Nonmanufacturing	39	37.5	380.00
Payroll clerks	226	39.5	266.00
Manufacturing	106	39.5	273.00
Nonmanufacturing	120	39.5	259.50
Key entry operators	867	38.5	223.00
Manufacturing	200	40.0	272.00
Nonmanufacturing	667	38.5	208.00
Key entry operators I	667	38.5	222.00
Manufacturing	131	39.5	276.00
Nonmanufacturing	536	38.5	209.00
Key entry operators II	200	38.5	225.00
Manufacturing	69	40.0	264.00
Professional and Technical Occupations—Men			
Computer systems analysts (business)	173	39.5	619.00
Manufacturing	111	39.5	641.00
Nonmanufacturing	62	38.5	580.00
Computer systems analysts (business) I	27	39.5	473.00
Computer systems analysts (business) II	83	39.5	596.50
Manufacturing	43	40.0	608.00
Nonmanufacturing	40	39.0	584.50
Computer systems analysts (business) III	63	39.0	711.00
Computer programmers (business)	153	39.0	441.50
Manufacturing	64	39.0	498.50
Nonmanufacturing	89	38.5	400.00
Computer programmers (business) II	103	39.0	453.50
Manufacturing	54	39.0	490.50
Nonmanufacturing	49	38.5	412.50
Computer programmers (business) III	33	39.5	447.00
Manufacturing	26	40.0	414.00
Computer operators	197	38.5	323.00
Manufacturing	80	39.5	407.00
Nonmanufacturing	117	39.5	265.50

Sex, Occupation, and Industry division	Number of Workers	Weekly Hours (standard)	Weekly Earnings (in dollars)
Computer operators I	101	38.0	265.50
Manufacturing	31	39.5	326.50
Nonmanufacturing	70	37.5	238.00
Computer operators II	82	39.0	369.50
Manufacturing	36	39.5	454.00
Nonmanufacturing	46	38.5	304.00
Drafters	275	40.0	474.50
Manufacturing	268	40.0	474.50
Drafters III	91	40.0	381.00
Manufacturing	86	40.0	373.50
Drafters IV	59	40.0	465.50
Manufacturing	59	40.0	465.50
Drafters V	106	40.0	595.50
Manufacturing	106	40.0	595.50
Electronics technicians	219	40.0	442.00
Manufacturing	70	39.5	454.00
Nonmanufacturing	149	40.0	436.50
Transportation and utilities	148	40.0	437.50
Electronics technicians II	77	39.5	418.50
Electronics technicians III	126	40.0	478.50
Nonmanufacturing:			
Transportation and utilities	102	40.0	472.50
Professional and Technical Occupations—Women			
Computer systems analysts (business)	66	39.5	515.50
Manufacturing	27	39.5	547.00
Computer systems analysts (business) I	32	39.5	543.50
Computer programmers (business)	59	39.5	403.00
Manufacturing	36	39.5	413.00
Computer programmers (business) II	41	39.5	418.50
Manufacturing	30	39.5	425.00
Computer operators	180	38.0	283.50
Manufacturing	50	39.0	330.50
Nonmanufacturing	130	38.0	265.00
Computer operators I	125	38.5	258.50
Manufacturing	42	39.0	313.00
Nonmanufacturing	83	38.0	230.50
Computer operators II	51	37.5	343.50
Manufacturing	44	37.5	328.50
Registered industrial nurses	58	39.5	451.50
Manufacturing	57	39.5	452.00

Source: *Area Wage Survey: Louisville, KY, Metropolitan Area*, U.S. Department of Labor, Bulletin 3020-56 (November 1983): 7.

possess? These are two of the most difficult questions faced by personnel managers. Over-staffing causes excessive costs, but understaffing causes quality to suffer and opportunities to be missed. Thus, *human resources planning,* also called *manpower planning,* can be important in holding down costs while providing a productive work force.[6] No firm can rely on obtaining critical, highly skilled personnel at a moment's notice.[7]

A survey of over 2,000 chief executives showed that 82 percent thought that human-resources planning was their organization's most important personnel function. Yet many companies have virtually no such planning or provide it only for top administrative positions. Why? Human resources planning has been called a problem waiting for a solution. Practitioners say it has seldom been successful, has proven cumbersome and expensive, and lacks specialists in the personnel field.[8]

Forecasts

Determining the future supply and demand for human resources is a first step in developing a manpower plan. The *supply forecast* is the result of direct interviews with employees and the use of standard personnel data, such as work histories, skills acquired, job progression, and demographics. Modern computerized personnel systems have simplified the process of generating supply reports, such as the one in Figure 4–1.

The estimate of the total number of employees needed as well as the skills required is known as the *demand forecast.* Planners find difficulty in developing precise demand forecasts for various reasons, such as changes in sales patterns, technological innovations, and company reorganizations. Precise demand forecasts are not as important when there is great flexibility in an organization's work force, when employees are mobile and multi-

skilled, and (most importantly) when workers are easily found and hired. Why, then, bother with forecasting? Because people are geographically less mobile today than in the past, employees are retiring earlier, and jobs have often become too specialized to be learned quickly.[9]

Demand forecasts are developed from two main sources: standard statistical data and knowledgeable personnel. Statistical techniques, such as correlation analysis, can be used to detect significant relationships between staffing levels and such variables as the economic climate, the unemployment rate, the competition, and sales levels. But all statistical approaches contain a bias—they predict the future based solely on the past. Thus, critical factors may be omitted. Such factors might include a plan for a new product line, the introduction of new machinery, the loss of an important contract, or a change in government regulations. Thus, knowledgeable personnel must be involved in decisions about future needs.[10] Once the information has been gathered and analyzed, demand reports, such as the one in Figure 4–2, are generated with the help of the computer.

Once the demand and supply forecasts have been made, personnel administrators can plan on how to address projected shortages or surpluses. Specialized training, early-retirement incentives, and increased outside recruitment are a few of the techniques available to address an organization's needs. Keep in mind that the forecasts are not "airtight": not all mismatches are cause for action. It may be preferable to wait for further information or to see if projected changes take place.

Management succession planning (MSP) is commonly used to meet changes in mid- and top-level personnel. The process involves identifying projected vacancies and choosing replacement candidates for each position, estimating the promotability of

FIGURE 4–1

A supply report (Source: "Manpower Planning Systems: Part I," by Charles F. Russ, Jr., copyright February 1982. Reprinted with the permission of *Personnel Journal*, Costa Mesa, California; all rights reserved.)

Job Title, Name	Social Security	Date Assigned	EEO	Status	Status Date	Promotable To
Plant Superintendent Jackson, Ralph	123-45-6789	05-77		R	10-84	
Plant Engr. Mgr. Robinson, Larry	234-56-7891	08-79		P	10-84	Plant Super.
Plant Controller Brown, Sarah	345-67-8912	01-78	1F			
Supv. Process 1 Miles, Jack	456-78-9123	10-67	5M	Q	12-82	
Fleming, Mark	567-89-1234	02-69		R	10-84	
Pressler, Roy	678-91-2345	09-77		P		Plant Engr. Mgr.
Supv. Process 2 Johnson, Tom	789-12-3456	04-74		R	09-83	
Plant Pers. Mgr. Powers, John	891-23-4567	11-78		P	09-83	Supv. Process 2
Indust. Engr. Mgr. Rodriguez, Tom	912-34-5678	06-80	3M	P	06-85	Supv. Process 1
Safety Mgr. White, Judy	134-56-7891	02-79	2F	p	09-83	Plant Pers. Mgr.
Qual. Cont. Tech. Ling, Sam	245-67-8791	11-81	4M	S		

Status Codes

S = Satisfactory but not moving

P = Place/promote, hence moving

R = Replace/retire, hence moving

Q = Questionable: employee is on probation and is not moving

EEO Codes

F = Female
M = Male
1 = White
2 = Black
3 = Hispanic
4 = Asian
5 = American Indian

114

Job Title	New Position Needs						Turnover Needs						Promotion Vacancy Needs						Total Needs					
	'86	'87	'88	'89	'90	Tot	'86	'87	'88	'89	'90	Tot	'86	'87	'88	'89	'90	Tot	'86	'87	'88	'89	'90	Tot
Plant Superintendent									1			1								1				1
Plant Engr. Mgr.														1				1	1					1
Plant Controller		1				1													1					1
Supv. Process 1	1					1							1			1	1		1					2
Supv. Process 2		1				1													1					1
Plant Pers. Mgr.													1					1	1					1
Indust. Engr. Mgr.																1		1				1		1
Safety Mgr.													1					1	1					1
Qual. Cont. Tech.			1	1	1	3															1	1	1	3

FIGURE 4–2

A demand report (Source: ''Manpower Planning Systems: Part I,'' by Charles F. Russ, Jr., copyright February 1982. Reprinted with the permission of *Personnel Journal,* Costa Mesa, California; all rights reserved.)

each candidate, and, most importantly, identifying development and training needs to assure the availability of qualified personnel for future openings.[11]

Management succession planning is a method for career planning designed in part to satisfy Equal Employment Opportunity Commission and Affirmative Action (EEOC/AA) requirements. The MSP system generates three reports. First is the supply report (Figure 4–1), which classifies each individual listed as satisfactory but not ready for promotion or placement on another job, as promotable, as replaceable or retiring, or as questionable because of probation or some other status. Second is the demand report (Figure 4–2), which shows new positions due to expansion, turnover, or promotion. And third is the human resources report (Figure 4–3), which shows the supply-versus-demand equation, including the name, job, and location of all those suitable for promotion. The purpose of the manpower report is to develop a zero balance between projected career changes and expected demand changes.[12]

An excellent example of how human resource planning can be tied to a firm's strategic business planning is provided by Robbins and Meyers, Inc., a multiproduct manufacturer with over 2,500 employees. The company instituted an annual planning cycle starting in September, as shown in Figure 4–4. Managers were provided background material, and planning dates were set. The planning process comprised the following steps:[13]

Identify Strategic Issues Managers identified issues that would constrain or enhance a business plan.

Conduct Organizational Analysis Managers developed a one- to two-year organizational plan to meet structural changes.

Forecast Staffing Requirements Managers identified open positions caused by turnover or growth.

Develop Succession Plans Managers developed individual succession plans for important positions.

	1986 Needs	Var.	1987 Needs	Var.	1988 Needs	Var.	1989 Needs	Var.	1990 Needs	Var.
Plant Superintendent	0	0	0	0	Robinson, Larry 1	0	0	0	0	0
Plant Engr. Mgr.	0	0	0	0	Pressler, Roy 1	0	0	0	0	0
Plant Controller	0	0	1	−1	0	0	0	0	0	0
Supv. Process 1	1	−1	0	0	1	−1	Rodriguez, Tom 0	1 3M	0	0
Supv. Process 2	0	0	Powers, John 1	0	0	0	0	0	0	0
Plant Per. Mgr.	0	0	White Judy 1	0 2F	0	0	0	0	0	0
Indust. Engr. Mgr.	0	0	0	0	0	0	1	−1	0	0
Safety Mgr.	0	0	1	−1	0	0	0	0	0	0
Qual. Cont. Tech.	0	0	0	0	1	1	1	−1	1	1

FIGURE 4–3

A human resources report, which projects both supply and demand. For each year and position, the report lists both the projected needs and the projected variance between demand and supply (e.g., the safety manager position in 1987 has a need of 1 and a variance of −1, or one position more than an identified employee suitable for promotion. (Source: "Manpower Planning Systems: Part I," by Charles F. Russ, Jr., copyright February 1982. Reprinted with the permission of *Personnel Journal*, Costa Mesa, California; all rights reserved.)

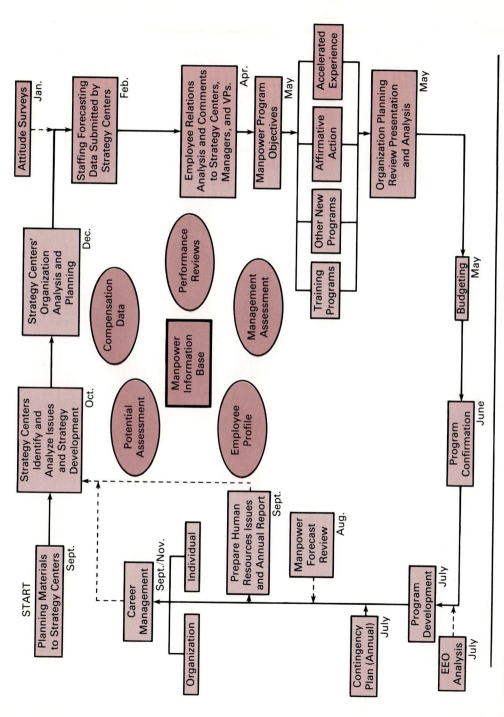

FIGURE 4–4

Robbins and Meyers of Dayton, Ohio, instituted human resources planning that was closely tied to the company's strategic business planning. As this flowchart shows, their annual planning cycle begins in September and proceeds through a number of specific steps. (Source: David R. Leigh, "Business Planning is People Planning," *Personnel Journal* 63 no. 5 (May 1984): 44–50. Used by permission.)

Identify Training Requirements Training managers developed programs based on individual and organizational needs.

Identify Development Plans for Selected Employees Those singled out in the succession plans were given individual development plans.

Conduct Organizational Review The human-resources plan of each division was reviewed by the president and manager of corporate planning.

Develop Budgets Approved plans were given budgeted expenses for implementation.

Management at Robbins and Meyers developed their human resources planning as a logical outgrowth of their strategic business planning. Their human resources planning constituted a continuous process—developing from the corporate business plan and helping that plan succeed.[14]

Entry-level Planning

Human resources planning for mid- and top-level positions focuses on specific individuals—their replacement upon retirement or their training, development, and promotion. Human resources planning is also used for entry-level positions, where the focus is not on career planning but on the forecasting of the number of entry-level applicants that will be needed at various times.

The personnel manager anticipates the company's needs, the training time that may be required, and employee turnover. As Figure 4–5 indicates, a personnel recruiter with a simple formula can estimate the number of applicants needed in order to fill various entry-level positions. The process can be used for each different entry-level position; thus, four or five different estimates may be made. If a firm typically hires a large number of entry-level clerical workers or sales representatives during the year, such estimates can minimize

FIGURE 4–5
Determining how many qualified entry-level applicants are needed annually

Formula

$$\text{Applicants Needed Annually} = \text{Current and Future Entry-level Positions Needed} \times \text{Turnover Rate} \times \text{Ratio of Applicants Needed to Every Applicant Hired}$$

Example

$$\text{Applicants Needed Annually} = 40 \text{ (clerical positions)} \times .5 \text{ (rate)} \times \frac{3}{1} \text{ (ratio)}$$

$$\text{Applicants Needed Annually} = 60$$

If training programs begin on the first of each month, then

$$\frac{60 \text{ Applicants}}{12 \text{ Months}} = 5 \text{ applicants needed to start each training program}$$

the time such positions are left open because of a lack of qualified trainees.

Personnel planning balances the long-run demand for employees with the long-run supply of internal and external applicants. Adjustments in training, the transfer of employees, and external recruitment can then minimize severe personnel shortages in future years.

There are a number of steps in determining the number of positions a company will need to fill. First, future customer demands are estimated by examining the market for products and services, the competition, and long-term growth potential. Once customer demands are estimated, decisions must be made regarding financial resource availability. Those resources determine the two critical inputs in the organization process, capital, and materials. Once financial determinations are made, the level of operation must be decided. Management estimates the required level of operation in future months and years so that it can economically purchase materials and equipment. Sometimes overlooked is an estimate of the level of operation and its effect upon personnel needs. Estimating the level of operation is critical to personnel planning because it involves not only the number of employees needed but also the different types of employees required for current and future positions.

RECRUITMENT SOURCES

Once management has determined an organization's staffing requirements, the recruitment process begins. The first decision made is whether a particular job opening should be filled by someone already employed or by an applicant from outside. Normally, firms recruit both internally and externally. In each case the advantages of recruiting outside the orga-

nization must be weighed against the advantage of recruiting inside the organization.[15] Table 4–2 shows a few advantages of each type of recruitment.

Internal Applicants

Of the several advantages to recruiting within the organization, probably of greatest importance is the increase in morale for employees who believe that the organization will reward successful performance and that they will be promoted to higher positions. The lack of possible promotion and advancement opportunities within an organization can be a major cause of turnover and dissatisfaction.

Managers recruiting within the organization also have the advantage of using personnel data maintained by the company. Interviews with supervisors and analysis of employee performance records can be added to the applicant's file during the recruitment process. At best, the organization can only guess at the completeness and objectivity of information received from other organizations. Only after years of interaction with the other organizations can a personnel officer be-

TABLE 4–2

The advantages of recruiting internally and externally

Internal Recruitment	External Recruitment
Increases morale of all employees	Applicant pool is greater
Knowledge of personnel records	New ideas, contacts
Chain effect of promotion	Reduces internal infighting
Need to hire only at entry level	Minimizes Peter principle
Usually faster, less expensive	

gin to measure the accuracy of external applicants' personnel files.

A promotion within the organization often leads to a vacant position, which can then be filled from within the organization. This chain effect on promotion means that two or more positions will often be filled at one time when internal recruitment is used. Thus internal promotions have a positive effect on employee morale because each promotion positively affects several employees.

When organizations promote from within, usually only entry-level vacancies are filled from the outside. The advantage of this approach is that it is not necessary to experiment with unknown people at high levels in the organization; individuals have a chance to prove themselves at lower positions first. Rewarding employees for successful performance also can be faster and less expensive than external recruitment. Therefore, because an organization uses its own records and sources of testing, internal recruitment can save money and time.

Employee Relocation Internal promotion with large companies often involves the relocation of an employee from one city to another. The work force of today may be less mobile than that of twenty years ago. The lure of a new home, better job, and higher salary has waned; instead, the prospect of locating in a new city often brings the anticipation of higher house payments, real estate hassles, and unhappy spouses who must find new jobs.

A study by the Equitable Relocation Management Group of Chicago concluded that the major reasons employees turned down attractive job offers that involved relocation were unenthusiastic spouses, anticipated difficulty in selling their homes, and higher interest rates on home mortgages.[16] Thus, successful recruitment of out-of-town applicants depends on the company's relocation policy

more than in past years. Two-career households and a fluctuating real-estate market have caused major changes in how employees view relocation.

Many companies have reevaluated their policies because of the increased likelihood that an employee will turn down an offer that involves relocation. Employers who recruit out-of-town applicants—whether they are internal or external applicants—can increase the likelihood that a candidate will accept a job that requires relocation if the following policies are instituted:[17]

- Providing relocation counseling about a new job for the spouse, school districts, good neighborhoods, and so on.
- Expediting the sale of a candidate's present home and the mortgage financing of a new one.
- Counseling with the candidate and family so that they view the location as a desirable place to live.

External Applicants

One of the greatest advantages of recruiting from the outside is that a greater number of applicants can be recruited than could normally be recruited internally. Outside applicants may bring new ideas, work techniques, production methods, or training to the organization, resulting in increased employee productivity.

External applicants also may have contacts that internal employees do not have. In sales, research and technology, and purchasing, for example, good external contacts are critical, and the recruitment of outside applicants with these contacts may be very helpful.

Recruitment of outside applicants for mid-level and higher positions will eliminate infighting by employees jockeying for promotion. Wherever infighting is severe, organizations begin to do more external recruiting to decrease internal dissension.

In recent years, organizations have sought applicants from the outside to minimize promoting employees to levels where they are unable to perform successfully. The concept that every employee will be promoted beyond his or her level of competence is called the *Peter principle*. This theory has validity; managers often have promoted employees who cannot perform as expected in their new jobs.[18] This theory may be a self-fulfilling prophecy for policymakers who blame the Peter principle for their own lack of good internal recruitment methods. However, any firm that promotes exclusively from within will experience the effects of the Peter principle to some extent.

One common method of avoiding the effects of the Peter principle—and the resulting dissatisfied employee—is the use of temporary titles. For example, an employee is promoted to "acting department head" for an unspecified period of time. If the employee is not capable of performing the job, a permanent department head can be recruited. Thus, the employee does not suffer the embarrassment of failing to handle the position; nor is a demotion or termination made part of the employee's permanent record. Whenever an acting department head proves capable, that employee can be made permanent department head.

Whether employees are recruited from inside or outside should be determined by the availability of qualified employees in the organization, the size of the organization, and the desire to keep up with contemporary ideas and methods. Employees should realize that external recruitment does not mean that no one is qualified to fill the position internally. Rather, it indicates the need for fresh ideas and new approaches to old problems.

METHODS OF RECRUITMENT

The two most common methods of internal recruiting are bidding and job posting. Bidding is common with unionized organizations; when an opening exists, qualified employees are notified that they may bid on the position if they wish to be considered for it. The employee with the most seniority receives the promotion. This structured process is usually specified in the union contract; promotions are based upon seniority and ability. There are a number of methods of external recruiting, including direct applications, employee referrals, campus recruiting, employment agencies, and overtime and temporary help.

Job Posting

One of the most popular methods of filling positions within organizations is job posting. A survey of over 6,000 companies indicated that job posting is the most common means of filling open positions. Posting has been used to fill over 75 percent of production openings, over 60 percent of clerical openings, and about 50 percent of professional and lower managerial positions.[19]

Although job posting is an effective, useful management tool, it can create severe employee morale problems if not handled properly. Managers should consider several aspects of the job-posting process.

First, the job-posting procedure should be clearly explained to the employees and should be followed to the letter each time a position is open. If the procedure varies according to the job or the particular employee applying for a position, employees may suspect that employer subjectivity is unfairly entering into the process.

Second, job specifications should be clear and should include the years of experience, skills, or training employees must have to apply for the posted position. This will make the decision process easier for management, assuming that strict seniority will not be used as the only criterion and that other factors such as an employee's personnel record and the results of interviews will be considered. When only a few job specifications are included in the posted position, the personnel specialist will have a larger number of applicants to review during the selection process.

A study of worker attitudes toward job-posting programs showed that vague or incomplete job requirements were a major source of employee dissatisfaction. Accurate job specifications that clearly detail the nature of the work, duties and responsibilities, and applicant requirements can significantly improve satisfaction with a job-posting program. This results in fewer and better applicants, fewer rejections, and less chance of employee resentment.[20]

Third, job-posting procedures should specify the exact period during which posted positions will remain open. For example, a position may remain open for fourteen working days after it is first posted, and applications will be taken until 4:30 P.M. on the fourteenth day. Also, the procedure should specify that employees on vacation or laid off will be notified by mail or employee publication of posted positions. The exact media to be used in the job posting process—that is, bulletin boards, employee newspaper, and so on—should not only be specified but also consistently used unless employees are notified about a change.

Fourth, the application procedure should be clear. For example, an employee may apply for a posted position through the personnel department or a supervisor. If the employee applies directly to the personnel department, supervisors feel that the chain of command has not been used. On the other hand, employees going through their supervisors some-

times feel that their supervisors may not wish them to receive the positions. A common compromise is to have employees submit written applications for a posted position to the personnel department with a copy to the supervisor. Finally, and perhaps most importantly, the personnel department should ensure that applicants receive adequate feedback once a selection is made. For example, when nine applicants apply for a posted position and one is accepted, the other eight employees may feel rejected. Although no amount of communication will entirely eliminate this feeling, it is imperative that the rejected employees receive feedback on the selection process. If not, the morale of one employee may increase while the motivation of eight other good employees may significantly decrease.

The rejected employees should be given a counseling interview by the personnel department or the hiring supervisor. The interview, which can help cushion the person's disappointment, should include the following:[21]

- Reasons for nonacceptance, but with emphasis on the person's qualifications and strengths that made him or her a strong candidate.
- Suggested remedial measures, such as training and education, needed to improve performance in the person's current job, possible new duties, and so on. Such counseling should be aimed at strengthening any weaknesses of the candidate.
- Information concerning possible openings they might apply for in the future.
- Assistance in the posting process, such as how to bid for a new job and how to conduct a job interview.

If properly used, job posting helps employees feel that they have some control over their future in the organization. Job posting often uncovers employee talent that supervisors would not voluntarily reveal. The supervisors may believe that the undue pressure on the department created by a good employee's loss outweighs the morale gained by having an employee promoted outside the department. Also, job posting avoids the awkward situation of an employee recommended for promotion who prefers to remain in his or her current job. When an unwanted promotion is offered by a supervisor, the employee may feel obligated to accept it or risk possibly never being asked again. Through job posting, employees not interested in positions do not apply.

Direct Applications

For most organizations, direct applications by mail or by individuals applying in person are the largest source of applicants. In the case of blue-collar jobs, walk-ins are often called *gate hires.* Direct applications can provide an inexpensive source of good job applicants to the organization, especially for entry-level, clerical, and blue-collar jobs. In relatively recent years, direct applications from new college graduates have been used to fill other entry-level positions.

The usefulness of direct applications will often depend upon the image the organization has in the community and, therefore, the quality of applicants who will apply directly to the organization. The size of an organization and its reputation determine whether applicants will seek out the organization rather than respond to other recruitment methods. Only the largest, best-known organizations in the labor market will receive a great quantity of direct applications. Organizations which receive many direct applications must develop an efficient means of screening those applications and keeping a current file of qualified candidates. While the cost of recruitment is low if large numbers of applications are received, the cost of screening and maintaining a file of applicants can be quite high. Medium-sized and smaller firms do not receive a large enough volume of direct applications to fill all their positions with available and qualified candidates without further recruitment methods.

Employee Referrals

In recruiting for exempt as well as nonexempt positions, employee referrals are one of the best means of recruiting applicants. Employees can be encouraged to help their employers locate and hire qualified applicants by rewards, either monetary or otherwise, or by recognition for those who assist the recruitment process.

Employees who recommend applicants place their own reputations on the line; therefore, they are usually careful to recommend only qualified applicants. When recommended applicants are hired, employees take an active interest in helping new employees become successful in their jobs.

Employee referrals are a quick and relatively inexpensive means of recruitment. In skilled, technical, or professional positions, employee referrals can help the organization pirate successful employees from other companies. Newly recruited employees from other organizations often bring new insights or new customers to the organization.

Some administrators avoid employee referrals because inbreeding and nepotism can cause employee morale problems, as well as a lack of successful and productive employees in future years. For example, friends of an employee rejected for promotion will also feel rejected. Naturally, employees who recommend applicants are dissatisfied when their applicants are not hired; they may show their dissatisfaction by not cooperating with the new employee. Typically, employee referrals do not help an organization recruit qualified minority candidates to meet equal employment requirements.

In past years the *old boy network* filled positions in some organizations with friends and relatives. This hiring of former college friends or neighborhood associates leads to a distorted mix of employees and usually an underrepresentation of minority groups in various job categories. However, today *networking* has replaced *old boy network,* both in name and in practice. The informal interpersonal network of professional contacts and resources that each employee establishes is an invaluable recruitment source. For example, *The Wall Street Journal* estimates that 70 percent of all executive positions are filled through personal contacts.[22]

Before taking advantage of the relatively inexpensive and easy method of recruiting employees through employee referrals, administrators should minimize possible problems by:

- Conducting objective recruiting, which will ensure compliance with EEO/AA guidelines.
- Ensuring that decisions about the hiring of applicants and their salaries are kept confidential. This process should always be confidential, but it is even more important when applicants are referred by current employees.
- Establishing specific policies on nepotism. For example, the company may not allow relatives to work in the same department or to supervise each other.

Campus Recruiting

Campus recruiting began to increase substantially in the mid-1980s as the number of college graduates began a projected long-term decline. The baby boomers have moved past their college years, and each succeeding class will be smaller than its predecessor until at least the year 2000. The decline in new college graduates began at a time when employers were increasing their recruitment due to the state of the economy in general and the shift to white-collar or professional industries in particular. Thus a new level of sophistication in campus recruiting began. Employers' prescreening of students has, in many cases, replaced the old method of selection from the placement office's resumé book. Prescreening programs are designed to identify the top students, often as juniors, and to begin to introduce them to employers. Professors often play a critical role in identifying such students. Citibank in New York, for example, hires professors to teach specific programs and involve their students where possible. Texas Instruments encourages company executives to teach at the university level, thereby identifying top students on the basis of firsthand experience. Employers in the expanding Sunbelt states who recruit in other states may carefully design recruitment brochures to emphasize quality-of-life factors and cost of living, as well as job-related information. Advanced word processing techniques also allow recruiters to send personal letters quickly to thousands of students. Recruitment videos, which can be used on campuses or for other recruitment efforts, have been effectively used by some employers who want to emphasize the quality of their work environment or community. The videos can be left at the university placement office for weeks and still provide students with a more realistic and personal view of the employer. Many campus recruiters still use the standard thirty-minute campus interview, handing students a copy of their annual report and playing a passive role in recruiting. These recruiters may be unhappy with their campus recruiting program, possibly because more aggressive recruiters have already signed the top students.[23]

Campus recruiting can be divided into two major sources:

- The trade or technical school that provides specialized education such as engineering or auto mechanics.
- The four-year college, which produces a wide variety of individuals with varying educational and skills levels. Compared to other forms of recruitment, campus recruitment is expensive and time-consuming for the organization. Usually the campus recruiter finds it very difficult to conduct in-depth, accurate interviews in the recruiting session. Often students who arrange for interviews later cancel or find that they are really not interested in the company or position after the interview has begun. Use of campus recruiting is dependent upon the condition of the economy and the job market.

A national survey of personnel departments that hired large numbers of college graduates investigated why recent college graduates are turned down after the initial campus interview. The reasons given, listed here in order of their occurrence, were the following:[24]

1. Undesirable personality traits, including lack of poise, poor presentation, no self-confidence, timidity, hesitant approach, arrogance, and conceit.
2. Poor scholastic record without a reasonable explanation for the low grades.
3. Poor personal appearance and careless dress.
4. Lack of enthusiasm and interest; no evidence of initiative.
5. Lack of goals and ambition, indecision, lack of interests.
6. Poor speech habits and expression.

7. Unrealistic salary demands, more interest in salary than in opportunity.
8. Lack of maturity; no leadership potential.
9. Lack of extracurricular activities without an adequate reason.
10. Lack of preparation for the interview; failure to get information about the company, resulting in inability to ask intelligent questions.
11. Lack of interest in the company and the type of job available.
12. Excessive interest in security and benefits: a "What can you do for me?" attitude.
13. Objection to traveling or moving out of town to a branch office.
14. Immediate or prolonged military service obligations.
15. No vacation jobs or work experience; no help in financing his or her education.

NCR College Recruiting Some primary disadvantages of college recruiting include the high cost per hire and the unwillingness of many graduates to relocate. Other disadvantages are the problems of decentralized hiring, the inconsistent standards at colleges, and the limited access to applicants. Such disadvantages have led some firms to decrease their campus efforts. But the National Cash Register (NCR) Company instituted a college-recruitment system that reportedly lowers the cost of college recruiting, increases the hire rate, and provides for decentralized hiring.

The heart of the system is a minicomputer at NCR world headquarters in Dayton, Ohio. Each year data on over 11,000 college graduates are made accessible to the thirty-five NCR locations nationwide, which hire 1,500 new graduates. The computer system ensures that local managers can scrutinize all job prospects. The current data on each includes a mini-resumé, school information, and interviewer notations. The system can also immediately generate personalized letters to students through the NCR word-processing system. NCR believes that its computerized college-recruitment system has produced these advantages over the traditional method of each department's recruiting on its own:[25]

- Improved quality of students hired because of wider access by all recruiters.
- Fewer on-campus visits needed to fill vacancies.
- Decreased cost per hire.
- Faster responses to students and universities, which improves working relationships.

Private Employment Agencies

Although personnel departments have increased their use of private employment agencies, some use private agencies only as a last resort, for the expense involved is usually prohibitive. Sometimes the employer pays 10 percent of the applicant's first-year salary as a fee to the agency. The pressure to recruit the best applicants from among the hundreds of applicants who would enable the organization to meet EEO/AA guidelines has enhanced the value of private agencies. In some cases, a good employment agency can save the personnel office valuable time by screening out unqualified applicants and locating qualified ones. Effective agencies may actually save the organization money by reducing recruitment and selection costs. Use of private employment agencies does not relieve personnel departments of any requirements under federal employment laws.

Only two or three competent agencies should be used by one organization; one specific agency should be used for a position when that agency typically has a good number of qualified applicants for that type of position. A *source trust* should be developed with

a particular agency counselor so that unqualified applicants are not sent. A counselor will work harder to retain repeat business than to fill just one immediate opening. Repeated contacts will help the counselor acquire a better understanding of the company and its requirements.[26]

Personnel managers should limit the applicants they allow an agency to send to four or five; this will keep them from being flooded with marginal applicants who probably could have been located without the agency. When limited to only four or five applicants, the agency counselor will do a better job of screening and will send only the people who have the best opportunity to be hired.

Advertising

A popular recruitment technique is employment advertising; in past years it has been primarily associated with newspaper classified ads. Many factors make advertising an attractive recruitment method. First, employers can attract employees from a wide geographic area. This has become necessary as employers seek to recruit through techniques other than the old boy network or gate hires. Second, many organizations find that they must recruit from nontraditional sources in order to meet EEO/AA goals. Third, employers have found that attractively designed and professionally developed recruitment advertising can be successful in attracting good applicants. Thus, personnel specialists have found that advertising can be just as important a tool in their field as in product marketing. The trend is toward an increasing use of professional advertising agencies.

Personnel recruiters can develop successful recruitment advertising for local newspapers, as well as trade and professional publications, by incorporating the elements of consumer advertising. Often an organization using advertising is not really trying to recruit the unemployed person, who will diligently follow up on most ads, but rather the under-employed person, who if given the right opportunity would welcome a change of jobs. To recruit this type of employee, the ad must be attractive enough to stimulate the employee to respond.

Recruitment advertising, still in its embryonic stage, has begun to use more of the marketing research tools common in consumer advertising. The current trend has been toward greater and more sophisticated local and regional recruitment advertising because of the high cost of relocating employees and, more importantly, the immobility of the work force. Two-career couples have made out-of-town recruiting far more difficult. According to George Rossi, corporate director of staffing and placement of the Digital Equipment Corporation, people tend not to want to relocate for technical and professional jobs, whereas people in the past often jumped at the chance to live in a new part of the country at a higher salary. To counter this immobility, Digital continued to recruit nationally but with a co-ordinated mixture of magazine, radio, television, and newspaper advertising. In addition, a job placement and assistance program for spouses was instituted at Digital.[27]

A successful recruitment advertisement is based on the answers to four questions, according to Bernard Hodes, president of a New York advertising firm. The four questions are:[28]

What Do You Want to Accomplish? Decide who you want to hire, how many people you want, and in what time frame. Develop accurate, current job descriptions, and summarize critical job functions to be included in an ad.

Who Do You Want to Reach? Estimate the demographics and motivations of those you want to respond. This helps select and shape the best media. Develop a psychographic profile of the target audience. The profile can be used to select benefits of the job or organization which would motivate a reader to respond.

What Should the Advertising Message Convey? Identify the facts which must be included, such as job duties and minimum qualifications. Also decide what image of the organization the ad should convey. Often the general advertising copy, logo, product lines, and the like can be incorporated into the ad so that the reader sees a connection between the common image of the company and the recruitment ad.

How and Where to Advertise? Decide which of the nine major types of advertising media should be used. One or more may be used after considering the strengths and weaknesses of each, as listed in Table 4–3. After one is chosen, a specific agent must be selected. For example, if a trade magazine is the medium, should *Engineering News-Record, Civil Engineering, Building Digest,* or some other agent be used?

For the job seeker, the number of recruitment ads in a local newspaper is not a reliable indicator of actual job opportunities. *Fortune* magazine editors closely scrutinized ads in a New York state newspaper and found that within a metropolitan area of about 273,000 people the classified ad section contained 228 employment ads. Of the 228 ads, only 131 (57 percent) offered full-time jobs in the immediate area. These ads included eight jobs offered through *blind ads,* which briefly describe a job at an unnamed organization, giving a box number to which an applicant must respond. Only 42 of 228 ads offered full-time jobs in the area to unskilled or semiskilled workers.[29] The number of employment ads in local newspapers has become less indicative of

TABLE 4–3

The advantages and disadvantages of the major types of advertising media

Type	Advantages	Disadvantages	When to Use
Newspapers	Short deadlines Ad size flexibility Circulation concentrated in specific geographic areas Classified sections well organized for easy access by active job seekers	Easy for prospects to ignore Considerable competitive clutter Circulation not specialized—you must pay for great amount of unwanted readers Poor printing quality	When you want to limit recruiting to a specific area When sufficient numbers of prospects are clustered in a specific area When enough prospects are reading help-wanted ads to fill hiring needs
Magazines	Specialized magazines reach pinpointed occupation categories Ad size flexibility High quality printing Prestigious editorial environment Long life—prospects keep magazines and reread them	Wide geographic circulation—usually cannot be used to limit recruiting to specific area Long lead time for ad placement	When job is specialized When time and geographic limitations are not of utmost importance When involved in ongoing recruiting programs
Directories	Specialized audiences Long life	Not timely Often have competitive clutter	Only appropriate for ongoing recruiting programs
Direct mail	Most personal form of advertising Unlimited number of formats and amount of space By selecting names by zip code, mailing can be pinpointed to precise geographic area	Difficult to find mailing list of prospects by occupation at home addresses Cost for reaching each prospect is high	If the right mailing list can be found, this is potentially the most effective medium—no other medium gives the prospect as much a feeling of being specially selected Particularly valuable in competitive situations
Radio and Television	Difficult to ignore; can reach prospects who are not actively looking for a job better	Only brief, uncomplicated messages are possible Lack of permanence;	In competitive situations when not enough prospects are reading your

TABLE 4–3
continued

Type	Advantages	Disadvantages	When to Use
Radio and Television (continued)	than newspapers and magazines Can be limited to specific geographic areas Creatively flexible; can dramatize employment story more effectively than printed ads Little competitive recruitment clutter	prospect cannot refer back to it (repeated airings necessary to make impression) Creation and production of commercials—particularly TV—can be time-consuming and costly Lack of special interest selectivity; paying for waste circulation	printed ads When there are multiple job openings and there are enough prospects in specific geographic area When a large impact is needed quickly; a "blitz" campaign can saturate an area in two weeks or less Useful to call attention to printed ads
Outdoor (roadside billboards) and Transit (posters on buses & subways)	Difficult to ignore; can reach prospects as they are literally traveling to their current jobs Precise geographic selectivity Reaches large numbers of people many times at a low cost	Only very brief message is possible Requires long lead for preparation and must be in place for long period of time (usually one to three months)	When there is a steady hiring need for large numbers of people that is expected to remain constant over a long period of time
"Point-of-Purchase" (Promotional materials at recruiting location)	Calls attention to employment story at time when prospects can take some type of immediate action Creative flexibility	Limited usefulness; prospects must visit a recruiting location before it can be effective	Posters, banners, brochures, audio-visual presentations at special events such as job fairs, open houses, conventions, as part of an employee referral program, at placement offices or whenever prospects visit at organization's location frequently.

Source: "Planning for Recruitment Advertising: Part II," by Bernard S. Hodes, copyright June 1983. Reprinted with the permission of PERSONNEL JOURNAL, Costa Mesa, California; all rights reserved.

The PQ Corporation's EEO/AA Recruitment Program

Paul Staley, president of the PQ Corporation, a chemicals manufacturer in Valley Forge, Pennsylvania, makes EEO/AA the responsibility of every manager. Not satisfied with the traditional EEO/AA recruitment emphasis on hiring goals and timetables, Staley made EEO/AA a part of the company's operating philosophy aimed at eliminating the type of work environment that many women and minorities find demoralizing—one in which they find a lack of support and respect.

Starting with this assumption, the personnel department developed a new staffing procedure. The procedure begins by developing a new position description based on a job analysis of each new opening. The description is posted internally, and candidate credentials are screened. The supervising manager then interviews selected candidates. The key to the new process is a two-part selection checklist that the supervising manager must complete for each candidate interviewed. The first part contains questions that determine how free the process was from possible discrimination. The questions include:

- Do you have a current job analysis for the position?
- Was the position posted internally?
- Is there a completed interview evaluation form?
- Were qualified minorities interviewed? Job-related reasons they were rejected?

The second part of the checklist correlates the job requirements and the attributes of each candidate. The checklists are designed to make managers think carefully about their selection decisions. The checklists are reviewed for possible discrimination. If a manager is perceived possibly to be discriminating, he/she must justify the decisions. Managers were told that the best decisions they could make would be documented, good, and legal.

Source: Adapted from Jeanne C. Poole and E. Theodore Kantz, "An EEO/AA Program That Exceeds Quotas—It Targets Biases," *Personnel Journal* 66, no. 1 (January 1987): 103–5. Used by permission.

the local economy because more companies are advertising positions not previously advertised. Some of these companies are advertising due to the increased success they have had with advertising positions; others advertise to comply with federal employment guidelines.

How much can an aggressive external recruitment program cost an employer? According to the Saratoga Institute of California, the 1986 median cost per hire for a new employee was $15,017. This included advertising costs, recruiter and candidate travel, referral bonuses, agency fees, relocation costs, and the recruiter's salary and benefits.[30]

Direct Mail   A relatively new tool for recruitment advertising is the direct-mail campaign. This technique is generally used to lure professionals who are employed but willing to consider a job with greater opportunities. For mid- and top-level management jobs, the best candidates may not respond to newspaper or trade-journal ads, because those candidates are not actively seeking jobs.

Direct-mail recruitment enables a recruiter to get the attention of desirable candidates and gives the employer an advantage over other employers looking for some prospects.[31] A highly successful direct-mail recruitment program was developed by the Martin Marietta Corporation. The company, which needed to staff a new program, had little success attracting experienced professionals with over two years of experience. Martin Marietta was looking for professionals who were successful in their current jobs, who were not actively looking in the market and thus not responding to conventional ads, and who would be motivated by a new and greater challenge. The Martin Marietta direct-mail program comprised primarily three steps:[32]

Obtain a Mailing List   From various list directories or other firms, a target mailing list

was obtained.[33] Martin used a 10,000-person list that concentrated on targeted disciplines within a 200-mile radius of Baltimore. For discretion, only home addresses were used.

Develop a Mail Package   Martin used a three-part mail package. First, the outer envelope was designed to capture attention. Second, the package contained an attractive company brochure, carefully designed to cover Martin Marietta's growth and technological successes, job descriptions for open positions, the company's location, and employee benefits. Third, the package contained a response card, a miniresumé requesting an applicant's name, address, present position, and college degree.

Follow Up Quickly   The response card was critical because it facilitated immediate response from individuals who were unlikely to have current resumés. A Martin Marietta representative telephoned each respondent quickly to keep interest high.

The results of Martin Marietta's program were typical of successful direct-mail programs: a high response rate of 4 to 5 percent, compared to a 2 percent industry standard; a low cost-per-hire ($700) for executive positions; and the filling of all open positions with highly qualified applicants.[34]

Hiring Alternatives

The three most immediate sources of additional labor are (1) current employees who work overtime, (2) temporary employees, and (3) leased employees. Assigning overtime to employees is an attractive alternative because it is a temporary rather than a permanent staff increase. Choosing overtime means using experienced, knowledgeable employees who do not require any additional training or orientation. But overtime also means additional fatigue for employees who have already worked their full shift and usually the expense of time-and-a-half or double-time pay.

Temporary help may be less costly than hiring new permanent employees, particularly for companies with great seasonal demands or for an unforecasted temporary absence of important personnel. In office administration, accounting, and engineering, temporary help can quickly be trained to be productive on the job with relatively low start-up costs.

The temporary service industry in the United States is booming. An estimated nine out of ten American companies use temporary services. Over 800,000 orders are filled *daily*. Why the demand from employers? Temporary services industry executives offer several reasons. The nature of their business forces them to provide trained personnel who are familiar with the latest office automation technology. Unsatisfactory temporary workers are quickly dismissed, and their companies are seldom contacted again. Thus, the temporary agency offers the employer trained, available personnel who can be put to work quickly and, if necessary, let go just as quickly. The cost and time associated with hiring permanent new employees make this an attractive alternative for many employers. Employers who have highly fluctuating staffing demands due to changes in the economy recognize temporary help as just that—a source of trained staff needed for only a temporary period of time.

Employers who use temporary services most often no longer view them as just a source of replacement secretaries. Certainly that is still a large portion of the business, but the downsizing of corporate America has provided temporary services with a large supply of highly trained individuals and many corporate clients, needing temporary manpower, that are wary of adding full-time personnel. Kelley Services, Inc., for example, has a program called Encore that actively recruits peo-

ple over age fifty. These individuals include many retired executives who can give an organization invaluable assistance without the costs of a full-time, high-level management position. Temporary services have enjoyed substantial growth in the small-business industry. The small entrepreneur who cannot afford or does not need full-time professional assistance can find it readily available on an as-needed basis.[35]

Employers considering using temporary services should review the following suggestions on how best to use the temporary service:[36]

- Develop a partner relationship with one service rather than a vendor relationship. Working primarily with one service allows them to learn your specific needs.
- Invite service representatives into your working environment to assess your needs before submitting orders.
- Before placing an order, compile as much information as possible about your needs—work experience, equipment, software, communication skills, and so on.
- Treat the temporary worker with the same courtesy as you would a permanent employee.

Leasing Employees

A new alternative to the traditional method of recruiting new employees is the practice of employee leasing. While the concept of employee leasing is not entirely new, there is a new breed of companies such as Contract Staffing of America, headquartered in Tustin, California. CSA hires workers and then contracts them out to employers that request employees with certain skills and abilities. Why the new interest in employee leasing? James Borgelt, general manager of Omnistaff, a Dallas leasing firm, believes his customers lease employees for several reasons. For example, small businesses cannot afford a pension program or other benefits that compete with those of large corporations. Thus they lose many good employees to large firms. However, Borgelt contends that his firm offers a competitive salary and benefits to its employees because it can take advantage of group rates. Omnistaff then leases the employees to small employers. Small employers also like not having the personnel administration duties such as payroll, W-2 forms, benefit claims, and so on, which are handled by Omnistaff.[37]

The costs of employee leasing are generally 5 to 10 percent of the payroll. However, when pension and other benefits are offered at a lower cost, the employer may find that leasing costs even less than 5 percent of the payroll. Ronald Pilenyo, president of the American Society for Personnel Administration (ASPA), warns that factors other than costs should be considered by employers. If the leasing company and the employer cannot come to an agreement on pay raises, for example, the employer may suddenly need to

hire a whole new set of employees. The leasing company becomes a third party in the employer-employee relationship, which may cause conflict. Common law requires the leased employee to be a *true* employee of the leasing firm, which therefore has ultimate administrative control.[38]

COST-BENEFIT ANALYSIS OF RECRUITMENT

The basic goal of recruitment is to locate, at the least cost, qualified applicants who will remain with the organization. Therefore, underqualified individuals who will later be terminated should not be hired; neither should overqualified individuals who will experience frustration and eventually leave the organization.[39]

A cost-benefit model illustrates the decision-making aspects of recruitment and stresses the economic implications of selection decisions. In the recruitment process, four outcomes are possible for each applicant, as shown in Figure 4–6. Quadrants I and III indicate correct

FIGURE 4–6
Four possible outcomes in the recruitment process

Applicant/ Employee Performance	Selection Decision	
	Reject	Hire
Successful Applicant/Employee	Incorrect Decision (False Negative) II	Correct Decision (Hit) I
Unsuccessful Applicant/Employee	Correct Decision (Hit) III	Incorrect Decision (False Positive) IV

Rate of success (hit rate) is computed as follows:

$$\text{Hit Rate} = \frac{\text{Hits (I + III)}}{\text{Hits (I + III)} - [\text{False Negatives (II)} + \text{False Positives (IV)}]}$$

Global Recruiting at IBM

IBM is a good example of the way in which the multinational enterprise can make effective use of its personnel. IBM has a policy of recruiting and developing host-country nationals for both research and management positions. It even decentralizes much of its R and D, using local technicians, engineers, and managers, while retaining centralized control over the ultimate use of the R and D. IBM also engages in local purchasing and attempts to keep a balance of trade by nation. It has host nationals, including local political figures, on its boards, and it attempts to act as a good corporate citizen in each host nation.

This geocentric concern for the social and economic welfare of all its managers and workers has resulted in an extraordinary loyalty to IBM among its personnel at all levels. There are excellent management-labor relations and a common corporate culture. Managers identify with the mission of IBM as the leader in the computer industry. Partly because of this method of human resource management, IBM has been successful in retaining its world share in the face of ever-increasing global competition.

Source: Alan M. Rugman, Donald J. Lecraw, and Laurence D. Booth, *International Business* (New York: McGraw-Hill, 1985), p. 400.

decisions: hiring applicants who eventually become successful employees and not hiring applicants who would have eventually become failures as employees. In quadrants II and IV, however, management makes incorrect decisions. In quadrant IV, a hired applicant is not successful on the job. In quadrant II, management rejects an applicant who would have been successful as an employee. The incorrect decision in quadrant IV is called a *false positive* because management was positive about an applicant who turned out to be unsuccessful. The incorrect decision in Quadrant II is called a *false negative* because management was negative about an applicant who would have been successful. In quadrants I and III, the managers scored a *hit* in correctly predicting the future performance of the applicant. Of course, management desires to maximize its rate of correct decisions, or *hit rate*, which is its percentage of correct predictions about future performances of employees.

In order to accomplish a cost-benefit analysis of the recruitment program, several estimates must be made. The cost of the two types of errors that can be made in the recruitment selection process should be considered. The actual dollar costs include advertising positions, reviewing applications, interviewing applicants, and testing a large group of applicants. Also, the cost of orientation and training of new applicants who are unsuccessful (false-positive decisions) must be included.

Perhaps more important than direct costs are the potential costs, which cannot be easily measured. False positives include the potential costs of an employee's becoming disenchanted with the organization and spreading low morale. The costs associated with false-negative decisions are also very difficult to estimate. Organizations often do not know, except in extremely costly situations, how much potential they have lost when they reject an applicant who could have been a successful employee. For example, what did it cost the professional baseball team whose scouts originally rejected the young Pete Rose?

Generally, the firm should develop a cost-benefit analysis to weigh the alternative of recruiting more individuals, which increases recruiting costs, against the cost of recruiting fewer individuals and possibly not locating a successful employee. A training program can be developed that identifies the potential employment capabilities of false-negative and false-positive applicants.

A perfect recruitment process, of course, would identify which of the four quadrants an applicant falls into and enable the recruiter to choose only those applicants who would be successful employees. Managers can estimate the success of their recruitment by looking at their hit rates and how the rates have changed. The most important cost-benefit analysis associated with recruitment focuses on the sources of recruitment (employee referrals, ad responses, and so on). Each source will produce a different percentage of successful job candidates at differing costs. Managers can easily relate the costs of using a source to the number of applicants located. The disadvantage of compiling direct dollar recruitment costs in this manner is that there is no accounting for the costs to an organization of losing a star performer because one source of

recruitment was not utilized. However, that unusual situation should not discourage cost-benefit analysis of recruiting.

INTERNATIONAL HRM: STAFFING

One of the more challenging issues facing multinational firms is staffing. Should a firm relocate home country staff to its foreign operations or hire host country personnel?[40] The multinational firm can choose to relocate experienced personnel from the United States (i.e., home country) or employ and train nationals (i.e., citizens of the host country). The choice is often determined on the basis of trade-offs between technical expertise that may be available only from the home country and the firm's need to adapt to local customs.

If the type of employee needed to staff the overseas operation is technically or professionally unique (e.g., computer engineer), chances are high that the person will be transferred from the United States. However, this strategy is very expensive.

The cost of sending personnel overseas (including Central and South America) is estimated at around half a million dollars for a three-year assignment for executives.[41] Of course, this cost will vary in terms of hardship to the employee, distance from the United States, and family obligations. Big-ticket expenditures for relocating personnel may include bonuses for hardship, education of children, visits back to the United States, and additional expenses to maintain an American standard of living. The high cost of expatriates is a major reason why fewer and fewer companies continue this personnel practice.

By and large, international firms are depending more on local labor sources to meet their staffing needs.[42] It is less expensive and, with the exception of a few countries, there is usually an adequate and available labor pool

TABLE 4-4

Recruiting Non-Americans: How to Screen for Loyalty

Loyalty is not defined in terms of patriotism or nationalism, but in terms of how well that person will understand, empathize with, and relate to the company and its global mission.

Whom do we hire when we take the plunge overseas? Here are eight measures to consider in selecting "locals":

1. How does the applicant view the United States?

If the person is unable to respond to provocative questions about his own nation without becoming defensive, don't go any further. Dedication and loyalty to the motherland are to be desired, but not the inability to put them in perspective with the company's historical U.S. orientation.

2. Has the applicant had previous foreign experience?

If this person has not had personal or professional experience outside the native land, take another look: firsthand experience may be critical to your success.

3. Does the applicant demonstrate clear mental flexibility?

Are this person's ideas open to change? Does this person wait to listen to other's ideas before responding, and in responding, does he show understanding of what the other person has said and why? If not, look elsewhere.

4. Can the applicant change his or her behavior in different environments?

Is this person's behavior open to change? Can this person respond to different signals and change behavior? Anyone without this flexibility goes on the waiting list.

5. Does the person have firsthand experience in the United States ?

Better get someone who's had personal experience here. You wouldn't want to move a person who'd spent five years in Nairobi to New York unless you were sure he understood the differences between them.

6. Does the person display international savvy in general?

Does the applicant show that he has learned how to assess the local ground rules before acting in *any* country? This is the sign of the real professional: someone who knows how to learn from experience in another country—*fast*.

7. Can the applicant recognize when behavior is influenced by cultural expectations, as in negotiating situations?

Does the applicant really demonstrate a general awareness and understanding of the patterns of cultural differences in human behavior? If applicant believes that "all people are the same," don't touch!

8. Does the applicant respond to verbal and nonverbal signals from someone different from himself? If he doesn't hold back and wait to find out what the other person is really intending, don't hire.

Source: Adapted from Henry Ferguson, *Tomorrow's Global Executive* (Homewood, IL: Dow Jones-Irwin, 1988), p. 72.

from which to recruit. An added advantage is that it creates career opportunities, goodwill, and loyalty to the company. It may also be politically astute since governments have been known to impose constraints on the number of foreign managers and specialists brought into their countries.

Recruiting productive and loyal local residents is just as challenging as in the United States—maybe even more so.[43] Perhaps the most sensitive issue is how to screen applicants for loyalty. Everyone who watches the evening news is aware that more and more countries are being swept up in a wave of nationalistic fervor. Certainly patriotism to one's own country is understandable and commendable, but it could cause the company embarrassment sometime in the future. To minimize the potential of a mismatch, a company recruiter might ask applicants the questions found in Table 4–4.

CONCLUSIONS AND APPLICATIONS

- Recruitment requires the personnel specialist to acquire a pool of available and qualified applicants. The recruiters can use a variety of sources including current employees, advertisements, the unemployed, and employees of other organizations who feel they are underemployed.
- Personnel planning can be a key method by which the personnel department can hold down recruitment costs and mini-

mize the time positions remain vacant. By developing demand and supply forecasts, the personnel specialist can initiate training programs, retirement incentives, management succession planning, and other techniques to aid future recruitment efforts.

- College-campus recruitment has decreased in recent years due to the higher cost per hire and the economy. Innovative firms such as NCR, however, have found that effective, low-cost college recruitment is possible using a computer data system.
- Effective recruitment advertising has increased due to the use of common marketing research tools. The need for advertising has increased because of two-career couples and a general unwillingness to relocate on the part of professional and technical employees. Current employees are the most common source of applicants for higher-level positions. They offer the organization several advantages over external applicants and give all employees the incentive of knowing that they may be promoted as a reward for hard work.
- Overtime and temporary help are immediate sources of additional labor and are considered alternatives to hiring permanent employees. Depending on the number of hours and skills needed, these recruitment sources may be more desirable than hiring permanent employees.

CASE STUDY
Song, The Accountant

Victor Chavez, president of Acme Quonset Huts, decided last June that the firm's three-person accounting staff must be increased to four. He knew that there were only six other nonproduction employees in the company, and believed that none of them was interested in accounting.

The local university offered a full accounting program, so Chavez called the placement director and asked for the names of all recent accounting graduates who were in the job market. After making several phone calls, four interviews were arranged. Two weeks later Chavez offered the job to Eudora Song, who had ten days to reply.

Two days after making the offer Chavez mentioned Song and the offer to Wendell Hardy, the personnel officer. Hardy became very upset because he knew nothing about hiring an additional accountant. After much discussion Chavez agreed to list the position through normal procedures, even though he felt it was a waste of time because the job required an accounting degree and he already had a good candidate in Song.

One week after Song was given the job offer, she called Chavez at 10:00 A.M. to accept it. At 9:00 A.M. that same day Sandy Ostermiller, a production employee for three years, came to Hardy's office to discuss the accounting position:

Ostermiller: "I noticed that an opening for an accountant position was advertised in yesterday's paper."

Hardy: "Yes, I am very proud of that because, off the record, old man Chavez did not want to list it. He thinks this place is still in the 1950s, with seven employees."

Ostermiller: "Well, good! My best friend, Emily Laurel, and I are considering applying."

Hardy: "You can't—you must have an accounting degree."

Ostermiller: "That's why we're so excited about it. Next week we both finish summer school at UC, where we're accounting majors."

Hardy: "That's really good news. We like to give our own employees a chance to move up. Here are two applications."

Ostermiller: "Well, that is what we thought, but we didn't know the policy about promoting people from inside."

Hardy: "To tell the truth, there isn't a written policy or anything. In my five years here, I've always given our people first chance at a job if they are qualified. As soon as I can, I'll tell Chavez, I know he will be happy that you two have worked so hard at night school."

Ostermiller: "Thank you. We both like it here, but we really don't want to work on the line for thirty more years."

Hardy: "Very good! Bring back the applications as soon as possible."

Questions

1. What has caused this difficult situation?
2. How can such future problems be avoided?
3. If Song is hired, can the firm be sued for discrimination?
4. If you were Hardy, how would you handle this situation?

EXPERIENTIAL EXERCISE
Effective Help-Wanted Ads

Purpose

To understand the criteria for evaluating help-wanted recruiting advertisements and the effectiveness of several actual help-wanted ads.

Introduction

What are the characteristics of effective help-wanted ads? Consider the following questions and dos and don'ts.

Who Do You Want?

Important information that you'll need *before* you write your ad includes:

- How many people do you need?
- What skills and abilities are required?
- Is this person likely to be working, and if so, where?
- What publications are they likely to read regularly?
- Which job rewards—compensation, benefits, career opportunities, and so on—are they likely to be looking for?
- How competitive is the market for this person?
- What is the likely level of job satisfaction the person has with his or her present job?

Once you've answered these basic questions, you'll need to create a strategy for effectively communicating the challenges and opportunities of the available job.

Some Dos and Don'ts

- *Headlines are important.* Use a distinctive headline to *sell* the job to the candidate. Don't just list the job title.
- *Use graphics carefully.* Ad graphics vary widely, ranging from the simple to the complex. Graphics that are confusing or misleading are worse than no graphics at all, so make sure that graphics make sense. A basic question to ask: Do the graphics convey a message that you want to communicate?
- *Don't use an idea only because it's clever or creative.* Cleverness and creativity are fine as long as they apply to the position being advertised.
- *Don't misrepresent the job.* Don't make promises you can't keep. Be honest about opportunities for advancement, challenge, responsibility, and so on. Honesty is the best policy.
- *Don't be vague.* Be specific about the job and the qualifications that are needed for a particular opening.
- *"Sell" the employee.* Without tooting your own company horn *too* loudly, make sure the ad contains the benefits of working for your firm.
- *Avoid sterotypes.* Beware of sexism, racism, and other stereotypes. Make sure it won't be seen as offensive to anyone.
- *Help prospective candidates identify themselves.* To avoid sifting through countless resumes, define the qualifications you are looking for. You'll cut down

1

THE ___ HAS IMMEDIATE OPENING FOR AN ADVERTISING SALESPERSON

The Classified Advertising Department of ___ is seeking an enthusiastic individual with above average written and oral communication skills to sell advertising by telephone on a full time basis.

1. Good telephone personality.
2. Enjoy working with the public.
3. Be goal oriented.
4. Type 40 w.p.m.
5. Have good grammatical skills including spelling and punctuation.
6. Previous advertising sales experience preferred.

This is an excellent opportunity for a career oriented individual to grow with a long established company.

Please apply in person between 9 a.m. and 4 p.m. Wednesday, March 23, 1988 or Monday, March 28, 1988.
Human Resources Department

Equal Opportunity Employer

2

Drivers Wanted

Express

A company that cares about its employees & owner/operators. We manage with that "small company" personal touch. We have a compensation package equal to any but believe that other things are important to you;

• Time at home
• New retirement plan
• Commitment to improving the Quality of Your Work Life

Drivers & owner/operators who are at lest 23 years old with 1 year OTR experience.

3

LOOKING FOR SUPPLEMENTAL INCOME?

DO YOU . . .
Enjoy dealing with the general public?
Enjoy convincing and persuading?
Enjoy making money for every sale you sell?

CAN YOU . . .
Speak clearly with good grammar and diction?
Politely and courteously deal with the public?
Use a telephone and communicate effectively?

WOULD YOU . . .
Be able to work Monday through Friday from 5:30 p.m. to 9 p.m. & Saturdays from 10 a.m. until 9 p.m.
Could earn up to $6.00 an hour? (some of our sales people are making much more than this!)

IF SO . . .
Come to ___ Bring a social security card or birth certificate and drivers license for proper identification and fill out an application.
Additional benefits are provided. They will be discussed in the interview.

SALES AND TELEMARKETING EXPERIENCE PREFERRED BUT NOT REQUIRED

An Equal Opportunity Employer

4

NURSING   male/female

ASSISTANT DIRECTOR OF NURSING (RN)

• 126 bed long term care facility
• 3-5 year long term care experience required
• Knowledge of Medicare & Medicaid
• Management experience preferred
• Energetic & creative must have love for geriatrics
Contact

5

HAIR DRESSERS. Wanted with or without following.

6

REGISTERED NURSES MALE/FEMALE SERVING THE DEVELOPMENTALLY DISABLED

Are you looking for a new challenge? We offer a unique transdisciplinary approach to resident care that is guaranteed to please. We can offer you full time employment with NO FLEXIBLE HOURS. No sending you home in the middle of the day. In addition, we offer an excellent continuing education program, paid holiday & vacation package, deferred compensation & retirement program. Min. requirements: must be licensed as a registered nurse or possess a valid work permit issued by the Ky. Board of Nursing. If you are interested contact:

7

PRODUCT DEVELOPMENT SPECIALIST

Product Research & Development Lab

Will handle assignments in the area of new products development in product improvements. Also will provide technical service to other departments. Will guide technicians in their work in the above areas.

QUALIFICATIONS: Bachelors Degree in Food Science, Biology, Chemistry, or related field is very desirable. Experience in product development and/or quality control in the beverage, dairy, food, or flavor industries is required. Competitive salary and benefits.

Send resume in confidence to:

Human Resources Department

COMPANY

Louisville, KY 40201

An Equal Opportunity Employer

Criterion*

Advertisement

Criterion	1	2	3	4	5	6	7
Distinctive headlines							
Effective graphics							
Clever and creative							
Avoids sounding too glamorous							
Specifies nature of job and qualifications							
"Sells" the employee							
Avoids stereotyping							
Helps candidate identify self							
Uses space economically							
Effective typeface							
Proper recruitment media							
TOTALS:							

Ranking (most effective to least effective)

1.
2.
3.
4.
5.
6.
7.

---

*Rank each ad for each criterion using the following scale:
5 = Excellent; 4 = Very Good; 3 = Satisfactory; 2 = Below Average; 1 = Very Poor

considerably on unqualified applicants if you'll specify the required education, experience, employment background, and personal and professional traits you expect.

- *Use advertising space economically.* Space cost is not cheap. Don't use a full-page ad when a half-page will do the job just as effectively. Don't use too many graphics and too little prose; conversely, don't use a space so small that the applicant will get eyestrain from reading. The size of the ad should be in proportion to the size of the firm, importance of the position, number of candidates sought, and so on.
- *Select a legible typeface.* Some typefaces are attractive but difficult to read. Fancy typeface may be acceptable for headlines, but if job hunters can't read the copy, they'll lose interest in the ad and the job.
- *Select recruitment media carefully.* Study the reading habits of potential candidates to determine what they read. Also study the readership demographics of the various media you are considering. A great-looking ad is no good if the right people aren't reading it.
- *Remember the final review.* After finalizing the ad, set it aside for a few days, time permitting, and return to it with a critical eye. With an uncluttered mind, you may see a problem you overlooked while initially working on the ad.

The Task

Illustrated on page 140 are several help-wanted advertisements. All were taken from the same Louisville, Kentucky, newspaper on the same Sunday morning. Using the criteria just listed, evaluate each ad, using the grid on page 141. Your instructor will lead you in a discussion of the results of your analysis.

From "Recruitment Ads at Work," by Margaret Magnus, copyright August, 1985. Reprinted with the permission of Personnel Journal, Costa Mesa, California; all rights reserved.

KEY TERMS AND CONCEPTS

Employee relocation
False negative
False positive
Gate hires
Hit rate
Human resource planning
Job posting
Labor force participation rate
Labor reserve

Leasing employees
Management succession planning
Networking
Peter principle
Pirating
Source trust
Underemployed
Unemployment rate

REVIEW QUESTIONS

1. Discuss hourly and professional applicants' knowledge of labor markets.
2. What are the advantages of recruiting applicants internally? Externally?
3. Why might a recent college graduate be quickly rejected during a campus interview?
4. Has advertising increased as a recruitment technique in recent years? Why?
5. Why might hiring temporary help be preferable to assigning overtime or hiring new employees?
6. How can U.S. firms successfully recruit local residents in foreign nations?

DISCUSSION QUESTIONS

1. If you were an underemployed MBA, what steps would you take to find a more satisfactory position?
2. From an inexperienced job applicant's point of view, which recruitment method is more attractive? From the point of view of an applicant with twenty years' experience?
3. How should applicants prepare for job interviews? What questions should they expect to answer?
4. What are the steps in a good job-posting procedure?
5. How should a personnel director compare alternative recruitment sources?

ENDNOTES

1. "Older Workers Rapidly Becoming a New Force in the Labor Market," *Resource* (August 1987): 2.
2. Pat O'Connor, "As the U.S. Grows Up, More Firms Turn to Older Workers," *The Courier-Journal* (July 13, 1987): B12, 7.
3. Margaret Magnus, "Is Your Retirement All It Can Be?" *Personnel Journal* 66, no. 2 (February 1987): 54–63.
4. Mitchell S. Novit, *Essentials of Personnel Management* (Englewood Cliffs, NJ: Prentice-Hall, 1979), pp. 60–64.
5. Paul Greenlaw and William Biggs, *Modern Personnel Management* (Philadelphia: Saunders, 1979), pp. 121–27.
6. Richard Frantzreb, "Human Resource Planning: Forecasting Manpower Needs," *Personnel Journal* 60, no. 11 (November 1981): 850–51.
7. Norman Scarborough and Thomas W. Zimmerer, "Human Resources Forecasting: Why and Where to Begin," *Personnel Administrator* 27, no. 5 (May 1982): 55–56.
8. Charles F. Russ, Jr., "Manpower Planning Systems: Part I," *Personnel Journal* 61, no. 1 (January 1982): 40–41.
9. Frantzreb, "Human Resource Planning," pp. 850–54.
10. Ibid.
11. Kendrith M. Rowland and Scott L. Summers, "Human Resource Planning: A Second Look," *Personnel Administrator* 26, no. 12 (December 1981): 73–80.
12. Russ, "Manpower Planning," pp. 44–45. For a complete discussion of commitment manpower planning see Charles F. Russ, "Manpower Planning Systems: Part II," *Personnel Journal* 61, no. 2 (January 1982): 119–123.

13. David R. Leigh, "Business Planning Is People Planning," *Personnel Journal* 63, no. 5 (May 1984): 44–45.

14. Ibid.

15. *Employee Promotion and Transfer Policies*, PPF survey no. 120 (Washington, DC: Bureau of National Affairs, Inc., 1978), pp. 2–4.

16. Edward Snow, "Spouse's Attitude Influences Move," *Personnel Journal* 63, no. 11 (1984): 30–31.

17. William S. Gault, "Real Estate Realities of Relocation," *Personnel Journal* 63, no. 11 (November 1984): 30–31.

18. Lawrence J. Peters and R. Hull, *The Peter Principle* (New York: Bantam Books, 1969), pp. 55–57.

19. Harriet Gorlin, "An Overview of Corporate Personnel Practices," *Personnel Journal* 61, no. 2 (February 1982): 126.

20. Lawrence Kleiman and Kimberly Clark, "Users' Satisfaction with Job Posting," *Personnel Administrator* 29, no. 9 (September 1984): 104–8.

21. Lawrence S. Kleiman, "An Effective Job Posting System," *Personnel Journal* 63, no. 2 (February 1984): 20–25, 81–84.

22. Gloria Glickstein and Donald C. Z. Ramer, "The Alternative Employment Marketplace," *Personnel Administrator* 3, no. 2 (February 1988): 100–4.

23. Maury Hanigan, "Campus Recruiters Upgrade Their Pitch," *Personnel Administrator* 32, no. 11 (November 1987): 55–58.

24. Frank S. Endicott, *The Endicott Report* (Evanston, IL: Northwestern University Press, 1977), pp. 10–11.

25. James E. Lubbock, "A Look at Centralized College Recruiting," *Personnel Administrator* 28, no. 4 (April 1983): 81–84.

26. Erwin S. Stanton, *Successful Personnel Recruiting and Selection* (New York: AMACOM, 1977), pp. 53–55.

27. Margaret Nemec, "Recruitment Advertising—It's More Than Just 'Help Wanted,'" *Personnel Administrator* 26, no. 2 (February 1981): 57–60.

28. Bernard S. Hodes, "Planning for Recruitment Advertising: Part II," *Personnel Journal* 62, no. 6 (June, 1983): 492–99.

29. Herbert E. Myer, "Jobs and Want Ads: A Look Behind the Words," *Fortune* (November 20, 1978): 88–96.

30. Margaret Magnus, "Is Your Recruitment All It Can Be?" *Personnel Journal* 66, no. 2 (February 1987): 55.

31. Richard Siedlecki, "Creating a Direct Mail Recruitment Program," *Personnel Journal* 62, no. 4 (April 1983): 304–7.

32. Rick Stoops, "Direct Mail: Luring the Isolated Professionals," *Personnel Journal* 63, no. 6 (June 1984): 34–36.

33. Siedlecki, "Creating a Direct Mail Program," p. 307. *Direct Mail List Rates and Data*, published by Standard Rate and Data Service, Inc., 5201 Old Orchard Road, Skokie, IL 60077, or contact *Direct Mail/Marketing Association* (DM/MA), 6 E. 43rd Street, New York, NY 10017.

34. Stoops, "Direct Mail," pp. 34–36.

35. "The Temporary Services: A Lasting Impact on the Economy," *Personnel Administrator* 33, no. 1 (January 1988): 60–65.

36. Ibid.

37. "Leasing Employees," *Changing Times* (May 1985): 50–54.

38. Ibid.

39. Greenlaw and Briggs, *Modern Personnel Management*, pp. 122–27.

40. This section draws on A. V. Phatak, *International Dimensions of Management* (Boston: Kent Publishing Company, 1983), pp. 90–96.

41. For more information on the costs of expatriates, see W. E. Green and G. D. Walls, "Human Resources: Hiring Internationally," *Personnel Administrator,* 29 (July 1984): 61–66. Also, see R. J. Stone, "Compensation: Pay and Perks for Overseas Executives," *Personnel Journal* 65 no. 1 (January 1986): 64–69.

42. For some staffing issues associated with expatriate managers, see G. M. Galiga and J. C. Baker, "Multinational Corporate Policies for Expatriate Managers: Selection, Training, Evaluation," *SAM Advanced Management Journal* 50, no. 4 (Autumn 1985): 31–38.

43. For a more thorough treatment of screening foreign employees, see Henry Ferguson, *Tomorrow's Global Executive* (Homewood, IL: Dow Jones-Irwin, 1988), pp. 70–74.

Chapter Five

Personnel Selection

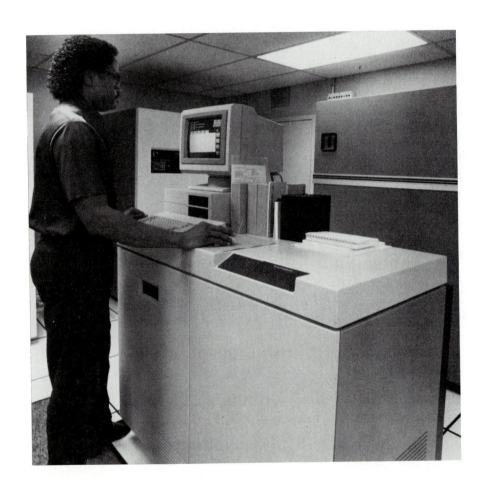

Chapter Outline

SELECTION DECISIONS
A Personnel Responsibility
Evaluating Ability and Motivation

FEDERAL LEGISLATION
Equal Pay Act
Civil Rights Act
Sexual Harassment
Age Discrimination in Employment Act
Separation Agreements
Vocational Rehabilitation Act
Vietnam Era Veterans Readjustment Act
Immigration Reform and Control Act

AFFIRMATIVE ACTION
Program Development
Required Records
Program Implementation

UNIFORM GUIDELINES ON EMPLOYEE SELECTION PROCEDURES

SIGNIFICANT COURT CASES
Racial Discrimination
Reverse Discrimination
Age Discrimination
Seniority and Affirmative Action

THE SELECTION PROCESS
Initial Screening
Application Blank
Testing
Interviews
Background Checks
Negligent Hiring
The Selection Decision

INTERNATIONAL HRM: EXPATRIATE RIGHTS

CONCLUSIONS AND APPLICATIONS

Chapter Objectives

1. To explain the personnel department's role in the selection process.
2. To develop a selection decision process.
3. To describe the purpose and requirements of the 1964 Civil Rights Act.
4. To know the procedure for developing an affirmative action plan.
5. To construct an effective sexual harassment policy.
6. To identify employer responsibilities under the 1986 Immigration Reform and Control Act.
7. To cite useful application-blank information.
8. To develop a structured employment interview.
9. To distinguish among different types of preemployment tests.
10. To understand the need for complete background checks.
11. To explain how the final selection decision is made.

Affirmative Action Reaffirmed by U.S. Supreme Court

The United States Supreme Court in 1986 and 1987 upheld and extended the general principles of affirmative action as they have evolved since the 1960s. In three related decisions in 1986, the Court ruled that minority-preference hiring and promotion plans are not limited to actual victims of job discrimination, and employment goals by employers may be used. In 1987, the Court ruled that employers may favor women and minorities over better qualified men and whites. The landmark cases include *Wygant* v. *Jackson Board of Education,* U.S. Supreme Court, 1986, 40 FEP Cases 1321; *Local 28, Sheet Metal Workers* v. *EEOC,* U.S. Supreme Court, 1986, 41 FEP Cases 107; *Local 93, Firefighters* v. *City of Cleveland,* U.S. Supreme Court, 1986, 41 FEP Cases 139; *Johnson* v. *Transportation Agency,* U.S. Supreme Court, 1987.

In *Wygant* the Court held that affirmative action plans need not be victim specific and may benefit individuals who did not suffer actual discrimination. Also the Court endorsed the concept that underuse of minorities or women can justify establishing an affirmative action plan. Actual discrimination need not be found. Affirmative action goals in hiring are allowed because no one has a right to a job, and such affirmative action would diffuse the impact of preferences. Affirmative action goals in promotion are allowed if strictly tailored to specific jobs, but affirmative action in layoffs is allowed only under the most stringent set of circumstances. The Court generally upheld the use of a seniority system in layoff situations.

In *Sheet Metal Workers,* the Court said a court may order a union to use quotas to overcome a history of discrimination. Also, black and hispanic applicants can benefit even if they personally were not victims of past union bias. The Court also pointed out the benefits of a flexible affirmative action plan rather than the rigid application of a color-blind policy.

And in *Firefighters* the court upheld a consent decree even though the promotional goals caused the seniority of white firefighters to be ignored. It upheld a voluntary agreement between a union and a public employer to promote minorities on a one-to-one basis.

In *Johnson* the Court ruled that employers may voluntarily correct a "manifest imbalance" in the work force through an affirmative action plan. In this case Diane Joyce, a road maintenance worker in Santa Clara County, California, received a promotion over Paul Johnson, another road worker, who had scored higher on an interview. The transportation agency decided to promote Joyce due to a shortage of women in its work force. A federal district court had declared illegal the affirmative action plan used by the agency when Johnson sued the county. The Supreme Court, however, ruled that the county could hire a woman over a better qualified man as part of an affirmative action program. This was the Court's first decision upholding hiring goals based on sex rather than race.

In summary, the Court upheld court-ordered or voluntary affirmative action plans, including numerical standards, to address underuse even if such a plan benefits nonvictims of discrimination. Within their affirmative action plan, private and public employers may hire or promote women and minorities over more qualified white men. Union-negotiated seniority systems, however, may be followed in layoff-recall situations even though they do not follow affirmative action goals.

Source: Michael R. Carrell and Christina Heavrin, *Collective Bargaining and Labor Relations,* 2nd ed. (Columbus, OH: Merrill Publishing Co., 1988) pp. 369–70. Used by permission.

THE personnel selection process begins when there are more qualified and available job applicants than there are positions open. It may be necessary to fill one particular position or several positions as they become open, or to fill positions continuously through training programs so that people are ready to take jobs as they become vacant. In large organizations, which continuously recruit and select job applicants for future job openings, the time positions remain vacant is minimized.

SELECTION DECISIONS

Personnel selection is the process of choosing qualified individuals who are available to fill positions in an organization. In the ideal personnel situation, selection involves choosing the best applicant to fill a position. After the position opens, the personnel manager reviews the available, qualified applicants and fills the position from that pool. The ideal situation, however, seldom occurs. The selection process involves a "best guess" process of determining that an individual probably can do a job and will be successful on the job.

There is no fail-safe method of determining the best person to fill any position. Many subjective factors are involved in the selection process because there is no perfect test or gauge of applicants. But there are objective techniques available which increase the validity of the process. The selection process is, perhaps, the heart of an organization's human resource program. If the selection process is well administered, the employee will be able to achieve personal career goals and the organization will benefit from a productive, satisfied employee.

A Personnel Responsibility

The selection process is usually centered in the personnel department, though it involves many individuals from other departments. Particularly in larger organizations, centralizing the recruitment and selection process in the personnel department is both efficient and effective. Both current employees and job applicants have one place to apply for jobs,

149
Personnel Selection

transfers, or promotions, as well as to inquire about related personnel matters. In most situations, the cost of recruiting and selecting employees is minimized with centralization because personnel specialists can perform these functions more effectively than managers in different departments. The trained personnel specialist can also save money by ensuring that an organization's personnel selection practices comply with federal laws and restrictions. In addition, the personnel manager can ensure that the selection process is objective. Centralizing the selection function minimizes the bias of department managers or others who may wish to promote employees or hire applicants who are not the best qualified.

While the personnel department usually is responsible for selection, individual managers are often involved in the interviewing process. Frequently, the applicant's second or third interview is with the department manager, who has valuable insights about work methods and departmental goals and can evaluate the applicant's qualifications. The selection process also relies on managers to assist in developing job specifications and writing job descriptions, which are critical in determining the needs for a particular position and the best-qualified applicants.

The centralization of the hiring process within the personnel department and the sharing of decision making with line managers have evolved over many years. As outlined in Table 5–1, hiring procedures have been greatly altered by outside influences, such as World War II, federal legislation, and new technology. Many common techniques—such as testing, employee training, and test validation—are the direct result of social movements and government statutes. Yet despite the increased role of the personnel department, the final selection decision is often made by line management, not personnel officers.

Evaluating Ability and Motivation

Maximizing employees' future performance is the objective of the selection process. An employee's performance on the job depends on the employee's ability and motivation to perform the job. The entire selection process hinges on determining which applicants have the best ability and the greatest motivation to be successful employees.

Often failure on the job is not due to a lack of skill or ability to perform the job adequately, but to a lack of motivation. Skills and abilities can be developed in employees through training inside and outside the organization, but motivation cannot be developed to the same extent. For example, 85 percent of the persons who failed to be successful sales representatives in one company did so from a lack of motivation rather than a lack of ability. The single most important indicator of how a job applicant will perform appears to be past performance. Therefore, during the selection process, obtaining an accurate and verifiable record of the applicant's past job performance is critical, though this is very difficult to do.[1]

FEDERAL LEGISLATION

From the mid-1960s through the mid-1970s, personnel administrators were bombarded with federal legislation and court cases involving the recruitment and selection of employees. Reflecting the mood of society, Congress and the courts initiated reforms to ensure that all individuals have an equal chance of being selected for employment and that they will be treated equally once they are hired. Special emphasis was given to veterans and to minorities, who had experienced discrimination in past decades. The various acts of Congress that apply to recruitment and selection must be understood in detail by personnel administrators and line managers.

Equal Pay Act

Because of many publicized cases of female employees' being paid substantially less than their male counterparts while performing identical work, the Equal Pay Act was passed by the U.S. Congress in 1963. The act requires organizations of all sizes to pay men and women substantially the same wages for *substantially equal* work or approximately equal "skill, effort, responsibility, and working conditions." Substantially equal is the basis upon which jobs should be compared. In practice this means that jobs do not have to be identical to command the same basic wage; neither do employers have to pay a different wage for each different job. They must pay equal wages for substantially equal work.

When an employer has employees in two or more establishments (separate businesses or locations), there need not be comparison of employees of the different establishments for purposes of pay comparisons. But if the employer centrally controls all employees and their work is integrated, then under the act employees should be compared for purposes of pay equity. The Equal Pay Act is administered by the Equal Employment Opportunity Commission (EEOC).[2]

The Equal Pay Act has had wider application than any other employment legislation because the act does not stipulate a statutory minimum number of employees. The act applies to all organizations with two or more employees.[3]

Of particular importance are the exceptions allowed by the Equal Pay Act: differences in pay can be based on seniority, merit, quality of work, or quantity of work. Therefore, paying different wages to men and women performing the same job can be justified by these differences.

This act has caused many organizations to develop a wage and salary system based on formal job evaluation plans. Under such plans, employees are paid according to the jobs they are performing and not other factors, such as sex or supervisory bias. Organizations which adopt or amend their wage and salary plan cannot, according to the Equal Pay Act, reduce the wage rate of any employee in order to comply with the act.[4]

Civil Rights Act

The primary federal law that regulates employment practices is the Civil Rights Act of 1964, an act passed while the nation mourned the death of John F. Kennedy. Only months before his assassination, the nation had witnessed civil rights demonstrations throughout the country as minorities demanded recognition of their civil rights. The act requires employment and compensation of employees without discrimination:

> *Title VII, Section 703* It is unlawful for an employer to discriminate against an individual with respect to his compensation, terms, conditions, or privileges of employment because of such individual's race, color, religion, sex, or national origin; or to limit, segregate, or classify his employees in any way which would deprive or tend to deprive any individual of employment opportunities or otherwise adversely affect his status as an employee, because of such individual's race, color, religion, sex, or national origin.

Two kinds of employment discrimination have been recognized by the courts and federal agencies. One kind, *disparate treatment,* occurs when an individual has suffered direct and deliberate discrimination. An example might be a job applicant being turned down because a supervisor "can't work with older women." The second kind, *disparate impact,* occurs when a group of people has suffered discrimination because of a personnel policy or procedure. An example might be a hiring

TABLE 5–1

A chronology of hiring practices and influences in the United States

Event or Innovation	Date	Explanation or Significance
First Personnel Department	1890s	John H. Patterson, president of the National Cash Register Co., Dayton, Ohio, establishes the first personnel department.
Scientific Management	1912	Frederick Taylor testifies before a special U.S. House committee on the principles and virtues of scientific management. This approach would reduce waste by hiring the right people and simplifying their jobs. Extremely popular for many years, by the end of the 1920s it was no longer in favor.
Testing	1918	The first group intelligence test, *Army Alpha,* is developed by personnel managers and psychologists to "match each enlisted man to a job." Shortly after World War I industry and the Civil Service Commission adopt testing as a breakthrough in hiring practices—each job could be scientifically filled with the right person.
	1920s	The first professional journal in personnel, *The Journal of Personnel Research* (forerunner of *Personnel Journal*), describes in issue after issue the profession's infatuation with testing as the means of making hiring decisions with objective and scientific information.
Staff Designation	1923	Line managers believe personnel should stay out of day-to-day decisions (including hiring), but personnel offices continue to take over the employment function to make it more scientific. In 1923 the National Personnel Association, in support of line management's views, changed its name to the American Management Association.
Great Depression	1930s	Massive unemployment stops almost all hiring and cruelly shows America that work is not appreciated until it is gone.
Wagner Act	1935	The once unified field of industrial relations is split into two, personnel and labor relations, in the years following the Wagner Act and the growth of union membership.
World War II	1940s	Organizations rapidly grow in size, and supervisors' preoccupation with production demands often forces them to relinquish all hiring and government-regulations concerns to personnel departments.
		The War Manpower Commission assumes control of most industrial hiring and introduces widespread use of manpower planning and training programs, which remain long after the war. Universities are encouraged to develop "industrial education" personnel programs.

TABLE 5–1
continued

Event or Innovation	Date	Explanation or Significance
		Nondiscriminatory hiring orders are first issued by President Roosevelt. By 1945 women account for 36 percent of the workforce due to the shortage of men. Both managers and women themselves are confronted with the fact that women are successful in jobs previously closed to them.
The Age of Sputnik	1950s	The combination of the G.I. Bill and the national "space race" with the U.S.S.R. ignites a trend for organizations to hire college graduates in unprecedented numbers, particularly scientists, engineers, and businessmen.
Federal Laws	1960s	The movement toward "fair and open" hiring practices begun during World War II crystalizes into federal legislation: The Equal Pay Act of 1963, The 1964 Civil Rights Act, Affirmative Action (1965 ex. order 11246), and the Age Discrimination in Employment Act of 1967.
		The new hiring legislation forces personnel managers to consider the validity and reliability of selection methods; the use of written tests and the "old boy network" decline as structured interviews, nondiscriminatory application blanks, assessment centers, and weighted application blanks grow in use.
The New Employee	1970s	"Matching the needs of the person with those of the organization" becomes the common hiring practice. A new wave of better educated, less-loyal employees armed with employment laws demands flexible working hours, quality circles, increased leisure time, compressed workweeks, quality of working life, and so on.
		Employers, because of court decisions, become more concerned that their hiring practices must be defensible to their employees and government.
Reagan Administration	1980s	Employers perceive a swing of the government-regulation pendulum in their direction. The Supreme Court and federal agencies, inspired by the 1978 EEO hiring guidelines, order less stringent government regulation of hiring practices, except in cases involving age discrimination, due to new "teeth" in the 1978 amendment to the 1967 ADEA. Unions suffer several setbacks from the NLRB and the courts.

Adapted from A. S. T. Blackburn, Sam Ervin, Jonathan Glassman, Martha Harris, and John Thelin, "Sixty Years of Hiring Practices," *Personnel Journal* 59, no. 6 (June 1980): 462–482.

policy that requires all police officers to be six feet tall and weigh 190 lbs. The indirect impact of that policy would be that a significantly smaller percentage of women would be hired.

The act also established the *Equal Employment Opportunity Commission (EEOC)*. The EEOC was given the authority to investigate employee complaints of job discrimination. Where the EEOC finds such complaints justified, it cannot directly order organizations to make personnel changes. But it can bring suit in federal courts against employers if job discrimination is suspected.

Under Title VII, the EEOC is empowered to investigate employee complaints and to act as their attorney. The employer is obligated to show personnel records and other requested material to the EEOC. In addition, all employee applications must be kept for three years in case they are needed in an EEOC complaint or other action. Typically, a discrimination complaint is processed in the following steps:

1. The employee's *inquiry* is filed with the EEOC or a state commission dealing with human rights. The employee is interviewed by a professional, who ascertains all facts of the case. The EEOC then reviews the facts and determines if the case warrants further investigation.

2. If the EEOC finds that there may be *probable cause*—a reasonable possibility—of discrimination, the commission requests the employer's records. These records may include application blanks, interview results, or test results. The EEOC then determines if there was probable cause for the complaint.

3. The EEOC arranges a *conciliation meeting* with the employer to discuss the employee's complaint if the EEOC feels that it has probable cause. The purpose of the conciliation meeting is to arrive at a mutual agreement that will satisfy both the employer and the aggrieved employee. If this is not possible, then the EEOC weighs the severity of the complaint and discusses alternative actions with the employee.

4. If there is no satisfactory conciliation agreement, the EEOC may issue a *right to sue* to the complainant, indicating that the commission does not feel that the case should be taken to court. Therefore, the complaining employee does have the right to sue with a private attorney. Many times this action is an indication that the EEOC does not feel that the complainant has a strong case. The alternative of giving the complainant a right to sue is for the EEOC to take the case of the complainant to court. Title VII covers attorney fees for complainants if the EEOC takes the case to court.

Court Procedures If the discrimination complaint is taken to court, the case usually proceeds in a predictable fashion. A well-known example is the *McDonnell-Douglas* v. *Green* case that was litigated in 1972.[5] The complainant must generally prove all of the following:

Minority or Female Status In most cases this is not difficult, though proving that one is of American Indian or Hispanic origin may be difficult in some situations.

Qualification for the Position The complainant must demonstrate minimum qualifications for the position specified in the employer's position announcement or recruitment ad.

Failure to be Hired Usually this is easily proved except in cases of ongoing recruitment where the complainant may still be under consideration for selection.

Someone Less Qualified Was Hired This is often a difficult and debatable aspect of a discrimination case. Using the company's own records, the complainant must prove that he or she is better qualified than the person hired. The complainant cannot claim discrimination if the employer hires one minority instead of another minority since both are equally protected under the Civil Rights Act.

The organization may put forward one of a number of defenses. For instance, the organization may claim that the employee did not have the requisite *bona fide occupational qualification (BFOQ)*. Title VII provides that in certain instances religion, sex, or national origin is a BFOQ if such qualification is reasonably necessary to the normal operation of the organization. BFOQ is a vague and seldom-used defense for discrimination cases. An example of a BFOQ might be a firm's hiring a male to serve as a men's room attendant or a church's refusing to hire someone of a different religion to serve as a minister. The courts have ruled that it is not a BFOQ for flight attendants to be female. Title VII also states that an organization must make reasonable accommodation for employees of specific religious beliefs or with handicaps. Exactly how much is "reasonable accommodation" is subject to interpretation.

Another defense is that it was a *business necessity* not to hire the complainant. If safety or profitability requires hiring a specific person, then discrimination could be defended under Title VII. For example, if a company hired an individual to work specific hours during the week, and after being hired the individual could not work those hours due to personal circumstances, management may claim a business necessity as a defense. An-

other example is a dress shop which claims that it is a business necessity to hire young females as salesclerks so that they may better meet the public they are serving.

Still another defense is that the person hired is better qualified for the job than the complainant. This is the most common defense for an organization charged with employment discrimination. Personnel records should prove that the results of the tests or interviews indicate that the person hired was better qualified. Personnel departments with standardized and documented records, using proper selection techniques, have a strong defense. If, however, their defense is based solely upon what they remember about a case or what they believe occurred, then they have a weak defense.

The EEOC usually hears complaints from applicants who were discriminated against in the process of hiring or promotion, not in matters of unequal pay. Under Title VII, employment discrimination refers to much more than the initial hiring process; it encompasses all "terms, conditions, or privileges of employment" and includes selection, promotion, transfers, or employee training. Therefore, all organizational decisions which relate to an employee's job classification are included under the Civil Rights Act.

Equal Employment Opportunity Act In 1972 the Civil Rights Act of 1964 was amended by the Equal Employment Opportunity Act. The amendment effectively changed Title VII of the 1964 act to include all private employers and labor unions with fifteen or more employees or members, state and local governments, and public and private educational institutions. More importantly, the Equal Employment Act considerably strengthened the 1964 act by giving the EEOC power to bring suits directly to federal courts when conciliation efforts proved unsuccessful. Previously, the EEOC did not have such power and relied upon employers to comply voluntarily with conciliation efforts. State and local EEOC offices were established to provide local-level counseling for complainants who felt they had suffered discrimination.

Pregnancy Discrimination Act A type of sex discrimination openly practiced in the past is one based not entirely on sex but on so-called *sex plus*.[6] A typical example of sex-plus discrimination occurred when a manager openly told all women with small children that they would not be hired because of their child-care responsibilities. The courts found the policy illegal because it was not equally imposed on men.[7] Sex-plus discrimination has also been used against pregnant women. The U.S. Supreme Court had held that such discrimination was legal. But the Pregnancy Discrimination Act of 1978, an amendment to the 1964 Civil Rights Act, prohibited sex discrimination, including but not limited to pregnancy, childbirth, or related medical conditions. The 1978 act also required employee medical insurance to cover pregnancy as fully as it covers other long-term disabilities.[8]

Sexual Harassment

Sexual harassment has developed into one of the most controversial, complex, and perhaps widespread human resource problems in the United States. One of the first attempts to measure the extent of sexual harassment was undertaken by *Redbook* magazine in 1976. Of the 9000 women workers who responded to a survey, 80 percent reported that they had experienced some form of unwanted attention on the job.[9] A study concerning women employed by the United Nations showed that 49 percent experienced sexual harassment at work. Another study showed widespread harassment among female employees of the Illinois state government. Of the 1,495 respondents to a random-sample survey, 49 percent said they had experienced one or more incidents of sexual harassment on the job.[10] Clearly, the magnitude of the problem demands that human-resource administrators seek ways to minimize sexual harassment in their organizations.

In 1980, the EEOC set forth guidelines which declared sexual harassment a form of illegal sex discrimination, because sexual harassment constitutes a form of behavior directed toward an employee specifically because of his or her sex. (Most incidents of sexual harassment are directed toward women, but research shows that male employees are also sexually harassed on the job, though such incidents are few compared to the problems reported by women.) The EEOC also issued guidelines that set forth a working definition of sexual harassment:[11]

> Unwelcome sexual advances, requests for sexual favors, and other verbal or physical conduct of a sexual nature constitute sexual harassment when (1) submission to such conduct is made either explicitly or implicitly a term or condition of an individual's employment, (2) submission to or rejection of such conduct by an individual is used as the basis for employment decisions affecting such individual, or (3) such conduct has the purpose or effect of unreasonably interfering with an individual's work performance or creating an intimidating, hostile, or offensive working environment.

Sexual harassment may include verbal abuse, sexist remarks, patting, pinching, or brushing against the body, leering or ogling, demand for sexual favors in return for a job or promotion, and physical assault.

The number of sexual harassment complaints under Title VII rose 70 percent from 1981 to 1985. A study sample of the cases filed in Illinois revealed that only 31 percent of the individuals filing complaints received favorable outcomes. The chances of a favorable court decision or out-of-court decision, however, were greatly enhanced (1) if the sexual harassment behavior involved sexual assault, unwanted physical contact, or propositions linked to employment, (2) if witnesses supported the charge, and (3) if management was previously notified of problems by the complainant. Complaints that courts have agreed to hear generally have involved clear-cut instances. Less serious behaviors such as crude jokes, offensive language, or unwanted gestures, stares, or whistles have generally not received favorable court litigation.[12]

Measuring and Researching Sexual Harassment Because of the sensitivity of the subject, it may be difficult to get an accurate reading of the extent of sexual harassment within an organization. Nonetheless, certain techniques may provide personnel administrators with estimates about the nature, extent, and location of sexual harassment. These include:

- Grievance data.
- Oral complaints to management and personnel officials.
- Exit interviews.
- Survey data.

Perhaps the most accurate and comprehensive technique for measuring sexual harassment is a well-designed anonymous employee survey. An example of a survey to discover the extent of sexual harassment is shown in Figure 5–1.

Reducing Sexual Harassment Court decisions, in addition to the progressive actions of many employers, have provided a number of guidelines and procedures for reducing the incidence of sexual harassment. Actions that

are important for controlling the problem include the following:[13]

- Establish clear policies defining and prohibiting sexual harassment and an explicit code of conduct for all employees. The code will serve as a basis to judge complaints, and issuance of such standards will help deter harassment.
- Establish an internal grievance system to handle complaints. Experience has shown that a properly administered and fair internal grievance system will encourage internal settlements and eliminate the need for employees to seek justice outside the organization, including the courts. It is important that all employees feel that their complaints will be handled promptly, fairly, and confidentially. The system should also serve to protect managers and other employees from unfounded or frivolous charges.
- Recognize and accept that sexual harassment is occurring in your organization. The absence of complaints does not mean that you have nothing to be concerned about. It probably means that you have not set up procedures to uncover the problem. Many women do not complain because they do not know how to file a grievance or they fear retaliation. It is probably valid to assume that sexual harassment is present in the work place and is a problem.
- Establish good lines of communication. Managers must realize that making sexual favors a condition of employment is not only wrong, it is also illegal. Rank-and-file employees must learn to use internal grievance procedures. All employees must know what the organization's policies are and how to seek redress for complaints. Policies and grievance procedures should be communicated through

Sexual Harassment Questionnaire
(Circle the best response listed after each question. Please answer each question.)

1. Are you aware that sexual harassment has been deemed illegal by guidelines set forth by the Equal Employment Opportunity Commission?

    a) yes
    b) no

2. Which of the following do you feel constitutes illegal sexual harassment? (circle all letters that apply)

    a) sexually offensive comments
    b) sex-oriented jokes
    c) staring or leering
    d) touching, grabbing, pinching

    e) sexual propositions
    f) rape
    g) other forms of sexual harassment
    h) none of the above constitutes sexual harassment

3. Which of the following have you experienced on your job from co-workers or supervisors? (circle all letters that apply)

    a) sexually offensive comments
    b) sex-oriented jokes
    c) staring or leering
    d) touching, grabbing, pinching

    e) sexual propositions
    f) rape
    g) other forms of sexual harassment
    h) have not experienced sexual harassment

4. How many times in the last twelve months have you personally experienced sexual harassment in the organization where you are presently working?

    a) none
    b) 1–2 times
    c) 3–4 times

    d) 5–6 times
    e) more than 6 times

5. How did you react to a co-worker or supervisor's sexual advances?

    a) ignored it
    b) enjoyed it
    c) ask them to stop

    d) reported it to a company official or government agency
    e) have not received sexual advances

6. If you reported sexual harassment to a supervisor or union representative, what do you think would most likely happen?

    a) nothing
    b) an investigation would be made, but no actual results obtained
    c) an investigation would be made, and action would be taken to stop it

    d) I would be transferred
    e) I would be fired

7. Have you ever used your sexual attractiveness at work for any of the following?

    a) to gain a promotion
    b) to get in good with the superior
    c) to obtain other advantages
    d) not applicable

FIGURE 5–1
A survey to discover the extent of sexual harassment in an organization. All respondents remain anonymous.

8. How has sexual harassment affected you? (circle all letters that apply)

    a) economically
    b) work opportunities
    c) mental and physical health

    d) self-esteem
    e) have not experienced any sexual harass-
       ment

9. You would hesitate to report sexual harassment because you:

    a) feel it would not do any good
    b) would be afraid of being punished in some way
    c) would fear the publicity
    d) would not hesitate to report it

10. Which sex do you feel has a problem with sexual harassment?

    a) women only
    b) mostly women and very few men
    c) women and men about equally

    d) mostly men and very few women
    e) sexual harassment is not a problem

11. Which individuals in your organization are most involved with sexual harassment?

    a) an immediate supervisor harasses a subordinate
    b) a company representative harasses a prospective employee
    c) a co-worker harasses another co-worker
    d) an employee harasses another employee who is neither a subordinate or co-worker
    e) a subordinate harasses a superior
    f) sexual harassment is not a problem

12. To what extent do you consider sexual harassment a problem in your organization?

    a) Sexual harassment is a frequent, troublesome part of the organization's working environ-
       ment. Organizational effectiveness is definitely affected by sexual harassment problems.
    b) Sexual harassment is an occasional problem with sexual harassment situations occurring
       only periodically. Organizational effectiveness is affected only to a minor degree.
    c) Sexual harassment is a minor problem with sexual harassment situations occurring infre-
       quently. Organizational effectiveness is affected hardly at all.
    d) Sexual harassment is not a problem in this organization. It does not affect the organization's
       effectiveness.

Please feel free to write below any additional comments you have on sexual harassment. We are particularly interested in learning about any situations in which you have personally experienced sexual harassment. Please do not sign your name or identify your employer. Thank you for your cooperation.

_____

_____

_____

FIGURE 5–1
continued

in-house newspapers, employee orientation, or employee counselors.

- Training courses can be used to alert managers and supervisors to the problem and to teach workers how to deal with harassment. The primary goal of these efforts is to create an awareness of the problem and to show organizational commitment to eliminating sexual harassment.

Age Discrimination in Employment Act

The Age Discrimination in Employment Act (ADEA) was passed in 1967 and amended in 1978 and 1986. The act makes it illegal for employers with twenty or more employees, governmental bodies, and labor unions to discriminate against individuals over age forty. Employers cannot refuse to hire or discriminate in terms of compensation, promotion, or other conditions solely due to an individual's age. Nor can age be used as a preferential criterion in recruitment.

Section 4(f) of the ADEA allows employers to discipline or terminate an employee for a job-related reason such as incompetence, theft, or some other just cause that is "not age related." The courts have upheld employers' age policies where health and safety are of concern. In a landmark case, *Hodgson* v. *Greyhound Lines, Inc.,* a court of appeals upheld Greyhound's policy of barring applicants over the age of thirty-five for the job of bus driver.[14]

The 1986 amendment prohibits any mandatory retirement age for workers (previously set at age seventy [1978 amendment] and originally at age sixty-five [1967 act]). Public safety employees of state and local governments are exempt until 1994, a measure intended to allow the EEOC adequate time to determine the validity of mental and fitness tests in such areas as police, fire, and emergency medical services. The 1986 amendment also requires employers to continue the same group health insurance for employees over age seventy that is offered to younger employees. The elimination of the mandatory retirement age has received ardent support from senior citizens, labor leaders, and civil rights groups.[15]

At least three areas of personnel costs may be significantly affected by the 1986 amendment. First, the requirement that employers continue to provide health coverage for older employees will most likely increase health care costs significantly. Medical plan rating manuals show increased claims for older workers; thus, health care premiums can be expected to rise. A critical factor will be how many employees choose to work beyond the normal retirement age. Conceivably, the amendment's requirement that employers continue health care coverage for older employees could influence their decision to continue working beyond the age at which they would like to retire. Thus, the new amendment gives them an additional incentive to continue working. A second area likely to be affected by the amendment is pension funding. In theory, if employees work longer, their retirement base and, therefore, their pension checks will be increased. However, if the average age of Americans does not continue to increase, choosing to work longer may mean that the future retirees will collect retirement pensions for fewer years. It may well be the year 2000 before the actual impact on pension costs is known, and then the results may differ from organization to organization.[16]

The third area affected will likely be Social Security. The Congressional Budget Office concluded that Social Security retirement benefits and Medicare may decrease by $25 million annually due to employees choosing to work longer. They will be contributing a greater amount and withdrawing less from the Social Security system, which should slow the rise in Social Security tax rates for both employers and employees.[17] Jerome Rosow, president of the Work in America Institute, Inc., supported the 1986 amendment by predicting that it will decrease the threat of intergenerational conflict if older workers continue to pay into the Social Security system longer and reduce the number of years they withdraw benefits.[18]

The 1978 amendment to the ADEA transferred the enforcement responsibility to the EEOC and provided for jury trials. The change to jury trials greatly increased the number of cases which go to court. Jurors tend to be sympathetic to individuals who are generally the same age as themselves, and they are often prejudiced against large corporations. At the same time, companies began "retiring" many older employees due to economic pressures. By 1985, 36 percent of the labor force was 40 years of age or older, a record in the United States. Increased pressure from the baby-boom generation to make room for their upward mobility also put pressure on companies to force early retirement of older workers.[19]

How can employers help their employees plan their retirement? An American Society for Personnel Administration survey of American employers found that they provide:[20]

- Early retirement options. In addition, early retirement incentive programs (ERIPS) may be offered to encourage eligible employees to volunteer for early retirement by speeding up their benefits.
- Written retirement planning information for employees of all ages. Of particular value is retirement program design and administration, as well as key personal issues such as Social Security, health, legal, and emotional adjustment.

- Postretirement benefits. In addition to monthly retirement checks, retirees may receive health insurance, life insurance, special activity discounts, and retiree newsletters. In recent years, more employers have also provided part-time and consulting work.

The result of these different forces has been a large increase in age-discrimination cases. The typical complainant in ADEA cases is a managerial or professional employee over age fifty. Most cases involve mandatory retirements, demotions, or direct terminations.[21] An analysis of over 300 cases filed in the early 1980s showed that while the EEOC was involved in less than 25 percent of the cases, it was able to win 79 percent of the cases it chose to pursue. Employees generally had a greater likelihood of winning cases that contested mandatory retirement and pension-related employer actions. Age-conscious remarks by employers can help an employee's case, as discussed in the feature "Age-Conscious Remarks That Can Be Used Against You." Employers can increase their chances of winning age-discrimination cases if they:[22]

- Make all decisions on the basis of documented performance appraisals.
- Eliminate organizational policies that might indirectly be age discriminatory and formalize personnel policies that are anti–age discriminatory.
- Train managers and other personnel to refrain from making references to age, especially in front of potential witnesses.
- Chart ages and any other employee characteristics protected against discrimination and analyze any possible age discrimination.
- Document employee responses to early retirement programs that may be needed as evidence of their voluntary participation.

PERSONNEL IN THE NEWS

Age-Conscious Remarks That Can Be Used Against You

In 1985 the EEOC reported a record number of age-discrimination charges against employers. Employees have clearly become more aware of employer age-discrimination practices—and they know their rights under the Age Discrimination in Employment Act (ADEA). Unlike most race-discrimination cases, age-discrimination cases are decided by juries, which may be more sympathetic to the worker. Age-conscious remarks by managers can influence a jury's decision.

Examples of age-conscious communications that have been found to be discriminatory included:

- A piece of paper with the official reason for layoff that says: "Lay off—too old."
- Memo recommending a reduction in [the work] force to promote "a younger image."
- Job advertisements seeking: "college student," "recent college graduate," or "retired person."
- Direct comments by supervisors who affect employment decisions: "for men your age, there isn't going to be a future in the new (company)"; or the company was "going to get rid of the 'good old Joes' and get some younger folks in."

In lawsuits involving age discrimination the employee must prove that age . . . was a determining factor in an employment action—but age need *not* have been the sole reason for the action taken. Employers can avoid liability by eliminating age-conscious remarks in official communications and by documenting a well-organized campaign to sensitize all managers to the need to avoid age-conscious remarks and thinking.

Source: John J. Coleman, III, "Age-Conscious Remarks: What You Say Can Be Used Against You," *Personnel* 62, no. 9 (September 1985), pp. 22–29. Used by permission.

Separation Agreements

An employer and an employee may both benefit from the employee's early retirement. In fact, employers often offer "retirement windows" to employees close in age and seniority to retirement. The window is a fixed period of time, usually a month, during which the employee must decide whether or not to accept and sign a separation agreement that provides enhanced retirement benefits such as continued health care coverage or a higher monthly pension. The 1986 ADEA amendment requires early retirement programs to be voluntary.

In a landmark case, *Sullivan* v. *Boron Oil Company* (1987),[23] an employee's written separation agreement was upheld as legal and binding. In this case, an employee of the Standard Oil of Ohio (SOHIO) Company signed an agreement titled "Release of Claims," which stated that "In consideration of the benefit provided me . . . , I release the Standard Oil Company . . . from all claims." The employee claimed age discrimination because he was mentally and physically fatigued when he signed the release. The U.S. Court of Appeals applied a five-part test to determine the validity and fairness of the agreement and found that (1) the release was clear and unambiguous, (2) the plaintiff knew his rights as stated in the agreement, (3) the plaintiff understood the agreement, (4) the plaintiff had an opportunity to negotiate, and (5) the plaintiff accepted the release for personal compensation. This decision provides employers with specific guidelines for developing voluntary early retirement plans that can be legally executed without fear of successful litigation.

Vocational Rehabilitation Act

Under the Vocational Rehabilitation Act of 1973, employers with government contracts of $2,500 or more must have approved affirmative-action programs for the handicapped. Programs include special recruitment efforts for the handicapped, as well as procedures to promote and develop the handicapped within the organization. Employees are also required to make environmental changes, such as adding ramps to make their businesses more accessible to the handicapped. The act is administered by committee members from the Civil Service Commission, the Administration of Veterans' Affairs, the U.S. Department of Labor, and the U.S. Department of Health and Human Services. Handicapped individuals who feel that their rights have been violated

under the act may file complaints with the U.S. Department of Labor.

Although the term *handicap* is usually associated with physical impairments, the act also covers such mental impairments as retardation and emotional disorders. In addition, the act covers certain illnesses sometimes used by employers as grounds for rejecting applicants, including diabetes, heart disease, epilepsy, and cancer. Individuals who are alcohol or drug users are included unless their illness affects their ability to perform their job.[24] In practice, the Department of Labor's guidelines for contractors require them to make a "reasonable accommodation" for the handicapped, which generally include:[25]

Job Accessibility Adding wheelchair ramps, braille signs on elevators, air conditioning for workers with respiratory problems, and so on.

Job Design Eliminating tasks that a handicapped person cannot perform but that are not really necessary to do the job.

Qualifications Eliminating unnecessary job specifications, such as a physical exam that might limit the entry of handicapped applicants.

Unprejudiced Treatment Eliminating hiring decisions based on people's fear or uneasiness about handicaps, such as about epilepsy or speech impairment.

Vietnam Era Veterans Readjustment Act

This act was a special effort to help Vietnam War veterans who had particular difficulty in securing jobs when they returned to the United States. The Vietnam Era Veterans Readjustment Act of 1974 requires all organizations holding government contracts of

Job Design and Selection

$10,000 or more to hire and promote veterans of the Vietnam War era. The act is administered by the Veterans Employment Service of the U.S. Department of Labor. Employers holding government contracts are required to list their job openings with local state employment offices in order that these offices may contact unemployed veterans as well as other individuals. One side effect of the act has been a demonstrated increase in job openings listed by state employment offices, which has increased their effectiveness in many communities.

Immigration Reform and Control Act

Congress in 1986, after years of debate, passed a comprehensive federal immigration control law. In effect, the Immigration Reform and Control Act (IRCA) shifted much of the burden of immigration enforcement from the federal government to employers. This shift was accomplished by making it illegal for an employer to hire, recruit, refer for a fee, or continue to employ an alien whom the employer knows is not eligible to work in the United States. Employers are required to verify and maintain records of each new employee's identity and work eligibility for three years of employment or for one year after termination. Thus, in practice, employers will require of all new employees one of the following as documentation of legal employment status:[26]

- Social Security card or certificate of birth with current driver's license.
- Alien Registration Receipt Card (green card).
- Valid United States passport.
- Valid certificate of citizenship or United States identification card.
- Valid certificate for naturalization.
- Unexpired Immigration Naturalization Service (INS) work permit.

- Unexpired foreign passport bearing an appropriate unexpired endorsement of the United States Attorney General.
- Resident alien card.
- Form I-94 bearing an employment authorization stamp.

A second major feature of the IRCA makes it unlawful for employers to discriminate against individuals who are "foreign looking" or "foreign sounding" but are legally in the United States. This section of the act was passed in response to concerns of Hispanic-American groups and others who feared that the new employer requirements might lead to unintentional employmemt discrimination.[27] Specifically, Section 274B(a)(1) of the act provides the following:

> It is an unfair immigration-related employment practice for a person or other entity to discriminate against any individual (other than an unauthorized alien) with respect to the hiring, or recruitment or referral for a fee, of the individual for employment or the discharging of the individual for employment—
> (A) because of such individual's national origin, or
> (B) in the case of a citizen or intending citizen . . ., because of such individual's citizenship status.

The preamble to the regulations emphasizes that personnel policies such as "English-only" rules, lengthy residence requirements, or unnecessary documents for employee verification can be challenged if adopted for discriminatory purposes.

Employers of four or more employees are covered by the act. The Department of Justice is charged with its enforcement. The act requires employers to refuse employment to unauthorized aliens after November 6, 1986. Legally, an employer can retain any employee hired and working before that date even if the individual was known to be an illegal alien, but the INS can apprehend such aliens at a later date. It is unlawful to continue to employ individuals whom the employer knows are using fraudulent documents or whose temporary work authorization has expired. The act specifically excludes union hiring halls from any documentations or certification requirements. Employers of union referrals, however, are covered by the act.

The act includes civil penalties of $250 to $2,000 per alien for the first offense of knowingly hiring an unauthorized alien. Subsequent offenses may bring penalties of $2,000 to $5,000. Penalties of $100 to $1,000 can be imposed on employers who fail to comply with the documentation requirements. Employers who engage in a ''pattern or practice'' of violations may be charged with additional fines and up to six months' imprisonment.[28]

Another major provision of the act is amnesty for aliens who entered the country illegally before January 1, 1982, and have resided here continuously since that time. The act allows ''brief, casual, and innocent absences'' from the United States without loss of amnesty, but not absences due to lack of work or vacation. Employers may assist individuals seeking to obtain amnesty by offering payroll records as evidence of continuous residence.

AFFIRMATIVE ACTION

By Executive Order 11246, President Lyndon B. Johnson created what is known today as *affirmative action*. Since 1965 this order has been amended several times by later presidents. An *executive order* is not a law and, therefore, does not have the wide impact of federal laws such as the Civil Rights Act of 1964. An executive order directly affects only governmental agencies and contractors or subcontractors of federal government programs. But organizations may be ordered by a court to develop an affirmative-action plan.

Unlike the previously discussed laws passed by Congress, which may be referred to as *neutrality laws* because they only require that organizations obey them, executive orders relating to affirmative action require that certain organizations take specific positive actions to improve the employment opportunities of minorities.

The U.S. Supreme Court reaffirmed and clarified the principles of affirmative action in 1986 and 1987 landmark decisions. See the chapter-opening article for a complete summary.

Program Development

Development and administration of an affirmative-action program usually requires an organization to perform specific acts. First, an organization must give a copy of the equal employment opportunity (EEO) policy to all employees and applicants. The policy must specify a commitment to EEO and affirmative action. The organization must reaffirm these commitments in all ads and employee notices.

Second, an organization must give a specific, top-ranking company official the authority and responsibility for affirmative-action program implementation. This manager or coordinator should have the authority to secure necessary information and demand assistance in developing and carrying out an affirmative-action plan. This person must receive complete support from top management to engender cooperation from lower-level employees, who may not place affirmative-action problems at the top of their daily agenda.

Third, an organization must complete a *work force analysis* of the organization. The first step in completing a work force analysis is to do a ''head count'' of the employees in the organization by number and percentage of minorities and females in each major job classification. The next step is to determine if the

Why Employer Sanctions in Immigration?

Immigration is an expression of one of the most fundamental human aspirations: the desire for a better life, a new start, a clean slate.

And, as long as people see these opportunities lying just across a border, they will continue to move toward them, whether someone says it is legal to do so or not.

This phenomenon of migration is a central element of the American experience and of our heritage. In recent years, however, a lack of control of illegal movement across our national borders—allowing the unfettered entry of millions of illegal aliens—has strained our national patience and placed at risk the long-standing American tradition of a fair, humane, and generous welcome for legal aliens.

It also highlighted the patent unfairness of an immigration system that allowed a flood of illegal entries into the United States but that allowed only a comparative trickle of legal aliens.

Finally, uncontrolled illegal immigration created an "underclass" in the United States: a class of law-abiding persons who had been in the United States for many years, but whose illegal status made them afraid and fearful of asserting their legal and moral rights lest they be deported. This class was especially vulnerable to the most shameful and degrading exploitation.

It was quickly clear to those of us on congressional panels with jurisdiction over immigration that the magnitude and complexity of the illegal immigration problem were such that a single solution was not possible.

A multifaceted approach was needed if the problems as well as the benefits posed by illegal immigration were to be dealt with by our government in a balanced, effective way.

This approach had to be stern enough to end illegal entry into the United States. At the same time, it had to be generous enough to legitimize the status of many of the undocumented who were already in the country, in keeping with the magnanimous and humane traditions of the United States.

The multifaceted, many-layered approach Congress eventually embraced—after almost continuous debate during a six-year period starting in 1981—took the form of the Immigration Reform and Control Act of 1986 (IRCA).

The act has three major components, with one component having a major subdivision.

First is the legalization program. Under it, undocumented persons of otherwise good character who had been in the United States since 1982 and have good work records and no criminal record could come out of the shadows of illegality, could legalize their immigration status, and could even become citizens of our nation.

Second, there is a labor section in the Immigration Reform Act that streamlines the H-2 program—already on the nation's statute books—allowing foreign workers to come into the United States for limited periods of time to do seasonal agricultural work.

A subsection of the labor provision is a program—the Special Agricultural Workers Program (SAW)—to legalize certain illegal aliens who had worked in agricultural pursuits in the United States between 1985 and 1986.

Both of these labor provisions were designed to deal with possible labor shortages caused by enactment of this immigration reform legislation.

Third, and perhaps the linchpin of immigration reform, is a section establishing penalties for employers who knowingly hire persons not authorized to work in the United States. Employer sanctions require that most U.S. employers verify the residency status of all prospective employees.

This verification procedure is designed to halt illegal immigration at its source by reducing or eliminating the employment incentive that inspires so many undocumented aliens to enter the United States for work.

Woven into employer sanctions is a protection against any discrimination that might be directed against prospective employees. It is precisely to avoid this possibility of discrimination that employers must ask all prospective employees to show the proper documentation—not just those who look or sound "foreign," but all employees. Employees and prospective employees are further protected from employment-related discrimination by a special counsel of the Justice Department.

Employer sanctions are a key element in the comprehensive strategy and national policy to control illegal immigration into the United States and to do justice to the illegal aliens who are already here.

It is hoped that by reducing the incentive for the undocumented aliens to enter, by enhancing the security of our borders to stop those who remain undeterred, and by providing a clean slate for certain illegal aliens who have already established themselves here in the United States, the new Immigration Act can help resolve the problem of illegal immigration in a pragmatic, principled way.

Thus, with the cooperation of employers and employees across the country, the borders of the United States will be made more secure, legal immigration policies will continue to be humane and generous, the American labor force will be protected from job displacement and depressed wages, and undocumented aliens can become full-fledged, productive members of U.S. society.

Source: Unpublished paper by U.S. Congressman Romano L. Mazzoli (D–Ky.). Used by permission.

organization has *underuse* of minorities and females in any job classification. Underuse can be defined as having fewer minorities or women in a particular job category that would be found in the relevant labor market. The EEOC job categories are shown in Figure 5–2. The next step for the organization is to compare its own employment figures with those of the Standard Metropolitan Statistical Area (SMSA). These data are available from the local U.S. Department of Labor office. The work force analysis should also identify any concentration of minorities or females in a particular job category. A *concentration* takes place when more of a particular minority group is located in a job category than would be expected when compared to the labor market figures. The final step of the work force analysis is to determine which job categories have an underuse or concentration of minorities or females. If either underuse or concentration occurs, then management must take affirmative actions in order to end the discriminatory activities that caused the underutilization or concentration.

Fourth, an organization must establish goals and timetables. Once managers have determined where an organization may have discriminated in the past, they can develop specific goals and timetables to improve performance in those job categories. Managers then determine if any discrimination barriers may have limited minority and female participation in certain job categories and also determine how to ensure that sufficient minori-

ties and females will be hired in the future. As Figure 5–3 illustrates, the goals should establish specific numbers and percentages to be hired in specific job categories, and the timetable should set dates when these goals should be accomplished.

And fifth, an organization must develop recruitment plans. Such plans may include advertising at colleges and universities which traditionally have large minority and female enrollments. Current minority and female employees are usually good sources of information about reaching interested female and minority applicants.

Required Records

Adequate records must be kept to meet EEOC requirements. Even if the organization's statistics show no problems with underutilization or concentration, these records can provide a defense in court cases or in compliance reviews by federal agencies. The EEOC recommends that the following records and supporting data be kept for affirmative-action purposes:[29]

- Most recent SF-100 (EEO-1) report and previous three years' reports (see Figure 5–4).
- Number of applications for each major job category and hires by sex and minority group for the previous twelve months (Form P).
- Chronological list of all hires by name, sex, minority group, job, rate of pay, and

Officials and Managers Occupations requiring administrative personnel who set broad policies, exercise overall responsibility for execution of these policies, and direct individual departments or special phases of a firm's operations. Includes: Officials, Executives, Middle Management, Plant Managers, Department Managers, and Superintendents, Salaried Foremen who are members of Management, Purchasing Agents and Buyers, and Kindred Workers.

Professional Occupations requiring either college graduation or experiences of such kind and amount as to provide a comparable background. Includes: Accountants and Auditors, Airplane Pilots and Navigators, Architects, Artists, Chemists, Designers, Dietitians, Editors, Lawyers, Librarians, Mathematicians, Natural Scientists, Registered Professional Nurses . . . and Kindred Workers.

Technicians Occupations requiring a combination of basic scientific knowledge and manual skill which can be obtained through about 2 years of post high school education, such as is offered in many technical institutes and junior colleges, or through equivalent on-the-job training. Included: Computer Programmers and Operators, Draftsmen, Engineering Aides, Junior Engineers, Mathematical Aides, Licensed, Practical or Vocational Nurses . . . and Kindred Workers.

Sales Occupations engaging wholly or primarily in direct selling. Included: Advertising Agents and Salesmen, Insurance Agents and Brokers, Real Estate Agents and Brokers, Stock and Bond Salesmen, Demonstrators, Salesmen and Sales Clerks, Grocery Clerks and Cashier-Checkers, and Kindred Workers.

Office and Clerical Includes all clerical-type work regardless of level of difficulty, where the activities are predominantly nonmanual though some manual work not directly involved with altering or transporting the products is included. Includes: Bookkeepers, Cashiers, Collectors (Bills and Accounts), Messengers and Office Boys, Office Machine Operators . . . and Kindred Workers.

Craftsmen (Skilled) Manual workers of relatively high skill level having a thorough and comprehensive knowledge of the processes involved in their work. Exercise considerable independent judgment and usually receive an extensive period of training. Includes: The Building Trades, Hourly Paid Foremen and Leadmen who are not members of management, Mechanics and Repairmen, Electricians, Engravers, Job Setters (Metal), Motion Picture Projectionists . . . and Kindred Workers.

Operatives (Semiskilled) Workers who operate machine or processing equipment or perform other factory-type duties of intermediate skill level which can be mastered in a few weeks and require only limited training. Includes: Apprentices (Auto Mechanics, Plumbers, Bricklayers, Carpenters, Electricians, Machinists, Mechanics, Building Trades, Metalworking Trades, Printing Trades, etc.) Operatives, Attendants (Auto Service and Parking), Blasters, Chauffeurs, Deliverymen and Routemen, Dressmakers and Seamstresses (Except Factory), Dryers, Furnacemen, Heaters (Metal), Laundry and Dry Cleaning Operatives, Milliners, Mine Operatives and Laborers, Motormen, Oilers and Greasers (Except Auto) . . . and Kindred Workers.

Laborers (Unskilled) Workers in manual occupations which generally require no special training. Perform elementary duties that may be learned in a few days and require the application of little or no independent judgment. Includes: Garage laborers, Car Washers and Greasers, Gardeners (Except Farm) and Groundskeepers, Longshoremen and Stevedores, Lumbermen . . . and Kindred Workers.

Service Workers Workers in both protective and nonprotective service occupations. Includes: Attendants (Hospital and Other Institutions, Professional and Personal Service, including Nurses Aides, and Orderlies), Barbers, Charwomen and Cleaners, Cooks (Except Household), Counter and Fountain Workers, Elevator Operators, Firemen and Fire Protection, Guards . . . and Kindred Workers.

FIGURE 5–2

A description of the job categories used by the Equal Employment Opportunity Commission (EEOC) (Source: Instructions for Filing Employer Information Report EEO-1, U.S. EEOC [Washington, DC: U.S. Printing Office, 1965], pp. 1–12.)

Each manager will establish goals and timetables to rectify underutilization of minorities and women. This is the heart of each unit's affirmative-action program. Goals should be significant, measurable, and attainable given the commitment of the organizational unit and its good faith efforts. The internal work force analysis and the analysis of the relevant external labor area provide the basic data on which goals and timetables are formulated, in combination with the company's goals and timetables. Goals and timetables must meet the following descriptions:

1. Goals and timetables will be determined for women and minorities separately.
2. In establishing timetables to meet goals, each organizational unit will consider the anticipated expansion, contraction, and turnover of its work force.
3. Specific goals and timetables for women and minorities will be established for each category of employment (e.g., office, factory, apprenticeship, college, professional).
4. Specific goals and timetables for women and minorities will be established for each promotional category (e.g., hourly to exempt, office, factory, professional).
5. The nature of the goals and timetables established are a function of:
   a. The degree of underutilization within the specified job family.
   b. The scope of the relevant recruitment area.
   c. The availability of qualified or qualifiable minorities and women in the area.
   d. The number of job openings available, determined by turnover, expansion, etc.
   e. The commitment of the organizational unit to correct underutilization of minorities and women.
   f. The AAP and EEO policy of the company.
6. The one year and five year goals will be recorded on Form XX, by completing Columns 37–61 per the instructions.

FIGURE 5–3
EEOC instructions to organizations about goals and timetables (Source: Adapted from *Affirmative Action and Equal Employment, A Guidebook for Employees,* U.S. EEOC [Washington, DC: U.S. Government Printing Office, 1974], p. A-14.)

recruitment source for the previous twelve months (Form P).

- List of schools, date, name, sex, and minority group of those interviewed (if there is a college recruitment program), indicating those to whom offers were extended and the disposition (Form P).
- List of all promotions and transfers, giving the date, name, sex, minority group, previous job department and pay, and new job department and pay for the previous twelve months (Form Q).
- List of all terminations by department for the previous twelve months, giving the name, sex, minority group, job and department, date of hire, date of termination, and reason (Form S).
- List of various ongoing or completed training programs during the previous twelve months, with the name, sex, minority group of participants, date of completion, and job and pay before and after training (Form R).
- Copies of any agreements pursuant to investigations of charges of discrimination by federal, state, or local agencies and copies of any outstanding charges and present status.

Standard Form 100
(Rev. 12-76)
Approved GAO B-180541 (R0077)
Expires 12-31-78

EQUAL EMPLOYMENT OPPORTUNITY

EMPLOYER INFORMATION REPORT EEO-1

Joint Reporting Committee

• Equal Employment Opportunity Commission
• Office of Federal Contract Compliance Programs

Section A — TYPE OF REPORT
Refer to instructions for number and types of reports to be filed.

1. Indicate by marking in the appropriate box the type of reporting unit for which this copy of the form is submitted (MARK ONLY ONE BOX)

(1) ☐ Single-establishment Employer Report

Multi-establishment Employer:
(2) ☐ Consolidated Report
(3) ☐ Headquarters Unit Report
(4) ☐ Individual Establishment Report (submit one for each establishment with 25 or more employees)
(5) ☐ Special Report

2. Total number of reports being filed by this Company (Answer on Consolidated Report only) _____

Section B — COMPANY IDENTIFICATION (To be answered by all employers)

OFFICE USE ONLY

1. Parent Company
   a. Name of parent company (owns or controls establishment in item 2) omit if same as label

Name of receiving office	Address (Number and street)	a

City or town	County	State	ZIP code	b. Employer Identification No.	b

2. Establishment for which this report is filed. (Omit if same as label)
   a. Name of establishment

Address (Number and street)	City or town	County	State	ZIP code	c

b. Employer Identification No.	(If same as label, skip.)	d

3. Parent company affiliation
   (Multi-establishment Employers
     Answer on Consolidated Report only)
   a. Name of parent—affiliated company   b. Employer Identification No.

Address (Number and street)	City or town	County	State	ZIP code

Section C — EMPLOYERS WHO ARE REQUIRED TO FILE (To be answered by all employers)

☐ Yes ☐ No 1. Does the entire company have at least 100 employees in the payroll period for which you are reporting?

☐ Yes ☐ No 2. Is your company affiliated through common ownership and/or centralized management with other entities in an enterprise with a total employment of 100 or more?

☐ Yes ☐ No 3. Does the company or any of its establishments (a) have 50 or more employees AND (b) is not exempt as provided by 41 CFR 60-1.5, AND either (1) is a prime government contractor or first-tier subcontractor, and has a contract, subcontract, or purchase order amounting to $50,000 or more, or (2) serves as a depository of Government funds in any amount or is a financial institution which is an issuing and paying agent for U.S. Savings Bonds and Savings Notes?

NOTE: If the answer is yes to ANY of these questions, complete the entire form, otherwise skip to Section G.

FIGURE 5–4

Employer information report EEO-1, which private employers must complete annually
(Source: *Mission, 5,* EEOC [Washington, D. C.: U. S. Printing Office, 1977], p. 13.)

Section D — EMPLOYMENT DATA

Employment at this establishment--Report all permanent, temporary or part-time employees including apprentices and on-the-job trainees unless specifically excluded as set forth in the instructions. Enter the appropriate figures on all lines and in all columns. Blank spaces will be considered as zeros.

JOB CATEGORIES	OVERALL TOTALS (SUM OF COL B THRU K) A	MALE					FEMALE				
		WHITE (NOT OF HISPANIC ORIGIN) B	BLACK (NOT OF HISPANIC ORIGIN) C	HISPANIC D	ASIAN OR PACIFIC ISLANDER E	AMERICAN INDIAN OR ALASKAN NATIVE F	WHITE (NOT OF HISPANIC ORIGIN) G	BLACK (NOT OF HISPANIC ORIGIN) H	HISPANIC I	ASIAN OR PACIFIC ISLANDER J	AMERICAN INDIAN OR ALASKAN NATIVE K
Officials and Managers											
Professionals											
Technicians											
Sales Workers											
Office and Clerical											
Craft Workers (Skilled)											
Operatives (Semi-Skilled)											
Laborers (Unskilled)											
Service Workers											
TOTAL											
Total employment reported in previous EEO-1 report											

(The trainees below should also be included in the figures for the appropriate occupational categories above)

Formal On-the-job trainees	White collar											
	Production											

1. **NOTE:** On consolidated report, skip questions 2-5 and Section E.
2. How was information as to race or ethnic group in Section D obtained?
   1 ☐ Visual Survey   3 ☐ Other — Specify ....
   2 ☐ Employment Record   ....
3. Dates of payroll period used —

4. Pay period of last report submitted for this establishment

5. Does this establishment employ apprentices?
   This year? 1 ☐ Yes 2 ☐ No
   Last year? 1 ☐ Yes 2 ☐ No

Section E — ESTABLISHMENT INFORMATION

1. Is the location of the establishment the same as that reported last year?
   1 ☐ Yes 2 ☐ No 3 ☐ Did not report last year 4 ☐ Reported on combined basis

2. Is the major business activity at this establishment the same as that reported last year?
   1 ☐ Yes 2 ☐ No 3 ☐ No report last year 4 ☐ Reported on combined basis

OFFICE USE ONLY

3. What is the major activity of this establishment? (Be specific i.e., manufacturing steel castings, retail grocer, wholesale plumbing supplies, title insurance, etc. Include the specific type of product or type of service provided, as well as the principal business or industrial activity.

Section F — REMARKS

Use this item to give any identification data appearing on last report which differs from that given above, explain major changes in composition or reporting units, and other pertinent information.

Section G — CERTIFICATION (See Instructions G)

Check one
1. ☐ All reports are accurate and were prepared in accordance with the instructions (check on consolidated only)
2. ☐ This report is accurate and was prepared in accordance with the instructions.

Name of Certifying Official	Title	Signature	Date

Name of person to contact regarding this report (Type or print)	Address (Number and street)		

Title	City and State	ZIP code	Telephone Area Code	Number	Extension

All reports and information obtained from individual reports will be kept confidential as required by Section 709 (e) of Title VII.

FIGURE 5–4
continued

- Copies of all current labor agreements.
- Seniority lists or computer printouts showing all employees by name, sex, minority group, date of hire, other job-related dates, original job, date of last promotion, present job and category, rate of pay, and (if available) education or special training or both. Data must be provided in seniority order within departments, along with all interpretive materials, including organization charts, promotional sequences, and lines of progression. Those on layoff status should be designated.
- Affirmative-action plan goals, along with current status of attainment.
- Material on testing.
- Written job descriptions and qualifications.

Program Implementation

Many managers and employees still do not recognize the importance and impact of anti-discrimination laws. Often EEO coordinators and affirmative-action program managers do not get complete cooperation from department heads and employees. Sometimes coordinators must resort to coercion to get information and assistance from employees.

The affirmative-action program manager may find it more productive to implement three basic strategies. First, try to make the recruitment and selection of employees more job related rather than trying to change employees' attitudes toward the recruitment and selection of minorities and females. Second, encourage participation in the design and implementation of the program from all levels of management. Third, relate organizational goals to each department's goals and timetables.[30] A specific letter of instruction to department heads concerning goals and timetables may help to accomplish this third strategy.

UNIFORM GUIDELINES ON EMPLOYEE SELECTION PROCEDURES

After 1966, federal agencies began issuing separate, sometimes conflicting, guidelines, leading to enforcement problems as well as to severe criticism from private industry. The early guidelines were complex and difficult for practitioners to understand. One consequence of the confusion was that many firms abandoned employment testing, which was believed to be greatly limited by the early guidelines. In some cases subjective selection procedures were often adopted, and minority candidates were hired to avoid charges of noncompliance.[31]

In 1978, the Uniform Guidelines on Employee Selection Procedures were adopted by four federal agencies: the Equal Employment Opportunity Commission, the Civil Service Commission, the U.S. Department of Labor, and the U.S. Department of Justice. In order to comply with suggested practices and avoid potentially costly litigation, both managers and personnel practitioners must be familiar with the guidelines' basic principles. The more significant sections are printed here and then interpreted in light of practical experience.

Section 2. B. Employment Decisions These guidelines apply to tests and other selection procedures which are used as a basis for any employment decision. Employment decisions include—but are not limited to—hiring, promotion, demotion, membership (for example, in a labor organization), referral, retention, and licensing and certification to the extent that licensing and certification may be covered by federal equal employment opportunity law. Other selection decisions, such as selection for training or transfer, may also be considered employment decisions if they lead to any of the decisions listed above.

Remember that guidelines apply to tests of the paper-and-pencil variety and "other selection procedures.'' Thus, the guidelines apply to any reference check, interview, application blank, or other selection instrument utilized by an organization. In recent years, due in part to the guidelines, the use of written tests has declined and the use of interviews in selection has increased. Ironically, the interview, which may be subject to even more personal bias, is just as vulnerable to EEO pressures.[32]

Section 3. Discrimination Defined Relationship between use of selection procedures and discrimination. Procedure having adverse impact constitutes discrimination unless justified. The use of any selection procedure which has an adverse impact on the hiring, promotion, or other employment or membership opportunities of members of any race, sex, or ethnic group will be considered to be discriminatory and inconsistent with these guidelines, unless the procedure has been validated in accordance with these guidelines, or the provisions of section 6 . . . are satisfied.

In Section 3 the guidelines link discrimination directly to adverse impact. *Discrimination* occurs when an individual who has an equal probability of being successful on a job does not have an equal probability of getting the job.

An *adverse impact* on an employment practice causes members of any race, color, sex, religion, or national origin to receive unequal consideration for employment. If an employer's selection procedure, such as an interview, results in an applicant's not having an equal chance to be hired or promoted, then that procedure caused the organization to discriminate against that applicant. A selection procedure or policy which has adverse impacts on the employment opportunities of any race, sex, or ethnic group is normally illegal under Title VII unless the employer can offer a legal defense.

Section 3 states that a properly validated selection procedure is not discriminatory. *Validity* in testing occurs whenever a test actually measures what it is intended to measure. If a test is valid, then the employer knows that it is directly measuring the applicant's ability to perform the job and not measuring something else. A valid test is not influenced by personal bias. For example, a person measuring a sapling with a yardstick and finding it to be 38 inches high thinks that is a valid measurement. The yardstick could not measure a friend's ability to estimate the height of the same tree correctly. The friend's point of view—size and proximity to the tree—influences the guesstimate. The same type of influence occurs when individuals' points of view consciously or unconsciously influence decisions concerning job applicants. Since there once were no standard means available to measure the validity of employment tests, the guidelines offer standards for test validity.

Section 5. General Standards for Validity Studies. A. Acceptable types of validity studies. For the purposes of satisfying these guidelines, users may rely upon criterion-related validity studies, content validity studies or construct validity studies in accordance with the standards set forth in the technical standards of these guidelines. B. Criterion-related content and construct validity. Evidence of the validity of a test or other selection procedure by a criterion-related validity study should consist of empirical data demonstrating that the selection procedure is predictive of or significantly correlated with important elements of job performance. Evidence of the validity of a test or other selection procedure by a content validity study should consist of data showing that the content of the selection procedure is representative of important aspects of performance on the job for which the candidates are to be evaluated. Evidence of the validity of a test or other selection procedure through a construct validity study should consist of data showing that the procedure measures the degree to which candidates have identifiable characteristics which have been determined to be important in successful performance in the job for which the candidates are to be evaluated.

Criterion-related validity can be established by collecting data from job applicants and employees. This form of validation correlates test scores with employee success on the job. There are many measures of employee productivity that may be used, such as absenteeism, sales levels, supervisory evaluations, or quantity of production. Two primary methods of establishing criterion-related validity are predictive validation and concurrent validation.

Predictive validity, preferred by the EEOC, is usually the most difficult to determine. Establishing predictive validity requires testing the entire pool of job applicants, hiring them, and then correlating their test scores with their criterion scores.

For example, to determine the predictive validity of a test given to applicants for sales-representative positions, all applicants during the previous month are tested. All applicants are then hired, given equal training, and assigned to sales routes. After one year, the total commission sales of the new employees (the criterion of job success) are correlated with their test scores. The resulting figure, called a *correlation coefficient,* can vary from -1 to $+1$. For example, if the correlation coefficient *(r)* is .67, then the test is valid for sales representatives because individuals' test performances have been shown to be related to job performance.

If the comparison of the applicants' test scores with their criterion scores produces a high correlation coefficient, then the organization may use the test for future applicants because it has evidence that the test is a valid predictor of employee performance.

Concurrent validity is similar to predictive validity in that test scores are compared to job-performance measures. But to establish concurrent validity, both test scores and performance measures are collected at the same time.

This is accomplished by testing current employees, for whom the organization already has performance scores, such as supervisory ratings. The major difference between predictive validity and concurrent validity is that the former concerns applicants and the latter concerns present employees. This difference is very important because in establishing predictive validity the firm gets test scores from the total range of individuals who might apply for the job. By contrast, in establishing concurrent validity, the firm tests only those individuals who have been kept as employees. For practical reasons, establishing concurrent validity is preferable. One important reason is that administrators do not like to hire all applicants, some of whom very likely will fail as employees. Another reason is time. Concurrent validity can be established within a few weeks; predictive validity requires at least six months to a year to be established.

Content validity is a nonempirical (non-statistical) approach to validation. To establish content validity, the organization shows, often through job analysis, that the content of the test is actually a sample of the work performed on the job. For example, a typing test could be given to applicants for clerical positions which require typing. Another example would be testing bank-teller applicants' speed and accuracy with figures.

Construct validity is another nonempirical approach to validation. This type of validation is based on the theoretical relationship between a test and a construct, a characteristic in that an employee should have to be successful. Giving store manager applicants a general IQ test because management believes they need a certain level of intelligence to be successful might be an example of construct validity. Giving sales clerks ''personality'' tests to determine if they will work well with customers could be considered construct validation.

In general, the EEOC gives the greatest preference to predictive validity and the least to construct validity. Both empirical validations, predictive and concurrent, are strong because they involve empirical data collection and statistics, which generally are not discriminatory. Content validity is at least a direct test of individuals' ability to perform some—usually not all—of the tasks required on the job. Construct validity is often management's last choice and may be hard to defend in court.

> *Section 4.D. Adverse Impact and the Four-fifths Rule* A selection rate for any race, sex, or ethnic group which is less than four-fifths (4/5) (or eighty percent) of the rate for the group with the highest rate will generally be regarded by the federal enforcement agencies as evidence of adverse impact, while a greater than four-fifths rate will generally not be regarded by federal enforcement agencies as evidence of adverse impact.

The *four-fifths rule* or *80 percent rule* in the 1987 guidelines raised serious questions by private industry. The rule provides a quantitative definition of adverse impact, not a legal definition.[33] For example, if eight out of fifty white male applicants (16 percent) and three out of twenty black male applicants (15 percent) were hired, the four-fifths rule has been met because four-fifths of 16 percent (12.8 percent) is less than the 15 percent hiring rate for blacks. No evidence of adverse impact is present.

The word *generally* in the four-fifths rule has caused some concern. The guidelines provide that a more stringent standard may be applied if there is evidence that the employer has discouraged minority or female applications.[34] Employers who want a more explicit definition of adverse impact are disappointed with the extensive use of the term *generally*.[35] That an employer has met the four-fifths rule

does not rule out the possibility of a federal agency finding adverse impact."[36]

> *Section 1.B. Purpose of Guidelines* These guidelines do not require a user to conduct validity studies of selection procedures where no adverse impact results. However, all users are encouraged to use selection procedures which are valid, especially users operating under merit principles.

These sections of the guidelines permit one component of the selection process to have adverse impact if the total selection procedure does not produce adverse impact. If an employer's total selection process meets the four-fifths rule but the interview, one of several components, violates it, the federal government usually will not take action or require validation of the interview process as part of the entire selection procedure.

> *Section 4.A. Information Required* Records concerning impact. Each user should maintain and have available for inspection records or other information which will disclose the impact which its tests and other selection procedures have upon employment opportunities of persons by identifiable race, sex, or ethnic group . . . in order to determine compliance with these guidelines. Where there are large numbers of applicants and procedures are administered frequently, such information may be retained on a sample basis, provided that the sample is appropriate in terms of the applicant population and adequate in size.

The guidelines require that certain records be kept by employers. Private employers must annually complete the EEO-1 form, shown in Figure 5–4; it includes the number of applicants and employees by minority group and sex. The format is quite similar to that required in affirmative-action reports.

The employer must indicate on the EEO-1 form if the selection process for any job has had an adverse impact on any group which constitutes 2 percent of the relevant labor force.[37] This section means that employers are not required to maintain records for minority groups that constitute less than 2 percent of the relevant labor force. Therefore, some employers will only be concerned with adverse impact against females and blacks, since many sections of the United States do not contain 2 percent of other minority groups.

SIGNIFICANT COURT CASES

Federal statutes passed by Congress and executive orders issued by presidents have had their impact. Personnel officials must also be concerned with various court decisions. A few of the most significant will be discussed here.

Racial Discrimination

Griggs v. *Duke Power Co.*
401 US. 424 (1971)
Supreme Court of the United States

The question at issue was if Title VII of the Civil Rights Act prohibits employers from requiring that applicants have a high school education or pass a standardized general intelligence test. In this case, neither condition of employment was shown to be significant for successful job performance. Both requirements disqualify black applicants at a substantially higher rate than white applicants, and the job in question was formerly filled only by white employees.

The Duke Power Company contended that its general intelligence tests were permitted by the Civil Rights Act because the act authorizes the use of any professionally developed test that is not designed, intended, or used to discriminate. The EEOC, however, contended that the Civil Rights Act and Congress intended only job-related tests to be authorized.

The Court noted that neither the high school completions requirement nor the general intelligence test had been shown to be directly related to successful performance of the jobs for which they were required. A company official had testified that the requirements were chosen because the company believed they would improve the quality of the work force. The Court stated that if an employment practice which excludes blacks cannot be shown to be related to job performance, it is prohibited by the Civil Rights Act.

The Civil Rights Act does not command that any person be hired simply because of the former discrimination or minority-group membership. The act does try to remove artificial, arbitrary, and unnecessary barriers to employment which discriminate on the basis of race, color, religion, sex, or national origin.

In this landmark case concerning Title VII of the Civil Rights Act, the Supreme Court's decision provided critical direction to the interpretation of the act. The decision established that (1) the employer must prove that any employment requirement is job related; (2) the absence of discriminatory intentions does not absolve an employer who has discriminated in practice; (3) even professionally developed, widely adopted tests must be shown to be significantly related to an applicant's ability to perform on the job successfully.

Reverse Discrimination

United Steelworkers v. *Weber*
443 U.S. 193 (1979)
Supreme Court of the United States

Weber alleged that the filling of craft trainee positions under an affirmative-action program, which reserved 50 percent of the openings for blacks, had resulted in junior black employees receiving training preference to more senior white employees. Weber contended that Congress intended in Title VII to make it illegal to "discriminate . . . because of . . . race" in hiring, promotions, transfers, and the selecting of apprentices for training programs. This is seen as a literal interpretation of the Civil Rights Act.

The Court noted that while the argument made by Weber was "not without force," it did not consider the spirit of the 1964 Civil Rights Act. Congress's primary concern was with "the plight of the Negro in our economy." Prior to the act, blacks were largely relegated to unskilled and lower-level jobs. Congress intended to open employment opportunities to blacks in occupations previously closed to them. Given the legislative history of the Civil Rights Act, the Court contended that it could not agree that Congress intended to prohibit the private sector from accomplishing the goal of the act. The Court noted that it is a "familiar rule, that a thing may be within the letter of the statute and yet not within the statute, because [it is] not within its spirit, nor within the intention of its makers."

The Court concluded that the adoption of the affirmative-action plan falls within the area of discretion left by Title VII to the private sector to adopt plans designed to eliminate conspicuous racial imbalance.

The Weber case is viewed by many to be the landmark case on *reverse discrimination*. In effect, it may have voided the concept of reverse discrimination in employment practices when a firm is following an approved affirmative-action plan. The concept of reverse discrimination had been the major issue in a 1978 Supreme Court decision in *Bakke* v. *University of California*.[38] In that case, Bakke, a white male, claimed reverse discrimination when denied admission to the University of California at Davis Medical School. Bakke had been denied admission even though he had scored higher on tests than some of sixteen minority students who were admitted because

the school had reserved sixteen positions for them. In a five-to-four decision the Supreme Court ruled that Bakke should be admitted even though race could be considered in a school's admission plan. The ambiguity of the Bakke decision may have encouraged the Supreme Court to hear the Weber case the following year in order to address the question of reverse discrimination.

The Weber decision established that (1) the Civil Rights Act cannot be literally interpreted but must be considered in light of its historical perspective; (2) Title VII permits employers to establish race-conscious affirmative-action plans, although it does not require them to do so; and (3) such affirmative-action plans can require that a certain number or percentage of positions be filled by minorities or women.

Age Discrimination

Coates v. *National Cash Register Co.*
433 F.Supp. 655 (1977)
U.S. District Court (WD of Va.)

In 1975 the National Cash Register Company (NCR) reduced its staff of field engineers because of deteriorating economic conditions. The Age Discrimination in Employment Act states that it is unlawful for an employer to discharge or to discriminate against any individual "because of such individual's age."

NCR stated that its decision to discharge certain individuals was not based on age but on the training of the individuals. The court found the evidence in the case established that the relative training levels of NCR employees were directly related to their age. Therefore, by using the training level as the basis of the discharge decision, NCR indirectly discharged the plaintiffs because of their ages. The age discrimination need not be direct or intentional; the court held that the plaintiffs were discharged "because of their ages."

The Coates case clearly determined that the Age Discrimination in Employment Act has "teeth" since (1) the court held that just because an employer's action does not directly discriminate on the basis of age, if age is a "determining factor'" the employer may be guilty of age discrimination; (2) individuals who have been subjects of age discrimination may be awarded back wages, reinstatement, and damages for pain and suffering.

Seniority and Affirmative Action

Firefighters Local 1784 v. *Stotts*
No. 82–206 (1984)
Supreme Court of the United States

The city of Memphis, Tennessee, like most other large cities and private employers, had entered into consent decrees that provided affirmative-action hiring and promotion goals in several departments, including fire.[39] The city also had a seniority system in the collective bargaining agreement with the fire fighter's union. In the event of layoffs, the policy was typical of most seniority systems, providing "last hired, first fired." Faced with a severe budget crisis in 1981, Memphis implemented a reduction in personnel. The reduction would have laid off the most recently hired fire fighters first, even though about 50 percent were black because of the city's affirmative-action plan. A federal district judge stopped the planned layoff because the action would have countered the effect of the earlier consent decree by decreasing the percentage of black fire fighters. Instead, the judge ordered the layoff of more senior white employees, an action contrary to the collective bargaining agreement and seniority policy of the city. Both the city and the union appealed the decision to the U.S. Supreme Court.

The Supreme Court overturned the decision of the federal judge. The Court emphasized that a court may not grant preferential treatment to any group or individual simply because they belong to a protected class adversely affected by a seniority system.[40]

The decision strongly reaffirmed earlier decisions by the Court that a bona fide seniority system cannot be altered by a lawsuit based on affirmative action or employment discrimination. The decision, most experts believe, affected neither the Weber decision nor the use of affirmative-action goals and timetables in hiring employees. The decision was narrow, affecting only layoff or recall actions that take place within a seniority system.[41]

THE SELECTION PROCESS

As Figure 5–5 indicates, the selection process pulls together organizational goals, job designs, and performance appraisals, as well as recruitment and selection. The first element in the selection process is the setting of organizational goals, which must include the general hiring policy of the organization. Management can either employ the best people in the marketplace for particular jobs—often incurring high individual salaries and benefits—or pay relatively low wages and salaries, unconcerned with employee turnover or dissatisfaction about wages, benefits, and working conditions. Policymakers must determine how the employees fit into the overall framework of the organization and must establish the relationship among the employees in the organization.

The second element, job design, involves determining what duties and responsibilities each job will entail. How motivating or repetitous each job becomes greatly affects the performance of employees on that job. The performance of employees will be affected by their ability and motivation. The job design will greatly affect both of these factors.

The third element involves the measurement of job success. The discovery of which

FIGURE 5-5

Basic elements in the selection process (Source: Mitchell S. Novit, *Essentials of Personnel Management,* © 1979, p. 70. Reprinted by permission of Prentice-Hall, Inc., Englewood Cliffs, N.J.)

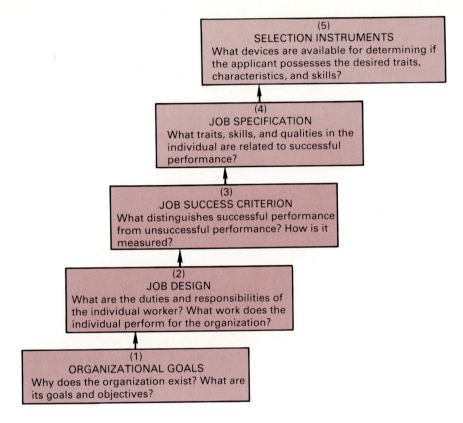

(5)
SELECTION INSTRUMENTS
What devices are available for determining if the applicant possesses the desired traits, characteristics, and skills?

(4)
JOB SPECIFICATION
What traits, skills, and qualities in the individual are related to successful performance?

(3)
JOB SUCCESS CRITERION
What distinguishes successful performance from unsuccessful performance? How is it measured?

(2)
JOB DESIGN
What are the duties and responsibilities of the individual worker? What work does the individual perform for the organization?

(1)
ORGANIZATIONAL GOALS
Why does the organization exist? What are its goals and objectives?

employees are successful will determine what kinds of employees to recruit and select in the future.

The fourth element, job specifications, comes from the job analysis, which specifies what traits, skills, and background an individual must have to qualify for the job.

Finally, policymakers must determine which combination of interviews, tests, or other selection devices to use in the selection process. There is no magical combination of selection instruments that will minimize the cost of selection and facilitate choosing the best candidates available. Although there are few new selection techniques in modern personnel management, there have been improvements in particular areas. There are also restrictions caused by federal guidelines and

other influences.[42] The steps in the selection process are outlined in Figure 5-6. They may change from one organization to another, but all of the steps are normally completed at one time or another. The sequence may vary within organizations according to the types of jobs being filled and the size of the organization. The process usually begins by reviewing current applications gathered through the organization's recruitment effort. The EEOC has warned that because minorities and females will not be fairly represented in a recruitment procedure that relies strictly on word-of-mouth or walk-in applicants, these methods may constitute discriminatory practices.[43]

Applicants who appear to be qualified for the position are then screened. Initial screening looks for the minimum requirements still

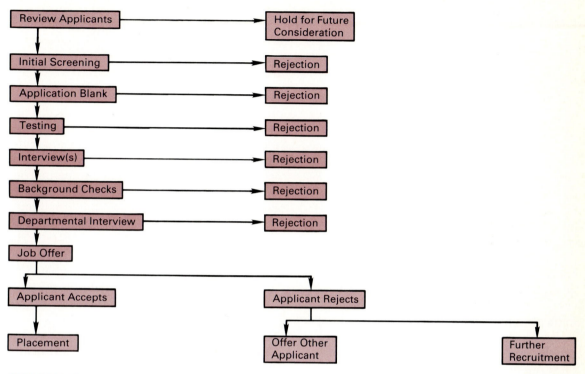

FIGURE 5-6
The steps in the selection process

available in the job market as determined by the job specifications. The third step is to have the applicants compete an application blank, which standardizes information about all of the applicants to be considered. Any tests relevant to the job and validated by the organization are then administered to applicants. The next step is usually to interview applicants within the personnel department. The background of desirable applicants is checked next, especially their references and employment history. Finally, the few applicants remaining are interviewed by the departmental supervisor or department head. During this in-depth interview, job requirements are discussed so that the applicant as well as the supervisor will be able to judge each other's interest in the job. At this point, a job offer can

be made to the applicant best qualified for the job. If that applicant rejects the offer, management can either contact other qualified applicants or begin the recruitment process again if there are no other qualified applicants available. When the applicant accepts the offer, the process of placing the applicant in the organization begins.

Initial Screening

Initial screening minimizes the time the personnel department must spend during the selection process by removing obviously unqualified or undesirable applicants. For most jobs, many of the applicants do not deserve the serious attention and time of the personnel specialist, particularly if many applications are blind resumés or walk-ins. To maintain a favorable corporate image, every applicant must be given courteous treatment. Primarily, the initial screening determines if the applicant possesses the critical job specifications and expedites the departure of the unqualified applicants to minimize the total cost of the selection process.

In reviewing resumés or letters from applicants, the personnel officer must determine which applicants have the minimum qualifications indicated in the job description. Qualified applicants are then queried about their interest in the position. If the initial screening can be done by direct contact with the applicant, then the interviewer may pursue a number of strategies. First, the interviewer should perform a visual screening, rejecting any totally unfit applicant—one who is under the influence of alcohol, unable to fill out an application, and so on. Next, the interviewer should ask so-called knockout questions. Such questions may indicate quickly if an applicant is unqualified. For instance: What are your salary requirements? Can you work weekends or nights? Can you work shift hours? Can you stay out of town three nights per week? Do you have a specialized degree? Are you registered in this state? How fast can you type and take shorthand? Finally, the interviewer should give a brief job description. Many applicants will not be interested once they learn the exact nature of the job, salary, or hours.[44]

Applicants who are rejected at this point in the selection process or at any other point must be included in an *applicant flow record.* The EEOC requires that companies with federal contracts record for each job applicant the name, race, national origin, sex, reference source, dates of application, and position applied for. The applicant flow record should also indicate whether a job offer was made to the applicant and the reason why an offer was not made or rejected. Applicant flow records provide data to be reported in quarterly reports and annual EEO-1 reports.[45]

Application Blank

An application blank is a formal record of an individual's application for employment. This record is later used by the personnel department and may be reviewed by governmental agencies. The application blank, which provides pertinent information about the individual, is used in the job interview and in reference checks to determine the applicant's suitability for employment. An example of an application blank appears in Figure 5–7. The Agreement section at the end should be read carefully. Applicants should be prepared to answer all questions and should always provide correct information.

Discriminatory Practices In recent years, the greatest changes in application blanks have come about after consideration of what questions should be eliminated from the application or very carefully worded. Primarily these questions concern:

Race, National Origin, Religion Employers have been warned by the EEOC and the courts that application forms which indicate race, national origin, religion, and sex often have been used to discriminate against minorities. Employers eliminated this information from personnel records (including the application blank) only to find that to comply with EEO/AA requirements this information had to be gathered in the application process. The EEOC advised that these data should be kept separate from the individual personnel files. Such information can be coded, incorporated into payroll or other records, and kept separate from the individual's personnel file. Requesting such information on application blanks is not a violation of the Civil Rights Act *per se,* but such information recorded on application forms would be carefully reviewed should discrimination charges be filed.[46]

Age, Date of Birth   The ADEA prohibits discrimination against applicants over age forty. Therefore, asking the date of birth or age of an applicant is unlawful. However, applicants may be asked if they are of minimum age in order to comply with state and federal child work laws. The employer may also ask if the individual is over age forty.

Marital Status   Asking if applicants are married or have children may constitute discrimination. Because such questions can be used to discriminate against women and rarely relate to job performance, they are violations of the Civil Rights Act of 1964.[47] Such information is needed for Social Security and tax records. It may be obtained after the applicant has been employed, but not during the selection process.

Education   The Supreme Court has prohibited establishing an education requirement as a condition of employment if such a requirement is not job related. The necessity of requiring a diploma certificate, or college degree should be determined through job analysis.[48]

Arrest Record   The courts have ruled that requesting arrest records is an unlawful selection consideration unless it can be proven to be a business necessity. This ruling was made because a greater proportion of minority-group members are arrested than nonminority members. Therefore, making decisions regarding employment on the basis of arrest records would discriminate against minority members.[49] Federal courts have also ruled that a felony or misdemeanor conviction should not be an absolute criterion for rejecting a job applicant. Instead, the employer should consider the nature of the offense and its relationship to the position.[50]

Credit Rating   Any inquiry into an applicant's credit record is unlawful. Since, on the average, minority applicants have poorer credit records than nonminority applicants, using credit records as a basis for employment would have an adverse impact on minority groups.[51]

Photograph   Since a photograph would identify an individual's sex, race, or national origin, it can be used to discriminate against minority applicants. The photograph does not provide any job-related information about the applicant. An employer may request a photograph of an employee for identification purposes after the employee is hired.

Height and Weight Requirements   Court decisions have determined that height and weight requirements discriminate against Hispanics, Asian-Americans, and women because many in these groups are shorter and slimmer than white males. Height and weight requirements should be made only if they are shown by the employer to be a business necessity or a BFOQ.[52]

Some state EEO laws are more rigid than the federal requirements. An employer could easily be in compliance with federal regulations but not state regulations. A major cause of this problem is the use of application forms from national printing firms that generally comply with federal regulations but contain questions that are illegal in some states. Selection officers are sometimes not aware of state laws. Failure to comply with state laws could be costly to employers. The chief of legal operations for the Ohio Civil Rights Commission, for example, has stated that such violations could lead to employers' being ordered to award back pay to all wronged parties who had completed the application forms.[53]

The local branch of the EEOC or the state civil rights commission will review application forms to be sure that any possible discrimina-

KFC Management Company — KFC Corporation

Employment Application

MO	DAY	YR

All Applicants Will Receive Consideration Without Regard To Age, Race, Color, Religion, Sex, National Origin, Handicap, Or Military Status

PLEASE COMPLETE ALL SECTIONS—FRONT AND BACK

PERSONAL

Last Name	First Name	Middle Name	Social Security#

Present Street Address	City	State	Zip	No. Yrs.	Home Phone (Including Area Code)

Last Address	City	State	Zip	No. Yrs.	If Under 19 Years Of Age, Date Of Birth:

Are You Legally Eligible To Work In The United States? ☐ YES ☐ NO   Have You Ever Been Convicted Of A Felony? ☐ YES ☐ NO   If Yes, Please Explain:

Notify In Emergency: State Name, Complete Address And Phone (Including Area Code):

Minors Indicate Parent or Guardian

JOB INTEREST

Position (Type of Work) Desired: Starting Monthly Salary Expected: $ Have You Ever Previously Applied To Our Firm? ☐ YES ☐ NO

Date You Can Start Work: List Any Relatives Or Acquaintances Working For Our Company:

Type Of Employment Desired:
☐ Full Time   ☐ Permanent Part Time   ☐ Temporary Full Time   ☐ Temporary Part Time   ☐ Summer

Are There Any Times When You Are Unavailable For Work? If So, Please Specify: Are You Known To Schools/References By Another Name? If Yes, By What Name:

Special Interests Or Qualifications That May Help Us In Considering Your Application:

EDUCATION

Circle Highest Grade Completed In Each School Category:

	Grade School	High School	College	Graduate School
	1 2 3 4 5 6	7 8 9 10 11 12	1 2 3 4	1 2 3 4

Schools	Name And Address	Dates Attended From	To	Diploma Or Degree	Grade Average	Areas Of Specialization
High School						
College						
Graduate School						
Other						

HEALTH

Do You Have Any Physical Disability Which Would Limit Your Ability To Perform The Job For Which You Are Applying? ☐ YES ☐ NO

While Working, Is There Anything To Prevent You From: ☐ Standing   ☐ Lifting

If Yes To Any Of The Above, Explain:

VETERANS AND DISABILITY INFORMATION

Answering the questions in this section is completely voluntary and will not affect your chances for employment with the company. They are being asked because the federal government requires the company to maintain records of Vietnam era veterans, disabled veterans, and handicapped individuals seeking employment. The answers to these questions will help fulfill our responsibility in this area, and the company would appreciate your help.

Did you serve in active military duty 180 days or more between August 5, 1964 and May 7, 1975? ☐ YES ☐ NO

Were you released from active military duty between August 5, 1964 and May 7, 1975 because of a service connected disability? ☐ YES ☐ NO

Are you a disabled veteran? ☐ YES ☐ NO

Do you have an emotional or physical handicap (disability)? ☐ YES ☐ NO

If you have a handicap and/or disability, please explain and list accomodations you feel are necessary. _____

HR015-REV7/83   **PLEASE CONTINUE ON REVERSE SIDE**

FIGURE 5–7

An excellent example of a complete application blank from Kentucky Fried Chicken Corporation. Used by permission.

184

EMPLOYMENT RECORD:

List Each Job Held Starting With Your Present Or Last Job. Include Military Service, Summer Employment and Volunteer Activities. If You Need Additional Space, Please Continue On A Separate Piece Of Paper.

Name Of Company	Type Of Business	From (MO & YR)	To (MO & YR)
Address (Including City And State)		Starting Salary	Last Salary
Name And Title Of Supervisor	Telephone	Titles And Duties:	
Reason For Leaving:			

Name Of Company	Type Of Business	From (MO & YR)	To (MO & YR)
Address (Including City And State)		Starting Salary	Last Salary
Name And Title Of Supervisor	Telephone	Titles And Duties:	
Reason For Leaving:			

Name Of Company	Type Of Business	From (MO & YR)	To (MO & YR)
Address (Including City And State)		Starting Salary	Last Salary
Name And Title Of Supervisor	Telephone	Titles And Duties:	
Reason For Leaving:			

Name Of Company	Type Of Business	From (MO & YR)	To (MO & YR)
Address (Including City And State)		Starting Salary	Last Salary
Name And Title Of Supervisor	Telephone	Titles And Duties:	
Reason For Leaving:			

Name Of Company	Type Of Business	From (MO & YR)	To (MO & YR)
Address (Including City And State)		Starting Salary	Last Salary
Name And Title Of Supervisor	Telephone	Titles And Duties:	
Reason For Leaving:			

REFERENCES

List Names And Addresses Of People Who Have Known You Over 3 Years. (DO NOT LIST RELATIVES.)

Name	Address	Occupation	Phone

AGREEMENT

I certify that all statements given on this application are correct, and understand that falsification or misrepresentation in this or any other personnel record can result in my dismissal if I am employed by the company. If requested to do so, I agree to submit to a physical examination which I must successfully pass as a condition of being accepted for employment. I agree to provide proof of age upon notification of hire. I authorize my former employers and other individuals to give the company information concerning me, whether or not it is part of their written record, and I release them and their companies from any liability whatsoever on account of such information furnished to KFC. I understand that the above noted examination and reference inquiries will be kept confidential and will not be released to anyone by KFC without my written consent. Also, I agree that if I am offered employment by KFC and accept, my employment will be employment at will, that my employment and compensation can be terminated, with or without cause, and with or without notice, at any time, at the option of either KFC or myself. I am hereby informed and I understand that no representative of KFC, other than the Chief Executive Officer, has any authority to enter into any agreement for employment for any specified period of time or to make any agreement contrary to the foregoing and that any such agreement must be in writing and must be signed by the Chief Executive Officer of KFC.

Public Law 91-508 requires that we advise you that a routine inquiry may be made during our initial or subsequent processing which will provide application information concerning character, general reputation and credit, personal characteristics and mode of living. Upon written request, additional information as to the nature and scope of the inquiry, if one is made, will be provided.

Signature:_____ Date: _____

WE APPRECIATE YOUR INTEREST AND THE TIME YOU HAVE TAKEN TO PREPARE THIS APPLICATION.

FIGURE 5–7
continued

185

tory practices are eliminated. Although future court decisions may alter the items that can lawfully appear on applications blanks, those questions which can appear on the application blanks concern:

- Applicant's name.
- Applicant's address and telephone number.
- If the applicant is of minimum working age.
- If the applicant can speak or read and write foreign languages (if job-related).
- Applicant's educational background (if job-related).
- Applicant's work history, including dates of employment, salary progression, job responsibility and duties, and reasons for leaving.
- If the applicant can meet special job requirements, such as evening work hours.
- Applicant's military experience.
- If a health problem will impair the applicant's job performance.
- Applicant's arrest record (if job-related).
- Applicant's willingness to travel.
- Applicant's special skills or training.
- How the applicant heard about the position opening.
- Membership in professional organizations.
- Names of relatives employed by the company.
- Other current employment, either full-time or part-time.

Uses of the Application Blank   The application blank is a permanent record of the applicant's qualifications for a job. In addition to providing information required for the selection process, the application supplies input for the EEO/AA report. Personnel specialists use the application to develop background checks and interview questions. An important part of the selection process is verification of the applicant's past work history and references. Applicants and their previous employers sometimes disagree about the duties, responsibilities, and importance of previous jobs, length of employment, salary levels, and especially the reason for leaving employment. In an effort to obtain accurate, complete information from the applicant, the personnel specialist starts with the application and follows through with background checks and an interview. During the interview some applicants will give different accounts of prior experience as well as skills from what they provided on their application blanks.

Application blanks can also be used as screening devices to generate *global assessments*, wherein the personnel specialist reviews the total applications and determines the general desirability of each applicant. A very subjective technique, global assessment is often used when many applicants are being considered and those lacking an appropriate background or skills can be quickly screened out.

A more objective screening technique using application blanks is to have the personnel specialist rate each applicant on particular job-related areas, such as the level of specific skills or experience in particular work areas or in supervisory positions. Such rating would change from job opening to job opening as different skills and background requirements become more relevant. Generally, if one particularly relevant job specification does not appear on completed application blanks, then these applicants can be screened out.

Testing

Testing, once the cornerstone of the selection process, has come under attack since the formation of the EEOC guidelines. The federal courts and the EEOC have alleged that most tests lack validity and that test specialists have manipulated different testing problems and test scores to apply to a single model of test validation. Tests have been given more than their weight in the selection process, and sometimes the entire hiring decision relies upon an individual's test score. Although the validity of aptitude tests and other specialized intelligence tests can be determined, it is much more difficult to determine the validity for other types of employee tests.[54]

In the past, part of the problem has been the use of general tests for purposes they were not developed for and the lack of specific validation by the organization utilizing them. The EEOC has emphasized that any test that adversely affects the employment status of groups protected by Title VII must be professionally validated within the organization using it. In 1974 the EEOC emphasized that testing was a major area for review and action by employers. If employers believe that tests are necessary in the employment process, they should validate them in accordance with EEOC guidelines. In the past, the use of intelligence, aptitude, and other tests having no proven relationship to successful job performance has had a major disproportionate effect on the rejection of minority job applicants. An EEOC alternative allows employers to compensate for adverse impact by using methods that permit a reasonable proportion of minority candidates to pass selection tests. Test scores may be used as a criterion for selection if the selection rate for minorities is 80 percent of the rate of other applicants. Employers have the option of substituting probationary periods for written tests as a means of evaluating the abilities of new employees.[55]

Employee personnel testing is generally far more objective than other selection procedures; testing has often proved to be the most valid selection procedure. An EEOC staff psychologist has noted the common misconception that the use of selection testing is the fastest way to incur trouble from the EEOC.[56] In fact, one of the most rigorous and complete studies of employment testing concluded that, in general, standardized tests do not discriminate against blacks; blacks and whites with similar test scores do equally well in job performance. Although blacks, Hispanics, and native Americans as groups do not score as well as white applicants, those differences are mostly due to less education and other social factors not caused by the standardized tests. Most importantly, no better alternative to a standardized test has been developed. Thus, at least some of the cynicism about testing in recent years has been unfair.[57]

However, a survey of over 7,000 personnel managers nationwide revealed that most

TABLE 5–2

Pre-employment testing by employers*

Type	Frequency of Employer Use
Achievement and work samples	55%
Clerical and word processing	31%
Physical strength	6%
Writing	6%
Equipment operation	4%
Assessment centers	3%
Personality and psychological	20%
Drug and alcohol abuse	18%
Polygraph	11%

Use of Test Results	Frequency
Reject applicants who refuse test	52%
Rate test results	35%
Passage required for position	20%

*Responses of 142 organizations surveyed.

Source: Adapted from Paul L. Blocklyer, "Preemployment Testing," *Personnel* 65, no. 2 (February 1988): 66–68.

do not use any pre-employment tests. The reason is the EEO requirement for validation. Most companies claim they do not have the time or the money for test validation. Of the tests still in use, job-skill or work sample and psychological tests are the most common. In general, entry-level positions receive more job-skill testing, while higher-level positions receive more psychological testing. Financial officers and sales managers received the most polygraph testing before a 1988 law was passed restricting the use of polygraphs. In the past the banking industry accounted for over one-third of all polygraph tests; the wholesale/retail, mineral extracting, and health care industries were also big users.[58]

General Intelligence Tests Decades ago, general intelligence tests were developed to predict the success of young children in school. Test scores are measures of the ability to do well in a traditional school setting[59] Testing the success of young school children in their academic careers is still what general intelligence tests are best suited for and should be utilized for.

Research has shown a consistent relationship between occupation or income level and general intelligence. Intelligence tests are useful to roughly categorize possible occupations for job applicants, because general intelligence minimums are required for each occupation.[60] But though intelligence and occupation are related, the results of intelligence tests do not predict potential success or failure in an occupation with a great deal of accuracy. Predicting success in an occupation requires testing that is much more specific to the particular requirements of the occupation. The person with higher general intelligence would, however, have a greater range of occupations which could be successfully pursued.[61]

Aptitude Tests Natural ability in a particular discipline or the ability to learn quickly or to understand a particular area reveals an aptitude for that area or discipline. Aptitude tests indicate the ability or fitness of an individual to engage successfully in any number of specialized activities.[62]

As the official U.S. Employment Services aptitude test, the General Aptitude Test Battery (GATB) is recognized as the basic denominator in estimating aptitude requirements. It is the aptitude test by which jobs are categorized in the *Dictionary of Occupational Titles (DOT)*. Also, all state employment agencies use the GATB, which tests:[63]

- General intelligence
- Verbal ability
- Numerical ability
- Spatial perception
- Form perception
- Clerical perception
- Motor coordination
- Finger dexterity
- Manual dexterity

The GATB consists of twelve timed tests (parts)—eight paper-and-pencil tests and four apparatus tests. Each part requires performance of familiar tasks such as name comparisons, arithmetic computations, reasoning, pegboard manipulations, and so on. Employer use of the GATB in employee selection has increased due to the U.S. Employment Service. The Employment Service conducted validity studies of the GATB over a forty-five-year period and found three general abilities (cognitive, perceptual, and psychomotor) to be valid predictors of job proficiency. The Employment Service then began implementing the testing in local Job Service (unemployment) offices. Employers can use the GATB scores as valid predictors of employee success.[64]

Personality and Interest Tests Both personality and interest tests seek to measure an individual's motivation in particular fields.

Personality tests, such as the Bernreuter Personality Inventory, measure neurotic tendency, self-sufficiency, introversion and extraversion, sociability, and self-confidence. The Thematic Apperception Test (TAT) is a common projective personality test in which the subject is asked to interpret certain situations. The TAT assesses the individual's need for achievement and has been successful in predicting individual motivation. Other personality tests, such as the California Psychological Inventory (CPI) and the Thurstone Temperament Survey (TTS), have been developed to assess specific personality aspects. However, the validity of using personality tests as useful indices of applicants' possible work motivation is highly questionable.

Although the use of personality tests has declined, a survey of university graduate students reported about 20 percent had taken a paper-and-pencil personality test. The primary problems of personality tests are threefold. First, they are generally not reliable or valid predictors of job performance. Second, to be useful, such tests assume that job applicants have sufficient insight to describe themselves accurately—often an unjustified assumption. Third, in a desire to perform well, candidates may give false responses to produce what they believe to be the desired "test score," despite there being no "right or wrong" answers on personality tests. For example, a study of applicants found that the same applicant appeared to be highly introverted when applying for a librarian's job and highly extroverted when applying for a sales job. Some tests include lie scales, which developers claim eliminate faked responses. But research evidence shows that applicants can evade such scales.[65]

Interest tests generally are designed to measure individuals' activity preferences. For example, individuals are asked if they would rather watch a baseball game on television, read a novel, or attend a local little league game on a Saturday afternoon. Interest tests such as the Strong Vocational Interest Blank (SVIB) have been found to predict the occupations people will enter with reasonable accuracy. By matching the interests of individuals successful in different occupations, the SVIB indicates to applicants which fields most closely match their interests. The SVIB has shown that within professions people's interests have been fairly stable. While interest tests are particularly useful for students considering many careers or employees deciding upon career changes, they are not particularly valid in selecting a specific employee for a job.

Achievement Tests Aptitude tests assess a person's capacity to learn, whereas achievement tests assess the degree to which a person has learned. Because achievement tests measure current behavior, they may be the best predictor of future employee behavior. Therefore, personnel departments may use achievement tests to determine whether a person can do the job and aptitude tests to measure whether or not someone can be trained to do the job. Through a job analysis for a specific occupation, a list of questions can be developed that will test an applicant's occupational experience. The U.S. Employment Service has developed a series of trade tests that measure an individual's knowledge of the behavior, tools, and equipment of a particular job. For example, electricians might be required to read wiring diagrams.[66] Because achievement tests can be validated, they are useful predictors of job performance where specific knowledge or experience is necessary to perform in a skilled occupation.

Work Samples One step beyond the achievement test, which measures knowledge of a particular job or occupation, is the use of a work sample, in which the applicant performs part of the job as a test. Examples of work samples are typing tests for secretaries, assembly tests for production-line workers, and trial-balances computation tests for accountants. Work samples are generally valid predictors of job performance since they measure those behaviors required for successful job performance. But work samples have limited use due to their specific nature; that is, they can only test an individual's ability on certain duties within the job setting. Other criteria are measured by other selection devices. Work samples are usually limited to jobs which are physical rather than mental in nature. In the future, more work samples for conceptual jobs can be expected.

When selecting a work sample, skills required by the test, ease of administration in scoring test results, and the abilities demonstrated on the test should be considered. For example, of the three major typing tests, the Typing Test for Business (TTB) has been found to be much easier to administer and has a higher demonstrated reliability than the SRA Typing Skills Test or the National Business Entrance Test.[67]

Polygraph Tests　The polygraph is a device which measures the emotions of an individual by directly measuring galvanic skin response, blood pressure, and breathing rate. A sampling of 400 firms on *Fortune* magazine's list of the largest companies reveals that polygraph use in corporations falls into three common areas: (1) verification of employment application information; (2) periodic surveys to determine employee honesty and loyalty; and (3) investigation of a specific instance of theft within the company. About 20 percent of those companies that responded to the survey used the polygraph in some capacity; 50 percent of the commercial banks and retail companies used polygraph examinations. Transportation and industrial firms also indi-

cated heavy use of the polygraph examination.[68]

The polygraph has come under severe criticism; in fact, many states have passed laws to severely restrict or eliminate its use. The legal considerations involve an employee's self-incrimination and invasion of the right to privacy. However, even some critics feel that the polygraph examination should be available to the applicant or employee who chooses to use it to prove innocence of a specific theft or to speed up the selection process.[69] In some situations, employees request a polygraph test to prove their innocence if a theft or other incident has occurred that might adversely influence their later promotion within the company. If the guilty party was not found in such a situation, management would be hesitant to promote anyone within the department who could have been guilty.

The future of the polygraph test appears to be in the hands of Congress. The Employee Polygraph Protection Act was passed by the U.S. House of Representatives and referred to the Senate in 1986. The purpose of the act is to ''prevent the denial of employment opportunities by prohibiting the use of lie detectors by employers.'' The act would further prohibit the use of the polygraph in cases involving theft or to determine employee loyalty or honesty.[70] In 1988 the U.S. Congress passed the act, which places strict limits on employment-related uses of the polygraph. However, polygraph tests would be permitted during investigations of theft, embezzlement, or other kinds of unlawful acts.

Graphology Tests　A graphology test is administered by a trained graphologist, who examines handwriting and determines the personality traits of the writer. Like polygraph examinations, graphology is a fairly young field, without legal status or professional licensing procedures. Employers find it difficult to validate the results of graphology tests. As in the case of polygraph examinations, the future of graphology in the personnel area will most likely be determined by the courts and the government.

Interviews

"I dread it."

"Every time we have a vacancy I fall three weeks behind in my own work."

"I never know what I can say because of all this affirmative-action stuff."

"We spent over an hour talking . . . but I'm having second thoughts now that he's been here for a week."

Managers realize that the selection process is critical to their organization, yet they often really do dread the process—particularly the interview. The comments above are typical of managers' thoughts about interviewing.[71]

The purpose of the interview is to determine three things about the applicant: (1) Does the applicant have the ability to perform the job? (2) Will the applicant be motivated for a sufficient length of time? (3) Will the applicant "fit in" with the organization? According to a nationwide survey, interviewing is the most widely used selection method. Some companies have reacted to EEOC and court decisions regarding testing by using fewer tests and turning to the interview as the primary selection technique. Ironically, interviewing is just as vulnerable to EEOC guidelines as the written test. The interview, however, has not received as much criticism as the written test.[72]

Research has constantly shown that the selection interview is low in both reliability and validity. Reliability is a particular concern with interviews because the interview technique does not have the consistency of form

that the written test or the reference check may have. Thus, the interview is not as consistent or reliable a selection technique as other methods.[73]

For many reasons there is low reliability or consistency in the interview process. First, interviewers must constantly work to reduce personal biases. Even when interviewers recognize their personal biases, an interviewee's sex, race, religion, school, or hobbies may influence the final decision. Biases can be positive as well as negative. The sex of the interviewer or the interviewee affects the total evaluation of the interview situation. This even occurs with trained, experienced interviewers.[74]

Second, all interviews are different, as are all interviewees. The content of interviews changes because no two interviewees have the same background and experience; different aspects of the individuals, their skills, and work histories must be discussed with each individual.

Third, the setting of the interview may affect the outcome. If one interview takes place early in the morning when the interviewer is fresh and the next interview is conducted late in the afternoon when the interviewer is in a hurry to leave, the second interviewee may receive little regard when the interviewees are compared. For another example, an applicant interviewed right after the most impressive applicant the interviewer has ever seen is more likely to get a less positive interview evaluation than normal, but an applicant following one of the worst applicants the interviewer has seen may get higher scores than normal.

Fourth, if the company has established a maximum number of people to interview and a deadline for filling the position, additional pressure is placed on the interviewer. The last applicant to be interviewed may be offered the position if the interviewer is in a hurry to fill it. Thus, the applicant may fill a position that otherwise would not have been offered.

Primarily, conducting good interviews is a two-step process. The first step is to create a good interview setting before the applicant actually arrives for the interview. The second step is to establish a useful questioning period during the interview. These steps encompass the following characteristics of interviewing:

Setting Prepare a setting which will put the applicant at ease and provide consistent surroundings for each interview. Allow thirty to sixty minutes for an adequate interview.

Documentation Prepare a system of written records and formalized procedures for the interview. Determine how the interview will be documented at its conclusion to provide a formal record of the outcome.

Standardization Standardize the interview format. Determine a line of questioning that includes the applicant's prior work history, military history, skills, and educational background. This will provide a framework for consistency in the information-gathering process.

Scoring Determine how the interview will be scored. That is, how will the applicant ultimately be evaluated as a result of the interview process? An applicant may be scored in each different area relevant to the job description, as well as on the basis of the applicant's response to questioning.

Reviewing Job Specifications Review the job description and job specifications for that particular job before each interview. Since the interviewer may see applicants for different jobs, the particular, important aspects of each job must be fresh in the interviewer's mind.

Reviewing The Application Blank Review the application before the interview, looking

for possible problem areas that require additional information and areas of possible strengths and weaknesses that should be gone into in more detail during the interview.

Training The Interviewer Train the interviewer to recognize personal biases and other possible detriments to interview reliability.

Job-Related Questions Prepare a line of questioning which keeps the interview job related and does not waste time by straying from the subject or delving into personal areas, which could be seen as discriminatory.

Conducting an interview is an art as much as a science. Only through experience and training can an interviewer thoroughly question a job applicant and get maximum information in minimum time. Table 5–3 contains some of the dos and don'ts of effective job interviewing.

The end of the job interview is a critical time. At the end the applicant should be able to ask questions concerning the job, pay, or working conditions. The interviewer should ask when the applicant will be available to work and tell the applicant when the job will be filled. If more people will be interviewed or there will be a waiting period for a final decision to be made, the applicant should be given an estimate—such as ten days or two weeks—of when a decision should be reached. The applicant should also be told whether to call to find out the results of the job decision or to wait for notification. Interviewers should be positive toward all applicants, even those who may have to be ruled out, because applicants may be available and suited for other positions at a later date.

Although the interview concentrates on verbal cues, much nonverbal information is given by the candidate that influences the interviewer's perception. Interviewers allow

TABLE 5–3
The dos and don'ts of effective interviews

DO	DON'T
Ask open questions: Why did you apply here? What specific skill do you have?	Ask all closed questions: Could you work here three to five years? Do you enjoy working with figures?
Ask job-related questions: Can you work the 3 to 11 shift? What COBOL experience do you have?	Ask personal questions: Does your husband work? Are your parents Spanish?
Ask reflective or follow-up questions: You said you didn't work the counter. Why? How could you accomplish that?	Ask broad or vague questions: Do you like people?
Open the interview by putting the applicant at ease—discuss an easy topic such as the last job or education.	Do all the talking. Let the applicant talk as much as possible.
Look for areas the applicant is uneasy about and find out why.	Ask judgmental questions: Don't you like flextime? I think a good health insurance plan is critical, don't you?
Ask positive questions: What was your reason for leaving XYZ Company?	Be impatient, constantly hurry the applicant, or look at the clock.
Use summary statements to ensure your understanding: Then you did train employees in COBOL programming?	Ask more than one question at a time: Why did you choose accounting? What courses did you like, dislike?

firmness of the handshake, physical appearance, and eye contact during the interview to affect their selection decisions. Body language is a *nonverbal cue* that can greatly influence the interviewer. Candidates who appear nervous or apprehensive do not make a positive impression. The lack of eye contact during the interview can have a strong negative impact on the selection decision if it is interpreted to indicate a person's lack of self-confidence or inability to communicate. Survey information indicates that some interviewers make a tentative decision about an applicant within a few minutes, largely because of impressions about dress and appearance, eye contact, or other nonverbal cues.[75]

A board or panel interview could replace the traditional one-on-one interview technique. The panel interview minimizes individual bias since all panel members score the applicant. The final evaluation for each applicant is an average of several individuals' evaluations, and, therefore, balances out one individual's bias. The panel technique also forces interviews to become more structured and to the point. The obvious disadvantage of the panel interview is the increased cost to the organization of having more than one interviewer and the increased discomfort for some interviewees.[76]

The Structured Interview A structured or patterned interview requires the interviewer to ask a series of predetermined job-related questions. The answers are often scored on a set scale such as: 1 for poor, 2 for marginal, 3 for acceptable, 4 for above average, 5 for outstanding. The interviewer, shortly after the interview is completed, completes an evaluation form, such as the one in Figure 5–8, and includes a brief rationale for the evaluations.

The structured interview can greatly increase the reliability and accuracy of the traditional informal or nonstructured interview.

A structured interview usually shows the following characteristics:[77]

Questions The interviewer asks questions exclusively concerned with job duties and requirements critical to the job.

Applicant Evaluation Form

Applicant's name _____ Pat Wing _____

Date _____ March 15 _____

Requirements (skills, knowledge, and personal traits)	How applicant demonstrated ability	Weight (importance of skill)	Rating of Applicant	Weight × Rating
Ability to supervise.	Was promoted to manage 15 professionals because of success in supervising two paraprofessionals.	5	4	20
Ability to speak before groups.	Evaluated by seminar participants as outstanding; spoke well during interview.	4	5	20
Knowledge of learning theory.	Unable to discuss theory, but had reasonable instincts; diversifies training design.	5	3	15
Knowledge of management theory.	Able to discuss major theorists.	5	5	25
Ability to cooperate in team environment.	Co-trained a few times; usually works independently.	4	3	12
Ability to deal with hostile participants.	Cited specific examples that indicated a great deal of skill.	5	4	20
			TOTAL	112

FIGURE 5–8

An evaluation form used in a structured interview

Scored Responses The interviewer is provided typical answers to questions on a five-point rating scale.

Interview Committee Responses are discussed and rated by a number of people to minimize bias.

Consistency All applicants for a position are asked the same questions, evaluated with the same scoring method, and reviewed by the same people.

Questions asked in a structured interview are of four types:

Situational Questions The applicant must respond with what he or she would do in a certain situation. For example: "How will you assign daily work when two employees are absent?"

Job-Knowledge Questions These are questions that concern the job knowledge the applicant must have before being hired. For example: "Describe a typical boiler and steam turbine operation."

Job-Simulation Questions These are questions that approximate the content of the job. For example: "What are the steps involved in replacing drum-type brakes?"

Worker-Requirement Questions These are questions that concern the applicant's willingness or availability for certain working conditions. For example: "Are you willing to relocate after a six-month training program?"

Background Checks

In recent years, thoroughly checking the backgrounds of prospective employees has become increasingly necessary. Such an investigation can be both an energy-saving procedure and a cost-efficient means of screening out undesirable applicants. Because applicants tend to misrepresent themselves on their applications or during interviews, checking references has become a common practice in personnel. Between 7 and 10 percent of applicants do not have the experience and background they claim. More persons claim to have graduated from the Harvard School of Business than have ever been enrolled there. Thus, employers are turning to a confidential investigation of applicants' backgrounds before proceeding through the selection process.[78]

Falsifying information on job applications is not limited to entry-level applications. In fact Humana, Inc., the national hospital chain, found that thirty-nine (5 percent) physicians seeking jobs during a nine-month period had lied on their job applications. Some doctors who had dropped out of residency training programs claimed that they had completed them. Others falsified board certifications, which indicates that they passed an exam in a particular medical specialty.[79]

There are several methods of checking references. The personnel specialist can personally visit previous employers or friends of the applicant. This method should be reserved for candidates being considered for high-ranking positions because of the extra time and expense incurred. A second method is to check references by mail. This method has two distinct disadvantages: several days to weeks are required, and it lacks the depth of information that a personal phone call can accomplish. In addition, most employers are increasingly wary of putting their perceptions about former employees in writing. The third method, the telephone call, is a time-efficient, accurate means of getting complete information on applicants. Previous supervisors and employers are more likely to give complete information regarding a candidate's background over the phone. The personnel specialist can go into detail or ask particular questions concerning the applicant. A final method for checking references involves the use of outside services, which for a fee will investigate the background of applicants. Such services conduct interviews with former employers and check criminal records, credit files, and educational credentials.

Personnel specialists generally prefer to gather information by telephone. They can be specific in their questioning and, most importantly, can receive immediate clarification of significant issues. A ten-minute phone conversation can usually cover more useful information than a two-page letter. The least preferred technique is the "to whom it may concern" letter; it is by nature too general and does not allow for discussions with other personnel specialists. Nonetheless, such letters are useful for the applicant who has relocated recently. Overall, from a cost-benefit perspective, the phone conversation is the most attractive method, providing the most useful information at a very low cost. When employers use written reference checks, they will often develop reference forms which specify the type of information desired and the relationship of the applicant and the respondent.[80]

Negligent Hiring

An employer's liability for the negligent hiring and retention of employees who engage in criminal or other illegal acts is a question of significant importance. In negligent hiring cases, the courts have generally found the employer's liability to depend on the soundness of the employer's investigation into the employee's background. If the employee was hired for a job that might include a risk of injury or harm to customers or co-workers, the employer's liability is particularly great. Negligent liability cases are generally decided by a jury, which determines if the employer should bear all or part of the cost associated with injury or harm to a third party.[81]

In one case, the parents of a young boy received an out-of-court settlement of $440,000 from the employer of the boy's murderer. The employer knew of the employee's extensive criminal background, including a second-degree murder conviction. The employee was hired to provide security in a construction skills training program, where he met the young boy.[82] In another case, a homeowner was assaulted in her home by an employee of a pest control company. An appellate court ruled that the homeowner had the right to sue for damages on the basis of negligent hiring and retention.[83] Pinkerton's Security Company lost a $300,000 suit for the negligent hiring of a security guard who was convicted of theft. Pinkerton's was found liable because it failed to check adequately the employee's references and previous employers.[84]

How can employers avoid negligent hiring liability? Unfortunately, there are no certain answers. However, following the reasoning of the courts in such cases, employers should:[85]

- Conduct reasonable-effort background checks, particularly if there are suspicious factors such as gaps in employment or admission of past criminal convictions.
- Request police records on applicants for security or other high-risk jobs.
- Reject applicants with criminal records (not arrest, but conviction). State laws vary, but most allow employers to deny employment to all persons with criminal records.

Personal References   Many employers continue to request that applicants list the names, occupations, and addresses of three or more individuals who are not previous employers or relatives but who can attest to the applicants' suitability. In reality, almost all applicants list individuals who will say something very positive about them and give good recommendations. Realizing this, the personnel specialist does not use a good recommendation to determine the applicant's suitability for the position. A realistic use of personal recommendations includes:

- Verifying the data received on the application blank or during the interview. Often personal recommendations can verify information on the application blank. For example, individuals did attend certain schools, do have certain work experiences, or lived at certain addresses for certain periods of time.

- Evaluating the quality of the personal recommendation. Applicants who give professional people or business executives as references have a definite advantage over applicants who use their next-door neighbors or former high school classmates as references.

- Determining the degree of knowledge the person has concerning the applicant. A personnel specialist may call a personal reference and find that the person has little or no knowledge of the applicant other than that the applicant lives down the street or went to the same high school. In some cases the references do not even give applicants good recommendations, simply saying that they really do not know much about the person. A lukewarm recommendation by a personal reference is certainly an indication of the applicant's lack of suitability for a position.

Previous Employers The most important reference check involves the previous employer, co-workers, and supervisor. The use of reference data in the selection process has led to a number of legal challenges under equal employment laws questioning the fairness of such techniques.[86] Thus, many employers have declined to give information to other prospective employers or only provide dates of employment for previous employees. The two legal areas that affect reference checking are equality and privacy. The three relevant federal laws and their major provisions are:[87]

The Privacy Act (1974) This act applies to federal employees only, though several private organizations have adopted policies similar to those specified in the act. Under the act, individuals may review company records that pertain to them, obtain copies, and have relevant information added to the file. Civil suits may be filed for damages that result from willful action which violates the act.

The Fair Credit and Reporting Act (1970) Individuals are given the right to know the nature and substance of their credit file. A person has a right to know when an investigative consumer report on his or her credit has been compiled and has a right to have access to the information compiled.

The Family Education Rights and Privacy Act (1974) Students are given the right to inspect their education records. This act also prevents universities from disclosing education records without prior consent.

Employers can legally provide factual and accurate information that would be useful to other prospective employers. But to protect themselves and the legal rights of former employees, they should follow the guidelines in Figure 5–9. In reality, there are few legal entanglements in reference-checking practices; privacy laws restrict employers from releasing information only in certain areas. Employers can release accurate, verifiable information

1. Don't volunteer information. Respond only to specific company or institutional inquiries and requests. Before responding, telephone the inquirer to check on the validity of the request.

2. Direct all communication only to persons who have a specific interest in that information.

3. State in the message that the information you are providing is confidential and should be treated as such. Use qualifying statements such as "providing information that was requested", "relating this information only because it was requested", or "providing information that is to be used for professional purposes only." Sentences such as these imply that information was not presented for the purpose of hurting or damaging a person's reputation.

4. Obtain written consent from the employee or student, if possible.

5. Provide only reference data that relates and pertains to the job and job performance in question.

6. Avoid vague statements such as: "He was an average student." "She was careless at times." "He displayed an inability to work with others."

7. Document all released information. Use specific statements such as: "Mr. _____ received a grade of C—an average grade." "Ms. _____ made an average of two bookkeeping errors each week." "This spring, four members of the work team wrote letters asking not to be placed on the shift with Mr. _____."

8. Clearly label all subjective statements based on personal opinions and feelings. Say "I believe . . ." whenever making a statement that is not fact.

9. When providing a negative or potentially negative statement, add the reason or reasons why or specify the incidents that led you to this opinion.

10. Do not answer trap questions such as: "Would you rehire this person?"

11. Avoid answering questions that are asked "off the record."

FIGURE 5–9
Guidelines for defensible references from organizations (Source: J. D. Bell, J. Castagnera, and J. P. Young. "Employment References: Do You Know the Law?" *Personnel Journal* 63, no. 2 [February 1984]: 32–36.)

about previous employees in the following areas: dates of employment; job progression; job titles, duties and responsibilities; performance appraisals by employees' supervisors; or other objective measures of employee performance, such as absenteeism, quantitative production, or sales.[88]

Increasingly, employees are suing former employers, contending that they have been defamed in a job reference. Many employers have become so concerned over such lawsuits that they will only provide a former employee's dates of employment and job title. This has made the process of checking references by previous employers difficult for personnel specialists. Unfortunately, good job applicants can be hurt by their previous employer's reluctance when they cannot prove their previous work records. The law is actually on the side of previous employers. The fundamental legal principle is that neither true statements nor statements of opinion can be defamatory. Employers are generally found liable for defamation only if they knowingly or recklessly spread false information. So, why are employers concerned about defamation cases? Bad publicity and legal fees—whether they win or lose.[89]

Employers should not release the following information without written consent: credit information, medical records, school records or other information, and results of polygraph or graphology tests.

Employers should never release false or unverified reference information, or information that is vague or misleading. For example, a past supervisor's feelings that the applicant did not get along with other employees due to personality conflicts should not be included as reference information. Also, if information would have an adverse impact on a protected class of individuals, then it should not be given as reference information. For example, a supervisor might have commented: "She couldn't handle the job; it was too rough for a woman." Such caution does not preclude or limit most background checking by employers. In fact, only rarely is a discrimination case based upon background checks successful, unless the information released was completely false or vague and misleading.[90]

Employees' privacy in the work place promises to be a major employee-relations issue during the next decade. How employees and employers feel about employees' rights to see their own personnel files and the right employers have to that information is a subject of discussion. A study of personnel executives of the *Fortune* 1,000, 77 members of Congress, and over 1,500 employees provided some interesting results. A majority thought that asking questions of job applicants in several areas is improper. The survey showed that employees, employers, and members of Congress strongly believed that employees should be notified before previous employers release personal information. Only in the area

of access to a supervisor's personal notes concerning employees did the employees and employers differ substantially concerning employees' access to their personnel records. Most employees did not believe their employers were engaged in improper collection and use of their personal data.[91]

The Selection Decision

Deciding which applicant should be offered the position may be accomplished by one of two processes: *compensatory selection* or *multiple hurdles* selection. The multiple hurdles selection process is the one shown in Figure 5–6. In this process the successful applicant must pass each hurdle: initial screening, application blank, testing, interview, background checks, and departmental interview. In the compensatory selection process, all applicants who pass the initial screening complete the application blank and are tested; each applicant is interviewed before the final choice is made. The applicants are then compared on the basis of all of the selection information. In compensatory selection, an applicant may score low in one area, but the score might be offset by a very high mark in another area. This is particularly beneficial to candidates who receive low interview scores because they are very nervous and lack self-confidence during interviews but perform very well on aptitude and background checks. The disadvantage of compensatory selection is its cost; a larger number of candidates must be processed through the complete selection procedure before a final decision is made. Primarily due to the cost factor, the multiple hurdles selection technique, in which a candidate might be rejected at each stage of the process, is more common.

When the selection decision results in the hiring of an employee who is successful on

PERSONNEL
IN THE NEWS

The Unfavorable But Positive Recommendation

For the person who desires to send a letter of recommendation that sounds positive yet contains unfavorable information, Robert J. Thornton of Lehigh University developed the Lexicon of Inconspicuously Ambiguous Recommendations (LIAR):

- To describe a candidate who is woefully inept: "I most enthusiastically recommend this candidate with no qualifications whatsoever."
- To describe a candidate who is not particularly industrious: "In my opinion you will be very fortunate to get this person to work for you."
- To describe a candidate who is not worth further consideration: "I would urge you to waste no time in making this candidate an offer of employment."
- To describe a candidate with lackluster credentials: "All in all, I cannot say enough good things about this candidate or recommend him too highly."
- To describe an ex-employee who had difficulty getting along with fellow workers: "I am pleased to say that this candidate is a former colleague of mine."
- To describe a candidate who is so unproductive that the position would be better left unfilled: "I can assure you that no person would be better for this job."

Any of the above may be used to offer a negative opinion of the personal qualities, work habits, or motivation of the candidate while allowing the candidate to believe that it is high praise. In any case, whether perceived correctly or not by the candidate, the phrases are virtually litigation-proof.

Source: Robert J. Thornton, "I Can't Recommend the Candidate Too Highly: An Ambiguous Lexicon for Job Recommendations," *The Chronicle for Higher Education* 33 (February 25, 1987): 42. Copyright 1984, The Chronicle of Higher Education. Reprinted with permission.

the job, then the cost of the selection decision is the normal cost of filling a vacant position. But if an erroneous selection decision is made, then additional costs are incurred. Management can make two types of errors in the selection process: selecting someone for a position who fails on the job (false positive) and rejecting an applicant who could have been successful on the job (false negative). Expenses associated with hiring the wrong employee involve the cost of replacing that individual, termination costs, costs of undesirable job behavior, and costs incurred by a lack of morale or cooperation with other employees. These costs must be weighed against the cost of rejecting the individual who could have been successful on the job. Included in these costs are the opportunity costs of having a successful employee who could have added to the productivity of the organization and the competitive disadvantage lost if the individual is hired by a competing firm. The cost of recruiting an additional applicant to replace the rejected individual also must be considered.[92]

Although it is difficult to attach dollar values to some of those costs, the decision boils down to estimating the possible losses incurred due to hiring poor employees in comparison with the costs incurred in rejecting employees who could have been successful. Attached to the latter cases are additional recruitment and selection costs.

INTERNATIONAL HRM: EXPATRIATE RIGHTS

When Ali Boureslan, a naturalized American citizen, was fired by his Saudi Arabia–based American employer, he sued for discrimination. What began as a relatively straightforward case involving one man, one company, and one incident has evolved into an important test case in international law. For the time being, at least, Boureslan's complaint is no longer the central issue. Whether he was discriminated against is no longer the relevant question. Boureslan, a Lebanese native and Moslem, was hired by Armco in the United States. After he was transferred to Armco's Saudi Arabian operation, he reported that a British co-worker was harassing him because of his religious obligations. The co-worker was eventually fired. Boureslan, however, was later laid off, along with other Armco employees in Saudi Arabia. His suit claims that

his termination was really part of the harassment that began with his co-worker.

The issue now concerns the administration of personnel policies by American companies with overseas operations. Does Title VII of the Civil Rights Act of 1964 apply to expatriate Americans who are working for U.S. companies? The answer to this question now facing the U.S. Court of Appeals could determine not only whether Boureslan's case will be tried, but it could also affect the competitiveness of American companies operating outside U.S. boundaries.

"The internationalization of the world's economy does not require or even suggest that the domestic social practice of this country or any country be made the standard of practice around the world" said attorney Lawrence Z. Lorber, who argued the case on the American Society for Personnel Administration's (ASPA) behalf. . . . ASPA earlier had filed a friend-of-the-court brief supporting Armco's position in the suit.

". . . While we can learn from our colleagues and adapt different personnel practices to our own culture, we cannot impose our standards around the world or compel our businesses to ignore the sovereignty and cultural mores of those nations in which and with which we conduct business," Lorber said.

Boureslan's attorney, James Tyson, agreed that there might be inequality in the treatment of workers of different nationalities, but that is not sufficient argument, he said, to deny American workers their rights under Title VII. One argument has been used by both sides to support their cases: the chilling effect on Americans' careers if they are guaranteed or denied civil rights protection overseas. Without Title VII protection, said Tyson, few American workers would be willing to accept overseas assignments and expose themselves to the capriciousness of their supervisors and foreign cultures.

On the other hand, Lorber said that with the protection—and almost certain resulting cultural conflict—of combined American law and local law, American companies operating abroad would hesitate to hire American workers. This would place an unfair limitation on qualified American employees for whom an overseas assignment would benefit their careers. Lorber added that the combined legal burden would undermine the competitiveness of foreign-based American companies and create unfair conditions that would favor American workers on the job site.

"Applying Title VII in foreign countries may have deleterious effects on U.S. foreign relations," Lorber said. "The purpose of the American trade treaties is to assure that nationals of one country would not be discriminated against within the territory of the other country. Extraterritorial application of Title VII would give Americans abroad more favorable employment conditions than the nationals in the host country. Such a result may subvert the U.S. foreign relations policy manifested in many commercial treaties."[93]

CONCLUSIONS AND APPLICATIONS

- The selection process generally centers on the personnel office. It is one of the most critical functions in personnel, because an organization's effectiveness depends on the employees. The selection process is not, however, one of scientific precision. Instead of finding the one best person, managers strive to select an applicant who has the ability and motivation to perform the job for many years.

- Federal laws and court decisions have greatly affected the selection process. Employers must ensure that their hiring practices in general are nondiscriminatory and that each applicant is given an equal opportunity.

- In recent years, many more discrimination suits have been filed under the ADEA. Employers have had to increase their efforts to guard against age discrimination by making employment decisions on the basis of documented performance data and by offering early retirement programs only on a voluntary basis.

- Affirmative-action programs by employers seek to determine areas of female and minority underuse. Employers establish goals and timetables to increase recruitment and selection of females and minorities in underused job categories.

- Selection screening devices, such as the interview and the application blank, each have advantages and disadvantages. Employers must carefully design each device to be valid and reliable.

- The interview tends to be the most commonly used and decisive selection technique. Subject to reliability problems, the structuring of the interview questions and the scoring of answers can greatly improve reliability and usefulness of the interview as a decision tool.

- Use of selection tests has greatly declined in the last twenty years because of questions about validity. Reference checking has increased in use but has been subjected to legal challenges. Employers can legally provide factual and accurate information, but they should be able to verify any job-related information they release.

CASE STUDY
Minority Candidates

Harry Lee, the personnel director of a 200-employee firm, Decisions Unlimited, was uncertain about hiring an accounts manager. Lee and the accounting department manager, Bob Roberts, reviewed the three top candidates. The first candidate, Mary Gronefeld, had six years of excellent experience with a firm in a nearby city. She had moved recently because her husband had accepted a new position. The second candidate, Archie Vernon, was a young college graduate looking for his first permanent job. Vernon scored the highest on the company's validated written test. The third candidate, Paul Joseph, scored nearly as high on the test as Vernon (0.5 percent difference) and had two years' experience with a local firm that employs about fifty workers. Joseph was also a Vietnam War veteran, which Lee and Roberts believed was important.

Lee: "The problem is that we have three great candidates!"

Roberts: "Yes. They are all good, and they interviewed well."

Lee: "But we only have one female who is not an hourly employee, and our affirmative-action plan says we will hire more females."

Roberts: "Wait a minute! Joseph is a veteran; doesn't the government say something about that?"

Lee: "Yes, that's true. But Vernon scored the highest on the test, so I think we should hire him."

Questions

1. How could Decisions Unlimited legally defend hiring each of the three candidates?
2. Who would you hire? Why?
3. What would you tell those not hired?

EXPERIENTIAL EXERCISE
Is This Application Blank Lawful?

Purpose

To recognize the legal issues surrounding the use of application blanks and to analyze an actual application blank for potentially unlawful items.

The Task

Illustrated on page 204 is an actual application blank currently in use by a retail clothing chain. How many potentially illegal items on the application blank can you identify? Following your analysis, your instructor will lead you in a discussion concerning this exercise.

APPLICATION FOR EMPLOYMENT

We are an equal opportunity employer, dedicated to a policy of non-discrimination in employment on any basis including race, creed, color, age, sex, religion or national origin.

PERSONAL INFORMATION

	DATE
	SOCIAL SECURITY NUMBER

NAME _____
                LAST   FIRST   MIDDLE

PRESENT ADDRESS _____
            STREET   CITY   STATE

PERMANENT ADDRESS _____
            STREET   CITY   STATE

PHONE NO. _____   REFERRED BY

DATE OF BIRTH	HEIGHT	WEIGHT	COLOR OF HAIR	COLOR OF EYES

MARRIED	SINGLE	WIDOWED	DIVORCED	SEPARATED

NUMBER OF CHILDREN _____ DEPENDENTS OTHER THAN WIFE OR CHILDREN CITIZEN OF U.S.A. YES ☐ NO ☐

IF RELATED TO ANYONE IN OUR EMPLOY, STATE NAME AND DEPARTMENT   REFERRED BY

EMPLOYMENT DESIRED

POSITION _____ DATE YOU CAN START SALARY DESIRED

ARE YOU EMPLOYED NOW? _____ IF SO MAY WE INQUIRE OF YOUR PRESENT EMPLOYER?

EVER APPLIED TO THIS COMPANY BEFORE? _____ WHERE? WHEN?

EDUCATION	NAME AND LOCATION OF SCHOOL	YEARS ATTENDED *	DATE GRADUATED *	SUBJECTS STUDIED
GRAMMAR SCHOOL				
HIGH SCHOOL				
COLLEGE				
TRADE, BUSINESS OR CORRESPONDENCE SCHOOL				

* The Age Discrimination in Employment Act of 1967 prohibits discrimination on the basis of age with respect to individuals who are at least 40 but less than 65 years of age.

GENERAL

SUBJECTS OF SPECIAL STUDY OR RESEARCH WORK _____

WHAT FOREIGN LANGUAGES DO YOU SPEAK FLUENTLY? _____ READ WRITE

U.S. MILITARY OR NAVAL SERVICE _____ RANK PRESENT MEMBERSHIP IN NATIONAL GUARD OR RESERVES

[CONTINUED ON OTHER SIDE]

LAST   FIRST   MIDDLE

KEY TERMS AND CONCEPTS

Achievement tests

Adverse impact

Age Discrimination in Employment Act

Application blank

Aptitude tests

BFOQ

Civil Rights Act

Discrimination

EEOC

Equal Pay Act

Executive Order 11246

Four-fifths rule

Graphology

Immigration Reform and Control Act

Intelligence tests

Interest tests

Negligent hiring

Polygraph

Probable cause

Reference checks

Reverse discrimination

Separation agreements

Sexual harassment

Substantially equal

Title VII

Types of validity

Underuse of minorities

Vietnam Era Veterans Readjustment Act

Vocational Rehabilitation Act

REVIEW QUESTIONS

1. Why is the selection process usually centralized in the personnel department?
2. Should the personnel office ask an applicant for date of birth, marital status, or a photograph?
3. How does the personnel specialist use the application blank?
4. What are the real uses of an applicant's personal references?
5. Which types of tests are the most useful in employee selection?
6. Which organizations are affected by the Civil Rights Act? What is its primary purpose?
7. Why should young employees be concerned with the Age Discrimination in Employment Act?
8. How can a firm get cooperation from managers in implementing an affirmative-action program?
9. What should managers have learned from the *Griggs* v. *Duke Power Company* and *United Steelworkers* v. *Weber* cases?
10. Why was the Immigration Reform and Control Act passed?

DISCUSSION QUESTIONS

1. What inappropriate personality traits would overshadow an employee's skills and abilities enough to cause the dismissal of the following persons: a food-store checkout clerk, a research assistant, an elementary school teacher?
2. If you inherited a shoe factory that had a history of high turnover and low wages, would you attempt to attract only the best workers by raising salaries or continue a minimum wage policy and disregard employees' dissatisfaction? What factors would influence your decision?

3. While interviewing two well-qualified applicants for an accounting manager's position, you notice that one applicant has had one job for seven years and the other has had five jobs in ten years, each change involving a salary increase. Would this information affect your decision?

4. Why should age and sex biases not color a personnel specialist's choice of persons to fill positions as car-wash employees, tool makers, receptionists, or sanitation workers?

5. You work in a department store's personnel department. The owner requests that all of the store's employees take polygraph tests periodically to minimize employee theft. Employees find this approach insulting and demand that you do something. What would you do?

6. If you believed you were discriminated against, under what circumstances would you contact the local EEOC or let the situation ride? Why?

7. Is affirmative action still important to employers?

ENDNOTES

1. Arthur Within, "Commonly Overlooked Dimensions of Employee Selection," *Personnel Journal* 59, no. 7 (July, 1980): 573–75.

2. Paul S. Greenlaw and John P. Kohl, "The EEOC's New Equal Pay Act Guidelines," *Personnel Journal* 61, no. 7 (July 1982): 517–21.

3. George Wendt, "Should Courts Write Your Job Descriptions?," *Personnel Journal* (September, 1976): 442–44.

4. Ibid., pp. 443–50.

5. *McDonnell-Douglas Corp.* v. *Green*, 441, U.S. 792 (1972), SEPD.

6. James Ledvinka, *Federal Regulation of Personnel and Human Resource Management* (Boston, MA: Kent, 1982), pp. 62–63.

7. *Phillips* v. *Martin Marietta*, 400 U.S. 542 (1971).

8. Public Law 95–955, 92 Stat. 2076–77 (1978).

9. C. Safran, "What Men Do to Women on the Job: A Shocking Look at Sexual Harassment," *Redboook* (November 1976): 419.

10. T. L. Leap and E. R. Gray, "Corporate Responsibility in Cases of Sexual Harassment," *Business Horizons* (October 1980): 58.

11. Equal Employment Opportunity Commission, *1980 Guidelines.* Washington, DC: Government Printing Office, 1980.

12. David E. Terpstra and Douglas D. Baker, "Outcomes of Sexual Harassment Charges," *Academy of Management Journal* 31, no. 1 (March 1988): 185–94.

13. See E. C. Collins and T. B. Blodgett, "Sexual Harassment: Some Get It, Some Won't," *Harvard Business Review* (March–April 1981): 77–78; K. A. Thurston, "Sexual Harassment: An Organizational Perspective," *Personnel Administrator* (December 1980): 59–64; and O. A. Ornati, "How to Deal with EEOC's Guidelines on Sexual Harassment," *EEO Compliance Manual* (Englewood Cliffs, NJ: Prentice-Hall, 1980).

14. *Hodgson* v. *Greyhound Lines, Inc.*, 499 F. 2d 859, 7th Circuit (1974).

15. Michael R. Carrell and Frank E. Kuzmits, "Amended ADEA's Effects on HR Strategies Remain Dubious," *Personnel Journal* 66, no. 5 (May 1987): 111–20.

16. Ibid.

17. "Retirement Age Law to Keep 200,000 on Job," *Resource* (November 1986): 3.

18. Edmund R. Hergenrather, "The Older Worker: A Golden Asset," *Personnel* (August 1985): 56.

19. Nicholas J. Mathys, Helen La Van, and Frederick Schwerdtner, "Learning the Lessons of Age Discrimination Cases," *Personnel Journal* 63, no. 6 (June 1984): 30–32.

20. Malcolm H. Morrison and M. Kathryn Jedrziewski, "Retirement Planning: Everybody Benefits," *Personnel Administrator* 33, no. 1 (January 1988): 74–80.

21. Herbert Field and William Holley, "The Relationship of Performance Appraisal System Characteristics to Verdicts in Selected Employment Discrimination Cases," *Academy of Management Journal 25*, no. 2 (March 1982): 392–406.

22. Mathys, La Van, and Schwerdtner, "Learning the Lessons," pp. 30–32.

23. *Sullivan* v. *Boron Oil Co. et al.*, No. 86–00076 (3rd Cir. 1987).

24. Ledvinka, *Federal Regulation*, pp. 71–81.

25. Ibid.

26. Bruce D. May, "Law Puts Immigration Control in Employers' Hands," *Personnel Journal* (March 1987): 106–111.

27. Lawrence Lorber and Craig Freger, "Employment Discrimination Under the Immigration Reform and Control Act of 1986," *HRM Legal Report,* American Society for Personnel Administration (Winter 1987): 4–7.

28. May, "Law Puts Immigration Control in Employers' Hands," p. 108.

29. U.S. Equal Employment Opportunity Commission, *Affirmative Action and Equal Employment, A Guidebook for Employers* (Washington, DC: U.S. Government Printing Office, 1974), pp. 47–48.

30. David Brookmore, "Designing and Implementing Your Company's Affirmative Action Program," *Personnel Journal* (April 1979): 232–37.

31. C. Paul Sparks, "Guidance and Guidelines," *The Industrial-Organizational Psychologist* 14, no. 3 (May 1977): 30–33.

32. Robert Gatewood and James Ledvinka, "Selection Interviewing and EEO: Mandate for Objectivity," *The Personnel Administrator* (May 1976): 15–18.

33. "Uniform Guidelines on Employee Selection Procedures (1978)," *Federal Register* (August 25, 1978): 38291.

34. William A. Simon, Jr., "A Practical Approach to the Uniform Selection Guidelines," *The Personnel Administrator* (November 1979): 75–80.

35. David E. Robertson, "New Directions in EEO Guidelines," *Personnel Journal* (July 1978): 360–62.

36. Simon, "A Practical Approach," pp. 78–80.

37. Ibid., p. 77.

38. *Bakke* v. *University of California,* 438 U.S. 265 (1978).

39. Louis P. Britt III, "Affirmative Action: Is There Life After Stotts?" *Personnel Administrator* 29, no. 9 (September 1984): 96–100. Note: Louis P. Britt III served as staff attorney for the City of Memphis and represented the city in the Stotts case.

40. Ibid.

41. Lawrence Z. Lorber, "Employers Should Not Take Precipitous Action in Affirmative Action Cases," *Personnel Administrator* 29, no. 9 (September 1984): 101–02.

42. Mitchell S. Novit, *Essentials of Personnel Management* (Englewood Cliffs, NJ: Prentice-Hall, 1979), pp. 70–74.

43. U.S. Equal Employment Opportunity Commission, *Affirmative Action and Equal Employment—A Guidebook for Employers,* vol. A (Washington, DC: U.S. Government Printing Office, 1974), pp. 29–30.

44. Erwin S. Stanton, *Successful Personnel Recruiting and Selection* (New York: AMACOM, 1977), pp. 73–84.

45. U.S. EEOC, *Affirmative Action,* pp. 29–30.

46. Ibid., pp. 40–60.

47. *Sprogis* v. *United Air Lines,* 444 F. 2d 1194 (7th Cir. 1971).

48. *Griggs* v. *Duke Power Company,* 401 U.S. 424 (1971).

49. *U.S.* v. *Bethlehem Steel Corporation,* 446 F.2d 652 (2nd Cir. 1971).

50. *Griggs* v. *Duke Power Company,* 401 U.S. 424 (1971).

51. EEOC Decision 72-0427 (1971), *CCH Employment Practices Guide,* para. 6312 (New York: Commerce Clearing House, 1970); *Parham* v. *S. W. Bell Telephone Company,* 433 F.2D 421 (1970).

52. *Castro* v. *Beecher,* 459 F.2d 725, C.A. 1, (1972); *CCH Employment Practices Guide,* para. 6231, 6286.

53. Jeremiah Bogert, "Learning the Applicant's Background Through Confidential Investigation,"*Personnel Journal* 55 (June 1976): 272–75.

54. L. Robert Ebel, "Comments on Some Problems of Employment Testing," *Personnel Psychology* 30 (1977): 55–63.

55. U.S. EEOC, *Affirmative Action,* pp. 43–45.

56. Ibid., p. 575.

57. Dale Yoder and Paul D. Standohar, "Testing and EEO: Getting Down to Cases," *Personnel Administrator* 29, no. 2 (February 1984): 67–74.

58. John Aberth, "Pre-Employment Testing Is Losing Favor," *Personnel Journal* 65, no. 9 (September 1986): 96–104.

59. Robert M. Guion, *Personnel Testing* (New York: McGraw-Hill, 1965), pp. 169–74.

60. Benjamin Schneider, *Staffing Organizations* (Pacific Palisades, CA: Goodyear, 1976): pp. 79–83.

61. Ibid., pp. 80–83.

62. The Reader's Digest Association, *The Reader's Digest Great Encyclopedic Dictionary* (Pleasantville, NY: Funk and Wagnalls, 1968), p. 73.

63. Schneider, *Staffing Organizations,* pp. 83–85.

64. Robert M. Madigan, K. Dow Scott, Diana L. Deadrick, and Jil A. Stoddard, "Employment Testing: The U.S. Job Service Is Spearheading a Revolution," *Personnel Administrator* 31, no. 9 (September 1986): 102–12.

65. Tony Keenan, "Recruitment On Campus: A Closer Look at the Tools of the Trade," *Personnel Management* 12, no. 3 (March 1980): 43–46.

66. Ibid., pp. 168–70.

67. H. Birdie Holder, "A Critique of Three Current Typing Tests," *Personnel Journal* 58 (May, 1979): 291–94.

68. John A. Bolt and Peter B. Holden, "Polygraph Usage Among Major U.S. Corporations," *Personnel Journal* 57 (February, 1978): 80–86.

69. G. Philip Benson and S. Paul Kreis, "The Polygraph in Employment: Some Unresolved Issues," *Personnel Journal* 58 (September 1979): 616–21.

70. Elaine Hobbes Fry and Nicholas Eugene Fry, "Information vs. Privacy: The Polygraphy Debate," *Personnel* 65, no. 2 (February 1988): 57–60.

71. Barbara Felton and Sue Ries Lamb, "A Model for Systematic Selection Interviewing," *Personnel* 59, no. 1 (January–February 1982): 40–48.

72. Robert Gatewood and James Ledvinka, "Selection Interviewing and EEO: Mandate for Objectivity," *The Personnel Administrator* (May, 1976): 15–17.

73. Ray Forbes, "Improving the Reliability of the Selection Interview," *Personnel Management* (July, 1979): 36–67. R. D. Arvey, "Unfair Discrimination in the Employment Interview: Legal and Psychological Aspects," *Psychological Bulletin* 86 (1979): 736.

74. Gerald Rose, "Sex Effects on Managerial Hiring Decisions," *Academy of Management Journal* 21 (1978): 104–12.

75. John Hatfield, "Nonverbal Cues in the Selection Interview," *The Personnel Administrator* (January 1978): 30–33.

76. Forbes, *Improving the Reliability,* pp. 36–37.

77. Elliot D. Pursell, Michael A. Campion, and Sarah R. Gaylord, "Structured Interviewing: Avoiding Selection Problems," *Personnel Journal* 59, no. 11 (November 1980): 907–12.

78. Carl Camden and Bill Wallace, "Job Application Forms: A Hazardous Employment Practice," *Personnel Administrator* 28, no. 3 (March 1983): 31–32, 64.

79. William A. Schaffer, Frank David Rollo, and Carol A. Holt, "Falsification of Clinical Credentials by Physicians Applying for Ambulatory-Staff Privileges," *New England Journal of Medicine* 318, no. 6 (1988): 356–58.

80. Bruce D. Wonder and Kenneth S. Keleman, "Increasing the Value of Reference Information," *Personnel Administrator* 29, no. 3 (March 1984): 98–103.

81. Ronald M. Green and Richard J. Reibstein, "It's 10 P.M. Do You Have to Know Where Your Employees Are?" *Personnel Administrator* 32, no. 4 (April 1987): 71–76.

82. *Henley* v. *Prince George's County,* 305 Md. 320, 503, A. 2d 1333 (1986).

83. *Abbot* v. *Payne* 457 So. 2d 1156, Fla. Dist. Ct. App. (1984).

84. *Welsh Manufacturing* v. *Pinkerton's, Inc.,* 474 A. 2d 436 R.I. (1984).

85. Green and Reibstein, "It's 10 P.M.," pp. 75–76.

86. J. D. Baxter, B. Brock, P. C. Hill, and R. M. Rozelle, "Letters of Recommendation: A Question of Value," *Journal of Applied Psychology* 66, no. 3 (March 1981): 296–301.

87. James D. Bell, James Castagnera, and Jane Patterson Young, "Employment References: Do You Know the Law?" *Personnel Journal* 63, no. 2 (February 1984): 32–36.

88. Edward L. Levine, "Legal Aspects of Reference Checking for Personnel Selection," *The Personnel Administrator* (November 1977): 14–17.

89. "When a Boss Says Too Much . . . ," *Denver Post* (December 6, 1987): G1, 6.

90. Ibid., pp. 15–77.

91. Allan Westin, "What Should Be Done About Employee Privacy?," *The Personnel Administrator* (March 1980): 27–30.
92. Marvin D. Dunnette, *Personnel Selection and Placement* (Belmont, CA: Brooks-Cole, 1966): 173–75.
93. Martha I. Finney, *Resource* Vol. 1, No. 14 (Alexandria, VA: American Society for Personnel Administration, December 1987), p. 1.

Bordon Electric Company: Part 1

The Bordon Electric Company is a small regional public utility in Bordon County, western Kentucky. It serves approximately 50,000 customers in three communities and the surrounding rural area. Electricity is generated at a central plant or purchased from a large utility in Louisville, Kentucky. Each community has a substation and its own work crew. The company presently employs 346 people.

The company is not unionized. The employees appear to be satisfied with their working conditions. While wages are not as high as in the larger urban areas, they are perceived by employees as equitable when compared to those paid for similar jobs in the surrounding vicinity.

The small utility has never had a professional human resources manager. Job analysis, recruitment, selection, orientation, performance appraisal, and other personnel functions have traditionally been the responsibility of each substation superintendent and central plant manager. There has been no companywide attempt to plan for the future in terms of human resource needs. But the utility has grown rapidly and profitably in both revenue and number of employees, making it imperative for the president, Tom Byrd, to hire a qualified human resource professional.

Tom Byrd is a strong professional executive who believes in affirmative-action programs and is concerned about Bordon's lack of progress in this area. Also, Tom is getting signals that a union may try to organize the craft employees.

Because of these anticipated problems and pressures, Tom realizes that he must begin to build a top management team that can help him manage this rapidly growing public utility. As part of this team, Tom wants to attract a top-notch director of human resources. He has appointed a search committee of five people from across the company and asks you to serve as consultant to this committee.

The search committee started the process by preparing a draft of the job description and the writing of the position announcement. The committee spent time discussing minimum qualifications, experience, and what they hoped the new person would accomplish once on board. The committee wanted you to determine where and how the position announcement should appear.

Position Announcement
Bordon Electric Company
Director of Human Resources

Dynamic Western Kentucky utility company seeks proven executive who can build, operate, and improve modern human resource systems in a non-union company. Must be able to influence line and staff managers in a public sector environment. Must be flexible and serve needs but maintain control over systems. The director will be responsible to the president for all human resource activities, which serve all company personnel. Duties include employee relations, staff recruitment, fringe benefits, negotiations with the state department of personnel, training, and affirmative action. A bachelor's degree is preferred, but persons with unusally strong experience will be considered. Experience must include a demonstrated administrative ability in personnel, a demonstrated high level of interpersonal skills, and a commitment to affirmative action. Pay is competitive and negotiable, depending upon the candidate's background. The company is located in a resort area surrounded by many lakes and wilderness areas. Send resume and cover letter by June 1, 1989, to Search Committee, Bordon Electric Company, P.O. Box 2010, Muray, KY 44444.

One day following the close of the application period, the search committee counted over 150 applications. The five top candidates and a summary of their resume credentials are:

1. Richard Banks
    Age, 29 years
    Married, one child
    Excellent health
    Education: MBA from Northwestern University (1986)
    　　　　　　 BS in commerce from Michigan State (1979)
    Experience: 2 years, assistant to the vice-president, Northwestern
    　　　　　　 University.
    　　　　　　 3 years, Colorado Outward Bound School (summers)
    General: Love the outdoors
    　　　　 Excellent management potential
    　　　　 Member of MENSA (top 1 percent of the population in
    　　　　 intelligence)

2. William Husker
    Age, 40 years
    Married, two children
    Good health
    Education: BS in education from Eastern Kentucky Univ. (1971)
    　　　　　　 Master's degree in labor relations (1986)
    　　　　　　 Attended numerous management training programs

Experience: Currently employed with Louisville Gas and Electric as
industrial relations officer for past 15 years
General: Excellent knowledge of utilities
Extensive experience with unions
Grew up in small town

3. Helen Horn
Age, 43 years
Divorced, one child (in college)
Excellent health
Education: Bachelor of Arts in English from Bellarmine College
(1988)
Experience: 8 years, personnel manager, United Parcel Service
(UPS)
3 years, secretary, UPS
9 years, housewife
General: Attended college at night while raising daughter
Graduated with highest honors
Strong recommendations from UPS regional office
Member ASPA—certified as a Professional in Human Re-
source Management

4. Windell Jones
Age, 35 years
Married, two children
Excellent health
Education: Grambling University, public administration (1977)
Experience: 5 years, affirmative action coordinator, Tennessee State
Government
5 years, State Personnel Office
General: Attended college on athletic scholarship
Strong leadership credentials
Extensive public-speaking experience

5. Jim Miller
Age, 37 years
Married, four children
Good health
Education: Some college (still attending at night)
Completed GED while serving in Marine Corps
Experience: 17 years, Bordon Electric Company
10 years, supervisor in special construction
7 years, business office manager

General: Internal applicant
  Solid knowledge of firm's accounting practices
  Thorough knowledge of utility industry and company
  Expects to complete college degree this year
  Hard-working, precise, well liked

Discussion Questions

1. Prepare a job description for the position of director of human resources. Identify where (i.e., newpapers, professional publications, etc.) the position's announcement should have been publicized.
2. As the consultant to the search committee, what procedures would you recommend the committee follow to increase the reliability and validity of the selection process?
3. Whom would you select for the position of director of human resources at Bordon Electric and why?

Part Two   Appraisal, Training, and Development

Chapter Six

Appraisal of Human Resources

Chapter Objectives

1. To explain the evaluative and developmental objectives of performance appraisal.
2. To recognize common appraisal problems.
3. To describe the major performance appraisal methods.
4. To develop an effective appraisal interview.
5. To design and evaluate a program of performance appraisal.
6. To discuss who should perform the appraisal.

Performance Appraisal at Control Data Corp

At Control Data Corporation, performance appraisal is far more than an employee review. The international computer and financial services company developed a comprehensive appraisal program that includes (1) job-related appraisal forms; (2) an appraisal process that includes the establishment of work levels, revision of expectations when necessary, salary actions, and performance documentation; and (3) a monitoring system to ensure that the system is used as intended. Over 15,000 jobs were evaluated by job analysts and grouped into thirteen *job families,* including management, engineer, customer-engineer, programmer-analyst, data processing operations, sales, and so on. About 15 percent of the employees in each job family then identified the performance factors that are necessary for success in each of the thirteen job families. Then the total appraisal model in the accompanying figure was developed in order that several desired functions be included.

In step one, for example, the manager and employee discuss key objectives to be accomplished and their method of evaluation. The agreed-upon goals are then formalized into a work plan to be achieved during the following period. The second step consists of the manager's constantly monitoring the employee's progress against agreed-upon goals; this step is called *coaching.* The third step requires the manager to complete the appraisal form using the agreed-upon goals as the standards. The manager must also describe how the employee achieved the objectives and why this performance was below, equal to, or above expectations. In step four, the manager and employee formally discuss the step-three appraisal. The purpose of the discussion is to develop a specific plan for improving ability where necessary. In step five, salary adjustments based on performance appraisals are made. Finally, step six requires the manager to discuss with the employee the firm's pay philosophy and the factors which determined the salary decision.

Employee brochures and managerial appraisal guides were then written and distributed in order that everyone understood the system. Surveys of employee and manager attitudes were then administered and revealed a high level of satisfaction with the total system and level of manager-employee communication.

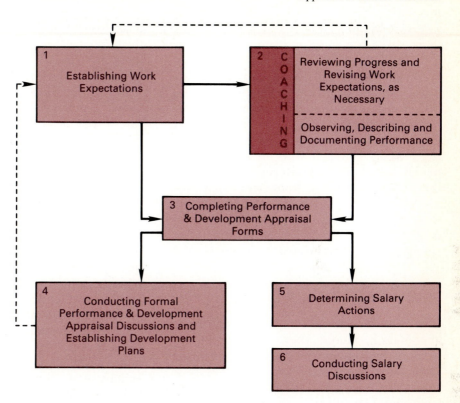

Control Data Corporation's performance-appraisal process (Source: Luis R. Gomez-Mejia, Ronald C. Page, and Walter W. Tornow, "Improving the Effectiveness of Performance Appraisal." Reprinted from the January 1985 issue of *Personnel Administrator* © 1985; The American Society for Personnel Administration, 606 North Washington Street, Alexandria, VA 22314.)

PERFORMANCE appraisal is a process of evaluating the behavior of employees in the workplace, normally including both the quantitative and qualitative aspects of job performance. Performance appraisal is one of the basic personnel functions; it is also called *performance review, employee appraisal, performance evaluation, employee evaluation, merit evaluation,* and *personnel rating.* All of these terms refer to the same process.

Performance appraisal is an entirely different process from job evaluation. Performance appraisal concerns how well someone is doing an assigned job. Job evaluation concerns how much a job is worth to the organization and, therefore, what range of pay should be assigned to the job. For example, a performance appraisal may show that someone is the best computer programmer the organization has ever had. The job evaluation is used to make sure that the programmer receives the maximum pay a computer programmer's position is worth to the organization.

Even though supervisors are the most integral part of the performance-appraisal process, many complain that appraising their employees' behavior is the most difficult and unpleasant task they must perform. In fact, supervisors often find ways to avoid performance appraisals. Almost everyone agrees that it is important to know how well employees are doing their jobs. But few people want to be involved in the actual analysis of employees' performance or the discussions of strengths and weaknesses with employees.

PERFORMANCE APPRAISAL

Why should management use performance appraisals if, indeed, they are such an unpleasant and often time-consuming process? There are several important objectives of a performance-appraisal program that cannot be achieved by any other method.

Performance appraisals are a key element in the use and development of an organization's most vital resource—the employees. Appraisals are used for a wide range of administrative purposes, such as making decisions relative to pay, promotion, and retention. Effective appraisals can significantly contribute to the satisfaction and motivation of employees—if they are used correctly.[1] For the most part, the objectives of performance appraisal fall into two categories: evaluative and developmental.

Evaluative Objectives

The most common decisions based on evaluative objectives concern compensation, which includes merit increases, employee bonuses, and other increases in pay. As far as employees are concerned, this is one of the primary objectives of performance appraisals. Thus, the term *merit review* or *merit evaluation* can be found in organizations using the performance appraisal to determine pay increases. Performance appraisal normally has a two-part effect on employees' future pay. In the short run, it may determine merit increases for the following year; in the long run, it may determine which employees receive higher-paying jobs.

Staffing decisions constitute a second evaluative objective of performance appraisal, because the managers and supervisors must make decisions concerning promotions, demotions, transfers, and layoffs. Past performance appraisals normally help determine which employee is most deserving of a promotion or other desirable job change.

Performance appraisals can be used to evaluate the recruitment, selection, and placement system. The effectiveness of these functions can be partially measured by comparing employees' performance appraisals with their test scores as job applicants. For example, management may find that applicants who scored approximately equally on selection tests show quite a difference in performance after one year on the job; thus, the tests may not accurately predict behavior. Such analysis not only validates selection techniques but also determines the strengths and weaknesses of the selection process as well as the appraisal process. As Table 6–1 illustrates, the evaluative objectives of compensation decisions (merit increases, bonuses) and staffing decisions (promotion, termination, succession planning, transfer, personnel planning) dominate the common uses of performance appraisal systems, with seven of the top ten uses.

Developmental Objectives

The second objective of performance appraisal encompasses developing employee skills and motivation and providing performance feed-

TABLE 6–1

A ranking of the uses of performance appraisal from a survey of 256 companies

Rank	Function of Appraisal	Percentage
1	Merit increases	91
2	Performance results/feedback/job counseling	90
3	Promotion	82
4	Termination or layoff	64
5	Performance potential	62
6	Succession planning	57
7	Career planning	52
8	Transfer	50
9	Manpower planning	38
10	Bonuses	32
11	Development and evaluation of training programs	29
12	Internal communication	25
13	Criteria for selection procedure validation	16
14	Expense control	7

Source: Charles J. Fombrun and Robert L. Laud, "Strategic Issues in Performance Appraisal Theory and Practice," *Personnel* 601, no. 6 (November-December 1983): 23–31. Used by permission of the American Management Association.

back. Because the employee has input into the appraisal, the process becomes more time-consuming than when a supervisor simply fills out an appraisal form.

Performance feedback is a primary developmental need, because almost all employees want to know how their supervisors feel about their performances. They want to know whether the results are satisfactory and if they are behaving as expected. As employees pursue their careers, periodically taking stock of how the organization views their performance is important. Their motivation to improve their current performance increases when they receive feedback that specifies goals, which in turn enhances future career moves.[2]

Developmental performance appraisal also involves giving employees direction for future performance. This feedback recognizes strengths and weaknesses in past performances and determines what direction employees should take to improve. Employees want to know specifically how they can improve. Because performance appraisals are designed to cope with the problem of poor employee performance, they should be designed to develop better employees.[3]

Appraisal results influence decisions concerning the training and development of employees. Below-average evaluations may signal areas of employee behavior that may be strengthened through on- and off-the-job training. Of course, not all performance deficiencies may be overcome through training and development. Supervisors must differentiate performance problems resulting from lack of a critical skill or ability from those caused by low morale or some form of job dissatisfaction.

THE APPRAISAL PROCESS

In creating and implementing an appraisal system, administrators must determine which process should be used. This decision is just as important as how the appraisal is conducted or the actual content of the appraisal. If employees believe the appraisal was undertaken lightly or if management is sloppy in its administration, then employees will take the appraisal process less seriously than they should. Possible legal ramifications exist wherever management is not uniform in its performance-appraisal procedures. Even if discriminatory performance appraisal practices by supervisors and managers do not lead to lawsuits, the loss of morale and employee productivity resulting from poorly administered performance appraisals can be detrimental to an organization's success.

Determining Performance Requirements   In the first step of the process, administrators must determine what skills, outputs, and accomplishments will be evaluated during each performance appraisal. These may be derived from specific job descriptions or they may be a uniform set of employee requirements included in all performance appraisals. For example, managers may determine that requirements fall into broad categories, such as quality of work, cooperation with other employees, and dependability. Or managers may decide that specific requirements should be set for each employee or for each job. Policymakers must determine exactly what areas of performance are going to be reviewed and how these areas are related to the organization's goals.

Choosing an Appropriate Appraisal Method   Several methods may be used to appraise performance; no one method is best for all organizations. The method of performance appraisal should be carefully chosen because most often it becomes the focal point of involvement between the supervisor and the employee. The manner in which a supervisor conducts the performance appraisal is greatly determined by the method. Within an organization, separate appraisal methods might be used for different groups, such as production employees, sales employees, and administrative employees.

Training the Supervisors   A critical step in performance appraisal is training of supervisors so that they do not commit errors during performance appraisal. Such errors may result in charges of discrimination, loss of employee morale and productivity, or inaccurate performance appraisals, which lead to poor compensation or staffing decisions.

Discussing Methods with Employees   Supervisors should discuss with employees the method that will be used. This discussion should specify which areas of performance are evaluated, how often, how the evaluation takes place, and its significance to the employee. The use of appraisals varies greatly; some organizations tie pay and promotion directly to performance appraisal; others conduct appraisals only in a perfunctory manner to meet some broad goals or policies. Understanding the significance of the performance appraisal, how it is conducted in the particular organization, and what consequence it may have are germane to the employee's future in the organization.

Most employees are anxious about the evaluation even under the best circumstances. Preparing employees for their role in the process can help reduce their anxiety and produce a more productive interview. Employees should be encouraged to prepare themselves by (1) documenting specific examples of their performance and bringing a log of such examples to the interview; (2) objectively reviewing both their strengths and weaknesses during the appraisal period so that legitimate criticism will not come as a complete surprise; and (3) expecting to participate in the process—not just agree to everything they hear from managers. Employees should be encouraged to ask reflective questions such as: "Why do you feel this way?" "Can you give me a specific example?" "Have you considered . . .?"[4]

Appraising According to Requirements The performance appraisal should evaluate the employee's work according to predetermined work requirements. Comparison with specific requirements indicates what the employee has or has not done well. The supervisor's feelings about the employee should not affect the appraisal. Feelings cannot be evaluated; they are only mental constructs and may be biased. By discussing the employee's behavior that has been observed and documented, the supervisor focuses the appraisal on concrete, actual performance by the employee.

Discussing Appraisal with Employees In some organizations, appraisal discussions are omitted whenever specific evaluative objectives for merit raises or promotions have been met. The general trend, however, is to make sure that supervisors discuss the appraisal with their employees, allowing employees to discuss areas of agreement and disagreement. The supervisor should emphasize positive work performance, those areas in which the employee has met or exceeded expectations, as well as areas that need improvement. In most cases, discussion of salary or promotion should not be mixed with the appraisal discussion. Mixing the two may divert the employee's attention from development of future performance goals or review of past performance.

Determining Future Performance Goals A critical aspect of performance appraisal is the use of goal setting.[5] How specifically or rigidly these goals are to be pursued is deter-

mined by the method of performance appraisal. Even if goals are only broadly discussed, setting goals for the employee's future appraisal period is critical because it gives the employee direction for continued or improved performance. Leaving the appraisal discussion, the employee feels comfortable knowing how past performance has been viewed and what needs to be accomplished to improve future performance.

Legal Considerations

The entire performance appraisal process has come under scrutiny by the EEOC and federal courts, which have warned employers about the possible discriminatory effects of their performance appraisals. The burden of proving the validity of a performance-appraisal instrument is clearly on the shoulders of the organization. Thus, policymakers must be cognizant of EEOC and court decisions in this area.

An analysis of court decisions involving charges of discrimination has revealed that performance appraisals are more likely to be illegal if:[6]

- Supervisors who evaluate employee performance are not given specific written instructions and training on how to complete appraisals.
- Job analysis is not used in the development of the content of the appraisal, as required by the EEOC *Uniform Selection Guidelines*.
- General, vague criteria are used in appraisals instead of specific, objective criteria.
- Employees are not provided direct feedback from the appraiser so that they are given a chance to improve their performance.

Personnel managers can best avoid legal entanglements if their performance appraisal processes include:

Documentation of All Appraisals Documentation ensures that management can defend its appraisal and consequential outcomes, such as decisions for promotion or pay based on actual appraisals. Documentation should include written, dated, signed appraisals and all performance records.

A Standard Appraisal Process Standardization ensures that all employees are given equal and consistent treatment. This will avoid possible claims of discrimination based on unequal conditions.

Job Relatedness Managers should be sure that the content and the focus of the appraisal process are on actual aspects of the job performed and not on biases or attitudes of supervisors or co-workers. The areas included in the process should be as specific to the job as possible.

Common Appraisal Problems

Appraisal problems should be recognized and minimized by trained supervisors, who should not only become aware of problems but should also learn how to avoid committing common appraisal errors. All methods of performance appraisal are subject to error, but through training management can minimize appraisal errors and problems.

Supervisory Bias The most common error which exists in any appraisal method is conscious or unconscious supervisory bias. Such biases are not related to job performance and may stem from personal characteristics such as age, sex, or race or from organization-related characteristics such as seniority, membership on an organization's athletic team, or friendship with top administrators. For example, a supervisor may give an undeserved high rating to the bowling-team captain. Managers need to eliminate the biases that they may

have for individual subordinates or set such biases aside during the appraisal process.

Halo Effect When a supervisor lets one particular aspect of an employee's performance influence the evaluation of other aspects of performance, a halo effect has occurred. For example, the manager who knows that a particular employee always arrives at work early and helps to open the business may let the halo caused by that employee's dependability influence the appraisal of other areas, such as quality of work or job knowledge. Thus, even though the employee may be only mediocre in terms of quality or quantity of performance, the employee receives all high ratings because he or she is dependable and arrives at work early.

Negative halos also exist. Resenting the fact that an employee shows no initiative in learning new aspects of the work within the department, a supervisor may give the employee low evaluations in all areas of performance even though the employee performs capably. Halo errors are minimized when the appraisal process is open to review by employees, who will point out that they are not particularly weak in areas in which they have been rated poorly. Employees with positive halos seldom point out, however, that they did not perform as well as their supervisors had indicated. Thus, positive halos are more difficult to minimize.

Central Tendency Supervisors may find it difficult and unpleasant to evaluate some employees higher or lower than others, even though performances may reflect a real difference. Central tendency results when they evaluate everyone as average. The problem of central tendency also occurs when supervisors cannot objectively evaluate employee performance because of a lack of familiarity with the work, a lack of supervisory ability, or fear that they will be reprimanded if they evaluate individuals too highly.

Leniency Inexperienced or poor supervisors may decide that the easiest way to appraise performance is simply to give everyone a high evaluation. The supervisor may believe that employees will feel that they have been accurately appraised, or that even if they know they have been inaccurately appraised, it will be to their benefit. Employees cannot complain about their appraisals if they all receive high appraisals. Thus, everyone is evaluated highly in almost all areas of performance. However, leniency seldom creates good feelings among all employees. The best performers in the department will complain about such supervisors because those who are working hard receive no more credit than fellow employees who are not.

The emphasis on salary considerations in the appraisal process will often lead managers to inflate appraisals to justify pay raises for their employees. But truly superior employees who are given glowing reviews receive only modest pay increases because virtually everyone received high evaluations; thus the superior employee becomes unhappy and may leave.[7] Lack of accurate appraisal can lead to turnover among the best employees, who go to organizations that can appraise their performance accurately and give them their justified recognition. Thus, supervisors' intentions of creating good feelings by giving all employees high evaluations may result in losing the very best employees.

Strictness Sometimes supervisors consistently give low ratings even though some employees may have achieved an average or above-average performance level. Strictness is the opposite of leniency. Problems of strictness are not nearly as widespread as problems of leniency.

Supervisors are often guilty of strictness in ratings because they feel that not one of the subordinates is "living up to standards of excellence." Unreasonable performance expectations that employees find impossible to achieve can be demoralizing. Failure to give recognition when due can quickly result in serious damage to supervisor–subordinate relationships.

Recency When organizations use annual or semiannual performance appraisals, there may be a tendency for supervisors to remember more about what their employees have done just before the appraisal than in prior months. It is human nature for supervisors to remember recent events more than events in the distant past.[8] Where severe recency problems occur in the appraisal process, managers may conduct more frequent appraisals, monthly or quarterly. Or they may require that supervisors keep a running log of employee behaviors to help avoid the recency distortion.

Overall Ratings Many appraisal forms require the supervisor to provide an overall rating of an employee's performance in addition to evaluations of specific performance areas. Often the supervisor must rate the employee as "outstanding," "definitely above average," "doing an average job," "substandard but making progress," or "definitely unsatisfactory." It is difficult at best for a supervisor to combine all the separate performance dimensions into an accurate overall rating.[9] Behavioral research indicates that supervisors are not consistent in this process. Thus, two employees who receive identical evaluations on every specific performance area could nevertheless receive entirely different overall ratings—which most likely will be used for merit and promotion considerations. In addition, employees are often not sure how evaluations of specific areas are weighed to produce an overall evaluation. Some supervisors may weigh all areas as equal, whereas others may only consider two to three items important in determining an overall rating.[10] When such problems occur, the validity of the appraisal process is jeopardized even if the specific areas evaluated are highly job related and the employees have been fairly rated in those areas.

Solutions to appraisal problems focus on two areas: the appraisal system and supervisory training. Appraisal systems should be based on a job analysis which specifies the content of the job. Specific performance criteria for each content area can then be developed. An employee's job performance is then measured against these criteria. Effectively training the persons, usually supervisors, who perform the appraisal can minimize appraisal problems such as leniency, the halo effect, and recency.[11]

APPRAISAL METHODS

The method of appraisal dictates the time and effort spent by both supervisors and employees and determines which areas of performance are emphasized. Ideally, an appraisal method is objective, accurate, and easy to perform.

Work Standards

In the past, setting work standards and comparing employees to those standards was often thought to be the ideal appraisal method. Work standards established the normal or average production output for employees on the job. Standards were set according to the production per hour or the time spent per unit produced. This standard allowed firms to pay employees on a piece-rate basis, but setting the standard rate of output for employees was a difficult task. Time studies can be used to set output criteria for persons on particular jobs. Work sampling, a statistical technique for setting standards of production based on random sampling, can also be used to set work standards. When the average production of the work group is used as a standard in a group piecework plan, members of the group receive pay based on the average pay earned by members of the group.[12]

Few modern organizations use only a production standard as a performance appraisal technique. In some cases, production standards are still used as part of the appraisal process, usually when employees are paid on a piece-rate basis. Quantity of production is only one aspect of job performance; other aspects should be included in the appraisal process. Use of piecework records as the sole performance criterion creates problems when decisions on promotions and salaries are made by comparing employees to one another. Further, fewer and fewer jobs can be measured solely by production levels. One employee's output is at least partially dependent upon the performance of other employees. If the production line stops moving or if other members of the team are not successful, individual production is severely hampered. Most modern jobs do not entail tasks which simply produce a certain number of units per hour. Instead, they involve other duties and responsibilities which cannot be directly measured. Therefore, other methods of performance appraisal are much more common.

Rating Scales

The rating scale compares employees to some cognitive standard, such as a high level of cooperation with fellow employees. The rating scale is one of the oldest and most common methods of performance appraisal. As shown in Figure 6–1, rating scales itemize job attributes that describe an employee's perfor-

Employee's Name _____ Date _____

Evaluator's Name _____ Period of Evaluation _____

Directions: Circle the number on each scale that best approximates the employee's performance.

	Poor	Below Average	Average	Above Average	Excellent
Job knowledge	1	2	3	4	5
Quality of work	1	2	3	4	5
Quantity of work	1	2	3	4	5
Cooperation	1	2	3	4	5
Customer courtesy	1	2	3	4	5
Company loyalty	1	2	3	4	5
Ability to learn	1	2	3	4	5
Dependability	1	2	3	4	5
Safety habits	1	2	3	4	5
Ability to follow directions	1	2	3	4	5

FIGURE 6–1
An example of the graphic form of rating scales

mance. Each item is followed by a scale on which the supervisor rates an employee somewhere between poor and excellent. The rating scale is, perhaps, one of the most popular appraisal methods because supervisors find it fairly easy to complete and because the scale takes less time to learn and utilize than other methods.

The rating scale achieves the goals of appraisal because it produces a numerical evaluation for each employee which is the total of the employee's ratings on each of the attributes. The total can easily be transferred to a scale of merit increases or used to compare employees for promotion decisions.

The rating scale in Figure 6–1 is the *graphic form*. Shown in Figure 6–2 is the *nongraphic form*. A nongraphic scale is usually more valid than a graphic scale because the former contains a brief description of each point on a scale rather than simply low and high points of a scale. The supervisor can give a more accurate description of the employee's behavior on a particular attribute because a description clarifies each level of the rating scale. On the graphic scale, supervisors arbitrarily decide what various points represent about an attribute; for example, what is "below-average" cooperation? Most rating scales are nongraphic because of their inherent abil-

Name: _____ For period ending: _____

Department: _____ Job title: _____

Instructions:

Listed below are a number of traits, abilities, and characteristics that are important for success. Place an "X" mark on each rating scale, over the descriptive phrase which most nearly describes the person being rated.

ACCURACY is the correctness of work duties performed.

Usually accurate; makes only average number of mistakes	Makes frequent errors	Requires absolute minimum of supervision; is almost always accurate	Requires little supervision; is exact and precise most of the time	Careless; makes recurrent errors

ALERTNESS is the ability to grasp instruction, to meet changing conditions and to solve novel or problem situations.

Requires more than average instructions and explanations	Slow to catch on	Exceptionally keen and alert	Grasps instructions with average ability	Usually quick to understand and learn

CREATIVITY is talent for having new ideas, for finding new and better ways of doing things and for being imaginative.

Continually seeks new and better ways of doing things; is extremely imaginative	Has average imagination; has reasonable number of new ideas	Frequently suggests new ways of doing things; is very imaginative	Rarely has a new idea; is unimaginative	Occasionally comes up with a new idea

FRIENDLINESS is the sociability and warmth which an individual imparts toward customers, other employees, the supervisor, and persons supervised.

Approachable; friendly once known by others	Extremely sociable; excellent at establishing good will	Very distant and aloof	Very sociable and outgoing	Warm; friendly; sociable

PERSONALITY is an individual's behavior characteristics or personal suitability for the job.

Very desirable personality for this job	Personality unsatisfactory for this job	Outstanding personality for this job	Personality satisfactory for this job	Personality questionable for this job

PERSONAL APPEARANCE is the personal impression an individual makes on others. (Consider cleanliness, grooming, neatness, and appropriateness of dress on the job.)

Very untidy; poor taste in dress	Generally neat and clean; satisfactory personal appearance	Unusually well groomed; very neat; excellent taste in dress	Sometimes untidy and careless about personal appearance	Careful about personal appearance; good taste in dress

PHYSICAL FITNESS is the ability to work consistently and with only moderate fatigue. (Consider physical alertness and energy.)

Energetic; seldom tires	Tires easily; is weak and frail	Excellent health; no fatigue	Meets physical and energy job requirements	Frequently tires and is slow

FIGURE 6–2

An example of the nongraphic form of rating scales (Source: Used with permission of the Kentucky Department of Education in Frankfort, Kentucky.)

ATTENDANCE is faithfulness in coming to work daily and conforming to work hours.

| Always regular and prompt; volunteers for overtime when needed | Often absent without good excuse and/or frequently reports for work late | Very prompt; regular in attendance | Lax in attendance and/or reporting for work on time | Usually present and on time |

DEPENDABILITY is the ability to do required jobs well with a minimum of supervision.

| Requires close supervision; is unreliable | Requires absolute minimum of supervision | Usually takes care of necessary tasks and completes with reasonable promptness | Requires little supervision; is reliable | Sometimes requires prompting |

JOB KNOWLEDGE is the information concerning work duties which an individual should know for a satisfactory job performance

| Lacks knowledge of some phases of work | Has complete mastery of all phases of job | Understands all phases of work | Poorly informed about work duties | Moderately informed; can answer most common questions |

QUANTITY OF WORK is the amount of work an individual does in a work day.

| Volume of work is satisfactory | Very industrious; does more than is required | Does just enough to get by | Superior work production recorded | Does not meet minimum requirements |

STABILITY is the ability to withstand pressure and to remain calm in crisis situations.

| Thrives under pressure; really enjoys solving crises | Goes "to pieces" under pressure; is "jumpy" and nervous | Tolerates most pressure; likes crises more than the average person | Has average tolerance for crises; usually remains calm | Occasionally "blows up" under pressure; is, easily irritated |

COURTESY is the polite attention an individual gives other people.

| Always very polite and willing to help | Sometimes tactless | Inspiring to others in being courteous and very pleasant | Agreeable and pleasant | Blunt; discourteous; antagonistic |

OVERALL EVALUATION in comparison with other employees with the same length of service on this job:

| Definitely Unsatisfactory | Substandard but making progress | Doing an average job | Definitely above average | Outstanding |

Signature of Supervisor   Date   Signature of Employee   Date

Signature of Reviewing Officer   Date   Signature of Personnel Officer   Date

Remarks:

FIGURE 6–2
continued

ity to be more job related and specific to employee behavior.

In general, rating scales are quick, easy, and less difficult for supervisors to use than many other methods of performance appraisal. Also, decision makers find rating scales to be satisfactory for most evaluative purposes because they provide a mathematical evaluation of the employee's performance, which can be used to justify compensation or job changes and to validate selection instruments. For example, if the rating scale contains twenty attributes with a 5-point scale for each attribute, employees can receive 100 points if they perform perfectly. Any percentage of that total can be directly related to a merit increase or promotion probability.

Rating scales have several disadvantages. Using the scale, supervisors can easily make halo or central-tendency errors. Since everyone can quickly be rated very high or very average on most items, supervisors who want to use central tendency or leniency in their appraisals can easily do so. Most rating scales have the disadvantage of not being related to a specific job. The attributes of the scale are so broad that they may apply to all jobs in the organization and are not developed to apply to any particular job. Rating scales also allow supervisory bias and the halo effect to enter the appraisal process.

Forced Choice

In a forced-choice performance appraisal, the supervisor must choose one statement (sometimes two) out of a possible three or four that best describes the employee's performance in a particular area. The supervisor may find that all of the statements describe the employee's performance; however, only the one or two that best describe the employee's behavior can be chosen. Unlike a rating scale, the phrases top management considers positive or nega-

tive evaluations of performance are not obvious. Therefore, the supervisor does not know if an employee's appraisal is low, high, or average. Adopting the forced-choice method will usually keep supervisors from making central-tendency, leniency, halo, or other common errors of appraisal.

As illustrated in Figure 6–3, the forced-choice method can use specific job behaviors or broad descriptions that might apply to all employees throughout an organization. Like the rating scale, the forced-choice method results in a mathematical total for the evaluation and is fairly quick and easy for supervisors to complete.

The forced-choice method contains some serious disadvantages. Supervisors may try to guess which descriptions the personnel office weighted positively and which negatively. Also, a good supervisor who wants to use performance appraisal as a developmental tool cannot use the forced-choice method because no feedback is given to the employee. The supervisor completes the form and then sends it to personnel or top administration for evaluation purposes; therefore, the forced-choice method is difficult to use for developmental purposes.

Ranking

Ranking employees from the most effective to the least effective is another appraisal method. Problems of central tendency and leniency are eliminated by forcing supervisors to evaluate employees over a predetermined range. The ranking method is comparative; supervisors judge employees' performances in relation to each other instead of against a standard, as is the case with rating scales.

Supervisors usually rank their employees from most effective to least effective in total job performance. This results in as many different rankings as there are departments or

FIGURE 6–3

An example of the forced-choice method used in the performance appraisal of sales representatives

INSTRUCTIONS: For each set of phrases choose one statement. Circle the letter preceding the phrase which *best* describes the behavior of the employee.

1. a. Returns customers' calls quickly.
    b. Learns new products on schedule.
    c. Does not anger easily.
    d. Tires of same route.

2. a. Is accurate with figures.
    b. Cooperates with supervisor.
    c. Does not waste time on telephone.
    d. Keeps automobile clean.

3. a. Prefers to stay on own route.
    b. Is friends with local politicians.
    c. Usually exceeds sales goals.
    d. Doesn't complain.

4. a. Obeys orders without arguing.
    b. Is loyal to the company.
    c. Is intelligent.
    d. Requires minimum supervision.

5. a. Seldom critical of company rules.
    b. Stays within expense account.
    c. Socializes with other employees.
    d. Maintains good appearance.

6. a. Turns in reports on time.
    b. Obeys traffic laws.
    c. Requires little prompting.
    d. Receives high customer praise.

7. a. Respects opinions of other salespersons.
    b. Adds new customers to route.
    c. Liked by others.
    d. Follows OSHA regulations.

8. a. Active in civic affairs.
    b. Keeps route sheets current.
    c. Customers know by first name.
    d. Does not lose route customers.

9. a. Handles customer complaints well.
    b. Has friendly personality.
    c. Active in company sports.
    d. Willing to accept new customers.

10. a Restores 1956 Chevrolets.
    b. Knows competitors' lines.
    c. Good communication skills.
    d. No serious traffic violations.

FIGURE 6–4
An example of ranking employees by department

Sales	Office	Warehouse	Records
1. Meehan	1. Vahaly	1. Ngo	1. Black
2. Garcia	2. Nelson	2. Brown	2. Gupta
3. Lickteig	3. White	3. Henderson	3. Manuel
4. Lopez	4. Tanaka	4. Ehrler	4. Chan
5. Smith	5. Sharbrough	5. Coe	
	6. Abramson		
	7. Heavrin		
	8. Ward		

areas within the organization, as in Figure 6–4. Some managers try to combine departmental rankings into a ranking for the total organization. Such ranking is very difficult, if not impossible, because employees have not been compared to any common standard. Instead, employees have only been compared to each other. Assuming that an employee ranked second in one department is equal to one ranked second in another department is an unfair assumption on the part of the administration. Usually when rankings are used, comparisons among departments are not made. However, when a total organizational ranking is used, employees receiving the highest rankings receive the highest merit increases or promotion considerations.

The advantage of ranking is that it is fast and easy to complete. A numerical evaluation given to the employees can be directly related to compensation changes or staffing considerations. In addition, ranking completely avoids problems of central tendency or leniency.

There are, however, serious disadvantages. Ranking is seldom developmental because employees do not receive feedback about performance strengths and weaknesses or any future direction. Also, ranking assumes that each department has employees who can be distributed fairly over a range from best to worst. This method does not recognize that

one department may have all excellent employees, while another has many poor employees. When ranking is used, there is no common standard of performance by which to compare employees from various departments since employees in each department are compared only with each other. This makes it difficult to use ranking for purposes of comparing employees in different departments who might be considered for the same promotion or other staffing change.

Forced Distribution

Forced distribution is another comparative method of performance appraisal. Similar to ranking, forced distribution requires that supervisors spread their employee evaluations in a predescribed distribution. As Figure 6–5 illustrates, the supervisor places employees in classifications ranging from poor to excellent. Like ranking, forced distribution eliminates central tendency and leniency biases. However, forced distribution has the same disadvantages as ranking. Forced distribution can be considered a specific case of ranking whereby employees are placed in certain ranked categories but not ranked within the categories. Often administrators will use forced distribution to compare employees from different departments. However, this is

Department ___Sales___ Supervisor ___Carrera___

Date ___April 17___ Period of Evaluation ___January–April___

Directions: Begin with the excellent classification then proceed to the above average, etc. List the names of the employees who fall into the classification; the total number within each category may not exceed the percentage allowance for the classification.

Poor 10%	Below Average 20%	Average 40%	Above Average 20%	Excellent 10%
Heavrin	Coe	White	Meehan	Vahaly
Ward	Manuel	Tanaka	Black	Ngo
	Smith	Lickteig	Nelson	
	Chan	Sharbrough	Garcia	
		Gupta		
		Brown		
		Lopez		
		Henderson		
		Abramson		
		Ehrler		

FIGURE 6–5

An example of forced distribution

valid only if there are in each department an equal number of excellent employees, above-average employees, and so on. That assumption is very difficult to make.

Paired Comparison

Another comparative method of performance appraisal involves paired comparison, in which supervisors pair employees and choose one as superior in overall job performance. As illustrated in Figure 6–6, this method results in giving each employee a positive-comparison total and a certain percentage of the total positive evaluation. This percentage of positive comparisons gives paired comparison an advantage over ranking and forced distribution. Paired comparison does not force distribution of employees in each department. For

example, if a department has two outstanding employees and six average employees and paired comparison is correctly used, then those two employees will receive a much higher percentage of positive comparison than the other six. Alternatively, if all employees have about the same performance except one poor performer, that employee may have a much lower total percentage of positive comparisons than the other employees in the department. Thus, the actual distribution of employees in the department is based on performance; that distribution may be reflected in the percentage of positive comparisons if the supervisor was accurate in the comparison.

Like ranking and forced distribution, paired comparison is quick and fairly easy to use if few employees are involved. In fact, su-

Instructions: Assign each employee's name a different capital letter on a separate sheet of paper. Example: A-Smith, B-Jones, etc. Then, develop a chart such as the one below and for each plotted pair, write in the letter of the employee who, in your opinion, has done the superior job overall.

Example:

	A	B	C	D	E
A		A	A	A	A
B			C	D	E
C				C	E
D					E
E					

To compute employees' positive evaluations:

$$\frac{\text{Number of Positive Evaluations}}{\text{Total Number of Evaluations}} \times 100 = \text{Employee's \% Total Positive Evaluations}$$

Employee A	Employee B	Employee C	Employee D	Employee E
$\frac{4}{4} \times 100 = 100\%$	$\frac{0}{4} \times 100 = 0\%$	$\frac{2}{4} \times 100 = 50\%$	$\frac{1}{4} \times 100 = 25\%$	$\frac{3}{4} \times 100 = 75\%$

FIGURE 6–6

An example of paired comparison of employees

pervisors may prefer paired comparison to ranking or forced distribution because they compare only two employees at a time rather than all employees to one another.

A particular problem associated with paired comparison is the rapid increase in comparisons that must be made as the employees within a department increase. The number of comparisons required equals $N(N - 1)/2$. Therefore, for 20 employees, 190 comparisons would be necessary $[(20 \times 19)/2 = 190]$. Thus, this technique is time-consuming with large numbers of employees.

Another disadvantage of paired comparison is that employees are compared to each other on total performance rather than on specific job criteria. Although paired comparison does not completely eliminate the possi-

bility of central tendency or leniency, those problems are minimized. And the advantages of not forcing the employee evaluations into set distributions make paired comparison an attractive alternative to ranking and forced distribution.

Critical Incidents

Several modern performance-appraisal methods employ the use of critical incidents to make the appraisal process more job-related than some of the other methods. The critical-incident methods of performance appraisal use specific examples of job behavior that have been collected from supervisors or employees or both. Normally, several employees and supervisors compile a list of actual job experiences involving extraordinarily good or bad employee performances. Neither normal procedures nor average work performance are included. Outstandingly good or bad job performances separate the better employees from the average employees and the poor employees from the average employees. Thus, the emphasis is on specific actions as critical examples of excellent or poor behavior. Once a list of critical-incident appraisals is finalized, a particular method of utilization may be chosen.[13]

Annual Review   One form of the method is for the supervisor to keep an ongoing record of employees' critical incidents during each period of appraisal. The supervisor annually reviews each employee's record as a determination of the employee's behavior. The outstandingly good or bad examples represent the employee's performance for the period of time. Employees who have little or no record during the year are doing their jobs satisfactorily, not performing much above or below job expectations. The advantage of the annual review is that it is usually very job specific. With specific dates and incidents included in the annual performance appraisal, the supervisor is less affected by bias.

The main disadvantage of using an annual review is the difficulty in keeping an accurate record. With other interests taking a much higher priority, maintaining records for employees is often not given adequate time. Such incompleteness may be due to supervisory bias or simply to a lack of time and effort. If management can train supervisors to keep a complete, objective record of employees' critical incidents, the process can be used for developmental purposes as well as evaluative purposes. Another disadvantage of the annual review is the lack of comparable data about employees; it is very difficult to compare the performances of different employees using records of critical incidents.

Checklist of Critical Incidents   Critical incidents may be used in performance appraisal by developing a checklist of critical behaviors related to an employee's performance. Such an appraisal form may have twenty or thirty critical items for one specific job. The supervisor simply checks if the employee has performed in a superior manner in any one of the incidents. Outstanding employees would receive many checks, indicating that they performed in a good fashion during the appraisal period. Average employees would receive few checks because only in a few cases do they perform outstandingly well.

The checklist method of critical incidents often involves giving different weights to different items in the checklist to indicate that some are more important than others. Often the weights are not revealed to the supervisors who complete the appraisal process. After the items checked on an employee's checklist are totaled, a numerical total evaluation for that employee can be made, making the appraisal process evaluative. The checklist method of critical incidents is fairly fast and easy to use since it can produce a mathematical total for employees. And it is evaluative as well as developmental. But the checklist is time-consuming and expensive to develop since checklists for each different job in the organization must be produced.

Behaviorally Anchored Rating Scales (BARS)   The most common use of critical-incident performance appraisals is in combination with rating scales. Instead of using broad employee attributes, the points on the rating scale are critical incidents. For example, a behaviorally anchored rating scale (BARS) is quick and easy to complete. Such scales are evaluative because mathematical totals can be easily related to merit increases and promotion probability. They are also job-related and more developmental than typical rating scales because the items being evaluated are items which are critical to good performance.

The Ohio State Highway Patrol developed a BARS appraisal system consisting of four stages. Stage one involved a detailed task analysis of the job of state troopers. The critical tasks were determined from interviews with troopers and supervisors. Stage two entailed assigning weight to each task according to how critical the task was in relation to the patrolman's job and how frequently it was required. Descriptions of "excellent," "average," and "poor" performance levels of each task were developed in stage three. The fourth stage included a statistical validation of the appraisal instrument, as discussed in chapter 5. As an example, the critical task "secure accident scenes" was given the following three levels of evaluation:[14]

- Uses available equipment and solicits any available assistance to secure scene of accident quickly and efficiently. (Excellent)
- Generally secures scene adequately before beginning accident investigation. (Average)
- May fail to adequately secure the scene before beginning accident investigation. (Poor)

BARS systems have been favored by federal agencies and personnel researchers because they are job-related. As with the other critical-incident systems, the primary disadvantage of a BARS system is the time and effort involved in adapting critical incidents to a rating-scale format. A BARS system requires a separate rating scale for each different job involved in the organization. This does not mean a different rating scale for each employee because many employees might be performing the same job. Examples of two BARS are given in Figure 6–7.

Essay

A performance appraisal primarily created for employee development is the written essay. The supervisor writes an essay describing the employee's performance, specifying examples of strengths and weaknesses. Because the essay method forces the supervisor to discuss specific examples of performance, it can also minimize supervisory bias and the halo effect. By asking supervisors to enumerate specific examples of employee behavior, this method also minimizes central tendency and leniency problems because no rating scale is being used.

The essay method often has a distinct disadvantage: the time the supervisors must spend writing separate essays about each employee can be formidable. Also, essays are not very useful for evaluative purposes; 200 essays describing different employees' performances cannot easily be linked to merit increases and promotion because there is no common standard. The essay method is best used in small organizations or small work units where the primary purpose is to develop employee skills and behavior.

Management by Objectives

One of the most widely discussed performance appraisal methods is management by objectives (MBO). Some of the companies that have implemented MBO reported excellent results, others disappointment, and many ambivalence. Generally, the MBO process is as follows:

- The subordinate and supervisor jointly determine the goals to be accomplished during the appraisal period and what level of performance is necessary for the subordinate to satisfactorily achieve particular goals.
- During the appraisal period, the supervisor and employee update and alter goals

Behaviorally anchored rating scale for the performance dimension 1a: Organization of Checkstand

Behaviorally anchored rating scale for the performance dimension 1b: Knowledge and Judgment

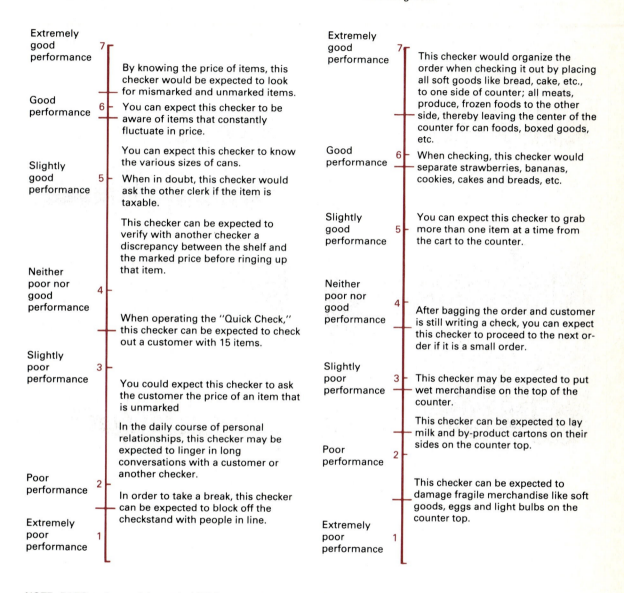

Dimension 1a: Organization of Checkstand

- Extremely good performance — 7
- Good performance — 6
- Slightly good performance — 5
- Neither poor nor good performance — 4
- Slightly poor performance — 3
- Poor performance — 2
- Extremely poor performance — 1

By knowing the price of items, this checker would be expected to look for mismarked and unmarked items.

You can expect this checker to be aware of items that constantly fluctuate in price.

You can expect this checker to know the various sizes of cans.

When in doubt, this checker would ask the other clerk if the item is taxable.

This checker can be expected to verify with another checker a discrepancy between the shelf and the marked price before ringing up that item.

When operating the "Quick Check," this checker can be expected to check out a customer with 15 items.

You could expect this checker to ask the customer the price of an item that is unmarked

In the daily course of personal relationships, this checker may be expected to linger in long conversations with a customer or another checker.

In order to take a break, this checker can be expected to block off the checkstand with people in line.

Dimension 1b: Knowledge and Judgment

- Extremely good performance — 7
- Good performance — 6
- Slightly good performance — 5
- Neither poor nor good performance — 4
- Slightly poor performance — 3
- Poor performance — 2
- Extremely poor performance — 1

This checker would organize the order when checking it out by placing all soft goods like bread, cake, etc., to one side of counter; all meats, produce, frozen foods to the other side, thereby leaving the center of the counter for can foods, boxed goods, etc.

When checking, this checker would separate strawberries, bananas, cookies, cakes and breads, etc.

You can expect this checker to grab more than one item at a time from the cart to the counter.

After bagging the order and customer is still writing a check, you can expect this checker to proceed to the next order if it is a small order.

This checker may be expected to put wet merchandise on the top of the counter.

This checker can be expected to lay milk and by-product cartons on their sides on the counter top.

This checker can be expected to damage fragile merchandise like soft goods, eggs and light bulbs on the counter top.

NOTE: BARS go beyond the typical MBO action planning to achieve goals (ends) and specifies within these activities the job-specific behaviors that are known to result in more or less effective performance (goal achievement).

FIGURE 6–7

Using BARS for a grocery clerk (Adapted from Fogli, Hulin and Blood, "Development of First-Level Job Criteria," *Journal of Applied Psychology* 55 [February 1971]: 3–8. Copyright 1971 by The American Psychological Association. Reprinted/adapted by permission of the author.)

as necessary due to changes in the business or environment.

- Both the supervisor and the subordinate decide if goals were met by the employee and discuss the reasons for any failures. Taken into consideration is the cause of deviation from expected performance, such as a strike, market change, or labor dispute.
- New goals and performance objectives are determined by the supervisor and employee for the next period.

The advantages of the MBO method are many. Both the supervisor and the employee participate in the appraisal process. The focus of the appraisal process is on specific goals and not broad personality traits such as dependability or cooperation. What is unique about the MBO procedure is that goals and objectives are determined before the appraisal period begins.[15] Previously discussed methods of appraisal take place after the employees' performance has occurred. Since the MBO process gives employees direction before the appraisal period begins, it is developmental in defining the direction employees should take and the expected level of achievement. The goal-setting orientation of an MBO program is also fairly unique among performance-appraisal systems. The disadvantage of the MBO procedure is the time and effort that must be spent by both the supervisor and the subordinate in the appraisal process.

Numerous studies of organizations' experiences with MBO show that for an MBO program to be successful several guidelines should be considered before the process begins.[16] First, an independent review committee of management and employees should be set up as an appeals mechanism. Thus, if an employee feels that a supervisor is setting unrealistically high goals or if a supervisor feels that employees are making excuses about goals not met, there is an independent body

to which they can appeal for a decision. Second, objectives and goals should be mutually accepted by the employee and supervisor. Generally, four or five specific objectives that are measurable in terms of dollars or units of time should be established. Whenever possible, objectives should be constructed with allowances for individual differences, though they should still be realistic and feasible.[17] Third, if possible, there should be a target date for completion of each specific objective. Several target dates for different objectives can be established at the beginning of the appraisal process.

Figure 6–8 is a good example of an MBO appraisal form because there is adequate room for position objectives and results. The employee and supervisor sign and date each objective as it is achieved. They also appraise the performance. In general, the MBO objectives should be specific, giving a time frame, a priority ranking, and a plan of action.[18]

Combination Methods

Employers often decide to use an appraisal method which combines some of the advantages of an evaluative form and a developmental form. Figure 6–9 is a good example of a combination form. The Kentucky Fried Chicken appraisal is a seven-attribute rating scale with three points ("excellent," "satisfactory," "unsatisfactory"). In addition, there is an overall performance rating. The form also requires short essay explanations for the rating given on each attribute. The appraisal form is different from most such forms because a "team member" is evaluated instead of an employee, stressing KFC's emphasis on teamwork as well as individual achievement.

Appraisal Schedule

How often to appraise employee performance is an important and difficult question. Probably the most common answer fixes a specific

Managerial Job Objectives

John Atkins	7/2	SUPERINTENDENT
Prepared by the manager	Date	Manager's job title
F. W. Crawford	7/2	PLANT MANAGER
Reviewed by his supervisor	Date	Supervisor's job title

Statement of Objectives Col. 1	Priority Col. 2	Date Col. 3	Outcomes or Results Col. 4
1. TO INCREASE DELIVERIES TO 98% OF ALL SCHEDULED DELIVERY DATES	A	6/31	
2. TO REDUCE WASTE AND SPOILAGE TO 3% OF ALL RAW MATERIALS USED.	A	6/31	
3. TO REDUCE LOST TIME DUE TO ACCIDENTS TO 100 MAN-DAYS/YEAR	B	2/1	
4. TO REDUCE OPERATING COST TO 10% BELOW BUDGET	A	1/15	
5. TO INSTALL A QUALITY CONTROL RADIOISOTOPE SYSTEM AT A COST OF LESS THAN $53,000	A	3/15	
6. TO IMPROVE PRODUCTION SCHEDULING AND PREVENTIVE MAINTENANCE SO AS TO INCREASE MACHINE UTILIZATION TIME TO 95% OF CAPACITY	B	10/1	
7. TO COMPLETE THE UCLA EXECUTIVE PROGRAM THIS YEAR.	A	6/31	
8. TO TEACH A PRODUCTION MANAGEMENT COURSE IN UNIVERSITY EXTENSION	B	6/31	

FIGURE 6–8

An example of an MBO appraisal form (Source: From *Managing by Objectives* by Anthony P. Raia. Copyright © 1974 by Scott, Foresman and Company. Reprinted by permission.)

interval between appraisals, such as one year or six months. The schedule provides consistency in the evaluation process, because all employees are evaluated for the same period of time. A variable-interval process can be used when a goal-setting approach establishes specific time periods to achieve certain goals.

Thus, at the end of each time period, an appraisal determines the achievement level for a particular goal. When goal achievement does not have to be tied to a specific time period, it can be linked with the company's standard appraisal period in order to maintain appraisal consistency.

FIGURE 6–9

An example of a three-point rating scale requiring short essay explanations. Used by permission.

At the end of a probationary period, new employees are informed if they have achieved a level of proficiency that would justify changing their status from probationary to permanent. This appraisal should be combined with an annual fixed-interval method that includes all employees. The most important question, then, is how long a time to allow between appraisals. Twelve- or six-month periods are most commonly used, though monthly and quarterly reports ensure that recency in the appraisal process will not affect the accuracy of the employee's evaluation.

For performance appraisal to be of significant value, the appraisal process should be conducted at regular intervals, such as quarterly or semiannually. This provides a series of appraisals that supply useful comparative information to managers.

Supervisors as Appraisers

The person in the best position to observe the employee's behavior and determine whether the employee has reached specified goals and objectives is the best person to conduct the appraisal. In a great majority of cases, the employee's direct supervisor or manager should conduct the appraisal. Generally, only that person has directly and constantly observed the employee's performance and knows what the level of performance should be. Supervisors would often prefer to avoid the appraisal process because uncomfortable face-to-face confrontations often result. Even so, policymakers should ensure that appraisals are conducted in a professional manner because performance appraisals of subordinates are a legitimate and critical part of supervision. In fact, most managers believe that supervisors who cannot accurately and honestly appraise and discuss employee behavior cannot be effective supervisors.

In some situations, if an employee is working very closely with other employees in a noncompetitive, work-group environment, then peers may be in the best position to evaluate a co-worker's performance. Peers can, in some situations, provide information that the organization could not get from the employee's supervisor due to a lack of direct contact between the supervisor and employee. These subordinates, however, often will not give objective, honest appraisals because of possible retaliation.

For jobs where outside clients are affected by the performance of an employee, evaluations by customers can add a dimension to the appraisal process. They can comment either in person or in writing about the employee's contact with them and the service provided. However, outside clients cannot give a total performance appraisal because they view only a small portion of the employee's activity.

In most situations, an employee's direct supervisor should complete the performance appraisal. Only in situations where that person cannot give objective, complete appraisal due to lack of information or lack of constant direct observation should peers or outside individuals be included in the appraisal process. Supervisors must be aware that their performance in the appraisal process will affect how they are rated by their superiors.

THE APPRAISAL INTERVIEW

One of the final—and most important—steps in the appraisal process is discussing appraisals with employees. Most administrators require that these interviews take place to provide performance feedback for employees. Thus, employees learn where they stand in the eyes of the organization and are coached and counseled about how performance may be improved.

Both parties generally perceive the appraisal interview as a stressful event. Even well-constructed, job-related appraisal forms

How Xerox Improved Its Performance Appraisals

In 1983 Xerox replaced its twenty-year-old performance appraisal system with a significantly different approach. The old appraisal system included many elements found in most systems; annual appraisals, employees documented their accomplishments, the manager assigned a numerical rating to each factor, and a summary overall rating from 1 to 5 in a forced distribution that determined merit pay increases. Surveys of employees and managers pointed out their extreme dislike of the system. Their complaints were not unfamiliar to most personnel managers: (1) lack of equity—95 percent of all employees received an overall rating of 3 or 4 on the 5-point scale; (2) merit increase figures were within 1 to 2 percent for each overall rating, hardly motivating; (3) anyone receiving less than a 4 believed they were second-class citizens; (4) the appraisal interview focused almost entirely on the overall rating and merit increase.

Management decided to address these concerns with the system. A task force of senior personnel managers and middle managers used employee attitude surveys to develop a new process entitled Performance Feedback and Development (PF & D). The new PF & D system provided:

- Objectives set by manager and employee at the beginning of the year. They are approved by higher management.
- A six month interim review. The manager and employee evaluate the employee's progress toward the agreed upon objectives and sign a written summary of their analysis.
- Merit increase decisions are made about one to two months after the six month review. The increase is based upon performance toward objectives.
- Year-end written narrative of the year's performance. Overall ratings were eliminated.
- At the beginning of a new cycle the manager and employee agree upon personal and developmental goals in addition to task objectives. A personal development goal, for example, might be better time management achieved through a new order-handling method.

A letter from the president accompanied a videotape that explained the problems of the old system and the operation of the new one. How does PF & D work? Employee survey results showed that after one year, 81 percent better understood their work group objectives; 72 percent understood the merit increases; and 77 percent considered the new system "a step in the right direction."

Source: Adapted from Norman R. Deets and D. Timothy Tyler, "How Xerox Improved Its Performance Appraisal," *Personnel Journal* 65, no. 4 (April 1986): 50–52. Used by permission.

can only reduce what is inherently a stressful process. Important to the success of the interview—that it affect the employee's future behavior—is the supervisor's behavior during the interview. Subordinates carefully evaluate each supervisor's behavior, including oral and written communication, as indices of their own ability and future with the organization.[19] The supervisor seldom has any more enthusiasm for the appraisal process than the employee. The interview, the most important element of the whole process, may be more effective if the evaluative and developmental aspects are separated. In so doing, the employee feels evaluated fairly on past performance before the focus shifts to specific areas for improvement.[20]

Problems with the Appraisal Interview

The appraisal interview is a very troublesome and difficult obligation for a great many managers. Some managers devise ways to avoid the interview even though it may be required by company policy. In other cases, the interview is glossed over or conducted in a mechanical fashion; its value then is highly suspect.

Playing God In a classic 1957 article, behavioral scientist Douglas McGregor pointed out that many managers who view the appraisal as playing God are uncomfortable in simultaneously playing helper and judge. According to McGregor:[21]

> The modern emphasis upon the manager as a leader who strives to help his subordinates achieve both their own and the company's objectives is hardly consistent with the judicial role demanded by most appraisal plans. If the manager must put on his judicial hat occasionally, he does it reluctantly and with understandable qualms. Under such conditions it is

unlikely that the subordinate will be happier with the results than will be the boss. It will not be surprising, either, if he fails to recognize that he has been told where he stands.

Constructive Criticism In appraisal interviews, supervisors must evaluate the performance of each employee. Many supervisors, however, have difficulty giving criticism constructively, and many employees have difficulty accepting criticism even though it may be given with sensitivity and diplomacy. One important study showed that defensiveness and poor performance can result from criticism given during the appraisal interview. About half the time, employees became defensive when criticized; a majority of employees felt they performed more favorably than their supervisors' assessments indicated.[22]

Personality Biases During the appraisal interview, the focus should be on performance and achievement of the goals and objectives, duties, and responsibilities that constitute the employee's job. Some supervisors assume roles as amateur psychologists and attempt to bring about personality changes that may improve job performance. But such an approach is unwise, according to Douglas McGregor. In citing the advantages of the objective-oriented appraisal process, whereby the supervisor and subordinate set performance targets, McGregor states:[23]

> Consider a subordinate who is hostile, short-tempered, uncooperative, insecure. The superior may not make any psychological diagnosis. The target setting approach naturally directs the subordinate's attention to ways and means of obtaining better interdepartmental collaboration, reducing complaints, winning the confidence of the men under him. Rather than facing the troublesome prospect of forcing his own psychological diagnosis on the subordinate, the superior can, for example, help the

individual plan ways of getting "feedback" concerning his impact on his associates and subordinates as a basis for self-appraisal and self-improvement.

Specific Feedback For the appraisal interview to be a truly developmental process, the employee must receive specific feedback on areas in need of improvement. All too often, supervisors cloak criticism in vague, subjective terms and phrases. Some examples:

- Your communication skills need improving.
- Your absenteeism rate is too high.
- Your output has not been up to par lately.
- You need to dress a little more conservatively.
- Your quality of work could stand a little upgrading.

Comments such as these provide little basis for positive behavior change; supervisors are responsible for making their expectations clear to employees. For example, do not say, "Your absenteeism rate is too high." It would be much more constructive to state, "You have accumulated six unexcused absences in the past three months and we expect no more than one unexcused absence per month. Can you suggest ways you may be able to achieve this standard in the future?"

Interview Format

The various problems associated with interviews may be minimized by following a planned, standardized approach. Although the precise interview format will vary to some extent from employee to employee, these steps should be generally covered:

Prepare for the Interview Preparation is important in a successful appraisal interview. During preparation, the supervisor should gather and review all relevant performance records. These normally include all data regarding work output and quality, schedules made and missed, absenteeism and tardiness, and so on. For supervisors using an objective-oriented appraisal system, all performance goals should be reviewed to determine which were met and which were not. The supervisor must be able to support the appraisal with facts. The supervisor may then want to make note of the specific items to be discussed during the interview. Finally, preparation includes setting a date for the appraisal interview that gives the employee plenty of lead time to prepare for the interview and develop a list of items to discuss.

State the Purpose of the Interview The employee should be told if the interview will cover compensation and staffing decisions (merit increase, promotion, transfer, etc.) or employee development or both. Some managers, however, avoid mixing compensation and staffing decisions with employee development issues in the same appraisal interview, contending that this would be "mixing apples and oranges." For example, it may be very difficult to motivate an employee to undertake new responsibilities if he has just been told he is not receiving a salary increase because of mediocre performance.

Indicate Specific Areas of Good Performance and Those That Need Improvement Supervisors generally begin the discussion of performance by highlighting areas of good performance. Appreciation and recognition for good work are important parts of the appraisal interview. Areas of performance in need of improvement are discussed next. Again, supervisors must be as specific as possible about performance needing improvement and avoid straying onto personality issues. The focus must remain on job performance.

Invite Participation After an employee's performance record is reviewed, the employee should be invited to comment. This enables the employee to "let off steam" and tell why certain performance problems exist. This is also an opportune time to clear up any misunderstandings which may still exist about job expectations. When supervisors have done a good job in communicating job goals, objectives, and standards, employees should not receive any surprises during the interview.

Focus on development The next step involves setting up the employee's development program. Employees are much more likely to be committed to developmental programs if they agree with the supervisor that the program is necessary to improve job skills and abilities. Employees who feel that performance problems exist or that a program of development is unnecessary to promote career goals will be minimally committed to development. Supervisors must clearly show their employees how development is related to job success.

Problem-solving Interviews

In many cases, a developmental program involves various kinds of on- and off-the-job training, development programs, and exercises.

Throughout this chapter, we have emphasized that one of the primary purposes of the performance appraisal is to enhance employee development. Most managers and administrators agree that a well-planned and implemented appraisal system can contribute enormously to employees' growth and enhance skills. According to Norman R. F. Maier, the problem-solving interview lies at the core of the employee development process. To conduct a problem-solving interview successfully, a supervisor must assume a certain role and possess certain attitudes and skills. Table 6–2

illustrates characteristics of the problem-solving method by comparing it to two other popular (but often ineffective) appraisal interviewing techniques.

AN EFFECTIVE APPRAISAL PROGRAM

Organizations have traditionally chosen evaluative appraisal forms such as rating scales and forced distributions over developmental appraisal techniques. In particular, rating scales have consistently been the most popular form. In the 1960s and 1970s a strong movement toward developmental forms occurred, including the introduction of MBO and BARS systems. But in the 1980s there was a significant shift back to the more traditional evaluative appraisal forms. Several *Fortune* 500 firms changed to rating scales or forced distributions because those methods are quantitative in nature and are believed to be more secure from legal challenges. Personnel managers seem to favor evaluative forms because they provide greater organizational equity when one form is consistently used. Top management in particular is not comfortable with nonstandard developmental forms.[24]

In general, performance appraisal systems are designed to (1) determine merit increases or bonuses, (2) comply with the law, and (3) be easily administered.[25] Jobs that are highly routine in nature and require little employee decision making or individual initiative are possibly best appraised by evaluative systems. But jobs that require a variety of tasks and greater employee decision making may require a developmental appraisal, which can focus on individual goal setting and feedback.[26] Thus, at higher levels in an organization, appraisal systems should rely more on individually tailored, goal-oriented systems of evaluation. In contrast, entry-level jobs

TABLE 6–2

The characteristics of three interviewing techniques are compared in this table

Characteristic	Tell and Sell	Tell and Listen	Problem-solving
Objectives	Communicate evaluation Persuade employee to improve	Communicate evaluation Release defensive feelings	Stimulate growth and development in employee
Psychological Assumptions	Employee desires to correct weaknesses if known Any person who desires to do so can improve A superior is qualified to evaluate a subordinate	People will change if defensive feelings are removed	Growth can occur without correcting faults Discussing job problems leads to improved performance
Role of Interviewer	Judge	Judge	Helper
Attitude of Interviewer	People profit from criticism and appreciate help	One can respect the feelings of others if one understands them	Discussion develops new ideas and mutual interests
Skills of Interviewer	Sales ability Patience	Listening and reflecting feelings Summarizing	Listening and reflecting feelings Reflecting ideas Using exploratory questions Summarizing
Reactions of Employee	Suppresses defensive behavior Attempts to cover hostility	Expresses defensive behavior Feels accepted	Problem-solving behavior
Employee's Motivation for Change	Use of positive or negative incentives or both Extrinsic: motivation is added to the job	Resistance to change reduced Positive incentive Extrinsic and some intrinsic motivation	Increased freedom Increased responsibility Intrinsic: motivation is inherent in the task
Possible Gains	Success most probable when employee respects interviewer	Develops favorable attitude toward superior, which increases probability of success	Almost assured of improvement in some respect
Risks of Interviewer	Loss of loyalty Inhibition of independent judgment Creates face saving scenes	Need for change may not be developed	Employee may lack ideas Change may be other than what superior had in mind
Probable Results	Perpetuates existing practices and values	Permits interviewer to change views in light of employee's responses Some upward communication	Both learn, because experience and views are pooled Change is facilitated

Source: Reprinted from Norman R. F. Maier, *The Appraisal Interview: Three Basic Approaches.* San Diego, CA: University Associates, 1976. Used with permission.

tend to be evaluated with rating scales or specific work standards. According to a survey of *Fortune* 1300 firms, in some cases there is no formal method.[27] An appraisal process with a developmental focus should contain the following:[28]

Defined Results and Goals   Employees need to understand how organizational goals relate to their job and to specific task goals.

Means and Ends of Goals   Employees need to be informed exactly how they can improve their performance and exactly what results are expected.

Career Development   Employees should be counseled on their current job performance as it relates to possible future promotions; thus, they are on the right track if certain performance levels improve.

Employee satisfaction with the appraisal system is largely determined by (1) the equality of the appraisal interview, (2) the method chosen (rating scale, forced choice, MBO, etc.) and its perceived relevance to performance, and (3) the system's usefulness in providing specific directions for the employee to improve his or her future performance.[29] Although management should not be overly concerned about whether every employee perceives the appraisal process as satisfactory, general employee dissatisfaction could easily lead to morale and turnover problems, especially among the best employees.

Design Input

In creating an appraisal system, or redesigning an existing program, the participation of line managers and employees is beneficial. Often the employees who will use the system are able to make valuable suggestions and contributions to strengthen the program. Further,

they may be able to see problems that are hidden from the personnel specialist.

Aside from gaining technical input, participation brings psychological benefits. Behavioral scientists have long recognized that those who participate in the development of a program are more likely to accept it. Users of the new system must support it and be committed to its success; soliciting the advice and recommendations of managers and employees is likely to result in their endorsement.

Trained Appraisers

No one is born with the ability to appraise others' performance accurately, and experience does not, of itself, prepare one to conduct performance appraisals. Rather, formal training is the most effective way to prepare managers and supervisors to conduct successful employee appraisals. Appraisal processes and techniques are often included in training programs for new supervisors. One-day training seminars sponsored by various personnel and management associations or schools of business are attended by large numbers of supervisors and middle managers. Topics normally included in appraisal training are:

- The purposes of performance appraisal.
- How to avoid problems—halo, bias, central tendency, and so on.
- How to conduct nondiscriminatory appraisals.
- The ethics of appraisals.
- How to conduct effective appraisal interviews.

Supervisors can significantly increase the accuracy of their appraisals if they receive the training. Practice exercises can help supervisors make independent evaluations of employees' behaviors. Common appraisal problems such as leniency, strictness, and especially the halo effect can be reduced through proper supervisor training. [30]

Formal and Informal Methods

Many supervisors think about the appraisal process only annually or semiannually—whenever the personnel department notifies them that an employee's anniversary date is approaching and the appraisal must be completed. Feeling greatly relieved upon completing the mandatory appraisal, some supervisors do not tackle the often painful subject of performance until it is time to complete another appraisal form. This mechanical approach to performance appraisal may facilitate decision making about pay increases, but by and large it neglects the fact that performance feedback for developmental purposes is a continuous responsibility of supervision. Regular informal appraisal sessions let employees know how they are doing and how they can improve their performances. Then, too, good work should not go unnoticed, and frequent supervisory recognition is an important technique for sustaining high levels of employee motivation.

APPRAISAL SYSTEM EVALUATION

An organization's performance appraisal program is generally created and implemented to satisfy certain stated objectives. Detailed listings of the goals and purposes of an organization's appraisal program are found in the company's personnel policy manual. Many organizations fail to assess periodically if those objectives are being achieved. Often appraisal programs are set in motion and left to function—sometimes dismally—without a thorough examination. In extreme cases, ill-conceived and poorly implemented appraisal programs may contribute to negative feelings between employees and management, perceptions of unfairness, hindered career development, and discriminatory (and illegal) employment practices. The periodic evaluation of the organization's appraisal program indicates good management, and makes good sense.

How can an appraisal system be evaluated? One company with approximately 20,000 employees followed these assessment procedures:

- Interviews. Managers from various departments were interviewed. Discussions focused on strengths and weaknesses of the present system and recommendations for improving the system.
- Analysis of employees' records. A random sample of almost 200 performance appraisal forms was selected to uncover possible discrimination. The forms were also examined to spot errors such as central tendency, leniency, and the halo effect.
- Analysis of the relationship between the employees and their ratings. Employee ratings were correlated with certain personal and work factors (such as age, tenure, and race). And employees were asked whether appraisal results were discussed with them.
- Analysis of appraisal systems in comparable settings. The organization's appraisal was compared to the systems used by thirty-nine similar organizations.

The evaluation pinpointed problem areas that were corrected through the design of a new appraisal system, which included:

- Development of two separate appraisal forms, one for nonmanagers and one for managers and professional employees.
- Meeting the legal requirement of job relatedness by having managers weigh various rating factors according to their relevance.
- Defining rating factors in behavioral terms to make the appraisal more objective.

■ Design of a MBO system for managerial and professional employees under which employees and their supervisors jointly determined performance goals. Employee performance was appraised by examining the degree to which these goals were met.

One method of evaluating the appraisal system is for top management to provide feedback to managers. Providing feedback to managers about the quality of their performance appraisals has several advantages. It is relatively easy and inexpensive, and managers are aware that their performance as appraisers will be evaluated. Most importantly, when managers are shown the ratings of other managers, the leniency error can be significantly reduced in their own ratings. Without such information, managers cannot know how lenient or strict they are as evaluators.[31]

The individual manager's appraisal of his or her employees can sometimes be supplemented by a group appraisal process, because in many work situations the individual employee's performance is substantially affected by the work group. The supervisor may gain valuable information if the employees are given the opportunity to evaluate one another's performance. The supervisor can then use the results to assess the accuracy of his or her own evaluation of the individual employee. If peers are given the opportunity to rate each other anonymously, the evaluations tend to be more candid because they do not have to face the other persons. The group appraisal provides a supervisor who may be out of touch with a "perception check." Another advantage is that group opinions cannot be discounted by the employee as just the supervisor's opinion.[32] Also, peer evaluations have been proven to be valid predictors of employee performance in higher positions.[33] Usually, some common patterns are seen in

peer appraisal. Employees who are rated low by others will rate themselves and everyone else lower. Thus, the low achiever sets lower expectations and standards than the high achiever.[34]

INTERNATIONAL HRM: PERFORMANCE APPRAISAL

In U.S. organizations, performance appraisal is a fundamental management tool that can, on its own, be useful as a basis for such functions as:

■ Making administrative decisions regarding personnel actions (e.g., pay-for-performance, promotions and transfers, and support for taking disciplinary actions and terminations).

■ Providing feedback to employees regarding their performance.

■ Coaching employees in improving areas of weakness and building upon areas of strength.

Its value can be further increased by linking it to other basic management tools such as performance planning, ongoing performance monitoring, and employee development. Overall, the performance appraisal process helps to clarify performance expectations, provide a framework for progress reviews, and identify developmental needs. It would be correct to conclude that for most U.S. employees, performance appraisal is an inherently natural management practice—even when it is not well done.

This conclusion may not hold for the manager working in Latin America, the Middle East, or any number of non-Western countries. Asian companies, for example, use a variety of performance appraisal methods much like those used in the United States. In Taiwan and Japan, MBO is often used for

International HRM: Assumptions That Underlie Our Leadership Concepts

Motives, aspirations, attitudes toward work, personal obligations are all shaped by the culture in which we were reared. As a result, one of the most subtle and stubborn problems . . . global managers face is leadership of their polyglot personnel.

We can illustrate this problem by a brief look at a few of our own cultural assumptions that are not shared by many people in other parts of the world.

Confident belief in self-determination.   Most Americans believe that they exercise considerable choice in what they do and, through this, in what happens to them. To be sure, we may run into "bad luck," but even here we are inclined to place at least part of the blame on ourselves.

This belief in self-determination is in sharp contrast to a fatalistic viewpoint found in some Moslem countries. It also differs from a mystical view that holds that events are determined by perhaps the capricious influence of spirits that must be appeased. Whatever the explanation, the critical issue is whether people believe that events will occur regardless of what they do, or whether they share with Americans and most Westerners the belief that they can help shape future events.

Results come from persistent hard work.   Both our lore and our experience underscore the necessity for hard work if objectives are to be achieved. Even if one does not accept the Puritan ethic that hard work is a virtue in itself, there is a strong belief that persistent, purposeful effort is necessary to achieve high goals. Hard work is not considered to be the only requisite for success; wisdom and luck also play their part. Nevertheless, the feeling is that without hard work a person is not only unlikely to achieve desired objectives, but also that any expectation of achieving them under these circumstances is unjustified.

This belief in the efficacy of hard work is by no means worldwide. Sometimes a fatalistic viewpoint makes hard work seem futile. In other instances, one needs merely to curry the favor of the right person, and in still other situations hard work is "unmanly."

Time is a crucial aspect of performance.   To an American, timing is an important factor. Effective use of one's own time and effective scheduling of independent activities requires precise timing. . . .

Virtually all studies of comparative management have noted the wide variation in attitude towards time in various cultures. Part of the charm of some Latin American cultures is their relaxed view of the clock and the calendar. People in many other parts of the world fail to understand why the normal rhythms of life should be twisted to fit a schedule.

Remove "second-raters."   The underlying assumption (in the United States) is that if a person is not continuing to perform well, he should be replaced with someone who will. The cost to the enterprise of poor performance, especially the poor performance of an executive, is far greater than the person's salary; this poor performance complicates the task of people whose work interrelates, and may undermine the effectiveness of the entire operation.

In a number of countries, the removal of a person from a recognized position involves so much loss of prestige that the action is rarely taken. This is particularly true when the appointment was initially made on the basis of family or friendship. Poor performance is an inadequate excuse for disgracing a relative or friend.

Source: Adapted from W. H. Newman, E. K. Warren, and A. R. McGill, *The Process of Management*, 6th ed. (Englewood Cliffs, NJ: Prentice-Hall, 1987), pp. 562–63.

evaluating managers. A variation of the critical incidents method is used for employees in a Chinese company. But in none of these examples is the performance appraisal used as evidence for promotion and merit pay decisions. Seniority (time on the job) is considered the most important determinant when it comes to these decisions.[35]

When evaluating employees of the host country, the process can be extremely frustrating to someone who is not familiar with the local culture's expectations for the roles of boss and subordinate. Different cultures have their own ideas and beliefs about work and even about what the culture defines as incompetent, mediocre, and excellent work performance. (See the accompanying feature "International HRM: Assumptions That Underlie Our Leadership Concepts.") In the United States it is performance that counts. In Islamic countries, for example, it may be the subordinate's personality and social behavior—not job performance—that matter.[36]

CONCLUSIONS AND APPLICATIONS

- Employees generally dislike and fear performance appraisal, and even supervisors find the process stressful. Employees will tend to be satisfied with the process if the appraisal interview is constructive and the chosen method is job-related and provides specific direction for future performance.

- The appraisal process generally has two goals: (1) the evaluation of employees' past performance for salary and selection decisions and (2) the improvement of future performance as a part of career development. The evaluative objective tends to dominate specific organizational uses of performance-appraisal information.

- To pass scrutiny by the EEOC and the courts, the appraisal process should contain certain features. A standardized process should evaluate all employees in a consistent manner. Job analysis should be used in the content development to assure job relatedness. Supervisors should be trained in the process and should provide employees with direct written feedback from the process.

- Certain appraisal problems, such as supervisor bias, halo effect, or recency, can only be minimized; others, such as leniency or central tendency, can be eliminated. But forms that eliminate these problems generally contain their own problems. Each appraisal method has unique advantages and disadvantages, but rating scales continue to be most often used by personnel managers.

- The appraisal interview is the most important element in the whole process.

Supervisors who dislike "playing God" find it hard to act simultaneously as judge and friend. Supervisors need to be trained for and give adequate attention to the appraisal interview. Employee preparation can also help them to provide useful input into the discussion as well as be psychologically prepared for any possible negative feedback.

- Organizations can benefit by periodically evaluating their appraisal program. The personnel department can provide feedback to supervisors about the quality of their appraisals and check for rater problems, such as the halo effect or leniency. Peer appraisals among employees may be used as supplemental information to supervisors as a check on their perceptions.

CASE STUDY
Centralized Performance Appraisal

The performance-appraisal policy of a private service organization is uniformly applied to the 300 professional employees of twelve regional offices as well as the home office. The firm provides professional technical assistance to clients in a three-state region. In five years, twelve regional offices were added to the home office.

Once a year, all professional personnel are evaluated by the same rating scale. Top management has required separate evaluations from the department head, division chairman (the employee's immediate supervisor), co-workers, and each of over 100 clients. The results from the clients are totaled to produce an average score for each rating scale item.

Each employee's appraisals are tabulated by a formula known only to the home office. The final evaluation is an overall rating of "excellent," "superior," "satisfactory," or "marginal," which is transmitted by letter to the department head of the local office. The department head informs employees of their overall evaluations and salaries for the following year as directly determined by the home office's formula.

At one regional office the professional staff, who are the organization's only contact with its clients, complained bitterly about the three-year-old appraisal process. They met with their department head, Steve Quigley, to discuss their concerns. Quigley only reinforced their complaints because he knew nothing more than the overall evaluation and salary figures he was given by the home office. Therefore, the professional staff pursued the issue with the home office. The reply from the home office was an immediate, large, across-the-board pay raise for all employees.

The next year, evaluations were carried out just as they had been in prior years. The professional staff began to complain again, claiming that they received no useful feedback and saw no justification for their individual salary adjustments. In one case, Quigley was told by the home office to reevaluate an employee he had rated as marginal. The vice-president instructed Quigley that the company ''had no marginal employees.''

Questions

1. Why would top management benefit from separate evaluations from department heads, co-workers, clients, etc.?
2. If the organization has used the same appraisal process since it began, why are employees only now complaining?
3. How can the employees complain again when they received a large across-the-board pay increase?
4. Should the appraisal process be altered? If so, how? If not, why?

EXPERIENTIAL EXERCISE
It's Great to Be Loyal . . . But What Does It Mean?

Purpose

To recognize the difficulty of performing a valid performance appraisal using a trait-oriented form that includes vague and subjective personal traits such as ''loyalty.''

The Task

Listed below are a number of traits taken from performance appraisal forms used in a variety of organizations today. Write a one-sentence definition for each trait that pertains to performing a job. As an example, the first item, ''initiative,'' has been completed. When you are finished, your instructor will lead a discussion concerning your definitions.

1. Initiative: Seeks better ways to do the job without being asked.
2. Cooperation:
3. Judgment:
4. Sensitivity:
5. Effort:
6. Dependability:
7. Attitude:
8. Leadership:
9. Tact:
10. Loyalty:

KEY TERMS AND CONCEPTS

Behaviorally anchored rating scale (BARS)

Central tendency

Critical incidents

Essay method

Forced choice

Forced distribution

Graphic rating scales

Halo effect

Leniency

MBO

Nongraphic rating scale

Paired comparisons

Performance appraisal

Ranking

Recency

Strictness

Supervisory bias

Work standards

REVIEW QUESTIONS

1. What are the major purposes of performance appraisal?
2. What are the steps in the performance-appraisal process?
3. Describe the major methods of performance appraisal.
4. What are the major problems that surround many performance-appraisal programs.
5. Describe some of the performance-appraisal practices in use by organizations today.
6. What are the conditions necessary for an effective performance-appraisal program?

DISCUSSION QUESTIONS

1. Think of two instructors you have had—one very good and one very poor. What specific behaviors distinguish the two instructors? If you were the dean who had to conduct performance appraisals for the instructors, what method would you use to gather performance data?
2. Write five MBO objectives for an individual selling vacuum cleaners door to door. How would you weigh each objective in terms of the overall performance of the salesperson?
3. A small number of organizations have subordinates rate the performance of their supervisor. What advantages do you see in doing this? What problems may occur?
4. Supervisors may ask employees to furnish a self-rating at the appraisal interview for discussion. What are the benefits and drawbacks of this procedure?
5. What method or methods would you use to appraise the performance of the following kinds of employees: keypunch operator, first-line supervisor in a manufacturing plant, professor of management, airline pilot, office clerk in large government office, and policy officer?
6. When the process of evaluating employees is viewed as purely perfunctory, supervisors show little or no interest in completing the forms and conducting the interview. In some cases, the appraisal interview is not conducted. Why do these problems exist? What can be done to reduce them?

7. As a personnel administrator who is developing a performance-appraisal system for department store sales personnel, you have decided to implement the BARS method. Write three behavioral statements that illustrate good performance and three that describe poor or mediocre performance.

ENDNOTES

1. Roy W. Regel and Robert W. Hollmann, "Gauging Performance Objectively," *Personnel Administrator* 32, no. 6 (June 1987): 74–78.
2. Beverly L. Kaye, "Performance Appraisal and Career Development: A Shotgun Marriage," *Personnel* 61, no. 2 (March–April 1984): 57–66.
3. Guvenc Alpander, "Training First-Line Supervisors to Criticize Constructively," *Personnel Journal* (March 1980): 216–21.
4. Beverly L. Kaye and Shelley Krautz, "Preparing Employees: The Missing Link in Performance Appraisal Training," *Personnel* 59, no. 3 (May–June 1983): 23–29.
5. Harold Koontz, "Making Managerial Appraisal Effective," *California Management Review* (Winter 1972): 46–55.
6. William H. Holley and Hubert S. Field, "Will Your Performance Appraisal System Hold Up in Court?" *Personnel* 59, no. 1 (January–February 1982): 59–64.
7. T. A. Rodman, "Make the Praise Equal the Raise," *Personnel Journal* 63, no. 11 (November 1984): 73–78.
8. Paul Greenlaw and William Biggs, *Modern Personnel Management* (Philadelphia: Saunders, 1979), p. 187.
9. P. Slovic, B. Fischoff, and S. Lichenstein, "Behavioral Decision Theory," *Annual Review of Psychology* (1977): 1–39.
10. Charles J. Holson and Frederick W. Gibson, "Capturing Supervisor Rating Policies: A Way to Improve Performance Appraisal Effectiveness," *Personnel Administrator* 29, no. 3 (March 1984): 59–68.
11. Stephen B. Wehrenberg, "Train Supervisors to Measure and Evaluate Performance," *Personnel Journal* 67, no. 2 (February 1988): 77–81.
12. Richard Henderson, *Compensation Management* (Reston, VA: Reston, 1979), pp. 237–39.
13. Greenlaw and Biggs, *Modern Personnel Management,* p. 198.
14. G. Rosinger, L. B. Myers, G. W. Levy, M. Loar, S. A. Mohrman, and J. R. Stock, "Development of a Behaviorally Based Performance Appraisal System," *Personnel Psychology* 35, no. 1 (Spring 1982): 75–88.
15. Dallas de Fee, "Management by Objectives: When and How Does It Work?," *Personnel Journal* (January 1977): 37–39.
16. Jack Bucalo, "Personnel Directors . . . What You Should Know Before Recommending MBO," *Personnel Journal* (April, 1977): 176–78.
17. Richard Steers, "Achievement Needs and MBO Goal-Setting," *Personnel Journal* (January 1978): 26–28.
18. Mark McConkie, "A Clarification of the Goal Setting and Appraisal Processes in MBO," *Academy of Management Review* 4, no. 1 (1979): 29–40.
19. R. H. Finn and P. A. Fontaine, "Performance Appraisal: Some Dynamics and Dilemmas," *Public Personnel Management* 13, no. 3 (Fall 1984): 335–43.

20. H. Kent Baker and Philip I. Morgan, "Two Goals In Every Performance Appraisal," *Personnel Journal* 63, no. 9 (September 1984): 74–78.

21. Douglas M. McGregor, "An Uneasy Look at Performance Appraisal," *Harvard Business Review* (May–June 1957): 89–94.

22. H. H. Meyer et al., "Split Roles in Performance Appraisal," *Harvard Business Review* (January–February 1965): 127.

23. McGregor, "An Uneasy Look at Performance Appraisal," pp. 91–94.

24. Robert L. Taylor and Robert A. Zawacki, "Trends in Performance Appraisal: Guidelines for Managers," *Personnel Administrator* 29, no. 3 (March 1984): 71–80. See also *Business Week* (May 19, 1980).

25. Douglas B. Gehrman, "Beyond Today's Compensation and Performance Appraisal System," *Personnel Administrator* 29, no. 3 (March 1984): 21–33.

26. Taylor and Zawacki, "Trends in Performance Appraisal," p. 80.

27. Charles J. Frombrun and Robert L. Laud, "Strategic Issues in Performance Appraisal: Theory and Practice," *Personnel* 60, no. 3 (November–December 1983): 23–31.

28. Gehrman, "Beyond Today's Compensation and Performance Appraisal System," p. 25.

29. Michael K. Mount, "Comparisons of Managerial and Employee Satisfaction with a Performance Appraisal System," *Personnel Psychology* 36, no. 1 (Spring 1983): 99–109.

30. David E. Smith, "Training Programs for Performance Appraisal: A Review," *Academy of Management Review* 11, no. 1 (January 1986): 22–40.

31. Brian L. Davis and Michael K. Mount, "Design and Use of a Performance Appraisal Feedback System," *Personnel Administrator* 29, no. 3 (March 1983): 47–51.

32. Peggy Lanza, "Team Appraisals," *Personnel Journal* 64, no. 3 (March 1983): 47–51.

33. Gary P. Latham and Kenneth N. Wexley, *Increasing Productivity Through Performance Appraisal.* (Reading, MA: Addison-Wesley 1982), p. 85.

34. Lanza, "Team Appraisals," p. 48.

35. Stephen J. Carroll, "Asian HRM Philosophies and Systems: Can They Meet Our Changing HRM Needs?". In *Readings in Personnel and Human Resource Management,* edited by R. S. Schuler, S. A. Youngblood, and V. L. Huber (St. Paul, MN: West, 1988), p. 448.

36. Lennie Copeland and Lewis Griggs, *Going International* (New York: Random House, 1985), p. 135.

Chapter Seven

Employee Training

Chapter Outline

ASSESSMENT
    Selecting a Method
    Training Objectives

TRAINING AND DEVELOPMENT
    On-the-job Training
    Off-the-job Training
    On- or Off-the-job Training?
    Program Implementation

EVALUATION
    Level 1: How Did Participants React?
    Level 2: What Did Participants Learn?
    Level 3: How Did Participants Change Behavior?
    Level 4: What Organizational Goals Were Affected?
    Applying Evaluation Strategies

PRINCIPLES OF LEARNING
    Motivation
    Participation
    Feedback
    Organization
    Repetition
    Application

LEGAL ISSUES

RESPONSIBILITY FOR TRAINING

INTERNATIONAL HRM: TRAINING

CONCLUSIONS AND APPLICATIONS

Chapter Objectives

1. To cite the major purposes of the training function.
2. To recognize the importance of understanding the training function from a systems perspective.
3. To underscore the importance of the training needs assessment function and to identify major needs assessment techniques.
4. To recognize the advantages of training human resources both on and off the job and to describe the major on- and off-the-job training techniques.
5. To identify the legislation that affects the training function and to describe how organizations may ensure that training is conducted in a nondiscriminatory fashion.
6. To cite the principles of learning that must be incorporated into the training function in order for training to be maximally effective.
7. To understand the importance of conducting a scientific evaluation of the training function and to describe the major training evaluation methods.

Kentucky Fried Chicken: Back to Basics

Before April, 1978, Kentucky Fried Chicken (KFC) had used a variety of training approaches, each with mixed results. Peer training was the most common method. Formal programs when used were often just a "quick fix"; the focus was usually on a temporary problem. They lacked systematic integration with other programs and were often quickly replaced by a new priority. This "program of the month" approach resulted in inconsistent execution from market to market and even store to store.

But that has all changed now. Kentucky Fried Chicken has one of the most sophisticated training operations of all fast-food franchise operations, including a full-scale training store located near its headquarters in Louisville, Kentucky. KFC believes strongly that training is critical in employee productivity. Their beliefs are embodied in KFC's "back to basics" training philosophy. Every training system operates with a philosophy—a set of beliefs concerning people, productivity and profits. KFC believes that:

- The moment an employee is hired, training takes place—planned or unplanned . . . controlled or uncontrolled. Training should be done through proven, systematic methods rather than hunch, intuition, or neglect.
- Training should take place as close to the job as possible. Training programs should be practical, consistent, cost effective, available when and where needed, and adapted to the nonprofessional trainer.
- Training must lead to measurable improvement in productivity and profits.
- Training is no longer a luxury. It is a necessary investment in people. In today's competitive market you win or lose by your training efforts.

Source: Adapted from the *Kentucky Fried Chicken Training Manual.*

DECISION makers are always looking for ways to make their organizations more effective. Managers of privately owned companies must enhance their organization's profits and their stockholders' returns by increasing sales or reducing operating costs or both. Government administrators at all levels have come under increasing pressure to provide more effective and efficient services. Leaders of voluntary organizations, such as the American Cancer Society and United Way, likewise seek ways to grow and prosper as critical financial resources become more and more difficult to obtain. The need to achieve goals as effectively as possible is common to all organizations, public and private, large and small. There are six major purposes of training:

To Improve Performance Employees who perform unsatisfactorily because of a deficiency in skills are prime candidates for training. Although training cannot solve all problems of ineffective performance, a sound training program is often instrumental in minimizing those problems.

To Update Employees' Skills Managers in all areas must always be aware of technological advances that will make their organizations function more effectively. Technological change often means that jobs change. Thus, employee skills must be updated through training so that technological advances are successfully integrated into the organization.

To Promote Job Competency Sometimes a new or newly promoted employee will not possess the skills and abilities required to be competent on the job. First, employee selection systems are not perfect. Even when tests, interviews, and other data indicate a high probability of job success, an applicant may prove incompetent on the job. No selection device is able to predict success or failure all the time, and training is often necessary to fill the gap between the new employee's predicted and actual performance. Second, managers knowingly hire and promote employees who need training to perform at standard levels. When the number of job openings exceeds the number of applicants, management has little choice but to hire or promote an applicant with few or no job skills and to remedy that lack through training. Third, many times

management hires employees who possess the aptitude to learn and then trains them to perform specific tasks. For example, in hiring new employees for its manufacturing operation in Louisville, Kentucky, the General Electric Company uses an aptitude test that measures general manual dexterity and motor coordination skills. To learn a specific assembly job, new employees undergo company-provided training that may last for periods ranging from a few hours to several days.

To Solve Problems Managers report they must achieve their goals through both scarcity and abundance: a scarcity of financial, human, and technological resources and an abundance of financial, human, and technological problems. Managers are expected to attain high goals in spite of personal conflicts, vague policies and standards, scheduling delays, inventory shortages, high levels of absenteeism and turnover, union–management disputes, and a restrictive legal environment. Organizational problems are addressed in many ways. Training is one important way to solve many of those problems. Training courses may concern personnel, marketing, accounting, finance, manufacturing, purchasing, information systems, and general management. Training personnel, universities, and training consultants assist employees in solving problems and performing their jobs effectively.

To Prepare for Promotion One important way to attract, retain, and motivate personnel is through a systematic program of career development. Developing an employee's capabilities is consistent with a personnel policy of promotion from within, and training is important in a career-development system. Training enables an employee to acquire the skills needed for a promotion and eases the transition from an employee's present job to one involving greater responsibilities. Organizations that fail to provide such training often lose their most promising employees. Frustrated by the lack of opportunity, achievement-oriented employees often seek employment with organizations that provide training for career advancement. By developing and promoting its human resources through training, management can supervise a qualified, motivated, and satisfied work force.

To Orient New Employees   During the first few days on the job, new employees form their initial impressions of the organization and its managers. These impressions may range from very favorable to very unfavorable and may influence their job satisfaction and productivity. Therefore, many administrators make an effort to orient new employees to the organization and the job.

New employees may experience surprise or even shock when events do not conform to their expectations. As a result, they may seek information about organizational realities and their preconceived assumptions. Their immediate need is to reduce any uncertainty about the job and find out how to fit in socially. The orientation process can reduce the difficulties encountered by new employees through effective orientation programs.[1] Orientation may be brief and informal, focusing only on such traditional topics as company benefits, holidays, vacations, and pay. Or it may be a one- or two-day program involving a company tour, meetings with managers and personnel officials, and discussions about a variety of subjects, including organizational objectives and philosophy, employee expectations, and relevant legislation.[2] Figure 7–1 shows the many topics that may be covered in a wide-ranging orientation.

Both line and staff managers share the responsibilities for orientation. Personnel or industrial-relations representatives may discuss company history, benefits, and personnel policies. The employee's immediate supervisor usually discusses job-related topics such as job rules and regulations, safety procedures, co-workers, and performance standards.

The time and effort invested in a well-planned orientation program may reap many returns. Research shows that orientation programs can reduce employees' anxiety, save supervisory and co-workers' time, develop positive attitudes toward the company, and create realistic job expectations.[3] In an oft-cited research study conducted at Texas Instruments, Inc., new employees were divided into two groups. One group attended the company's traditional two-hour orientation program, which focused on employee benefits and performance requirements. An experimental group attended both the traditional two-hour program and a six-hour program devoted to social orientation, which covered (1) why they would probably succeed on the job, (2) how the company grapevine worked and what to expect from it, (3) how to take the initiative in requesting help from supervisors, and (4) how individual supervisors operated. Compared to the control group, employees in the expanded session required less training time and fewer training costs, and their records later showed reduced absenteeism, tardiness, waste, and product rejects.[4]

Training is the systematic process by which employees learn skills, information, or attitudes to further organizational and personal goals.[5] The thought of training often brings to mind a trainer, participants, and traditional training techniques: a film being shown, workbooks being completed, or a chalkboard-assisted lecture. To the army veteran, the thought of training may conjure up not-so-pleasant memories of basic training, replete with long hours of marching, physical training, and military-science lectures. But such implementation of training is only a small part of the training process. Successful training involves considerable effort both before and after the trainer and trainees are brought together. In other words, training is best thought of as a complex system that involves a number of distinct but highly inter-related phases. A training systems model is shown in Figure 7–2. The three major phases of training are (1) assessment, (2) training and development, and (3) evaluation.

ASSESSMENT

In some cases, the determination of training needs is a fairly straightforward process that may be conducted without an extensive analysis of the organization. For example, all new employees normally undergo orientation training. An impending technological change such as the introduction of new computer hardware will automatically require the need for training those affected. On the other hand, determining training requirements to resolve deficiencies in skills or to address career developmental needs necessitates much greater analysis by training personnel. To identify the training needs that result from performance problems, the trainer must systematically collect and analyze employees' output, product quality, and attitudes.

Training needs may be gathered using a variety of methods. Some of the more common include the following.[6]

Advisory Committees Advisory committees generally comprise various levels of management, and some organizations create multiple committees to represent the various functions, such as production and accounting. Committees often determine whether a particular problem is a training problem and establish training priorities.

Assessment Centers Used mostly for management development, the assessment center requires participants to undergo a series of ex-

ercises and tests to determine their strengths and weaknesses in performing managerial tasks. Although the assessment center is used primarily to predict success in a managerial role, its use in measuring training needs is increasing.

Attitude Surveys Attitude surveys are most effective in measuring the general level of job satisfaction, but the data gathered may show various areas where training needs exist.

Group Discussions This method generally involves meeting with employees who represent a specific work area. A primary benefit of group discussions is that the employees are emotionally committed to the training as a result of the active participation in the assessment process.

Employee Interviews This method generally involves a discussion between the trainer and an individual employee. Although employee interviews are good for specifying individual training needs, they are also time-consuming. This method is little used compared to other less-costly methods.

Exit Interviews A high turnover rate may spell organizational problems and a need for training, particularly in the area of supervision. The validity of exit interviews greatly depends on an unbiased and skilled interviewer and on honest answers from the employee who is leaving.

Management Requests Occasionally, a member of management may request that an employee or employees receive training. With this approach, care must be taken to ensure that the problem is actually a training problem and that the training needs have been accurately diagnosed.

Observations of Behavior Trainers or supervisors may directly observe employees' behav-

Appraisal, Training, and Development

NAME OF
EMPLOYEE _____

STARTING
DATE _____

DEPARTMENT _____ LOCATION _____

ITEMS COVERED BY PERSONNEL RELATIONS DEPARTMENT OR BRANCH OFFICE ON FIRST DAY
OF ORIENTATION: (45 minutes)

PART I—Organization and Personnel Policies & Procedures

☐ 1. XYZ Company Organization
☐ 2. Basic Insurance Benefits *(Paid in full by the company)*
    ☐ A. Hospitalization
    ☐ B. Short-Term Disability
    ☐ C. Basic Life Insurance
    ☐ D. Travel Accident
☐ 3. Optional Insurance Benefits *(Paid for by you and the company)*
    ☐ A. Comprehensive Medical
    ☐ B. Contributory Life Insurance
    ☐ C. Long Term Disability

☐ 4. Vacations
☐ 5. Holidays
☐ 6. Probationary Period
☐ 7. Compensation
☐ 8. Performance Appraisal
☐ 9. Medical Absence
☐ 10. Personal Status Change Notice

☐ 11. XYZ Company News
☐ 12. Tuition Refund Plan
☐ 13. Building Facilities
☐ 14. New Building
☐ 15. XYZ Company and You
☐ 16. Equal Opportunity Employment

APPOINTMENT FOR SECOND MEETING: (45 minutes)

DATE _____ TIME _____

*IMPORTANT: BE SURE TO BRING THIS FORM BACK WITH YOU, SIGNED BY YOUR MANAGER
WHEN YOU COME TO YOUR SCHEDULED SECOND MEETING.*

PART II—Personnel Policies & Procedures

☐ 1. Review & Questions on Part 1
☐ 2. Retirement Program
☐ 3. College Gift Matching Plan
☐ 4. Time Off the Job
☐ 5. Award for Recruiting
☐ 6. Credit Union

☐ 7. XYZ Company Investment Plan
☐ 8. U.S. Savings Bonds
☐ 9. Employee Activities
☐ 10. Suggestion System
☐ 11. Personnel Inventory

_____
PERSONNEL RELATIONS STAFF REPRESEN-
TATIVE

_____
DATE

FIGURE 7–1
Orientation checklist for personnel representatives and supervisory personnel

ITEMS TO BE DISCUSSED BY DEPARTMENT HEAD OR SUPERVISOR WITH NEW EMPLOYEE:

FIRST DAY OF EMPLOYMENT
- ☐ 1. Introduction to Co-workers
- ☐ 2. Information on Location of Facilities
    - ☐ A. Coat Room
    - ☐ B. Cafeteria
    - ☐ C. Wash Room
    - ☐ D. Bulletin Board
    - ☐ E. Coffee Service
    - ☐ F. Provision for Lunch

RULES AND POLICIES
- ☐ 3. Hours: starting, lunch, dismissal time, hours per week
- ☐ 4. Pay: when, where, and how paid—overtime policy
        (Explain deductions when 1st check is received.)
- ☐ 5. Holidays and Vacations in Detail
- ☐ 6. Probationary Period
- ☐ 7. Absences:
- ☐ 8. Organization of Department
        Corporation—Division—Department—Section
- ☐ 9. Rules on:
        Tardiness, Telephone Coverage, Behavior, etc.

DURING FIRST TWO WEEKS OF EMPLOYMENT
- ☐ 10. Accident:
        Reporting accident or injury on job
- ☐ 11. Employee's Discount on XYZ Company products
- ☐ 12. Salary Check—Explanation of Deductions
- ☐ 13. Salary Reviews
- ☐ 14. Employee Appraisal Plan
- ☐ 15. Suggestion System
- ☐ 16. Reporting Change in Address, Name, Phone, etc.
- ☐ 17. Invite Questions and Help on Problems

As indicated by check marks, all of the above items have been discussed with the employee.

The employee has been advised as to the time and extent of 1st vacation as shown by the Table on last page of this form.

Employee has been instructed to attend the second scheduled meeting and to bring this check list with him.

_____
DEPARTMENT HEAD OR SUPERVISOR

_____
DATE

FIGURE 7–1
continued

FIGURE 7–2
A training systems
model (Source:
*Training: Program
Development and
Evaluation,* by I.
Goldstein. Copyright ©
1974 by Wadsworth
Publishing Co., Inc.
Reprinted by
permission of Brooks/
Cole Publishing
Company, Monterey,
Calif. 93940.)

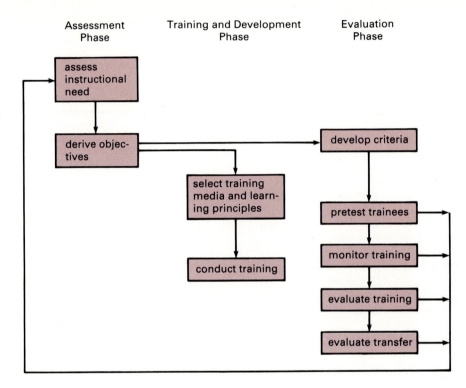

ior to identify training needs. This method is generally limited to the assessment of technical skills and behaviors. Its primary drawback is that it is time-consuming and thus costly.

Performance Appraisals A valid, job-related appraisal system will point out strengths and weaknesses in employee performance and may indicate training and development needs. Time and cost are low since the data are regularly gathered. And because both the employee and supervisor are involved, an emotional commitment to training is often an additional benefit of this method.

Performance Documents Most organizations regularly gather data on employee performance, such as productivity, absenteeism, accidents, and turnover. Such information is

generally accurate and may be used to point out training needs. A major shortcoming of this approach is that the data simply indicate the existence of a problem and do little to specify its cause. Only a careful analysis will determine whether or not training will solve that problem.

Questionnaires Some organizations use questionnaires to identify training needs. The employees themselves are generally the respondents. The questionnaire generally specifies important skill areas, the importance of the skill, and the employee's perception of training need for each area. The cost of this technique is relatively low because a great deal of data may be collected in a relatively short time. An example of such a questionnaire is shown in Figure 7–3.

POSITION: Clerical

Employee _____   Department _____

Supervisor _____   Date _____

INSTRUCTIONS:

In column A, rate the skill necessary for the employee to perform the job. Use the following ratings: 1—very important; 2— moderately important; 3—not important.

In column B, rate the need for training for each skill area which received a rating of 1 or 2 in column A. In assessing training needs, use the following ratings: 1—no need for training; 2—moderate need for training; 3—immediate, critical need for training.

Skill	A How important is the skill?	B Employee's need for training
Ability to read and comprehend rough-draft material		
Typing speed		
Typing accuracy		
Proofreading skills		
Ability to use office machinery		
Filing skills		
Ability to compose letters and memos		
Oral communications		
Ability to organize daily routine		
Human relations skills		

FIGURE 7–3

An example of a questionnaire for identifying training needs

Appraisal, Training, and Development

Skills Test A test of necessary skills, such as typing, computer programming, or driving, may also be used to measure training needs. When using skills tests for needs assessment, it is critical that the tests be job-related and measure those skills and abilities required for successful job performance.

Selecting a Method

Several criteria may be used in selecting a needs-assessment method.[7] First, *employee involvement* is important because a feeling of participation in the assessment process enhances employee motivation to undergo training. Employee perceptions about a training program before it begins can affect the effectiveness of the training. When employees are provided a realistic preview of training programs and have some choice of which program (or training method) they enter, the outcome of the training is improved. Employees given a preview of programs and some choice will generally make a stronger commitment to attend the program, learn more from the training, and are more satisfied with the program. Why? Perhaps employees who have chosen a particular program because they desire the training are more motivated to learn.[8]

Second, *management involvement* is important because supervisors generally have accurate information about their employees' performance and are in a prime position to assess the need for training within the work group. Third, the *time required* is always important in considering any form of a data collection, and needs assessment is no exception. And since time is generally a scarce commodity, trainers often favor methods that do not involve large investments in time. Fourth, the *cost* of the assessment method, in terms of personnel and materials involved, is an important consideration. Training budgets rarely afford the selection of training processes and activities with-

TABLE 7-1

A comparison of the various methods of needs assessment using the five selection criteria

Methods	CRITERIA				
	Employee Involvement	Management Involvement	Time Required	Cost	Relevant Quantifiable Data
Advisory committees	Low	Moderate	Moderate	Low	Low
Assessment centers	High	Low	High	High	High
Attitude surveys	Moderate	Low	Moderate	Moderate	Low
Group discussions	High	Moderate	Moderate	Moderate	Moderate
Employee interviews	High	Low	High	High	Moderate
Exit interviews	Low	Low	Low	Low	Low
Management requests	Low	High	Low	Low	Low
Observations of behavior	Moderate	Low	High	High	Moderate
Performance appraisals	Moderate	High	Moderate	Low	High
Performance documents	Low	Moderate	Low	Low	High
Questionnaires, surveys, and inventories	High	High	Moderate	Moderate	High
Skills tests	High	Low	High	High	High

Source: J. Newstrom and J. Lilyquist, "Selecting Needs Analysis Techniques," *Training and Development Journal* 33, 1979. With permission.

out financial consideration. Fifth, the needs-assessment information must be *relevant* and *quantifiable*. Vague or subjective opinions about training needs will do little to generate the support from top management needed for a successful training program.

How do the various assessment methods measure up to the selection criteria? Table 7–1 shows how each method is evaluated using the five criteria. The table shows that there is no one best method and that each method has its own strengths and weaknesses. In selecting a particular method or combination of methods, trainers must carefully consider the merits and drawbacks of each and make their selections in light of the conditions and constraints within their own organizations.

Training Objectives

Following an assessment of training needs, training objectives are written to reflect what the participant should be able to do upon the completion of training. Thus, a link between the assessment phase and the evaluation phase is formed. Training objectives indicate the kinds and levels of skills, abilities, knowledge, and attitudes the participant should possess after the program has been completed. Well-written objectives will benefit training in at least three important ways:

- Training objectives help determine which methods are appropriate by focusing on the areas of employee performance that need to change.
- Training objectives clarify what is expected of both the trainer and the participants.
- Training objectives provide a basis for evaluating the program after its completion.

What are the qualities of good training objectives? A well-written training objective will have three parts: (1) a statement of terminal behavior, that is, what the learner will be able to do upon completion of training; (2) a description of the conditions under which terminal behavior is expected to occur; (3) a statement of the minimum level of achievement that will be accepted as evidence that the learner has accomplished what was required. Table 7–2 shows a few examples of what should be included in written training objectives.

TABLE 7–2
Three sample training objectives.

Terminal Behavior	Condition	Minimal Achievement
To type	Given a standard key-punch operator's examination	No fewer than ten cards per minute with an error rate no higher than 3 percent
To perform maintenance	Given a standard set of tools	Preventive maintenance on a lathe within thirty minutes according to company standard
To locate and correct errors	Given a business letter containing grammatical errors	Locate 95 percent of all errors after studying the letter for no more than five minutes

Corporate Classrooms

Company on-site classrooms have traditionally focused on job-specific training for new employees. In recent years, however, some corporations have begun offering academic courses in basic math, writing, science and even advanced degree programs in business and technology.

In 1984 Aetna Life & Casualty Company opened an eight story, $42 million training institute in Hartford, Connecticut. The facility includes a 269-room hotel, cafeteria, and computerized library. Course offerings range from word processing to advanced management courses for top executives. New employees with little formal education take courses in remedial reading, oral communications, and writing. Why this major investment in an on-site comprehensive educational program? Motorola, Inc., which operates a similar Training and Educational Center in Schaumburg, Illinois, believes that corporate classrooms are a response to rapidly changing technology. They found that their work force largely had skills that were outdated. Even new, entry-level workers do not have sufficient basic math skills. Similar programs can be found at Eastman Kodak, Westinghouse Electric Company, and NCR Corporation.

Source: Adapted from Constance Mitchell, "Corporate Classes: Firms Broaden Scope of Their Educational Programs," *The Wall Street Journal* (September 28, 1987): 1. Reprinted by permission of The Wall Street Journal, © Dow Jones & Company, Inc. 1987. All Rights Reserved.

TRAINING AND DEVELOPMENT

The focus of the assessment phase is on determining how and to what degree employees must change their behavior to achieve organizational and personal goals. The next phase concerns the selection of training techniques that will be most effective in changing behavior. A wide variety of training techniques exist, and care must be taken to ensure that training techniques are effectively matched with training needs and objectives. Training personnel must avoid the temptation to select a program or technique simply because it is popular, entertaining, or in vogue. Unless a particular training technique is based on a valid need—as indicated by a well-planned needs assessment—the organization will gain few, if any, returns for its training dollars.

Training techniques may be performed on or off the job. Specific kinds of on- and off-the-job training will be briefly discussed, along with the advantages and disadvantages of each.

On-the-job Training

On-the-job training is job instruction normally given by an employee's supervisor or an experienced employee. The Bureau of National

Affairs reports that 90 percent or more of all training is performed on the job.[9] On-the-job training may involve learning how to run a machine, to complete forms and paperwork, to drive a vehicle, to conduct an interview, or to sell the company's product. Both new and existing employees at all job levels—unskilled, skilled, clerical, management, and staff—are often trained on the job. Some common on-the-job training techniques include job rotation, enlarged job responsibilities, job instruction training, learner-controlled instruction, and apprentice training.

Job Rotation   Also referred to as *cross-training,* job rotation involves placing an employee on different jobs for periods of time ranging from a few hours to several weeks. Skilled, unskilled, or clerical employees who undergo job rotation usually learn such specific tasks as how to run a machine or how to perform a routine assembly or clerical process. At that job level, job rotation normally consumes a short period, such as a few hours or one or two days. At higher job levels, job rotation may consume much larger periods, because staff trainees often learn complex functions and responsibilities during the rotation.[10] For example, on-the-job training for a bank lending officer may consist of one or two months in each department, including loan operations and collections, bookkeeping, trust operations, data processing, and commercial lending.

Enlarged Job Responsibilities   Giving an employee added job duties, responsibilities, and assignments is another way to train an employee on the job. Rather than simply giving an employee more of the same work to perform, this popular form of job training involves delegating more decision making to the employee through challenging job assignments and problem solving. This technique is widely used in training managers, professional staff, and skilled clerical employees, but it has seen limited use in the blue-collar manufacturing ranks.

Job Instruction Training (JIT)   Faced with massive training needs during World War II, the federal government developed job instruction training (JIT) to enable supervisors to train their employees quickly and effectively. In essence, JIT is a series of steps for supervisors to follow when training their employees. Because of its simplicity and commonsense approach, JIT remains a popular tool for many modern trainers. The steps in the JIT system are the following:[11]

Preparation   After putting the learners at ease, find out what they know and do not know about their jobs. Motivate them to learn more about their jobs.

Presentation   Convey knowledge and operating skills by telling, showing, and illustrating. Go slowly; be patient. Go over each point individually. Question learners' understanding and repeat if necessary.

Performance Tryout   Ask learners to perform the job. Query apprentices about why, who, when, and where. Watch their performances closely. While correcting errors, repeat instructions as often as necessary.

Follow-up   Allow learners to work independently, and check back frequently to make sure that they can do their jobs correctly. Reduce direct supervision gradually as satisfactory performances are reached.

Learner-Controlled Instruction   Often considered a more effective and improved form of on-the-job training is learner-controlled instruction (LCI). With its origins in the hotel/motel and restaurant industries, LCI

Appraisal, Training, and Development

is a results-oriented training technique that incorporates many of the elements of effective training. LCI may be used to train both non-management and management employees. The five elements of LCI, as shown in Figure 7–4, are the following:

Actual Working Environment LCI incorporates the primary advantage of on-the-job training. By learning in his or her working environment, the employee reduces training time and costs through an efficient use of material, facilities, and instructional personnel.

Competency-based Learning Before training begins, employee competencies and standards of performance are determined and clearly specified. LCI training is centered on those competencies, which are also used to evaluate training and assess the trainee's progress in learning skills and abilities.

Individualized Instruction With traditional classroom training, each participant is fed the same material over a fixed number of hours. As a result, quick learners get bored and slow learners may be left behind. With LCI, the individual differences of each trainee are accommodated as the learner proceeds at his or her own pace. Training time may be expanded or contracted depending on the learner's aptitude for acquiring new skills and abilities.

Results-oriented Feedback Throughout LCI training, the learner receives results-oriented feedback, the purpose being to offer praise and recognition whenever new skills are learned and to help overcome any difficulties the learner may experience. Once the learner demonstrates mastery of a skill or ability, training in that particular area of competency is completed.

FIGURE 7–4
A model of LCI

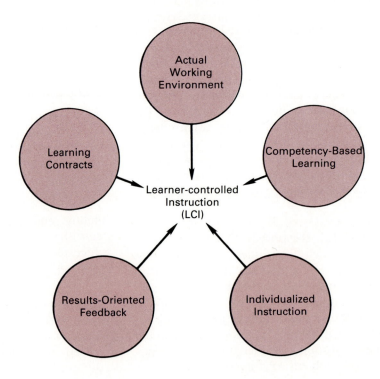

Learning Contracts The learning contract is a written document that normally contains four parts: (1) results-oriented behaviors the trainee is expected to learn, (2) training resources that will help the employee learn, (3) the criteria on which the training evaluation will be based, and (4) a certification section indicating who will be responsible for conducting the training evaluation. An example of a learning contract used by a medium-sized restaurant chain is shown in Figure 7–5.

Does LCI work? According to the training director of one company that uses LCI, the time needed to train new managers dropped from an average of 16 weeks to 11 weeks with the introduction of the technique. The Marriott Corporation reported significant reductions in training first-level supervisors in its hotel division, and Allied Supermarkets claimed reductions in training time with assistant supermarket managers. In all likelihood, the use of LCI in training managers and supervisors will continue to increase.[12]

Apprentice Training A combination of on- and off-the-job training, apprentice training is widely used in the skilled trades, such as barbering, carpentry, printing, welding, and plumbing. Apprentice training involves cooperation among employees, the government, educational institutions (usually vocational or technical schools), and labor unions. The U.S. Department of Labor regulates apprentice training programs and determines the length of apprenticeships and the minimum requirements for classroom instruction. Certain conditions of employment and training may also be negotiated with individual unions.

Apprenticeship programs do not escape criticism. Some critics suggest that union control of entry into apprenticeship programs results in labor shortages and high wage rates.[13]

Other critics hold that apprenticeship programs discriminate against women and blacks.[14] (It should be pointed out that many unions have antidiscrimination clauses and that discrimination in apprenticeship programs is illegal under the Civil Rights Act.)

On-the-job Training: The Balance Sheet
The widespread use of on-the-job training is, no doubt, due to the many benefits it offers. Among the potential assets of this type of training are:

- The employee is doing the actual work, not hypothetical or simulated tasks.
- The employee receives instructions from an experienced employee or supervisor who has performed the task successfully.
- The training is performed in the actual work environment under normal working conditions and requires no special training facilities.
- The training is informal, relatively inexpensive, and easy to schedule.
- The training may build cooperative relationships between the employee and the trainer.

Among the potential liabilities of on-the-job training are:[15]

- The trainer may not be motivated to train or to accept the responsibility for training; thus, training may be haphazard.
- The trainer may perform the job well but lack the ability to teach others how to do so.
- The trainer may not have the time to train and may omit important elements of the training process. While the employee is learning on the job, resources will be inefficiently used, performance (at least initially) will be low, and costly errors may be made.

COMPETENCY: The ability to evaluate employee performance	
LEARNING STRATEGIES	EVALUATION GUIDES

1. While mastering this competency, determine the following:
  a. What is the employee evaluation system?
    (1) Formal periodic system
    (2) Daily on-going evaluation
  b. When and how is the evaluation system used?
  c. What is the purpose of the periodic evaluation and the purpose of daily evaluation?
  d. How should follow-through on evaluation be handled?
    (1) Counseling and coaching
    (2) Disciplinary actions
    (3) Raises or promotions
  e. Who has the authority to terminate employees and under what conditions?
2. Observe and assist as necessary to learn how to conduct:
  a. Employee counseling sessions
  b. Employee disciplinary sessions
3. Observe and assist management personnel to develop an understanding of procedures for evaluating employees to include:
  a. Daily evaluation
  b. Periodic evaluation
4. Review any problems encountered in evaluating employee performance with the contractor and/or training advisor and determine how each problem could have been avoided or overcome.
	Trainee performed as follows:
	_____ Answered all questions in Strategy #1.
	_____ Explained management's responsibility for employee evaluation and feedback about performance.
	_____ Described the importance of objectivity and fairness in evaluating employee performance and in giving feedback to employees.
	_____ Displayed a positive attitude about performance evaluations.
	_____ Explained how employee evaluations are essential to employee motivation and morale.
	_____ Found a satisfactory solution to all problems encountered.

FIGURE 7–5

An example of a learning contract (Source: F. Kuzmits, "Train Your New Managers with LCI," *Personnel* [April 1985]. Used with permission.)

RESOURCES	CERTIFICATION
-Personnel Manual: #430 Employee Relations #432 Grievances #434 Performance Appraisal and Review for Operations Management	I agree to assist the learner in developing mastery of the competency described in this Training Contract _____ _____ Signed Contractor Date I certify that in my judgment the learner has demonstrated mastery of the competency described in this Training Contract. _____ _____ Signed Contractor Date _____ _____ Approved • Training Advisor Date

FIGURE 7–5
continued

Off-the-job Training

Off-the-job training is any form of training performed away from the employee's work area. Two broad forms of off-the-job training programs exist: (1) in-house programs are coordinated by the employee's organization and conducted within a company training facility; (2) off-site programs are held away from the organization and sponsored by a professional association, educational institution, or independent training firm. A wide variety of training methods is employed to train employees off the job; these range from lecturing to using relatively new techniques that involve expensive and sophisticated audiovisual techniques.

Lecture   The lecture remains the most popular technique for providing factual information to many people at the same time, but it only involves one-way communication. Students will testify that overuse of the lecture can quickly result in boredom and frustration.

Lectures are particularly effective when used sparingly and combined with other training techniques.[16]

Conference/Discussion   Many training programs focus on organizational problems, innovative ideas, and new theories and principles. Discussing problems and critical issues permits a dialogue between the trainer and trainee, as well as among the trainees. This two-way communication provides trainees with immediate feedback on their questions and ideas and heightens motivation for the learner.

Audiovisual   This method employs sight or sound to assist the trainer.[17] Modern audiovisual techniques include using videotape and closed-circuit television; traditional techniques include using chalkboard, films, slides, and flip charts. Audiovisual techniques work best when used with other training methods; the

Flight Trainer Simulates Vertigo

To train fighter pilots to handle the dizziness and spatial disorientation caused by strong accelerations, Environmental Tectonics Corp. (ETC) in Southampton, Pa., has developed a specialized flight simulator called Gyrolab. The simulator generates up to two times the force of gravity (G) by spinning at the end of a short planetary axis; it also rotates on three axes to simulate the roll, pitch, and yaw of an aircraft.

Spatial disorientation occurs when pilots execute rapid turns, experiencing accelerations of up to 9 Gs. If the pilot turns his head to one side, the G forces disturb the vestibular system of the inner ear. These disruptions give rise to severe dizziness and distorted perceptions, such as not knowing the difference between up and down. Spatial disorientation is blamed for 40 percent of the crashes involving high-performance aircraft.

Training on the Gyrolab teaches pilots to recognize the onset of spatial disorientation and to fly by relying on their instruments rather than on their distorted perceptions. The system costs from $750,000 to $1.5 million, depending on features, and can be customized to simulate different aircraft, such as the F-16 and the F-18. ETC recently sold the first Gyrolab to the United Arab Emirates Air Force.

Source: "Flight Trainer Simulates Vertigo," *High Technology* (March 1985), p. 7. With permission.

---

trainer must bear in mind that sophisticated equipment is no substitute for a well-planned training program.

Vestibule In a training area created to resemble the employee's actual work area, vestibule training is performed with the aid of an instructor, who demonstrates on the same kinds of machines and uses processes the trainee will use on the job. Vestibule training has been successfully used for a variety of skilled positions, including retail sales personnel, bank tellers, machine operators, and aircraft pilots. An example of how this form of simulation can be used to train fighter pilots is discussed in the feature "Flight Trainer Simulates Vertigo."

Programmed Instruction This method involves self-instruction without the presence or participation of the trainer.[18] In programmed instruction, the material to be learned is presented in text form or through a computer terminal. Programmed instruction that uses computer technology is called *computer assisted instruction (CAI)*. In programmed instruction, information is broken down and presented to the trainee in small, logical steps. After receiving a small piece of information, the trainee answers a question about the material by writing in the text or, if a machine is used, pushing a button on the machine. The trainee is immediately informed if the answer is correct. When the answer is correct, the trainee receives new information. An incorrect answer, however, usually results in the trainee's being presented with remedial material.

Programmed instruction offers advantages not found in other training methods. To begin with, it recognizes individual learning differences by allowing each of the trainees to learn at an individual pace. In addition, learning is enhanced through active participation by the trainee and through immediate feedback on responses to questions. Finally, its highly individualized nature offers flexibility in scheduling training by eliminating the need to assemble large groups of trainees at the same time.

Off-the-job Training: The Balance Sheet

Among the potential assets of off-the-job training are:[19]

- Cost-efficient training, because groups rather than individuals are usually trained.
- Trainers, usually full-time instructors or training personnel, are likely to be more competent trainers than on-the-job trainers, who normally spend only a fraction of their time training.
- More planning and organization often go into off-the-job training than into on-the-job training.
- Off-the-job training enables the trainee to learn in an environment free from the normal pressures and interruptions of the work place.
- Off-site courses and seminars enable small companies with limited resources to train employees without the formidable expenses of a large training staff and training facilities.

Among the potential liabilities of off-the-job training are:

- Employees attending off-the-job training are not performing their jobs. This is an added expense of training, though training benefits should exceed costs in the long run.
- Off-the-job training often has problems of transfer of learning. Sometimes off-the-job training is of limited practical value to the trainee—particularly when the training is conducted away from the organization. Because it is impossible for the trainer to customize a course for each participant, off-the-job programs normally contain limited applications for a trainee's specific problems and situations. This is the greatest potential drawback to off-the-job training.

On- or Off-the-job Training?

It would be naive to suggest that either on-the-job or off-the-job training programs will always be the most effective type of training to use. Because each organization has its own set of assets and liabilities, selection of a particular training technique should be made after closely examining the organization's specific training environment.[20]

First, training needs and objectives must be considered. If the trainee's job contains relatively uncomplicated tasks and if immediate production by the employee is an important objective, then on-the-job training may be preferable. On the other hand, if employees need exposure to new concepts, tools, and techniques, then off-the-job training may be preferable.

Second, resources often play an important role in deciding between on- and off-the-job programs. Managers of organizations that have few or no training resources—facilities, equipment, and qualified on-the-job train-

Seminar: _____ Date(s): _____

Speaker: _____ Time: _____

Speaker: _____ Facility: _____

No. of participants: _____ Meeting room: _____

Luncheon room: _____

LUNCHEON MENU:

1st day: _____

2nd day: _____

3rd day: _____

COFFEE BREAK TIMES AND MENUS:

Registration: _____

Morning break: _____

Afternoon break: _____

AUDIOVISUAL AIDS FOR SPEAKERS: PHYSICAL SETUP:

_____Flip chart and markers   _____Proper posting in lobby

_____Overhead projector   _____Proper storage for equipment

_____35 mm projector   _____Proper lighting

_____Screen   _____No phone calls

     _____No piped-in music

FIGURE 7–6
An example of a training checklist

DIAGRAM OF SEATING ARRANGEMENTS:

MATERIALS FOR PARTICIPANTS:

_____Name tags   _____List of participants

_____Pens   _____Handout material

_____Pencils   _____Textbooks

_____Notebooks   _____Evaluation forms

_____Filler paper   _____Upcoming seminar brochures

_____Legal pads

ADVERTISEMENTS: CONCLUSION OF MEETING:

  Publications and dates: Collect:

NEWS RELEASES: _____Evaluation forms

  Publications and dates: _____Excess materials

  Radio stations and dates: _____Audiovisual equipment

FIGURE 7–6
continued

ers—often have little choice but to look to off-site programs for training employees.

Third, the money available for training significantly determines training activities. On-the-job training becomes increasingly attractive as training budgets shrink. Many administrators are simply unable to afford off-the-job training offered by professional associations and private training groups, because the cost per participant of a three-day seminar, including travel, food, lodging, and seminar fee may run well into four figures. For the small, financially strapped organization, on-the-job training and low-cost off-the-job programs (such as university and govern-ment-sponsored courses) are often the only economically feasible training alternatives.

Program Implementation

The implementation of training brings the trainer and trainees together. Implementation involves careful planning and consideration, because the structure and environment of the program will also affect its overall success. To ensure that all necessary arrangements have been made for an off-the-job training program, some organizations use a checklist as an aid in planning the program. An example of this type of form is shown in Figure 7–6.

EVALUATION

The purpose of evaluation in the training process is to determine whether trainees actually learned new skills and attitudes or a body of knowledge as a result of the training program. In the eyes of the trainee, training ends when trainer and trainee go their separate ways. Upon returning to the job duties, the employee hopes to perform more effectively or, perhaps, be better prepared for promotional opportunities. When direct involvement in the program has ended, as far as the employee is concerned, training is over. But though the instruction has ended, the training process has not yet run its full cycle.

One very important question remains: Was the training effective? This often overlooked question involves the third and final phase of training—evaluation. Over $100 billion a year are spent nationwide on training activities, and the cost of training to large organizations can run into the millions of dollars. With training costs often consuming a sizable portion of the personnel budget, any prudent manager should ask: Are we getting our money's worth?

One popular evaluation strategy includes four different levels of evaluation. In fact, it comprises four separate evaluation strategies. The designer of this system, D. L. Kirkpatrick, advocates applying each level of evaluation to a program. He suggests measuring the participants' reaction, participants' learning, change in participants' behavior, and impact of the program upon organizational effectiveness.[21]

Level 1: How Did Participants React?

Throughout training, each trainee formulates opinions and attitudes about the overall effectiveness of the program. Perhaps the trainee is favorably inclined toward the content of the program but thinks that the trainer is too cold or too impersonal. Or the trainee may like the instructor but thinks that the program is too long or too short. Probably some aspects of the program will be both liked and disliked by the participants. At this level of evaluation, the trainee normally completes a questionnaire about the adequacy of training facilities, the skill of the trainer, the quality of the program content, and the relevancy of training techniques. After the questionnaires are tabulated and reviewed, the program's quality is judged on the basis of the overall responses.

This first level of evaluation is highly subjective, and training administrators must ensure that the participants are not responding favorably simply because they enjoyed the program or instruction. Figure 7–7 is a questionnaire used for evaluating training programs offered through the University of Louisville's Center for Management Development.

Level 2: What Did Participants Learn?

Training is an educational experience. Without exception, each participant is expected to learn some skill or some body of knowledge. This level of evaluation examines the extent of learning that took place as a result of training and involves more effort and sophistication than simply measuring the participants' reaction to training.

Learning is often assessed by testing a trainee both before and after a program. For example, if a program is designed to teach BASIC (a computer language), the trainee would be expected to score significantly higher on a test after training than before training. This second level of evaluation is easily conducted if tests are readily available to measure learning, but the absence of valid tests makes such evaluation difficult to administer. In addition, it is difficult to create a test

Participant Evaluation Form

	Very Little	Some	Quite A Bit	A Great Deal
1. To what extent did this seminar present material that met my needs?	1	2	3	4

Comments: _____

_____

	Very Little	Some	Quite A Bit	A Great Deal
2. To what extent were the handouts and reference materials appropriate for this program?	1	2	3	4

Comments: _____

_____

3. To what extent did the seminar leader:

	Very Little	Some	Quite A Bit	A Great Deal
a. present the material in an organized manner;	1	2	3	4
b. present important content;	1	2	3	4
c. solicit questions from the group;	1	2	3	4
d. make the seminar interesting;	1	2	3	4
e. provide a forum for group discussion?	1	2	3	4

Comments: _____

_____

4. How can this seminar be improved? _____

_____

_____

5. In the future, I would like to see the Center of Management Development offer the following seminars and workshops:

_____

_____

_____

Signed (optional)

FIGURE 7–7

An example of an evaluation form given to trainees at the end of a seminar.
This is an example of Level 1 evaluation.

to measure many behavioral skills, such as communication skills, interpersonal relations, and leadership skills.

Level 3: How Did Participants Change Behavior?

Participants in training are expected to learn a skill or body of knowledge that results in a positive change in job behavior. Learning time-management techniques, for example, is purely an academic—and costly—ability unless behavior is changed on the job, that is, unless learning is *applied*. The important question to ask concerning this third level of evaluation is whether learning was transferred from training to the job.

Level 4: What Organizational Goals Were Affected?

Ultimately, training is expected to result in a more effective organization. The fourth level of evaluation examines the impact of training on organizational goals of productivity, quality, and job satisfaction, as well as decreased turnover, accidents, and grievances. Although this level of evaluation is appealing in both theoretical and practical terms, it is not always possible or relevant to do. Where it is difficult to connect acquired skills directly to organizational goals, the administrator must implement a less-sophisticated evaluation strategy, that is, one of the other levels.

Applying Evaluation Strategies

Training effectiveness can be evaluated by the simple and uncomplicated process of measuring participants' reactions or by sophisticated, time-consuming strategies that compare training costs and benefits and measure organizational results. Flexibility should be the key to evaluating training programs; training personnel should apply the most sophisticated strat-

egy that is relevant and economically feasible.[22] Combining the four levels of training evaluation with a cost-benefit strategy would certainly enable management to ascertain whether a program was contributing to the effectiveness of the organization, but this approach would involve considerable time and money. At the very least, measurable objectives should be written during the assessment phase and evaluated after training has been completed. If the costs and benefits of training may be estimated with little difficulty, a cost-benefit analysis should be undertaken in addition to other strategies that may be implemented.[23]

PRINCIPLES OF LEARNING

As indicated earlier in this chapter, training is a form of education. Whether training takes place on or off the job, employees are expected to learn and apply new skills and abilities to benefit both the organization and its employees. Because training is a type of learning, trainers can benefit from applying certain principles of learning when designing and implementing training programs.[24] Because neglect or misapplication of principles of learning could easily result in training that fails to achieve results, it is important that trainees become familiar with the basics of adult learning.[25]

Motivation

Sometimes the need for training is not clear to employees. They may consider training a waste of time and resist being taken away from their jobs. One effective way to motivate trainees is to show employees how training will help accomplish organizational or personal goals.[26] These goals may include improved job performance and increased opportunities for promotion. Trainers should not automatically assume that all employees want to be trained, and training personnel must make trainees aware of how they will benefit from training.

Participation

Another way to inspire trainees is through active participation in the training process. Although direct involvement is an integral part of on-the-job training, off-the-job training—especially in the classroom—sometimes fails to consider this important principle of learning. Lecturing is certainly a valuable training technique, but reliance on lecturing alone will result in boredom and apathy. Active participation in the learning process through conferences and discussion enables trainees to become directly involved in the act of learning.

Feedback

Most college students want to know at all times where they stand in their courses. Professors sometimes joke that students demand test results before the ink on their papers has dried. Feedback on progress in courses reduces anxiety and lets students know what they must do to improve. Similarly, employees taking part in a training program want to know how they are doing and how their progress compares to training objectives. Giving the employee feedback is usually an informal part of on-the-job training, and close communication between the trainer and trainee helps the feedback process.[27] Feedback in short courses and seminars is usually less frequent, and normally consists of informal comments by the instructor or a discussion of the results of tests.

Organization

Training must be presented so that segments of materials build on one another; gaps, contradictions, or ambiguities in the material must be avoided. For example, in organizing a course about the operation and maintenance of a large printing press, the safety precautions that must be taken should be presented first. Next, the major parts of the machine and the functions of each should be explained. Then, a competent operator could be observed running the machine, followed by hands-on experience with several uncomplicated tasks, and so on. The final portion of training may involve preventive maintenance and minor repairs. In this example, each part of training flowed into another without inconsistencies or gaps.

Repetition

A wealth of behavioral research shows that frequent practice during training helps the learning process. Practice is important whether the skills being learned are technical (e.g., operating a lathe or computer) or behavioral (e.g., communication or interpersonal skills). Including practice sessions in technical training is relatively easy, but practicing interpersonal skills presents challenges to the trainer. Frequently, role-playing techniques are used to practice such skills.

Application

Time and time again graduates complain: "The real world is different from school. I can't apply the theories I learned in class." Similarly, job training is useless unless learning can be applied at work. This transfer-of-learning problem is particularly troublesome in off-the-job instruction. The problem is less severe for technical training (especially with the vestibule technique), because the technology used on the job should be identical to that used during training.

Minimizing transfer-of-learning problems poses a challenge to trainers. The trainer must study the job environment of prospective trainees and create settings that resemble each trainee's own job environment as much, as possible.[28] When constructing the training environment, consideration must be given to the physical setting, the technology of the work, intergroup and interpersonal relationships, and supervisory styles. The following are specific ways in which a positive transfer of learning may take place.[29]

- Maximize the similarity between the training and the job.
- Provide as much experience as possible with the task being taught.
- Provide for a variety of examples when teaching concepts or skills.
- Label or identify important features of a task.
- Make sure that general principles are understood.
- Make sure that the training is rewarded on the job.
- Design the training so that trainees can see its applicability.
- Use questions to guide the trainee's attention.

LEGAL ISSUES

As explained in chapter 5, the Civil Rights Act forbids discrimination in any term or condition of employment because of race, color, religion, sex, or national origin. The act covers training activities, just as it does any other personnel activity. Anyone involved in training employees must understand how EEOC guidelines apply.[30] In general, federal employment legislation affects training and development in five ways.[31]

- Training required to obtain a job or a promotion must be job related.
- Selecting employees for a training or de-

velopment program must not be done in a discriminatory manner.
- The training process itself must not be discriminatory. For example, to comply with federal legislation, AT&T redesigned pole climbing so that women could successfully complete the pole-climbing training course.[32]
- If career decisions are made by management on the basis of success during training, it should be shown that the training was job related. For example, if preferred job assignments are given to employees who performed effectively during training, a correlation between training success and subsequent job success should be shown.
- Preferential treatment for training minorities is legal if an affirmative-action program exists. Such treatment was supported in the Supreme Court case *United Steelworkers* v. *Weber* in 1978. The Supreme Court ruled that affirmative-action programs involving training *are* legal where evidence of racial imbalance exists. The Court also upheld the use of dual seniority systems for admitting employees into training.[33]

RESPONSIBILITY FOR TRAINING

Like many staff functions, responsibility for training is shared between line management and staff administrators. Effective training requires that line and staff are able to work closely together on all phases of the training process, and that both parties understand and recognize their shared authority.[34] Trainers or line managers unwilling to approach the training process cooperatively find that training does not help their organizations. Although the responsibility for various functions

TABLE 7–3
Line and staff responsibilities in the training process

Training Phases	Training Staff's Role	Line Management's Role
Phase 1—Analyzing needs and setting objectives	Conduct actual needs analysis; design tools that may be used to survey needs; determine personnel who need training; write training objectives.	Supply training personnel with necessary performance data; review and approve needs analysis and training objectives.
Phase 2—Designing the program	Determine the type of program and training techniques.	Review and approve training program and techniques; if applicable, perform on-the-job training (or supervise on-the-job training if conducted by a nonsupervisory employee)
Phase 3—Evaluating the program	Perform the evaluation; present findings to line management.	Supply trainer with necessary performance data; review evaluation results.

of training will differ from organization to organization, certain responsibilities are usually reserved for either line managers or staff personnel. Table 7–3 illustrates some of the training activities and responsibilities normally carried out by line and staff.

INTERNATIONAL HRM: TRAINING

In their book *Going International,* authors Lennie Copeland and Lewis Griggs tell how Motorola lost out in France to the Japanese when France's Thomson group chose the Oki Electric Industry Company to expand the French

company's semiconductor business. After working with Motorola for six years, a Thomson group executive said: "We may just have more in common with the Japanese than we do with the Americans." He explained, "We both attach great importance to form and style."[35]

How can a gap as large as the one between Motorola and Thomson be bridged? And what caused the gap in the first place? The reasons for the gap can be summed up in two words: *cultural ignorance.* Generally speaking, the American manager is hurried, abrupt, direct, and objective. Managers in most other countries have opposite traits. The

British and Japanese, for example, pay much more attention to the formalities of communication and interpersonal behavior than Americans do. They are less hurried, more personal, less direct, more diplomatic, and conscious of form and style as much as substance.

The best solution for closing the gap lies with intercultural preparation. The objective is not to make U.S. managers behave like people from other cultures; rather, the objective is to help managers (and other expatriates) cope with unexpected events in a new culture. In Saudi Arabia, for example, it is important for a male to avoid getting into an elevator when it is already occupied by a Saudi female. Intercultural preparation will enable expatriates to communicate better and to understand their hosts so that they can do business in an atmosphere of mutual respect, understanding and appreciation.

While there are a large number of training techniques available for preparing expatriates for overseas assignments, they can be categorized into five groups:[36]

1. Area studies, or documentary programs, which expose people to a new culture through written materials on the country's sociopolitical history, geography, economics, and cultural institutions.
2. Cultural assimilator, a programmed instruction method that exposes trainees to specific incidents critical to successful interaction with a target culture.
3. Language preparation.
4. Sensitivity training, in which people's self-awareness is increased.
5. Field experiences, or exposing trainees to mini-cultures within their own country during short field exercises.

For the most part, intercultural training is currently limited to providing general information about the target culture. For example, trainees will hear about religious practices, politics, and economics and currency facts, but will not often hear about differences that separate Americans from the rest of the world.

Evidence is only now appearing that intercultural training is "best achieved by making trainees aware of how their culture relates to a target culture at both general and specific levels."[37] Training that gives attention to problems of pace (e.g., time is money), conduct (e.g., form over substance), communication (verbal and nonverbal), and relationships (individual vis-à-vis group) will deliver a proper global orientation.

CONCLUSIONS AND APPLICATIONS

- Training is important in the achievement of organizational objectives. Through training, employees gain skills, abilities, knowledge, and attitudes that help them perform more effectively in present and future jobs. As such, training may be considered an investment in human resources that will provide many important benefits and returns to the organization.
- Training serves the organization by providing a number of important functions: (1) improving performance, (2) updating employee skills, (3) promoting job competency, (4) solving problems, (5) preparing for promotion, and (6) orienting new employees.
- The training process includes three distinct but related phases: assessment, training and development, and evaluation. Each phase is important for successful training and none can be omitted.
- Training involves close cooperation between line and staff personnel, and each must recognize their shared authority.

- Training must reflect certain principles of learning to be successful. The following principles hold: the trainee must be motivated, the trainee must get feedback on his or her progress, the material must be well organized, the trainee must be able to practice, and learning must transfer to the job environment.

- To be successful, training must be effectively managed. Applying the basics of good management to the training function, training administrators must promote cooperation between line and staff, receive top management support for the training function, ensure that personnel who conduct on-the-job training know how to train, and are rewarded for their training efforts, build flexibility into the scheduling process, recognize performance problems that can—and cannot—be solved through training, design an objective training evaluation system, and periodically audit the overall training function through an outside consultant.

- Training and development administrators should make every effort to evaluate training. Only through a sound evaluation will trainers obtain support from top management and show how training improves organizational effectiveness. Major training efforts should include the following levels of evaluation: reaction, learning, behavior change, and results. Evaluation should focus primarily upon how the trainer's performance improves after completion of training.

- Both line and staff trainers must be aware of the legal environment surrounding the training and development function. Race, religion, sex, color, national origin, or age must not be a factor in determining who receives training or who is selected to be developed for promotional opportunities. The only exception to this rule is where an organization has an approved affirmative-action program. In this case, preferential treatment for minorities may be legal.

CASE STUDY
Mayflower Manufacturing Corporation

Bob Cosenza is personnel manager for the Mayflower Manufacturing Corporation, a small manufacturer of gas heating equipment and fireplace fixtures located in Jeffersonville, Indiana. Mayflower employs about 150 people. The industry is very competitive, and Mayflower strives to keep costs at a minimum.

During the past several months, the firm lost three major customers because of defective products. Further investigation found that defects were running at 12 percent, compared to an overall plant standard of 6 percent. In discussion with Tim Metcalf, vice-president and general manager, Cosenza decided that the problem was not in engineering but in a lack of proper training in quality control for machine operators. Cosenza convinced Metcalf that a training program in quality control would reduce manufacturing defects to acceptable levels, and received Metcalf's approval to design and implement a program for operators. Because Metcalf was concerned that the course might cause production scheduling problems, Cosenza emphasized that the training program would consume no more than eight working hours and would be broken into four two-hour segments, with one segment held every week.

Cosenza began designing the course. First, he assessed training needs and created training objectives. Cosenza contacted James Farrell, an engineering professor from a nearby state university, about conducting the project. Farrell was highly regarded as an expert on quality control and had written a widely used text. Farrell gave Cosenza a brief outline of a prospective course, in which he included factors affecting product quality, production standards, inspection techniques, and safety procedures.

Next, Cosenza sent a memo to all first-line supervisors urging them to review their records, determine which employees had quality problems, and schedule these employees for the program. A copy of the professor's course outline was attached to the memo. As a final design step, Cosenza wrote the following training objective for the program: "To reduce the current levels of product defects to standard plant levels of 6 percent within a six-month period."

Farrell's training program consisted of lectures, discussions, case studies, and an occasional film. In preparing for the course, the professor drew heavily from his text, which was given to each participant, so that chapters could be assigned to prepare trainees for each session. Trainees spent a considerable portion of the training program discussing the questions and cases following the chapters in the text.

Because of a lack of space, the training sessions were held in the company's cafeteria. The training was scheduled to take place between breakfast and lunch, while cafeteria personnel were preparing the luncheon meal and washing breakfast dishes.

About fifty employees were expected to attend each session, but average attendance was closer to thirty. In checking, Cosenza heard many supervisors say, "If I let everybody go who's supposed to attend, I won't make my quota this week. Then I'll really be in hot water. Sorry, but production comes first." Cos-

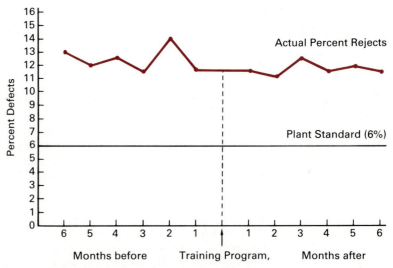

Product defects before and after the training program

enza also heard comments from some of the trainees that "the employees who really need to be here are still back in the shop."

Cosenza decided that the best way to evaluate the course would be to determine if the training objective was met by closely observing the product defects that occurred after the training program. The resulting chart of monthly trends for total product defects before and after the program was not encouraging.

Upon reviewing the evaluation data, Cosenza was dismayed and frustrated that the program had failed to achieve results. Six months after the program, defects were still running well above standard—almost as high as before the program was implemented. The pressure on Cosenza was really mounting; he was not looking forward to meeting with Metcalf to review the results of the training evaluation.

Questions

1. What are the flaws in the design of Cosenza's training program? What are the problems involved with each phase of the training process?
2. How would you assess training needs?
3. Would you write training objectives any differently?
4. Would you consider training methods and techniques other than those used by Farrell?
5. Would you make any changes in the training evaluation strategy?
6. Are problems in quality control always solvable by employee training? Discuss.

**EXPERIENTAL EXERCISE
Job-Instruction Training (JIT)**

Purpose

To participate in demonstrating or observing one of the most popular and effective forms of on-the-job training: JIT.

The Task

A student will be asked to demonstrate the JIT technique in teaching another student one of the following tasks (or one created by the instructor or students). Students not involved in the actual training should evaluate how effective the student trainer performs the JIT (observe closely to see if the trainer covers all four JIT steps). Following this exercise, your instructor will lead a discussion of JIT and on-the-job training in general.

1. Build and fly a paper airplane.
2. Self-defense techniques (disarm an armed attacker; karate technique, etc.).
3. Athletic endeavor: proper baseball hitter's stance, how to throw a forward pass, how to shoot a jump shot or free throw, and so on.

4. Tie a sailor's knot.
5. Popular (or 1950s or 1960s) dance: stroll, frug, hitchhiker, alligator, monkey, mashed potatoes, continental, hully-gully, twist, pony, locomotion, fly, hucklebuck, popeye, skate, bristol stomp, limbo, and so on. Your instructor may have to be the trainer on this one!

KEY TERMS AND CONCEPTS

Apprentice training

Audiovisual

Conference/discussion

Employee orientation

Job instruction training (JIT)

Job rotation

Learner-controlled instruction

Lecture

Legal issues in training and development

Levels of training evaluation

Off-the-job training

On-the-job training

Programmed instruction

Training evaluation

Training feedback

Training needs assessment

Training objectives

Training systems model

Transfer of learning

Vestibule

REVIEW QUESTIONS

1. What are the major purposes of training?
2. Of what value is a strong employee orientation program?
3. Describe the activities involved in each phase of the training.
4. Distinguish between on- and off-the-job training techniques, and describe the advantages and disadvantages of each.
5. Describe the various levels for evaluating training effectiveness.
6. Distinguish between line and staff responsibilities in carrying out training.
7. Discuss the principles of learning as they apply to the training function.
8. Discuss the management principles that are important to training.
9. Discuss the legal issues involved in training and development.

DISCUSSION QUESTIONS

1. Below are listed several training situations and several potential methods. How would you match them?

   A. Train fifty new employees to run a small printing press.

   B. Train twenty personnel administrators on the federal legislation as it applies to EEO hiring, firing, promotions, and training.

   a. Off-the-job university-sponsored seminar

   b. On-the-job instruction

   c. Apprentice training

   d. Vestibule training

   e. Programmed instruction

   f. Lecture

    C. Train one new receptionist how to run a copy machine and an automatic collating machine, and the proper techniques for handling incoming calls.

    D. Train six personnel interviewers in the techniques of employee interviewing.

2. Do you believe that the principles of learning are effectively applied by professors in college and university classrooms? Which principles are most effectively applied? Least effectively?

3. "Training is not a luxury. It is a critical process that has a major impact on organizational goals." Comment.

4. If you were a newly appointed training director for a medium-sized manufacturing company (750 employees), how would you communicate the importance of training to top management?

5. Some managers feel that training is more important in some organizations than others. For example, it could be argued that training is more important in a computer-components manufacturer than in a corrugated-box manufacturer employing approximately the same number of employees. Do you agree? Why or why not?

6. Prepare an orientation program for pledges selected by a fraternity or a sorority. What should be covered?

7. Often, college and university faculty are evaluated by means of a student opinion questionnaire upon completion of the course. What are the advantages and disadvantages of this type of evaluation procedure?

8. Think of a simple task that can be performed in the classroom, such as how to build a paper airplane. Using JIT, list the steps involved and train a classmate to perform the task. Ask for feedback from the trainee concerning your effectiveness as a trainer. Create another simple task and switch roles with your classmate.

ENDNOTES

1. Gareth R. Jones, "Socialization Tactics, Self-Efficacy, and Newcomers' Adjustments to Organizations," *Academy of Management Journal* 29, no. 2 (June 1986): 262–79.

2. See W. D. St. John, "The Complete Orientation Program," *Personnel Journal* (May 1980): 373–378. and D. C. Feldman, "A Socialization Process That Helps New Recruits Succeed," *Personnel* (May-June 1980): 183–91.

3. B. W. Marion and S. E. Trieb, "Job Orientation: A Factor in Employee Performance and Turnover," *Personnel Journal* (October 1969): 799–804.

4. Earl R. Gomersall and M. Scott Myers, "Breakthrough in On-the-job Training," *Harvard Business Review* (July–August 1966): 62–71.

5. In this chapter, the focus is primarily upon the training nonmanagement personnel. The development of managerial potential is discussed in the following chapter.

6. J. W. Newstrom and J. M. Lilyquist, "Selecting Needs Analysis Methods," *Training and Development Journal* 33 (1979): 178–82. See also K. N. Wexley and G. P. Latham, *Developing and Training Human Resources* (Glenview, IL: Scott, Foresman, 1981), chapter 3; F. L. Ulschak, *Human Resource Development: The Theory and Practice of Need Assessment* (Reston, VA: Reston, 1983).

7. Newstrom and Lilyquist, "Selecting Needs Analysis Methods," pp. 180–81.

8. William D. Hicks and Richard T. Klimoski, "Entry into Training Programs and Its Effects on Training Outcomes: A Field Experiment," *Academy of Management Journal* 30, no. 3 (September 1987): 542–52.

9. "On-the-job Training," *Personnel Management*, BNA Policy and Practices series (Washington, DC: Bureau of National Affairs, 1975), p. 205.

10. See T. Fransworth, *Developing Executive Talent* (London: McGraw-Hill, 1975).

11. Methods for modernizing the JIT method are discussed in Fred Wickert, "The Famous JIT Card: A Basic Way to Improve It," *Training and Development Journal* (February 1974): 6–9.

12. See F. E. Kuzmits, "Train Your New Managers with LCI," *Personnel* (April 1985), 69–72.

13. Wexley and Latham, *Developing and Training Human Resources*, p. 113.

14. G. Strauss, "Union Policies Towards the Admission of Apprentices," Reprint no. 357 (Berkeley, CA: University of California, 1971).

15. For a detailed discussion of the potential pitfalls of on-the-job training, see I. L. Goldstein, *Training: Program Development and Evaluation* (Belmont, CA: Wadsworth, 1974), pp. 142–43.

16. Criticisms of the lecture technique are outlined in B. M. Bass and J. A. Vaughan, *Training in Industry* (Belmont, CA: Wadsworth, 1966).

17. For details regarding the use of video tape in training, see Thomas F. Stroh, *The Uses of Video Tape in Training and Development*, AMA Research Study 93 (New York: American Management Association, 1969). A discussion of the various kinds of audiovisual techniques is included in Wexley and Latham, *Developing and Training Human Resources*, pp. 131–34. See also J. E. Holbrook, "How to Sell Your Ideas for Audiovisual Training Programs to Top Management," *Personnel Administrator* (July 1981): 47–54.

18. Effective applications of programmed instruction are discussed in J. Murphy and I. Goldberg, "Strategies for Using Programmed Instruction," *Harvard Business Review* (May–June 1964): 115–32. Applications of computer-assisted instruction are discussed in J. Patrick and R. Stammers, "Computer Assisted Learning and Occupational Training," *British Journal of Educational Technology*, 8, no. 3 (October 1977): 253–67.

19. Wexley and Latham, *Developing and Training Human Resources*, pp. 126–27.

20. The question of on-the-job training versus off-the-job training is dealt with in William McGehee and Paul Thayer, *Training in Business and Industry* (New York: Wiley, 1961), pp. 184–92.

21. D. L. Kirkpatrick, "Four Steps to Measuring Training Effectiveness," *Personnel Administrator* (November 1983): 19–26. See also K. Bunker and S. Cohen, "The Rigors of Training Evaluation, A Discussion and Field Demonstration," *Personnel Psychology* 30 (1977): 525–41; and K. Bunker and S.

Cohen, "Evaluating Organizational Training Efforts: Is Ignorance Really Bliss?" *Training and Development Journal* 32 (1978): 4–11.

22. Issues dealing with the complexities of training evaluation are discussed in J. S. Monat," A Perspective on the Evaluation of Training and Development Programs," *Personnel Administrator* (July 1981): 25–27.

23. For a detailed discussion of cost-benefit analysis of training evaluation, see T. Cullen et al., "Cost Effectiveness: A Model for Assessing the Training Investment," *Training and Development Journal* (January 1978): 24–27.

24. The relationship between training and learning principles is described in Craig E. Schneier, "Training and Development Programs: What Learning Theory and Research Have to Offer," *Personnel Journal* (April 1974): 288–300. See also Lee Hess and Len Sperry, "The Psychology of the Trainee as Learner," *Personnel Journal* (September 1973): 781.

25. An excellent overview of the importance of learning principles is given in Wexley and Latham, *Developing and Training Human Resources,* chapter 4.

26. The value of goal setting and its impact on motivation is discussed in G. P. Latham and E. A. Locke, "Goal Setting: A Motivational Technique That Works," *Organizational Dynamics* (Autumn 1979): 68–80.

27. Research shows that trainees will accept negative feedback as long as it is not seen as punitive. See D. R. Illgen, C. O. Fisher, and M. S. Taylor, "Consequences of Individual Feedback on Behavior in Organizations," *Journal of Applied Psychology* 64, no. 4 (May 1982): 349–71.

28. For a study involving the problems of learning transfer, see H. Baumgartel and F. Jeanpierre, "Applying New Knowledge in the Back Home Setting: A Study of Indian Managers' Adoptive Efforts," *Journal of Applied Behavioral Science* 8 (1972): 674–94.

29. Wexley and Latham, *Developing and Training Human Resources,* pp. 75–77.

30. C. J. Bartlett, "Equal Employment Opportunities in Training," *Human Factors* 20 (July 1978): 179–88.

31. Wexley and Latham, *Developing and Training Human Resources,* pp. 22–27.

32. E. I. Smith, *Small Climber Development* (Basking Ridge, NJ: AT&T, 1978).

33. For details of the Weber case, see J. Ledvinka, *Federal Regulation of Personnel and Human Resource Management* (Belmont, CA: Wadsworth, 1982), pp. 121–23.

34. D. F. Michalak and E. G. Yager, *Making the Training Process Work* (New York: Harper & Row, 1979), p. 3.

35. Lennie Copeland and Lewis Griggs, *Going International* (New York: Random House, 1985), p. xvii.

36. P. Christopher Earley, "Intercultural Training for Managers: A Comparison of Documentary and Interpersonal Methods." *Academy of Management Journal* 30, no. 4 (December 1987): 686.

37. Ibid., p. 697.

Chapter Eight

Management Development

Chapter Outline

DEVELOPMENT VERSUS TRAINING
Managerial Skills
The Development Process

ASSESSMENT
Current Needs
Long-range Needs

PROGRAM DESIGN
On-the-job Development
Off-the-job Development
Implementation

EVALUATION

WOMEN MANAGERS
Obstacles to Upward Mobility
Stereotypes About Women Managers
The Old Boy Network
Role Conflict
The Dual-Career Couple
Development for Women Managers

SUCCESSFUL PROGRAMS
Performance Appraisal
Long-range Planning
Top Management Support
Shared Responsibility
Environments for Change
Professional Staff
Problems of Management Development

INTERNATIONAL HRM: EMPLOYEE DEVELOPMENT JAPANESE STYLE

CONCLUSIONS AND APPLICATIONS

Chapter Objectives

1. To recognize the differences that exist between the training and management development functions.
2. To describe how both short- and long-range management development needs may be assessed.
3. To identify common on- and off-the-job management development techniques and to describe the conditions under which their effectiveness may be maximized.
4. To discuss the unique development problems faced by women managers and to recognize how the obstacles that women face in pursuing top management careers may be removed.
5. To describe the organizational conditions that are necessary for management development to be successful.
6. To understand the cultural differences in training employees by discussing how employee development takes place in Japan.

Getting Maximum Productivity from the Fast-Trackers

Most employees, after some training and experience on the job, develop into productive, reliable workers. Based on a learning curve, the majority of employees are fairly predictable in the amount of time training takes and in the rates of productivity that can be expected over their careers. But what happens with young managers who enter training like balls of fire, who learn everything quickly, then take on their job responsibilities, successfully, with astounding capabilities? Management of these people is complex, and often frustrating, but if dealt with properly, the payoff for their employers can be as great as the payoff for the employees themselves.

This type of employee, the "fast-tracker," is an achiever, eager to learn, highly self-motivated, and often at odds with the bureaucracy and red tape characteristic of most organizations. The fast-tracker is independent, likes work that is challenging, and is superbly productive, as long as nurturance and freedom are present. Fast-trackers present problems in that they do not need the same type of supervision as do other employees. This raises the suspicions and jealousies of other employees, and also makes insecure executives nervous about these "comers" stepping on toes to advance through the organizational ranks.

Assigning mentors is often an effective alternative for the nurturing that fast-trackers need. But to keep these employees working at their full potential, some other recommendations are:

- Making sure recruiters don't raise the expectations of fast-trackers too high in order to prevent disappointment
- Giving fast-trackers the opportunity to come in contact with high-level managers, thus providing role models while at the same time providing the chance for upper management to get to know the fast-trackers
- Permitting as much autonomy as possible as an incentive for innovation and creativity.

It is important, above all else, that fast-trackers not be allowed to just fend for themselves. When given directions and allowed to progress at top speeds, fast-trackers can become truly productive, enriching parts of organizational life.

Source: Adapted from "Getting Maximum Productivity from the Fast Trackers," *ABA Bank Personnel News* (February 1985): 3.

WHAT is the most critical element in an organization's success? There is little argument that the effectiveness of an organization depends upon the quality of its management. The absence of high-quality management guarantees, at best, mediocre organizational performance. At worst, the organization will not survive over the long run.

Management development is a systematic process by which persons acquire the skills, knowledge, and abilities to lead and manage organizations successfully. That process is critical in cultivating young, well-educated management trainees and then keeping them in the organization. A well-planned and well-implemented development effort can satisfy a number of organizational objectives:

To Ensure That Managers at All Levels Can Perform Effectively In highly complex and rapidly changing organizations, very few people are able to assume management jobs without adequate preparation. Through developmental activities, managers acquire the tools and techniques necessary to achieve their objectives.

To Avoid Managerial Obsolescence Organization obsolescence may be defined as not keeping pace with new methods and processes that enable employees to remain effective. Rapidly changing technical, legal, and social environments have affected the way managers perform their jobs, and management personnel who failed to adapt to these changes become obsolete and ineffective.[1]

To Provide for Managerial Succession A manager's career may involve six or seven promotions with a single organization. A manufacturing vice-president, for example, may have held positions of first-line supervisor, superintendent, assistant plant manager, plant manager, and assistant vice-president. Each new position requires a new set of skills, and developmental activities are often implemented to ease the transition into jobs involving greater responsibilities.

To Satisfy Personal Growth Needs Most managers are achievement oriented and need to face new challenges on the job. Management development can play a dual role by providing activities that result in both greater organizational effectiveness and increased personal growth.

DEVELOPMENT VERSUS TRAINING

Management development is closely related to the training of lower-level employees described in chapter 7. Both training and management development stress the processes by which employees acquire the skills that make them competent and prepare them for future responsibilities. Historically, the term *training* has been used to designate the acquisition of technically oriented skills by nonmanagement personnel. The term *management development* is normally associated with the methods and activities designed to enhance the skills of managers or future managers.

Training and management development are also different in other ways. First, management-development activities tend to focus on a broad range of skills, whereas training programs focus on a smaller number of technical skills. For example, a training program for printing-press operators would be designed to enable operators to upgrade technical skills, such as printing speed and accuracy. In contrast, a development program for printing managers may focus on a wide variety of interpersonal and managerial decision-making skills, such as planning, organizing, leading, communicating, motivating, and scheduling.

Second, management development is usually aimed at the long run, whereas training often concentrates on the short run. Developmental activities should take place continually throughout a manager's career and be an integral, ongoing part of the manager's job. In many organizations, a strong commitment to management development means that a manager may spend many weeks each year in both on- and off-the-job developmental programs and activities.

Management-development activities have received increased attention from management in recent years. This emphasis is illustrated by the estimated $30 billion spent annually for development programs in the United States alone. Development effectiveness is usually determined by (1) trainee satisfaction with the program, (2) knowledge or skills acquired, (3) behavior change (on the job), and (4) direct organizational improvements such as lower absenteeism, fewer accidents or grievances, and so on.

The attitudes, interests, values, and expectations of the trainees, as well as the program itself, can affect the success of the program. In particular, the trainees should be internally motivated to participate in the program, not forced by someone. Also, they should be externally motivated to transfer their learning to the job; management should provide a supportive climate which will allow them to practice new knowledge and skills.[2]

Managerial Skills

Each manager, regardless of the position in the hierarchy, uses a mix of technical, conceptual, and human-relations skills.[3] Figure 8–1 illustrates how the mix of these skills varies according to the level of the management job.

Technical skills include knowledge of equipment, work methods, and work technologies. These skills are much more important for first-level managers than for middle- and top-level managers. First-level managers often conduct on-the-job training for employees and troubleshoot problems with the organization's technology. In addition, some first-level managers are "working supervisors" and on occasion perform their subordinates' jobs.

Conceptual skill is the ability to view the organization as a whole and to coordinate and integrate a wide array of organizational func-

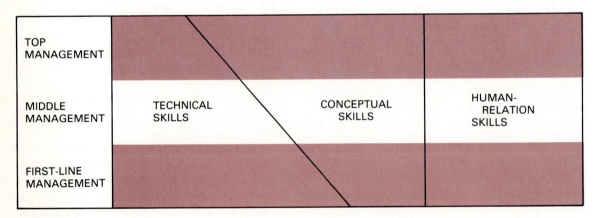

FIGURE 8–1
A different mix of skills is required at each level of management

tions, activities, goals, and purposes. For example, the manager of a large manufacturing plant must integrate production, marketing, engineering, and financial functions and objectives so that departmental and organizational goals are achieved. The need for conceptual skills becomes increasingly critical as the employee progresses from first-level management to top management.

One popular definition of manager is "one who accomplishes his or her work through others." In this sense, every manager is a leader, and *human relations skills* are equally important for managers on all organizational levels. Important human relations skills include the ability to communicate with employees, the ability to establish strong interpersonal relations, and the ability to build cooperative, satisfying relationships among work-group members.

The Development Process

In some organizations, management development takes place on a very informal basis. Managers may attend a seminar, join a professional association, or subscribe to professional journals in order to keep abreast of new tools and techniques. At times the manager may be solely responsible for his or her own development, and the organization may play a passive role in creating developmental activities. Such informal approaches to management development are seldom planned, coordinated, or evaluated on a systematic basis. Therefore, their overall effectiveness is open to question. A formal, planned approach is more likely to result in successful and satisfying management development for the organization and the individual.

The management-development process parallels the training systems model discussed in chapter 7. The three major phases of development are (1) assessment, (2) program design, and (3) evaluation.[4]

ASSESSMENT

Organizations are rare, indeed, in which each member of management is motivated, competent, and fully qualified. An organization's managers will possess widely varying skills, motives, and abilities. Some managers will consistently turn in a superlative performance, far surpassing organizational expectations. Others may fail miserably, indicating an obvious mismatch between the individual and the job. Another group of managers, perhaps the majority, will fall into above-average, average, or marginal categories. Managers in those categories—particularly managers in the last category—are obvious candidates for management development because they have room for improvement. Managers in the marginal category may be new managers, promoted from nonmanagement ranks, who are strong in technical skills but lacking experience and expertise in interpersonal and conceptual skills, such as leadership, communication, planning, organizing, and control. Many newly appointed first-level supervisors require a considerable amount of development early in their management careers. Other candidates for management development are obsolete managers, those who are out of touch with new managerial tools and techniques. Managers at any level or stage in their career can fall victim to obsolescence, particularly in highly dynamic industries such as the computer, communication, or health-care industries.

Current Needs

Current developmental needs of managers are assessed using several of the methods discussed in chapter 7. Considerable use is made of surveys, interviews, performance-appraisal data, and assessment centers. Because current developmental needs are tied directly to prevailing levels of performance, a well-planned and administered performance-appraisal system is important in an organization's assessment efforts. Personnel administrators must ensure that the organization's performance-appraisal system includes a description of developmental activities that may strengthen areas where performance problems exist. Further, by relating needs assessment to performance appraisal, the link between management development and managerial effectiveness becomes clear to the superior who conducts the appraisal. Figure 8–2 illustrates how needs assessment can be tied directly to the appraisal process.

Long-range Needs

Over a period of years, the composition of a company's management will undergo many significant changes. A small number of managers may be fired; others will quit to seek better opportunities elsewhere. Some will remain in the same position, and a certain percentage will climb the organizational ladder to upper-level management positions. For some, the ascent will be slow and arduous; for others, the climb will be swift and spectacular.

The likelihood of numerous management changes, particularly when the organizational objectives include rapid growth, creates career opportunities for the aspiring, motivated manager or the employee who strives to join management ranks. The processes of organizational growth and change create heavy demands for managerial expertise, and efforts must be made to ensure that managers are adequately prepared to assume their new jobs and responsibilities. Few managers are able to tackle increasingly challenging positions without exposure to formal developmental activities.

Assessing long-range development needs begins with a forecast of the demand for man-

agers. The prediction in the medium-sized company, for example, may be that the size of the management team must increase by 10 percent per year for the next five years to satisfy its optimistic plans for business expansion. To a significant degree, the company's continued growth hinges on its ability to ensure a continual supply of competent managers. Where will it get the managers it needs? Basically, two alternatives exist. First, the organization may hire new managers from the external labor market. External recruitment may prevent stagnation by bringing fresh, innovative ideas to the company. In addition, recruitment from the outside lessens the need for strong internal management development and its associated operating expenses. Second, the organization may choose to develop existing personnel, that is, follow a policy of promotion from within. Despite the advantages of external recruitment, most companies choose the second alternative.[5]

If the organization satisfies most personnel demands from inside, the promotion potential of current managers must be determined. Strengths and weaknesses are closely examined to predict how managers will perform if promoted. During this assessment, managers with considerable skills and exerience may be considered promotable without formal development. A certain percentage of managers may have "peaked" in their present jobs and thus be deemed unpromotable. Others may be judged promotable but only after further preparation. For the last group of managers, an analysis must be made of the specific skills and abilities they will need in order to be successful after being promoted.

To assist in making that analysis, some organizations prepare a personnel planning tool called a *management* or *executive succession chart*. Succession charts indicate successors for

THE KENTUCKY OIL COMPANY
ANNUAL PERFORMANCE REVIEW FOR THE PERIOD _____ to _____

EMPLOYEE: Herb Satterlee
JOB TITLE: Superintendent, Foundry

SUPERVISOR: Ralph Pedigo
DATE: January 14, _____

OBJECTIVES	RESULTS
1. Meet production quotas with 95% reliability	96.3% reliability
2. Reduce reject rate to 4% of all products manufactured	3.8% reject rate
3. Reduce waste and spoilage to 5% of materials used	4.3% waste and spoilage
4. Reduce unexcused absenteeism to 3% annually	5.2% unexcused absenteeism
5. Reduce employee turnover to 10% annually	19.5% annual turnover
6. Reduce grievances to 1 per 15 employees annually	3.7/15 employees

PRINCIPAL ACCOMPLISHMENTS

Herb has done an excellent job in increasing the foundry's productivity and reducing rejects, waste, and spoilage. His technical and problem-solving skills have been a great asset in accomplishing the objectives.

AREAS OF PERFORMANCE IN NEED OF IMPROVEMENT

Herb would benefit greatly from developing a more people-oriented leadership style. Also, Herb needs to sharpen his skills in employee motivation and corrective counseling procedures. With these improvements, there is a good chance that he will achieve his goals concerning absenteeism, turnover, and grievances.

SPECIFIC ACTIONS PLANNED TO IMPROVE PERFORMANCE

Herb and I have agreed that the following developmental activities will help him achieve personal and organizational goals:

1. Attend university-sponsored seminars on leadership, employee motivation, absenteeism control, and corrective counseling procedures.
2. Continual coaching on my behalf that focuses specifically on the reduction of employee-related problems.
3. Become a temporary member on the committee on employee absenteeism and turnover to learn more about these problems and how to control them.

Signature of Supervisor _____

Signature of Employee _____

Employee's Comments:

_____

_____

FIGURE 8–2

An example of how one company directly ties needs assessment to performance appraisal

each position in the management hierarchy and often combine current performance data with a judgment of promotion potential. Although the primary focus of a succession chart is upon an organization's current structure, the performance and promotion data on the chart are valuable for a growing company in determining promotions in the future. (Figure 8–3 illustrates the information normally contained on a typical management succession chart.

The assessment of development needs—whether to improve current performance or prepare employees for promotion—should re-sult in an individualized program for each employee. No two management jobs are exactly alike; nor is the performance of any two managers identical. An assessment of one plant supervisor may find weaknesses in counseling employees, conducting performance appraisals, and leading committee meetings. Another supervisor may need development in quality control, preventive maintenance, or interviewing skills. Yet a third supervisor, who is performing excellently, may be considered strong promotion material and thus may need development in various middle-management planning and control techniques.

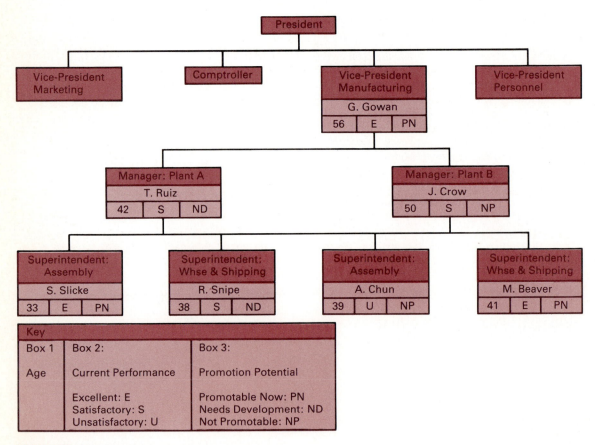

FIGURE 8–3
A typical management succession chart

Trends suggest that managers are participating in the design of their developmental activities, resulting in individualized programs that satisfy both organizational and personal needs. A sales manager, for example, may desire to attend a continuing education seminar on ''reducing executive stress'' or ''life planning.'' Although the immediate payoff to the organization may not be apparent in terms of increased sales or profits, the manager's boss may finance the seminar to acknowledge the individual's personal goals of growth and development. The argument can be easily made that personal growth enhances the manager's overall worth to the organization. In sum, a tailor-made program is likely to be more effective in maximizing both current and future organizational and personal goals.

PROGRAM DESIGN

The increased emphasis upon management development has led to a proliferation of management-development techniques, resulting in a wide choice of developmental strategies. Like employee-training activities, management-development techniques may be grouped into two broad categories: on-the-job techniques and off-the-job techniques.

On-the-job Development

How does one learn the difficult task of management? What may organizations do to ensure that their managers possess a healthy mix of technical, conceptual, and human-relations skills?

To turn young, inexperienced, but ambitious men and women into skilled and confident managers, most organizations put a great deal of time and trust into on-the-job development techniques. Managers essentially learn by doing: on-the-job techniques enable managers to practice management skills,

make mistakes, and learn from their mistakes under the guidance of an experienced, competent teacher. If properly planned and implemented, on-the-job techniques can be powerful teaching devices.[6] Most organizations make extensive use of these methods.[7]

Coaching   As in athletics, the organizational coach assumes the role of helper and teacher. The coach—often the new manager's boss—achieves developmental objectives by setting goals, by providing assistance in reaching goals, and by giving timely and constructive performance feedback. The coach answers questions, lets the employee participate in making decisions, stimulates the employee's thinking, and helps when problems occur.[8] Trust, cooperation, and mutual respect are imperative for coaching to be helpful. Properly done, coaching can be an extremely effective way to develop employee confidence and build strong supervisory-subordinate relations.[9]

Coaching, however, is not problem-free. According to psychologist Harry Levinson, coaching will fail unless there is a rapport conducive to learning created between the manager and the supervisor. Levinson suggests that the coach must be willing to give sufficient time to the development process and allow the subordinate to assume some risks and make mistakes.[10] Another problem is that coaching may perpetuate management styles in need of change. In such situations, coaching simply promotes managerial obsolescence and thus may do more harm than good.[11]

Job Rotation and Lateral Promotion
Job rotation enables an employee to learn new skills and abilities by performing different jobs and is commonly used at all organizational levels.[12] Job rotation for managers usually involves temporary assignments that may range from several months to one or more

years in various departments, plants, and offices. Job rotation for management trainees usually involves several short-term assignments that teach a variety of skills and give the trainees a greater understanding of how various work areas function. Management trainees are usually college graduates or employees promoted from the blue-collar or clerical ranks into first-level management.

Job rotation benefits management trainees in other ways. By being able to compare the rewards and satisfactions gained from working in different jobs and environments, management trainees get a feel for the kind of position they would like to fill on a permanent basis. For example, a manufacturing management trainee may spend a few months each in the assembly, warehouse, and shipping departments and then have a significant role in choosing which department is to be his or her permanent job assignment.

For middle- and upper-level management, job rotation serves a slightly different function. At these levels, job rotation assignments normally involve *lateral promotions,* which may last for one or more years. In contrast to a vertical promotion, where an employee takes over a supervisor's job, a lateral promotion involves a move to a different work environment so that the manager may develop competence in general management decision-making skills. Much like the short-term job rotation assignment, a lateral promotion allows the manager to be exposed to many organization operations and management styles.[13]

Although both lateral promotion and short-term job rotation enable managers and management trainees to broaden their organizational knowledge and develop decision-making skills, these methods are not without flaws. First, some organizations need managers with specialized skills in technical areas rather than in general management skills. Second, for upper-level managers, job rotation and lateral promotion often involve an expensive and emotional move to another part of the country. Although companies generally bear such moving costs, managers are forced to pull up stakes, leaving behind close personal relationships and other community ties. More and more, managers are turning down promotions that involve relocating to a new city. Promotions were accepted with little question years ago, but one study showed that 42 percent of the companies sampled employed managers who had refused transfers.[14] Third, a job rotation or lateral promotion may force managers to take short-term views of their jobs. For example, a colonel assigned to battalion headquarters for a one-year tour of duty may focus on short-range programs with immediate payoffs and thereby neglect planning and policy decisions that would not generate benefits for three or four years—long after the officer has been reassigned.

Mentoring A mentor is an experienced, productive manager who relates well to a new employee and facilitates his or her personal development.[15] Mentoring is often used with young professional employees who have high career aspirations. Their mentors are usually eight to fifteen years older and are considered successful. Mentorships may be formally established by the organization as part of an employee's orientation program, or they may form informally. Formal mentor programs are increasing in popularity and usually receive top management support and participation. Typically, a program emphasizes the development of realistic expectations by the protege, scheduled meetings between the mentor and protege, and stated topics to be discussed.[16]

The possible benefits of mentoring to both the employer and protege include the following:

- The mentor may advance the career of the protege by nomination for promotion or sponsorship of membership.
- The mentor may provide the protege visibility in the organization or profession through joint efforts.
- The mentor may protect the protege from controversial situations and provide coaching by suggesting work strategies.
- The mentor may provide counseling with regard to work and personal problems.
- There is better job performance and longer service with the organization from proteges who develop more skills and self-confidence.

While women can benefit from mentoring the same as men, female mentors are often lacking. In many organizations, there are few women in mentor positions. And unfortunately, the development of cross-gender mentorships has been inhibited by a number of factors.[17]

Committee Assignments A great deal of a manager's time (many think too much time) is spent in committees, which permeate all levels of management. Committees are formed to solve current problems, plan for the future, and discuss and act upon issues critical to the organization.

Serving on a committee and participating in decision making enable a manager to strengthen a variety of skills. For example, a newly appointed production foreman may be asked to formulate recommendations to solve a quality-control problem. While working on this committee assignment, the foreman may gain a greater understanding of the issues involved in quality control, meet and discuss the problem with personnel from other departments, and develop an appreciation for good working relationships among quality-control inspectors, production managers, supervisors, and line employees.

Off-the-job Development

In most organizations, management development takes place both on and off the job. Off-the-job activities enable a manager to get away from the day-to-day pressures of the work environment and devote full attention to strengthening managerial skills. Off-the-job development often occurs in formal courses and seminars, conducted either in-house or off-site by a university, consulting group, or nonprofit association, such as the American Management Association, American Society for Training and Development, or American Society for Personnel Administration.[18]

The length and breadth of these courses vary considerably. A one- and two-day seminar normally focuses on a specific management technique or problem, such as time management or executive speaking. One- or two-week courses may focus on a wide variety of managerial methods and processes. For example, the American Management Association's popular five-day course "Developing Supervisory Leadership Skills" covers leadership, communication, discipline, employee development, job satisfaction, and morale.

Some universities sponsor advanced management programs that closely resemble a highly concentrated master's degree program in business administration. One of the most popular courses of this nature is the Harvard Business School's Advanced Management Program. Other colleges and universities offering similar programs include the University of Chicago, UCLA, Wharton, Carnegie-Mellon, Indiana University, and Stanford.

Several large, progressive organizations have created in-house educational programs to satisfy their needs for skilled management talent. Many corporate programs, which closely resemble those sponsored by universities, offer managers and executives instruction in timely issues and topics involving management theory and practice. Large companies that have established their own management development centers include IBM, General Motors, Exxon, and General Electric.

The organization with the greatest management-development need is the largest single employer in the United States—the federal government. With millions of civilian and military employees to manage, a development program is imperative, and the federal government offers extended management programs for managers in both the civilian and military sectors. Most of this training takes place at the U.S. Army War College and the Federal Executive Institute. Some occurs at smaller training facilities located throughout the world.

Managers who participate in off-the-job programs are exposed to a variety of teaching techniques. Several of the techniques, especially lecture, conference/discussion, and audiovisual devices, are quite similar to techniques used in training, as was discussed in chapter 7. The techniques discussed here are exclusively or primarily used in the development of managers.

Case Study   A case study is a written description of an organizational problem. The case method was developed at the Harvard Business School in the 1920s and remains a popular teaching technique there and in many other universities. Case studies require participants to identify and analyze specific problems, develop alternative courses of action, and recommend the best alternative. A case study may be analyzed by individuals or groups. In development programs, participants often form teams to study cases and then present their recommendations to other teams for discussion and analysis. Cases may cover a wide variety of typical management topics, including business policy, finance, marketing, and personnel.

The primary purpose of the case study is to enhance problem-solving skills.[19] Partici-

pants practice defining problems, generating solutions, and deciding upon optimal solutions. Working in a group gives members insight into group dynamics and group decision-making processes. For maximum effectiveness, cases should be written to simulate a manager's real-life problems, constraints, and working environment.[20]

Role Play   During role play, participants act out, or play the role, of those involved in an organizational problem. Usually there are no scripts, and participants have limited data on which to base their roles. For example, assume that managers are receiving instruction in the use of employee counseling. One member of a group may play the role of an employee who has been tardy and absent several times. Another member plays the role of the employee's supervisor. With as much realism as possible, the two players act out their roles in front of the instructor and other participants. Discussion normally follows role play, which lasts only a few minutes. Role play may be videotaped and viewed in segments for an in-depth analysis of the roles and how they were acted out.

The primary goals of role playing are to analyze interpersonal problems and develop human-relations skills. Role play is commonly used to develop skills in interviewing, job counseling, disciplining, performance appraisal, sales, and other job duties that involve interpersonal communication.[21] For this technique to be successful, the instructor must ensure that the situations are credible and that each role player performs realistically.[22]

Management Games   Management games are designed to replicate conditions faced by real organizations and usually involve competing teams that both make decisions concerning planning, production, finance, and control of a hypothetical organization.[23] The winner is typically the team that achieves the highest net profit at the completion of the game. More complex games involve the use of a computer.[24] In those games, teams receive a printout detailing the overall impact of their decisions on the effectiveness of the enterprise.

A number of benefits may be derived from playing a management game. First, as a team member, the participant is able to study group dynamics: conflict resolution, communication patterns, and development of interpersonal relationships. Second, the trial-and-error process of game playing enables participants to learn from mistakes without jeopardizing a real organization. Third, participants can examine how various areas of an organization interrelate—how advertising expenditures affect sales volume or how various levels of research affect long-range profits. Finally, participants find that games are fun and interesting. Team players eagerly await the computer printout, which disinterestedly judges the strengths and weaknesses of their collective decision making. The winning team often takes great pride and satisfaction in victory.[25]

In-basket Exercise The in-basket exercise is designed to develop the analytical and problem-solving skills of lower-level managers. The technique centers on a series of hypothetical problems that a supervisor may find in a typical in-basket. Examples of items the in-basket may contain include:

- A letter from an EEOC representative who wants to talk about alleged discrimination in the work unit.
- A note from an employee who wants a six-week leave of absence to stay with his sick mother. Without his work, production goals probably would not be met.
- A note from a trusted and valuable employee who will quit if she doesn't get a 10 percent raise.

- A letter from the personnel director stating that he is unable to find qualified candidates for five vacant positions in your work unit.

The in-basket exercise forces the trainee to make immediate decisions and to determine priorities. The participant must quickly think through alternative courses of action, select the best solution, and determine how it should be implemented. After completing a series of in-basket exercises, participants discuss their decisions and receive feedback on their performances from the instructor.

Sensitivity Training Through sensitivity training (also called *T-group*—"T" for training), individuals become more aware of their feelings and learn how one person's behavior affects the feelings, attitudes, and behaviors of others. An open and honest "no holds barred, tell it like it is" discussion of participants' conduct is an important part of the training experience. Perhaps for the first time, many participants learn how their behavior is perceived by others. For some participants the experience is a tremendous emotional high; others leave the training session depressed and demoralized. The general goals of sensitivity training include:

- To become more competent in personal relationships.
- To learn more about oneself as a person.
- To learn how others react to one's behavior.
- To learn about the dynamics of group formation, group goals, and group growth.

Sensitivity training has many opponents.[26] They argue—justifiably—that there is very little documentation that performance in the organization improves as a result of participation in sensitivity training. Some opponents contend that openness, sensitivity, and trust are not always productive or appropriate behavior in organizational situations. Further, some opponents assert that innermost feelings and beliefs are highly personal and that sensitivity training is an invasion of privacy.

Does sensitivity training result in greater managerial effectiveness? Research has proven inconclusive.[27] According to the studies, sensitivity training can produce such behavioral changes as greater openness, trust, and respect for the feelings of others. It has not, however, been demonstrated that behavioral change has led to more effective job performance. Because its impact upon an organization's effectiveness is questionable, sensitivity training has lost much of the popularity that it enjoyed in the past.

Membership in Professional Organizations   One informal way to keep abreast of new theories, principles, methods, and techniques in a field is through membership in a professional organization. Regardless of the occupation or interest, there is probably a group that meets periodically to discuss the important issues that apply. Hundreds of such associations exist, with memberships varying from a handful to several thousand.

Membership in a professional organization helps develop managers in various ways. During monthly meetings and at conventions, members socialize with their colleagues, exchange ideas, and discuss common problems. They listen to a variety of speakers and learn about advances in their field. Many companies encourage their managers to join professional organizations and to attend meetings regularly. Often the company pays membership dues and travel expenses to annual meetings. As an additional benefit, some large professional organizations publish journals for their membership. Examples include the American Society of Personnel Administration's monthly *Personnel Administrator*, The Industrial Management Society's *Industrial Management*, and the American Management Association's *Management Review*, *Supervisory Management*, and *Personnel*. These journals feature articles about new ideas, trends, issues, and problems in the management and personnel fields.

Behavior Modeling   Behavior modeling is a classroom-oriented technique generally used to teach problem-solving skills to first-level supervisors. The technique focuses on individual "skill modules" that address a common problem most supervisors face, such as absenteeism, tardiness, or employee orientation. Each module contains the following elements.[28]

- Trainers introduce the topic (e.g., employee orientation).
- A model of effective supervisory behavior is illustrated, usually by film or video tape. A discussion of key learning points follows the film.
- The training group discusses the model of effective behavior.
- Trainees practice desired behaviors, using role play, as other trainees observe (each participant acts out the desired behaviors).
- Trainees receive feedback on the effectiveness of their behavior from the observers.

Studies of the effectiveness of behavior modeling generally show support for the technique. In two studies involving trainees at AT&T and General Electric, supervisors who had received training through behavior modeling performed their jobs significantly better than those who received no training.[29] Behavior can change in a positive way when trainees are given a model to follow, are provided with a set of learning points, are given an opportunity to practice and perfect skills, are provided feedback on their progress in acquiring new skills, and are given praise when new skills are learned.[30]

Assessment Center   The assessment center is an off-the-job technique that requires managers to participate in activities designed to identify their job-related strengths and weaknesses. The technique is used primarily as a device to select new managers, but it has seen increasing use with existing managers.[31]

During an assessment center, which normally lasts one and a half or two days, a small group of six or seven participants are observed and evaluated by trained assessors, who evaluate the participants on qualities considered important for effective management. Some of those qualities may include oral and written communication skills, sensitivity, ambition, energy, planning ability, and decision making. Exercises used to measure and evaluate those qualities include interviews, leaderless group discussions, role play, and in-basket exercises. Following the exercises, participants normally receive detailed and specific feedback about their performance and their developmental and growth needs. Suggestions for development may include such off-the-job activities as courses, readings, and seminars and such on-the-job activities as task-force and committee assignments, coaching, and counseling.[32]

Implementation

Implementation of a manager's individual developmental plan will vary considerably, depending on the number and kind of skills that need improving and the particular stage of a manager's career. Classroom activities, such as seminars and courses, usually last for a day or two—several weeks at the most. Coaching, job rotation, lateral promotion, understudy assignment, committee assignments, and professional memberships may encompass months or, perhaps, several years. Lateral promotions and transfers, for example, may consume a major portion of a manager's entire career. For such long-term developmental strategies, the distinction between management development and the manager's actual job duties is blurred.

Development should be viewed as a permanent part of the manager's job rather than as a knee-jerk reaction to the problems of aspiring young managers or obsolete executives. Personnel administrators should work with line managers to create and implement developmental plans that prevent managerial performance problems. Progressive organizations view management development as a continuous process, not simply a one-shot program or activity. Strong, competent managerial talent rarely results from a smattering of one- or two-day seminars every year or disjointed on-the-job coaching.

EVALUATION

Management development should be viewed as an investment that will return dividends in the form of a stronger and healthier organization. Because an investment in management development can involve significant time and money, efforts should be made to determine whether or not certain expenditures are justified. Perhaps managerial skills could be obtained more efficiently in other ways—for example, through a policy of bringing in experienced managers from the outside. The effective personnel administrator will make every effort to ensure that development dollars are wisely spent.[33]

Strategies for evaluating management development programs are basically the same as those for evaluating employee training, as discussed in chapter 7. Evaluative strategies should focus on measuring four levels of evaluation through the analysis of participant reaction, participant learning, changes in participant behavior, and changes in organizational effectiveness.[34] Evaluating management development by examining these four levels would certainly enable the personnel executive to make a valid judgment of the worth of the developmental activities. But training personnel often feel that such a strategy is too time-consuming and costly for all management-development activities. Research shows that most organizations measure participants' reactions but fail to assess changes in the manager's job behavior.[35]

WOMEN MANAGERS

Since the beginning of the industrial era, female employees have actively participated in all sectors of the economy. But traditionally, women have been restricted almost exclusively to low-paying, monotonous jobs involving little responsibility and few opportunities for advancement. Rarely did a woman's role in an organizational setting include management, and when it did, her pay was often lower than that of her male counterpart. Even though equal employment opportunity and affirmative-action programs have led to more women managers, statistics indicate that women are still lower paid and underused in management positions. In 1988 women made up 48 percent of the total labor force. But only 16 percent of all professional employees were women, and females constituted only 9 percent of all executive, administrative, and managerial employees.[36] One need only peruse the photos of management and board members in corporate annual reports to see which sex dominates the executive suites.

Obstacles to Upward Mobility

The underrepresentation of women in high-level managerial ranks, sometimes referred to as the *glass ceiling* because of the invisible bar-rier that blocks women from top jobs, results from a variety of problems and issues. To a large extent, these problems stem from both long-held cultural attitudes and organizational practices.

Stereotypes About Women Managers

One set of obstacles are the stereotypes of women that workers frequently encounter in the world of work. Generally, these stereotypes hold that a woman's place is in the home and that women lack the mental and physical makeup to perform a management job. Negative stereotypes of working women include the following:[37]

- Women work merely to supplement the family income; they do not need equal pay or benefits because men support families.
- Women do not want to be managers because it would involve an extra workload, which would interfere with family obligations.
- Women are unable to meet certain work demands for emotional toughness and stability because of their psychological makeup. They tend to take things personally, to respond to anger and frustration by crying, and to be insufficiently hard-nosed in making difficult decisions.

There are several strategies for dealing with the negative stereotypes that many female managers must confront. The first is a vocal and assertive stance by top management that recognizes the workplace rights of minority employees. Top management must enact a policy which demonstrates that the organization is serious about equal opportunity for women and that antifemale attitudes will not be tolerated. Second, training and development for all managers should focus on the legal rights of women, with specific emphasis upon the dos and don'ts of managing and promoting women. Third, employees whose antifemale attitudes result in unsatisfactory behavior should be counseled and, if the unsatisfactory performance continues, disciplined. This action sends a message throughout the organization that antifemale stereotypes, or at least the behaviors that often result from them, are inappropriate and may possibly lead to disciplinary action.

The Old Boy Network

Another prevalent obstacle to the development of women managers is the old boy network, the informal advice and assistance that often facilitate upward mobility into management ranks. The fast track on which many male managers have swiftly traveled has been greased by membership in an old boy network. For example, at a Rotary Club luncheon, one member may ask another if he is interested in a job opening. By belonging to this club, the aspiring manager becomes privy to inside information: who to know, important positions coming up, job assignments that count, and other valued information that increases both visibility and credibility. One particularly important aspect of the old boy network is the patronage of a sponsor or mentor, who may open the way to upper management ranks. Because of the paucity of females among top executives, few women are able to provide guidance and advice to women at lower management levels. Many women, however, are forming their own career-related information communication systems through *networking*. Networking provides a means to disseminate and collect valued information on jobs available, jobs becoming available, and other information helpful to career-oriented women.

Role Conflict

How does a good manager behave: masculine, feminine, or androgynous (possessing both masculine and feminine characteristics)? Several studies show that good managerial behavior is described—by males and females alike—in such masculine terms as self-reliant, independent, assertive, forceful, and willing to take risks.[38] Obviously, perceptions that describe appropriate managerial behavior in masculine terms create an inevitable conflict that focuses on the following issues: First, because good managers are defined in masculine terms, should women seek other, more traditionally "feminine" careers such as nursing or teaching? And second, do the research results suggest that women should adapt to masculine standards, as did the women in one study?[39] Perhaps in time, as more and more women reach the ranks of upper management, the characteristics of effective managers and executives will take on less of a masculine definition and more of an androgynous one.[40]

The Dual-Career Couple

A dual-career couple is defined as "two persons engaged in a lifestyle in which each individual pursues a separate career role along with a committed love relationship."[41]

The good news about this relationship is that each partner of the dual-career couple is able to pursue his or her career goals while experiencing a satisfying personal relationship with the other that often includes marriage and children. The dual-career couple, at least in theory, eschews the traditional 1950s Ozzie and Harriet family in which the husband "brings home the bacon" while the wife assumes total responsibility for managing the household and raising the children.

More good news for the dual-career couple: financial independence. The combined income of a husband and wife who are both managers, professionals, or executives may easily total $100,000 a year, and possibly much more. With that kind of income, the material dreams of the dual-career couple are often possible: a BMW and a Volvo station wagon, a four-bedroom, three-bath house in the suburbs, tuition for the children at the finest private schools and colleges, closets full of designer clothes, frequent weekend trips and annual vacations to Europe, and perhaps even a vacation home on a lake or in the mountains.

Is it too good to be true for the dual-career couple? Perhaps. The personal and organizational problems of the dual-career couple, particularly for the female on the fast track, are well documented.

First, the potential personal problems:[42]

- Family versus work: Who assumes responsibility for raising the children when both the husband and wife hold professional jobs that may require working evenings and weekends? More specifically, who stays home when the children are sick? Who attends the PTA meetings? Who helps with the homework in the evenings?

- "Baby panic": Should the dual-career couple have children, and if so, when? Sometimes referred to as the "thirty-year baby panic," this problem is inevitably faced by professional couples who postpone having children in their twenties for the sake of their careers.

- Managing the household versus work: Who shops for the groceries? Who washes the dishes and takes out the garbage? Who assumes the basic responsibility for managing the house?

- Relationship conflicts: Is the dual-career couple able to rise above the tensions that might occur when the wife's career—and salary—leap ahead of the husband's?

Second, the organizational problems:

- Inflexible working hours: The traditional working hours of 8:00 A.M. to 4:30 P.M. often conflict with child-raising responsibilities, which may require picking up the children from school at 3:30 or 4:00 P.M.

- The "trailing spouse": What happens when the husband or wife is offered a promotion that requires relocation to another city? The trailing spouse is the spouse who is either forced to remain behind or to move and seek a new job. Both options present problems. If the trailing spouse keeps his or her job and stays behind, the dual-career couple is forced into a commuting marriage on weekends, assuming that the marriage survives. But if the trailing spouse follows, he or she must begin a job search and face the prospect of finding a job which is not as challenging or financially rewarding as the one left behind.

Today, more and more companies are helping the dual-career couple manage both the personal and organizational problems they often face. These coping strategies include a loosening of transfer and nepotism policies, and seminars and workshops for the dual-career couple. The career problems of dual-career couples are dealt with in more detail in chapter 9.

Development for Women Managers

Each member of an organization must recognize the responsibility to eliminate inequities that may exist for female employees. EEO is not solely the personnel department's job; it is the responsibility of every worker, regardless of position or level. Management-development personnel, however, are in a unique position to push for true EEO opportunities for employees of both sexes. Some of the ways management-development administrators can facilitate the movement of women into management ranks include the following:

- Ensure that performance-appraisal data used for development decisions are free of bias against women. For example, if a woman's performance appraisal includes statements such as "not fit for promotion into management" or "performing unacceptable work as a manager—recommend demotion to a nonsupervisory role," be sure that the reasons for these assessments are valid.

- Include a presentation about prejudice and discrimination in all developmental programs for new managers and supervisors. Programs should include discussions of relevant EEO guidelines, what discrimination is and how to avoid it, and how to conduct fair and impartial performance appraisals.
- Implement special programs that deal solely with discrimination and EEO. Examples are "Positive Approaches to EEO and Affirmative Action," "What First-line Supervisors Must Know About EEO," and "Developing Minority and Female Employees."
- Create programs especially for aspiring women managers. Studies of the problems of women managers suggest that women would greatly benefit from developmental activities that focus on their particular problems and needs. For example, it has been stated that new women managers need to enhance their self-esteem, to learn new behaviors for managing interpersonal conflict, and to develop team-building skills. They also often need help with career planning.[43]

SUCCESSFUL PROGRAMS

Modern facilities, expensive equipment, abundant staff administrators, and an ample training budget will not guarantee the success of management-development efforts. The true value of management development lies in its results, including a steady stream of competent, motivated managers able to meet current and future organizational goals. To achieve these results, a number of conditions must be satisfied.

Performance Appraisal

The developmental needs of current managers are most effectively pinpointed through objective, results-oriented appraisal techniques. A vague, subjective appraisal system, such as a graphic rating scale, will offer little help in uncovering specific deficiencies in managerial skills and abilities. Results-oriented systems, such as MBO, remove many of the obstacles in conducting a thorough, valid assessment program.

Long-range Planning

Management-development activities must be based on future needs of managers and on the skills required to fulfill job responsibilities. For example, potential changes in technology, government legislation, and other internal or external variables must be analyzed and incorporated into developmental activities to prevent managerial obsolescence in the future. Ideally, administrators responsible for planning development also play an active role in the organization's long-range planning.

Top Management Support

An organization's management development must receive a strong endorsement from top management. Without this support, development programs may be viewed as a form of entertainment or a second-rate, marginally effective activity. Support also means a sufficient budget to carry out a full program of development. The tendency to slash development activities during hard times must be avoided.

Management-development personnel, however, should not expect an automatic

Stay Away from Politics

Training for all staff who will be personally interacting with non-Americans should include two elements of political preparation. First, the staffer should be briefed on the politics of the country to which he or she will be assigned or with whose nationals he or she will be working. Basic governmental structure, names of key leaders and parties, and the principal issues of the day are important for executives, managers, and other interface staffers to know.

Second, training should be provided in what those people think of the United States, both as a society and as a political power. I was in the United Kingdom when Britain, France, and Israel invaded Egypt in 1956. Incredulous that such an outdated imperial policy could have been adopted, I pestered my British friends with provocative questions. Their response was to explain the countries' action without including their own political views of it. I first began to learn how to handle cross-national tensions on a personal level.

The Bay of Pigs taught me an important lesson: irrespective of how I felt about the policies that led to that disaster, as an American I had to represent those policies to my Indian hosts. I learned to suppress my political opposition and to interpret the events judiciously for those who were curious. I have since returned to the United Kingdom following our involvement in the Vietnam War, and while our government was funding and training Contras in Nicaragua. Each of these was difficult to handle under provocative, somewhat unfriendly questioning.

From these events, I also learned a lesson that everyone should learn: be ready for the obvious hostile questions, but be ready for the second and third questions, too, for the people who are interested will ask you and they tend to be very well informed about the United States.

Source: Adapted from Henry Ferguson, *Tomorrow's Global Executive* (Homewood, IL: Dow Jones–Irwin, 1988), pp. 66–67.

stamp of approval by top management. This support must be earned by demonstrating how programs are contributing to the goals of the organization. Because of the importance of the bottom line, demonstrating the cost-effectiveness of development may well be the most productive way to gain the support of top management. Unfortunately, that form of evaluation is the most difficult to demonstrate.

Shared Responsibility

Successful management development involves a cooperative effort. The company, the managers, and their bosses all share in the responsibility for development. The employer has a responsibility to provide a supportive environment and resources for development, such as company-paid courses and seminars as well as tuition assistance. Supervisors should encourage managers to take advantage of development resources the company provides. Supervisors can also create meaningful on-the-job activities, such as job rotation and the assignment of special projects. Finally, development will not take place unless managers are self-motivated. Managers cannot be forced or pressured to develop themselves. Each must recognize the link between management development and the achievement of organizational and personal goals.

Environments for Change

During development, managers are often exposed to innovations that may involve unfamiliar techniques or new ways to approach the decision-making process. For development to be fully realized, managers must be able to apply new skills and abilities in the work environment. Therefore the work environment must be receptive to new ideas and techniques, allowing managers to depart from well-established but ineffective ways. Problems of transfer of learning become significant when managers attempt to apply new ideas in rigid, uncompromising environments.

One classic problem of transfer of learning involved a widely used human-relations training program for supervisors. Testing before and after the program revealed that supervisors underwent an attitude change about people-oriented leadership. Supervisors' on-the-job behavior changed, however, only when

their new attitude was supported by their bosses.[44]

In the end, the environment has a significant effect on performance. Management development cannot be effective if it conflicts with existing norms, values, beliefs, and customs. In assessing needs and designing activities staff members must pay close attention to conditions at the work place and ensure that what is learned can be transformed into on-the-job behavior.

Professional Staff

During the 1970s and 1980s, the design of development programs was revolutionized. There are now new technologies for needs assessment and program evaluation, and there has been a virtual explosion of new developmental techniques and devices. Further, management development has expanded to include managers from all organizational levels. Thus, management-development professionals must be able to design programs to strengthen a variety of managerial skills and abilities not only for supervisory personnel but also for top management and executive personnel.

Management development has matured in other ways. The modern management-development staff often not only designs but also implements developmental activities. Thus, those professionals must possess strong conceptual skills while being technically able to conduct development activities. Training professionals must be familiar with the great variety of developmental activities available and be able to select activities to satisfy myriad development needs.

In short, management-development personnel must be talented, competent professionals. They must know their own job as well as the jobs of managers at all levels of the organization. These professionals must also understand how the culture of an organization's employees affects managerial decisions and be able to design programs that complement that culture—rather than clash head-on with unbending norms, values, and customs.

An organization creates a professional management-personnel staff primarily by recruiting and hiring individuals with a proper blend of education and job experience. A sound professional base would be provided by a degree in personnel or a related field. Naturally, the staff must continually develop themselves to avoid obsolescence within their own ranks. They must keep abreast of advances in developmental technologies, methods, and processes. Membership in professional associations, such as the American Society for Training and Development and the American Society for Personnel Administration, help achieve this goal. Also, short courses and seminars—such as "Train the Trainer" or "Skills and Techniques for the Management Development Specialist"—are particularly important for employees new to management development.

Problems of Management Development

Successful programs avoid the common problems of development. Some of these problems are caused by placing unqualified individuals in charge of the program. These persons may lack the technical skills to perform management development, such as how to assess developmental needs, how to match needs with techniques, or how to evaluate management development activities. Further, trainers may be deficient in conceptual skills and fail to understand how management development must be coordinated with other organizational activities and functions. Finally, interpersonal problems, particularly between line managers and the management-development staff, may result in less than optimal management devel-

opment. For example, line and staff may have strong differences of opinion over the content of a course, or they may disagree over how the authority and responsibility for management development should be divided. Figure 8–4 is a list of the ten most serious mistakes in management development.

INTERNATIONAL HRM: EMPLOYEE DEVELOPMENT JAPANESE STYLE

The Japanese regard human resources as the critical ingredient for success. Management methods operate to build a solid foundation of employee relations through their influence on the quality of the individual–organization relationship. The centerpiece of this comprehensive approach to human resource management is the tradition of career employment. Because Japanese employment is based on matching the organization and the workers, job tenure until retirement is a logical consequence as long as the firm survives. Other personnel processes are integrated in such a manner that they can be understood as adaptations to this policy; length of service is a significant criterion for employee differentiation. As the most valuable corporate asset, the work force is regarded as an indispensable resource, not merely dispensable hirelings. The pervasiveness of this attitude is illustrated by the practice of "eternal employment," whereby some companies actually have built tombs for their employees! If employees are considered the firm's most valuable asset, it follows that great care is taken to select the best applicants. If only good employees are recruited, lifetime employment is a rational management policy. In Japan, a prospective full-time employee (seldom female) is normally hired directly on graduation from school. Career potential and intellectual capacity are more important in selection decisions than narrowly

1. *Fixing the primary responsibility for development on the staff.* Executives must recognize that the responsibility to develop human resources belongs, ultimately, to each line manager. The staff should assist line managers in achieving this goal.

2. *Lack of instruction in training for trainers.* Line managers must possess the specific skills and abilities that are necessary to develop their subordinates. The management development staff should see that managers are trained in these skills.

3. *Hasty or shallow needs analysis.* Programs must be built upon the particular developmental needs of each individual. Further, programs must focus only on those needs which may be met through developmental activities—and not, for example, needs that can be most effectively met through policy revisions or reorganizations.

4. *Substituting training for selection.* Developmental processes cannot take the place of good selection techniques. A skill or ability cannot be developed where basic aptitudes are nonexistent.

5. *Limiting the planning of development activities to courses.* The greatest opportunities for learning exist through work experiences. While seminars and courses are important, on-the-job development through techniques such as job rotation, committee assignments, and coaching are superior mechanisms for fostering personal growth.

6. *Overconcern with personality.* Attempts to modify an individual's basic personality through training and development are not only of questionable effectiveness, but also raise many moral and ethical issues. Programs that include a self-examination and critique of one's own behavioral patterns are certainly important, but efforts to restructure one's personality are not within the domain of management development.

7. *Lumping together training and development needs.* Each individual manager has a unique set of developmental needs. While some of a manager's needs may be the same as others, no two developmental programs will be identical.

8. *Preoccupation with mechanics.* Management development activities sometimes center around a trainer's favorite training techniques—such as videotape or role playing—rather than the real needs of the participants. Developmental methods should be selected after specific needs have been defined and the program objectives have been set.

9. *On again, off again crash programs.* To achieve consistent results, management development must be applied in a regular, uninterrupted manner. Subordinates cannot be expected to maintain an interest in development unless they perceive it as an important, ongoing part of running the organization.

10. *Lack of provision for practical application of the training.* Individuals must be able to utilize their newly learned skills and abilities back on the job. Relating management development to the learner's working environment is a key consideration in writing developmental objectives and planning developmental activities.

FIGURE 8–4

Ten serious mistakes in management development (Source: J. W. Taylor, "Ten Serious Mistakes in Management-Training Development," *Personnel Journal* [May 1974]: 357–62. Reprinted with permission of *Personnel Journal,* Costa Mesa, CA © May 1974.)

defined job skills. Hiring compatible, flexible individuals is necessary when people are expected to work together over a long period of time, to develop a broad set of relevant talents, and to have the ability to work hard for mutual benefit.[45]

The philosophy inherent in the Japanese employer–employee relationship is reflected in the systematic development of the whole person. There is a mutual commitment to and by the organization for a lifetime of work. Like the U.S. military, training and work are the same process, and both are part of the regular rotation of employees in the firm. Continuous, multi-functional training occurs throughout one's career and creates opportunities for advancement. In a permanent employment system, the company is not reluctant to invest in training for fear that employees will be hired away by other firms. Given the immobility of employees in the job market, promotions occur slowly by seniority. The individual receives instruction not only for one job, but for many jobs at the same level. For example, a new worker who is assigned to the shop floor will be encouraged to learn to operate as many different machines as possible. In short, great value is placed on education in Japan, where learning is treasured; "training is the way," according to a popular book by a seventeenth-century samurai warrior.[46]

CONCLUSIONS AND APPLICATIONS

- Strong management development is important to an organization's success. Effective management-development activities help ensure a continual supply of competent, satisfied managerial personnel.
- Many managers have strong drives for recognition, responsibility, and personal growth. Management-development activ-

ities can play a dual role by helping to satisfy both organizational needs and manager's personal needs.

- All management-development personnel should become familiar with the behavioral patterns of obsolescent managers and determine the extent to which the problem pervades the organization. Obsolescence poses a greater threat to organizations in dynamic environments than to those that operate in more stable surroundings.
- Technical, conceptual, and human-relations skills provide the foundation for all management jobs, though the mix of the three skills will vary considerably by management level. Training and development administrators should become knowledgeable about how the skills and abilities for effective management vary among low-, middle-, and top-management levels.
- A well-conducted needs assessment provides a strong base for successful management development. A results-oriented performance-appraisal system, such as the performance review processes included in MBO, will provide valuable data for assessing current managerial development needs. Effective long-range personnel planning provides valuable data for determining both the number of managers needed in the future and the skills they must possess to be successful.
- Effective management development includes a balance of both on- and off-the-job activities. Individual programs should be created for each manager and should be built upon current strengths and weaknesses, career potential, and personal needs.
- Activities should be selected and created with the manager's environment in mind. For example, role play, manage-

ment games, in-basket exercises, and case studies should be custom built to simulate as closely as possible the situations and problems that make up the manager's real working conditions.

- Evaluating management development poses a challenge for the personnel administrator. Evaluative techniques should assess the extent to which the managers' objectives are more effectively achieved through participation in management development.

- Historically, women have faced formidable obstacles in their advancement into managerial ranks. Management development can play a dual role in removing these obstacles by (1) developing special courses dealing with discrimination in the advancement of women and (2) creating management-development programs to meet the particular needs of women workers.

CASE STUDY
Cincinnati Trust Bank

With over 900 employees and assets of over $2 billion, Cincinnati Trust Bank (CTB) is the city's largest bank in terms of human and financial resources. Offering a wide range of banking services, CTB has twenty-seven branches located throughout the city. Its growth and profit figures are impressive, and the bank's outlook appears bright.

For over two decades, the bank has operated a formal training department for clerical and operative personnel. New tellers, clerks, receptionists, and other kinds of lower-level administrative personnel usually spend their first one or two weeks of employment in the bank's training department at the home office downtown. After being permanently assigned to a branch or home-office department, employees usually receive on-the-job training from their supervisors.

About a year ago, the vice-president for personnel sensed a need for a more formal development of managerial personnel and created the position of Manager, Supervisory and Executive Development. Before the creation of this position, management development consisted primarily of informal on-the-job coaching and job rotation. Occasionally managers would attend seminars or short courses if they desired and if budget monies were available.

Keith McCloud was hired to fill the manager's job. McCloud had an MBA with a personnel concentration and five years' experience as a training and development manager with a medium-sized bank in Indianapolis, Indiana. He was charged with the overall responsibility of assessing management-development needs at all levels of the management hierarchy and implementing, coordinating, and evaluating developmental efforts.

McCloud's first assignment was to create a comprehensive developmental program for the bank's entire first level of supervision. Some of these supervisors were the head teller, accounting supervisor, operations officer, and keypunch supervisor. McCloud began by conducting an assessment of developmental needs. Because the bank did not have a formal personnel planning function, he was unable to get a firm fix on the future need for managers or who the managers might be. In turning his attention to the assessment of current supervisory development needs, McCloud ran into another problem. The bank's performance-appraisal system focused on the use of a general, trait-oriented appraisal system. The appraisals were virtually worthless in determining developmental needs. McCloud then determined that he had to rely on other techniques to assess needs; he interviewed supervisors and their bosses. He implemented a morale survey for all nonsupervisory employees to get a feel for the supervisory-related problems they experienced. Based on his interviews and the survey, McCloud uncovered these problem areas experienced by large numbers of supervisors:

- A lack of knowledge about the budgeting process—how to create a budget and use it to control financial resources.
- Inability to hold effective performance-appraisal interviews.
- Inability to delegate authority effectively.
- Lack of knowledge about different techniques to motivate employees.
- Inability to manage time and plan effectively on a day-to-day basis.
- Lack of skills in selecting new employees.
- Inability to manage meetings effectively.
- Lack of understanding about how a supervisor's leadership style affects employee productivity and morale.
- Inability to define clear expectations for subordinates.
- Lack of understanding concerning the role of the supervisor.
- Inability to write clear and concise letters and memos.
- Employee dissatisfaction with pay, health benefits, and the bank cafeteria.

Questions

1. Of the problems uncovered by Keith McCloud, which ones may be classified as technical skills? Conceptual skills? Human-relations skills?
2. Which problems are solvable through management-development activities and which are not?
3. Which problems should be dealt with during on-the-job developmental activities? Off-the-job activities? Both on- and off-the-job activities?
4. In addition to the list of problems McCloud developed, what other problems must he deal with and how can they be remedied?

EXPERIENTIAL EXERCISE
Supervision: A Basket Case?

Purpose

To understand how the in-basket technique for developing managers works by participating in an in-basket exercise.

Introduction

The in-basket is a simulation consisting of notes, letters, memos, and other information that is typical of the kind of printed material that crosses a manager's desk daily. The term *in-basket* is derived from the fact that supervisors and managers face a constant barrage of written requests, questions, concerns, and problems that must be attended to—the kinds of things that often end up in a manager's in-basket. This management development technique forces the manager to make decisions: more specifically, decisions about how to act upon (if at all) the things that land in the in-basket. The exercise itself teaches the training participant how to act upon a variety of problems that confront managers daily.

The Task

Assume that you supervise twenty-five blue-collar employees in a mid-sized manufacturing company (1,200 employees) and that you are participating in a management development program that uses the in-basket technique. Listed below are brief descriptions of items that are sitting in your in-basket. For each item, answer the following two questions:

1. How important is this item? (Assign one of the following numbers: 1: not important at all; 2: somewhat important; 3: important; 4: very important; and 5: extremely important.) Be prepared to explain and defend your answer.
2. What specifically should be done with this item? Some options to consider (you may develop others) are: 1: act upon the item immediately; 2: postpone acting upon it until a later date (specify how much longer); 3: delegate the item to someone else to act upon (assume you have a secretary or an assistant and that the organization you work for has a normal line/staff organization structure with staff assistance from the human resource department, etc). If you chose this option, specify *who* should act upon the item; 4: seek more information about the item (specify *what* information you would seek); and 5: do nothing (place the item in the circular file). Be prepared to explain and defend your answer.

In-basket Items

1. A letter from an employee that requests three days' sick leave to visit a sick aunt in a distant city. Current policies do not provide for sick leave to visit or care for sick relatives. She is an excellent employee.
2. A request from a company to provide a work reference on a former employee you supervised. The employee was a machine operator. He worked for you for about a year and, overall, did satisfactory work, but nothing exceptional.
3. A telephone message to call your spouse immediately.
4. An anonymous letter, signed "concerned female employee," who complains of sexual harassment in your work group. A male employee who is one of your subordinates is named as the harasser.
5. A letter from an excellent employee who wishes to set up an appointment to discuss her future with the company. She states that she is "burned out" in her job and wants a promotion to a more responsible job. She insinuates that she will look for other employment if she is not promoted soon. There are no job opportunities in your work unit, and only a handful in other areas of the company.

6. A letter from the human resource manager, who expresses concern about the plant's becoming unionized. He wants to meet with you to discuss specifically what you can do to stop "all this talk about a union."

7. A letter from the vice-president of manufacturing, who wants to talk to you about the possibility of using quality circles in the plant to improve product quality. He notes that because you are a recent business school graduate, you "probably know more about quality circles than anyone else at the plant."

8. A letter from an EEOC representative who wants to talk to you about a complaint filed against your company by a former employee of yours. She (a black female) alleges that you fired her not because of poor performance (as you stated to her) but because she was black.

9. An anonymous letter stating that alcohol and illegal drugs are being consumed in cars and vans in the company parking lot during the lunch hour.

10. A note from your boss that a supervisory position will be open in a few months. He wants to know who, if anyone, among your current nonsupervisory employees might be a good candidate for the job.

KEY TERMS AND CONCEPTS

Case study	Management development
Coaching	Management games
Committee assignments	Managerial obsolescence
Conceptual skill	Mentoring
Executive succession chart	Professional organizations
Human-relations skills	Role play
In-basket exercises	Sensitivity training
Job rotation and lateral promotion	Technical skills

REVIEW QUESTIONS

1. What is management development, and what are its major purposes?
2. Discuss how both current and long-range development needs can be assessed.
3. Describe the major phases of management development.
4. Describe the various kinds of on-the-job and off-the-job development techniques.
5. Discuss the importance of creating an individual development plan for each manager.
6. Discuss an effective strategy for evaluating a management-development effort.
7. Describe the problems of career development for women, and explain how management-development activities facilitate the upper mobility of females in management ranks.
8. Enumerate some of the key mistakes in carrying out management development.
9. List the major considerations for conducting management development.

DISCUSSION QUESTIONS

1. It is often said that management development should take place throughout a manager's career, not just in the initial stages. Do you agree? Explain the meaning behind this statement.

2. Write a brief job description for a position titled director of management development. List some of the major duties and responsibilities of the position.

3. In line with question 2, write a brief job specification for the position of director of management development. What skills and abilities should the director have? What formal education and job experience would you expect the director to possess?

4. Management development involves a partnership between line management and staff administration. How does the role of director of management development differ from the role of line manager in carrying out management development?

5. In practice, it is often very difficult to conduct an accurate assessment of management-development needs. Why is this so?

6. Assume that you are the head of a personnel department in a large hospital that employs 125 first-level, middle, and top managers. At present, management development takes place on a very informal basis, and you feel that the hospital needs to formalize the development function by creating the position of director of management development. What argument would you use to get the position approved?

7. You are the head of your organization's development function. Your boss calls you into his office and makes the following statements: "You have requested a $250,000 management-development budget for the coming fiscal year. Can you prove that we are getting our money's worth?" What would you tell your boss?

8. One occasionally hears the old adage, "you can't make a silk purse out of a sow's ear." Do you see any relationship between this cliché and management development?

ENDNOTES

1. See Elmer Burack and Gopal Pati, "Technology and Managerial Obsolescence," *MSU Business Topics* (Spring 1970): 49–56; and Herbert Kaufman, *Obsolescence and Professional Career Development* (New York: AMACON, 1974).

2. Raymond A. Noe, "Trainees' Attributes and Attitudes: Neglected Influences on Training Effectiveness," *Academy of Management Review* 11, no. 4 (October 1986): 736–49.

3. E. Mandt, "A Basic Model of Manager Development," *Personnel Journal* (June 1979): 395–400.

4. Details of the systems approach to management development are discussed in R. School and W. Brounell, "Let Management Development Score for Your Organization," *Personnel Journal* (June 1983): 486–91, and R. Walters, "How to Develop Managers for the Future—A Systems Approach," *Personnel Administrator* (August 1980).

5. Newman Peery and Y. K. Shetty, "An Empirical Study of Executive Transferability and Organizational Performance," *Proceedings* (Kansas City, MO: Academy of Management, 1976).

6. Considerations for developing in-house management development programs are discussed in S. Truskie, "Guidelines for Conducting In-house Management Development" *Personnel Administrator* (July 1981): 25–27; and E. Jennings, "How to Develop Your Management Talent Internally," *Personnel Administrator* (July 1981): 28–32.

7. Bureau of National Affairs, "On-the-Job Training," *Personnel Management: BNA Policy and Practice Series* (Washington, DC: Bureau of National Affairs, 1975).

8. A certain amount of risk taking is important for effective management. See A. Hill, "How Organizational Philosophy Influences Management Development" *Personnel Journal* (February 1980): 118–20.

9. See the Woodlands Group, "Management Development Roles: Coach, Sponsor, Mentor," *Personnel Journal* (November 1980): 918–21; and J. Yeager, "Coaching the Executive: Can You Teach an Old Dog New Tricks?" *Personnel Administrator* (November 1982).

10. Harry Levinson, "A Psychologist Looks at Executive Development," *Harvard Business Review* (November–December 1962), pp. 69–75.

11. Chris Argyris, "Puzzle and Perplexity in Executive Development," *Personnel Journal* 39 (1969): 463–65.

12. T. Farnsworth, *Developing Executive Talent: A Practical Guide* (London: McGraw-Hill, 1975).

13. For a detailed discussion of the advantages and disadvantages of job rotation, see Yoram Ziera, "Job Rotation for Management Development," *Personnel* (July–August 1974): 25–35.

14. See "Taking the Jolts Out of Moving," *Nation's Business* (November 1975): 36–38; and "Moving on Loses Its Glamour for More Employees," *The Wall Street Journal* (August 3, 1976): 1.

15. K. E. Kram, *Mentoring at Work: Developmental Relationships in Organizational Life* (Glenview, IL: Scott, Foresman, 1985).

16. E. Lean, "Cross-Gender Mentoring—Downright Upright and Good for Productivity," *Training and Development Journal* 37, no. 5 (May 1983): 60–65.

17. Ibid.

18. For a description of the off-the-job courses and seminars, see "More Executives Take Work-Related Courses to Keep Up, Advance," *The Wall Street Journal* (March 3, 1980): 1.

19. K. Wexley and G. Latham, *Developing and Training Human Resources* (Glenview, IL: Scott, Foresman, 1981), p. 193.

20. Ibid., p. 194; see also C. Argyris, "Some Limitations of the Case Method," *Academy of Management Review* 5 (1980): 291–98.

21. The various forms of role playing are outlined in W. Rohlsing, "Role Playing" in R. Craig, ed., *Training and Development Handbook* (New York: McGraw-Hill, 1976).

22. For applications, see J. Maxwell Towers, *Role Playing for Managers* (Oxford: Pergamon Press, 1974).

23. C. Craft, "Management Games," in R. Craig, *Training and Development Handbook*.

24. The distinction between computer-based and manually operated games is discussed in L. Coppard, "Gaming Simulation and the Training Process," in R. Craig, *Training and Development Handbook.*

25. While interest in management games usually runs high, there is little empirical evidence supporting their effectiveness. See Janet Schriesheim and Chester Schriesheim, "The Effectiveness of Business Games in Management Training," *Training and Development Journal* (May 1974): 14–18, and Wexley and Latham, *Developing and Training Human Resources,* pp. 205–206.

26. For detailed criticisms of this form of training, see John R. Kimberly and Warren R. Nielsen, "Organization Development and Change in Organization Performance," *Administrative Science Quarterly* (June 1975): 191; and Martin Lakin, "Some Ethical Issues in Sensitivity Training," *American Psychologist* (October 1969): 923–28.

27. John P. Campbell and Marvin D. Dunnette, "Effectiveness of T-Group Experiences in Managerial Training and Development," *Psychological Bulletin* (August 1968): 73–104; and Robert J. House, "T-Group Education and Leadership Effectiveness: A Review of the Empiric Literature and a Critical Evaluation," *Personnel Psychology* (Spring 1967): 1–32.

28. Wexley and Latham, *Developing and Training Human Resources,* p. 178.

29. W. Byham and J. Robinson, "Interaction Modeling: A New Concept in Supervisory Training," *Training and Development Journal* (February 1976): 20–23.

30. Favorable reactions to the behavior modeling approach are also reported in G. Latham and L. Saari, "The Application of Social Learning Theory to Training Supervisors Through Behavior Modeling," *Journal of Applied Psychology* 64 (1979): 163–68. See also S. Wehrenberg and R. Kuhnle, "How Training Through Behavior Modeling Works," *Personnel Journal* (July 1980): 576–80.

31. W. Byham, "The Assessment Center as an Aid in Management Development," *Training and Development Journal* (December 1971).

32. Ibid.

33. See F. Hoy et al., "Are Your Management Development Programs Working? *Personnel Journal* (December 1981): 953–57.

34. D. Kirkpatrick, "Evaluation of Training," in R. Craig, *Training and Development Handbook.*

35. Ralph Catalanello and Donald L. Kirkpatrick, "Evaluating Training Programs," *Training and Development Journal* 22, no. 5 (1968): 2–9.

36. U.S. Bureau of Labor Statistics, *Handbook of Labor Statistics* (Washington, DC: U.S. Government Printing Office, 1988).

37. Rosalind Loring and Theodora Wells, *Breakthrough: Women Into Management* (New York: Van Nostrand Reinhold, 1972). See also E. Mirides and A. Cote, "Women in Management: The Obstacles and Opportunities They Face," *Personnel Administrator* (April 1980).

38. G. N. Powell and D. A. Butterfield, "The 'Good Manager': Masculine or Androgynous?" *Academy of Management Journal* 22, no. 2 (June 1979): 395–403.

39. Ibid., p. 401.

40. For a discussion on the meaning and measurement of androgyny, see S. L. Bem, "The Measurement of Psychological Androgyny," *Journal of Consulting and Clinical Psychology* (May 1974): 155–62.

41. M. Parker, S. Peltier, and P. Wolleat, "Understanding Dual Career Couples," in B. A. Stead, ed., *Women in Management,* 2nd ed. (Englewood Cliffs, NJ: Prentice-Hall, Inc., 1985), p. 75.

42. For an excellent overview of dual-career couple problems and issues, see F. S. Hall and D. T. Hall, *The Two-Career Couple* (Reading, MA: Addison-Wesley, 1979).

43. Ibid.

44. Edwin A. Fleishman, "Leadership Climate, Human Relations Training, and Supervisory Behavior," in Edwin A. Fleishman, ed., *Studies in Personnel and Industrial Psychology* (Homewood, IL: Dorsey Press, 1967), pp. 250–63.

45. James S. Bowman, "The Rising Sun in America," *Personnel Administrator* 31, no. 9 (September 1986): 65–66, 114–115.

46. Ibid.

Chapter Nine

Internal Staffing and Career Management

Chapter Outline

PROMOTION
    Recruiting for Promotion
    Official Promotion Criteria
    Unofficial Promotion Criteria

OTHER INTERNAL MOVES
    Demotion
    Transfer
    Layoff

INTERNAL-STAFFING POLICIES
    Assistance for Laid-off Employees
    Equal Employment Opportunity

CAREER MANAGEMENT
    Benefits to the Organization
    Organizational Career Planning
    Individual Career Planning
    Integrating Plans
    Implementing Programs
    Evaluation of Career Programs
    Career Problems

CONCLUSIONS AND APPLICATIONS

Chapter Objectives

1. To recognize the various kinds of internal staffing decisions that have an impact upon the personnel/human resource function and to describe how these decisions may be effectively made.
2. To discuss the importance of making sound promotional decisions and to describe both effective and ineffective criteria for making these decisions.
3. To understand the inherent dangers in making promotional decisions solely on the basis of past performance.
4. To identify the personnel/human resource department's role in assisting the laid-off employee to gain employment as quickly as possible.
5. To understand the legal issues that surround the internal staffing process.
6. To explore a career management model and to illustrate the elements necessary for a successful career management function.

Dow Jones Program of Career Development

Kevin Litz was a delivery driver at Dow Jones in Naperville, Illinois. After five years in that job he completed an MBA degree and a CPA certificate. Many companies would have lost Kevin, a loyal, hard-working employee, because now he wanted a career change. However, Kevin let Dow Jones know he "druther be working as an accountant" through the Dow Jones career development program called the "Druthers" Program. Kevin was now qualified for a new job and had a good work record at Dow Jones. He was selected for an accountant position in South Brunswick, New Jersey.

Dow Jones employs about 4,500 people in the United States. Several factors convinced top management that it needed an innovative career development program. First, the old traditional program did not help retain good employees. Employees applied for openings and were treated [like] other candidates. Second, the union and employees were pressuring for job posting. Third, and most importantly, management believed that (a) career development should emphasize employees playing a major role, (b) career development should be based on merit and not seniority or favoritism, and (c) managers should be actively involved in employees' career development.

The Druthers Program was created from management's philosophy. The employees initiate the program by writing their manager a letter expressing an interest in a job change. Where possible they specify why they are ready and qualified for a change, their career objective, and the next job desired. The letter also indicates if the employee is willing to relocate or travel. The hiring manager decides who is hired for open positions, but under the program the Druthers file is first checked to determine if any inside candidates have expressed an interest. When possible they are hired first.

If an employee seeks a job outside their present department, their request is placed on a national Druthers list. Each regional manager receives an updated list each month and through conference calls discusses openings and candidates with the national coordinator. Employees may remain on the list for up to twelve months and may reapply if not placed within that time.

Seminars on career planning and self-assessment are provided to employees. They explain job requirements, career options and self-presentation skills. A handbook on the Druthers Program is also provided to interested employees. The company's educational assistance program is designed to help employees achieve the necessary educational qualifications. The program pays full tuition, and lab and registration fees. Costs are paid before registration. The results of the program include an average of three placements per month and employees active in their own career development. While generally successful, the program did incur problems. Some employees blamed the program if they were not selected for a particular job. Managers resisted losing valued employees, especially if they could not fill the vacancy due to budget limits. Some employees feared that their supervisor might see them as disloyal for showing an interest in moving. Dow Jones, however, believed that these problems could be partly addressed through training, and recognized that similar problems would surface whenever turnover occurred.

Source: Richard K. Broszeit, "If I Had My Druthers," *Personnel Journal* 65, no. 10 (October 1986): 84–90. Used by permission.

THE typical organization chart, with neatly drawn and labeled boxes connected by horizontal and vertical lines, often fails to convey the great amount of movement by personnel that takes place in modern enterprises. People are shifted up, down, across, and out in organizations of all kinds and sizes. These decisions about *internal staffing*, involving promotions, demotions, transfers, and layoffs, represent an important area of personnel policy and management. Effective internal-staffing plans, policies, and procedures will promote the achievement of both organizational and personal goals. But mismanagement of internal staffing may result in a great deal of job dissatisfaction and reduced organization effectiveness. In this chapter, we will discuss internal-staffing decisions and the issues connected with them. In chapter 5, the primary concern was with external hiring. The focus here will be on the staffing decisions that affect the firm's internal human resources.

The last part of this chapter concentrates on a concern associated with internal staffing: career management. Many modern personnel professionals have designed programs and procedures that enable employees to progress upward in a planned and systematic way. Successful career management leads to an improved quality of working life and maximum utilization of employee skills.

Several important factors influence internal-staffing decisions. These include:

Creation of New Jobs Business or government expansion generally results in filling new positions by promoting existing employees. Increases in the number of new positions are particularly commonplace for companies in growth industries, such as computers and home entertainment.

Reorganization A major restructuring of an organization may result in various types of personnel actions. For example, while Jimmy Carter was the governor of Georgia, the state government reorganization plan included centralization of many staff services, such as purchasing and employee training. The reorganization brought about many transfers and promotions, as well as some demotions.

General Business Trends One consequence of major economic downturns is that a significant number of workers will temporarily or permanently lose their jobs. Companies that manufacture durable goods, such as automobiles and home appliances, are particularly vulnerable to fluctuations in the business cycle. Companies that produce services, such as health care and nondurable items, are sometimes said to be "recession proof" and may enjoy a stable or growing labor force through both good and bad economic times.

Resignations, Terminations, and Retirements Voluntary and involuntary turnover and retirement create vacancies that may be filled by promoting or transferring existing personnel. Employee reductions that result from termination, resignation, retirement, and death are collectively referred to as *attrition*.

PROMOTION

A promotion involves the reassignment of an employee to a higher-level job. When promoted, employees generally face increasing demands in terms of skills, abilities, and responsibilities. In turn, employees generally receive increased pay and (sometimes) benefits as well as greater authority and status.

Promotions serve many purposes and provide benefits to both organizations and employees. First, promotions enable organizations to use their employees' abilities to the greatest extent possible. An effective system of promotion permits an organization to match its continuous need for competent personnel with the employees' desires to apply the skills they have developed. Second, promotions can encourage excellent performance. Employees may perform at high levels if they think that high performance leads to promotion.[1] Third, there is a significant correlation between opportunities for advancement and high levels of job satisfaction.[2] In sum, an effective system of promotion can result in greater organizational efficiency and high levels of employee morale.

Recruiting for Promotion

Two main approaches are used to recruit employees for promotion. The more common approach is the *closed promotion system,* which places the responsibility for identifying promotable employees with the supervisor of the job to be filled. In addition to reviewing the past performance and assessing the potential of subordinates, a supervisor may inquire in other departments about employees who may be qualified for the job. A drawback to the closed promotion system is that many employees who may be qualified and interested in promotion are often overlooked. For example, the vice-president of a large bank with an opening for a commercial loan officer in its home office may be unaware of qualified or interested employees in branch offices. In such cases, the job may be filled by an employee known to the executive but less qualified than other employees. An approach that overcomes this problem is known as the *open promotion system,* more popularly known as *job posting.* With job posting, job vacancies are publicized on bulletin boards and internal communication systems so that all interested employees may apply. Job posting enhances participation and equal opportunity, but it also increases administrative expenses and takes time. A survey by the Bureau of National Affairs showed that open promotion systems are used mostly at the clerical and blue-collar levels in government and unionized companies, that open and closed systems are used about equally for professional and technical employees, and that closed systems are used almost exclusively for managerial personnel.[3]

Official Promotion Criteria

For many employees, a promotion is a highly sought prize. Climbing the organizational ladder has long been a part of the American dream. Status, satisfaction, and financial rewards accrue to those who are able to rise in an organization. But frustration, stress, and even severe depression may occur when personal goals of upward mobility are unheeded by an organization—particularly when an employee feels passed over for a deserved promotion. Because organizational effectiveness and job satisfaction are influenced by the way promotions are made, it is important for organizations to gather reliable data for making decisions about promotions. There are a number of criteria that organizations officially examine in deciding which candidates to promote.

Seniority Many organizations place significant weight upon an employee's seniority when making a promotion decision. Seniority is directly related to an employee's length of service and has long been important in American industry. For generations, a senior employee has expected and often received a greater share of organizational rewards than a junior employee. Salaries and benefits, such as vacation time and sick leave, are often tied to seniority.

Students of management often think that seniority should be given very little or no weight in promotional decisions, holding that seniority is anathema to private enterprise because length of service rather than performance is rewarded. But there are sound arguments for using seniority as a criterion in promoting employees. First, seniority avoids the problems of biased managers, who may promote favorite employees. Second, seniority is a quick, easy, and painless way to make a promotion decision. Third, there is often some correlation between seniority and perfor-

mance: up to a point, employees usually become more competent at their jobs as they gain experience. And fourth, seniority rewards the loyal employee who has perhaps labored for many years to produce the organization's products or services.

A *seniority system* is a set of rules governing the allocation of economic benefits and opportunities on the basis of service with one employer.[4] It is by far the most commonly negotiated means of measuring service and comparing employees for promotion and employment decisions.

Seniority is perhaps the most important measure of job security to employees, and the issue of seniority is popular among unions and viewed as critical to job security. Seniority is highly visible because it is so easy to define and measure. Normally, it is calculated in terms of days, beginning with the employee's date of hire, and, with a few exceptions, continues over the years during the employee's tenure. Union negotiators vehemently claim that management, in the absence of a job seniority system, will make promotion, layoff, and other decisions based solely upon possible short-run cost savings or individual biases rather than the objective criteria that seniority easily provides. These criteria include the employee's loyalty to the company and the skills and productivity that increase with time spent on the job.

Management may argue that time worked on the job is only one measure and that the employee's performance record, as well as other criteria, should be considered, especially performance appraisals completed by supervisors. However, performance appraisal systems, even at their best, are heavily dependent upon supervisor's objectivity and ability to evaluate individual performance honestly and thoroughly, something that is often very difficult to do. Therefore, performance appraisals are subjective and do not guarantee employees the objectivity and consistency they expect when promotion or layoff decisions are made.

In nonunionized organizations, it certainly is not unheard-of for employers to terminate or lay off senior employees who have worked into higher pay grades or other junior employees who have unjustifiably suffered a supervisor's contempt. A seniority system provides a means of job security and requires that if a supervisor feels an employee is unproductive or unable to produce successfully, the supervisor must defend and subject the decision to an agreed-upon process. Also, the seniority system uses a basic and fair premise that employees who have stayed with the organization longer and provided more service should be given first preference when all other aspects of the employment decision are equal.

To define the concepts of seniority fully, it may be helpful to distinguish between unionized and nonunionized employer-employee relationships. Seniority provisions are not required by federal laws, nor is it an inherent right of employees. However, seniority is a mandatory subject in the collective bargaining process. Strict formal seniority systems are commonplace in virtually all unionized organizations but are rare among nonunion employers. The latter employer typically maintains total decision-making control in all aspects of employment that are partially or totally governed by seniority systems in the unionized organization.[5] A Bureau of National Affairs survey of over 400 labor contracts found that 88 percent of the agreements provided for the seniority system, including 95 percent in the manufacturing industries and 76 percent in the nonmanufacturing industries. In most of the contracts surveyed, seniority played a critical role in the determination of promotion and layoff decisions.[6]

Depending on the particular labor agreement, seniority rights are vested within a variety of different employee units. The most common unit would be *plantwide seniority*, where an individual employee receives credit that become applicable whenever that employee competes with any other employee from another unit for the same position. Other common seniority units include departmental, trade, classification, and companywide. For example, in a *departmental seniority* system, employees accrue seniority according to the amount of time they worked within a particular department, and that seniority credit is valid only within that department.[7] For example, an employee with eleven years of seniority in department x could not successfully compete with an employee with seven years in department y for an open position in department y.

In situations involving layoffs, seniority systems often use *bumping;* that is, employees with greater seniority whose jobs have been phased out have the right to displace employees with less seniority. Such bumping rights may be limited to departmental or job classification seniority instead of plantwide seniority. In a combined seniority system, plantwide seniority is frequently used to determine bumping rights.[8]

Management often disagrees with the use of seniority as the sole determinant of promotion decisions. The Bureau of National Affairs estimates that seniority is a determining factor in promotional policies as provided by collective bargaining agreements in 67 percent of labor contracts. However, only 9 percent call for promotion decisions based upon seniority as the sole determiner. Another 33 percent provide that the most senior individual will receive promotion if he or she is qualified for the job.[9] In most promotional policies, seniority is treated as a determining factor along with employee skill and ability.

What weights are given to seniority and ability in actual promotion decisions? Is there a difference between union and nonunion employers? An analysis of over 700 U.S. firms indicated that 60 percent give the person with greater seniority a preference in promotion decisions. In practice both union and non-union employers reported giving length of service more weight in promotion decisions than required by written policy or union contract. While union employers reported using seniority to a greater extent, the difference in comparison with nonunion employers was not significant.[10]

Nonunion organizations often have promotion policies based primarily upon promoting from within to boost employee morale and assure individuals that they can work hard and get ahead. Like union organizations, they hesitate to promote a less senior employee unless there is concrete evidence to show that a more senior employee is less capable. The effect of such a promotion upon general employee morale, as well as upon the individual involved, also needs to be determined. Therefore, in nonunion organizations, seniority is weighed carefully along with the employee's past record and demonstrated skills.[11]

Performance Because of the drawbacks in using seniority as the sole promotion criterion, many organizations strongly consider current performance when promoting employees to jobs of increased responsibility, especially in management and professional jobs. Seniority is given little or no weight in such cases. Instead, a candidate's performance appraisals, training and development history, formal education, special awards, and other performance data are often combined with an informal judgment of the employee's chances for success in a higher-level job. Using this approach, the chances that the organization will make an effective promotion decision are relatively good when both the candidate's present job and the higher job require similar skills and abilities. Examples of such promotions include:

- Receptionist to secretary
- Police sergeant to police captain
- Bookkeeper to accounting assistant
- Foreman to superintendent
- Regional plant manager to district plant manager

In these examples, past work performance is a fairly good predictor of future success. But past performance is not always a valid indicator of future performance, particularly when the employee is promoted to a job that requires skills and abilities considerably different from those used in the previous job. A common situation involves the promotion of a lower-level employee to supervisor, such as advancement from assembly-line worker to first-line supervisor. Supervisory skills are almost totally different from those required for successful assembly-line work; and many organizations have committed grave errors by promoting an employee into supervisory ranks solely because of technical expertise. As one recently promoted employee put it:[12]

> I really looked forward to my promotion from printing-press operator to print-shop manager. The job was given to me because I was the best operator in the shop. I got a big pay increase and my own office. My family and friends really bragged about me. But it didn't take long to realize that I didn't like supervision. I don't feel I'm one of the gang anymore and I find it difficult to give orders to men I used to joke and drink beer with. I really wish I could have my old job back but don't have the guts to admit I can't hack it as a supervisor.

The problem inherent in the print-shop employee's promotion is very common in organizations today. Employees are often promoted because of talents that bear little resemblance to the talents needed in the new job. Promotion into sales management is a good example. The top salesperson, demonstrating a unique ability to sell effectively, may be promoted to sales manager. Top management may believe that a good salesperson is also a good manager. But the sales manager often becomes frustrated by having to work with subordinates rather than with customers; motivating employees to sell is much different and perhaps much more difficult than persuading customers to buy. Management and nonmanagement jobs involve different skills, and many employee-job mismatches have resulted from promotions which have ignored this fact.

Many examples in the sports world illustrate that success or mediocrity in one job does not automatically spell success or mediocrity in another. Bill Russell, Ted Williams, and Bart Starr performed brilliantly as professional athletes but enjoyed much less success as coaches. Both John Wooden and Adolph Rupp had lackluster college basketball careers, but their achievements as basketball coaches are legendary. Frank Tarkenton, O. J. Simpson, Alex Karras, and Bruce Jenner have all carried their successes from the athletic world into the field of entertainment.

Assessment Center To improve the chances of making successful promotional decisions—particularly from nonmanagement to management—many organizations are using assessment centers. Job candidates are brought to assessment centers for evaluation of their promotability, as measured by a series of exercises. These exercises focus on the kind of skills and abilities required to effectively perform the higher-level jobs that the candidates seek.[13]

The purpose of the assessment center may be better understood if an operating center is described. American Telephone and Telegraph's (AT&T) assessment-center program is one of the largest and most sophisticated. AT&T has over fifty assessment centers across the United States. Each assessment center takes place in a conference room or seminar area, away from the work site.

The primary purpose of the assessment center is to improve an organization's selection of managers, particularly at the first level of management. A secondary purpose is to increase the pool of employees from which managers are selected. An AT&T employee may ask to attend an assessment center, or a supervisor may feel that an employee is supervisory material and suggest that the employee attend. In either case, the final decision to participate is the employee's.

Roughly a dozen participants undergo exercises designed to determine their potential as successful managers. Common exercises during the two and one-half day program include:[14]

- An in-depth interview concerning career goals and plans
- A test of general mental ability
- A test of reasoning ability
- A test of knowledge about current affairs
- A series of in-basket exercises
- A management game involving the start-up and operation of a toy company
- Role playing

Throughout the session, six assessors and a director observe and evaluate each participant. They are experienced, successful line managers who volunteered to be trained as assessors. The job of assessor is a temporary assignment which usually lasts about six months.

After the sessions are over, the participants return to work. The assessors pool their evaluations and place each participant into one of the following categories: more than acceptable, acceptable, less than acceptable, and unacceptable. These ratings become important criteria for selecting managers in the future, though the ratings are not the sole criterion used for making a promotion decision. Traditional promotion criteria—such as past performance and supervisory recommendations—are also used.

AT&T participants may request full reports concerning their performances at the assessment center, and about 85 percent of the participants make that request. Receiving a rating of "less than acceptable" or "unacceptable" is not the "kiss of death" for participants. These employees may still get promoted into management with the help of a persuasive supervisor or mentor.[15]

AT&T placed the cost of each participant in an assessment center at about $400 in 1967. No doubt costs are considerably higher now. But the important question is whether the benefits exceed the costs, and AT&T thinks without a doubt that they do. Beginning in the late 1960s, AT&T conducted a number of sophisticated studies on effectiveness of their program. The results show that the assessment center is a more effective selection method than such traditional practices as performance reviews, interviews, and supervisory recommendations.

Although assessment centers vary somewhat from company to company, AT&T's are fairly typical. Other firms using assessment centers include Standard Oil of New Jersey, IBM, General Electric, Sears, and the Brown and Williamson Tobacco Company. Because of the costs involved, only large firms have been able to afford permanent assessment-center operations. Generally, smaller organizations do not have enough promotions to justify the expenses and thus usually rely on traditional selection methods.

Studies show that the assessment-center approach improves the odds that a correct promotion decision will be made.[16] In comparing the method to traditional methods, one researcher stated that "the average validity of the assessment center is about as high as the maximum validity attained by use of . . . traditional methods."[17]

Unofficial Promotion Criteria

A common retort to a presentation of official criteria used in promotion decisions is this: "What you say about making promotional decisions is all well and good. But it's all theory. Where I work, promotions depend on who you know, not what you do." The statement contains a good deal of truth. All too often, a gulf exists between theory and practice when promotions are considered. Rational criteria such as seniority, performance, and assessment-center ratings may be cast aside for political reasons. Unofficial criteria may influence or even dominate a promotion decision.

Personal Characteristics Together, Title VII of the Civil Rights Act and the Age Discrimination Act prohibit discrimination in all terms and conditions of employment on the basis of age, race, color, religion, sex, or national origin. All internal-staffing decisions fall under the domain of these acts, just as external recruiting, selection, and placement practices do. Although almost all organizations profess to abide by EEOC guidelines and include "Equal Opportunity Employer" at the bottom of their help-wanted advertisements, not all organizations practice what they preach. Certain personal characteristics of the candidate may either help or hinder progression into the upper levels of the organization. Being of the "wrong" sex, race, or religion may create a real though unspoken obstacle to advancement. Such practices are not only immoral and unethical but also clearly illegal.

Prejudice causes a sizable pool of valuable human talent to be overlooked and wasted.

Nepotism Being of a certain bloodline sometimes helps one's progression into a higher level job. Nepotism, from the Italian *nepotismo* ("favoring of nephews"), is the showing of favoritism or patronage to relatives. Nepotism is often criticized because family members get desirable jobs and promotions primarily by virtue of their lineage.[18] Nepotism is still practiced at many well-known firms, such as Ford and Toyota Motor Companies, Brown and Williamson Tobacco Company, IBM, and Playboy Enterprises.

Employers may restrict nepotism with a written policy prohibiting the hiring of applicants who are related to current employees. However, the possibility of two unrelated employees marrying must also be considered in a nepotism policy. Since such a situation may involve two current, valued employees, it becomes a more difficult policy question. A common policy requires that if two employees within the same department marry, the junior employee must accept a transfer. A U.S. court of appeals upheld such a policy even though a female employee claimed sex discrimination. The court approved a policy forbidding married couples from working in the same department because it had been applied consistently to all married couples.[19]

Social Factors Membership in a certain club or political party, graduation from the right university, and participation in the right sport (traditionally golf, perhaps now jogging, tennis, or racquetball) are important in getting promoted in some organizations, particularly at the upper-management and staff levels. One classic account of the importance of these factors in decisions of promotion was published by sociologist Melville Dalton. Dalton conducted in-house research on managerial practices at several large companies, asking, "What are the things that enable men to rise in the plant here?" This response came from a fifty-three-year-old foreman:[20]

> I'm surprised that anybody who's been around here as long as you have would ask that question. You know as well as I do that getting in and running around with certain crowds is the way to get up. Nearly all the big boys are in the yacht club, and damn near all of 'em are Masons. Hell, these guys all play poker together. Their wives run around together, and they all have their families out to the yacht club hobnobbing together. That's no mystery. Everybody knows it. It's the friendships and connections you make running around in these crowds that makes or breaks you in the plant.

Although there is no doubt that management is much more enlightened now than when Dalton conducted his research, few would disagree that the right connections often play an important role in reaching the executive suite.

Friendships In organizations of all forms and sizes, strong informal bonds are created between employees who share common interests, ideals, values, beliefs, and attitudes. In turn, such informal bonds between decision makers and candidates for promotion may play a significant role in deciding who gets promoted and who doesn't. Particularly at the top organizational levels, executives prefer to work with people whose thoughts and perceptions mirror their own. In a sense, this personal chemistry may be just as important as ability in getting ahead.

OTHER INTERNAL MOVES

Promotions are not the only way an employee may move in an organization. For many reasons, employees may have to be moved down, over, or even out. Thus, personnel administrators must be prepared to deal with demotions, transfers, and layoffs.

Demotion

Many people join organizations with the hope of periodically progressing upward through promotions. Others seek "just a job" and desire to stay at the jobs for which they were hired. But very few people begin working with the expectation that they will be forced downward through a demotion.

A demotion is the reassignment of an employee to a lower job with less pay, involving fewer skills and responsibilities. Demotions may take place for reasons beyond the control of the employees. Such major changes as reorganizations, company mergers, or business contractions may result in fewer jobs, forcing some employees to accept lower positions. In these cases, both blue- and white-collar employees may be demoted. The common union practice of bumping normally results in the employee with the least seniority being demoted to a lower-paying job. In these cases, the stigma attached to the demotion may be minor. Although employees will no doubt suffer anxiety and frustration over being demoted, they may rationalize the situation by claiming to be "simply in the wrong place at the wrong time—it could have happened to anybody."

In other situations, employees may be demoted for inability to perform their jobs according to acceptable standards. In such cases, demoted employees' frustration, resentment, anger, and fear can continue for a considerable length of time. When demotion is viewed as a devaluation of personal worth, the psychological damage can be significant.

Many managers and personnel administrators agree that demotion is not an effective way to handle disciplinary problems. Demo-

tion will not improve the behavior of an employee who has a long record of poor work habits, such as chronic absenteeism, insubordination, or drinking on the job. Those problems are most likely to be remedied by supervisory counseling, corrective discipline, and employee rehabilitation. In some situations involving unsatisfactory performance, employees may be the recipients of a rather common aberration of personnel management: the promotion-demotion. Here, employees are "kicked upstairs" to higher-paying jobs which typically involve little authority or responsibility. Demotion-promotion is a common way of dealing with a loyal long-term employee (generally near retirement) who has become obsolete or untrainable in the job. A more meaningful and equitable approach would be to keep the employee in the present job but reassign a portion of the authority and responsibilities to others.

Transfer

A transfer is the reassignment of an employee to a job with similar pay, status, duties, and responsibilities. Whereas a promotion involves upward movement, a transfer involves horizontal movement from one job to another.[21]

Transfers take place for several reasons. First, because personnel placement practices are not perfect, an employee-job mismatch may have resulted. A transfer moves the employee to a more suitable job. Second, an employee may become dissatisfied with the job for one or a variety of reasons: serious conflicts with co-workers or a supervisor that appear unresolvable, or a dead-end job from which a transfer would advance career goals. Third, organizations sometimes initiate transfers to further the development of the employee, especially at management and staff levels. The transfer may involve a job with the same or similar title but in an environment with new co-workers or unique problems. A different atmosphere is often a broadening experience for any employee. Fourth, organizational needs may require that employees be transferred. Voluntary or involuntary turnover, promotions, demotions, and terminations may result in job vacancies that may be filled most effectively through transfers.

Layoff

In good economic times, business and government expand, sales go up, jobs are plentiful, and unemployment drops. But economic downturns create economic woes, and the action that hits workers the hardest is the layoff.

A layoff cuts surplus employees from the payroll. If the need for human resources increases after a layoff, some or all of the employees who have been laid off may be *recalled*. If the demand for the organization's products or services does not increase, then the layoff becomes permanent and employees are formally separated from the firm.

Normally, layoffs involve hourly, blue-collar workers in the manufacturing and production centers of the organization. In unionized organizations, layoff and recall procedures are spelled out in great detail in the labor–management agreement. Typically, the contract specifies the maximum period in which laid-off employees may be recalled and the rights and privileges that employees hold while laid off. Seniority plays a major role in determining the order of layoffs. For example, a contract between Joseph E. Seagrams & Sons, Inc., and the Distillery, Rectifying, Wine, and Allied Workers' International Union of America included the following layoff and recall provisions:

Article XII, section 1
The employee's length of service for the purpose of determining seniority rights shall be deemed to have commenced on the first day of employment with the employer. In all cases of promotion or recall, seniority rights of employees shall govern. The principle of seniority shall govern in all cases, including the filling of vacancies occurring in shifts or new positions created. If vacancies occur in a higher rated position, seniority including the ability to perform the work shall be the controlling factor in the selection of employees to fill such vacancies.

Generally, union contracts mandate so-called bumping privileges that enable an employee to bump, or displace, an employee with less seniority. Under most union agreements, an employee may bump another employee with less seniority whether a layoff is imminent or not. Because widespread bumping reduces the efficiency of a company's operation, management usually restricts bumping provisions. For example, the contract may state that only employees qualified to hold the new job may bump other employees.

Production employees are usually among the first to be laid off, but managers, staff administrators, and other skilled employees are not immune to layoffs. Usually, a layoff at these levels is an admission that an organization is in very serious financial trouble. Administrators generally strive to avoid laying off management and staff employees because the firm has spent a great deal of time and money recruiting them and developing their skills and abilities. However, faced with the realities of survival, management may have little choice. Because managers and staff administrators are not union employees, no formal, written agreement covers the terms and conditions of their layoff. Usually employee performance plays a major role in deciding which upper-level employees to lay off; other criteria include seniority, age, family obligations, and political considerations.

Legal Issues in Layoffs By the 1970s, a great deal of controversy had arisen concerning the role of seniority in laying off minority employees. Women and blacks have only relatively recently made significant gains in many union-dominated jobs. As a consequence, most have less seniority than white males. Thus, layoffs of union employees have generally had an adverse impact on minorities. But the federal courts have long upheld the validity of the *bona fide seniority system (BFSS)*, holding that it is not illegal to make layoffs using a seniority system unless the seniority system was intentionally designed to discriminate. For example, in 1969 the Crown Zellerbach Company was ordered by the U.S. Court of Appeals to revise its seniority system because labor–management provisions only enabled employees to progress within certain job lines. The effect of this provision was to keep minorities out of departments with high-paying jobs. Crown Zellerbach was ordered to revise its system of promotion and adopt a plantwide seniority system.

Several court decisions in the early 1980s led to an erosion of the BFSS concept, particularly in government jobs involving police officers, fire fighters, and teachers. A federal judge in 1981 barred the city of Boston from reducing the fire department's 14.7 percent level of minority fire fighters achieved through the city's affirmative-action plan. The result was that 83 white males with greater seniority were laid off in place of minority workers. Similar court rulings have taken place in Memphis, Cincinnati, Toledo, and Jackson, Michigan. As might be expected, relations between protected and nonprotected workers have been severely strained where such rulings have taken place.[22]

The concept and practice of a seniority system was upheld under a precedent-setting 1984 Supreme Court decision, *Firefighters Local 1784* v. *Stotts*.[23] The Court decided that the affirmative-action goals of a consent decree requiring the hiring and promotion of black employees cannot be given greater protection than the seniority system in the event of unanticipated layoffs. The Court said that an award of competitive seniority can be made only to actual victims of discrimination.

A city agreed to a consent decree to settle charges of race discrimination in the fire department. When the city later responded to a budget crunch by preparing to lay off fire fighters based on their seniority, the district court enjoined any layoffs that would decrease the percentage of blacks in the department.

On appeal, the Supreme Court differed with the district court's ruling. The injunction's interference with a collectively bargained seniority system cannot be justified as an effort to enforce the decree, the Court said, because the decree, to which the union was not a party, mentioned neither layoffs nor an intent to depart from the lawful seniority system. Nor could the district court grant competitive seniority to black employees as a "modification" of its decree, the Court explained, because there was no finding that any of the blacks protected from layoff had been victims of discrimination.[24]

INTERNAL-STAFFING POLICIES

Sound internal-staffing policies and practices will often resolve many personnel problems for the organization. When employees think that their skills are being disregarded or underused, dissatisfaction and turnover are likely to occur. When employees think they are being treated unfairly or discriminated against in promotion, transfer, or layoff decisions, dissatisfaction may lead to turnover. An employee who thinks he or she was discriminated against may file a complaint with the EEOC or another equal-employment agency. Management may lay off employees with little concern for the workers' interests, creating considerable ill will with labor or in the community. Each of these problems reflects a lack of concern for human resources and reduces the organization's overall effectiveness. Therefore, administrators must create and implement internal-staffing practices that are fair and that make the greatest use of employees' abilities.

The most prudent approach to filling job vacancies is to follow a policy of promotion from within but maintain enough flexibility to tap the external labor market when employees within the organization are not qualified. To support a policy of promotion from within, administrators need tools to predict the promotability of employees, particularly when decisions concern the promotion of personnel from nonmanagement to management positions. In these situations, assessment centers and job-related interviews should prove valuable.

The quality of staffing decisions depends on the quality of the information used to make those decisions. Managers must ensure that their performance-appraisal systems generate data that accurately reflect the candidates' achievements. Yet many firms still use vague, subjective, and biased rating systems which not only provide little meaningful performance information but also run the risk of being illegal. Often such systems permit politics to dominate staffing decisions. Such results-oriented appraisal systems as MBO and such behavioral systems as BARS eliminate much of the subjectivity and bias of rating scales and result in better decisions. Personnel administrators must create systems that provide accurate measures of employee performance.

Assistance for Laid-off Employees

Economic misfortunes may cause a firm to lay off great numbers of workers. Layoffs can be professionally managed to reduce the eco-nomic strains that laid-off workers and the community face when large numbers of jobs are temporarily or permanently eliminated. Providing assistance to employees during layoffs reflects a genuine concern for the organization's workers and is an act of social responsibility to the community. Laid off employees can be helped through notification of plant closings, severance pay, supplemental unemployment benefits, and out-placement assistance.

Notification of Plant Closings In 1988 the U.S. Congress passed a law requiring employers to provide workers with advance notice of plant closings and layoffs. The plant closings bill requires employers of more than 100 people to give workers and their communities 60 days' written notice of any closure or layoff involving 50 or more full-time employees. Major exemptions from this legislation include "unforeseeable circumstances" and the need to raise capital privately to keep a facility open.[25] President Reagan vetoed a similar bill earlier in 1988, but an election year allowed the bill to become law without his signature. The U.S. Chamber of Commerce was strongly opposed to the plant closings bill. However, company officials at the Ford Motor Company, Eastman Kodak Company, Whirlpool Corporation, and others noted that the law mandates less notice than most firms have voluntarily given workers.[26]

The biggest advantage of notification of an imminent layoff is that workers and communities are given time to prepare. For example, workers would have a chance to find new jobs. But many managers see problems in giving advance notice; they claim that advance notice of a plant closing may hurt their credit ratings and reduce new customer orders. They also worry about employee morale, motivation, and absenteeism as workers look for new jobs. One professor of industrial relations suggests learning from West Germany's experiences:[27]

> Of all the European countries, Germany appears to have the greatest success in achieving the growth and increasing the productivity that go with change, while also avoiding the political and social disruption that have occurred in France and Great Britain. German legislation requires that a firm give notice "in good time," which has usually been interpreted to be about three months.

Supplemental Unemployment Benefits In the 1950s, steel and automobile industry union leaders began negotiating *supplemental unemployment benefits (SUB)* plans. These plans provide additional income to supplement state unemployment benefits to employees who are laid off. Union negotiators normally contend that state unemployment benefits do not enable the employee to adequately maintain his style of living. SUB plans are designed to be directly supplemental; employees receive a certain percentage of their gross pay for a maximum number of weeks when unemployed. For example, if each employee subjected to a layoff during the period of the contract receives 75 percent of normal base pay, with the company providing the additional funds necessary to the employee's state unemployment benefits, an employee making about $266 a week would receive a total of $200. This 75 percent figure would include $150 per week of state unemployment benefits, with the remaining $50 being provided by the company.

Guaranteed Income Stream The relatively high unemployment rate and severe layoffs in the 1970s and 1980s caused job security to become a top priority for union negotiation and members.[28] Several innovative provisions in contracts have the intent of improving employment security. One of the

most interesting and publicized is the *guaranteed income stream* (GIS) plan in the auto industry.

The GIS plan is an alternative to the traditional SUB, although the goal of income maintenance for employees is the same. The typical GIS plan differs from SUB plans in three important areas. First, GIS plans furnish benefits to eligible workers until they retire and thus have been called a "guaranteed lifetime wage," whereas SUB plans end after a short period of time, usually two years. Second, qualification for a GIS plan is based on earnings and not employment, which encourages laid-off workers to seek other employment. Third, the benefits provided by a GIS plan are only partially offset by outside earnings until a breakeven point is reached. Under most SUB plans, benefits are completely offset by outside earnings—a deterrent to laid-off workers seeking outside jobs. Thus, GIS plans create incentives for laid-off workers, unlike SUB plans, which tie them to their former employer. Both sides may benefit from GIS plans. If laid-off workers find new jobs, the amount of GIS benefits paid by the former employer may be reduced as they are partially offset by the outside income. However, the employer is encouraged to avoid layoffs by the long-term eligibility aspect of a GIS plan. When layoffs are necessary, the employer has an additional financial incentive to help workers find new employment. The GIS plan may eventually replace SUB plans since both management and labor can realize important advantages.[29]

Severance Pay Severance pay, sometimes called *dismissal pay,* is income provided to employees who have been permanently terminated from the job through no fault of their own. While similar to SUB in its appearance and formula for provision in determining benefits, severance pay is given under quite different circumstances. SUB pay enables the employee who is temporarily laid off to feel minimum impact from the layoff and anticipate a return to work and full pay. Employees who receive severance pay, however, realize that they have no hope for future work with the company. It is not normally provided to employees who are terminated for just cause or who quit.

The purpose of severance pay is to cushion the loss of income due to plant closing, merger, automation, or subcontracting of work. Therefore, union negotiators contend that management should shoulder some of the financial burden while the employee is seeking other permanent work.

The amount of severance pay is usually specified by a formula guaranteeing a percentage of base pay determined by the number of years of service with the company. The percentage normally increases as the employee's number of years increases to a maximum percentage. To be eligible, employees are normally required to have a minimum number of years of service, usually one, except in a case of disability. In the case of a merger, plant closing, relocation, or the sale of the company, the liability for severance pay may become a most important issue. Court decisions have upheld the legal right of employees to receive severance pay from the parties involved. In such cases severance pay owed workers is generally regarded as a legal liability of the company.[30] Unions have a legal right to file suit on behalf of employees denied negotiated severance pay under the Labor Management Relations Act, Section 301.[31]

Out-placement Assistance In contrast to years past, many firms are providing a number of services to laid-off employees that involve job-placement assistance and training for new job skills. For example, when the Ford Motor Company closed its Milpitas, California, plant, it offered extensive out-placement services to laid-off employees. In cooperation with the United Auto Workers (UAW), Ford assessed the training needs of over 2,000 hourly workers, used idle portions of the plant to teach remedial English and math, and offered "vocational exploration" classes that encouraged employees to learn new skills, such as auto upholstery and forklift operations.[32]

A similar program was offered to hundreds of International Harvester (IH) employees laid off in Louisville, Kentucky. A joint IH-UAW program called the Out-placement Assistance Program included the following activities:[33]

Assessment Participants were asked to analyze all the skills they had acquired through formal training or experience at IH and through other activities that may have taken place off the job. The assessment phase also included the determination of skills that the participants liked to use and the jobs they would like to have.

Stress Counseling Participants took a test that measured their stress levels and then engaged in discussions that helped them come to grips with the hostility and frustration of being laid off.

Financial Counseling A portion of the course was devoted to tips on saving money and on working with creditors to get more time to pay bills.

Family Counseling Guest speakers discussed how to resolve marital and family problems that might arise as a result of unemployment.

Job Hunting The heart of the course was devoted to finding a job. Participants were encouraged to set up a "job squad" of friends, relatives, former bosses, and so on that would provide an informal network of job contacts.

They were also given advice on how to read help-wanted ads, with emphasis on determining if their skills might qualify them for the job. The counselors also provided assistance on filling out application blanks and on effective job interviewing.

What are the components of a model out-placement program? The Illinois AFL-CIO program is often used by employers to guide their efforts in developing programs for the soon-to-be unemployed. The program includes the following:[34]

Advance Notice   Advance notice of a plant closing of six months or a year will give "organizations time to organize their out-place-ment programs and permit employees to ad-just their own plans as well as consider the various employment options."[35]

Labor-Management Out-placement Commit-tees   A cooperative effort by labor and man-agement, enabling both parties to participate in setting out-placement goals, is believed to be the most effective way to implement out-placement activities.

Job-search Training   Such training is usually helpful, though the success rate is closely tied to the conditions in the labor market.

Job Clubs   A job club brings job seekers to-gether, provides a location for job-search training, and reduces the frustration and iso-lation that generally accompany job-hunting efforts.

Aggressive Job Development   These activities include contacting suppliers, customers, and the business community in general in an at-tempt to place laid-off workers.

Skills Training   Research shows that only about 20 or 25 percent of laid-off employees seek skills training, even though it is free. But skills training is important, and most organi-zations provide this service.

Personnel Assistance   During and after a plant closing, a small staff of personnel em-ployees should be maintained to assist unem-ployed workers through counseling, job assis-tance, and training.

Third Parties   Successful programs often in-clude the use of outside consultants who have expertise in creating and implementing out-placement activities.

Industrial Development   In most cases, a va-cant plant is turned over to industrial real-es-tate personnel with little or no thought about how the plant could be kept in operation by another company. In several instances, coop-erative efforts among management, local gov-ernments, federal redevelopment agencies, and labor have resulted in a closed plant being taken over by another firm. In many cases, a significant number of laid-off employees were employed by the new employer.

For managers and staff professionals, out-placement assistance often includes resumé preparation and job counseling. Some firms employ out-placement consultants to help laid-off executives find new jobs. Through counseling, these consultants help individuals gain self-confidence, sharpen interviewing skills, and develop job contacts. Generally, the company that laid off the employee pays the consultant's fee, which may amount to as much as 15 percent of a laid-off executive's annual salary.

Equal Employment Opportunity

Personnel policies should dictate that inter-nal-staffing decisions are made without re-gard to race, color, religion, national origin, sex, or age. Any personnel procedure or practice that adversely affects protected classes of employees is potentially illegal and may result in a complaint being filed against the organization.

Methods for making promotions should conform to EEOC guidelines, which require that objective job descriptions be used and that promotion procedures be valid and in writing. An affirmative-action program may require management to post promotional opportunities, to use skills inventories when recruiting promotion candidates, to implement formal employee appraisal systems, and to establish career counseling programs.

CAREER MANAGEMENT

People have varying expectations about the rewards and satisfactions they seek from their jobs. To some, work is purely a necessary evil, a painful mechanism for earning enough money to support one's self or one's family. These employees do not expect to be fulfilled in their work: they may, in fact, feel that working and enjoyment are totally incompatible. Other employees not only seek good salaries and benefits but also desire to satisfy certain human needs through their work. They want to work with agreeable and friendly coworkers and to receive ego satisfaction from performing their jobs. They may not, however, aspire to middle- or upper-level management or professional positions. These workers feel that management positions may involve stress, too much responsibility, pressure, long hours, and weekends at the office. A good family life with the time to pursue hobbies and other interests may be perceived as being just as important as—or more important—than a high status, high-paying job.

For other persons, work is the most significant part of their lives. Totally committed to their jobs, they receive a great deal of personal pride and satisfaction from their work.

A vice-presidency or presidency is the pot of gold at the end of the rainbow, and these overachievers are more than willing to invest long hours, weekends, and holidays in pursuit of their dreams. To these employees, the job comes first and everything else—family, hobbies, social obligations, and other interests—comes second.

On a continuum of career interest, work may be viewed as "just a job" on one end and a career on the other. In the past, managers did not try to clarify this distinction for their employees. Management has long felt that employees should take personal responsibility for defining their employment goals and aspirations. Managers assumed that those possessing extraordinary human talent and ambition would rise to the top, much like cream in a bottle of milk. Employees with lesser skills and more modest achievement drives would, mostly through personal choice, remain in lower-status jobs. In the end, people would naturally find the jobs for which their skills and abilities were best suited. Generally, management was interested but passive, making promotion and transfer decisions when necessary and leaving long-term occupational plans and strategies up to the individual.

Contemporary personnel professionals, however, are playing an increasingly active role in designing and implementing programs that help employees not only focus on career choices and objectives but also achieve the objectives they formulate. Such help originated with a concern for the quality of working life, an eye to EEO legislation, and a need to use the organization's human resources effectively. Programs have been created that draw upon both traditional personnel tools and contemporary methods designed specifically for the development of career paths. In general, all of these programs fall under the general heading of *career management*. Important terms and concepts in career management are the following:

Career A sequence of jobs held during a person's working life.

Career Management The process of designing and implementing goals, plans, and strategies that enable administrators to satisfy work-force needs and allow individuals to achieve their career objectives.

Individual Career Planning The process whereby each employee personally plans career goals.

Organizational Career Planning The process whereby management plans career goals for employees.

Benefits to the Organization

Well-planned and executed career programs will benefit both the organization and employees in a number of ways. These include:

Manpower Inventories Effective career management will help ensure a continuous supply of professional, technical, and managerial talent so that future organizational goals may be achieved.

Staffing from Within Because of the many potential advantages of promotion from within, most organizations like to promote employees when positions become available. But recruitment from within requires a strong career-management program to guarantee that employees can perform effectively in their new jobs. Promoting employees before they are ready to assume their new jobs will result in unsatisfactory performance, as predicted by the Peter principle.[36]

Solving Staffing Problems Certain staffing problems may be remedied through effective career management. First, a high rate of employee turnover may be caused, at least in part, by a feeling that little opportunity exists within the organization. Second, recruiting new employees may be easier if applicants realize that the company develops its employees and provides career opportunities. Many college graduates desire to work for organizations that will assist in career management.

Employee Needs The current generation of employees is much different from those of generations past. Higher levels of education have raised career expectations. And many workers hold their employers responsible for providing opportunities so that those expectations may be realized.

Enhanced Motivation Because progression along the career path is directly related to job performance, an employee is likely to be motivated to perform at peak levels so that career goals may be accomplished.

Equal Employment Opportunity The letter and spirit of federal EEO guidelines demand fair and equitable recruiting, selection, and placement policies, and the elimination of discriminatory practices concerning promotions and career mobility. Many affirmative-action programs contain formal provisions to enhance the career mobility of women and minorities, including the development of career paths and the design of formal training and development activities. Further, several court actions have forced organizations to strengthen such career-advancement procedures to remove obstacles to the career progression of minorities.

Four factors determine the success of an organization's career management efforts. First, career management must be planned; haphazard or ill-conceived attempts to manage careers will fail.[37] Line managers and personnel administrators who share the responsibility for effective career management must work together to ensure that line and staff efforts are coordinated. Second, top management must support career management. Such support comes from a climate that encourages promotion from within, the development of employee skills, and the use of valid performance criteria for promotion decisions. Third, administrators must not omit or neglect any of career management's many programs and processes. The career-management process will vary from organization to organization, but certain elements are central to every program. These include organizational career planning, individual career planning, integrating organizational and individual plans, implementation, and evaluation.

A fourth factor, *career match*, has been found to be the most critical factor in career-management programs. The program must seek to find a career match between the employer's plans for the employee and his or her personal aspirations. Programs that simply explain the organization's career plans to the employees, but do not assist them in clarifying their own goals and developing a match between theirs and the organization's, are likely to fail. The employee and employer should negotiate a mutually acceptable outcome. If the employer addresses employees' expectations early in their career, employees may willingly modify their expectations. However, if differences are ignored, the employee may develop incompatible career plans, which cause undesired turnover when they are not met by the employer.[38] In fact, today's workers are more willing to change jobs and even careers if their career objectives are not met.[39]

Organizational Career Planning

An important part of the human resource planning process involves the forecast of both long- and short-term human resource needs. During this process, the major changes the organization is likely to face are predicted (growth, decline, reorganization, new technologies), and their impact on the organization's labor force is assessed. Emphasis is placed on predicting changes in the numbers

and the kinds of employees that will be needed. But manpower plans must be flexible enough to adjust to such contingencies as rapid, unpredicted organization growth or decline.

Some organizations develop individual career plans for managers and for professional personnel. An executive succession chart (chapter 4) is sometimes used as an aid in career planning. Decision makers must develop individual plans based on future organizational needs, the employee's performance and promotability, and EEO considerations.

Individual Career Planning

Today an increasing number of individuals are plotting their own career goals and creating strategies to achieve them. Their actions are consistent with the attitude that emphasizes that individuals should take greater responsibility for the events that shape their lives. Many books have been published to assist in the planning and integrating of personal, social, family, and work goals.

Many progressive organizations offer counseling about career opportunities as a part of their career-management system. Usually, career counseling is voluntary and available to all employees. Typically, career counselors are in the personnel department; in smaller firms, a personnel administrator may conduct career counseling along with other personnel functions.

Whether employees conduct career planning through a course or seminar or through formal career counseling, the first step is the assessment of personal interests, aims, skills, and abilities. It is important that employees find out as much as possible about themselves—their ambitions, needs, values, strengths, and limitations. The second step is the collection of information about existing and future opportunities in an organization.

Career counselors are generally prepared to offer this kind of information. In addition, an organization's informal grapevine often contains valuable information about upward progression, such as what important jobs are likely to open up, who the good managers to work for are, and which departments or work projects have the highest growth potential. Many practicing managers and administrators have testified to the value of this informal network. Although many old boy networks have long been closed to women and minorities, many networking systems have been formed to provide minorities with helpful career information.

Based on self-assessment and evaluation of opportunities in an organization, employees must then set career goals, that is, realistic goals that have a high probability of being achieved. Not everyone who aspires to a top position or dreams of a six-figure salary can achieve such goals. Frustration and disappointment can be kept to a minimum, however, if the employee is realistic.

The final step in the individual planning process is the development of a strategy to achieve career goals. Strategic decisions are often informal, rarely put in writing, and subject to considerable adjustment as an employee progresses through a career. The realities of organizational life demand flexible planning because uncertainty and risk underscore any form of long-range planning. Usually, strategies combine work experience and formal education. Previous education and expertise strongly influence the work experiences employees seek. Formal long-term education strategies often include earning an advanced degree such as a master's degree in business administration, health care, management science, or industrial psychology. Short-term educational strategies may include participation in short courses or seminars. Frequently, employers will reimburse some or all of the tuition and other expenses, particularly if the employee's work is related to the additional education.

Getting to the top of the organizational hierarchy takes much more than experience and education. Sheer ability, a great deal of fortitude, political savvy, foresight, and boldness are among the characteristics of those who occupy executive suites. Some advice on staying on track to the executive suite is given in Figure 9–1.

Integrating Plans

To be effective, career-management efforts must strike a workable balance between the organization's human-resource needs and employees' career goals. In reality, this balance is difficult to achieve. The dynamic nature of organizational life sometimes makes it extremely difficult for each person to carry out career plans within specific time constraints. Business contraction, "dead wood," and company politics are some of the roadblocks and detours in the career paths of many employees. Unpredictable delays in career progression will inevitably result in disappointment, frustration, and turnover as employees leave to join organizations that promise to fulfill career objectives.

To a considerable extent, management can minimize employee frustration and turnover caused by career stagnation through practical career counseling that integrates organizational needs and individual career goals. With the aid of professional career counselors, employees can realistically appraise career goals and the organization's predicted human resource needs. In some cases, overly optimistic personal career goals may have to be trimmed back. In other cases, the counselor may suggest opportunities and, perhaps, alternative career paths to accelerate an employee's career aims. Regardless of the plan

FIGURE 9–1

Getting to the top
(Source: Adapted from
E. E. Jennings, *Routes
to the Executive Suite*
[New York: McGraw-
Hill, 1971]; and from
R. H. Buskirk, *Your
Career: How to Plan It,
Manage It, Change It*
[Boston: Cahners,
1976].)

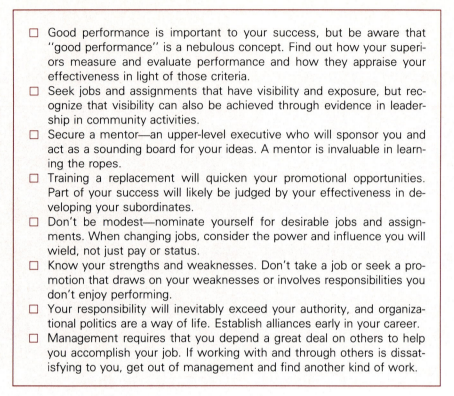

☐ Good performance is important to your success, but be aware that "good performance" is a nebulous concept. Find out how your superiors measure and evaluate performance and how they appraise your effectiveness in light of those criteria.

☐ Seek jobs and assignments that have visibility and exposure, but recognize that visibility can also be achieved through evidence in leadership in community activities.

☐ Secure a mentor—an upper-level executive who will sponsor you and act as a sounding board for your ideas. A mentor is invaluable in learning the ropes.

☐ Training a replacement will quicken your promotional opportunities. Part of your success will likely be judged by your effectiveness in developing your subordinates.

☐ Don't be modest—nominate yourself for desirable jobs and assignments. When changing jobs, consider the power and influence you will wield, not just pay or status.

☐ Know your strengths and weaknesses. Don't take a job or seek a promotion that draws on your weaknesses or involves responsibilities you don't enjoy performing.

☐ Your responsibility will inevitably exceed your authority, and organizational politics are a way of life. Establish alliances early in your career.

☐ Management requires that you depend a great deal on others to help you accomplish your job. If working with and through others is dissatisfying to you, get out of management and find another kind of work.

finally agreed upon, however, it must be evaluated and updated when organizational or personal factors necessitate changes.

Implementing Programs

Career development is a long-term process, spanning an employee's entire working career. Although minor (and occasionally major) adjustments in career paths are expected, effective career management enables career progression to proceed with regularity and predictability. The primary elements in implementing a career-management program include the publication of job vacancies, the implementation of employee performance appraisals, the establishment of training and

development activities, and the evaluation of career progression.

Job Vacancies Publicizing job vacancies (job posting) is an excellent way to disseminate career information and notify employees who may be qualified for a vacant job. Bulletin boards and internal company news bulletins are normally used for this purpose. Job announcements generally include the job title, a brief description of duties, necessary qualifications, starting salary, and location of the job.

Appraisal Data Sound employee performance appraisal data are particularly important for career development. Performance feedback by an employee's supervisor will include an analysis of strengths, weaknesses, and shortcomings so that any problems may be overcome. Continued inattention to or disregard of performance shortfalls will limit career progression. Thus, supervisors have the important responsibility of honestly telling employees whether their performance is satisfactory in light of their career goals. Further, personnel administrators play an important role by designing and implementing valid performance-appraisal systems.

Training and Development Experiences Perhaps the most meaningful aspect of career development is the accumulation of work experiences and off-the-job developmental activities that broaden employees' skills and abilities. Effective development enables the employee to assume increasingly challenging job responsibilities and to perform at higher job levels. Many training and development activities—for example, job rotation, coaching, committee assignments, and off-the-job educational strategies—are core components of career management for many organizations. Any serious attempt at career management must include well-planned and well-coordinated employee training and development.

Career Evaluation The final phase of the career-development process is evaluation of an employee's progress toward career goals. Evaluation usually takes place annually or biannually, possibly during a formal performance review. During evaluation, employees review the progress of their careers with supervisors and perhaps career counselors. Particular emphasis is placed on whether career goals and timetables have been reached. If progress has been less than expected, the reasons are explored and discussed. Shortfalls in

career progression may be remedied through additional work experiences and off-the-job development. When the initial career aims were unrealistic, the employee must revise career goals. Good counseling skills are particularly important for supervisors or counselors who deal with disappointed, frustrated employees facing career stagnation.

Personnel administrators should recognize that employees generally progress through *career stages*. Each stage represents a unique set of opportunities, problems, and circumstances, and the needs of employees change as they pass from one stage to the next. Research suggests that employees generally advance through four stages:[40]

Establishment At the beginning of a career, the employee faces anxiety and uncertainty over his or her performance potential and competency. During establishment, a supportive and caring superior is particularly important for assisting the employee to become a productive employee.

Advancement Next, the employee demonstrates competence and a knowledge of the politics of organizational life. Less guidance and supervision are needed than during the establishment stage. But coaching, counseling, role models, and friendships remain important at this stage.

Maintenance People generally have achieved their highest advancement during the maintenance stage, devoting a considerable amount of their energies to developing and guiding others with less experience. This stage brings a great deal of satisfaction to some—notably those who have achieved their career goals. But others find disappointment and frustration—especially those who have not been particularly effective or have failed to reach career objectives and must consider new directions.

Withdrawal Withdrawal begins as one retires or moves on to a new career. During this stage, the individual devotes greater time to leisure and to the family. Frustration, stress, and boredom may also characterize this stage because the retiree loses his or her job identity and the social contacts enjoyed at work.

Evaluation of Career Programs

Because career development exists to serve several needs, evaluation must consider a number of different criteria. The degree to which career programs are established to solve staffing problems (e.g., providing a continuous supply of skilled workers or an effective internal promotion system) will influence what criteria are used in the evaluation process. Criteria include internal versus external hiring rates, turnover rates, exit interview results, and analysis of EEOC reports and audits.[41]

Even though a great deal of time and expense are expended on career development programs, few organizations formally evaluate their efforts. One research study involving forty corporations found only fifteen with formal evaluation systems, eight with informal methods, and seventeen with no evaluation whatsoever.[42]

Career Problems

Not unlike most large and complex human resource programs, career development systems must overcome several obstacles before they become effective. One of the most significant problems involves the question of employee expectations. Some employees think the organization should bear the major responsibil-

ity for employee development. But most organizations cannot afford the time and cost of planning the career of each employee and expect employees to assume some responsibility for development, such as attending evening graduate programs or funding their own trips to seminars and workshops.

Another problem is the impatience and frustration employees feel when advancement opportunities are few and far between. This problem is common in a declining economy, when promotional opportunities shrink. Having established career plans and goals and completed a number of developmental activities, employees often become alienated and cynical when promotions fail to materialize. To a degree, frustration can be minimized through candid career counseling and by communicating to employees that promotions are not automatic outcomes of career programs.

A particularly severe problem in managing career programs concerns the role of the supervisor in the career system. The supervisor is the employee's most important career counselor.[43] But an American Management Association study showed that in a sample of 225 companies the majority of supervisors surveyed thought that (1) career planning was a burden, (2) career planning for subordinates was not part of their job, and (3) they were not equipped to assist employees in career planning and counseling.[44] Because of the importance of supervisory participation in the development of careers, it is critical that they receive training in the skills required for career management and that they are rewarded for helping advance the careers of their subordinates.

Dual-career Couples Based on Labor Department statistics, about 60 percent of all working women are living with employed husbands. This represents about 46 million working men and women (out of about 100 million in the U.S. labor force) who are included in a growing segment of today's society: the dual-career couple. In the past, organizations largely ignored the problems of the dual-career couple, leaving them to solve the problems that their situation brought about. Faced with a large and growing number of dual-career couples, employers have begun to create policies and services that address the problems of those couples. Some of the problems that dual-career couples face include:[45]

Conflicting Alternatives Advancing the husband's or the wife's career often means moving in different geographical directions, often resulting in a crisis over whose career is most important.

Lack of Preparation Most dual-career couples lack the skills necessary to manage two careers and fail to develop plans to resolve conflicts between careers and family.

Lack of Experience in Conflict Resolution Many couples lack the skills necessary to solve crises, such as when to begin a family or how to divide the family responsibilities of shopping and cooking.

Reluctance to Approach the Company Many dual-career couples see their employer's policies as rigid and are reluctant to discuss their problems with a boss. They may feel that openness about their career problems may harm their chances of advancement.

Employers have instituted various programs to help couples with their problems. Authors Francine and Douglas Hall suggest that an effective program will contain the following characteristics:[46]

Dual-career Audit An audit, performed through a company survey, should be a starting point for a company to recognize the extent of the problem. Areas the audit should address include the number of dual-career employees, the conflicts they face, how effective they perceive present company policies and opportunities to be, and how competent they think they are to manage their careers.

Special Recruiting Techniques By giving a potential employee and his or her spouse a realistic view of the company's work load, travel, and career opportunities, employers may be able to avoid a potentially poor job match. Some companies offer new employees "couple counseling" immediately after hiring to help identify potential problems and conflicts and to explore coping skills.

Revision of Transfer Policies In many companies, advancement inevitably means a geographical move. But in many cases, relocation results in crises for the dual-career couple. Employers are now finding ways to enhance their employees' careers without permanent geographical transfer. Alternatives include temporary relocation assignments (two or three months) and more effective use of local training and development activities.

Revision of Nepotism Policies Employment policies often forbid an employee's spouse to work for the company. Most employers are revising their policies to allow both spouses to work for the company, as long as an employee does not supervise a relative or participate in decisions concerning the relative's salary, performance, or advancement.

Assistance for Dual-career Couples Many employers are helping couples learn the process of managing their careers. Workshops and seminars enable participants to assess their opportunities, obstacles, potential conflicts, and developmental needs.

Layoffs India Style

When I arrived in New Delhi to manage the Center, it had been in operation just one year. The founder, who had managed it during its first year, was a man of many outstanding qualities, much admired among his colleagues. But he laid the foundation for most of my management troubles.

Using good American business practice, he had recognized that circumstances could change and that operations could be retrenched or the Center would close without much warning. In every employee's letter of appointment he included a clause that carefully stated that employment could be terminated at any time without cause. He assumed, when writing these letters, that the employee would recognize that his or her job would last only as long as U.S. government grants kept coming.

It was my bad luck that the federal funds began to dry up almost as soon as I arrived. With little regard for budgetary constraints, my predecessor had already hired thirty-two officers, clerks, messengers, and night watchmen. I now had money for only twelve to fifteen employees. That meant that I had to lay off employees to make the budget balance. This is not an uncommon American practice. It is not without its thorns, of course, but layoffs are familiar to any American executive and are always in the backs of employees' minds.

You wouldn't believe the hullabaloo when I told the employees of the layoff! Delegations from those employees who were kept on urged me to change my mind. Those laid off protested bitterly. As a new executive, I had some trouble wrestling with my own emotions on this one.

American workers would have spoken to the reporters outside the gates, filed grievances with the union, and tried to reverse the layoff decision, too. The Indian employees went further, totally discounting the warnings in my predecessor's letters of appointment and assuming that their employment (like any employment in India) was to last for life. Several of them went to a communist member of Parliament. They did not just protest being laid off—they told the M.P. that I was a spy! I was a spy because I typed some of my own letters (letters home, actually)—and I rode my bicycle to deliver these letters to the U.S. Embassy. (Actually, I was riding off to a nearby ruin where a lovely park made it possible to read my papers without telephone interruptions.) I learned about their reports when I picked up the morning paper and found myself a lead article: "Notorious U.S. Spy in Defense Colony."

My predecessor had wisely employed the daughter of the civil servant in charge of law and order in India, the Home Secretary. Knowing that the attack on me was really a veiled attack on him and his boss, the Home Minister, India's second most powerful person, the government of India discounted the story. But to find myself labeled "a notorious espionage agent" came as a considerable surprise to me, for I featured myself as an ordinary manager. Because I had played my political relations properly, this blew over very quickly, but the lesson should have been my predecessor's: do not hire Indian employees unless you intend to keep them for their working lives or unless you have carefully provided in advance a soft landing for them in another position of equal worth.

Fifteen years later, when I really had to close down the whole operation, we took greatest care to make certain that each and every employee had another job before we shut the doors. Layoffs are not expected in India.

Source: Adapted from Henry Ferguson, *Tomorrow's Global Executive* (Homewood, IL: Dow Jones-Irwin, 1988), pp. 85–86.

CONCLUSIONS AND APPLICATIONS

- Several factors result in a need for significant internal personnel changes: organizational growth, major reorganizations, changes in general business conditions, and resignations, terminations, and retirements. Personnel administrators should closely monitor these changes to ensure that internal-staffing decisions are as planned and orderly as possible and should strive to integrate both short- and long-range manpower needs.

- Decision makers should look closely at their mechanisms and practices for recruiting promotion candidates. An open promotion system enables greater use of employee skills and abilities as compared to closed systems.

- Criteria for making promotion decisions should be applied in a manner consistent with the nature of the work force and or-

ganizational goals. Seniority is a prime factor in making promotions among unionized employees; performance and promotability are important in promoting nonunionized employees. Political considerations, though impossible to eliminate, should be minimized. Assessment centers are valuable tools for identifying potential managers among nonmanagerial personnel.

- It is important that decision makers write sound personnel policies for making internal-staffing decisions. An important issue to clarify is whether to promote from within or hire from the outside. Normally, advantages of promoting from within far outweigh the other. Appraisal data for making promotional decisions must be objective and must accurately reflect an employee's performance and promotability. Assistance should be available for laid-off employees. Internal staffing should be performed with an eye toward equal opportunity for all employee groups. Long- and short-range planning decisions should be integrated as fully as possible. Line and staff personnel must agree on the nature of their respective areas of authority and responsibility on internal staffing issues.

- Career management involves integration of organizational manpower needs with the career goals and aspirations of individuals. To be effective, career management should be formal and planned, should receive support from top management, and should be recognized as a process that involves coordination of a number of separate yet interrelated personal tools and techniques.
- Once organizational manpower needs and personal career goals have been defined and integrated, a number of personnel practices can start a career in motion. These include job posting,

performance appraisal, and training and development activities.

- Decision makers should periodically assess the extent to which career-management efforts are actually resulting in benefits to the organization and individual employees. Some of these benefits may include reduction of employee turnover, attraction of high-quality job candidates, increased employee motivation, greater personal control over employee careers, and equal opportunity for all employee groups.
- Dual-career couples should be prepared to deal with problems that include potential conflicts over career paths and the division of family responsibilities. Assistance from organizations may include dual-career audits, special recruiting techniques, and special policies for dual-career couples.

CASE STUDY
Assessment Center at Piedmont Insurance

The Piedmont Insurance Company's personnel committee entered the executive conference room, took their seats, drank coffee from styrofoam cups, and chatted amiably among themselves. Each of the organization's six major departments was represented, typically by the department head. They included Kathy Morris, claims manager, Allen Mazula, manager of personal lines, and Lynn Snead, manager of group insurance. They were waiting for Jerry Smyth, head of Piedmont's personnel department and chairman of the personnel committee. The committee members had only a vague notion of what the meeting was all about; the memo calling the session spoke sparingly of "problems with promotion decisions" and a need to develop "a system for making more effective promotion decisions."

The Piedmont Insurance Company is a medium-sized, rapidly growing insurance company based in Durham, North Carolina. Piedmont Insurance is one of eighteen insurance companies owned by Tidewater, Inc., a large insurance holding company. Offering a variety of personal, home, and life insurance coverage, Piedmont has recently captured a sizable niche in the group insurance market. Piedmont's labor force totals about 4,500 employees, including about 600 line managers and staff administrators.

Smyth, about five minutes late, hurriedly took his chair at the end of the conference table. After uttering a brief apology for his tardiness, he got to the point:

Smyth: "This afternoon we need to discuss a serious personnel problem that we've had in this organization for some time. As I'm sure you are all aware, we have recurring performance problems at the first level of management. Deadlines are frequently missed and quality control is almost nonexistent. Turnover among the clerical staff and sales personnel is about twice what it should be. And our annual employee attitude surveys show that our supervisors are in dire need of both work-oriented and people-oriented skills. We have much job dissatisfaction at the clerical and salesperson level, and all fingers point to supervision. Besides, the productivity audit conducted last year by our management consultants, Van Auken and Associates, confirmed that our first level of supervision was one of the organization's weakest links. To make a long story short, we need to consider alternative ways to strengthen our first-line supervision."

Morris: "But Jerry, each new manager is required to attend a forty-hour supervisory training program offered by your department. Isn't the program having any impact?"

Smyth: "Well, we haven't been satisfied with the results of our evaluation studies. Currently we're looking at ways to improve our management training."

Mazula: "Jerry, you don't turn someone into a supervisor in one week. What else are we doing to develop the skills of our new managers?"

Smyth: "Several things. First, we generally pay for an employee to attend a seminar as long as it's related to the job. Second, we reimburse employees for expenses they receive in getting a college degree. And as you know, we also encourage all middle managers to work closely with their supervisors to develop skills through on-the-job coaching."

Snead: "Besides taking a closer look at our training and development programs, what else can we do to improve our supervision?"

Smyth: "I think we need to make some significant changes in the way we make promotion decisions, particularly when promoting a nonmanagement employee into the first level of management. We're presently promoting about seventy-five employees a year into supervision. Historically, we've promoted someone because of a high degree of technical skills. But technical skills only play a minor role in supervision. And I'm afraid we've tried to make supervisors out of a good number of people who simply don't have the aptitudes to be successful managers. And we're probably overlooking a lot of employees who have the basic qualities that it takes for successful supervision."

Snead: "And how do we deal with these problems?"

Smyth: "A couple of months ago I sent to each of you a memo and several current journal articles that described the assessment-center concept. I think this is the real key to long-run improvements at our lower management levels. I've been toying with the idea of going ahead with the project for some time and decided to make a formal request to top management. I'm going to propose that we begin an assessment center for selecting first-level managers, and I want to discuss with you several different strategies for getting the program into action.

"One approach is to put our own assessment staff together under my direction. We could study other programs, select our own tests and exercises, train our own assessors, and periodically conduct our own assessment, say every three months or so. Another alternative is to hire an outside consulting firm to come in and do the assessments. And a third approach is to persuade the corporate personnel office at Tidewater to put together a program that could be used by each company. The economies of scale of this approach would be tremendous; with the great number of promotions that are made annually in the Tidewater system, a full-time professional staff would easily keep busy the year around."

Snead: "Hold on, Jerry. We all realize that a lot of successes have been recorded for the assessment-center concept, but it's not a perfect system. It won't guarantee success. Besides, it's pretty costly. How will we know we're getting our money's worth? To improve the quality of our supervision, maybe we should consider some other alternatives to the assessment center. We could beef up our supervisory training. Or we could make our promotion decisions much more carefully than we do now, perhaps by a formal committee. And to get more candidates, we could use job posting for the first level of supervision. That way all interested personnel would be welcome to apply.

"But if we do finally decide to go with the assessment center, let me strongly encourage that we start slowly at first with a pilot program in one department. That way we can iron out the bugs in the system before we go any further with it."

Questions

1. Evaluate the following alternatives for improving Piedmont's first level of supervision: (1) more supervisory training for new supervisors, (2) promotion decisions made by a promotion committee, and (3) implementation of an assessment center.

2. If you recommend an assessment center for Piedmont, who should conduct it—Piedmont's personnel department, Tidewater's corporate personnel office, or an outside consulting group? Should the program begin on a pilot-study basis?

3. Are the training and the assessment-center approaches mutually exclusive strategies for improving the quality of supervision? Discuss.

EXPERIENTIAL EXERCISE
What Are You Going to Do with Your Life?

Purpose

To get you to start thinking about career goals, personal strengths and weaknesses, and strategies for achieving career goals.

The Task

Listed below are several areas which are normally the focus of career planning workshops for employees and students. After you complete all questions, your instructor will lead you in a discussion concerning career planning.

Goal Setting

I. *Career Goals*

Let's begin by outlining a few career goals. How much thought have you given to what you want to be? How much money you want to make? The kind of organization you would like to work for? The industry? Geographical location? Think about these questions, and complete the following section.

A. Job

What *specifically* would you like to be doing in five years?

_____

B. Salary

How much money would you like to be making? (Of course, your salary goals should be tied directly to your job goal.) Be realistic!

$_____ per year

C. What size company would you like to work for?

1. Small (less than 300 employees) _____

2. Medium (300 to 1,000 employees) _____

3. Large (1,000 employees or more) _____

D. Which industry would you prefer to work in?
1. Government

Local _____

State _____

Federal _____

2. Construction _____

3. Mining _____

4. Manufacturing _____

(which kind?—automobile, etc.) _____

5. Agriculture _____

6. Transportation _____

7. Wholesale/retail trade _____

8. Services _____

(which kind?—banking, health care, etc.) _____

E. Where would you like to live?

1. Northeast _____

2. Southeast _____

3. Midwest _____

4. Central Plains _____

5. Southwest _____

6. Northwest _____

7. Doesn't matter _____

II. *Strengths and Weaknesses*

Right now, you have several strengths—skills and abilities—that will be assets in achieving your job goal. You will probably also need to acquire *new* skills to realize your job goal. In addition, you may have some weaknesses that you need to overcome before achieving your goals. In relation to your job goal, think about your strengths and weaknesses and complete the following section.

A. Strengths

List your strengths—include all skills and abilities, organization skills, technical skills such as your college major, and human skills (e.g., communication, motivation, etc.).

B. Skills to develop

Think about the job you would like to have, the skills you presently possess, and the skills you think you'll need to obtain to be competent in the job you want. Needed skills may include decision making, technical, and human relations skills. List these skills.

C. Obstacles

Now think of all the obstacles that you must overcome to realize your job goal. Obstacles relate not so much to skill deficiencies (listed before) as to external considerations, such as a reluctance to relocate if it is a condition for a promotion, or perhaps the difficulties (time and money) you would face in getting an MBA at night.

D. Soul search

Consider all your thoughts thus far: job and salary goals, strengths, areas that need to be developed, and obstacles. In light of your shortcomings and obstacles that need to be overcome, how *realistic* are your job and salary goals? How likely is it that your goals can be achieved? Write a statement about the likelihood of meeting your job goal in five years. Be honest!

KEY TERMS AND CONCEPTS

Assessment center

Bumping

Career development

Career management

Career stages

Closed promotion system

Demotion

Dual-career couple

Guaranteed Income Stream (GIS)

Individual and organizational career planning

Internal staffing

Layoff

Nepotism

Open promotion system

Out-placement assistance

Promotion

Seniority System

Severance pay

Supplemental unemployment benefits (SUB)

Transfer

REVIEW QUESTIONS

1. What are the benefits of an effective system for making promotion decisions? What are the various criteria that may be used for making promotion decisions?
2. What are the major causes of employee demotions, transfers, and layoffs?
3. What are some important personnel policies and practices that have an impact on internal-staffing decisions?
4. What are the benefits that may be gained from a career-management program?
5. What are the problems of two-career couples and how may they be overcome?

DISCUSSION QUESTIONS

1. In many organizations, it is customary to place new employees on probation for three to six months. If the new employee doesn't work out, he or she may be terminated without the right to appeal the firing. Do you think a similar probationary period should be enforced for employees who receive promotions? Can you think of any arguments for and against this proposal?

2. Seniority is a common criterion for deciding who to lay off among the blue-collar work force. Should seniority be the major factor in deciding upon white-collar layoffs? Defend your reasoning.

3. Most organizations used closed promotion systems when selecting candidates for promotion, though it is generally recognized that this approach minimizes the pool of candidates from which an employee may be selected. Why do organizations continue to use the closed promotion system?

4. An oft-cited advantage of using seniority as a criterion for making promotions is that it eliminates supervisory bias that may accompany a supervisor's promotion recommendations. Are there any ways to reduce the possibility of supervisory bias while using performance-related criteria in making promotion decisions?

5. The personnel literature generally holds the assessment center in high regard. Can you think of reasons why an organization would not adopt the assessment center in gathering promotion data?

6. Usually there is a tremendous stigma against an employee who admits, "I received a promotion and I am failing on my new job. I would like a job with less authority and responsibility." How can this stigma be eliminated?

7. If an employee receives a promotion and fails, whose fault is it—the organization's or the employee's?

8. In this chapter, we mentioned that advanced notice of plant closings is required by law in some European countries. Would you favor similar legislation in the United States? Why or why not? If you support such legislation, how much advance notice do you feel should be given?

9. Compare the predictors that are used to make external and internal staffing decisions. In general, which staffing decisions do you feel are more effectively made—external or internal?

10. Assuming you were employed full-time, what would you perceive as some of your immediate supervisor's responsibilities in the career-management process?

11. How would you evaluate your college's or university's efforts at preparing you for a career in the world of work? Cite your school's strong and weak areas.

ENDNOTES

1. This thesis is supported by the *expectancy theory* of job motivation, which suggests that an employee will be motivated to perform if (1) he or she values a certain outcome or (2) expects that high performance will lead to the outcome. See J. Richard Hackman and Lyman W. Porter, "Expectancy Theory Predictions of Work Effectiveness," *Organizational Behavior and Human Performance* (November 1968): 417–26.

2. See Frederick Herzberg et al., *The Motivation to Work* (New York: Wiley, 1959).

3. Bureau of National Affairs, *Employee Promotion and Transfer Policies,* Personnel Policies Forum survey no. 120 (Washington, DC: Bureau of National Affairs, 1978).

4. Maryellen Kelley, "Discrimination in Seniority Systems: A Case Study." *Industrial and Labor Relations Review* 36, no. 1 (October 1982): 40–41.

5. Stephen Cabot, *Labor Management Relations Manual* (Boston: Warren, Gorham, Lamont, 1980), chap. 15, p. 2.

6. Bureau of National Affairs (BNA) Editorial Staff, *Grievance Guide* (Washington, DC: Bureau of National Affairs, 1978), p. 2.

7. Cabot, *Labor Management,* chap. 15, p. 4.

8. Ibid., chap. 15, pp. 4–5.

9. BNA Editorial Staff, *Grievance Guide,* pp. 173–74.

10. Katherine G. Abraham and James L. Medaoff, "Length of Service and Promotions in Union and Nonunion Work Groups," *Industrial and Labor Relations Review* 38, no. 3 (April 1985): 408–20. Also D. Quinn Mills, "Seniority versus Ability in Promotion Decisions," *Industrial and Labor Relations Review* 38, no. 3 (April 1985): 421–25.

11. Michael R. Carrell and Christina Heavvin, *Collective Bargaining and Labor Relations,* 2nd ed. (Columbus, OH: Merrill, 1988), 239–45.

12. Conversation with the author.

13. As indicated in a previous chapter, the assessment center may also be used to assess management development needs and strengthen managerial skills. See L. C. Nichols and J. Hudson, "Dual Role Assessment Center," *Personnel Journal* (May 1981):380–87; and F. Enzs, "Total Development: Selection, Assessment, Growth," *Personnel Administrator* (February 1980).

14. Walter S. Wikstrom, "Assessing Managerial Talent," *The Conference Board Record* (March 1967). Assessment center procedures and exercises are also outlined in C. Jaffee and J. Sefcik, Jr., "What Is an Assessment Center?" *Personnel Administrator* (February 1980): 35–39.

15. Wikstrom, "Assessing Managerial Talent."

16. See F. Frank and J. Preston, "The Validity of the Assessment Center Approach and Related Issues," *Personnel Administrator* (June 1982): 87–94; and C. Millard and S. Pinsky, "Assessing the Assessment Center," *Personnel Administrator* (February 1980): 40–44.

17. S. D. Norton, "The Empirical and Content Validity of Assessment Centers vs. Traditional Methods for Predicting Managerial Success," *Academy of Management Review* 2 (1977): 442–53.

18. This point may be debated. It can be argued, and often is, that the family member is the most qualified person for the job.

19. *Fitzpatrick* v. *Duquesne Light Company,* U.S. Court of Appeals, Third Circuit, No. 85–3103 (1985).

20. Dalton Melville, *Men Who Manage,* (New York: John Wiley, 1959), p. 154.

21. Upper-level transfers (and promotions) sometimes require the professional to relocate to a new area. For a discussion of the problems and coping mechanisms related to the relocation issue, see the September 1980 and April 1984 issues of *Personnel Administrator.* Both issues are devoted to the topic of employee relocation.

22. S. Wermiel, "Court Orders That Shield Minorities from Layoffs Generate Bitterness," *The Wall Street Journal* (March 23, 1983): 33.

23. *Firefighters Local 1784* v. *Stotts* no. 82–206 U.S. (1984).

24. "Blacks Hired Under Consent Decree Subject to Seniority-Based Layoffs." *U.S. Law Week* 52, no. 49 (June 19,1984): 1193.

25. "Reagan, Succumbing to Politics, Decides Against Vetoing Plant Closings Measure," *The Wall Street Journal* (August 3, 1988): 3.

26. Ibid.

27. "Plant Closing Bills: Labor Takes a Beating," *Business Week* (August 20, 1984): 20.

28. D. Quinn Mills, "When Employers Make Concessions," *Harvard Business Review* (May–June 1983): 103–13.

29. Peter Cappelli, "Auto Industry Experiments with the Guaranteed Income Stream," *Monthly Labor Review* 107, no. 7 (July 1984): 37–39.

30. Martin Joy Galvin and Michael Robert Lied, "Severance: A Liability in Waiting?" *Personnel Journal* 65, no. 6 (June 1986): 126–31.

31. *UAW* v. *Roblin Industries,* 114 LRRM 2428 (D.C. Mich., 1984).

32. "A Ford Plant Closing May Prove a Model of Labor-Management Cooperation," *The Wall Street Journal* (October 11, 1983): 1.

33. "At Closed Harvester, a Program Tries to 'Retool' Workers," *Louisville Courier-Journal* (January 2, 1983): G-1.

34. W. L. Batt, Jr., "Canada's Good Example with Displaced Workers," *Harvard Business Review* (July–August 1983).

35. G. Shultz and A. Weber, *Strategies For Displaced Workers* (New York: Harper & Row, 1966), p. 190.

36. See L. Peter and R. Hull, *The Peter Principle* (New York: William Morrow, 1969).

37. M. Vosburgh, "The Annual Human Resource Review: A Career Planning System," *Personnel Journal* (October 1980): 830–37.

38. Cherlyn S. Grawrose and James D. Portwood, "Matching Individual Career Plans and Organizational Career Management," *Academy of Management Journal* 30, no. 4 (December 1987): 699–720.

39. M. J. Driver, "Career Concepts—A New Approach to Career Research," in R. Katz, ed., *Career Issues in Human Resource Management* (Englewood Cliffs, NJ: Prentice-Hall, 1982), pp. 23–32.

40. L. Baird and K. Kram, "Career Dynamics: Managing the Superior/Subordinate Relationship," *Organizational Dynamics* (Spring 1983): 46–64.

41. J. Dowd and J. Sonnenfeld, "A Note on Career Programs in Industry," in J. Sonnenfeld, *Managing Career Systems* (Homewood, IL: Richard D. Irwin, 1984), p. 325.

42. T. Gutteridge and F. Otte, "Organizational Career Development: State of the Practice," unpublished monograph (October 1982), p. 23.

43. J. Walker and T. Gutteridge, "Career Planning Practices: An AMA Report" (New York: AMACOM, 1979).

44. Ibid., p. 13.

45. F. Hall and D. Hall, "Dual Careers—How Do Couples and Companies Cope with the Problems?" *Organizational Dynamics* (Spring 1978): 57–77.

46. Ibid.

Bordon Electric Company: Part Two

Helen Horn joined the Bordon Electric Company eight months ago as director of human resources. Bordon Electric is a small regional public utility serving 50,000 customers in three communities and the surrounding rural area. Electricity is generated at a central plant, but each community has a substation and its own work crew. The total labor force at the central plant and three substations, exclusive of administrative and clerical personnel, numbers 280 people.

Horn designed and introduced a Performance Evaluation and Review System (PERS) shortly after joining Bordon. This system was based upon a similar system she had developed and administered in her prior position with a small company. She thought that the system had worked well and that it could be easily adapted for use at Bordon.

The purpose of PERS, as conceived by Horn, is to provide a positive feedback system for evaluating employees that would be uniform for each class of employees. Thus, the system would indicate to employees how they were performing on the job and help them correct any shortcomings. The plant supervisors and field supervisors are responsible for administering the system for the plant workers and the substation crew workers, respectively. The general supervisors are responsible for the plant/field supervisors. Employees get personal PERS reports monthly informing them of their current status, and there is a review and evaluation every six months.

PERS is based on a point system in an attempt to make it uniform for all workers. There are eight categories for evaluation, with a maximum number of points for each category and a total of 100 points for the system. The eight categories for the plant and crew workers, and the maximum number of points in each category, are as follows.

Categories	*Points*
1. **Quality of work** Points are deducted if the job must be redone within 48 hours of completion.	15
2. **Productivity** Points are deducted if the work was not completed within the time specified for the type of job.	15
3. **Safety on the job** Points are deducted if the employee does not use safe work habits on the job to protect himself and others.	15

4. **Neatness of work area or repair truck**   15
   Points are deducted if the work area or truck is not clean
   and neat.

5. **Cooperation with fellow workers**   10
   Points are deducted if an employee does not work well
   with others.

6. **Courtesy on the job and with the public**   10
   Points are deducted if an employee is rude and unpleasant
   when there is contact with the public.

7. **Appearance**   10
   Points are deducted if an employee does not wear standard
   work clothing or if the clothing is sloppy and dirty at the
   beginning of each day.

8. **Tardiness/excess absenteeism**   10
   Points are deducted if an employee arrives late or is absent
   for causes other than illness or death in the immediate family.

Total Points   100

    The list of categories used to evaluate the plant/field supervisors is slightly different.

    Each employee begins the year with 100 points. If an infraction in any of the categories is observed, 1 to 5 penalty points can be assessed for each infraction. Notification is given to the employee indicating the infraction and the points to be deducted. A worker who is assessed 25 points in any one month or loses all the points in any category in one month is subject to immediate review. Likewise, anytime an employee drops below 40 points, a review is scheduled. The general supervisor meets with the employee and the employee's plant/field supervisor at this review.

    If an employee has no infractions during the month, up to 12 points can be restored to the employee's point total—2 points each for categories 1–4 and 1 point each for categories 5–8. However, at no time can a worker have more than the maximum allowed in each category or more than 100 points in total.

    When Horn first introduced PERS to the general supervisors, they were not sure they liked the system. Horn told them how well it had worked where she had used it before. Horn's enthusiasm for the system and her likable personality convinced the general supervisors that the system had merit.

    There were a few isolated problems with the system in the first two months. However, Larry Cox, a crew worker, is very unhappy with the new system, as evidenced by his conversation with Bob Cambron, a fellow crew worker.

Cox: "Look at this notice of infraction—I have lost twenty-two points! Can you believe that?"

Cambron: "How did your supervisor get you for that many points in such a short time?"

Cox: "It's all related to that bad storm we had two weeks ago. He disagreed with me on the work at Del Park and Madeline Court. It was dangerous, and I probably did fly off the handle. It was late at night after I had been working fifteen to sixteen hours straight. Look what he got me for: five points for lack of cooperation, five points for a dirty uniform, five points for a messy truck, including lunch bags and coffee cups in the cab, four points for slow work, and three points for being ten minutes late the next morning. Can you imagine that—being docked for ten minutes when I worked a double shift the day before. I didn't get home until 1:00 A.M. I even cleaned the truck up after he left that night—on my own time, no less!"

Cambron: "At least you won't get reviewed."

Cox: "Sure, but I bet he planned it to come out less than twenty-five points."

Cambron: "Boy, we worked ourselves to a frazzle that night and the next two days. You know, one of the guys over in substation 3 told me that his supervisor adds back points to their PERS reports over and above the normal monthly allowances."

Cox: "Well, don't that tell you what a screwy deal this whole PERS system is?"

Discussion Questions

1. Without regard to Larry Cox's recent experience with the system, evaluate the PERS in terms of its
   a. Design for a performance review and evaluation system.
   b. Value as a motivational device.
2. What problems might occur in the administration of the PERS system, and how might these administrative problems affect employee motivation? Explain your answer.

Part Three

Compensation and Health

Chapter Ten

Compensation Systems

Chapter Objectives

1. To recognize the relationship between a pay system and the process of attracting and retaining employees.
2. To identify the legal considerations of a pay system.
3. To explain the link between pay, motivation, and performance.
4. To explain the purpose of a wage survey.
5. To describe the major methods of job evaluation.
6. To develop a time-based pay system using pay grades and steps.
7. To understand piece-rate incentive systems.
8. To recognize gainsharing and profit-sharing group incentive plans.
9. To identify executive compensation methods.
10. To explain the current issues of comparable worth, two-tier wage systems, and COLA versus merit pay increases.

Raise the Minimum Wage?

The debate over what should be the national minimum wage has continued since it was set at $.25 per hour by the Fair Labor Standards Act in 1938. Opponents usually claim that raising the minimum increases inflation by increasing the cost of goods and services. They also believe that a higher minimum wage will raise unemployment as employers lay off employees to contain their payroll costs. Supporters of a higher minimum wage discount these claims by noting that any such negative effects on inflation or employment are only temporary.

In March 1987, Senator Edward Kennedy of Massachusetts and Representative Augustus F. Hawkins of California introduced bills to increase the national minimum wage from $3.35 to $4.65 per hour by 1990. Representative Hawkins defended the proposed increase on the basis of social and economic reasons: (1) From 1981, when the minimum was raised to $3.35 per hour, to 1987, the cost of living rose by about 27 percent; (2) in 1988 12.5 million American workers earned less than $4.00 per hour—which would not provide a poverty level income for a family of three; (3) minimum wage earners as a group are the best consumers, since they spend more on basics and thus help the private sector; (4) inflation and unemployment are affected far more by other federal economic factors, such as interest rates, the trade deficit, business taxes, and federal training program cuts, than by the minimum wage.[*]

What do personnel executives, the people who may directly experience the effects of a change in the law, say about it? In a survey conducted by *Personnel Journal*, 61 percent favored raising the minimum wage, while 36 percent were opposed. In addition, 66 percent predicted that the Kennedy–Hawkins proposed increase would have no effect on jobs in their organization, 15 percent predicted a reduction in jobs, and another 12 percent predicted a reduction in teenage employment. The executives also supported (57 to 41 percent) the concept of a *subminimum wage* for teenagers. One human resources director summed: "The current minimum wage doesn't motivate people to work and stay on the job." Another personnel manager with 1,350 employees added, "If Kennedy wants people to be paid more, he should focus his committee's efforts on ways to make them worth more to employers."[†]

[*]U.S. Representative Augustus F. Hawkins, "Increasing the Minimum Wage Makes Good Social and Economic Policy," *Personnel Journal* 66, no. 7 (July 1987): 12–16.

[†]Margaret Magnus, "Should the Minimum Wage per Hour Be Changed?", *Personnel Journal* 66, no. 6 (August 1987): 9–23.

ONE of the traditional personnel functions is determining employees' compensation. In the modern organization, with a variety of costly employee benefit programs, wage incentive programs, and structured pay scales, the compensation task is even more difficult and challenging for a personnel specialist. Employees' compensation affects their productivity and their tendency to stay with the organization. Although managers and researchers do not agree about the degree to which compensation affects productivity, compensation is of great importance. Employees' need for income and their desire to be fairly treated by the organization make developing the compensation program all the more important for the personnel department. Yet there is no exact, objective method of determining compensation for any one job or employee. Compensating employees for what they give the organization is to some extent as much an art as a science.

The term *compensation* is often used interchangeably with *wage and salary administration*; however, the term *compensation* actually is a broader concept. Compensation refers not only to *extrinsic rewards* such as salary and benefits but also to *intrinsic rewards* such as recognition, the chance for promotion, and more challenging job opportunities. The term *wage and salary administration* usually refers strictly to the monetary rewards given to employees. Figure 10–1 is a model of the total compensation system.

The compensation of people at work has become one of the most demanding problems facing management. In the past, payment for work performed was simple and straightforward. Paying for work not performed, such as paid vacations, was simply unheard of by management. For the most part, the employer displayed a "take it or leave it" attitude when making pay offers for employees. Although things have changed substantially, newer and

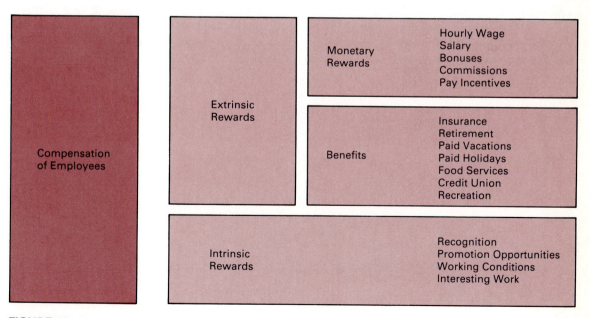

FIGURE 10–1

The total compensation system

Compensation and Health

better ways of compensating people are needed in personnel management.[1]

COMPENSATION OBJECTIVES

Organizations have many objectives in designing their compensation systems. The personnel specialist must keep in mind the goals of the system and what the organization needs to accomplish to obtain these goals. Primarily, the goals of any organization in designing a compensation system should be to attract and retain good employees. Also, the system should motivate employees and comply with all legal requirements. Figure 10–2 shows the objectives of any compensation system and how they are achieved.

Attracting Employees

Although most job applicants are not aware of the exact wages offered by different organizations for similar jobs within the local labor market, they do compare job offers and pay scales. Job applicants who receive more than one offer will naturally compare monetary offers. Since it is easier to compare dollars, job applicants often will put more weight on the salaries being offered than on other types of compensation, such as benefits and intrinsic rewards. Although one organization may make an offer $500 a year higher, that organization may provide less take-home pay than a competing organization which pays more of the benefit costs.

Some employers argue that wage level is not the important determinant of job choice; if that were the case, wage levels for similar jobs would be more similar within the same labor market. Employees would more readily leave lower-paying organizations and seek out higher-paying organizations. Indeed, a lack of market knowledge exists among job seekers. Given the limited knowledge job seekers often have about various employers, their general perceptions of the type of work they will perform and the exact salary being offered are the best factors they have to consider.[2]

A strategic pay decision by an employer is choosing a general pay level for the organization. In comparison to other employers within the same industry and labor market, management must decide whether to be a high pay-level employer, a low pay-level employer, or

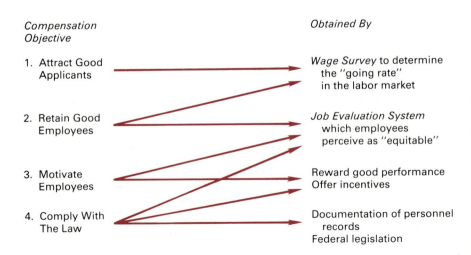

FIGURE 10–2
Objectives of a compensation system

Compensation Objective

1. Attract Good Applicants
2. Retain Good Employees
3. Motivate Employees
4. Comply With The Law

Obtained By

Wage Survey to determine the "going rate" in the labor market

Job Evaluation System which employees perceive as "equitable"

Reward good performance
Offer incentives

Documentation of personnel records
Federal legislation

a competitive pay-level employer. A *high pay-level strategy* may be chosen because management believes that if it maintains high salaries, the company will attract and retain the best employees within the geographic area, industry, or profession. Sometimes management will expect more from employees because the company pays higher than average salaries. A *low pay-level strategy* may be chosen because management decides to expect and live with the increased turnover and morale problems that may result. The savings in total personnel costs may be estimated to outweigh the disadvantages associated with low morale and high turnover. Employers may choose this strategy simply because the organization cannot afford to pay more. Small employers and those operating in highly competitive markets are likely to choose the low pay-level option. The *competitive pay-level strategy* may be chosen if management believes that the additional costs associated with this strategy cannot be justified or are simply not affordable. At the same time, management may believe that if the company's pay level is competitive within the labor market, the employee problems associated with the low pay-level strategy can be largely avoided.

Most employers will try to remain competitive within the local labor market by offering salaries that are similar to those offered by competing employers. Usually this means determining what the going rate is for jobs within the local labor market. This entails using *wage surveys,* which estimate average salaries for entry-level positions. The employer has two alternatives: the first is for the organization to conduct a wage survey and determine the going rate for jobs in the local labor market; the second is to use published market data.

Conducting a wage survey is a difficult, expensive process for an individual organization. The personnel specialist must determine

that employers have roughly comparable positions within the local labor market. Job titles are no longer an acceptable means of proving comparability of positions. By comparing brief job descriptions, the specialist must determine if the job is similar to other organizations' positions at a particular wage level.

A further requirement for conducting wage surveys is determining which information about each job is necessary. The wages being paid for each job type included in the survey must be precisely defined. If possible, survey information should include salary ranges, incentives, normal wage changes such as cost of living increases, and specific wage policies and practices within each organization in the survey. Information about seniority provisions, paid vacations, sick leave, and the number of paid holidays per year is helpful. Also, any additional pay, such as a uniform allowance or bonus plan, should be reported. Lastly, a wage survey should include questions concerning unusual working conditions such as high levels of noise or fumes.[3] A typical wage survey data sheet is shown in Figure 10–3.

Organizations have turned more to published wage-survey information for a variety of reasons. First, published information can be obtained quickly, at low cost, and with little effort by the organization. Second, conducting wage surveys has become a science in recent years; few organizations have personnel capable of undertaking such a task. Third, using an organization's wage survey may cause problems in court cases. Opposing lawyers will try to prove that the survey caused the organization to perpetuate past discriminatory practices that occurred in the surveyed organizations. The abundance of market data in most large communities has made more effective wage and salary administration possible in most geographic areas; sufficient market data are available to price anywhere from 5 to

Name of participating company _____Code _____

Address _____Business _____

Survey No. _____Data furnished by _____Title _____Date _____

		SHOP	OFFICE	SALARY	INCENTIVE
1. Number of employees in your company		_____	_____	_____	_____
2. Minimum hiring rates		_____	_____	_____	_____
3. Do you use training rates for new employees?		_____	_____	_____	_____
4. Number of hours worked.	Per week	_____	_____	_____	_____
	Per year	_____	_____	_____	_____
5. What method of progression do you use					
	Within the range	_____	_____	_____	_____
	Automatic Increase	_____	_____	_____	_____
	Merit Increase	_____	_____	_____	_____
	Part Automatic—Part Merit	_____	_____	_____	_____
6. Are you granting rest periods	With pay	_____	_____	_____	_____
	Without pay	_____	_____	_____	_____
7. Do employees working on holidays receive					
	Straight hourly rate	_____	_____	_____	_____
	Time and one-half	_____	_____	_____	_____
	Double time	_____	_____	_____	_____
	Other compensation	_____	_____	_____	_____
8. What is the average percentage of base rate paid as supplemental wages?		___%	_____%	_____%	_____%
9. In percent of base rates how much do you pay for a 40-hour workweek?					
	Afternoon shift	___%	_____%	_____%	_____%
	Night shift	___%	_____%	_____%	_____%
	Saturday	___%	_____%	_____%	_____%
	Sunday	___%	_____%	_____%	_____%
	Holiday	___%	_____%	_____%	_____%
10. Do you supply work clothes and laundry?		_____	_____	_____	_____
11. Do you use a single rate (SR)	SR	_____	_____	_____	_____
or a rate range (RR) for each job?	RR	_____	_____	_____	_____

12. If you use an incentive plan, briefly explain the incentive method used _____
_____
_____

13. What are the average incentive earnings per hour as a percentage of base rate?	___%	_____%	_____%	_____%

FIGURE 10–3

A typical wage survey data sheet (Source: Herbert G. Zollitsch and Adolph Langsner, *Wage and Salary Administration* [Cincinnati: South-Western Publishing Co., 1970], pp. 337–38. Used by permission.)

		Shop	Office	Salary	Incentive

14. Do you pay supplemental wages (Fringe Benefits)?
Annual Bonus___ Attendance Bonus___ Christmas Bonus___ Profit Sharing___
Stock Purchase Plan___ Seniority Bonus___ Vacation with Pay___ Paid Holiday___
Other Payments _____

		Shop	Office	Salary	Incentive

15. Are you guaranteeing an annual wage?

Yes ____ ____ ____ ____

No ____ ____ ____ ____

If "yes," please explain amount and number of weeks per year, etc. _____
_____
_____

16. Which of the following holidays do you grant with pay?

	Jan. 1	Feb. 12	Feb. 22	May 30	July 4	Labor Day	Thanksgiving	Dec. 25
Shop	____	____	____	____	____	____	____	____
Office	____	____	____	____	____	____	____	____
Salary	____	____	____	____	____	____	____	____
Incentive	____	____	____	____	____	____	____	____

	Shop	Office	Salary	Incentive

17. Are vacations granted with pay

After 1 year employment	____ wks.	____ wks.	____ wks.	____ wks.
" 2 " "	____ "	____ "	____ "	____ "
" 3 " "	____ "	____ "	____ "	____ "
" 4 " "	____ "	____ "	____ "	____ "
" 5 " "	____ "	____ "	____ "	____ "

18. If you have employee benefit plans, excluding social security and workmen's compensation, who contributes—

	Company only	Employee only	Both Company	Employee
Accident Insurance	_____	_____	____%	____%
Life Insurance	_____	_____	____%	____%
Hospitalization Insurance	_____	_____	____%	____%
Pension	_____	_____	____%	____%
Savings	_____	_____	____%	____%

	Shop	Office	Salary	Incentive

19. If sick leave is granted with pay, how is it paid?

Full Pay	____	____	____	____
% of Base Rate	____%	____%	____%	____%

20. Attached are condensed descriptions of key jobs designated by our job numbers as indicated below. These jobs will also be used in repetitive surveys. Please fill in correct current data.

Job Code No.   Job Code No.   Job Code No.   Job Code No.

_____   _____   _____   _____
_____   _____   _____   _____
_____   _____   _____   _____

50 percent of comparable positions in many organizations. The relative availability of market data today has changed the basic approach to salary classification work. Employers can receive wage-survey information from local chambers of commerce, unions, trade services, and the U.S. Department of Labor.

Retaining Good Employees

After the organization has attracted and hired new employees, the compensation system should not hinder efforts to retain productive employees. While many factors may cause employees to leave an organization, inadequate compensation is often the cause of turnover. To retain good employees, the personnel manager must make sure that there is compensation equity within the organization.

If employees perceive that they are being treated inequitably by the organization, tension results. The perception of inequity causes an unpleasant emotional state that may cause employees to reduce their future efforts, change their perceptions regarding rewards for their work efforts, or, as often is the case, leave the organization.[4] Research has found that employee perceptions of equitable treatment were affected when an organization altered its pay system to increase the pay of about 50 percent of its employees. But the same employees reported diminished perceptions of inequity nine months after a change in pay systems. This suggests that such perceived inequity is short-term in nature; however, additional perceptions of unfair treatment may cause employees to leave the organization.[5]

Job satisfaction is often considered to be a strong determinant of turnover. However, employee perceptions of inequitable treatment have been found to be even stronger predictors of absence and job turnover than job satisfaction. If employees perceive that they will be more fairly or equitably treated by another organization, the probability of their leaving increases.[6]

To provide for equity among jobs, administrators usually create a systematic relationship among the pay scales for various jobs within an organization. This process is usually called job evaluation.

Job evaluation is the systematic determination of the relative worth of jobs within the organization which results in an organization's pay system. Primarily, jobs are compared on the traditional bases of skills required to complete the job, effort required to perform the job, responsibility of the job holder, and working conditions on the job. The primary purpose of job evaluation is to develop a system of compensation which employees will perceive to be equitable. Thus, job evaluation strives to obtain internal consistency among jobs, while wage surveys help the organization to maintain external consistency with other organizations in the local labor market.

No compensation program will keep all employees satisfied all the time. If management is able to minimize turnover and lost production due to perceptions of inequitable compensation, then its goal of retaining good employees has been achieved. Not only must an organization have a very fair and equitable system, but this system must be explained to its employees. Administrators must tell employees the various wage rates paid to different positions and how those wage levels are determined. Many managers involve employees in job classification and compensation matters. The most equitable and fair compensation system is useless unless employees perceive it to be equitable.

Motivation

Employees expect that their performances will correlate with the rewards received from the organization. Generally, that perceived relationship takes the form exhibited in Figure 10–4. Employees set expectations about rewards and compensation to be received if certain levels of performance are achieved. These expectations determine goals or levels of performance for the future. Employees achieving the desired level of performance expect a certain level of compensation. At some point, management evaluates and rewards the employee's performance. Examples of such rewards include merit increases, promotions, and intrinsic rewards such as recognition and increased status. Employees consider the relationship between their performance and the rewards related to that performance and then the fairness of that relationship. The final step in the process involves employees' setting new goals and expectations based on prior experiences within the organization.

If employees see that hard work and superior performance are recognized and rewarded by the organization, they will expect such relationships to continue in the future. Therefore, they will set higher levels of performance, expecting higher levels of compensation. Of course, if employees see little relationship between performance and rewards, then they may set minimum goals in order to retain their jobs but will not see the need to excel in their positions.

To safeguard this relationship of performance and motivation, which benefits the organization and the employee, the organization must provide:

Accurate Evaluation Management must develop a system of accurate performance appraisal in order to identify those employees who are outstanding performers, minimum achievers, and poor performers. Although developing an accurate performance appraisal is not easy, it is a critical link between employee performance and motivation.

Performance Rewards Management should identify which rewards relate to performance levels and tell employees that pay, increased benefits, change in hours or working conditions, or recognition will be directly related to high performance.

Supervisors' Feedback Supervisors must give complete and accurate feedback to employees when appraising their performances. Employees must be told what they are doing well and which performance areas need improvement.

Many managers have theories regarding the motivation of employees' performance; some believe that only one motivational theory is enough to develop productive employees. Others may claim that no technique

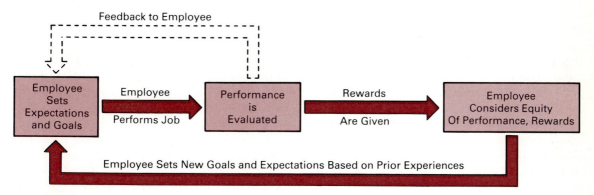

FIGURE 10–4

Motivation and performance model

works because employees are born either achievers or loafers. Undoubtedly no single theory will solve all motivational problems; however, something can be learned from each theory.

Maslow's Hierarchy of Needs Abraham Maslow has identified a five-level hierarchy of needs that all human beings share. In order of their importance, these needs are (1) physiological, (2) security, (3) social, (4) self-esteem, and (5) self-actualization.[7]

Physiological needs, according to Maslow, are the primary needs for food, shelter, and clothing. These needs can be directly satisfied by compensation; employees who are adequately paid can provide for their basic needs. Once the physiological needs have been satisfied, the safety or security need becomes a motivational factor. Many employees' most important security need is job security. Other security factors include increases in salary and benefits.

On the next level is the social need. At this level, employees desire social relationships inside and outside the organization. Peer group acceptance within the work force is often an important psychological need for employees. Once employees have friendships within the organization and feel a part of the peer group, the need for self-esteem takes precedence. Organizational factors such as job title, status items within the organization such as parking spaces or office size, and level of responsibility become important to the employee at this level.

Finally, the highest need is self-actualization. At this level, employees seek a fulfilling, useful life in the organization and in society. Employees will seek challenging and creative jobs to realize self-actualization. Maslow contends that individuals will climb the ladder of need fulfillment until they have become self-actualized. If any need is not fulfilled, the individual will continually strive to fill that need, which becomes a motivational factor. At any level, needs may be fulfilled outside the organization as well as within the organization.

Perhaps the most valuable aspect of Maslow's theory is its emphasis on employees' individual needs. The implication is that managers must accurately assess individuals' needs and link those needs to the organization's compensation methods.

Goal Setting Research has shown that job performance can be increased when individuals are given measurable goals rather than vague performance standards. If individuals are given specific goals which they perceive to be difficult but reasonable, they will be more successful in attaining these goals.[8] *Goal setting* is an integral part of MBO.

Positive Reinforcement The concept of positive reinforcement is central to most motivation techniques. The principal theory behind reinforcement is that behaviors rewarded by the organization are repeated by the employee more often than unrewarded or punished behaviors. The *law of effect* states that behavior that leads to a pleasant response will be repeated, whereas behavior that results in unpleasant experiences tends not to be repeated.[9] Reinforcement is at the heart of merit pay increases, which will be discussed later in this chapter. In order for reinforcement to continue to affect employees' future behavior, a manager must make certain that rewards are meaningful and desired by each employee. As Maslow points out, employee needs are different; therefore, the manager must tailor the reward, whether it be recognition, pay, or changing job requirements, to fit the employee. In addition, the manager must be sure that employees realize that rewards are contingent upon correct behavior.

Legal Considerations

A fourth major objective of the compensation system is to comply with federal legislation. Government has affected compensation by legislating pay levels and nondiscriminatory pay practices. As an employer in competition with private employers, the government also affects pay systems. At any time, government can increase its control over compensation by freezing wages; this occurred during the Korean War and from 1971 to 1974. A governmental *wage freeze* requires that federal regulatory bodies review wage increases. *Wage guidelines* are not strict wage controls but simply requests to employers to voluntarily comply with wage increase maximums.

Fair Labor Standards Act The major compensation legislation regulating employers is the Fair Labor Standards Act (FLSA) of 1938. This act has been amended by Congress several times to provide higher minimum wage levels. The provisions of this law include the following:

Minimum Wages Under the FLSA, employers must pay an employee at least a minimum wage per hour, as shown in Table 10–1. The minimum wage per hour in 1938 was $.25; in 1985, $3.35 (as set by the 1978 revision). Exempted from the act are small businesses whose gross sales do not exceed $362,500 (1981 ceiling). Also exempted are organizations which operate within one state. How-

ever, several states have minimum wage laws which parallel the federal minimum wage provisions; some have lower minimum wages.

Child Labor The FLSA prohibits hiring individuals between the ages of sixteen and eighteen for hazardous jobs, or employing individuals under sixteen in interstate commerce except in nonhazardous work for a parent or guardian. The act also requires individuals under eighteen to obtain temporary work permits to be given to their employers.

Overtime Compensation The FLSA stipulates that certain employees must receive overtime pay of one and one-half times the normal rate when they work over forty hours per week. Certain kinds of employees are *exempt* from the overtime provision of the act. Exempt employees normally occupy professional, technical, managerial, and supervisory positions; they are entitled to minimum pay under the act. All other employees are nonexempt.

Some organizations have tried to lower their overtime costs by classifying more employees as exempt. In effect, this possibly illegal act reduces total payroll costs, as exemplified in Figure 10–5. The restaurant, tourist, and medical industries are exempt from the overtime provision, as are agricultural workers. When calculating overtime, a workweek is 168 consecutive hours or seven consecutive days, not necessarily a calendar week. Special provisions allow hospitals to use a fourteen-day period instead of a seven-day period.

TABLE 10–1

U.S. minimum wage changes under the Fair Labor Standard Act as amended (wages per hour)

1938	1945	1950	1956	1962	1967	1974	1978	1979	1980	1985
$ .25	$ .40	$ .75	$1.00	$1.15	$1.40	$2.00	$2.65	$2.90	$3.10	$3.35

Example 1	Nonexempt employee receives $6.00/hr and works 48 hours in one week.

Normal pay   = 40 hrs × $6.00/hr = $240.00
Overtime pay =   8 hrs × $9.00/hr = $ 72.00
                          (1½ rate) $312.00 Total pay

Example II	Exempt employee receives $280.00/week salary but works 50 hours in one week, lowering the company's labor cost.

Normal hourly rate = $280 ÷ 40 hrs = $7.00/hr.
  (40 hrs)
Hourly rate = $280 ÷ 50 hrs = $5.60/hr.
  (50 hrs)

Example III	Exempt employee receives $160.00/week salary but works 53 hours in one week.

Normal hourly rate = $160.00 ÷ 40 = $4.00/hr.
  (40 hrs)
Hourly rate = $160.00 ÷ 53 = $3.02/hr.
  (53 hrs)

Total minimum wage for 53 hrs = (40 hrs × $3.35) + (13 hrs × $5.025) = $199.33. Thus, under the act it would be illegal to pay this employee only $160.00 for 50 hours.

FIGURE 10–5
Minimum-wage and overtime examples under the FLSA

The Wage and Hour Division of the U.S. Department of Labor has investigated thousands of cases of possible employer violation of the overtime provision. In 1987 a historic $2 million back pay settlement for hours worked over forty per week was awarded to station managers and assistants of Highway Oil, Inc.[10] The employer claimed that the employees were exempt from the overtime provision of the FLSA and were covered by a commission plan instead. If the commission plan had been correctly developed, the employees could have been exempt. The court decision covered 3,300 employees.

While the FLSA has been in existence for fifty years, the U.S. Department of Labor estimates that there are 73,000 compliance investigations annually. About half of them involve the overtime pay provision. In many cases, while the employer and most affected employees are happy with their compensation system, it is found to be in technical violation of the FLSA.

Many of the technical violations of the act result from newer compensation plans which include pay incentives such as attendance bonuses, productivity bonuses, and commissions. Employers are often unaware that such bonuses and commissions must be included in the regular rate of pay when computing the overtime rate of pay. As a general rule, the act requires that all compensation be included in the employee's regular rate of pay, with seven specific exceptions.[11]

- Gifts
- Christmas bonuses
- Special occasion bonuses

- Profit-sharing payments
- Thrift plan payments
- Savings plan payments
- Irrevocable contributions made to a bona fide trust

The most common mistake made by employers is the treatment of bonuses and commissions as discretionary income and not part of an employee's regular rate of pay, which is used to determine the overtime rate. The Department of Labor's regulations provide that if a bonus or commission is promised to employees by a specific policy or agreement, it is not discretionary income and must be included in the employee's weekly earnings. The total weekly earning is then divided by the number of bonus hours worked to determine an hourly rate for the week. The employee must then be paid one and one-half times the hourly rate for any hours worked over forty per week. If the payment of a bonus or commission cannot be made until after the employee is paid for the week, the employer may temporarily disregard it. However, once it can be determined and paid, any additional overtime must also be paid. For example, if an employee received a bonus of $100 for a week during which he worked fifty hours, the additional overtime due would be calculated as follows: $100/50 = $2/hour increase in hourly rate; thus, the employee is due $1 for each of ten hours of overtime, or $10. Employers may choose to base a bonus or commission on a percentage of total earnings if the percentage is increased to one and one-half for all overtime hours.[12]

The Davis–Bacon Act The Davis–Bacon Act of 1931 regulates employers who hold federal government contracts of $2,000 or more for federal construction projects. It provides that employees working on these projects must be paid the prevailing wage rate. In most urban areas the union wage is the prevailing wage for that particular geographic area. If the local union wage for plumbers is $10 per hour, then any plumbers hired to work on federal construction projects in the area must be paid $10 per hour. The reasoning behind the Davis–Bacon Act is that often governments will award contracts to the firm submitting the lowest bid for certain construction specifications. By requiring all employers in construction projects to pay the prevailing wage, the Davis–Bacon Act puts bidders on an equal basis and ensures that craft workers will not be underpaid.

Walsh–Healey Act The Walsh–Healey Act of 1936 covers employers with federal contracts of over $10,000. It requires employers to pay overtime for any hours worked over eight per day at a rate of one and one-half times the normal hourly rate. If an employee works days of more than eight hours within a forty-hour week, he or she will receive greater compensation for the same total hours worked (Figure 10–6).

Federal Wage Garnishment Act In 1970 Congress passed the Federal Wage Garnishment Act to limit the amount individuals can have garnisheed from their paychecks. Employees who do not pay outstanding debts are often taken to court by collection agencies or companies. The court may order their employers to deduct from employee's paychecks a certain amount of money, which is forwarded to the courts and then to the debtor. Under this act, the maximum *garnishment* of an employee's paycheck is 25 percent of take-home pay or thirty times the minimum wage per hour, whichever is smaller. The act also prohibits employers from firing employees who have had their pay garnisheed.

Example I	Nonexempt employee receives $6.00/hr and works 45 hours in one week.

Hours—Monday thru Wednesday = 11 hrs/day
Thursday and Friday   = 7 hrs/day

Pay Under Fair Labor Standards Act	*Pay Under Walsh-Healey Act*
Normal Pay =	Normal Pay =
40 hrs × $6.00/hr = $240	38 hrs × $6.00/hr = $228
Overtime Pay =	Overtime Pay =
5 hrs. × $9.00/hr = 45	9 hrs × $9.00/hr = 81
= $285	Total Pay = $309

Difference = $309.00/week − $285.00/week = $24.00/week.

Example II	Nonexempt employee receives $6.00/hr and works 40 hours in one week.

Hours—Monday, Tuesday, Wednesday, Friday = 10 hrs/day

Pay Under Fair Labor Standards Act	*Pay Under Walsh-Healey Act*
Normal Pay =	Normal Pay =
40 hrs × $6.00/hr = $240.	32 hrs × $6.00/hr = $192
Total Pay	8 hrs × $9.00/hr = 72
	Total Pay $264

Difference = $264.00/week − $240.00/week = $24.00/week.

FIGURE 10–6
Overtime examples under Walsh–Healey

Discrimination Laws

The discrimination laws discussed in chapter 5 also pertain to employee compensation. The *Equal Pay Act* of 1963 is an amendment to the 1938 FLSA. The act requires equal pay for equal work for males and females. Equal work is not interpreted to mean identical, but rather substantially equal in terms of skills, effort, responsibility, and working conditions. Thus, through job analysis, an employer can assign two different jobs to the same pay grade or classification (see Table 10–4) because they are substantially equal. Within the same pay grade, men and women may receive different pay rates if the differences are based on one or more of the following: (1) seniority, (2) merit, (3) quality of work, or (4) quantity of work.

Title VII of the 1964 *Civil Rights Act* provides that "It is unlawful for an employer to discriminate against an individual with respect to his compensation, terms, conditions, or privileges of employment because of such individual's race, color, religion, sex, or national origin." The *Age Discrimination in Employment Act* of 1967 (amended in 1986) prohibits discrimination in compensation against employees over age forty. Employers can generally protect their compensation practices against discrimination claims by developing a standardized system with jobs assigned to pay grades based on a job analysis procedure. In pay discrimination court cases, the burden of proof is on the employer to provide documentation that pay decisions were based on objective criteria.

JOB EVALUATION

Job evaluation is a process of systematically analyzing jobs to determine the relative worth of jobs within the organization. This analysis is the basis of a job hierarchy and pay ranges. The result is a pay system with the pay rate for each job commensurate with its status within the hierarchy of jobs.[13] Job evaluation should not be confused with performance evaluation, the process of determining how well employees are accomplishing their jobs. Job evaluation does not review the employees within a position but rather assesses the worth of the position to the organization. Thus, employees in positions of less worth to the organization are paid less than employees in positions of greater worth. For example, a systems analyst would not receive a higher salary than the director of data processing.

Through job evaluation, management can recruit productive employees to fill positions and maintain internal perceptions of pay equity by paying each position fairly in comparison with all other positions within the organization. Job evaluations may also be used to involve employees in the evaluation process. By understanding how the organization's compensation system is established and maintained, employees can ensure that the system is accurate and complete. Also, employee involvement will help communicate to other employees that the system is fair and equitable.

Job-evaluation Committee

The process of job evaluation is expensive and not completely objective. Primarily a problem-solving, subjective judgmental process, job evaluation requires the best input from individuals within the organization. Because it is impossible for one individual to have adequate knowledge of all the jobs in the organization, a job evaluation committee is necessary. The expertise and varying backgrounds of different committee members contribute to the accuracy of the evaluation process. The members of the committee should have adequate knowledge of all work areas within the organization and a basic familiarity with the jobs within each department. Members should be trained in the basic concept of job evaluation and specifically in the method chosen by the organization to develop job evaluation.[14] Organizations often maintain a permanent job-evaluation committee.

Once established, the job-evaluation system should be flexible and reviewed periodically. The job-evaluation committee can provide this review since those individuals are most familiar with the compensation system. For example, when supervisors ask that a job be reclassified, the committee would be able to make the determination faster and easier than an inexperienced committee made up of new members.

Outside Assistance

The first decision the job evaluation committee makes is whether the organization should produce a job-evaluation system or hire outside consultants. Outside consultants offer experience and expertise in the area because they are employed by many firms to produce similar systems year after year. Often faster and more objective than internal employees, outside consultants need substantial internal input to analyze jobs and make difficult comparison decisions. Many decisions critical to the job evaluation process can be made only by individuals familiar with the organization and its basic jobs. While over 70 percent of the organizations in this country are estimated to use job evaluation, less than 20 percent buy packaged evaluation plans from a consultant or other source.[15]

A better alternative is hiring an evaluation consultant to organize the evaluation process and train the job-evaluation committee. Once trained, the members do the decision making; the consultant can be brought in at the end of the process to make necessary adjustments.

Methods of Job Evaluation

Primarily, there are four methods of job evaluation: ranking, classification, point, and factor comparison. These four methods include the framework of most job-evaluation systems. These methods and all of their derivations can be characterized as either quantitative (point method and factor comparison) or nonquantitative (ranking and classification).

Ranking Method The oldest method of evaluating jobs is the ranking method, which requires the job-evaluation committee to rank all of the jobs in the organization according to their relative worth in comparison to each other. Ranking the jobs within their departments, as in Table 10–2, may be the easiest way to begin. The committee must come to a consensus regarding the ranking of the jobs within a department. The actual final ranking may be made by having each committee member rank the jobs within the department and then compute the average ranking for each job to determine the final rankings.

After the jobs are ranked within the department, the job-evaluation committee has one of two choices. First, it can develop separate compensation systems for each department. In the case of Table 10–2, three compensation systems are developed. Second, the committee may choose to produce a total ranking, as shown to the right in Table 10–2.

TABLE 10–2
Ranking method of job evaluation

Ranking by Department		Total Company Rankings	
Rank	Job	Rank	Job
Sales		1.	General Manager
1.	Sales Manager	2.	Asst. General Manager
2.	Route Foreman	3.	Production Foreman
3.	Route Sales Worker	4.	Sales Manager
4.	Trainee	5.	Route Foreman
		6.	Machinist
Office		7.	Lathe Operator
1.	General Manager	8.	Route Sales Worker
2.	Asst. General Manager	9.	Assembler
3.	Accounting Clerk	10.	Drill Press Operator
4.	Clerk Typist	11.	Accounting Clerk
5.	File Clerk	12.	Laborer
		13.	Clerk Typist
Shop		14.	File Clerk
1.	Production Foreman	15.	Trainee
2.	Machinist	16.	Janitor
3.	Lathe Operator		
4.	Assembler		
5.	Drill Press Operator		
6.	Laborer		
7.	Janitor		

To determine this total ranking, the committee compares the top-ranked jobs in each department. Thus, the production foreman would be compared to the general manager and the sales manager, and the job considered most important to the company would be ranked first. The process continues until all jobs in the company have been ranked by the committee. The ranking method requires that committee members objectively compare different jobs.

After the rankings have been completed, pay scales must be assigned to the ranked jobs. The first step in this process is to ensure external equity by comparing *benchmark jobs* with jobs of other organizations within the local labor market.

A benchmark job contains standardized characteristics that can be easily identified in jobs of a similar nature within other organizations. If, for example, the committee identified the sales manager, lathe operator, drill-press operator, and clerk-typist positions as benchmark jobs, they could identify the average wage paid for similar jobs in the local market and set pay scales for these jobs first. Once these pay scales were set, then the pay scales for jobs between benchmark jobs would have to be set according to their ranking; jobs ranked higher than the sales manager job obviously would be given higher pay, whereas jobs ranked lower would be given lower pay, which would still be higher than the next-ranked benchmark job.

Job evaluation determines the worth of each job in the organization, not each individual employee. In the example of Table 10–2, while there are sixteen jobs ranked, there may be forty or more employees in this particular organization, because several employees hold the same job.

Speed and ease of completion are the main advantages of the ranking method of job evaluation. Another advantage of ranking is that since it can be done in-house fairly easily, it is less expensive than some other methods of job evaluation. The ranking method also is easy to explain to members of the job evaluation committee, since the concept of ranking is familiar to most individuals.

The ranking method contains serious disadvantages. Due to its very nature, ranking is limited to smaller organizations where individuals are very familiar with various jobs and can have the complete knowledge of the jobs required to make an accurate comparison of jobs. Another serious disadvantage is the assumption of equal intervals between the rankings. For example, in Table 10–2, the assistant general manager is ranked one notch lower than the general manager and only one notch higher than the accounting clerk within the office department; but the assistant manager's job is worth more than the one notch indicates. This magnitude of difference is shown in the total company rankings when the assistant general manager is ranked second and the accounting clerk is ranked eleventh. However, the same problem may exist in the total company rankings; the difference between positions is not always equal to one interval.

The problem of unequal intervals becomes acute after the benchmark pay scales are determined from wage surveys, and the positions between benchmarks are assigned pay scales either more or less than the benchmark positions. Companies that use the ranking technique must realize that the intervals are not equal and try to create reasonable differences among the ranked positions in pay scales.

Another major disadvantage of ranking is that the method is a *global appraisal* of the worth of the jobs. Instead of evaluating the various factors of each job, ranking simply evaluates the job in its entirety and thus makes a global appraisal in comparing it to another job. While all job-evaluation techniques are subjective, ranking is more subjective than more discerning methods.

Another serious problem of the ranking method is the difficulty of defending it to employees. When employees ask why their jobs are not as highly paid as others', the personnel officer or supervisor who responds that these jobs were ranked two notches lower than other positions does not completely satisfy the employees. The ranking method should be used only by small organizations which can satisfactorily compare all the jobs and make accurate comparison decisions.

Classification Method The classification method, also called the grade description method, enables an organization to analyze its jobs and place them in broad class descriptions or grades. The U.S. Office of Personnel Management's General Schedule (GS) appears in Table 10–3. The classification method can be accomplished in the following steps:

Step 1. Review all jobs and create categories The job-evaluation committee first reviews the job descriptions and determines the duties and responsibilities of various jobs. The usual breakdown of job categories would be: supervisory or technical, factory or production, clerical, and sales.

Step 2. Determine the grades or classes for each category The larger the organization and the more jobs within each category, the more grades within each particular job category. The well-known Westinghouse Plan uses the following broad definitions for grades within each category:[16]

Grade 1. Unskilled The positions of this group, usually clerical, require accuracy and dependability but no extended training. Office worker, records clerk, and file clerk are examples.

Grade 2. Skilled The positions of this group, mostly clerical, require training of either physical or mental abilities. The group includes such positions as stenographer, production clerk, detail draftsperson, and bookkeeper. The nonclerical positions for this group would include laboratory assistants, plant operators, and draftspersons.

Grade 3. Interpretive The highest positions in this group would include chief clerk, office manager, and other positions which are mostly supervisory in nature. First-line supervisors would be the highest supervisory positions within this group.

Grade 4. Creative This group includes positions of a creative character such as engineer, salesperson, staff supervisor, designers, attorneys, and other technical and professional positions.

Grade 5. Executive Most positions at this level are executive and include department manager, sales manager, superintendent, foreperson, and assistant general manager. Generally, this is a function of departmental management.

Grade 6. Administrative The positions of this group involve responsibilities of large functional divisions. District sales manager, chief engineer, director of research, purchasing director, and treasurer, are examples of positions at this grade.

Grade 7. Policy This grade includes those positions held by the senior policy officers of the organization.

If the job evaluation committee decided to use Westinghouse's seven grades, then general job descriptions must be written for each job category.

Step 3. Write Grade Descriptions A broad job description must be written for each job in the

TABLE 10–3
U.S. Office of Personnel Management: Schedule of Annual Rates by Grade: 1987 General Schedule (GS)

Rates within Grade and Waiting Period for Next Increase

Grade	52 Weeks			104 Weeks			156 Weeks				Amount of within Grade Increase
	1	2	3	4	5	6	7	8	9	10	
1	9619	9940	10260	10579	10899	11087	11403	11721	11735	12036	Varied
2	10816	11073	11430	11735	11866	12215	12564	12913	13262	13611	Varied
3	11802	12195	12588	12981	13374	13767	14160	14553	14946	15339	393
4	13248	13690	14132	14574	15016	15458	15900	16342	16784	17226	442
5	14882	15316	15810	16304	16798	17292	17786	18280	18774	19268	494
6	16521	17072	17623	18174	18725	19276	19827	20378	20929	21480	551
7	18358	18970	19582	20194	20806	21418	22030	22642	23254	23866	612
8	20333	21011	21689	22367	23045	23723	24401	25079	25757	26435	678
9	22458	23207	23956	24705	25454	26203	26952	27701	28450	29199	749
10	24732	25556	26380	27204	28028	28852	29676	30500	31324	32148	824
11	27172	28078	28984	29890	30796	31702	32608	33514	34420	35326	906
12	32567	33653	34739	35825	36911	37997	39083	40169	41255	42341	1086
13	38727	40018	41309	42600	43891	45182	46473	47764	49055	50346	1291
14	45763	47288	48813	50338	51863	53388	54913	56438	57963	59488	1525
15	53830	55624	57418	59212	61006	62800	64594	66388	68182	69976	1794
16	63135	65240	67345	69450	71555	73660*	75765*	77870*	79975*		2105
17	73958*	76423*	78888*	81353	83818*						2465
18	86682*										

*The rate of basic pay payable to employees at these rates is limited to $72,500, the rate payable for level V of the Executive Schedule.

Source: *Salary Table No. 72, OPM Doc. 124-48-6* (Washington, DC: U.S. Office of Personnel Management, 1987).

organization. A broad description must be general enough to include the variety of jobs which fall into that description, yet specific enough so that employees will recognize their jobs being described. If descriptions are too broad, then individuals do not recognize their jobs and feel that the system is unfair or vague. If descriptions are too specific, it will be difficult to assign a number of jobs to a few grades. The definitions for each grade within each broad category should include such items as the type of work being accomplished, the degree of supervision required, the complexity of duties and decisions involved in accomplishing the job, education and experience necessary for performing the job, level of effort and responsibility demanded by the job, and contact with others.

Step 4. Assign Jobs to a Grade   After reviewing job descriptions of the various jobs and preparing the grade definitions, the committee can assign each job in the organization to a particular grade. Each job has peculiar duties or responsibilities that differentiate it from other jobs in the organization. However, using a classification system divides jobs within an organization into a hierarchy of grades so that employees performing jobs of similar worth to the organization will receive similar pay. Again, the committee members must have some knowledge of jobs to be able to assign jobs to the appropriate grades.

Step 5. Assign Pay Ranges to Grades   As in the ranking method, the evaluation committee should first compare its benchmark jobs to those of other organizations to be sure that the pay ranges assigned to each grade will keep the organization competitive in the local labor market. Then the committee determines pay ranges from starting pay levels to maximum pay levels for each pay grade. Usually the total range is broken into levels within the pay grade so that as employees receive merit

increases and acquire seniority they move to a higher pay level.

The primary advantage of the classification method is that it has been in use by federal, state, and local civil service bodies for many years. For this reason, employees in other organizations may accept it. This is also a good system for a very large organization with many offices located in several regions in the country. By being broad in nature, the classification method allows all plants and offices to be included in the same compensation plan. Cost-of-living adjustments can be made for different locations and still use the same classification plan. Of course, this is helpful in union negotiations and for employees transferring from one area to another within the organization.

Because the descriptions are broad and not specific to the jobs assigned to them, the system can last for many years without being changed substantially, which saves the company money and time in keeping the system functional. As jobs change slightly from one year to the next, their grade classifications will not be affected; more detailed systems, like those which follow in this chapter, require constant updating.

The major disadvantage to the system is that the descriptions are so broad that they do not relate specifically to jobs that are assigned to them. This can lead to abuse of the system by a job classification committee or a supervisor. It also causes many employees to question if there are specific reasons for their jobs being classified in a certain grade. Employees may not recognize how grade descriptions apply to their particular jobs. Often, after reading the grade descriptions, employees feel that their jobs are more similar to a higher grade than to the assigned grade. Some employees simply do not accept the system as a valid and objective means of job classification.

Point Method One of the most popular, basic systems of job evaluation today is the point method, which divides jobs into specific factors that the job evaluation committee believes are critical and valued by the organization. Rather than globally reviewing jobs, the point method breaks jobs down into their components, reviews each of the components, and compares the jobs by those components. There are countless variations of the point method; all are basically mathematical and compare jobs on factors chosen by the job evaluation committee. Because the point system specifically compares jobs according to their content and because it is quantitative, the point system is generally accepted by federal agencies and the courts. Most point systems follow these steps:

Step 1. Select Compensable Job Factors The evaluation committee identified factors that describe the fundamental elements of the jobs. The committee considers if one job requires more mental effort or more monetary responsibility than another job. Since the passage of the Equal Pay Act, many point systems have used factor categories indicating skill, effort, responsibility, and working conditions, as shown in Table 10–4. Although a limitless number of factors can be chosen, the more factors chosen, the more expensive the job evaluation becomes. Therefore, the evaluation committee generally chooses between eight and sixteen factors in the point system.

The committee should determine which factors make some jobs more valuable than others and which factors are common to all jobs in the organization. After the factors have been determined, they should be clearly defined so that others know exactly what each factor entails. The Allis–Chalmers Manufacturing Company has determined ten compensable factors, as shown in Figure 10–7.

Step 2. Divide Factors Into Degrees Once the factors have been chosen, the next step is to divide each factor into different degrees signifying the extent to which the factor exists in the particular job. Each degree must then be defined so that the evaluation committee agrees upon its specification. Usually between three and seven degrees will be utilized for each factor.

Step 3. Assign Point to Degrees The assignment of points to each degree within factors provides a system of weighting each factor within the point system. Therefore, more important factors will be given larger point totals than lesser factors. For example, in the Allis–Chalmers point plan, the degrees in the factor "monetary responsibility" constitute a larger point total than the performance factor.

There are various nonstatistical and statistical approaches to assigning points to each degree. The evaluation committee should consider three or four different systems and choose the one which best reflects the circumstances of the organization.

Step 4. Rate Jobs on Each Factor The evaluation committee begins with the first factor and evaluates each job on that factor. For each factor, the committee determines the degree that best defines the level required for the job. All of the jobs are rated on one factor before the committee moves on to a second factor. The reason for this is to maximize the objectivity of the decision process. Any biases a committee member may have concerning a particular job will be minimized if that job is not evaluated in total but is compared against other jobs as each factor is reviewed.

Step 5. Total Points for Each Job Once all the jobs have been assigned degrees and point totals on each factor, the committee can total the points for each job. Jobs are divided into clerical, production, and administrative areas,

TABLE 10–4
Compensable job factors

Skill

Accuracy of calculations	Education	Manual skill
Accuracy of measurement	Foresight	Math skill
Accuracy of reading	Ingenuity	Mechanical ability
Accuracy of selection	Initiative	Mental capability
Adaptability	Inventiveness	Mentality
Adjustability	Job knowledge	Motor accuracy
Analysis	Job skill	Originality
Analytical ability	Judgment	Personal requirements
Aptitude	Knowledge of equipment and tools	Physical skill
Artistic ability	Knowledge of materials	Precision
Attention to orders	Knowledge of methods	Previous training
Complexity	Knowledge of other operations	Resourcefulness
Cooperation	Leadership	Tact and diplomacy
Creativity	Length of schooling	Training time
Decision	Management ability	Versatility
Details	Manual dexterity	

Effort

Alertness	Honesty of effort	Physical effort
Application	Memory	Physical pace or energy
Concentration	Mental effort	Quickness of comprehension
Endurance	Mental stability	Strength
Exertion	Monotony of work	Visual effort
Fatigue	Muscular coordination	

Responsibility

Avoidance of shutdowns	Good will	Property
Company policy	Inventory	Quality
Confidential data	Maintenance of work pace	Safety of others
Cost of errors	Material	Reports and records
Effect on subsequent operations	Money	Supervision of others
Equipment	Production levels	

Working Conditions

Accident hazard	Discomfort	Health hazard
Clothing spoilage	Environmental deterrents	Nervous strain
Current expense	Eyestrain	Noise level
Danger	Fumes	Surroundings

	Points					
Factors	1st Degree	2nd Degree	3rd Degree	4th Degree	5th Degree	6th Degree
Skill						
1. Knowledge	7	17	30	47	70	100
2. Training and experience						
3. Complexity of duties	9	20	36	56	84	120
4. Contacts with others	7	17	30	47	70	100
Responsibility						
5. Responsibility for trust imposed	6	14	26	40	60	
6. Monetary responsibility	9	20	36	56	84	120
7. Performance	4	10	18	28	42	60
Effort						
8. Mental or visual	4	8	15	24	35	—
9. Physical	0	4	9	16	25	—
Job Conditions						
10. Work conditions	0	6	14	25	40	—

SELECTED FACTORS

1. Knowledge

Education provides the basic prerequisite knowledge that is essential to perform the job. This knowledge may have been acquired through formal schooling such as grammar school, high school, college, university, night school, correspondence courses, company education program, or through equivalent experience in allied fields. Analyze the requirements of the job and not the formal education of individuals performing it.

Points

1st Degree

Requires ability to read, write, and follow simple written or oral instructions, use simple arithmetic involving counting, adding, subtracting, multiplying, and dividing whole numbers, etc.

7

2nd Degree

Requires ability to perform work requiring advanced arithmetic involving adding, subtracting, dividing, and multiplying of decimals and fractions; maintain or prepare routine correspondence, records, and reports. May require knowledge of typing or elementary knowledge of shorthand, bookkeeping, etc.

17

FIGURE 10–7

Point plan of job evaluation for nonexempt salaried positions of the Allis–Chalmers Manufacturing Company (Source: *Compensation Management* by Richard I. Henderson, 1979. Reprinted with permission of Reston Publishing Company, Inc., a Prentice-Hall Company, 11480 Sunset Hills Road, Reston, Virginia.)

3rd Degree
> Requires specialized knowledge in a particular field such as advanced stenographic, secretarial or business training, elementary accounting or general knowledge of shop practice and manufacturing methods, blueprint reading, shop specifications, basic principles of production control, welding, chemistry, electricity, etc.   30

4th Degree
> Requires ability to understand and perform work requiring general engineering principles, commercial theory, principles of advanced drafting; knowledge and application of general accounting fundamentals. Originate and compile statistics and interpretive reports; prepare correspondence of a difficult or technical nature. Requires a broad knowledge of complicated shop procedures and processes, purchasing, accounting, general sales work, foreign trade, labor laws, time study, etc.   47

5th Degree
> Requires ability to understand and perform work of a specialized or technical nature. Examples are work involving use of all types of drawings or specifications in which application requires theory or analysis of design or principles involved; use of advanced formulas for determining relationships; apply highly specialized technical theory in determining causes of and correcting design or operating difficulties; knowledge of theory and practices in accounting and finance, business administration, chemistry, physics, journalism, and related technical or specialized fields.   70

6th Degree
> Requires knowledge in a highly advanced and specialized field in order to understand and perform work requiring creative endeavor.   100

2. Training and Experience

Experience is the length of time usually required by an individual with the specified knowledge to acquire the skill necessary to perform the duties of the job. Where previous experience is necessary, time spent in related work or in lesser positions, either within the company or with other organizations, shall be considered as contributing to the total experience required to effectively perform the job. This consideration will be based on continuous progress by an individual and will not include time spent on jobs due to lack of promotional opportunities.

Experience	Points
Up to and including 3 months	9
Over 3 months, up to and including 6 months	19
Over 6 months, up to and including 9 months	28
Over 9 months, up to and including 12 months	35
Over 1 year, up to and including 2 years	62
Over 2 years, up to and including 3 years	82
Over 3 years, up to and including 4 years	97
Over 4 years, up to and including 5 years	108

FIGURE 10–7
continued

Experience	Points
Over 5 years, up to and including 7 years	123
Over 7 years, up to and including 10 years	134
Over 10 years	140

3. Complexity of Duties

This factor appraises the complexity of job duties, such as the amount of judgment required in the making of decisions; analyzing problems and situations; planning of procedures and determining methods of action; and the extent to which initiative and ingenuity are required to successfully complete the job.

Points

1st Degree
  Work is routine, consisting of simple repetitive operations, such as filing, sorting, duplicating, copy typing, etc., performed under immediate supervision or where little choice exists as to method of performance. 9

2nd Degree
  Perform work from detailed instructions or where variation in procedures is limited. Work is semirepetitive requiring minor decisions and some judgment in analysis of data or situations from which an answer can readily be obtained. 20

3rd Degree
  Perform work where procedures are of a varied or diversified nature within a well-defined field under direct supervision. Requires initiative and independent judgment to analyze data or situations and determine solutions to problems within the limits of standard practice. 36

4th Degree
  Plan and perform complex work where only general policies or procedures are available in an established field requiring their application to cases not previously covered. Job duties involve working independently toward general results, devising new methods, and modifying or adapting standard procedures to meet new conditions. Requires analytical ability, initiative, and exercise of judgment to obtain solutions to problems and make decisions based on precedent and company policy. 56

5th Degree
  Plan and perform highly complex or technical work where no procedures or standard methods are available. Duties require a high degree of originality, initiative, and independent action to deal with complex factors difficult to evaluate or the making of decisions based on conclusions for which there is little precedent. 84

6th Degree
  Final analysis and judgment in planning and coordinating the work of a large group or department. Requires initiative and aggressiveness; original and creative planning and formulation of policy. 120

FIGURE 10–7
continued

and then jobs within each area are listed with point totals. Through routine checks the committee makes sure that there are no obvious mistakes. For example, a supervisory position should have a greater point total than the position supervised. Administrators may divide jobs into different functional areas (such as sales, production, professional) at this point in order to develop separate pay systems for each area. This process will ensure external equity as well as internal equity.

Step 6. Identify Benchmark Jobs Benchmark jobs should be compared to the other jobs in the organization to ensure that the point totals appear to be in line. After the system of tying in point totals to a pay structure is developed, these benchmark jobs will be compared to jobs of other organizations within the labor market to ensure external equity.

The most important advantages of the point method are that it is detailed and it is specific. Jobs are not globally assessed, as they are in the nonquantitative systems; they are compared on specific factors important to the organization. This makes the point method—and other quantitative methods in general—more valid because management cannot manipulate the method or allow intentional bias by a supervisor. In most cases, employees accept the point method because of its mathematical nature and complex, sophisticated methodology. Personnel specialists can explain to employees how the job was evaluated, what degree was allocated in the various factors, and therefore how the total points were derived and the pay scale determined. Another important advantage is that the system is easy to keep current and accurate as jobs change. If a job is given increased duties, the supervisor or employee can request that the job be reclassified. Reclassification is quite simple under the point method since the specific factors affected by the change in the job

can be reevaluated and possibly given a higher degree. Thus the total points allotted to the job change, and in some cases the job's pay grade must be changed. The point method's mathematical comparison of jobs makes it easy to assign monetary values to jobs, which have quantitative differences. Therefore, differences in point totals among jobs can be easily converted to differences in pay scales.

The obvious disadvantages of the point method are that it is much more time-consuming and costly to develop than the ranking or classification methods. The point method also requires a great deal of interaction and decision making by the job analyst and the job-evaluation committee. If the organization contains several hundred different jobs and several compensable job factors are chosen, then thousands of decisions regarding degrees and factors must be made by the committee.

The advantages of the point method—particularly acceptance by employees and governmental agencies—have made it more attractive than other methods. Most likely the point system will continue to gain popularity until a more sophisticated version of a quantitative system is developed.

Factor-comparison Method Developed in the 1920s by Eugene Benge, the factor-comparison method combines the ranking method and the point system. This method develops a wage scale for each factor in an evaluation process. The total wage rates for benchmark jobs are then compared to the local wage survey to ensure external consistency. Benge's method uses the following procedure:

Step 1. Select Benchmark Jobs Benchmark jobs comparable to other jobs in similar organizations within the local labor market are chosen. These jobs should be clearly defined in the minds of evaluation committee members, and represent a cross section of jobs in all departments of the organization.

Step 2. Choose Compensable Factors As in the point system, primary compensable factors of various jobs in the organization are chosen. Between four and seven factors are selected. Commonly, five factors are used: skill, effort, responsibility, working conditions, and physical requirements.

Step 3. Rank all Jobs on Each Factor The evaluation committee then ranks all of the benchmark jobs, one factor at a time. Comparing one factor at a time minimizes subjectivity or bias for the jobs.

Step 4. Allocate Wages to Factors Using current wage scales and wage surveys of the local labor market, each factor for each job is allocated a certain wage rate either on a per hour, per month, or annual salary basis. The factors can be weighted by giving one factor more total dollars than another factor.

Step 5. Determine Final Ranking Benchmark jobs may now be ranked according to their total wage allocation and compared to the external market to ensure that the organization is competitive. After this is done, other jobs can be added to the rankings and given a wage rate by judging the difference between each job and the nearest benchmark job. This is a very difficult and subjective process for the evaluation committee.

The end product of a factor-comparison method is shown in Figure 10–8. The Olympia Machine Tool and Die Shop developed the wage scale for five compensable factors: skill, mental demands, physical demands, responsibility, and working conditions. Ten benchmark jobs are selected for the job evaluation process. An evaluation committee ranked the

jobs, reviewed market surveys, ranked the benchmark jobs one factor at a time, totaled the rankings, and assigned wage levels. The committee did not use mathematical averages for rankings and wage scales, but discussed differences where they occurred and developed satisfactory compromise levels. These scales for the benchmark jobs can now be used to evaluate all other jobs within the organization. The committee members will analyze each of the other jobs, determine which benchmark job it most closely resembles, assign the corresponding monetary value, and finally total up the wage rate assigned to the job.[17]

Like the point system, the factor-comparison method has the advantage of evaluating jobs on a component basis rather than in their entirety. Also, like the point system, the method compares jobs one factor at a time, minimizing problems of bias or committee subjectivity. The factor-comparison system is usually easier to develop than the point method because it involves fewer factors. Also, the factor-comparison method is tied to the external market because wage surveys are used to determine rates for each factor consistent with other organizations.

The factor-comparison method has the disadvantage of being limited primarily to manufacturing organizations employing hourly workers. Other types of organizations would lack external market information to help them tie wage rates to some meaningful source; without such input, setting wage rates for individual factors of jobs would be difficult. Therefore, the factor-comparison method is used almost solely by manufacturing organizations.

The factor-comparison method is also more difficult to explain to employees, who are less likely to accept something they do not understand. Another disadvantage is that the factor-comparison method uses monetary

Dollars per Hour per Factor	Mental Requirements	Skill Requirements	Physical Requirements	Responsibility	Working Conditions
2.80	Electronic Tech. Tool Maker	Tool Maker Machinist			
2.65	Electrician			Inspector Electronic Tech.	
2.50	Machinist	Electronic Tech.		Tool Maker	
2.35	Inspector	Electrician		Electrician	
2.20					
2.05		Engine Lathe Oper.	Laborer	Machinist	
1.90		Turret Lathe Oper.	Assembler Fork Lift Oper.	Engine Lathe Oper.	Laborer Fork Lift Oper. Floor Sweeper
1.75	Engine Lathe Oper.		Turret Lathe Oper. Electrician		Assembler
1.60		Inspector	Machinist Floor Sweeper	Fork Lift Operator	Machinist Turret Lathe Oper.
1.45	Turret Lathe Oper.			Turret Lathe Oper.	Tool Maker Engine Lathe Oper. Electrician
1.30	Assembler Fork Lift Oper.		Toolmaker Engine Lathe Oper.		
1.15		Assembler Fork Lift Oper.		Assembler	Inspector
1.00			Inspector Electronic Tech.		Electronic Tech.
.85	Laborer				
.70	Floor Sweeper	Laborer		Laborer	
.55		Floor Sweeper		Floor Sweeper	

FIGURE 10–8
The factor-comparison method as used by the Olympia Machine Tool and Die Shop (Source: *Compensation Management* by Richard I. Henderson, 1979. Reprinted with permission of Reston Publishing Company, Inc. a Prentice-Hall Company, 11480 Sunset Hills Road, Reston, Virginia.)

comparisons of factors, in contrast to the point system, which uses abstract quantitative differences or points. Thus, the point system can be easily adapted to cost-of-living changes or merit increases, whereas the factor-comparison system cannot change as jobs change or as the industry changes.

Other Methods Countless varieties of each method of job evaluation have been developed by individuals and groups. Some of the methods have become widely used by particular industries and trades. Obviously, there is a distinct advantage in using a method that has been applied to other organizations; comparative information from other organizations is invaluable and saves a great deal of time and effort for the job-evaluation committee. Two of the most widely used systems for factory jobs were developed by the National Electrical Manufacturers Association and the National Metal Trade Association (now the American Association of Industrial Management). These systems use factors, subfactors, and degrees of factors as standards, similar to the point and factor-comparison methods.

Another popular method is the *Hay Guide Chart-Profile method*. The Hay method uses three compensable factors: (1) know-how, which encompasses the variety of tasks performed, depth of job or the complexity of tasks performed, and human-relations skills; (2) problem solving, which includes the degree of supervision received and the new situations that require creative thinking; and (3) accountability, which refers to freedom to act on the job and the job holder's ability to make work decisions.

The U.S. Office of Personnel Management developed a point-factor method called the *Factor Evaluation System (FES)*. As with most point-factor systems, job evaluators must compare the content of each job with compensable factors written in general terms which apply to all of the jobs of the organization. The system's written benchmarks relate to specific job content and describe an actual job situation that typically represents jobs within an occupation.[18]

PAY SYSTEMS

The method by which individuals are paid for performing their job constitutes the pay system of the organization. Generally, people are compensated for the *time* they contribute to the job or the *amount* of work they produce on the job. *Time-based systems,* the more common type, are used for jobs in which employees are paid by the hour worked (hourly) or

by the fraction of an annual rate of pay (salaried), such as a week or month. In general, nonexempt jobs, such as blue-collar and unskilled positions, are hourly so that the employer will comply with the FLSA. Exempt jobs are usually salaried; employees are paid monthly, semimonthly, or weekly. Jobs that pay employees according to their performance are often referred to as *performance-based systems* or *incentive pay systems*. They include piece-rate, sales-commission, and group-production plans.

Most employees in the United States are paid on the basis of time-based systems. Rates of pay are fixed by the hour, day, week, month, or year. Thus, gross pay is calculated by multiplying the rate by the units of time worked. Employers often prefer the time-based system because employee motivation is difficult to predict in a totally performance-based system. Employees often prefer the known pay level they receive in a time-based system, which makes it easier to make house, car, and other fixed monthly payments. But time-based systems have the disadvantage of paying people for unproductive time on the job as well as for productive time. Hard workers can be penalized because greater productivity may not show up in their paychecks.[19]

Time-based Systems

Most time-based systems use a schedule of pay grades and steps such as the one in Table 10–5. The matrix can include hourly rates or annual rates of pay depending on whether the jobs are hourly or salaried. Jobs are assigned to a particular pay grade depending on the results of the job evaluation, as discussed earlier in this chapter.

When job evaluation is completed, administrators must determine a final pay system to apply to jobs within the organization. Their decisions involve establishing minimum and maximum pay levels for each pay grade

TABLE 10–5

A sample schedule of hourly pay grades and steps

Pay Grade	Step 1	Step 2	Step 3	Step 4	Step 5	Step 6	Step 7
1	$ 3.35	$ 3.49	$ 3.62	$ 3.77	$ 3.91	$ 4.05	$ 4.18
2	3.85	4.01	4.17	4.33	4.49	4.65	4.81
3	4.42	4.59	4.75	4.92	5.09	5.26	5.52
4	5.08	5.29	5.50	5.71	5.93	6.14	6.35
5	5.84	6.08	6.32	6.57	6.81	7.06	7.30
6	6.71	6.98	7.27	7.55	7.82	8.10	8.38
7	7.71	8.03	8.35	8.67	8.99	9.31	9.63
8	8.86	9.22	9.60	9.96	10.33	10.71	11.07
9	10.18	10.60	11.03	11.45	11.87	12.30	12.72

and determining how individuals will advance in pay grades. A standardized pay system must be promulgated and documented in order to maintain internal as well as external *pay equity*. Also, management must be able to document and defend its pay system in court. Administrators have found it advantageous to develop pay grades and steps, or levels, which specify the annual amount paid salaried employees in a particular pay grade and step, and to use a monthly or hourly basis for other jobs.

If the organization has undergone job evaluation, then the pay system can be designed on a *scatter diagram* by first plotting the wage rate and pay grade for each current employee. Point totals should be shown if the point system of job evaluation was utilized. The scatter diagram in Figure 10–9 illustrates the use of equal-interval pay grades. That is, each pay grade has an equal number of points but has an unequal range as far as the total pay within the pay grade. While the dollar figures in each pay range are not increased equally, the actual percent increase of pay for each pay range is 25 percent. Thus, an employee with a 340-point job would find that job classified in pay grade four with a minimum pay of $5.08 and a maximum pay of $6.35 per hour.

Number of Steps   In developing a compensation system, the number of steps within each *pay grade* must be decided. Figure 10–10 illustrates how pay grade 5 could be divided into seven equal increases of approximately $.24 per hour. An alternative method is to give equal percentage increases for each step; thus employees receive a larger cents-per-hour increase with each step raise. Many organizations prefer that as individuals receive raises in their pay grades, the increases become larger.

Deciding how many steps should be included within each pay grade is a difficult decision. If too many steps are included, employees' motivation for good performance will be very small because the increase will be very small. Having few steps in each pay grade creates larger increases and motivates employees to work for merit increases. Employees reach the top of their pay grades more quickly when grades have few steps and, therefore, have no opportunity for advancement within the jobs they currently hold. Once individuals have reached the top of their pay grades, the practice is usually to keep them at that highest step, to transfer them to jobs in a higher pay grade, or to promote them. Organizations with relatively few opportunities for promotion, or with turnover so low that many indi-

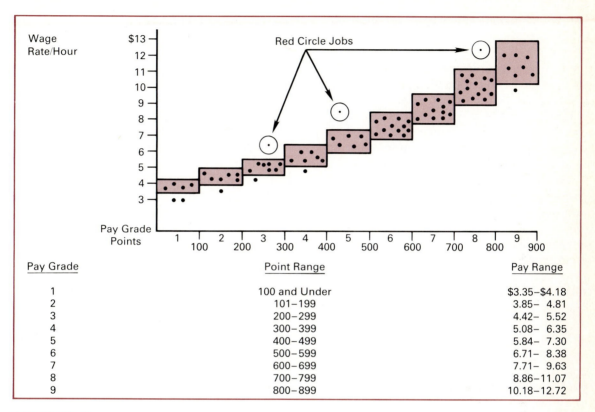

FIGURE 10–9
A scatter diagram

Pay Grade	Point Range	Pay Range
1	100 and Under	$3.35–$4.18
2	101–199	3.85– 4.81
3	200–299	4.42– 5.52
4	300–399	5.08– 6.35
5	400–499	5.84– 7.30
6	500–599	6.71– 8.38
7	600–699	7.71– 9.63
8	700–799	8.86–11.07
9	800–899	10.18–12.72

viduals stay within one pay grade for several years, find it wise to have many steps and, perhaps, even wider-ranging pay grades.

Figure 10–10 illustrates the practice of using two or more entry-level salaries for jobs within a particular pay grade. The reason for the practice is that while managers wish to be consistent and pay similar wages for similar jobs, allowances must be made for individual differences in job candidates who are hired. Candidates with more experience and skills can be hired in a higher step; a recruit who has just finished school and has no experience would logically be hired at step 1. In most situations this would not violate federal laws: consistency within the pay system could be proved since similar wages were paid for sim-

Pay Grade 5		
Step 7	$7.30	
Step 6	7.06	TOP LEVEL STEPS
Step 5	6.81	
Step 4	6.57	MID POINT
Step 3	6.32	
Step 2	6.08	ENTRY LEVEL STEPS
Step 1	5.84	

FIGURE 10–10
Pay grade 5 with internal steps

ilar work, making allowances for individual differences.

Red Circle Employees Another decision to be made by the evaluation committee is illustrated in Figure 10–9. Three individuals within the pay grade system have been red circled. A red circle indicates that this individual is currently being paid more than the maximum of that pay grade. Through seniority or for some other reason, the individual is currently being paid more than the organization planned to pay any employee to perform jobs of that pay grade. Red-circled individuals remain at the same pay level until either they are promoted to a higher pay grade or cost-of-living adjustments increase their pay grade salaries to equal or exceed the red circle rate. The Equal Pay Act of 1963 protects individuals from having their pay lowered through the job-evaluation process.

In Figure 10–9 one person in pay grade 4 and two in pay grade 1 are currently being paid less than the minimum of the pay grade. Those individuals normally have their pay increased to the minimum of their pay grade. When the compensation system is finalized, no individual will receive less pay than the minimum of the job grade; any individual currently receiving more than the maximum will be red circled until some time in the future.

Overlap of Grades The organization must also decide whether to overlap pay grades so that the maximum of one pay grade is higher than the minimum of the next higher pay grade. The compensation system in Figure 10–9 allows pay grades to overlap. One advantage is that employees can be transferred or promoted from one job to the next without necessarily being given pay increases. For example, an employee paid $6.90 per hour in pay grade 5 could be promoted to a job with a larger point total in pay grade 6 without an increase in pay.

Management has the option of not paying individuals higher salaries immediately but of offering them higher salaries if they prove themselves and receive merit increases, thus moving up in the pay grade. Another advantage of overlapping pay grades is that this gives grades a greater range with more steps of a meaningful size. Thus, employees are rewarded with merit and seniority increases while they stay in the same job and pay grade.

One disadvantage of overlapping pay grades is that a promotion may not bring a pay increase and could even bring a cut in pay. Also, overlapping grades makes it possible for an individual in a higher pay grade to supervise employees in a lower pay grade who receive higher paychecks than the supervisor. For example, when a new supervisor is placed in a department in which an employee is at the highest step of the next lower pay grade, the employee will receive higher pay than the supervisor. In manufacturing and construction organizations this is not unusual.

Pay Increases

Primarily two types of pay increases are made: *across-the-board increases,* where everyone in the organization receives an equal pay increase, and *merit* or *seniority* increases given to selected individuals.

Across-the-Board Increases These increase the employee's income due to the cost-of-living allowances or in order to make the organization's pay system compatible with the local labor market. An across-the-board *cost-of-living adjustment (COLA)* can be an equal percentage or equal dollars. Managers often prefer to give equal-percentage increases because COLAs are related to the cost of living, which is measured in percentages. Hearing that the cost of living has gone up a certain percentage, employees realize that their buying power has decreased. Therefore, they hope to receive a COLA at least equal to the increase in their cost of living.

Using equal percentages can be deceiving since employees must use increased wages and not percentages to purchase goods and services. Using cost-of-living figures can also be misleading because any individual's actual increase in cost of living depends on spending habits, cost of major assets such as automobile and home, and other factors. The national increase in the cost of living may have little bearing on individual employees' actual bills.

Management often prefers to give across-the-board COLAs in equal percentages. Equal-percentage increases mean that employees in higher pay grades will receive greater actual dollar increases than employees in lower pay grades. An across-the-board percentage increase simply changes the dollar amounts for each grade and step in the compensation system; it does not move any employee or job within the system. Therefore, if a 7 percent cost-of-living pay increase were given to the pay grades and steps in Table 10–5, all of the amounts would change but the pay grades and steps would not. In Figure 10–9, the pay grade configuration would become more sloped as the higher pay grades experienced greater dollar increases than the lower pay grades.

If an equal-dollar across-the-board increase is given as a cost-of-living allowance, the amounts in Table 10–5 would increase an equal dollar figure. In Figure 10–9, the scale on the left side would slide down because individuals in lower pay grades get a larger percentage increase than individuals in higher pay grades. Individuals in higher pay grades argue that this is unfair because they cannot keep up with the cost of living since their increase is not as great as that of individuals in

lower pay grades. In summary, equal-dollar across-the-board COLAs decrease the differentials in pay between jobs and pay grades.

Equal-dollar and equal-percentage increases have advantages and disadvantages. In previous years, percentage increases in COLAs have been more common. However, due to the effects that equal-percentage COLAs and rising inflation have upon employees in low pay grades, some administrators have reconsidered in recent years; they are giving greater percentage increases to lower pay grades or equal-dollar increases to the entire labor force.

Merit Increases Time-based pay systems are not completely void of a relationship between pay and performance. Instead, many include merit increases to employees. After a performance appraisal of their work, employees receive increases in pay if their work record is judged meritorious. Merit raises are designed to motivate employees by tying at least part of their pay to their performance. But organizations often find it difficult to design performance appraisal and reward systems that meet employee expectations and perceptions of equity. Merit pay has been the subject of a great deal of debate by personnel practitioners, though most agree on a number of points. The portion of pay determined by merit increase is usually small. For most salaried, non-union employees, job evaluations and salary surveys determine pay grade and level, which represent a large percentage of total salary.[20]

Merit pay systems rest heavily on three assumptions: (1) employee differences in performance can be accurately measured, (2) employees can effectively perceive pay differences as relating to performance differences, and (3) individuals will increase their future performance to gain more merit increases.[21]

Critics of merit systems, however, point out their frequent problems: (1) there is only a slight relationship between performance appraisals and percentage pay increases, and employees are quick to realize it, (2) supervisor bias remains more important in the appraisal process than employee productivity, and (3) employees simply do not perceive that merit raises are linked to their performance, true or not. Thus management must audit its merit system for these possible problems, and must simply assume that it is effective because it is well intentioned.[22]

Many managers believe that linking pay increases to performance is effective because of the *law of effect*: behaviors that are rewarded are more likely to be repeated; behaviors that are punished are less likely to be repeated. Also, rewards that are obtained as a result of one's performance will have greater value than rewards that are given to everyone. Thus, a 7 percent merit increase in an organization where the average is five percent will be more highly valued than if a 7 percent across-the-board increase was given.[23]

When employees receive merit increases, they do not change pay grades, since a pay grade is based on the point total of their jobs or their classifications. But employees who receive merit increases move up one or more steps within their pay grades. Administrators may give two-step increases to the top 5 percent of their employees and one-step increases to the next highest 20 percent of their employees. The amount of increase depends on the pay grade and step of each employee. Employees find this system fair since everyone gets an equal step increase even though the amount changes according to the job classification. How large the increases are in actual dollars and cents depends on the number of steps within each pay grade.

Some organizations give seniority increases to employees who have successfully performed their jobs for a certain length of time. These increases move employees up one or more steps within their pay grades. If the organization of Table 10–5 gave merit increases, the dollar amounts in each pay grade would stay the same but employees would move up one step. The same would be true for the organization of Figure 10–9.

Performance-based Systems

The use of performance-based systems has seen a resurgence. After critics had convinced many managers that such systems could not be accurate or motivational, some organizations at least have found that Frederick Taylor may have been right all along. Five surveys of over 4,700 companies show that after switching from time-based to performance-based pay systems, organizations reported average productivity increases of 29 to 63 percent.[24] IBM, for example, was able to increase labor productivity in typewriter manufacturing by nearly 200 percent over a ten-year period. The reason cited was the use of two policies: (1) pay for productivity, only for productivity and (2) promote for productivity, only for productivity.[25]

Individual Incentive Plans   Most individual incentive systems are *piece-rate* or related plans. Such plans include a guaranteed base rate of pay for individuals who fail to achieve a standard level of production. The guaranteed rate is usually an hourly rate determined through job evaluation. The standard, the output an average employee should be able to produce, is usually determined by industrial engineers using time and motion studies. The results, however, are usually open to debate between management and labor.

Straight piecework is the most common and easily understood individual incentive plan. If an employee is paid $.025 per unit produced and completes 100 units in an hour, then the hour's gross earnings would be $2.50. Variations of straight piecework include falling piece rate and rising piece rate.

Plans that use a *falling piece rate* involve a standard time and rate of production. If the employee produces more than the standard, the gain is shared between the employer and the employee. Table 10–6 is a comparison of the various piece-rate plans. For the falling piece-rate plan, the employee's hourly earn-ings increase with output above a standard of 100, but the rate per piece falls at various pre-determined levels. Thus, an employee who has produced 140 units (40 percent above standard) receives only $3.22 (29 percent more) and not $3.50, which would be the case if the .025 rate were maintained. The em-

TABLE 10–6

A comparison of piece-rate plans ($100 per worker overhead cost per hour)

Standard piece-rate plan

Number of Pieces	Piece Rate	Worker's Earnings	Per Piece Overhead Cost	Total Cost
100	$.025	$ 2.50	$1.000	$1.025
120	.025	3.00	.833	.858
140	.025	3.50	.714	.739
160	.025	4.00	.625	.650
180	.025	4.50	.556	.581
200	.025	5.00	.500	.525

Falling piece-rate plan

Number of Pieces	Piece Rate	Worker's Earnings	Per Piece Overhead Cost	Total Cost
100	$.025	$ 2.50	$1.000	$1.025
120	.024	2.88	.833	.857
140	.023	3.22	.714	.737
160	.022	3.52	.625	.647
180	.021	3.78	.556	.577
200	.020	4.00	.500	.520

Rising piece-rate plan

Number of Pieces	Piece Rate	Worker's Earnings	Per Piece Overhead Cost	Total Cost
100	$.025	$ 2.50	$1.000	$1.025
120	.030	3.60	.833	.863
140	.035	4.90	.714	.749
160	.040	6.40	.625	.665
180	.045	8.10	.556	.601
200	.050	10.00	.500	.550

Source: Leonard R. Burgess, *Wage and Salary Administration* (Columbus, OH: Merrill, 1984), pp. 241–242.

ployer receives the remainder of the gain, effectively lowering the overhead cost per piece.

Plans that use a *rising piece rate* also involve a standard time and rate of production. But as Table 10–6 illustrates, the worker who increases output by 40 percent has a greater than proportional increase in hourly earnings. After earning $2.50 for the first 100 pieces, the worker earns $2.40 ($4.90 − $2.50) for the next forty pieces, or 96 percent of the base hourly pay. The increase occurs because the worker earned $.025 per piece for the first 100 pieces and $.035 per piece for the next 40. Management benefits nevertheless: the total cost per piece still declines as more pieces are produced because the fixed overhead cost is spread out over more pieces.[26] Why would management agree to a rising piece-rate system? If the higher hourly earnings are sufficiently motivational, the total cost per piece could be lower than under a falling piece-rate plan. For example, if under the falling piece-rate plan of Table 10–6 the employee is only slightly motivated and averages 120 units per hour, then management has an average total piece cost of $.857. But if the rising piece-rate plan is slightly more motivational and the employee averages 140 units per hour, management averages $.749 total per unit cost, while the employee averages $4.90 per hour instead of $2.88 (falling rate of 120 pieces).

Piece-rate systems have the advantages of being easily understood, simple to calculate, and motivational. But most jobs do not easily lend themselves to such a pay system because the output of the employee cannot be directly and objectively measured. Also, most employees' output is affected by the output of others. Thus their productivity is not directly proportional to their input. Finally, employers and employees can seldom agree on what is a fair production standard.

Standard hour plans are similar in concept to piece-rate plans except that standard time is set to complete a particular job instead of paying the employee a price per piece. For example, an auto mechanic might be given a standard time of two hours to tune up an eight-cylinder car. If the worker's pay rate is $8.00 per hour and three eight-cylinder tune-ups are finished in six hours, then the employee earns $48.00. If a so-called Halsey 50/50 incentive plan is used, the worker and employer share equally in the time saved by the employee. Thus, if three tune-ups are completed in five hours, then the employee would be paid $52.00 ($48.00 + $4.00 [½ hour saved at $8.00/hour]), and the employer has an additional hour's work time.

Group Incentive Plans In the United States and most other countries, the trend has been away from individual incentive plans and toward group incentive plans. Group incentive plans tend to encourage employee cooperation, whereas individual incentive plans tend to foster competition.[27]

Rapidly changing technology has led to a redesign of many jobs. Most modern jobs do not emphasize individual effort but instead stress the effort of the entire group. Thus, if incentive plans are introduced in the modern work place, a group incentive plan is the first to be considered by management and the personnel administrator.

The *Scanlon plan* was developed by Joseph Scanlon, an official of the United Steelworkers Union. It has since become a basis for labor–management cooperation above and beyond its use as a group incentive plan. The plan contains two primary features: (1) departmental committees of union and management representatives meet together at least monthly to consider any cost savings suggestions; (2) any documented cost savings that result from implemented committee suggestions are divided, with 75 percent going to the employees and 25 percent to the company.

After five years with a Scanlon plan, the Rocky Mountain Data Systems, a dental profession service company, reported the following:[28]

- Profits were up 22 percent on assets, 11 percent on sales.
- Employee compensation was up 14 percent per year compounded.
- The "peak-out" phenomenon, whereby employees no longer could reach a maximum in their pay grade, was avoided.
- Labor-management hostility subsided as employees realized that they had a stake in the company because they shared in the gains and the losses.

At the Parker Pen Company the plant manager concluded that the Scanlon plan increased productivity because everyone participated. It generated an atmosphere in which people came forward with good ideas. A union leader at Parker Pen expressed his belief that the plan enabled the company to introduce new equipment without labor opposition and thus beat foreign competition.

Gainsharing A derivation of the Scanlon plan is gainsharing. Gainsharing systems emphasize employee involvement in managing the organization as well as sharing in its profits. Under a gainsharing plan, the performance of the entire organization is measured and a target productivity level for a future period of time is set. If the organization's performance exceeds the targeted level, employees equally share the "gain" in a bonus. The key to gainsharing is employee involvement. Small groups of employees meet, analyze production methods, present new ideas, and implement them. The process is similar to that of quality circles, with a notable exception: self-management. Gainsharing allows employees not only to implement their ideas but also to work without direct supervisors or quality inspectors. Employees are given a salary and production goals and told to select their own work methods. The objective is to create a work force in which all employees cooperate in establishing and working toward common goals. Can gainsharing work? It has at the Dana Spicer Heavy Axle Division's facility in Hilliard, Ohio. There are no supervisors or time clocks at Dana. After three years of gainsharing the employees (all salaried) are very content, labor efficiency is up 45 percent compared to that of the pregainsharing system, and quality problems are down 50 percent. During one six-month period, over 400 productivity ideas were contributed by the employees at Dana, and employees averaged monthly bonuses of 12 to 16 percent. The U.S. General Accounting Office estimates that about 1,000 American firms currently use gainsharing.[29]

Other group incentive plans involve programs that set expected levels of productivity, product costs, or sales levels for individual groups and then provide employee bonuses if the targeted goals are exceeded. One widely recognized example is the Nucor Corporation. In 1980 the company reported a staggering growth of 600 percent in sales and 1,500 percent in profits over ten years due to a production incentive program. The company actually developed four separate incentive programs: one each for production employees, department heads, professional employees, and senior officers. Their theory was that "money is the best motivation."[30]

Profit-sharing Plans

In a profit-sharing plan, employees receive a share of the company's profits. The profit share is paid in addition to employees' regular wages and is generally intended to increase employees' incentive to work. The annual or quarterly payments are usually a fixed percentage of the profits of the organization and are divided among employees equally.

Profit-sharing plans have increased in use in recent years because management prefers them to increases in salaries or wage rates, which become permanent increases in personnel costs. Profit-sharing bonuses, however, do not automatically carry over to future years. Instead they are paid only in those years in which the company earns a profit.

Profit-sharing plans have also increased in labor agreements in the 1980s.[31] Management favors replacing COLAs with profit sharing as a wage supplement for several reasons: (1) payments are made only if the company makes a profit and thus is usually financially strong; (2) unlike COLAs, payments are not tied to inflation, which is not related to the company's financial status and may require increases during difficult times; (3) workers' pay is linked to their productivity, as well as to the number of hours they work, giving them a direct incentive to make the company more profitable; (4) workers may feel more a part of the company and develop increased interest in reducing waste and increasing efficiency in all areas, as well as in their own jobs.

In 1986, for example, the Ford Motor Company distributed $224 million in annual profit-sharing checks to U.S. employees. The average worker received $1,200, a decrease from the 1985 average of $2,100, when Ford reported higher profits. Peter Pestillo, Ford's personnel chief and chief labor negotiator, noted, "We think it's money well spent. They get more, and they get more done. We think we get a payback in the cooperation and enthusiasm of the people." The 1984 Ford–United Auto Workers (UAW) master agreement was the first to contain a profit-sharing provision pushed by management as a means of avoiding the UAW-proposed 3 percent annual raises.[32] The concept of profit sharing within the auto industry is not new, however. Douglas Frasier, former president of the UAW, noted that the union first asked for a profit-sharing plan over forty years prior to the 1984 agreement and during several other negotiations, but neither of the U.S. auto giants became interested until they started losing money in the 1980s.[33]

Growth of Incentive Plans

A survey of 1,600 American companies showed that the use of performance-based systems doubled from 1982 to 1986. While only about 10 percent of all employers reported using any incentive system, another 7 percent expect to add systems in the near future. The most popular incentive system was profit sharing, used by 32 percent of the respondents with an incentive system. Lump-sum bonuses not tied directly to profits were reported by 30 percent, individual incentive programs by 28 percent, and gain sharing or small-group incentive plans by 14 percent. The new incentive plans generally replace across-the-board increases.[34]

Just how much can a change from a time-based to a performance-based pay system affect the bottom line of a company? Victor Kiam, chairman of Remington Products, Inc., the shaver company, credits the profit-sharing plan he initiated shortly after purchasing the company with its turnaround from a $5 million a year loser to profits of over $10 million a year in ten years. Kiam put "the whole company on incentive, from the maintenance guy to the chief financial officer." The average factory worker at Remington earns one-third of his income in bonuses based on company profits. Kiam also eliminated executive perks including separate washrooms, parking spaces, and dining rooms.[35]

EXECUTIVE COMPENSATION

In large, established companies, members of top management are paid differently than mid-level and lower-level managers. In general, executive pay comes in four forms: (1) base salary, (2) annual bonus, (3) long-term incentives, and (4) benefits and perquisites ("perks").[36] Base salaries, at the center of executive pay, are generally determined through job evaluation and serve as the basis for the other types of benefits.

Annual bonuses for executives include both cash and stock payments. Bonuses are usually tied to the performance of the company as a whole for the previous year or for division managers to their particular area. Although most executive compensation plans design such bonuses to be pay for performance, to some extent executives have come to rely on them to maintain their standard of living. An analysis of *Fortune* 500 showed no difference in giving bonuses between the companies with the best corporate performance and those with the worst.[37]

Long-term incentives are designed to allow the executive to accumulate wealth. The basic philosophy is that these individuals should have a stake in the long-term future of the firm. It is thought that they will make decisions more in line with the company's long-term future if they have a personal stake in that future. Executive benefits and perks range from the traditional executive automobile and dining room to the more unusual country-club membership, private use of company airplanes, and personal legal counseling.

The ability of a firm to reward executives effectively was greatly enhanced by the Economic Recovery Tax Act (ERTA) of 1981. The act provides for a reduced maximum tax rate (50 percent), favorable tax treatment for stock options, highly attractive maximum capital gains rates, and dramatic changes in the taxation of inherited wealth.[38]

Income Deferrals

The use of income deferrals in executive pay plans is a well-established practice. Some 40 to 45 percent of the *Fortune* 500 companies utilize them. The tax advantage of income deferrals is illustrated in Table 10–7. The example shows how an executive who receives a $10,000 bonus would benefit by deferring the income. But there are both advantages and disadvantages to deferral.[39] The major advantages are:

- Amounts deferred continue to appreciate on a pretax basis.
- Appreciation is taxable only at receipt, thus allowing full annual earnings to continue appreciating.
- Deferrals can be to years after retirement to supplement retirement income, when the retiree's tax bracket is sometimes lower.
- The company has the use of the money until it is paid.
- Deferral plans are not subject to burdensome reporting requirements.

The major disadvantages are:

- Deferred compensation cannot be included in the basis for calculating pension benefits. Thus, executives in a qualified pension plan whose basis is total W-2 earnings will have a significant loss in retirement income, more than offsetting the tax-sheltered appreciation of the deferred monies. Many companies, however, offset this loss of pension earnings by installing a nonqualified supplemental retirement income plan, but this can be expensive.

TABLE 10–7
The tax advantages of
income deferrals are
evident in this example
of one executive

Items	Personally Invested At 10%	Deferred Payment 10%
Initial Capital	$10,000	$10,000
Less: Taxes (50%)	− 5,000	
Net Capital	$ 5,000	$10,000
Annual Investment Income	$ 500	$ 1,000
Less: Taxes (50%)	− 250	
Net Annual Investment Income	$ 250	$ 1,000
Net Compounded Over 10 Years	$ 3,145	$15,940
Plus: Net Capital	+ 5,000	+ 10,000
Gross Value	$ 8,000	$25,940
Less: Taxes (50%)		− 12,970
Net Value	$ 8,145	$12,970
Difference (52%)		$4,825

Source: James T. Brinks, "Executive Compensation: Crossroads of the 80's," *Personnel Administrator* (December 1981): p. 27.

- Few executives under fifty-five will actually defer income because of their substantial demands for current income to meet mortgages, children's education, and so on.
- Unless the appreciation rates are high enough, the executive can lose against inflation. Therefore, the appreciation should be tied to inflation-sensitive interest equivalencies, such as the prime rate or Treasury bill rates.
- Any interest earned is taxable interest income to the company, and there is no offsetting compensation expense until the monies are actually paid out.
- The deferred income becomes part of the debt of the company. Thus, should the company default, the executive would have to join all other creditors for payment.

Stock Options

Stock options have become extremely important to most executive compensation plans. The gist of the stock option is that the execu-tive is given the right to buy the company's stock at an option price up to a fixed future point in time. The option price is usually the current market price. Thus, if an executive is given an option to buy stock at $20 a share and waits five years until the price has risen to $50 a share, then he or she has an unrealized capital gain of $30 a share.[40] Stock-option programs are a complex but critical part of executive compensation plans. It is thought that managers should profit from their efforts; if they cause the company's stock price to rise, they should share in the gain.

The most common form of stock option uses the so-called nonqualified approach. The executive is given the right to purchase the company's stock at the current price for up to five or ten years. The company can take a tax deduction on the "spread" between the option price and the current market price when the right is exercised. The tax deduction is taken without incurring a charge to earnings, which is an advantage for the company. But the executive must be able to raise the cash to exercise the option and pay the tax incurred, which is a major drawback for the executive.[41] Stock appreciation rights (SARs) give the executive the right to exercise a nonqualified stock option or receive the spread in cash. The executive thus avoids the need to raise the cash to exercise the option and is not required to hold the stock for any length of time.

The 1981 tax act restored favorable tax treatment to so-called qualified options called *incentive stock options (ISOs)*. ISOs the executive incurs no taxes at the time of exercise but is taxed upon sale of the stock. But the company receives no tax benefit, as it does under a nonqualified option.[42]

Another approach to long-term executive compensation is to closely relate incentive rewards to corporate performance through performance shares or performance units. With this approach, executives are promised a number of shares of stock or units if the company meets long-term growth targets. Usually the earnings per share of the company are used as the target.

Executive compensation has become a highly complex yet critical aspect of a corporate pay system. Top executive pay packages today usually include traditional base pay and executive benefits supplemented with short-term bonuses, stock options, and performance shares or units. Executives benefit by avoiding some taxes and providing for sizable wealth accumulation; companies are able to focus the executives' decision making on long-term growth and return on investment.

COMPENSATION ISSUES

Several important issues face personnel managers in the area of compensation. Inflation constantly decreases employees' disposable income, but they nevertheless have to pay higher Social Security and income taxes. Employers, however, are in no position to simply give away dollars to help employees; instead, employers must be innovative in their approach to compensation problems.

Wage Compression

Wage compression refers to decreasing the differentials between higher and lower pay grades. Faced with high turnover in low-paying jobs and with employees who cannot live within their means, employers have had to give greater increases to lower-paying positions than higher-paying positions. Pay differences between top- and middle-level jobs and middle- and lower-level jobs are decreasing. With the graduated income tax, salary differences after taxes will probably become even lower in the future.

Compression, however, takes a number of forms. A manager may find that the salary difference after taxes between his or her salary and those of subordinates is insignificant. A similar form of compression occurs when a recent college graduate with no experience finds little difference between his or her pay and that of a qualified, successful graduate with ten years of experience.

When the results of compression are fully perceived, employees complain of pay inequity. Naturally, this results in a loss of morale and a tendency to work less effectively. Qualified successful employees turn down promotions because the incremental increases in pay are not worth the extra responsibility or risk.[43]

Two-tier Wage Systems

A wage system that pays newly hired workers less than current employees performing the same or similar jobs is termed *two tier*. Following the institution of the historic first two-tier wage system in 1977 at General Motors' Packard Electric Division in Warren, Ohio, many more union–management negotiations have resulted in similar systems.[44] The basic concept is to provide continued higher wage levels for current employees if the union will accept reduced levels for future employees. Union leaders believe that they must accept the two-tier system or face greater layoffs in the future. Management usually claims that the system is needed to compete with non-union and foreign competition. The airline, copper, trucking, auto, food, and aerospace industries have negotiated two-tier systems.[45]

Examples of two-tier agreements include:[46]

- At American Airlines, a DC-10 pilot can make as much as $127,900 a year, but a recently hired pilot will make only about half as much. A certain class of flight attendants starts at $972 a month and peaks at $1,199 a month in their fifth year. Flight attendants hired before December 6, 1983, started at $1,194 a month and top out at $2,217 in their twelfth year.
- At Packard Electric, new hires are brought in at 55 percent of the wages of current employees.
- At General Motors' Delco Products plant in Rochester, New York, new assemblers earn up to $9.68 an hour. Those hired years ago earn up to $13.00 an hour.
- Newly hired journeymen at the Ingalls Shipbuilding Company in Pascagoula, Mississippi, earn $1.00 less than the senior employees. The wages of new hires catch up after 2,000 hours.

While a two-tier system is contrary to the historic union doctrine of equal pay for equal work or pay equity, when the system is first negotiated, the union representatives can claim that they have avoided disaster and have saved the jobs and/or wage levels of current members (who must vote on the contract). It is relatively easy to sell such a con-

cept since no workers at that point are accepting the lower tier. However, five or ten years later, when many workers are being paid lower wages for the same work as their fellow union members, if can become a source of conflict and resentment. In some cases, the lower-paid workers express their feelings with lower product quality and productivity records than their higher-paid counterparts. In these bargaining units, the conflict could present even greater problems to both union and management leaders as the number of lower-tier workers approaches 51 percent of the bargaining unit and they demand equity.[47]

Do employees hired into a lower-tier pay position perceive their treatment as equitable or not? A study of about 2,000 employees found that low-tier employees perceived the employer as being significantly lower in pay equity and perceived the union as less useful in obtaining fair pay for its members. In addition, the low-tier employees felt a lower level of commitment to their employer—which might affect their productivity and tenure with the organization. These perception problems can be controlled, the research results suggest, if low-tier employees are assigned to new work locations where there are few high-tier employees and/or if they are hired for part-time instead of full-time work. Employees hired under these conditions do not report equity perception problems.[48] Another method of minimizing the morale problems of low-tier employees is to provide eventual merging of the two tiers for each individual. American Airlines, for example, provides parity for low-tier employees after ten years of service.[49]

Unions continue to place a high negotiating priority on preserving jobs. Two-tier pay systems, lump-sum bonuses in lieu of merit wage increases, and health insurance cost-reduction plans are three major cost-saving approaches negotiated by management in exchange for a job security provision. Unions continue to resist two-tier systems because of morale problems that develop as more lower-tier workers are hired. However, when faced with wage cuts or layoffs as the only other means of significantly reducing employer payroll costs, two-tier systems appear more desirable to current members. Lump-sum payments typically appear in three-year contracts, for example, where the first year includes a specified base-wage increase followed by two lump-sum payments in the following years. The employer's cost savings occur due to the avoidance of compounding base wage increases and related benefits such as pensions, which use base wages in payment formulas.[50]

While two-tier systems may come under increasing pressure from employees and labor leaders, management in those industries where such systems have been adopted is not likely to grant the pay increases necessary to raise the lower tier to equality with the higher tier. Cost pressures from deregulation, non-union competition, and foreign competition are likely to increase, not decrease, in the future. Thus, labor and management often must consider the low-tier pay level a reality and adjust to it, or consider across-the-board pay or benefit cuts for high-tier employees which would produce equal cost savings. Such across-the-board concessions, combined with profit-sharing bonuses and job security, may easily appeal to low-tier employees, but can it be sold at the bargaining table to senior, high-tier employees?

It is likely that two-tier systems will continue to be considered by labor and management when faced with greater long-term competition. Before adoption, the pros and cons listed in Table 10–8 should be carefully considered.

COLA or Merit Increases?

Employers have been faced with the dilemma of using increased revenues to grant COLAs to all employees or giving merit raises to increase job performance. During highly inflationary periods, employers have stressed COLAs rather than merit increases; but when there seems to be no slowing of inflation, employers begin to change their thinking. Usually there is not enough in the company budget for increases that match COLAs as well as sizable merit increases to motivate the employees.

A survey revealed that employers were beginning to increase merit raises and stop automatic across-the-board COLAs for all employees. Continental Can, a large container producer, abandoned its merit pay system based on a "write-up from the manager stating why the increase was justified" and instituted special qualitative and quantitative performance criteria for merit increases. Marginal

TABLE 10–8

Pros and cons of the two-tier wage system

Pros	Cons
• Significantly reduced labor costs • Maintenance of higher employment levels • Relief from wage compression between senior and junior employees on the same job	• Resentment, low quality, and low productivity from low-tier employees • Higher absenteeism and turnover of low-tier employees • Intensification of the preceding problems as low-tier employees increase in number

Better Pay for Women Agenda

Why is U.S. Senator Barbara Mikulski (D. Md.) carrying a red purse in the halls of Congress? Because Mary Kay Oaken, national president of the Business and Professional Women's (BPW) Clubs, Inc., chose it as the symbol of the women's movement. Instead of social issues, pocketbook issues count to most women, claims Oaken. The purse is the best symbol "because we are talking about money, and red because working women in this country are financially in the red." The better pay agenda of BPW not only includes the issue of pay equity but also includes the issues of equal education, social security, pension and insurance reform, career training, boardroom barriers, and improved dependent care and family leave. (See box opposite.) Oaken encourages all working women to joint BPW's agenda—and carry red purses.

Source: Adapted from "Better Pay for Women Agenda," *National Business Women* 68, no. 3 (June–July 1987): 13. Used with permission. *National Business Women* is the magazine of Business and Professional Women (BPW/USA).

workers no longer receive merit increases, while outstanding workers may earn as much as a 12 percent increase. At International Multi Foods Corporation, employees and managers mutually set goals which determine merit pay increases.

Pitney-Bowes, Inc., a business equipment producer, allows a few employees each year to become eligible for a lump-sum merit increase of up to 15 percent of their base pay. The one-time extra incentive allows the company to give large motivational paid bonuses without being burdened with a permanently higher salary commitment. Company management reasons that yesterday's outstanding performance should not have to be paid for on a continuing basis into the future.[51]

Pay Secrecy

One compensation issue that has been debated in recent years is whether to have an open system—that is, one in which employees know the pay grade each job is classified in and the pay ranges for those grades. In a closed system, employees are told that pay is a personal matter and they are not to discuss other employees' pay levels. Many organizations still have a closed system of compensation.

Comparable Worth

According to Winn Newman, general council of the Coalition of Labor Union Women, the leading women's economic issue is pay equity, or comparable worth. The Equal Pay Act does not always enable women to obtain relief from discrimination because the act only guarantees women equal pay with men on jobs that have the same job classification. The average full-time female worker earns about 68 percent of the average male's wage—decades after the passage of the Equal Pay Act.[52]

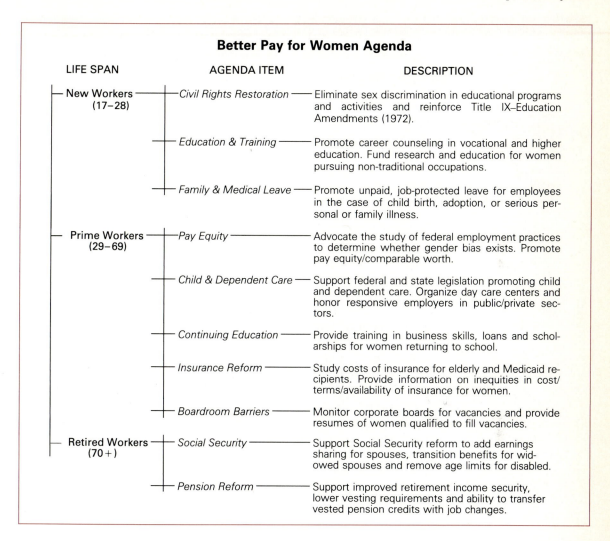

Better Pay for Women Agenda

LIFE SPAN	AGENDA ITEM	DESCRIPTION
New Workers (17–28)	Civil Rights Restoration	Eliminate sex discrimination in educational programs and activities and reinforce Title IX–Education Amendments (1972).
	Education & Training	Promote career counseling in vocational and higher education. Fund research and education for women pursuing non-traditional occupations.
	Family & Medical Leave	Promote unpaid, job-protected leave for employees in the case of child birth, adoption, or serious personal or family illness.
Prime Workers (29–69)	Pay Equity	Advocate the study of federal employment practices to determine whether gender bias exists. Promote pay equity/comparable worth.
	Child & Dependent Care	Support federal and state legislation promoting child and dependent care. Organize day care centers and honor responsive employers in public/private sectors.
	Continuing Education	Provide training in business skills, loans and scholarships for women returning to school.
	Insurance Reform	Study costs of insurance for elderly and Medicaid recipients. Provide information on inequities in cost/terms/availability of insurance for women.
	Boardroom Barriers	Monitor corporate boards for vacancies and provide resumes of women qualified to fill vacancies.
Retired Workers (70+)	Social Security	Support Social Security reform to add earnings sharing for spouses, transition benefits for widowed spouses and remove age limits for disabled.
	Pension Reform	Support improved retirement income security, lower vesting requirements and ability to transfer vested pension credits with job changes.

At the heart of the issue is the concept of comparable worth.

The doctrine of comparable worth requires that pay be equal not just for men and women performing the same job but for all jobs requiring comparable skill, effort, responsibility, and working conditions. According to supporters, the doctrine represents the spirit, if not the letter, of the Equal Pay Act. Opponents of comparable worth argue that the large percentage of women in such lower-paying jobs as secretary, nurse, and elementary school teacher is a result of women's attraction to those jobs and that their pay level is the result of the external marketplace, as verified by wage surveys. Furthermore, oppo-

International HRM: Why "Other" People Work

Americans perceive many foreigners as poor workers. "No work ethic," we say, meaning "lazy." Yet a universal concern of the Japanese, Swiss, and others who take over American firms or invest in the United States is that perpetual problem of getting the American labor force to produce.

"We ask them to use not just their arms and hands, but their brains," says the president of a U.S. tire manufacturing company. Yet his workers gripe that they are being overworked, and they are unenthusiastic about the 65 percent improvement in productivity since "foreigners" took over the plant. Those complaining are not disgruntled foreign laborers, however, but Americans, and the speaker is Kazuo Ishijure, president of Japan's Bridgestone Tire Manufacturing (U.S.A.), which acquired a Firestone Tire and Rubber Company plant in 1983.

The problem boils down not to laziness but to conflict between culturally different patterns of job behavior, management styles and the role that work plays in the employee's life.

In Japan, for example, employees are wedded to their company. Their attention and energies are concentrated on the company—their personal life is their company life, and its future is their future. Compared to Americans, who are job oriented rather than company oriented, the Japanese are generally much better informed about their company's business, and easily step outside their own tasks to help a colleague. American business is more segmented and cellular; parochial attitudes prevail. Americans "mind their own business" and feel little loyalty to a company. When we are displeased with our salary, company policy, or personalities, we resign.

The Latin American, on the other hand, tends to work not for a company or for a job, but for an individual. People strive for personal power. Relationships and loyalties are much more personalized, and managers can get performance only by effectively using personal influence and working through individual members of a group. Among Turks and Arabs, too, the individual is supreme, although inextricably integrated with family and society. Employees tend to be evaluated on their loyalty to superiors more than on actual job performance. In Islamic societies it is unclear where friendship ends and business begins, when socializing at the workplace stops and work begins. . . .

The Australians say they "go to work to get a vacation." They have the shortest working hours in the world and they need their frequent "smoke-ohs" (smoking breaks) during the day. To the French the quality of life is what matters. . . . The French cling to their free time and vacations: they resist working overtime and have the longest vacations in the world, by law a minimum of five weeks a year. German firms, too, are moving in this direction. However, both French and Germans usually work hard during work hours, and have a reputation for being productive and concerned with quality.

Source: Adapted from Lennie Copeland and Lewis Griggs, *Going International* (New York: Random House, 1985), pp. 127–28.

nents argue, the demand for comparable worth is not a demand for equal opportunity but a demand to be protected against one's career choice.[53]

The debate on comparable worth will most likely continue for many years. At stake are billions of dollars in employee wages. It is not an easy issue to decide: what is the worth of a secretary in comparison to a security guard? Even women's groups are split on just how the doctrine would be put into practice. A bill introduced in the Senate in 1983 that would have required comparable worth in federal jobs was not supported by the National Organization for Women.[54] Most labor and management representatives agree that the issue will be primarily pursued by labor unions, not the government. Labor unions active in the public sector, such as the American Federation of State, County and Municipal Employees (AFSCME), will most likely be taking the initiative. Public employers are the primary targets of advocates because they are legally more vulnerable and because (according to a leading labor attorney) they include the greatest pay inequities.[55] The courts have generally allowed for pay differences between males and females if they are based on (1) seniority, (2) merit, (3) performance (quantity or quality), or (4) other factors such as job evaluation or red circled employees.[56]

In 1985, the EEOC rejected the idea that comparable worth should be instituted as an interpretation of the Civil Rights Act. In a unanimous decision, the commission said that the doctrine should not be recognized as part of the act. The case involved administrative staff workers (85 percent female) and maintenance workers (88 percent male). The commission ruled that no "barriers existed to prevent males and females from moving between job categories—and thus no discrimination."[57]

Also in 1985, the U.S. Court of Appeals for the Ninth Circuit rejected the doctrine of comparable worth, despite a study by a state government which showed that women were paid 20 percent less than men for "jobs requiring the same skills and effort as those held by men." The court held that market factors should determine wage and salary levels.[58]

INTERNATIONAL HRM: COMPENSATION JAPANESE STYLE

Compatible with the view that experienced, trained workers are more reliable and productive than those that aren't, lifetime employment in Japan leads to seniority-based salaries, evaluations, and promotions—a quite rational and convenient policy when length of service is seen as an index of achievement. Not only is this approach in accord with the custom of respecting elders, but it also complements lifelong employment.

Upon joining the company, the employee expects a job for life, with steady career progression based on his sex, education, and length of service. The fact that advancement depends primarily on such personal attributes rather than on job performance is further evidence of the relative insignificance of the concept of a discrete job in Japanese culture. As employees advance, they, like U.S. military personnel, can predict how much they will receive and what rank they will hold 10 or 20 years ahead.

Congruent with a comparatively equitable distribution of national income and the strong group orientation of the Japanese, there are few pay classes and low salary differentials. This has the effect of lessening the importance of particular positions, so that issues such as comparable worth are less likely to emerge. Indeed, although the compensation of the managerial elite is high by Japanese standards, it is not high enough to enable most executives to accumulate personal fortunes. Recent changes in some corporations notwithstanding, individual differences in competence within age and educational classes are virtually ignored in the initial stages of a career, at least for pay purposes. This encourages employees to concentrate on long-term organizational goals without worrying about how much money their peers are making.[59]

The rationale for pay by age is maintenance of one's family, not economic reward; as in the U.S. government, compensation is primarily based on job tenure and living costs. Thus an employee is assured of earning enough to meet expenses during his career, and is prepared as a result to commit himself to the organization for a long period. Seniority pay means that frequent, formal personnel appraisals are unusual in Japan: the assumption is that each person will contribute the maximum to the organization, and the employees' best efforts provide the standard by which they will be evaluated. Performance, both of a technical and an interpersonal nature, is highly valued, particularly for top positions, and permanent employment promises that one's true contribution eventually will be recognized. A strict merit system would damage group harmony; length of service, with its subtle, implicit, long-run ratings, is more suitable.[60]

CONCLUSIONS AND APPLICATIONS

- Organizations use both extrinsic and intrinsic rewards to compensate employees for their time and effort. Pay systems are designed to attract, retain, and motivate employees while complying with state and federal laws.

- Job evaluation is used to evaluate jobs systematically and to assign them to pay grades. The personnel specialist strives to maintain a pay system that employees view as equitable both internally and externally. Standard methods of evaluation include ranking, classification, point, and factor comparison. Each offers different advantages to the organization.

- Pay systems are usually designed to compensate people for the amount of work they produce (piece work) or the time they spend on the job (hourly and salaried.) Most employees in the United States are paid through time-based systems because of the complexity of most jobs, which makes a performance-based system impractical.

- COLAs are designed to maintain the purchasing power of the salary employees receive. Whether COLAs are given on a basis of equal percentage or equal dollars can affect the relative difference between higher- and lower-paid employees.

- Merit pay increases are intended to tie employees' performances to their raises. Valid and effective merit systems require the organization to use accurate performance appraisals.
- Executive compensation has become a complex area of personnel functions. Top organization executives often receive compensation in as many as four areas, including salary, bonuses, long-term incentives, and benefits.

- The doctrine of comparable worth became hotly debated in the 1980s. Many supporters of the doctrine believe it is necessary because some new jobs and occupations are low-paying solely because they have historically been filled by women. Opponents argue that EEO laws are changing such disparity and that the marketplace should determine wage levels.

CASE STUDY
Job Evaluation

The Metropolitan Office Machines Company is located in a large northeastern city with a population of about 3 million. A three-employee operation in 1956, the firm has over 200 employees today. The work force includes industrial sales representatives, buyers, office personnel, and warehouse operators and drivers. Profits have been very good, and the firm recently moved into its new custom-designed facility. Generally, the employees have been very loyal to the firm and appear to be happy in their work. Since the late 1950s, Metropolitan has had a generous profit-sharing plan. Turnover has averaged less than 1 percent for the last ten years, and absenteeism has never been a problem.

At a recent board of directors meeting, some concern was expressed over the company's lack of a modern job-evaluation system tied to various pay grades and levels. Several board members mentioned that other organizations caught napping in this area had become involved in costly litigations as a result. In recent years the few employee complaints concerning pay had been dealt with by the grievance committee without much difficulty. The personnel director, an employee with twenty-two years in the company, challenged the need for a new system of job evaluation at the board meeting. His method of job rankings had worked well for over twenty years and been accepted by the employees. Once a year, a wage survey was conducted before COLAs were determined to keep Metropolitan's pay structure higher than the competition's.

The board members were not convinced; they held on to the issue with beaglelike tenacity. A few mentioned that the company offered almost no fringe benefits except a generous profit-sharing plan. Employees paid their entire premiums in the group health-insurance plan and group life-insurance plan. Although no pension plan was provided, employees could have a portion of their monthly pay deposited directly in Individual Retirement Accounts at local banks.

The board of directors could not reach a consensus. One member expressed concern that the company would be sued by someone claiming discrimination "because today everyone wants something for nothing." Other members were concerned that the pay and benefits plans be kept up to date.

Questions

1. Should a new job-evaluation system be adopted?
2. Should merit increases be offered instead of COLAs?
3. How should the board evaluate the effectiveness of the company's pay structure?

EXPERIENTIAL EXERCISE
How Should These Employees Be Paid?

Purpose

To examine the various ways of compensating people using incentive plans.

Introduction

While most employees are paid a salary for the period of time worked, there is an increasing trend toward a phenomenon known as *pay for performance*, whereby employees, in addition to their normal salary, are paid an incentive for high performance. The increasing use of incentive systems is primarily the result of organizational efforts to increase profits and competitiveness through increased employee productivity. Studies show that incentive plans, if well constructed and implemented, can have a dramatic effect on employee productivity.

Conditions Necessary for Using Incentive Systems

In reality, a relatively small percentage of the total labor force is paid on an incentive basis–about 15 percent. Why? Because an incentive pay system is impractical to administer unless certain key conditions can be met. Those conditions include the following:

1. The output must be measurable and suitable for standardization.
2. There must be a consistent relationship between the employee's skill and effort and the employee's output.
3. The output can be measured and credited to the proper individual or group.
4. The incentive system should lead to an increase in productivity.
5. The employees, the union (if one exists), and management must all support the incentive system.

The Task

Listed below are several jobs. For each job, complete the questions in the figure provided. Following this exercise, your instructor will lead a discussion on incentive compensation systems. Some jobs are appropriate for incentive compensation systems, while others are more appropriate for a wage or salary system.

Valerie McCloud—Forklift Driver
Valerie McCloud drives a forklift for a small metals manufacturer. She picks up parts that have been boxed and loaded onto pallets and delivers them to the

warehouse for shipping. She occasionally also performs odd jobs throughout the day at the request of her supervisor. McCloud is a member of the Teamsters' Union.

Jill Peters—Seamstress

Jill Peters works as a seamstress for a large textile firm in South Carolina. She works independently, using an industrial sewing machine. All day, she sews sleeves and pockets to men's shirts. Her output is tallied twice a day by her supervisor.

William Grant—Assembly-Line Worker

William Grant is an assembly-line worker for a large home appliance manufacturer. He attaches parts to washing machines as they reach his position on the line. Twenty-seven employees work on this particular assembly line in the plant. Daily output for the group is recorded by the employees' supervisor.

Claire Walker—Keypunch Operator

Claire Walker is a keypunch operator for a large state government agency. Her work varies from day to day, although much of it is very similar in nature. Weekly, her supervisor receives a computer printout that details each keypuncher's production rate and quality index.

Rick Fernstein—Accounting Instructor

Rick Fernstein is an assistant professor for a large urban university. He is responsible for activities involving teaching, research, and community service. Annually, he prepares a performance report covering all activities for the year. This report includes summaries of student course evaluations, publications, committee work, and other school-related activities. Fernstein's department head closely reviews the report and assigns an overall performance evaluation of "excellent," "good," "satisfactory," "below satisfactory," or "unacceptable."

Dennis Cuestick—Automobile Salesman

Dennis Cuestick is an automobile salesman for a Ford dealer in a midwestern town. Six days a week, he "works the floor." The company's sales personnel have an informal system for taking turns when customers enter the showroom or call to make inquiries about a car. Sales are recorded daily by the sales manager.

Paul McCleskey—Route Salesman

Paul McCleskey is a route salesman for a large cola manufacturer. His route covers a large rural area in central Georgia and consists primarily of servicing small mom-and-pop grocery stores, lounges, and restaurants. At the end of each day, McCleskey turns in a report to his supervisor, detailing his sales activity for each account.

Charley Bedeman—Farm Laborer

Charley Bedeman is a farm laborer for the Jiffy Orange Juice Company in Orlando, Florida. He rises daily at 6:00 A.M. and is in the groves picking oranges by 7:00 A.M. Using a centuries-old technology, he carefully places each piece of ripe fruit in his deep "picking bag" slung over his shoulder. He dumps a full bag into a box and starts all over until quitting time at 5:00 P.M.

Kathy Miller—Secretary

Kathy Miller is a secretary to the Dean of the Arts and Sciences School at a small, private liberal arts college. She types correspondence and reports, takes dictation, files, maintains the dean's schedule, and so on. Miller's work is evaluated by the dean annually, using a performance-evaluation form that includes quantity of work, quality of work, dependability, judgment, communication skills, ability to get along with others, and loyalty. For each of these traits, she is assigned a rating of "very good," "above average," "average," "below average," or "unsatisfactory." One of these ratings is also given to Miller to designate her overall performance for the year.

Sheldon Smedley—Attorney

Sheldon Smedley, a recent graduate of a prestigious eastern law school, works for a reputable Washington law firm specializing in corporate law. Smedley is assigned to the division that handles patent and trademark violations. He works directly with clients, researches cases, writes briefs, and represents clients in court. His performance is reviewed informally about every six months. No special forms are used to conduct these evaluations.

| Employee | COMPENSATION PLAN | | | | | INCENTIVE PLAN | |
	(A) Hourly only	(B) Hourly plus incentive	(C) Salary only	(D) Salary plus incentive	(E) Incentive only	1. If you checked B, D, or E, indicate the appropriate *form* of incentive (piecework, commission, merit increase, bonus, stock option, stock appreciation rights, performance shares, profit sharing, Scanlon plan).	2. If you have recommended some form of incentive, indicate the type of output (net sales, per item manufactured, per set of encyclopedias, etc.) that the incentive should be based upon.
Valerie McCloud							
Jill Peters							
William Grant							
Claire Walker							
Rick Fernstein							
Dennis Cuestick							
Paul McCleskey							
Charley Bedeman							
Kathy Miller							
Sheldon Smedley							

KEY TERMS AND CONCEPTS

Benchmark job

Classification method

COLA

Comparable worth

Compensable factors

Davis-Bacon Act

Degrees of factors

Executive compensation

Exempt/nonexempt

Factor-comparison method

Fair Labor Standards Act (FLSA)

Gainsharing

Garnishment

Goal setting

Global appraisal

ISOs

Job Evaluation

Merit pay increases

Pay grades and steps

Performance-based system

Point method

Profit-sharing plans

Ranking method

Red circle job

Stock options

Straight piecework

Time-based system

Two-tier wage systems

Wage survey

Walsh-Healey Act

REVIEW QUESTIONS

1. Outline at least four reasons why an organization needs a compensation system.
2. Which jobs might effectively use performance-based pay systems?
3. What steps should a personnel specialist take to maximize employee performance motivated by the organization?
4. What is the difference between employee evaluation and job evaluation?
5. When are employees' wages subject to garnishment?
6. In job evaluation, why should a committee be used instead of one person?
7. What are the comparative advantages of each of the four job-evaluation methods?
8. Should pay grades be allowed to overlap?

DISCUSSION QUESTIONS

1. If you were working on an assembly line, would you prefer receiving COLAs or merit increases? Why? If you were a supervisor, would your decision be the same? If you were the owner of a manufacturing plant?
2. You are the head of the newly established personnel department for a small company. The owner, who began the firm fifty years ago, refuses to allow employees to discuss their wages—and for good reason. The owner's relatives receive 10 percent more than other employees. Various employees have asked you why salaries have been kept secret, and you say . . .
3. Should federal and state governments be able to legislate minimum wages rather than adopting a laissez-faire attitude that would allow employers operating on a slim profit margin to pay only what they could afford?
4. What arguments would you offer to support the repeal of the Davis-Bacon Act?
5. Which method of job evaluation would you prefer if you were implementing one? What factors would influence your decision?

ENDNOTES

1. R. C. Pilenzo, "Compensation: The State of the Art," *Personnel Administrator* (September 1977): 11.
2. L. Dyer, D. P. Schwab, and J. A. Fossum, "Impacts of Pay on Employee Behaviors and Attitudes: An Update," *Personnel Administrator* (January 1978): 51–53.
3. David W. Belcher, *Wage and Salary Administration* (Englewood Cliffs, NJ: Prentice-Hall, 1962), pp. 106–13.
4. J. S. Adams, "Inequity in Social Exchange," in L. Berkowitz, ed., *Advances in Experimental Social Psychology,* vol. 2 (New York: Academic Press, 1965), pp. 422–36.
5. Michael R. Carrell, "A Longitudinal Field Assessment of Employee Perceptions of Equitable Treatment," *Organizational Behavior and Human Performance* 21 (1978): 108–18.
6. John E. Dittrich and M. R. Carrell, "Organizational Equity Perceptions, Employee Job Satisfaction, and Departmental Absence and Turnover Rates," *Organizational Behavior and Human Performance* 24 (1979): 29–40.
7. A. H. Maslow, "A Theory of Human Motivation," *Psychological Review* (1943): 370–96.
8. E. A. Locke, "Toward a Theory of Task Motivation and Incentives," *Organizational Behavior and Human Performance* 3 (1968): 157–80.
9. E. L. Thorndike, *Animal Intelligence* (New York: Macmillan, 1911), pp. 1–56.
10. *Brock* v. *Highway Oil, Inc.*, No. 81-4245 (D. Kan. 1987).
11. Gina Ameci, "Bonuses and Commissions: Is Your Overtime Pay Legal?" *Personnel Journal* 66, no. 1 (January 1987): 107–10.
12. Ibid.
13. Belcher, *Wage and Salary,* pp. 176–77.
14. Richard Henderson, *Compensation Management* (Reston, VA: Reston, 1979), pp. 231–33.
15. *Job Evaluation Policies and Procedures,* Personnel Policies Forum survey no. 113 (Washington, DC.: Bureau of National Affairs, 1976), pp. 1–8.
16. *Industrial Relations Manual* (Columbus, OH: Westinghouse Electric Corporation, 1940), p. 4.
17. Henderson, *Compensation Management,* pp. 491–95.
18. Ibid., pp. 203–5.
19. Belcher, *Wage and Salary.*
20. Nathan B. Winstanley "Are Merit Increases Really Effective?" *Personnel Administrator* 27, no. 4 (April 1982): 37–40.
21. William C. Mihal, "More Research Is Needed; Goals May Motivate Better," *Personnel Administrator* 28, no. 10 (October 1983): 61–67.
22. Frederick S. Hills et al., "Merit Pay: Just or Unjust Desserts?" *Personnel Administrator* 32, no. 9 (September 1987): 53–59.
23. Richard E. Kapeleman, "Linking Pay to Performance Is a Proven Management Tool," *Personnel Administrator* 28, no. 10 (October 1983): 61–68.
24. C. F. Vough, *Productivity: A Practice Program for Improving Efficiency* (New York: AMACOM, 1979), p. 2.
25. Leonard R. Burgess, *Wages and Salary Administration* (Columbus, OH: Merrill, 1984), p. 242.
26. Ibid., p. 249.

27. Robert J. Schulhof, "Five Years with a Scanlon Plan," *Personnel Administrator* 24 (June 1979): 55–62.

28. Burgess, *Wages and Salary Administration,* p. 251.

29. Larry Hatcher, Timothy L. Ross, and Ruth Ann Ross, "Gainsharing: Living Up to Its Name," *Personnel Administrator* 32, no. 6 (June 1987): 153–64.

30. John Savage, "Incentive Programs at Nucor Corporation Boost Productivity," *Personnel Administrator* 22 (August 1981): 33–36.

31. *Basic Patterns in Union Contracts* (Washington, DC: Bureau of National Affairs, 1986), pp. 122–23.

32. "Pay Day: Typical Ford Worker Gets $1,200 for Profit Sharing," *The Courier-Journal* (March 13, 1986): B8.

33. Douglas Frasier, speech at the University of Louisville, April 22, 1986.

34. "Non-Traditional Pay Plans Gaining Popularity, Study Shows," *Resource* (December 1986): 1, 6.

35. Speech by Victor Kiam at the University of Louisville, School of Business, February 26, 1987.

36. William J. Smith, "Executive Compensation After ERTA," *Personnel Administrator* (February 1983): 63–65.

37. James T. Brinks, "Executive Compensation: Crossroads of the 80s," *Personnel Administrator* (December 1981): 23–25.

38. Smith, "Executive Compensation," pp. 63–65.

39. Brinks, "Executive Compensation," pp. 26–27.

40. Burgess, *Wages and Salary,* pp. 298–300.

41. John McMillan and Sanford D. Hickok, "Taking Stock of the Options," *Personnel Journal* (April 1984): 33.

42. Smith, "Executive Compensation," p. 64.

43. Robert Gibson and Paul Dorf, "Compensation: New and Better Tools," *Personnel Administrator* (May 1978): 29–30.

44. "The Revolutionary Wage Deal at G.M.'s Packard Electric," *Business Week* (August 29, 1983): 54.

45. S. R. Premeaux, R. W. Mondy, and A. L. Bethke, "The Two-Tier Wage Systems," *Personnel Administrator* 31, no. 11 (November 1986): 93–100.

46. I. Ross, "Employers Win Big in the Move to Two-Tier Contracts," *Fortune* (April 29, 1985): 82–92; R. J. Harris, Jr., "More Firms Set Two-Tier Pacts with Unions, Hurting Future Hires," *The Wall Street Journal* (December 12, 1983): 34; D. Wessel, "Two-Tier Pay Spreads, But the Pioneer Firms Encounter Problems," *The Wall Street Journal* (October 14, 1985): 1.

47. Michael R. Carrell and Christina Heavrin, *Collective Bargaining and Labor Relations,* 2nd ed. (Columbus, OH: Merrill, 1988), pp. 169–70.

48. James E. Martin and Melanie M. Peterson, "Two-Tier Wage Structures: Implications for Equity Theory," *Academy of Management Journal* 30, no. 2 (June 1987): 297–315.

49. Agis Salpukas, "The Two-Tier Wage System Is Found to Be Two-Edged Sword by Industry," *New York Times* (July 21, 1987): 1, 47.

50. George Ruben, "Labor and Management Continue to Combat Mutual Problems in 1985," *Monthly Labor Review* 109, no. 1 (January 1986): 3–15.

51. James C. Hyatt, "More Firms Link Pay to Job Performance as Inflation Wanes," *The Wall Street Journal* (May 7, 1977): 1.

52. "Better Pay for Women Agenda," *National Business Women* 68, no. 3 (June–July 1987): 13.

53. Robert D. Hershey, "The Wage Gap Between Men and Women Faces a New Assault," *The Louisville Courier-Journal* (November 6, 1983): 1, 4.

54. Ibid, p. 4.

55. Newman, "Pay Equity Emerges," p. 50.

56. Elizabeth A. Cooper and Gerald V. Barrett, "Equal Pay and Gender: Implications of Good Cases for Personnel Practices," *Academy of Management Review* 9, no. 1 (January 1984): 84–94.

57. Pete Yost, "EEOC Rejects Comparable Worth as Means to Judge Discrimination," *The Louisville Courier-Journal* (June 19, 1985): B-1.

58. "U.S. Court Says 'No' to Comparable Worth," *Resource* pamphlet (1985).

59. James S. Bowman, "The Rising Sun in America (Part Two)" *Personnel Administrator* 31, no. 10 (October 1986): 81–82.

60. Ibid.

Chapter Eleven   **Benefits**

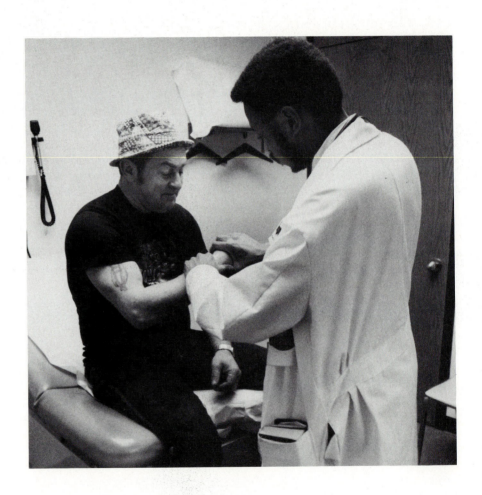

Chapter Outline

TYPES OF BENEFITS
Required Benefits

PENSIONS
Early Retirement
Pension Eligibility
Pension Plans
Employee Retirement Income Security Act
Unisex Pensions
Section 401(K) of the Internal Revenue Code

PAID TIME OFF
Vacations
Holidays
Personal Absences
Military Leave
Sick Leave
Maternity and Paternity Leave

PREMIUM PAY

INSURANCE
Group Dental, Legal, and Vision Insurance
Health-care Plans

EMPLOYEE SERVICES
Child-care Programs
Credit Unions
Individual Retirement Account (IRA)
Food Services
Education Expenses
Transportation Programs
Employee Stock Ownership Plans (ESOPs)
Social Activities
Work Environment

TOTAL BENEFIT PLANNING
Flexible Plans
Publicizing Benefits

INTERNATIONAL HRM: MANAGING BENEFITS

CONCLUSIONS AND APPLICATIONS

Chapter Objectives

1. To understand the growth of employee benefits and their organizational objectives.
2. To cite the benefits required by law.
3. To explain the major elements of pension systems.
4. To identify major paid time-off benefits.
5. To describe alternatives to traditional sick leave policies.
6. To identify premium pay benefits.
7. To reveal the various employee services provided by employers.
8. To recognize the types of insurance benefits offered by employers.
9. To explain the advantages of flexible benefit plans.
10. To understand the employer's need to publicize the benefit program.

429

Flexible Benefit Plan at Bell

Born out of the breakup of the old Bell system, Bell Communications Research Inc. (Bellcore) started a new life in 1984. With 7,500 employees Bellcore decided that as a new employer it was an ideal time to create a flexible benefits plan—something old Ma Bell was too big and tired to consider. A project staff of four benefit planners, whose "main purpose in life has been the implementation of a flex program effective January 1, 1987," had three years to design and implement the project.

First, they studied the demographics of the employees and found that most were young (two-thirds between the ages of twenty-six and forty-five), most were married (62 percent), highly educated, and 42 percent were female. Second, they made key policy decisions. They decided to cap the total cost of the benefit plan at the level which had been spent under the old Bell system—a considerable cost savings. A policy of strict equity in credit allocations with dependent neutral rates was developed. For example, the program included two flexible reimbursement accounts. Each employee had $3,000 in a health care account and $5,000 in a dependent care account, with unused portions paid out as taxable income. Benefits that could be chosen included a medical plan with four levels of coverage, a dental plan, vision care, home health care for elderly or ill dependents, hospice care, birthing centers, group life, paid time off, disability, savings plan, and a pension plan. In order to minimize administrative work and employee decision making, employees could change only one option per year or lifestyle change after the initial enrollment period.

The third stage of the program was the communication of the new "Flex '87" to the employees. The substantial communication process included:

- Articles on the general concept of flexible benefits.
- Written material on each specific benefit option.
- PC presentation of the entire program (over 1,500 employees asked for a copy of the disk).
- Two hotlines to answer employee questions (one with the carrier and one with the benefits staff).
- Departmental meetings with small groups of employees.
- Videotape of the entire program.

Flex '87 was very successful by all indications. Only 25 percent of the employees chose to keep their old medical plan, compared to an estimate of 76 percent based on other flexible programs. A large number of employees chose no coverage in several benefit areas due to coverage by a spouse—a large savings to both Bellcore and the employees. Few employees failed to return any form, the default option.

Source: Adapted from "Flex at Bell Communications Research," *Benefits News Analysis* 9, no. 6 (June 1987): 21–22. Used by permission.

T HE policy of awarding employee benefits increased dramatically in the United States during World War II. As governmental wage controls were imposed, employees and unions looked to benefits as a means of increasing the quality of working life. For many years, benefits were called *fringe benefits*. Today, between 25 and 40 percent of an organization's total payroll costs is usually made up of employees' benefits. The Bureau of Labor Statistics reports that the rate of growth of benefits substantially outpaced the growth of wages between 1940 and 1986, particularly toward the end of that period.[1]

Few organizations award benefits based on employee performance; instead, such benefits as paid vacations and pension plans are tied to factors other than performance (e.g., seniority). Benefits have not become a motivational tool because few employees realize the cost of benefits or appreciate many of their benefits until later years.

From 1980 to 1986, the cost of benefits jumped 51.5 percent, while wages and salaries grew 34.8 percent. During that time the average cost of benefits per employee increased to $10,283 per year.[2] The U.S. Chamber of Commerce has noted that the costs of benefits vary widely among industries, as shown in Table 11–1. The petroleum, public-utility, rubber, and metal industries pay the highest benefits for their employees. The lowest benefits are paid by the textile and apparel industries, department stores, and hospitals. Three benefit areas that have rapidly increased in recent years are medical insurance, pensions, and wages paid for time not worked (see Table 11–2). For example, coffee breaks, rest periods, wash-up time, and any other paid time on the job when the employee does not work, combined with paid vacations, holidays, and sick leave, increased from $1,005 in 1971 to $3,487 in 1986 (247 percent!).[3]

The amount of increase in benefits differs from one industry to another, but the rapid increase experienced by U.S. companies can be generally attributed to four causes:[4]

- Federal wage ceilings during World War II and again in the 1970s caused unions and all employees to look to benefits as a means of increasing compensation.

- Companies use benefits to gain employee compliance and loyalty. When employees have accumulated several years' seniority, they often find that taking a higher-paying job with a different organization would be a great loss because some of their benefits are based upon company seniority.

- Most employees' wages satisfy their basic needs; therefore, they have become interested in bargaining for more and greater benefits, especially in the area of health care and pay for time not worked, which satisfy other needs.

- Inflation and rising wage levels have created interest in using benefits as tax shelters. Employers can consider benefit costs a tax-deductible expense of doing business. Employees have found that it is cheaper for them if employers provide

TABLE 11–1
Average cost of
employee benefits by
industry in 1986

Industry	Cost per Employee, per Year
All Industries	**$10,283**
Manufacturing industries	**12,035**
Food, beverages and tobacco	7,580
Textile products and apparel	4,743
Pulp, paper, lumber and furniture	9,922
Printing and publishing	6,919
Chemicals and allied products	11,287
Petroleum	11,755
Rubber, leather and plastic	13,450
Stone, clay and glass	7,748
Primary metals	13,402
Fabricated metals (excluding machinery and transportation equipment)	8,497
Machinery (excluding electrical)	10,461
Electrical machinery, equipment and supplies	9,380
Instruments and miscellaneous manufacturing	10,403
Nonmanufacturing industries	**8,917**
Public utilities	12,712
Department stores	5,102
Trade (wholesale and retail other than department stores)	6,107
Banks, finance companies and trust companies	7,153
Insurance companies	8,315
Hospitals	7,172
Miscellaneous nonmanufacturing	9,494

Source: Reprinted by permission from *Nation's Business* (February 1988). Copyright 1988, U.S. Chamber of Commerce.

many benefits than if employees purchase identical benefits. Thus, the employer's tax burden is reduced and employees' disposable income increases.

Government influences employee benefits through regulations concerning employment opportunities, safety, health care, retirement and unemployment compensation, and workers' compensation. Even greater governmental influence is expected in the future. The government appears to be actively transferring the cost of welfare or social programs to private industries in the form of required employee benefits. To stem the tide of the rising costs of benefits, many personnel administrators believe that organizations must change their traditional approaches to employee benefits.[5]

In an effort to contain benefit costs, many employers have instituted a *coordination of benefits (COB) program.* Such programs are primarily established to guard against having to pay duplicate claims when more than one medical policy covers a claimant. The dra-

TABLE 11–2
Average annual cost of benefits per employee in 1986

Benefit	Cost per Employee, per Year
Old-age, survivors, disability and health insurance (FICA)	$1,588
Unemployment compensation	258
Workers' compensation	277
State sickness benefits insurance	211
Retirement and savings plans contributions	1,762
Life insurance and death benefits	127
Medical insurance (current employees)	1,604
Medical insurance (retirees)	157
Short term disability insurance	139
Long-term or salary continuation insurance	50
Dental insurance	148
Other medically related payments	86
Paid rest periods (coffee and lunch breaks, etc.)	879
Paid vacations, holidays and sick leave	2,608
Maternity and parental leave	48
Discounts on goods and services	63
Meals furnished	26
Education expenditures	41
Child care	159
Miscellaneous	53
Total benefits costs	**10,283**

Source: Reprinted by permission from *Nation's Business* (February 1988). Copyright 1988, U.S. Chamber of Commerce.

matic increase in two-income households has made this type of coverage common. The national average in savings of COB program is 4 to 5 percent of insurance costs. For example, Borden, Inc., saved over $1,613,000 in the first two years of its COB program simply by self-administration of health-care and major-medical insurance.[6]

Flexible benefit plans, as illustrated at the opening of this chapter, have also been successfully used by employers to contain benefit costs. An employer can set any maximum benefit allowance per employee, requiring the employee to pay any additional costs.

Another major method of reducing benefit costs is a *sick leave bank*. For example, employ-

ees who currently receive ten sick days per year are given only seven days, with the remaining three days placed in a combined employee pool. The use of the pooled sick days is determined by a panel of employees who review requests from employees. Thus employees can be covered against long-term illnesses by the pool, whereas before, they would likely have used up most of their personal sick days and been left without income. Peer pressure is used to control abuse by employees. The company benefits because the average number of sick days actually used by employees in a year decreases because the employee panel desires to build up the pool for legitimate needs.[7]

TYPES OF BENEFITS

The various benefits offered by employers can be divided into six types: (1) those that are required by law of the employer, (2) retirement benefits, (3) pay for time not worked, (4) premium pay, (5) insurance, and (6) employee services. Each type presents a different challenge for the personnel profession. Skyrocketing costs of insurance and retirement benefits have forced employers to reexamine the usefulness of those benefits and to evaluate whether benefits provided by the government should also be provided by the employer. At the same time, employees are demanding more days away from the work place with pay. Finally, employee services, which range from tuition reimbursement to out-placement counseling, have been increasing rapidly.

Required Benefits

Some employee benefits are required by law and therefore do not need to be negotiated with a union. Some benefit plans, such as supplemental unemployment benefits (SUB), are designed to supplement those required by law in order that the employee is guaranteed a greater level of benefit than provided by the government. A few union leaders have expressed opposition to government-imposed benefit programs, such as the Occupational Safety and Health Act of 1970, the Pension Reform Act of 1974, and the Health Maintenance Organization Act of 1973, because the federal government has provided to all employees benefits previously negotiated for union employees. Other union opposition has arisen because such federal legislation has taken from union negotiators the ability to bargain for benefits that might be preferable to those provided by government. Thus, benefits that are provided for all restrict negotiators'

ability to bargain for specific programs their membership might prefer.

Unemployment insurance, Social Security, and *workers' compensation* represent three important government-required benefits that are costly to management. Unemployment insurance originated in 1938. Government economists realized that unemployment insurance helps maintain the economy by stabilizing purchasing power and also helps workers bridge the gaps between jobs without having a significantly negative impact on their lives.[8] States are able to provide unemployed employees with benefits by imposing unemployment payroll taxes on employers. Normally, the amount paid by employers varies according to the unemployment rate within the state. To receive benefits, unemployed workers must have worked for a certain period of time and have registered for employment at a U.S. Employment office.

In 1935 Congress established the Social Security system to provide supplemental income to retired workers. Initially, Social Security was to provide retirees with an income that, when added to their retirement savings, would enable them to live their retirement years in dignity. The cost of the system is borne by both employers and employees; each group pays an equal amount of taxes into the system, which then uses the funds to pay benefits to currently retired individuals. Technically, Social Security taxes are Federal Insurance Contributions Act (FICA) taxes. It is often noted by management that employees pay half the cost of the system but receive all the benefits. That sentiment ignores the benefits to society that Social Security undoubtedly brings. In addition to Social Security, most labor agreements provide for a separate private pension plan.

The Social Security system is actually two separate systems: one to provide retirement benefits and one to provide disability, survivors', and Medicare benefits. To become eligible, workers must have contributed for ten years or forty quarters in the system.

Since the Social Security Revision Act of 1972, the benefits paid to recipients who are eligible to receive the retirement income increase each year by a percentage equal to the increase in the consumer price index (CPI) if the CPI increases by 3 percent or more. This automatic increase has been one of the causes of the periodic financial troubles of the Social Security system.[9] It also has given employers a strong argument not to provide for increases in employees' private pension dollars. The Social Security tax rate increased from 3.0 percent in 1960 to 7.65 percent for 1990.[10]

Laws requiring workers' compensation have been enacted by states to protect employees and their families against permanent loss of income and high medical bills in case of accidental injury or illness occurring on the job. The primary purpose of most state laws is to keep the question of the cause of the accident—whether the employer or employee was at fault—out of the debate. In most cases, the laws provide employees with assured payment for medical expenses or lost income due to injury on the job. Workers' compensation funds are primarily provided through employer contributions to a statewide fund. A state industrial board then reviews cases and determines eligibility for compensation.

Employees are often able to recover total medical expenses and up to two-thirds of lost income due to missed work or disability.[11] States may allow employers to purchase workers' compensation insurance from private insurance companies to augment state funds. Union leaders have played an important role in assuring that state laws are updated and employee interests are protected. Their efforts protect the interest not only of union workers but of nonunion workers as well.

PENSIONS

In the United States, individuals are expected to provide for their retirement through the "three pillars": Social Security, private pension, and personal savings. Together these three sources of income can replace an employee's preretirement disposable income, and thus can be considered to create the ideal pension system.[12] In general, the goal of such a system is to allow the retiree to maintain a standard of living reasonably consistent with the employee's preretirement standard of living. But it should be recognized that when employees retire they usually have lower living expenses than a working family because of the elimination or reduction of commuting costs, mortgage payments, and child-rearing costs. In addition, they gain eligibility for certain tax exemptions, for Medicare, and for other benefits made available to the aged.[13] Thus, retired workers do not normally need 100 percent of their preretirement income but only a portion of it. Employers thus often integrate an employee's pension income with Social Security. Private pension plans also normally provide for early retirement income to employees who lose their jobs because of disability. Approximately two-thirds of private employer pension plans provide immediate disability benefits; the remaining third defer benefits until retirement age. Employees under the latter plans are normally covered by disability insurance until they receive their pension payments.[14]

Early Retirement

Employers often at some point offer an early-retirement *window*. Such a plan is usually characterized by the employer's offering for a specified period of time (usually two to six months) special benefits to eligible employees who choose to retire early. Thus, for a short period employees have an alternative window to leave their employer. Employers have realized many benefits from early-retirement programs. They can reduce personnel costs and improve the organization's cash flow by replacing retiring employees with lower-paid employees. Employers can even cut the total cost of a vacated position by dividing the retiree's duties among other employees. During hard economic times, severe layoffs and pay cuts may be avoided with early retirements. Eliminating jobs that have become unneeded because of technology is easier if some employees choose early retirement. Younger employees gain from early-retirement programs because new promotion opportunities are created. Participation in an early-retirement program must be voluntary in order to comply with the Age Discrimination in Employment Act, as discussed in chapter 5.

A major disadvantage of window programs is that highly valued employees may choose to participate. Thus, the program must be carefully designed not to be too attractive to valued employees. Although window programs cost additional dollars to provide incentives for employees to retire early, properly designed programs can provide significant payroll reductions, as well as open up promotion opportunities for deserving younger employees.[15] However, the Age Discrimination Act makes it illegal for an early retirement program to have as its *sole* purpose the opening of positions for younger employees.

When do most employees choose to retire? This decision has been found to be largely determined by four variables:[16]

- Changes in the Social Security system and the value of its benefits
- Personal health
- General economic conditions (people retire earlier during good times)
- Mandatory retirement laws or policies

Therefore, the passage of the 1987 Age Discrimination in Employment Act (see chapter 5), which eliminated employer-mandatory retirement policies, combined with a generally healthier work force and the change in the Social Security retirement age to sixty-seven (with full benefits), will likely cause the average retirement age of employees to increase during the 1990s.[17]

Pension Eligibility

Private pension plans have become one of the most sought-after as well as one of the most expensive employee benefits. But only in the last twenty-five to thirty years have employers felt an obligation to provide income to employees beyond their productive years. This obligation occurred largely as a result of a 1949 decision by the Supreme Court, *Inland Steel Company* v. *NLRB*, in which the Court declared pension plans to be mandatory collective bargaining subjects. In the early stages of the pension movement in the United States, this benefit was recognized as discretionary on the part of an employer and as a source of motivation for senior employees. By 1980 the Bureau of Labor Statistics estimated that 66 percent of all nonfarm employees were covered by a private pension plan. Likewise, the number of private pension plans throughout the United States has increased dramatically since the 1949 decision. Fewer than 1,000 private pension plans were in operation in 1940; over 700,000 were in operation in 1982.[18]

Vesting   Vesting refers to an employee's right to receive retirement benefits paid into a plan by an employer. A vested employee can leave an employer and still collect a pension upon attaining retirement age. Employees always have a right to the contributions they have made; vesting refers only to employer contributions.

The Tax Reform Act of 1986 requires most employers to choose one of two vesting options: (1) 100 percent vesting after five years of service or (2) 20 percent vesting after three years, and an additional 20 percent each year, reaching 100 percent after seven years.[19]

Contributing to pension plans does not guarantee benefits. It is estimated that more than 10 million American workers who actively pay into pension plans will never collect from them. For example, one woman worked for more than 30 years for companies with private pension plans. But at the end of that time she was not eligible to receive a single penny in retirement benefits because she had never become vested with an employer for whom she worked. She worked for Liggett & Meyers Tobacco Company in Richmond, Virginia, for twenty-three years, but only seven years counted toward the pension plan by the time the company moved its operation in 1970—not enough to qualify her to meet the minimum requirement of ten years. After several odd jobs, she worked for eight and a half years for the American Tobacco Company in Richmond, but again she had not worked enough years to become eligible to receive company pension benefits. Therefore, at age fifty-three and after thirty-four years of work, she had no retirement income other than her Social Security.[20]

The reason so many American workers will not receive a private pension when they retire is simply that they leave an organization before becoming vested, that is, before meeting the organization's eligibility requirements. Many employees leave jobs frequently for various reasons during their productive years, and thus they miss being covered by any one company's pension plan. But for many other employees, loss of benefits is the result of a company that shuts down, lays off its workers, or dismisses workers before they become vested. A worker leaving behind a pension may forfeit several thousands of dollars of retirement income. Sizeable losses in vacation, insurance, and other benefits may also occur.[21]

Pension Plans

Employer-provided pension plans are designed to supplement the employee's Social Security benefits. Pension benefits, when added to Social Security costs, represent for employers the single most costly employee benefit. If an employer's pension plan qualifies under the Internal Revenue Code, the employer may deduct pension costs as a business expense and must meet the standards set by the Employee Retirement Income Security Act of 1974 (ERISA). The nature of a pension plan, or how good a pension plan is for employees, is determined by how the plan addresses several basic pension issues.

Supplemental or Flat-rate Supplemental pension plans are tied to Social Security benefits. A supplemental pension plan provides retirees with a fixed level of retirement dollars, to be provided by Social Security and a private pension. The intention is to have a guaranteed level of retirement benefits created by a pension that augments Social Security benefits. Therefore, as Social Security benefits increase each year, the amount employers must pay in pension benefits decreases.

Because Social Security benefits rose rapidly in the 1970s and 1980s; *flat-rate pension plans* are becoming more common. The flat-rate pension guarantees employees a certain pension income based on years of service and the level of pay. This amount is determined and paid by previous employers regardless of any other income employees may receive in retirement. The flat-rate system is usually requested by unions.

Financing Pension benefits received by employees are financed primarily through two plans. Under a *contributory plan* the employee and employer share the cost of pension benefits. The percentage contributed by the employer changes according to the type of contributory plan. A *noncontributory plan* is financed entirely by the employer. Employees and union representatives make strong arguments for noncontributory plans. They argue that because employers incur lower absenteeism and turnover costs with loyal employees who stay with the company due to the pension plan, the employer should pay the pension costs. Also, employers can charge their contributions to pension plans to the cost of doing business; therefore, employers do not pay the tax rate on pension costs that employees must pay. Employers, however, argue for a contributory plan because they feel that employees will value their pension plans more when they contribute something. Small employers believe that they cannot afford to provide pension plans when they must contribute to Social Security.

Funding Methods There are four general methods of funding pension plans. Each method may provide a particular advantage to management; in general, the methods are trusted plans, current-expenditure plans, insured plans, and profit-sharing plans.

Trusted or *funded plans* are those for which employers have created a separate account for funds and invested dollars annually to provide the future retirement benefits for employees. Employers assume liability for the fund. The fund is usually administered by a bank or separate board, which makes decisions about the investment of the funds and the payment of retirement benefits. Usually, the fund is kept financially sound by an actuarial study of the estimated financial liability of the plan, as well as of its expected value of current assets. If the actuarial study determines that the fund does not have enough money to guarantee benefit payments to both present and past employees who have earned them, then the employer adds the additional money necessary to keep the fund financially sound. This review of actuarial soundness is normally done annually. In some years, if the number of retired employees decreases and the number of new employees changes, it may not be necessary for the employer to add any additional money to the fund; in other years, employers may have to add substantial amounts.

Current-expenditure plans treat the retirement benefits paid to previous employees as a current expense. Therefore, such a plan is known as a *nonfunded* or *pay-as-you-go* plan. Current-expenditure plans are not actuarially sound and guarantee no fund available to current employees for retirement benefits in later years. Yet, for many employers the possibility of funding a trusted plan is very small because such plans usually require a large amount of capital to begin. In the current-expenditure plan, the employer simply meets the yearly retirement benefits due its previous employees as it meets other expenses. The largest nonfunded plan in the world is the U.S. Social Security retirement system.

Insured plans are pension plans provided to employers by insurance companies. The insurance company usually treats the provisions of the pension plan for the employer as it would any other type of collective insurance. That is, the employer is required to pay a premium, for which the insurance company administers the plan, pays out all benefits due, and assumes future payment liability. Although the employer may pay more to the insurance company than might be necessary under a trusted plan, the expertise and experience of the insurance company may be worth the additional fee for the small or medium-sized employer.

Profit-sharing plans are funded pension plans, with the funds provided by a percentage of company profits. A profit-sharing plan is a compromise between a current-expenditure plan and a trusted plan. Management hopes employees will be more interested in the profitability of the company if their pensions share in the risk of doing business. Companies that experience stable profitability and growth will have little trouble funding a pension plan through a profit-sharing approach. But if profits were to decrease substantially or become nonexistent over several years, the plan may eventually become financially unsound. Sears, Roebuck, & Company, as well as other firms in this country, have found profit-sharing pension plans to be quite successful.

Retirement Age The age at which employees can begin collecting pension benefits is an important aspect of any pension plan. Many plans stipulate that a minimum age must be reached before collecting pension benefits; in most cases it is sixty-five, though sometimes this has been reduced to sixty or even fifty-five. Some companies offer supplemental retirements to encourage early retirement. Other pension systems do not set a retirement age but require specific years of service, for example, "twenty and out" or "thirty and out." The advantage of pensions specifying a service requirement is that employees may collect one employer's pension while working for another employer and building up a second retirement income. For example, an employee who begins working for an employer at age twenty may be eligible to collect retirement benefits at age forty and then begin a second career with a different employer. At retirement from the second job, this employee will receive two full pensions, in addition to Social Security, and is sometimes called a *double dipper*.

Benefit Formula The many different private pension plans in use can generally be divided into two categories:[22]

- *Defined benefit plans.* Most retirement plans in the United States are described as defined benefit plans. These plans provide a specific monthly benefit determined by a definite formula. The retirement benefit is usually a function of the employee's average earnings over a specific number of years multiplied by the number of years of service (see Figure 11–1).

FIGURE 11–1

Determining retirement benefits through a benefit formula

EXAMPLE I
Base pay = Average pay for last three years worked.
25 years service × $18,000 base pay × 2.0% = $9,000/year or $750/month

EXAMPLE II
Base pay = Average pay for total years worked.
25 years service × $8,000 base pay × 2.0% = $4,000/year or $333/month

EXAMPLE III
Base pay = Average pay for total years worked.
35 years service × $6,000 base pay × 2.0% = $3,600/year or $300/month

- *Defined contribution plans.* In contrast to a defined benefit plan, which provides a known benefit, defined contribution plans provide a fixed or known contribution. The contribution is allocated annually to the employee's account, which accrues investment earnings. The account is usually converted into an annuity upon the employee's retirement. Employees have limited security because their future benefits are related to the employer's ability to continue making contributions. The plans, however, are never unfunded, as are some defined benefit plans.

Every defined benefit plan is based on a formula that determines the benefits employees will receive upon retirement. The amount of benefits received by employees is usually determined by multiplying the average pay figure by the years of service and then multiplying that product by a stipulated benefit percentage, such as 2 or 3 percent. Normally, systems use an average of the last three or five years of the employee's career as the average pay figure because inflation substantially lowers the average pay figure and, therefore, retirement benefits. As the years of service increase, the benefit amount increases to a maximum at thirty or thirty-five years of service.

Figure 11–1 illustrates how various average pay figures affect the determination of an individual's retirement benefits. In the first example, the employee's base pay is the average pay for the last three years worked. This amounts to $18,000, not an unusually high salary. An employee with twenty-five years' service and a 2 percent rate is eligible for $9,000 a year in retirement benefits, or $750 per month.

If, however, the average pay for total years worked is used, as in the second exam-

ple, the retirement benefit is substantially changed. Due to inflation, the employee's average pay for a total of twenty-five years is only $8,000. Therefore, with the same percentage and service figures, the retirement benefit is only $4,000 per year, or $333 per month. If that same employee had worked the previous thirty-five years, the average pay is even lower due to inflation.

Employee Retirement Income Security Act

Prior to 1974, private pension systems were criticized because in too many cases they were not providing employees with sufficient funds to live comfortably in retirement. In addition, many systems were cheating employees out of pension dollars to which they were entitled. Finally, some mismanaged pension systems did not increase the value of their benefit portfolios. In response to these complaints, Congress approved the Pension Reform Act of 1974, officially designated the Employee Retirement Income Security Act (ERISA), or Public Law 93–406. Congress accomplished the most complete overhaul of pension and benefit rules in U.S. history. The reform act affects virtually every pension and benefit plan. Responsibility for administering the complex, new employee benefit program is shared by the U.S. Treasury Department and the U.S. Department of Labor.[23]

The lengthy and complicated law primarily affects the following aspects of pension planning:

1. Employers are required to count toward vesting all service from age eighteen and to count toward earned benefits all earnings from age twenty-one. (Prior to the Retirement Equity Act of 1984, accrual toward vesting began at age twenty-two and toward earnings at age twenty-five.)

2. Employers must choose from among two minimum vesting standards.

3. Each year employers must file reports of their pension plans with the U.S. Secretary of Labor for approval. New plans must be submitted for approval within 120 days of enactment.

4. The Pension Benefit Guarantee Corporation (PBGC) was established within the Department of Labor to encourage voluntary employee pension continuance when changing employment. This is accomplished by providing *portability*—the right of an employee to transfer tax-free pension benefits from one employer to another. In addition, through employer premiums the PBGC ensures that benefits are paid to participants should a pension plan terminate.

5. Pension plan members are permitted to leave the work force for up to five consecutive years without losing service credit and are allowed up to one year off maternity or paternity leave without losing service credit.[24]

ERISA substantially reduced the number and scope of pension issues. The law has been criticized by employers because it is quite complex and may have encouraged some employers to provide no retirement plan at all.[25]

Unisex Pensions

In July 1983 the U.S. Supreme Court, in a landmark decision, sent shock waves through the insurance and pension industries. The court ruled that federal laws that prohibit sex discrimination in employment also prohibit sex discrimination in retirement plans. Pension plans must provide equal retirement payments to men and women. The ruling did soften the impact of the Court's decision on pension systems by denying retroactive relief to women currently receiving pensions and allowing for an August 1983 starting date for contributions to retirement plans to provide for equal payments. To comply with the decision, thousands of employers are faced with four options: (1) raise women's benefits to equal men's, (2) reduce men's benefits to equal women's, (3) strike an average between the two, (4) eliminate lifetime annuities, which guarantee retirees a monthly income for as long as they live and instead give employees their benefits in a lump sum when they retire.

Why had employers previously paid men higher benefits than women? The life expectancy of female employees is longer than that of male employees. Therefore, the insurance companies must pay them retirement benefits for a longer period of time. If, then, male and female employees earn the same total dollar value of benefits and female employees will collect those benefits over a longer period of time, their monthly payments must be less. Nathalie Norris, however, did not accept this reasoning and time honored practice—so she sued on the basis of sex discrimination and took her case all the way to the U.S. Supreme Court. Norris believed that since she had made the same monthly payments as her male counterparts, she should not accept a lower monthly benefit simply because she was a female. The U.S. Supreme Court agreed, and millions of American women will benefit from the historic 1983 decision.[26]

Section 401(K) of the Internal Revenue Code

Many small or medium sized organizations offer 401(K) retirement plans. Such plans are generally inexpensive and easily understood. Section 401(K) of the Internal Revenue Code first became effective in 1980. It provides for company-sponsored IRS-qualified retirement plans. Usually, such plans allow employees to

Lowering Pension Costs at MeraBank

Deregulation of the banking industry in the 1980s presented MeraBank of Phoenix, Arizona, with many new decisions and opportunities. Formerly a mutual savings and loan association, federal deregulation brought a loss of competitive advantage in the traditional savings institution's products but an opportunity to offer an array of new products as well as interstate banking. MeraBank began offering checking accounts, consumer loans, and business financing in Arizona and new operations in other states.

MeraBank quickly grew from 700 to 2,000 employees. The company had for many years offered an annual employer profit-sharing contribution of up to 15 percent to the employee pension plan. Employee voluntary contributions were permitted, but virtually no one participated.

To raise needed capital, MeraBank went public, and the new owners (shareholders) had a strong interest in net earnings. Thus, the human resources staff was asked to reevaluate the thirty-seven-year-old profit-sharing plan. The review concluded that the employer contribution of 15 percent was high and that some employees were concerned about the totally discretionary nature of the employer contribution.

The solution was Profit Plus, a new retirement plan. The new plan provided quicker vesting, a guaranteed annual employer contribution of 2 percent of wages, an employer matching contribution of 50 percent of the first 6 percent of employee contribution, and a pretax 401(K) plan match. The 401(K) match was contingent on the firm's return on equity. The employees especially liked the guaranteed 2 percent employer contribution and the fact that they could increase the employer contribution by increasing their own contribution. MeraBank used written materials, employee meetings and a video presentation to communicate the new plan. More than 70 percent of the eligible employees enrolled in the new plan, and an opinion survey indicated they were very satisfied with the new plan. MeraBank reduced the employer contribution by nearly a million dollars in the first year compared to the previous plan.

Source: Adapted from Carroll Roartz, "How MeraBank Lowered Pension Costs without Lowering Morale," *Personnel Journal* (November 1987): 63–71. Used by permission.

defer a portion of their salary as a payroll deduction and thus reduce federal and state tax liabilities. In addition, most employers increase the incentive for employees to save in 401(K) plans by offering a matching contribution, commonly 25 to 50 cents for each employee dollar saved.[27]

The plans have become popular with employees because they can be tailored to meet individual needs. The employee decides how much is deposited in the plan and when to change the level of contributions. Younger employees can use the plan to save for a car or home, whereas older employees can use it as a retirement income supplement. In comparison to traditional savings plans, 401(K) plans allow employees to make pretax instead of after-tax contributions. But access to the funds is limited to age fifty-nine and a half, separation from the employer, or to cover financial hardship. The dollar savings of the pretax 401(K) plan can be substantial but must be weighed against the disadvantage of the limited access.[28]

Under the 1986 Tax Reform Act, the maximum salary deferral to a 401(K) plan is $7,000 a year, to be increased as inflation increases. The act also requires 401(K) plans to meet a nondiscrimination test which prohibits highly paid employees from taking substantially greater advantage of this tax shelter than lower-paid employees. Employees' ability to make hardship withdrawals from 401(K) accounts is limited under the 1986 act to their own salary deferrals (not employer contributions), and withdrawals are subject to a 10 percent income tax.[29]

PAID TIME OFF

Employees expect to be paid for holidays, vacations and miscellaneous days they do not work. Employers' policies covering such benefits vary greatly. The most common examples of time off with pay are:[30]

- Holidays
- Vacations
- Jury duty
- Election official
- Witness in court
- Civic duty
- Military duty
- Funeral leave
- Family leave
- Marriage leave
- Maternity leave
- Sick leave
- Wellness leave
- Time off to vote
- Blood donation
- Lunch, rest, and wash-up periods
- Personal leave
- Sabbatical leave

Vacations

Employers have long believed that vacations increase employees' productivity on returning to the job. Employees who take strenuous vacations may not receive physical rest from the job but usually receive a mental break from the work place. Today virtually all organizations have a schedule of paid vacations based upon years of service with the organization. A typical system is shown in Table 11–3.

Employers often require employees to stagger their vacation dates throughout the warmer months to provide the organization with a steady flow of goods or services. Manufacturing and production industries may shut down during the summer, requiring all employees to take their vacations during the shutdown while the company retools or makes necessary repairs within the plant. The steel industry has utilized an unusual form of paid vacation termed a *sabbatical.* Sabbatical

TABLE 11–3
A typical schedule of paid vacations

Service	Vacation
1 year	1 week
2–5 years	2 weeks
6–10 years	3 weeks
11–15 years	4 weeks
16–20 years	5 weeks
Over 20 years	6 weeks

vacations are given to employees every five years to provide them with thirteen weeks of continuous paid vacation. Employees may not take second jobs during their thirteen-week vacations but must rest. A sabbatical vacation gives employees in particularly unhealthful and tedious work environments time away for a complete rest.

Holidays

Following World War II, unions and employees increased their demands for paid holidays; previously, many holidays were unpaid. The average number of paid holidays in 1950 was three; thirty years later, employees in most organizations received eight holidays. Employees required to work on normal holidays are often given double or triple pay. In the chemical, hotel, and restaurant industries, which operate every day, employees may get double pay for working on holidays, as well as another day off during the following week. Normally, when a holiday falls during an employee's paid vacation, the employee is scheduled for one extra day's vacation.

The *floating holiday*, which was first provided in the rubber industry, has increased in popularity as an employee demand. Floating holidays allow the selection of the day the holiday is observed to be left to the discretion of the employee or to be mutually agreed

upon by management and the employee. Employers have resisted the concept of a floating holiday on the theory that there is little difference between a floating holiday and an additional vacation day.

Many employers observe the practice of *Monday holidays* begun by the federal government. The observance of Monday holidays is, in theory, designed to give employees more three-day weekends during the year for additional rest and relaxation. But in practice the Monday holiday has increased the chief administrative problem caused by paid holidays—absenteeism. Employees can easily see that being absent on Friday or Tuesday would provide them a four-day weekend, or almost a complete week's vacation. To minimize this problem and other holiday-related absenteeism problems, a written personnel policy should provide for the following:

Eligibility   Requiring employees to work the last working day before the holiday and the first scheduled working day after the holiday, helps to minimize the problem of employees' stretching holiday periods.

Holiday Rate   If employees work on what is normally a paid holiday, they should receive premium pay.

Paid Holidays   The days determined to be paid holidays should be specified in writing, in advance.

Holidays on Nonwork Days   If a paid holiday falls on a nonwork day, such as Sunday, for example, will employees be given another day off? If so, which one?

Personal Absences

Employees may receive full pay for a number of personal absences, such as a summons by federal, state, or local courts to serve as jurors or witnesses. Employees are not counted absent and are paid during the period covered by the summons. Some employers require that employees reimburse them for any pay received from the court. When a death occurs in the immediate family (spouse, child, parent, sister, brother, or inlaws), employees are eligible to receive three to five days of funeral leave. Usually employees are not charged with vacation or other paid leave, nor do they lose any pay during funeral leave.

Military Leave

Military leave is provided for members of U.S. armed forces reserve units. While most employers do not charge leave time against vacation time, most also do not pay employees for military leave. Some employers do give employees full pay during military leave, and many employers pay the difference between the military pay and the employee's take-home pay.

Sick Leave

Sick leave is generally accrued by employees at a specific rate, for example, one day per month from the first day of employment. Many employers allow unused sick leave to be accumulated without any maximum. A doctor's certification is usually not necessary for short-term illnesses, but extended sick leave normally requires medical evidence. Sick leave pay provides income during personal or family illness. Sick leave normally should be taken only for illness; however, sick leave is often used for personal reasons other than illness.

Sick Leave Alternatives Reducing sick leave has become a high priority to most personnel directors. Both the work disruption and the cost of sick leave can be of concern to top management and supervisors. The good

intention of a typical sick-leave program often becomes subject to abuse by employees. Paid sick leave is often used for nonillnesses such as personal problems, weather, personal business, child care, hangover, transportation problems, and so on. The costs to the organization associated with sick-leave abuse include:[31]

- Salary and benefits paid to the absent employee.
- Extra work for other employees who "cover" for the absent employee, or wages paid to temporary or overtime help.
- Loss in productivity caused by less experienced personnel performing the work.
- Lower morale of employees who resent doing the work of others.

One of the first published alternatives to the traditional sick-leave plan was developed by a hospital. Their *paid-leave plan* combines the vacation days, holidays, and average number of sick days per employee into a total to be used at the discretion of the employee. The hospital's absenteeism was reduced considerably, and hospital employees preferred the paid-leave plan because they had increased control over their work schedules.[32]

Sick-leave banks provide another alternative to traditional programs, as discussed earlier in the chapter. This arrangement allows employees to pool some portion of their sick days into a common fund.[33] Absenteeism and sick-leave abuse are reduced due to employees' desires to protect the fund.

Well-pay programs have become increasingly popular alternatives to the traditional sick-leave plan. The concept is to provide positive reinforcement to employees for not being sick or absent. Employees are either given a bonus in dollars or paid time off for each week or month they are not absent. One organization after one year reduced the total sick leave used by employees by 46 percent. The well-pay program included:[34]

- Discontinuance of sick leave accrual.
- No pay for the first day of an employee's sick leave.
- A bonus paid to employees not absent at any time for four consecutive weeks, plus additional bonus for consecutive four-week periods without an absence.
- Disability pay for illnesses beyond one day for eligible employees.

Personal leave is an alternative that allows employees fewer days of leave without specifying why they miss work.

Maternity and Paternity Leave

Providing an expectant parent a leave of absence during the baby's first months at home has become an accepted personnel policy. The Pregnancy Discrimination Act requires employers to offer women maternity leave similar to other benefits for disabilities. Thus, most maternity-leave policies provide women up to six months of unpaid leave with a continuation of paid insurance and other benefits, as well as a guarantee of the same job once they return to work. Some men have requested paternity leave similar to the employer's maternity leave. Over 10 percent of the companies included in a Forbes Market Value 500 survey provided paternity leave.[35]

PREMIUM PAY

Many employers and virtually all labor agreements provide for special payments to employees for working under undesirable circumstances. The most common premium pay is for the Saturday or Sunday hours worked that are not part of the normally scheduled workweek. Other common examples of premium pay include *overtime* rates for time worked over eight

hours per day and *shift differentials,* which provide higher hourly rates to employees who work the least-desirable hours.

In the manufacturing and construction industries, *reporting pay* is the minimum pay guaranteed employees who report for work even though work is not available. For example, if employees have not been instructed by the company not to report for work within four hours before the start of their shift, they are guaranteed four hours of pay even if work is not available because of equipment failure.

Supplemental pay given to employees called back to work before they were scheduled to report is called *call-in pay.* Thus, employees who do not take their complete rest between scheduled workdays receive a lump-sum bonus for being called in before their next normal reporting time.

Dismissal pay, or *severance pay,* is usually awarded to employees who have been permanently severed from their jobs through no fault of their own. Such premium pay is most common in manufacturing or unionized industries. Dismissal pay includes payments to workers who lose their jobs due to technological change, plant closings, plant mergers, or disability. Employees who quit their jobs or refuse to take other jobs within the company are not covered. Nor does dismissal pay cover employees who are terminated for unsatisafctory performance. The amount of dismissal pay employees receive is determined by their years of service and past salary. The purpose of dismissal pay is to cushion the loss of income of loyal employees.

INSURANCE

Most companies provide employees with life and medical-insurance plans and pay part of the plans' costs. Health-insurance packages normally cover group life, accident and illness, hospitalization, and accidental death or dismemberment. The life insurance program is usually part of a *group plan,* which permits the business and the employee to benefit from lower rates based on the total value of the group policy. A good rule of thumb in determining the coverage needed for each employee is to provide twice the employees' annual salary in life insurance. Companies usually provide a base life insurance policy and allow employees to provide additional coverage at their expense. In addition to life insurance benefits, a fixed lump-sum benefit is usually paid when accidental death or dismemberment occurs. Employers generally provide some type of hospitalization plan that pays fixed cash benefits for hospital room and board as well as other routine hospital charges.

Group Dental, Legal, and Vision Insurance

Major group-insurance plans are also often provided by employers that would not have been provided before the 1970s. Few employers used to provide dental, legal, or auto insurance for employees. Such insurance plans have become common, and they are highly sought by employees. Comprehensive dental benefits have been developed to provide protection against the cost of basic types of dental care. Such plans include (1) schedule plans, (2) comprehensive plans, and (3) combination plans.[36] *Schedule plans* have no deductible and provide specific payments for each procedure covered. *Comprehensive plans* require an initial deductible and then provide a fixed percentage payment of covered expenses. Most *combination plans* provide a fixed fee schedule for routine dental procedures and a deductible on other procedures, with a coinsurance clause requiring the covered employee to pay a percentage of the fee.[37]

The provision of full legal services through negotiated group plans is relatively new. During the early 1970s, prepaid legal services first became common through a Supreme Court decision that upheld such a plan and declared such legal expenses to be nontaxable.[38] Two types of prepaid legal plans are commonly negotiated. One is a so-called open panel, which allows the employee to select any attorney who will perform the service at a stated fee. The other type is the so-called closed panel, which requires employees to use specific attorneys. Most plans require the employee to pay part of the annual fee.[39] Employees usually prefer the open panel because they can use their own attorneys. Companies, however, prefer closed panels, which can be more easily administered.

Routine eye examinations, glasses, and contact lenses are usually included in provisions for vision care. Employees may be given the choice of doctors or may be limited to certain ones who are retained under contract.

Health-care Plans

One of the most common employee benefits designed to provide income maintenance and insurance to employees is the health-care plan, whose general purpose is to help the covered employees maintain their standard of living when unexpected health-related problems occur. A variety of health-care insurance plans covering medical bills and related costs are often provided, in addition to such related health-care benefits as Medicare provided by Social Security, workers' compensation, and in-house medical services. Most employers provide for hospitalization and major medical insurance.[40]

Hospitalization plans normally take one of two forms: commercial insurance or a hospital service plan. *Commercial insurance* involves a contract between an employer and an insurance company that provides fixed cash benefits for hospital room and board, as well as for other hospital charges. The employer agrees to pay the premiums to cover the insurance provided by contract, and the insurance company assumes the liability of those employees who qualify to receive the benefits. Commercial insurance pays directly to the insured company, which then reimburses the hospital for the cost. Therefore, a plan can be tailored to the needs of the company as specified by an agreement.

Under a *hospital service plan*, a nonprofit organization such as Blue Cross–Blue Shield provides coverage for hospital services when needed, including room, board and other costs. The Blue Cross portion of the plan covers hospital cost; the Blue Shield portion covers physicians' fees. The primary advantage of a hospital service plan is that hospitals offer lower rates to the Blue Cross system. But such plans are usually less flexible than commercial insurance. The employer and union negotiators must choose from among the options available.[41]

Most health care plans provide for a $100 deductible to be paid by the employee and a maximum percentage, often 80 percent, to be paid by the employer for major medical expenses. Most plans also provide for a maximum figure. Because such benefits usually overlap with benefits provided by other sources, such as workers' compensation and other insurance, the insurance plan must specify whether benefit payments are made in lieu of any other benefits received or whether benefits received from other plans are to be deducted from the amount the employee is entitled to under the health insurance plan.[42]

Many employers think that health insurance costs are out of control. The biggest supplier to General Motors in 1985 was not U.S. Steel (now USX) but Blue Cross–Blue Shield. The health-care industry has become a supplier that determines its own supply of doctors, prescribes its own demand for services, and controls its own price levels. Over 50 per-

cent of the nation's total health-care costs are provided through health insurance programs paid for by employers. Many companies are beginning to deliver health care to employees with in-house plans. Employers have found that less reliance on outside insurance and governmental agencies and more reliance on internal company health programs can minimize their health-care insurance costs.

One of the most effective methods of controlling group health costs is employer *self-funding*. Employers who switched from an insurance company to self-funding report on an average cost savings of about 7 percent.[43] Self-funding allows a company to pay health claims out of its own funds; the employer acts as the insurance company. Improving the cash flow, reducing the costs of premiums and taxes, and eliminating the third party (insurance company) are the primary advantages of self-funding programs, which include the following: (1) the employer pays employee claims directly from revenues, like any other expense; (2) a trust is created under Section 501(c)(9) of the Internal Revenue Code. In the latter cases, funds held in the trust accumulate tax-free earnings, which are used to pay claims.[44] Other health care alternatives are discussed in chapter 12.

EMPLOYEE SERVICES

Employee services include a variety of employee benefits. Organizations vary greatly in the services they offer and the service costs they pay. Employee services have been developed to increase employee loyalty to organizations and decrease absenteeism and turnover.

Child-care Programs

One of the rapidly growing employer services is the provision of child care. Such programs include both on-site facilities and voucher systems, which reimburse employees for the use of outside private child-care centers. The history of employer-sponsored child care (or day care) in the United States begins in the nineteenth century. As early as 1854 there was some employer involvement in child care. The textile industry in the early to mid-1900s sponsored many centers as it greatly expanded its largely female work force.[45] But industrial interest elsewhere did not materialize until the 1940s, when World War II forced millions of married women into the labor force. That period's Lanham Act provided government financial support for over 2,800 day-care centers. But when the war ended, so did federal support, forcing the closing of centers; many working wives returned to domestic work.[46] Interest continued to be low until the 1960s, when tax laws and social attitudes made child care appear to be a profitable and responsible employee service. But the 1970s saw many of the new centers of the 1960s close. Reported reasons for closing included high expense (particularly for on-site facilities), administrative problems, and—most important—not enough employee use.[47] The 1980s brought strong renewed interest in employer-sponsored child care.

The provision of child-care programs can, some research has concluded, significantly reduce absenteeism and turnover. Labor statistics show an increase in participation by single parents and two-income families in the labor force; such trends should increase the demand for child-care programs.[48] But employer-provided on-site child-care programs are giving way to alternative means of assisting working parents. The national trend is for employers to say that they cannot afford to "take care of their employees." Employers often do not want to be accused of attempting to "bring up the nation's children."[49] Information and referral services are provided by some employers when established centers can accommodate the demand and when the employer wants to

use the least costly approach. By far the most useful option is the *voucher system*. Each employee selects his or her own child-care center; the employer reimburses all or part of the expense.[50] This option becomes more attractive if it is part of a package designed so that employees can choose their benefits, because employees without children can choose other benefits in place of child care. The employer does not favor those who need child-care facilities. For large employers who have available space and are not located in an area with adequate centers, an on-site facility remains a useful option.

The U.S. Department of Labor estimates that women and minorities will fill 80 percent of the 21 million new jobs which will be created by the year 2000. Employers, however, have been slow to realize that this new work force will demand family care benefits—primarily maternity/paternity leave and day care. "They have been reluctant to venture into this area because family care changes the whole atmosphere at work—forever," claims Dana Friedman, senior research fellow at the Work and Family Life Center of the Department of Labor. Working women do not want to be forced to choose between a career and raising a family. They want and should be able to choose both, says Friedman. The new breed of fathers also want to help raise their children without fear of losing their jobs.[51]

Credit Unions

Company credit unions are a long-established employee service provided by many organizations. Employees become members by purchasing shares of stock for a small fee. They may then deposit savings that accrue interest at rates higher than those provided by local financial institutions. Employees may apply for loans from their credit union at lower rates than those charged by many financial institutions. Normally administered by a separate board of directors, the credit union is an entity independent of the organization.

Individual Retirement Account (IRA)

The individual retirement account (IRA) is a relatively new employee service which was developed with the Pension Reform Act. IRAs allow all individuals to contribute to a personal retirement account and, therefore, participate in the tax advantages of deferred income. In the future, more and more companies will probably offer to set up IRAs for employees as an alternative to pension or profit-sharing plans. Small companies may find it especially advantageous to place part of employees' wages in IRAs, which benefit the company as a taxable deduction and also provide employees with some retirement income.[52]

The 1986 Tax Reform Act substantially reduced the desirability of IRAs. The new law restricts fully deductible IRA contributions to individuals who are not covered by an employer-sponsored retirement plan and whose income is below $35,000 (single return) or $50,000 (joint return).[53]

Food Services

Most companies provide some type of food facility to minimize the time taken for breaks and lunch periods. Food services vary according to the size of the company and the nature of the work. Some organizations may only provide vending machines and a few tables; others provide complete cafeteria services underwritten by the company. To minimize the time employees spend on coffee breaks, companies have experimented by placing coffee and soft drink stands in each department or by providing mobile coffee stands to bring doughnuts and coffee to individual employees. These alternatives minimize the time employees spend away from their work sites to take coffee breaks.

While managers recognize the benefits of corporate food service programs, they also know that just making food available is not enough. People are finicky eaters and, out of boredom or dislike, may still choose to eat elsewhere. Thus, the employer must market its food service to employees to keep their business. Here are a few examples of successful food service promotions:[54]

- *Greyhound.* Greyhound Food Management developed a "Fling into Spring" program in all its food service programs. The program offered customers a free frisbee with the purchase of a bacon cheeseburger. The results? A 40 percent increase in food sold overall and 33,000 frisbees given away. Why? "Everybody loves frisbees and the idea of springtime. Employees were more interested in getting a frisbee than going elsewhere for lunch," claimed Joseph K. Faisley, GFM president.

- *Interstate United.* Desiring to increase breakfast sales in its cafeterias, Interstate United began a "You Win" program. Randomly selected vending machine coffee cups carried a "You Win" sticker, which entitled the buyer to a reduced-rate breakfast. Vending machine sales increased by 17 percent and cafeteria breakfasts by 8 percent.

- *Cedar-Sinai Medical Center.* Each February and August, the Los Angeles Cedar-Sinai Medical Center holds a "Winners Program." The program is an employee recognition program for food and nutrition services nonmanagement employees. The program recognizes employee excellence in three specific, measurable areas. Employees receive points for their performance and may "cash in" their points for catalog gifts. They also receive T-shirts and jackets. The program reduced accidents by 56 percent and absenteeism by 23 percent.

- *Service America.* "Servomation Salutes . . ." a different country each month by featuring one of its popular dishes; this was Service America's promotion program. Colorful posters depicting the food in a typical national setting were displayed in the dining area to advertise the new month's selection. In addition, recipe cards and desserts were given away during the month. After two successful years, the salute to a country was changed to various other themes, such as health foods, fresh fruits, and Christmas ideas.

Education Expenses

Many organizations offer employees partial or total tuition reimbursement. Employees often use this highly sought benefit to prepare themselves for promotion opportunities. Generally, the portion of tuition that organizations reimburse depends upon the grades received in the classes taken. For example, the organization may pay 100 percent of the tuition costs for an A, 50 percent for a B, and 25 percent for a C. Employers may also require that employees take career-related courses to receive tuition reimbursement.

Transportation Programs

The higher energy costs of the 1970s caused employers to consider methods of helping employees get to work. Ride sharing, in use since World War II, is probably still the most common employee transportation program. The personnel department can assist employees who want to share rides by providing them the names of other employees who live nearby or by working with other employers to involve their employees.

New approaches to employer-sponsored transportation first surfaced in the 1970s for a variety of reasons, including higher gasoline prices and the high cost of parking. Also, some employers realized that tardiness and absenteeism could be lowered through ride-share programs. Seattle First National Bank in 1979 became the nation's first private employer to offer free bus passes to employees. The program, which attracted over 3,000 of the bank's 7,500 employees, cost $500,000, but it also enabled the bank to discontinue plans for an expensive new parking facility. At the same time, an overtaxed Seattle bus system was helped, and employees gained real savings in transportation costs. Another example is the 3M Corporation, which pioneered the nation's first "van pool." Because of mounting parking problems at the firm's Minnesota headquarters, the company offered employees monthly van fares of $39, and the original 6 vans in the program grew to over 150 vans. 3M saved $3.2 million by eliminating plans for a new parking facility. Similar programs at Conoco in Houston, Erving Paper Mills in Massachusetts, and the Tennessee Valley Authority in Knoxville enjoyed similar success. Most operate on a break-even basis, while the firm benefits by reducing parking needs, lower absenteeism and tardiness, and higher employee morale. Employees enjoy the social interaction as well as the real savings.[55]

Humana, the international hospital corporation, offers employees at their headquarters in Louisville, Kentucky, the choice of free bus tickets or a parking space. In Louisville, a downtown parking space costs at least $50 a month, while bus fare costs only $25 a month. Additional employer financial gains can be realized through the Environmental Protection Agency's (EPA) *marketable rights system* for pollution controls. The EPA has imposed growth constraints on urban development and thus has created a market for pollution rights generated by an employer's mass-transit subsidy program.[56]

Employee Stock Ownership Plans (ESOPs)

An employee service similar to profit sharing—with many of the same advantages and disadvantages—is stock ownership, sometimes called the employee stock ownership plan (ESOP). Millions of employees are becoming part owners of the companies they work for, and by the year 2000, 25 percent of all U.S. workers may have used an ESOP. The rapid increase is expected as a result of the 1984 Deficit Reduction Act passed by Congress, which provides lucrative tax incentives to employees. In fact, about 70 to 100 failing companies have used ESOPs to avoid hostile takeovers. A chemical company in Newark, Delaware, W. L. Gore & Associates, Inc., has about 3,000 employees who own 10 percent of the company's stock through an ESOP. The employees want the company to be successful because "I feel I'm a part-owner," says Robert Barclay. Employees generally supervise themselves, and the company has grown at a 25 percent annual rate.

A textile manufacturer in Danville, Virginia, Dan River, Inc., has about 8,000 employees who own 70 percent of the company's stock through an ESOP. But the union and many employees are not at all happy. Why? They have no voting rights or other control over the operation of the company. Control is held by the 30 percent outside investors and top management even though the employees are providing the capital. In fact, 85 percent of all companies with ESOPs do not allow worker-owners voting rights.

However, the ESOP trend may change if more employees develop the attitudes of those at Dan River. The U.S. Department of Labor,

however, does investigate reported abuses of ESOPs and can intervene in some cases. Advocates of ESOPs contend that their primary advantage is in raising employee productivity. In a study of 360 companies by the National Center for Employee Ownership (NCEO), companies with ESOPs had grown two to four times as fast as those without them. Advocates further claim that the U.S. system of capitalism is greatly enhanced by "turning workers into capitalists through stock ownership."[57]

Social Activities

One employee service that has been reevaluated in recent years is the company-sponsored social activity. Company picnics and athletic teams have provided employees with opportunities to satisfy their social needs in past decades. Increased community-sponsored recreation has made employers question whether employees really want company social activities, since often only a small percentage of employees participate in them.

Work Environment

In recent years, employers have found that many employees especially appreciate the attention given to improving the work environment. Employees have suggested changes in the work place to reduce noise levels, to create a more pleasant atmosphere by adding large windows overlooking the surrounding area, or to incorporate shower and sauna facilities. Allowing employees to determine their own office decors and eliminating the need to punch time clocks are other employee services which have increased the pleasantness of work environments.[58]

TOTAL BENEFIT PLANNING

With benefit costs increasing to up to 40 percent of total payroll costs, employers are reevaluating their total benefit packages. Many benefit packages have little effect on employee motivation and performance. Since many costly and expensive benefits are tied to seniority, such as vacation and retirement income, employers seldom link benefits to level of performance. Some personnel specialists believe that most employees do not truly understand the nature of their benefit packages, nor do they appreciate the total cost of providing them with benefits. When given the choice between additional benefits or disposable income, employees overwhelmingly choose additional disposable income. The organization may find it less expensive and more popular to offer employees fewer benefits and more wages.

Companies can best use their benefit dollars by assessing employees' needs and determining which benefits are truly demanded. Through meetings with employee representatives and union leaders, employers may find that the employees do not truly desire certain costly benefits and have a greater need for benefits that may be less expensive. The company's total benefit package should be reviewed as a whole and not as separate components.

Flexible Plans

The so-called cafeteria approach to benefit compensation allows employees to determine some of the benefits to be included in their compensation packages. Employees pick and choose from a ''menu'' of benefit items. The obvious advantage of such a flexible plan is that all employees do not have the same needs and desires. Younger employees with families, for example, may prefer to have complete hospitalization, dental, and vision care, with minimal retirement benefits. Older workers who can meet most living expenses are more concerned with retirement income that will allow them to meet the normal cost of living expenses in later years.

In a true *cafeteria* approach, employees might choose to expend a certain number of company dollars on increased vacation pay and extra life insurance or to provide daycare facilities for employees' children. In order to satisfy all employees' needs, the personnel specialist must incorporate a variety of benefits into the menu.[59] Figure 11–2 is an example of a benefits questionnaire in which employees can indicate their preferences. Such a program would be offered by a large company where many employees are involved and, therefore, benefits such as a day-care center are practical. Many companies have already made advances in cafeteria compensation by offering alternatives limited to a few benefits. Employees' appreciation of the cafeteria approach will be maximized when organizations limit the percentage of salaries which can be expended on employee benefits.[60]

Employers experimenting with the cafeteria approach have reported serious problems, which possibly have diminished its popularity. A major problem is the lack of appreciation and interest by employees in the program. When asked to make their choices, employees may respond that they are not capable of choosing between benefit plans because they cannot predict which benefits will be more beneficial to them in the long run. They may even criticize management for not making the decision in the best interest of employees and accepting the consequences. Employers have complained that the paperwork and time spent in designing and implementing cafeteria compensation are tremendous—possibly greater than the additional benefits derived from such an approach.

Cafeteria plans have had an ''on-again-off-again'' life. American Can was one of the early major employers to implement a serious flexible benefit plan, starting with 700 participating employees. A survey of the company's 9,000 participating employees disclosed that 92 percent thought they had substantially im-

1. In the space provided in front of the benefits listed below indicate how important each benefit is to you and your family. Indicate this by placing "1" for the most important, and "2" for the next most important, etc. Therefore, if Life Insurance is the most important benefit to you and your family, place a "1" in front of it.

IMPORTANCE		IMPROVEMENT
(5)	Dental Insurance.......	(18)
(6)	Disability (Pay while Sick)	(19)
(7)	Educational Assistance ..	(20)
(8)	Holidays	(21)
(9)	Life Insurance	(22)
(10)	Medical Insurance......	(23)
(11)	Retirement Annuity Plan	(24)
(12)	Savings Plan	(25)
(13)	Vacations.............	(26)
(14–15)		(27–28)
(16–17)		(29–30)

Now, go back and in the space provided after each benefit, indicate the priority for improvement. For example, if the Savings Plan is the benefit you would most like to see improved, give it a "1", the next a priority "2", etc. Use the blank lines to add any benefits not listed.

2. Would you be willing to contribute a portion of earnings for new or improved benefits beyond the level already provided by the Company:

(31) ☐ Yes   ☐ No

If yes, please indicate below in which area(s)

(32) ☐ Dental Insurance   (36) ☐ Retirement Annuity
(33) ☐ Disability Benefits   Plan
(34) ☐ Life Insurance   (37) ☐ Savings Plan
(35) ☐ Medical Insurance

3. As you know, in the past the Company has made certain employee benefit improvements each year, in addition to wage and salary adjustments. Which of the following statements reflects your view:

(38) ☐ a. Place more emphasis on improving wages and salaries and less on employee benefits.

☐ b. The current mix of benefit improvements and wage and salary adjustments is about right.

☐ c. Place more emphasis on improving employee benefits and less on wages and salaries.

In order that we may effectively analyze the replies, please check the appropriate boxes.

AGE:
(39) ☐ under 26   ☐ 26–35   ☐ 36–45
      ☐ 46–55   ☐ 56 & over

SEX:
(40) ☐ Male   ☐ Female

MARITAL STATUS:
(41) ☐ Single   ☐ Married   ☐ Other

YEARS OF SERVICE:
(42) ☐ under 1 year ☐ 1–4 years ☐ 5–9 years ☐ 10–14 years
      ☐ 15–24 years ☐ 25 & over

PAY GROUP:
(43) ☐ Hourly   ☐ Weekly   ☐ Foremen
      ☐ Monthly

DIVISION:
      ☐ Agricultural ☐ Central   ☐ Chemicals
                          Research
      ☐ Corporate HQ ☐ Cosmetics   ☐ Instrumentation
      ☐ Metals   ☐ Minerals   ☐ Pharmaceuticals
      ☐ Toiletries

LOCATION:
(Field Sales employees should check "FIELD" rather than the name of their distribution centers.)

☐ Atlanta	☐ Boston	☐ Chicago
☐ Dallas	☐ Field	☐ Green Bay
☐ Houston	☐ Los Angeles	☐ Manitowoc
☐ Milwaukee	☐ Newark	
☐ New York	☐ St. Louis	

FOR OFFICE USE ONLY Division (44–45)   Location (46–47)

WE'D LIKE TO KNOW . . . If you would like to take this opportunity to explain further any of your answers or comment on any other matter, please use the back of this form.

PLEASE RETURN THIS QUESTIONNAIRE IN THE ENCLOSED PREPAID ENVELOPE
(Compliments: Pfizer, Inc.)

FIGURE 11–2

A sample of an employee benefits questionnaire (Source: David Thompson, "Introducing Cafeteria Compensation in Your Company." *Personnel Journal,* [March, 1977], pp. 128–29. Reprinted with permission of *Personnel Journal,* Costa Mesa, CA. Copyright 1977.)

proved their benefits by producing the proper mix of benefits. Pepsi Cola and North American Van Lines were among major firms that followed with their own successful plans. Small firms (eight to twenty employees) have also reported employee and employer satisfaction with cafeteria plans.[61]

An important feature of a cafeteria plan is the opportunity for each employee to spend employer dollars as personally desired. By contrast, many so-called flexible plans are fixed, offering the employee the opportunity to choose among limited alternatives or offering a "take-it-or-leave" approach. For example, the employer offers to pay a portion of an employee's medical insurance if the employee pays the balance. But if the employee does not choose medical insurance (possibly because of a spouse's coverage), then the employer's contribution is lost. A true flexible plan credits the employee with the employer's share, which could be applied to another benefit.[62]

Types of Flexible Plans In reality there are three major types of flexible employee benefit plans. First, there is the *core cafeteria plan*, which provides employees a "core" (minimum) coverage in several areas and allows the employee to choose either additional benefits or cash, up to a maximum total cost

to the employer. In the core cafeteria plan of Figure 11–3, the employee has a choice of items 1 through 6 and cash. This plan strikes a balance between giving the employee complete freedom to choose among benefits and the employer's need to protect employees against poor decisions. Second is the *buffet plan,* which starts employees with their exact current benefit coverage and allows them to decrease coverage in some areas (life insurance, medical insurance, etc.) in order to earn credits for other benefits (dental care, day care, etc.). Third is the *alternative dinners plan,* which provides a number of packages ("dinners") to choose from. For example, one package might be aimed at the employee with

FIGURE 11–3
Flexible employee benefits plans (Source: "Flexible Benefits Are a Key to Better Employee Relations," by Albert Cole, Jr., copyright January 1983. Reprinted with the permission of *Personnel Journal,* Costa Mesa, California; all rights reserved.)

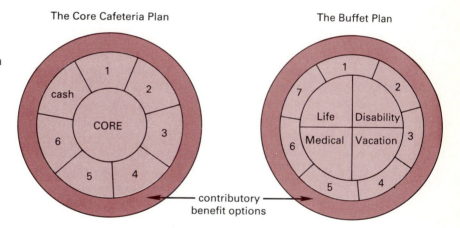

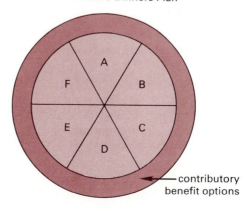

a nonworking spouse and children, another aimed at the single employee, and a third aimed at an employee with a working spouse and no children. The total cost of each dinner would be approximately the same.[63]

Advantages of Flexible Plans Four reasons explain the increased use of flexible plans: (1) employee benefits are an increasing percentage of the total compensation package, possibly reaching 50 percent by 1990; (2) life has changed radically since the 1960s, when cafeteria plans were first introduced (e.g., with both spouses employed, one medical-care coverage is sufficient); (3) employers recognize that standard nonflexible benefit programs may not meet an employee's needs and thus do not help motivate and retain good employees; and (4) employers want to communicate the cost of benefits to employees, and that can be more effectively accomplished through a flexible program.[64]

There has been considerable growth in the number of companies with flexible benefits plans. A survey of firms reported that only 6 percent offered cafeteria plans in 1982, but by 1985 25 percent expected to have implemented a plan.[65] That expansion of programs was not limited to any particular size or type of employer. Originally created as a means to better meet employees' individual needs, flexible plans can serve different objectives. Meeting the increasingly diverse needs of employees (working women, two-paycheck households, and older workers) is still a primary objective. But cost control of benefits and tax effectiveness have become equally important objectives. In the past, a company's costs for nonflexible benefits increased in direct proportion to increases in payroll and medical costs. But a company's commitment to provide flexible credits can be expressed in dollars with no automatic increase in costs. A company can then increase the cost per employee at a rate it can afford and at the same time involve the employee in the decision-making process. For example, a company offers employees two medical plans with differing levels of coverage, with one of the plans at a substantially higher premium.[66] Each employee then must decide if greater coverage is worth a higher premium—and thus a loss of other benefits for that employee. The company has not automatically absorbed the cost increase, as it would have in the past with a nonflexible plan. Instead, the benefit cost per employee can be kept at a constant level, with the employee choosing among the options available.

Employers can also better contain benefit costs with flexible programs because the automatic request from unions to match any program given to nonunion employees becomes very difficult to meet. A flexible plan with various options for each employee makes it far more difficult for unions to demand equal treatment.[67]

Implementation of Flexible Plans Companies that have experienced success with the cafeteria approach have begun by "dreaming big, but starting small." A small start in cafeteria planning can be successful if top management is aggressive in adopting the plan and is willing to involve employees.[68] The steps in adopting a cafeteria approach are:

- Review employees' total compensation needs and obtain top management support for the program.
- Develop a timetable for implementation within the benefits section of the personnel department.
- Survey employees to determine what their needs and desires are in the benefits area.
- Select two to four benefit items from which employees can choose.
- Allow employees to allocate small dollar amounts to various benefits initially.

- Review the plan with the IRS and appropriate state agencies.
- Design a data-processing system which will minimize additional paperwork and the cost of implementing the program.
- Communicate to employees the program's core coverage, which guarantees certain benefits, such as life insurance and hospitalization, that all employees will need.
- Discuss the program with insurance companies and other outside agencies.
- Implement the program through employee selection.

Publicizing Benefits

As employers reexamine benefit programs and question if they are cost-effective, they should determine if there exists a lack of communication with employees concerning the benefit programs. Without such communication, some employees cannot visualize the entire benefit program and its value to them. Since employers must report their pension program to employees under ERISA, the entire benefit program should be communicated.[69]

Studies have demonstrated that employees who give little thought to their benefits may not be able to recall 15 percent of the benefits they receive. Employers might be able to increase the productivity and the advantages of good employee benefits by making employees aware of what the company does for them that does not appear on their paycheck.

An example of one method of providing employees with this information is an employee earnings and benefits letter, as shown in Figure 11–4. This letter keeps employees informed and aware of what the company does in terms of benefits. Section A of the letter lists an employee's gross wages and breaks down the various costs of benefits included therein. Section B includes benefits that do not appear on an employee's W-2 earnings statement and, therefore, are not known to employees. Any benefit that does not show up on an employee's paycheck should be included in section B to make the employee aware of benefit costs. Considering companies' investments in providing benefits to employees, it is unusual that more companies do not do a better job of making employees aware of the costs of the benefits. Only when a company translates benefits into dollar values can employees appreciate the magnitude of what their company does for them.[70]

Communicating Benefits at American Express The employees in the main lobby of American Express Company's headquarters in New York City are not playing computer games. Instead the credit card firm has provided them with instant access to their personal benefit information through a personal computer. The company's Benefit Center allows employees to enter a code number and then ask a variety of questions about their benefit package. For example, they can check their balance in the company's thrift plan or ask more complicated questions, such as their level of vested pension benefits should they leave the company. The system even allows employees to facilitate a flexible benefits plan by self-enrollment in the system. The Metropolitan Life Insurance Company created the software program, which it is providing to corporate clients.[71]

INTERNATIONAL HRM: MANAGING BENEFITS

Benefit packages vary widely throughout the world. In Britain, for example, where health care is available at no cost to everyone, medical insurance coverage would be wasted and unappreciated.

The benefits offered to U.S. workers typically represent a higher percentage of the

COMPANY NAME
ADDRESS
DATE

Employee's Name
Address
Dear _____.

    Enclosed are your W-2 forms showing the amount of taxable income that you received from _____ during 1980. Listed below in Section A are your gross wages and a cost breakdown of various fringe benefit programs that you enjoy. In addition to the money you received as wages, the company paid benefits for you which are not included in your W-2 statement. These are fringe benefits that are sometimes overlooked. In an easy-to-read form, here's what _____ paid to you in 1980.

Section A—Paid to You in Your W-2 Earnings

Cost-of-Living Allowance   _____
Shift Premium   _____
Suggestion Award(s)   _____
Service Award(s)   _____
Vacation Pay   _____
Holiday Pay   _____
Funeral Pay   _____
Jury-Duty Pay   _____
Military Pay   _____
Accident & Sickness Benefits   _____
Regular Earnings   _____
Overtime Earnings   _____
Allowances   _____
      GROSS WAGES   _____

Section B—Paid for You and Not Included in Your W-2 Earnings:

Company Contribution to Stock Purchase & Savings Plan   _____
Company Contribution to Pension Plan   _____
Company Cost of Your Hospitalization Payments   _____
Company Cost of Your Life & Accidental Death Insurance   _____
Company Cost for Social Security Tax on Your Wages   _____
Company Cost of the Premium for Your Workers Compensation   _____
Company Cost for the Tax on Your Wages for Unemployment Compensation   _____
Company Cost for Tuition Refund   _____
Company Cost for Safety Glasses   _____
      TOTAL COST OF BENEFITS NOT INCLUDED IN W-2 EARNINGS   _____
      TOTAL _____ PAID
      FOR YOUR SERVICES IN 1980   _____

    You have earned the amount on the bottom line, but we want to give you a clearer idea of the total cost of your services to the company, and the protection and benefits that are being purchased for you and your family.

                                             Personnel Manager

FIGURE 11–4
A sample employee earnings and benefits letter

compensation package than they might in underdeveloped countries. Even Western European countries invest less in employee benefits than the United States. However, most of these countries provide extensive tax-supported social services that are comparable to employee benefits in U.S. companies. Perhaps an extravagant illustration is the case of Sweden, where the government taxes more than half of employees' annual earnings.

Benefit packages must be competitive in the host country if the global organization is to attract and retain the best people. Yet, too many U.S. firms still believe that people are—not withstanding some minor differences—basically the same. People may be biologically the same, but culturally they are different. In South America, for example, a U.S. mining company offered all kinds of perquisites—good meals, hot water, housing, movies, high wages, and more—to attract workers but lost out to a French mining company that offered none of these comforts. After weeks of costly investigations, the U.S. company learned the simple truth. All the locals wanted was time off—to come and go on their own terms—which the French were more than willing to give.[72] It is ironic that the U.S. mining company was prepared to offer extravagant employee benefits at enormous expense when they were neither needed nor appreciated.

Before deciding what benefits to offer, global firms must understand the culture and the competition. Since the former has been discussed in preceding chapters, nothing more need be said. The competition should be targeted and its benefits surveyed. As long as they are reasonable, benefits levels at competing organizations should be matched. Wages, pensions, time off, insurance, and perquisites should meet the needs of the host country's work force.

CONCLUSIONS AND APPLICATIONS

- Employee benefits are not just a fringe cost to employers; they represent a substantial percentage of the total payroll. Benefits are usually awarded on an equal percentage or seniority basis and seldom on the basis of merit.

- Certain benefits are required by law, including Social Security, workers' compensation, unemployment insurance, and overtime for nonexempt employees. These benefits, however, represent only 25 percent of total employer-paid benefit costs.

- Retirement income is provided through Social Security, private pension plans, and personal savings. Employers believe that they directly or indirectly provide all of these sources—which constitute the single most expensive benefit area. Many employees, however, receive only Social Security after retirement because either they do not save or they do not become vested with an employer.

- Insurance programs provided by employers have expanded to include dental, legal, and vision care, as well as the traditional life and hospitalization coverage. Employers are looking to self-funding and other measures to minimize insurance rate increases.

- Paid time off from work has increased as a percentage of the workweek.

- Transportation programs and child-care plans represent two types of employee services designed to meet changing employee needs.

- Flexible or cafeteria benefit plans have received great interest from employers because they help contain benefit costs and provide employees with more individualized programs.

CASE STUDY
Cafeteria
Planning

A few months back Dick Roberts, personnel manager of the Bel Air Insurance Company, returned to Passaic, New Jersey, from a two-day professional conference in Cleveland. Usually Roberts was not particularly impressed with seminars and workshops, but this time he was very excited about one session. During "Cafeteria Benefit Planning" the vice-president of human resources of a large manufacturing company explained that his company had initiated cafeteria planning six months earlier. Not only had they saved over $250,000 in benefits costs, but their employees were most satisfied.

Five months after returning from the conference, Dick had a cafeteria plan operating at Bel Air. President Patrick Hunt had been very supportive of Roberts, citing that possible savings could curb rising personnel costs. Bel Air employees were given a wider range of benefit alternatives than usual because the home office allowed great flexibility in the company's group life, major medical, auto, and home insurance plans.

Three months after Bel Air began its cafeteria plan, a tragic accident occurred. The wife of Roberts's best friend, Carlos Nomad, who was an employee of the data processing section, was struck by a taxi. After five months in the hospital, she died. Grief stricken, Nomad came into Roberts' office on his first day back at work. "Dick, I'll have to file for bankruptcy. I've lost Cathy, and the medical bills have taken all the money the kids and I had. I didn't put any hospitalization or major medical insurance in my plan; none of us had ever been sick."

Questions

1. Should the firm assist Nomad? How?
2. Was Bel Air partly responsible for Nomad's lack of insurance?
3. How can Roberts keep this situation from recurring? Should he do so?

EXPERIENTIAL EXERCISE
Flexible Benefits Plans: Decisions, Decisions, Decisions

Purpose

To gain an understanding of the philosophy behind cafeteria benefits plans by comparing your own benefits preferences to those of your fellow students.

The Task

Listed below are twenty kinds of benefits which employers may provide. From number 1 (most important) to number 20 (least important), rank-order each benefit in terms of its importance to you. Make any assumptions that you wish about your age, marital and family status, health, and leisure activities. Your instructor will lead a discussion about cafeteria plans once you have completed the exercise.

Benefits

- Pension plan (employer provided)
- Paid vacations
- Paid holidays
- Paid sick leave
- Guaranteed maternity or paternity leave
- Medical insurance
- Legal insurance
- Health maintenance organization health care option
- Vision care
- Subsidized child care
- Credit union
- Subsidized company cafeteria
- Tuition reimbursement
- Profit-sharing plan
- Company-sponsored social events (annual picnic, parties, etc.)
- Life insurance
- Disability insurance
- Dental insurance
- Free parking
- Suggestion program

Rank Order

Rank each benefit from most desired to least desired

1.	8.	15.
2.	9.	16.
3.	10.	17.
4.	11.	18.
5.	12.	19.
6.	13.	20.
7.	14.	

KEY TERMS AND CONCEPTS

Child-care programs

Contributory/noncontributory retirement plan

Coordination of benefits

Defined benefit retirement plan

Defined contribution retirement plan

Dismissal pay

Employee earnings and benefits letter

ERISA

ESOPs

401(K) plans

Flexible benefits

Funded/nonfunded retirement plan

Individual retirement account (IRA)

Maternity and paternity leave

On-call pay

Paid time off work

Portability

Premium pay

Reporting pay

Sick-leave alternatives	Transportation programs
Social Security system	Unemployment insurance
Supplemental retirement plan	Vesting
Supplementary unemployment benefits (SUB)	Workers' compensation

REVIEW QUESTIONS

1. How can employee benefits attract, retain, and motivate employees?
2. About how much of the total payroll cost consists of benefits?
3. What factors are important in determining the size of an employee's retirement benefit?
4. Why do some states require employers to pay more unemployment insurance taxes than others?
5. What are the traditional problems with paid sick leave? Solutions?

DISCUSSION QUESTIONS

1. If you were establishing your own business, which benefits would you be legally required to pay and which would you choose to offer?
2. Cite examples to prove that the cost of living for retired individuals increases as much as or less than the CPI increases. Therefore, should Social Security increase as the consumer price index rises?
3. In view of the fact that there are now fewer persons working to provide benefits for the Social Security system, would you agree that all state, federal, and local government employees and nonprofit association employees should enter the Social Security system?
4. Do you believe that the government will transfer support of welfare or social programs to private industries in the form of required benefits? If so, how soon?
5. Periodically, pension fund frauds involving the loss of retirement funds for thousands of employees are reported. How can persons and companies which have contributed to the pension fund safeguard their contribution to the future?
6. Should employers provide child care? What advantages can be realized?

ENDNOTES

1. Robert Frumkin and William Wiatrowski, "Bureau of Labor Statistics Takes a New Look at Employee Benefits," *Monthly Labor Review* 105, no. 8 (August 1982): 41–45.
2. Albert G. Holzinger, "The Real Costs of Benefits" *Nation's Business* (February 1988): 30–32.
3. James R. Morris, "A Brake on Benefits," *Nation's Business* 76, no. 2 (April 1984): 84–86. See also Holzinger, "The Real Costs of Benefits."
4. Richard I. Henderson, *Compensation Management,* (Reston, VA: Reston, 1979), pp. 321–22.

5. Richard Schulz, "Benefit Trends," *Personnel Administrator* (September 1977): 19–20, 35.

6. Thomas N. and Teresa N. Fannin, "Coordination of Benefits: Uncovering Buried Treasure," *Personnel Journal* 62, no. 5 (May 1983): 386–89.

7. Hoyt W. Dagel and John D. McMillan, "Are You Overlooking Employee Benefit Programs That Could Also Benefit the Company?", *Personnel Administrator* 25, no. 5 (May 1980): 54–56.

8. Evan Claque and Leo Kramer, *Manpower Policies and Programs: A Review 1935–1975* (Kalamazoo, MI: Upjohn, 1976), pp. 82–83.

9. Jerry Flint, "The Old Folks," *Forbes* (February 18, 1980): 51–56.

10. Dale Detlefs, *1984 Guide to Social Security* (Louisville, KY: Meidinger and Associates, 1985), pp. 6–9.

11. Michael P. Littea and James E. Inman, *The Legal Environment of Business: Text, Cases and Readings* (Columbus, OH: Grid, 1980), pp. 464–65.

12. Kenneth P. Shapiro, "An Ideal Pension System," *Personnel Journal* 60, no. 4 (April 1981): 294–97.

13. Vincent M. Tobin, "What Goes into a Retirement Income Policy?" *Personnel* 61, no. 4 (July–August 1984): 60–66.

14. Donald Bell and William Wiatrowski, "Disability Benefits for Employees in Private Pension Plans," *Monthly Labor Review* 105, no. 8 (August 1982): 36–40.

15. David H. Gravitz and Frederick W. Rumack, "Opening the Early Retirement Window," *Personnel* 60, no. 2 (March–April 1983): 53–57.

16. Kathryn H. Anderson, Richard V. Burkhauser, and Joseph F. Quinn, "Do Retirement Dreams Come True? The Effect of Unanticipated Events on Retirement Plans," *Industrial and Labor Relations Review* 39, no. 4 (July 1986): 518–26.

17. Michael R. Carrell and Frank E. Kuzmits, "Amended ADEA's Effects on HR Strategies Remain Dubious," *Personnel Journal* 66, no. 5 (May 1987): 111–120.

18. Lawrence Meyer, "Many Workers Lose Retirement Benefits Despite Reform Laws," *Washington Post* (September 7, 1982): 1.

19. Fredrick I. Schick, "Tax Reform's Impact on Benefit Programs," *Personnel Administrator* 32, no. 1 (January 1987): 80–88.

20. Meyer, "Many Workers Lose . . ."

21. Olivia S. Mitchell, "Fringe Benefits and the Cost of Changing Jobs," *Industrial and Labor Relations Review* 37, no. 1 (October 1983): 70–78.

22. Allen Stitler, "Finally, Pension Plans Defined," *Personnel Journal* 66, no. 2 (February 1987): 45–53.

23. *Pension Reform Act of 1974* (New York: Commerce Clearing House, 1974), p. 2

24. The Retirement Equity Act of 1984.

25. "When Pension Liabilities Dampen Profits," *Business Week,* (June 16, 1983): 80–81.

26. Tom Nicholson and Penny Wang, "A Blow to Unisex Pensions," *Newsweek* (July 18, 1983): 66.

27. Trisha Brambley, "The 401(K) Solution to Retirement Planning," *Personnel Journal* 63, no. 12 (December 1984): 66–67.

28. Marcia Lewis and Richard Sears, "How Do 401(K) and Traditional Savings Plans Compare?" *Personnel Administrator* 27, no. 10 (October 1982): 71–76, 92–93.

29. William M. Mercer-Meidinger, Inc., "How Will Reform Tax Your Benefits?" *Personnel Journal* 65, no. 12 (December 1986): 49–57.

30. Richard I. Henderson, *Compensation Management* (Reston, VA: Reston, 1979).

31. Barron H. Harvey, Judy A. Schultze, and Jerome F. Rogers, "Rewarding Employees for Not Using Sick Leave," *Personnel Administrator* 28, no. 5 (May 1983): 55–59.

32. F. C. Joran, "A Fair System for Time Off the Job: Combine Sick Days, Vacation Days and Holidays into Paid Days," *Modern Business Practice* (1974).

33. "A Low-Cost Fringe That Workers Appreciate," *Business Week* (March 13, 1978): 79.

34. Harvey et al., "Rewarding Employees," pp. 55–59.

35. Nancy Norman and James T. Tedeschi, "Paternity Leave: The Unpopular Benefit Option," *Personnel Administrator* 29, no. 2 (February 1984): 39–43.

36. J. F. Follman, Jr., "Dental Insurance," *Pension and Welfare News* (August 1983): 20–24, 72.

37. Henderson, *Compensation Management*, p. 323.

38. Sandy Dement, "A New Bargaining Focus on Legal Services," *American Federationist* 85 (May 7, 1978): 7–9.

39. Henderson, *Compensation Management*, p. 325.

40. Ibid.

41. Ibid.

42. K. Per Larson, "How Companies Can Rein in Their Health Care Costs," *The Personnel Administrator* (November 1979): 29–33.

43. Ronald Bujan, "A Primer Self-Funding Health Care Benefits," *Personnel Administrator* 28, no. 4 (April 1983): 61–64.

44. Ibid.

45. Sandra E. La Marre and Kate Thompson, "Industry-Sponsored Day Care," *Personnel Administrator* 29, no. 2 (February 1984): 53–65.

46. Thomas I. Miller, "The Effects of Employer Sponsored Child Care on Employee Absenteeism, Turnover, Productivity, Recruitment on Job Satisfaction," *Personnel Psychology* 37, no. 2 (Summer 1984): 277–87.

47. La Marre and Thompson, "Industry-Sponsored Day Care," pp. 53–65.

48. Stewart A. Youngblood and Kimberly Chambers-Cook, "Child Care Assistance Can Improve Employee Attitudes and Behavior," *Personnel Administrator* 29, no. 2 (February 1984): 45–46, 93–95.

49. La Marre and Thompson, "Industry-Sponsored Day Care," pp. 64–65.

50. Ibid.

51. James Fraze, "Preparing for a Different Future," *Resource* 7, no. 1 (January 1988): 1, 10

52. Schulz, "Benefit Trends," pp. 18–19.

53. William M. Mercer-Meidinger, Inc., "How Will Reform Tax Your Benefits?", pp. 52–53.

54. Margaret Magnus et al., "Dollars, Sense and Solutions," *Personnel Journal* 65, no. 3 (March 1986): 49–60.

55. Karen Debats, "Employer-Sponsored Transportation Programs," *Personnel Journal* 60, no. 4 (April 1981): 270–76.

56. Don R. Osborn and Margaret McCarthy, "The Economical and Ecological Advantages of Mass-Transit Subsidies," *Personnel Journal* 66, no. 4 (April 1987): 140–47.

57. John Hoerr et al., "ESOP: Revolution or Ripoff?" *Business Week* (April 15, 1985): 56–57.

58. Richard Woodman and John Sherwood, "A Comprehensive Look at Job Design," *Personnel Journal* (August 1977): 284–87.

59. David Thompson, "Introducing Cafeteria Compensation in Your Company," *Personnel Journal* (March 1977): 124–25.

60. Schulz, "Benefit Trends," p. 20.

61. Robert B. Cockrum, "Has the Time Come for Employee Cafeteria Plans?" *Personnel Administrator* 27, no. 7 (July 1982): 66–69.

62. Albert Cole Jr., "Flexible Benefits Are a Key to Better Employee Relations," *Personnel Journal* 62, no. 1 (January 1983): 49–53.

63. Ibid., pp. 51–53.

64. Cockrum, "Has the Time Come?" pp. 66–68.

65. Peter W. Stonebraker, "A Three-Tier Plan for Cafeteria Benefits," *Personnel Journal* 63, no. 12 (December 1984): 51–57.

66. Dale Gifford, "The Status of Flexible Compensation," *Personnel Administrator* 29, no. 5 (May 1984): 19–25.

67. Ibid.

68. Thompson, "Introducing Cafeteria Compensation," pp. 126–28.

69. Robert Krogman, "What Employees Need to Know About Benefit Plans," *Personnel Administrator* (May 1980): 45–46.

70. Jeffrey Claypool and Joseph Cangent, "The Annual Employee Earnings and Benefits Letter," *Personnel Journal* (July 1980): 563–65.

71. "Computer-Based Communications at American Express," *Benefit News Analysis* 8, no. 4 (April 1987): 4–6.

72. Lennie Copeland and Lewis Griggs, *Going International* (New York, Random House, 1985), p. 14.

Chapter Twelve   Health and Safety

Chapter Objectives

1. To understand the recent investment of employers in employee wellness programs.
2. To reveal the problems caused by employee alcohol and drug abuse.
3. To discuss policy issues surrounding AIDS in the work place.
4. To identify the purposes of employee assistance programs (EAPs).
5. To understand the general provisions of the Occupational Safety and Health Act (OSHA).
6. To recognize alternatives to traditional employer health care programs including health maintenance organizations (HMOs) and preferred provider organizations (PPOs).
7. To describe the federal right-to-know regulations.
8. To identify job stress warning signs and methods of care.
9. To discuss effective accident prevention programs.

Illegal Drugs at Work

A Long Island forklift operator steers his cargo into a door—after smoking a joint at lunchtime. In Houston a stoned quality control inspector causes an entire batch of pharmaceutical products to be contaminated. The use of illegal drugs by rock stars, professional athletes, and movie stars no longer raises eyebrows, but how about use in hospitals, courtrooms, nuclear plants, and on construction sites?

"Perfectly respectable professionals" in virtually all lines of work have dramatically increased their use of illegal drugs. It is such a widespread problem that the superintendent of the Boston Police Department notes that today undercover agents wear three-piece suits instead of hippie-type clothes. The total cost to the U.S. Economy is estimated to be $26 billion. Employees who use drugs on the job are estimated to be one-third less productive than their counterparts. The indirect costs such as theft by employees to cover their habits and angry customers cannot even be estimated. National Car Rental's personnel director calls it the greatest employee problem in industry today—nothing else is even in second place.

The problem is more difficult today because alcohol, still the most abused drug, can be detected by supervisors much more easily than most illegal drugs such as Percodan, Dilaudid, and Quaaludes.

Business is beginning to respond with employee assistance programs (EAPs) and supervisor training. Some are even using counteroffensives like the Boston Blue Cross–Blue Shield office that requested an undercover police investigation. The Mobay Chemical Corporation of Baytown, Texas, uses drug-sniffing dogs to search work areas. In Ontario, California, the Sunkist Products Company requires all new and "strange-acting employees" to take urine tests. Most EAPs, which once were only concerned with alcohol abuse, have quickly expanded to deal with all forms of chemical abuse by employees.

Source: Adapted from John Brecher et al., "Taking Drugs on the Job," *Newsweek* (August 22, 1983), pp. 54–60. Condensed from *Newsweek*. Copyright 1983, by Newsweek, Inc. All rights reserved. Reprinted by permission.

IN the United States there has occurred an unparalleled interest in health and fitness. Almost monthly, new low-calorie, low-sodium, or high-fiber "health" foods appeared on grocery store shelves. At the same time, more Americans are running or joining aerobic classes, health spas, and gyms in a desire to lose weight or get in shape. This new national interest in health and fitness also is felt in the work place. Employers in increasing numbers realize that they can reduce health-insurance costs and health-related employee problems by offering preventive employee health and safety programs.

Employee assistance programs designed to help employees overcome personal crises such as alcoholism, job burnout, or family problems have also become common. Such programs have proven that valuable, skilled employees who experience problems can be helped. Once they have dealt with their problems, those employees often provide many more productive years of service. In fact, employees may be particularly grateful to employers who lend assistance during a crisis.

EMPLOYER HEALTH-CARE PROGRAMS

General Motors spends more money for employee medical benefits than it spends for steel from its main supplier. Every year in the United States, employee illnesses and injuries cost over $25 billion in lost workdays. The annual rate of disability retirement is 170 percent higher than in the 1950s.[1] Employers pay half of U.S. health-care bills through insurance programs, which equals almost 10 percent of the gross national product.[2]

Such statistics alone give employers more than adequate reason to be concerned about employee health and safety. But other reasons include various legal requirements, employer

goodwill, and the increased employee productivity and morale that result from health programs. The array of programs available to employers seeking to reduce health-care costs include wellness programs, physical-fitness programs, preferred-provider organizations, smoking-cessation programs, preadmission certification, and expanded employee-assistance programs.

Wellness Programs

Employers have tried a number of approaches to address rising health costs and the poor fitness and health of employees. One approach is the establishment of wellness programs. The Health Insurance Association of America defines *wellness* as a "freely chosen life-style aimed at achieving and maintaining an individual's good health."[3] From management's perspective, employees are a company's greatest asset, and their state of health affects their contribution to the company in such measurable ways as absenteeism, productivity, fatigue-caused accidents, alertness and creativity, and health-care claims and insurance premiums. At the same time, employees indicate by their high degree of participation a great interest in wellness programs. Reasons include (1) the presumption that it is a quality program because it is company sponsored, (2) the perception that it is a fringe benefit and thus should be taken advantage of, and (3) the recognition that it is a convenient way to take care of health concerns.[4]

A U.S. Department of Health and Human Services 1987 survey confirmed that wellness programs are offered by a majority of American employers. Although such programs were once perceived to be a fad or a frivolous employee benefit, about 66 percent of U.S. employers with over 50 employees offer at least one wellness activity each year. What is the reason for the substantial growth rate in such programs? Employers report that they are an unqualified success. Employees who participate are more likely to have lower health-care costs and generally are healthier. The most common wellness activities offered by employers include:[5]

- Smoking cessation (36 percent)
- Health risk appraisals (30 percent)
- Back care (29 percent)
- Stress management (27 percent)
- Exercise/physical fitness (22 percent)
- Off-the-job accident prevention (20 percent)
- Nutrition education (17 percent)
- Blood pressure checks (17 percent)
- Weight control (15 percent)

One successful corporation wellness program was established by the Mesa Petroleum Company. Their program averaged $173 per participant in medical costs compared to $434 for nonparticipants.[6] General Motors' employee assistance program cut medical benefit payments by 60 percent after one year.[7] The Campbell Soup Company's colorectal cancer detection program recorded savings of $245,000 in medical payments.[8] And Burlington Industries reported that absenteeism decreased from 400 days to 19 days annually due to its "healthy back" program.[9]

Company Physical-Fitness Programs
One major employer-sponsored method of increasing employees' health is the company physical-fitness program (PFP). The National Industrial Recreation Association estimates that over 50,000 firms have PFPs. Such programs are relatively new in personnel; more than 70 percent of company PFPs have been started since 1975.[10] A leading authority on PFPs believes that all personnel departments should initiate such programs to develop employees mentally and physically. Most employees need up to three years to realize the full benefits from a program.[11]

PFPs vary greatly, from a basketball hoop in the employee parking lot to the Kimberly Clark Company's $2.5 million physical-fitness center. According to a survey of 226 program directors, 41 percent of PFPs have gymnasiums and exercise rooms, 34 percent have an entire building used exclusively for physical fitness, 10 percent have company-sponsored teams and 6 percent use YMCA facilities. In most programs, employees are encouraged to use the facilities and participation is voluntary. In 67 percent of programs, facilities are used on employee's own time; in 33 percent, on company time.[12]

Organizations that support PFPs generally expect them to be attractive to employees, to reduce the impact of stress, and to increase employee productivity. In addition, they are often expected to decrease absenteeism and turnover, as well as accidents and medical claims.[13] Documented improvements by employees who actively participate in a PFP include:

- Improved cardiovascular function, decreased body weight, and fat reduction.[14]
- Lower medical claims.[15]
- Smoking reduction and blood pressure normalization.[16]
- General physical fitness.[17]

Hard evidence that PFPs directly cause changes in the corporate bottom line is not readily available. Nevertheless, there continue to be increases in the development of PFPs because many believe that they positively affect both the employees and the organization. Table 12–1 shows the benefits thought to accrue from the establishment of such programs.

Employee Assistance Programs

Beginning in the early 1970s, employee assistance programs (EAPs) significantly increased in U.S. firms. The number continues to increase because many employers believe they

TABLE 12–1
Benefits of physical fitness programs

Physiological Improvements	Behavior Changes	Benefits to the Organization
Weight and body-fat loss Greater strength and endurance Better nutritional habits Less smoking Improved blood pressure and cardiovascular function Stress reduction	Less absenteeism Fewer fatigue-related accidents Higher productivity Enhanced mental alertness	Lower medical claims and insurance premiums Fewer disability claims Fewer losses due to accidents Lower workers' compensation costs Higher employee morale and productivity Lower overtime and temporary-worker salaries due to absenteeism reduction

can save money by helping employees resolve personal problems that affect job performance. EAPs also provide public evidence of management's concern for employees' well-being, which should be a strong boost to the employees' morale. But the primary reason that company-sponsored EAPs have increased is because they may enhance a company's profitability by reducing absenteeism, turnover, tardiness, accidents, and medical claims. It is estimated that a troubled employee costs the employer at least 5 percent of that employee's annual salary.[18]

A milestone in the growth of EAPs occurred in 1987. Over 800 EAP practitioners applied to take their first professional certification test. The test was developed and sponsored by the Association of Labor-Management Administrators and Consultants on Alcoholism (ALMACA). The certification program was designed to legitimize the EAP profession through standardization. Eventually state or federal laws as well as insurance companies may require EAP certification similar to that required by other professions.[19]

Many EAPs grew from alcohol-treatment programs. The typical program addresses psy-

chological and physical problems, including job stress, chemical dependency (alcohol and drugs), depression, marital and family problems, financial problems, health, anxiety, and even job boredom. The procedure in virtually all EAPs consists of (1) problem identification, (2) intervention, and (3) treatment and recovery. Program operations generally fall into two categories: internal programs that use a full-time staff of counselors and other employees, and referral centers that use a full-time specialist who identifies the problem and refers the employee to a community agency for treatment.

An example of a successful referral program is the EAP at the Bechtel Power Corporation in San Francisco. When a supervisor believes that an employee's performance has been adversely affected by personal problems, the supervisor phones the EAP office.[20] (An alternative first step is employee self-referral.) Once the supervisor and EAP specialist discuss the particulars of the situation—such as performance record, absenteeism, and so on—the supervisor is normally advised to suggest that the employee use the EAP. It is carefully explained to the employee that participation is voluntary and does not affect the discipline process, which may be implemented if required by poor work. Strict confidentiality is guaranteed. At some point the employee may be given the choice of termination or using the EAP.

When the employee calls the EAP office, a specialist then performs *triage*—the determination of the relative urgency of the case. A case may be (1) a life-threatening emergency such as a suicide attempt; (2) an urgent need such as extreme anxiety or crying; or (3) a routine need. In the first case, the counselor responds immediately; in the second, within hours; in the third, a counseling session is set up within days. At the counseling session a referral to a local agency is made and the follow-up process is started. Follow-up by the agency is continued for as long as needed, with particular attention given to the continuance and frequency of the employee's sessions.[21]

Internal programs are usually more expensive and therefore found mostly in larger organizations. Such programs provide a sense of security because the employee is not given a quick diagnosis and sent to an outside source. Instead, sessions with in-house counselors provide the needed treatment in most cases. Exceptions include cases of chemical abuse and various physical problems.[22]

EAP professionals generally agree on what components are essential for a successful program. Essentials for an effective EAP include:[23]

Confidentiality Employees must believe that all information about problems will be kept confidential by the counselor. Supervisors should only be informed that the employee is in fact continuing to receive assistance.

Normal Disciplinary Procedures No employee should receive lenient or harsh treatment due to participation (or lack of it) in an EAP. An exception occurs if a supervisor believes that an employee must be terminated but after due process grants the employee the chance to use the EAP as an alternative. Even then, the employee's work must show improvement.

Voluntary Participation Supervisors can strongly urge an employee to participate and even give termination as the alternative, but the employee must seek help voluntarily for any chance of success.

Job Security No employee will be affected by disciplinary or other action because he or she participated in the program.

Insurance Coverage Both inpatient and outpatient treatment must be covered by insurance.

Management Support Management must provide written assurance that the company is committed to the process.

Accessibility Employees must know how and for what types of problems they can receive assistance. A broad range of assistance ensures a better image and greater use.

Follow-up Some problems will take years to correct, though most can be rectified in a number of months. Periodic follow-up, whether by in-house counselors or outside agencies, is critical to a high recovery rate.

Separate Location The program should be located away from the work place to help assure privacy.

Alcoholic Employees

One of society's most persistent and devastating ills, alcoholism often leads to severe marital problems, family abuse, estrangement between parents and children, the loss of close friends and acquaintances, emotional illness, and ostracism by society. Statistics show that alcohol and other mood-altering substances increase violent crimes and traffic accidents that result in death. The societal burdens of alcoholism have long been of major concern to professionals in social work, medicine, and psychiatry.

Alcoholism has also received a great deal of attention from both management academicians and personnel practitioners. Much of this interest has been created by the publication of data that show that (1) an alarming percentage of American workers are alcoholics and (2) the alcoholic worker has many more work-related problems than a nonalcoholic worker. How many workers are alcoholics? While the exact numbers are impossible to pin down, most informed sources, including the National Council on Alcoholism (NCA), estimate about 10 percent of the labor force. Alcoholics are in business, government, the professions, sciences, voluntary agencies, and academia on all organizational levels. The National Institute on Alcohol Abuse and Alcoholism (NIAAA) estimates that 25 percent of alcoholic employees are white-collar employees, 30 percent are blue-collar workers, and 45 percent are managers and professionals.[24]

Although some alcoholic employees perform their work satisfactorily and meet job expectations, a great many cannot. The NCA reports that alcoholic employees are absent an average of two to four times more often than nonalcoholic employees and that on-the-job accidents are two to four times more frequent for alcoholic employees.[25] In addition to these costly problems, alcoholic employees may create other work-related difficulties:

- The alcoholic's negligence may cause accidents and injuries to other employees.
- The alcoholic may disregard job details, use poor judgment, and make bad decisions.
- The alcoholic may perform unevenly in terms of quantity and quality.

- The alcoholic may minimize contact with co-workers and supervisors and exhibit antisocial behavior.

The alcoholic employee's performance, including above-average absenteeism, injuries, accidents, and substandard levels of productivity and quality, all represent real costs to the organization. For large organizations, the costs can be staggering. The U.S. Postal Service estimates its losses in productivity from alcoholism at $186 million annually. United California Bank—California's fourth largest bank—estimates losing $1 million a year to alcoholism among its employees.[26] Nationwide, $25 billion is lost annually due to alcoholics' absenteeism, accidents, sick leave, decreased productivity, and poor work quality. A full-scale attack on alcoholism can be justified not only for social and moral reasons but for economic considerations as well.

What causes alcoholism? There is little agreement about the specific causes. Predicting precisely who will or will not become an alcoholic is impossible. Alcoholism does not discriminate against any particular social or economic class; this disease is as likely to victimize the middle manager as the assembly-line worker.

Nonetheless, researchers have isolated a mix of circumstances that greatly influence problem drinkers. The NCA suggests that the *problem drinker* is one who:

- Experiences intense relief and relaxation from alcohol.
- Has difficulty in dealing with and overcoming depression, anxiety, and frustration.
- Is a member of a culture in which there is pressure to drink and culturally induced guilt and confusion regarding appropriate drinking behavior.

According to the NCA, when these persons encounter problems with their families, spouses, jobs, loneliness, old age, and so on, their probability of becoming alcoholics increases significantly.

Researchers also recognize the possibility that certain work conditions may lead to alcoholism. In a U.S. Department of Health, Education, and Welfare (HEW) report entitled *Work in America,* the author stated:[27]

> Nonsupportive jobs in which the worker gets little feedback on his performance appear to cause the kind of anxiety that may lead to or aggravate alcoholism. Work addiction, occupational obsolescence, role stress, and unstructured environments (for certain personality types) appear to be other important risk factors for both alcoholism and drug addiction.

The HEW report's suggestion that organizations do have some control over whether an employee becomes a problem drinker is important. Decision makers are faced with a difficult choice involving moral and economic considerations. They may create an environment that produces satisfying human experiences and enhances mental and physical health. Or they may create an environment that leads to frustration, anxiety, and stress— one that compels a certain type of employee to seek relief through alcohol or, perhaps, other addictive chemicals. Faced with these alternatives, managers have a twofold responsibility: to create programs for employees suffering from alcoholism and to create a work climate that minimizes the conditions and circumstances that pressure an employee to seek relief in excessive drink.

Unlike job attitudes or opinions, alcoholism cannot be measured by traditional personnel tools such as surveys or questionnaires. First, many alcoholics are unwilling to admit that they have a problem; thus a general-purpose questionnaire—even though anonymous—would not generate much useful data on alcoholism within the organization. Sec-

ond, alcoholism can be defined only in the most general terms. For instance, the *American Heritage Dictionary* defines alcoholism as "a chronic pathological condition chiefly of the nervous and gastroenteric systems, caused by habitual excessive alcoholic consumption." In conducting research, it may be difficult to distinguish between heavy or excessive drinking and the various stages of alcoholism. Third, employees may perceive alcoholism as a sensitive personal issue. Many employees would no doubt feel that the collection of information about alcohol abuse is an invasion of privacy.

Even though alcoholism may be difficult to measure quantitatively, persons may determine if they have the symptoms of the problem. Both the NCA and Alcoholics Anonymous (AA) have developed checklists to help individuals decide if they may need help in combating alcohol. Although a checklist is not useful for research purposes, it may be part of an organization's alcoholism education program given to employees who inquire about the organization's rehabilitation services. The AA checklist is shown in Figure 12–1.

Because alcoholism is difficult to measure in an organizational setting, research will be limited. For example, it may be impossible to analyze which employees have the highest rates of alcoholism or what work conditions and environmental settings tend to aggravate the problem.

A researcher may be able to evaluate the organization's rehabilitation efforts with known alcoholic employees and determine how these employees behave differently. By analyzing the work histories of alcoholic employees, it should also be possible to discover how their absenteeism, accidents, injuries, productivity, and work quality differ from organizationwide norms. This information will help call management's attention to the seriousness of the problem.

One device used in some companies to help the alcoholic to appreciate the seriousness of his problem is to ask him to answer 20 questions relating to his drinking pattern. This test has been used, occasionally with modifications, in a number of industrial alcoholism programs. The test:

		YES	NO
1.	Have you lost time from work due to drinking?	( )	( )
2.	Has drinking made your home life unhappy?	( )	( )
3.	Do you drink because you are shy with people?	( )	( )
4.	Has drinking affected your reputation?	( )	( )
5.	Have you gotten into financial difficulties because of your drinking?	( )	( )
6.	Do you turn to lower companions and an inferior environment when drinking?	( )	( )
7.	Does your drinking make you careless of your family's welfare?	( )	( )
8.	Has your drinking decreased your ambition?	( )	( )
9.	Do you want a drink "the morning after"?	( )	( )
10.	Does your drinking cause you to have difficulty sleeping?	( )	( )
11.	Has your efficiency decreased since drinking?	( )	( )
12.	Has drinking ever jeopardized your job or business?	( )	( )
13.	Do you drink to escape from worries or troubles?	( )	( )
14.	Do you drink alone?	( )	( )
15.	Have you ever had a complete loss of memory as a result of drinking?	( )	( )
16.	Has your physician ever treated you for drinking?	( )	( )
17.	Do you drink to build up self-confidence?	( )	( )
18.	Have you ever been in an institution or hospital on account of drinking?	( )	( )
19.	Have you ever felt remorse after drinking?	( )	( )
20.	Do you crave a drink at a definite time daily?	( )	( )

When he takes the test, the employee is reminded that only he can determine whether or not he is an alcoholic. However, if the employee answers *yes* to as few as three questions, he can be reasonably certain that alcohol has become, or is becoming, a problem for him.

FIGURE 12–1

AA's checklist for alcoholism (Source: Alcoholics Anonymous, *A. A. and the Alcoholic Employee* [New York: Alcoholics Anonymous World Services, Inc., 1962], pp. 12–13.)

Reducing Alcoholism Because employee alcoholism may stem from both personal and work factors, the most effective strategy for combating alcoholism is to minimize the potential of alcoholism by keeping stress and anxiety at the lowest possible levels. Rehabilitation programs for employees currently suffering from alcoholism should be implemented.

Programs to minimize alcoholism in the work place may be most difficult for the personnel administrator to implement and control. Challenge, stress, and conflict seem to be inevitable in the jobs of many modern managers and administrators. Further, the personnel administrator has only moderate control over the work climate and goal-setting process for employees outside of the personnel department. Nonetheless, the personnel staff can educate top and middle managers about the potentially harmful effects of excessive job stress and anxiety. Through training and development activities, the personnel staff can make executives aware that the way people are managed and how their jobs are designed may significantly affect their mental and physical health.

The second strategy to fight alcoholism—the implementation of rehabilitation policies and programs—has become an important personnel responsibility in many larger organizations today. As management and labor continue to accept employee rehabilitation efforts, such programs will, no doubt, continue to expand.

Kemper Insurance Companies, one of the first organizations to implement a formal employee assistance program, has outlined its approach to employee rehabilitation in a pamphlet entitled *Management Guide on Alcoholism*.[28] Kemper's policies are shown in Figure 12–2.

Do employee assistance programs work? The answer is a qualified yes. The majority of alcoholic employees fully recover as a result of rehabilitation efforts. The NCA reports that business and industry success rates range from 65 to 80 percent and that Air Force and Navy success rates are 70 to 80 percent. A NIAAA research study reported that "72 percent of executives of *Fortune* 500 companies with occupational programs believe their firms have saved money as a result of these programs, and most of the executives are convinced of the effectiveness of the program."[29]

One of the most widely reported company success stories involves Oldsmobile Motor Di-

vision's employee assistance program. Oldsmobile's Employee Alcoholism Recovery Program involves a cooperative effort between General Motors and the United Auto Workers. The mechanics of the program are similar to the procedures outlined in Figure 12–2. An evaluation study showed that 117 program participants significantly reduced their absenteeism, accidents, grievances, and disciplinary actions during the year following their participation in the program. Preprogram costs due to lost wages were estimated at $84,616; lost wages were estimated at $43,336 after their involvement in the program. Oldsmobile reported that the economic benefits of the program far exceeded the costs and termed the program both profitable and worthwhile.[30]

Drug Abuse Control

Employers are becoming more and more concerned over the increase of drug abuse in the work place. As a result, testing has moved into almost every industry. In 1987 President Reagan's Commission on Organized Crime requested that all U.S. companies test their employees for drug use. Employee testing, the Commission believed, can create a safer work environment and reduce society's demand for illegal drugs. How serious are the problems created by a drug user? One company estimated, based on employee records, that the typical drug user, compared to the norm for the work unit:[31]

- Functions at about 67 percent of potential capacity.
- Is 360 percent more likely to be involved in an accident.
- Requires three times the average use of sick leave and benefits.
- Is five times more likely to file a worker's compensation claim.
- Is absent ten more workdays per year.
- Is more likely to file a grievance complaint.

FIGURE 12–2

Kemper's policies on employee alcoholism (Source: *Management Guide on Alcoholism* [Long Grove, IL: Kemper Insurance Companies, undated], pp. 6–11. Used with permission.)

Alcoholism Policy. In accordance with our general personnel policies, whose underlying concept is regard for the employee as an individual as well as a worker:

1. We believe alcoholism, or problem drinking, is an illness and should be treated as such.
2. We believe the majority of employees who develop alcoholism can be helped to recover and the company should offer appropriate assistance.
3. We believe the decision to seek diagnosis and accept treatment for any suspected illness is the responsibility of the employee. However, continued refusal of an employee to seek treatment when it appears that substandard performance may be caused by any illness is not tolerated. We believe that alcoholism should not be made an exception to this commonly accepted principle.
4. We believe that it is in the best interest of employees and the company that alcoholism be diagnosed and treated at the earliest possible stage.
5. We believe that the company's concern for individual drinking practices begins only when they result in unsatisfactory job performance.
6. We believe that confidential handling of the diagnosis and treatment of alcoholism is essential.

The objective of this policy is to retain employees who may develop alcoholism by helping them to arrest its further advance before the condition renders them unemployable.

Supervisory Practices. Supervisors are instructed that they should *not* attempt to identify alcoholic employees. Further, supervisors should not discuss "drinking problems" with their employees, except where drinking on the job or an intoxicated employee is observed (the diagnosis of alcoholism is the job of trained professionals). Rather, the supervisor's responsibility is to closely and accurately monitor employee *performance and work habits* and confront the employee whose performance problems persist with the warning that continued poor performance will lead to disciplinary action. . . .

Treatment facilities. Kemper, as do most companies which conduct employee assistance programs, uses a variety of alcoholism treatment sources. These include both private alcoholism consulting and treatment firms and not-for-profit organizations such as AA and Al-Anon, which provides support and assistance to the family members of an alcoholic.

Personnel policies requiring employee drug testing generally distinguish between preemployment and postemployment tests. Unless limited by a state law, employers may require any applicant to submit to a drug screening test. Employers claim that since they have a legal right to hire only qualified applicants, and drug use is related to job performance, they have a right to use drug screening. This concept was generally upheld by a U.S. Supreme Court decision in *New York City Transit Authority* v. *Beager*.[32] The Court ruled that the safety and efficiency of the public transportation system constituted a valid business necessity and a justifiable reason to require drug testing of bus driver applicants. The International Business Machine Company (IBM) began drug screening for all new employees in 1985. A preemployment test policy similar to that used by IBM and other companies might include the following:[33]

- Notify applicants of the screening on the physical exam questionnaire. This minimizes claims of privacy invasion.
- Do not allow an applicant to reschedule a test after he or she appears at the doctor's office and realizes that it is part of the physical exam. The person may be a substance abuser who will refrain from illegal substance use before the next physical exam.
- If test results are positive, repeat the test. This ensures test validity. Ensure that test samples are kept by the doctor's office for 180 days in case of litigation.
- Maintain confidentiality by recording positive test results only on the doctor's records. On personnel records, use a code if someone fails the test. Only the applicant should be made aware of the test results, and the person can simply be informed that they were unsatisfactory.

Postemployment testing of current employees presents more difficult policy issues. Unless limited by a collective bargaining agreement, an employer may test employees at random as a preventive measure. If a routine, random test is not used, an employee can be tested for "probable cause" if a reasonable suspicion of drug use occurs based on specific behavioral activities, poor job performance, or job absences.[34] In addition to the policy considerations for applicants discussed, postemployment policy considerations might include the following:[35]

- Consistent administration. Specify what drugs, including counterfeit and other drugs, are considered dangerous. Prescription drug use must also be considered. Obsolete prescriptions can be a source of problems.
- Substantive proof of drug use. While many supervisors can detect alcoholic intoxication, drug abuse is more difficult to determine. Laboratory testing is the only reliable method.
- Avoid disclosure of test results to anyone other than the employee, the EAP officer, or a person involved in a grievance or legal proceeding.
- Communication of the policy to employees. Emphasize that the policy is designed to discourage the use of drugs. However, employees should be warned that drug abuse will not be tolerated. Abusers must respond to treatment or be terminated.
- Possession of drugs. If aggressive drug searches with dogs or other methods are considered, first notify employees as to what substances will be included; second, involve law enforcement officials.

How does the general public feel about employee drug testing? A *Newsweek* survey reported very strong public support. Eighty-five percent of those polled supported testing for police officers, 84 percent for airline pilots, 72 percent for professional athletes, 72 percent for government workers, 64 percent for high school teachers, and 50 percent for all workers.[36]

Smoking in the Work Place

A 1986 report of the U.S. Surgeon General concluded that sidestream or passive smoking, the involuntary inhaling by nonsmokers of tobacco smoke, is dangerous to their health. The report stated that environmental tobacco smoke (ETS) causes 2,400 to 4,000 lung cancer deaths annually among nonsmokers. ETS is the combination of sidestream smoke, which comes from burning cigarettes between puffs, and mainstream smoke, which is exhaled by a smoker.[37] In addition, other reports indicate that nonsmokers exposed to ETS have a 1.3 to 3.5 times greater risk of developing lung cancer than unexposed nonsmokers.[38] Tobacco smoke is also a severe problem for allergy sufferers.

Legal restrictions on smoking in the work place are mostly found at the state and local levels. As of 1986, ten states had enacted laws regulating smoking in the private sector workplace.[39] Many local governments have also passed restrictions. The 1973 federal Rehabilitation Act was applied to work place smoking in a 1982 court case when an employee successfully claimed that he was handicapped as a result of inhaling the smoke of fellow employees.[40] The court found, however, that the employer only had to make "reasonable accommodations" for the employee and was not required to ban work place smoking.

Balancing the rights of smokers and nonsmokers is a difficult personnel policy issue. However, more employers have continued to develop new policies: 16 percent in 1980 to 57 percent in 1987.[41] In addition to the health considerations of nonsmokers, employers must consider that the employee who smokes costs the employer an average of $400 to $1,000 per year more than the nonsmoker in health insurance claims, absenteeism, maintenance, and productivity.[42] But there are conflicting opinions on the specific effects of employee smoking in the workplace. A nonaffiliated research group has published research results indicating that smokers are high achievers and among the most productive employees.[43] Employers have developed a number of policies on work place smoking:

- *Total ban.* In 1984 the Boeing Company in Seattle announced its intention to provide a smoke-free environment for all employees. With over 85,000 employees, Boeing became the largest U.S. company to ban smoking in the work place. According to the company's president, Malcolm Stamper, developing a smoke-free environment is an essential ingredient in providing a clean, safe, and healthy work environment.[44]
- *Work-station ban.* Restrict smoking to separate, ventilated smoking lounges.
- *Encouragement of no smoking.* A bonus or award may be given to employees who do not smoke. The City Federal Savings and Loan Association of Birmingham, Alabama, for example, awards $20 per month to employees who do not smoke at work.[45]
- *Dangerous area ban.* Allow smoking in all areas except near combustible materials or in other hazardous situations. This policy meets minimum federal Occupational Health and Safety Administration (OSHA) standards.
- *Reasonable accommodation.* Separate employees who complain of smoke from adjacent co-workers who smoke and improve ventilation.

Before establishing one of these policies, an employer should consider the following:

1. All employees, from the president down, must be included in formulating the policy.
2. Disciplinary actions to be invoked when violations occur should be included in any policy.
3. Allow a transition period of several months between the announcement and implementation of the policy. This will give smokers who must quit the time to adjust.

4. Provide smoking cessation classes for smokers if a total ban is imposed.

5. Inform new employees of the policy during the interview process.

"Once adopted, a smoking policy that is properly communicated and fairly enforced can greatly assist employers in protecting the rights of nonsmokers. Such a policy can also help avoid the many legal liabilities which may result from tobacco smoke in the work-place."[46]

The courts have upheld the legal right of employers to prohibit smoking in the work place, as well as to require job applicants to be nonsmokers. But the U.S. Supreme Court has not yet addressed the issue in a precedent-setting case. Personnel policy makers have many issues to consider—the rights of smokers and nonsmokers, the health and safety problems that may be caused by smoking in the work place, and a variety of policy options. The issue will likely continue to be one of the most controversial in the area of employee health and safety.

AIDS in the Work Place

In only a few years AIDS—acquired immune deficiency syndrome—has become a health issue that has captured the attention of all Americans. The reasons are obvious: it is fatal, and the number of cases diagnosed in the United States alone has doubled every year since 1981.[47] The concerns and fears concerning AIDS have spread to the work place. The issues confronting employers are complicated.

First, the employer should consider the legal environment. Title VII of the 1964 Civil Rights Act does *not* prohibit discrimination on the basis of "physical handicap" or "medical condition." Employers with federal contracts of $2,500 or more are covered by the 1973 Rehabilitation Act, which does prohibit discrimination against handicapped individuals.

AIDS is a physical handicap protected under the Rehabilitation Act according to most interpretations of a U.S. Supreme Court decision, *Arline* v. *School Board of Nassau County*.[48] In addition, many states and cities have laws prohibiting discrimination against individuals with a physical handicap or medical condition and are investigating AIDS cases under EEO guidelines. In practice, employers should hire and retain employees with AIDS just as they would any other employees with a physical handicap. As long as they can perform the job, they should be allowed to work. Employers are not required, however, to hire or retain employees who cannot perform their job. When the disease has reached the point where the employee is incapable of working, or requires prolonged absence from work, the employee may be placed on medical or disability leave.[49]

Employers are considering AIDS testing for current employees or job applicants. Medical experts contend that AIDS is not transmitted through casual or normal work place contact, and thus, employer testing is unwarranted. Labor lawyers stress that employer testing could invite legal action under handicap discrimination or privacy invasion. The only justification for testing would be if an employee's job responsibilities involved activities that could transmit the AIDS virus.[50]

According to three national surveys, only 2 to 9 percent of all employers have policies covering AIDS. Perhaps the number is small in spite of the national attention focused on the virus because there are major reasons for not issuing AIDS policy statements: (1) there is no need since AIDS should be treated like any other disease or condition; (2) issuing a policy statement may obligate an employer to follow a course of action that may prove unwise; (3) although the facts about AIDS are still rapidly changing, it is generally agreed that the virus cannot be transmitted by normal work place contacts. The notable exception would occur in organizations where there is a likelihood of blood contact with other persons.[51]

Some employers have, however, issued policies. Bank of America was one of the first U.S. employers to develop a policy on AIDS in the work place. Their program began with two principles: a safe work environment should be provided to all workers, and an employee's health condition is personal and confidential. The policy (see page 482) treats AIDS in a manner consistent with life-threatening illnesses in that the employer will make "reasonable accommodation" for employees, which might include a job transfer or disability leave.[52]

The progressive Bank of America policy also stresses education. Employees are told that AIDS is not treated differently from other medical conditions in terms of employee benefits. Employees with questions or concerns about AIDS are directed to AIDS hotlines and community organizations. The policy was also formed to provide all employees and customers with the facts about AIDS. Medical evidence indicating that AIDS is not spread via casual contact in the work place is highlighted in regular employee communications. However, if medical research evidence changes, Bank of America would likely change its policy. Nancy Merritt, vice president and program manager of personnel relations, explains: "If we were dealing with a disease that could be transmitted by casual contact in the workplace, we would not permit an affected employee to continue working. Also, if appropriate, we would tell employees what they had been exposed to."[53]

A difficult employment issue is the rights of co-workers of AIDS victims. OSHA requires every employer to provide a safe and healthy work place. The Secretary of Labor may take action against employers who fail to provide a safe working environment. Co-workers of an AIDS victim who might seek such action,

however, would need to prove that they are at risk of contracting the disease, a difficult task given current medical evidence. Federal OSHA regulations do provide that an employee may refuse to work if "a reasonable person would conclude [that] he faced an immediate risk of death or serious injury." Such action may not be considered reasonable by the Labor Department unless direct contact with blood or other body fluids were required by the job.[54]

Job Stress

In recent years, the issue of job stress has captured the attention of many human resource managers and organizational researchers. The reason for their interest and concern is simple: excessive job stress is said to result in low productivity, increased absenteeism and turnover, and an assortment of medical ills including alcoholism, drug abuse, hypertension, and a host of cardiovascular problems.

Another reason for concern over job stress is that stress-related workers' compensation claims have risen dramatically in the last decade, with some awards to individual employees amounting to thousands of dollars. About 14 percent of all occupational disease claims were stress-related in 1988, up from 5 percent in 1980. Stress-related claims, on average, are estimated at $15,000, twice as much as those for employees with physical injuries.[55]

But what exactly is job stress? Unfortunately, job stress is not easy to define or measure. Various definitions of job stress include:[56]

"Stress is the force or stimulus acting upon the individual that results in a response of strain" (stimulus definition).

"Stress is the physical or psychological response an individual makes to an environmental stressor" (response definition).

"Stress is the consequence of the interaction between an environmental stimulus and

Bank of America: Policy on AIDS

Bank of America recognizes that employees with life-threatening illnesses including, but not limited to, cancer, heart disease, and AIDS may wish to continue to engage in as many of their normal pursuits as their condition allows, including work.

As long as these employees are able to meet acceptable performance standards, and medical evidence indicates that their conditions are not a threat to themselves or others, managers should be sensitive to their conditions and ensure that they are treated consistently with other employees.

At the same time, Bank of America seeks to provide a safe work environment for all employees and customers. Therefore, precautions should be taken to ensure that an employee's condition does not present a health and/or safety threat to other employees or customers.

Consistent with this concern for employees with life-threatening illnesses, Bank of America offers the following range of resources available through Personnel Relations:

- Management and employee education and information on terminal illness and specific life-threatening illnesses.
- Referral to agencies and organizations which offer supportive services for life-threatening illnesses.
- Benefit consultation to assist employees in effectively managing health, leave, and other benefits.

Guidelines

When dealing with situations involving employees with life-threatening illnesses, managers should:

1. Remember that an employee's health condition is personal and confidential, and reasonable precautions should be taken to protect information regarding an employee's health condition.
2. Contact Personnel Relations if you believe that you or other employees need information about terminal illness, or a specific life-threatening illness, or if you need further guidance in managing a situation that involves an employee with a life-threatening illness.
3. Contact Personnel Relations if you have any concern about the possible contagious nature of an employee's illness.
4. Contact Personnel Relations to determine if a statement should be obtained from the employee's attending physician that continued presence at work will pose no threat to the employee, co-workers

or customers. Bank of America reserves the right to require an examination by a medical doctor appointed by the company.

5. If warranted, make reasonable accommodation for employees with life-threatening illnesses consistent with the business needs of the division/unit.

6. Make a reasonable attempt to transfer employees with life-threatening illnesses who request a transfer and are experiencing undue emotional stress.

7. Be sensitive and responsive to co-workers' concerns, and emphasize employee education available through Personnel Relations.

8. Do not give special consideration beyond normal transfer requests for employees who feel threatened by a co-worker's life-threatening illness.

9. Be sensitive to the fact that continued employment for an employee with a life-threatening illness may sometimes be therapeutically important in the remission or recovery process, or may help to prolong that employee's life.

10. Encourage employees to seek assistance from established community support groups for medical treatment and counseling services. Information on these can be requested through Personnel Relations or Corporate Health.

Source: Allan Halcrow, "AIDS: The Corporate Response," *Personnel Journal* 65, no. 8 (August 1986): 123–27. Used by permission.

the idiosyncratic response of the individual'' (stimulus–response definition).

A working definition used by many researchers takes into account the unique personality of each individual and recognizes that stressful events may be physical or mental: ''stress is an adaptive response, mediated by individual characteristics and/or psychological processes, that is a consequence of any external action, situation, or event that places special physical and/or psychological demands upon a person.''

Finally, here is a practical definition: ''stress is the body's way of reacting to normal and abnormal occurrences in order to keep the body functioning smoothly and to protect it from harm.''[57]

How is the job stress measured? The accurate measurement of job stress is critical for researchers who desire to determine where and to what extent job stress exists in an organization. Measuring job stress is usually the first step in designing programs to reduce and control the problem.

The most common and accurate method of measuring job stress is a paper-and-pencil job stress survey. A job stress instrument requires employees to respond to questions about possible *stressors* in their jobs.

As an example of how the survey process works, the Armstrong Transfer & Storage Company suffered a serious problem with stress-related workers' compensation claims. The Memphis, Tennessee, company saw its claims rise from $93,000 in 1984 to $272,000 in 1986.

To determine the extent of work place stress, Armstrong's consulting firm gave questionnaires to its 500 employees. The results showed, for example, that employees were worried about worn-out loading equipment but failed to report it for fear that they would have to pay for it.

In response to the survey results, Armstrong's management repaired or replaced broken equipment and held weekly meetings to allow employees to air their grievances. Following the stress-reduction program, accidents fell from 65 to 10 per year, and a follow-up survey showed that perceived stress had dropped significantly.[58]

Without question, human resource managers should take the issue of work place stress seriously and implement programs to monitor and control it. In addition to the regular measurement and collection of job stress data, both organizational and personal strategies should be employed to control stress.[59]

Organizational strategies to control stress include:

- Preventive management. With this approach, managers identify potential problems that may become serious stressors and take steps to reduce or eliminate them. Surveys and employee/group interviews are important tools in this process.

- Changes in organizational climate. The term *organizational climate* refers to the elements in the work environment (penalties, rewards, leadership style, job satisfaction, etc.) and the employees' attitudes toward them. Changing the organizational climate to reduce stress involves identifying the ideal climate (from the employees' viewpoint) and working to create it.

- Management by objectives. Management by objectives (Chapter 6), a performance appraisal technique that identifies employee goals, clarifies roles and responsibilities, and strengthens communication, may also reduce stress by eliminating the uncertainty in critical aspects of the employee's job.

- The physical environment. Reducing stress in the physical environment requires management to undertake one of two different strategies (or both). The first strategy is to alter the physical environment (reduce noise, institute better control of temperature, etc). The second strategy is to protect employees from the environment (with improved safety equipment, etc.)

- Provide employee facilities. An increasing number of companies are providing recreation and physical fitness facilities to improve employee health and morale and to reduce stress. Many such facilities include exercise equipment and programs such as aerobics, weight training, racquet sports, and running. More sophisticated programs (the previously discussed wellness programs) include health testing and counseling by medical professionals.

In addition to organizational approaches, individuals should undertake their own stress management programs. Which strategies employees do select depends, of course, on their personal preferences, needs, and life-styles. Some personal approaches to stress reduction include:

- Meditation. While many forms of meditation exist, one of the more popular is transcendental meditation (TM), introduced in the United States by the Maharishi Mahesh Yogi around 1960. Using TM, the participant utters a mantra—a word or sound that the meditator concentrates on—to enter a state of mental and physical relaxation. While detractors of TM are easily found, research shows that meditation can reduce anxiety and improve work performance and job satisfaction.

- Exercise. One of the least expensive and potentially most effective stress-reduction strategies is exercise—jogging, racquet sports, fitness classes, bicycling, swimming, and so on. Research shows that a sound program of physical fitness can improve mental health as well as physical well-being.

Many other personal strategies exist for controlling stress. Some that have been reported in the literature and offered by students include proper diet, legal drug use, walking, the "primal scream," owning a pet, sleeping or napping, alcohol, and sex. Perhaps the formula for stress reduction is as simple as "do what works for you."

HEALTH-CARE COSTS

One of the most rapidly rising personnel costs is health care. K. Per Larson, health economist at the American Health Foundation and a nationally recognized expert on health care, identified the following reasons why health-care costs have risen far faster than any other personnel-related cost:[60]

Inflation   Even the lower inflation rates of the 1980s failed to cut the increases in health-care costs. In 1982 the consumer price index for all items was 292.4, but for a hospital room the index was 588.5. One essential problem has been the "pass-along" policies of the insurance industry. Increased competition, self-funding, and greater attention to the causes of cost increases can significantly lower premium costs.

Price   The same surgery can vary in price up to 400 percent. Medicare and Medicaid funds have encouraged large price increases in services for the poor and elderly. The price influenced by many factors, including the type of insurance an organization purchases.

Intensity   Supply determines demand, and medical professionals are prescribing more and more services. For example, the use of in-patient radiology and pathology increased six times from the late 1960s to the late 1970s, and elective surgery grew at a rate three times that of population growth. Screening of prescribed services beforehand and careful claims review can reduce system abuse.

Volume   The oversupply of hospital beds has increased patient stays. Prepaid group clients stay 30 percent fewer days for the same services, indicating that the average length of stay can be decreased. Employers can use peer review organizations (PROs) to decrease unnecessary extra days.

Population   The medically costly over-65 age group is growing at a tremendous rate.

Capital   Most of the nation's hospitals need reconstruction, and consequently tomorrow's medical costs will contain large increases in capital expenses.

Cost Shifting   The increase in employer and government cost-containment measures such as *diagnostic-related groups (DRGs),* which provide services for specified fees, will force hospitals to shift costs to other patients.

Health-care services for employees will continue to escalate into the 1990s. The possible savings through cost containment programs are substantial and will grow in future years. At the same time, the diversity of cost-containment strategies grows every day. Increasing employee deductibles and co-payments will likely reduce only coverage, not costs. Instead, employers must consider and carefully evaluate new providers' self-insurance and other alternatives to the traditional health insurance plan.

Employers can also significantly lower health care costs through employee awareness and incentives. For example, a study of two

---

PERSONNEL IN THE NEWS

How to Tell If You're Stressed—And What to Do About It

Only recently have consultants and psychologists begun to study workplace tension in depth. They've discovered the most trying professions are those involving danger and extreme pressure—or that carry responsibility without control. The symptoms of stress have been found to range from frequent illness to nervous tics and mental lapses. The most common tips for dealing with it focus on relaxation. But sometimes the only answer is to fight back—or walk away.

10 Tough Jobs	Warning Signs	Ways to Cope
Inner-city high-school teacher	Intestinal distress	Maintain a sense of humor
Police officer	Rapid pulse	Meditate
Miner	Frequent illness	Get a massage
Air-traffic controller	Insomnia	Exercise regularly
Medical intern	Persistent fatigue	Eat more sensibly
Stockbroker	Irritability	Limit intake of alcohol and caffeine
Journalist	Nail biting	
Customer service/ complaint department worker	Lack of concentration	Take refuge in family and friends
Waitress	Increased use of alcohol and drugs	Delegate responsibility
Secretary	Hunger for sweets	Quit

Source: Annetta Miller et al., "Stress on the Job." From NEWSWEEK, April 25, 1988, © 1988, Newsweek, Inc. All rights reserved. Reprinted by permission.

---

urban hospitals found that 78 percent of their admissions were related to personal habits that caused health problems that could have easily been avoided. Many typical group health-care plans encourage overuse because employees perceive that the benefits have been "earned" and therefore should be "spent." Employers can establish incentives to reward employees who do not spend their health care benefits. Examples of such incentives include:[61]

- Financial rebates to employees who have not used their health care benefits by the end of the year.
- Extra vacation time for employees who have not used their health care benefits, for participation in disease detection or wellness programs, for weight control, for smoking cessation, and so on.
- "Wellness" discounts in insurance rates for employees who meet certain standards, such as nonsmoking, measurable

physical fitness, percentage of body fat, good blood pressure, and so on.

- Lower co-insurance liability (the percentage of medical bills paid by the employee, usually 20 percent) for employees who choose out-patient surgical services, preadmission testing, home health services for shorter hospital stays, and so on.
- Lotteries for prizes such as paid vacation trips and appliances for employees who qualify by passing medical or dental tests.

Health Maintenance Organizations (HMOs)

Due to years of frustration with typical health insurance plans offered to employers and employees, in 1973 Congress passed the Health Maintenance Organization Act. The act sets standards for private individuals to qualify for federal financial assistance in the creation of a health maintenance organization (HMO). The federal government provides financial assistance to establish an HMO as a means of providing employees with an alternative to other health care delivery systems. Once HMOs are established, they should become self-sufficient through income received from the employees and employers they serve. Generally, HMOs provide employees with more comprehensive care, particularly preventive medicine, which includes normal visits to a physician. This care is not included in most private health-care plans. HMOs are designed to provide total health-care maintenance to the employee and family at a lower annual cost. At first, private insurance companies such as Blue Cross–Blue Shield and Delta Dental were not affected by HMOs. However, HMOs are steadily increasing and have made a significant impact in the employee health care field.

According to the 1973 act, employers with twenty-five or more employees who currently offer a medical benefit plan must offer the HMO option to employees if a federally approved HMO exists in the local area. Primarily a prepaid group health insurance plan, the HMO provides for the family's total health care. An HMO is a local hospital and clinic to which employees may take their families for routine checkups, shots, and treatment for injuries or illnesses. There are a number of advantages to the use of HMOs:

Fixed Costs An HMO provides a specified list of health services for a specified maximum annual cost; therefore, unexpected health costs to the employees are minimized. The services are generally more comprehensive than those offered by private health insurance plans.

Minimum Administration Costs The employers' formerly cumbersome and expensive claim-review process is replaced by a monthly check sent to the HMO. No other financial transactions or vouchers are necessary.

Standard of Quality HMO facilities and personnel are selected according to federal training and experience requirements.

Cost Savings One goal of the HMO act is to minimize the cost of hospital care, the most expensive part of any health-care program. HMO physicians have a financial stake in preventing unnecessary hospitalization costs, because every dollar spent on health care means a corresponding cost to them. One major American industry with 5 percent of its employees enrolled in HMOs is estimated to save about $2 million per year in health-care costs.[62]

Less Production Loss Since HMOs are open on evenings and weekends, employees are absent less frequently. And because HMOs strive to prevent disability and serious illnesses, employees incur fewer disability days.

Unique Services Many HMOs provide a wider range of health services than other health-care systems. HMOs may include a human relations department that provides health counseling for smoking withdrawal, weight reduction, abortion, and sterilization. That department may also provide education about diet, diabetes, and hypertension.[63] An exam-

ple of HMO services provided in Louisville, Kentucky, is shown in Figure 12–3.

HMOs are not without their disadvantages. The major problem in employees' ac-

Benefit	Maxicare	Humana Plan 100	Partners
Hospital Services (Inpatient)	100%	100% Covered at Network Hospitals	100% Covered at Network Hospitals
Inpatient Surgical Physician Services	100% with participating physicians	100% with participating physicians	100% with participating physicians
Outpatient Surgery	100% with participating physicians	100% with participating physicians	100% with participating physicians
Physicians Office Visits	100% with participating physicians	100% with participating physicians	100% with participating physicians
Psychiatry/Mental Nervous			
• Inpatient	10 days at 100% plus 20 days at 50%/yr.	80%; 30 days per calendar year.	20 days at 100%/yr.
•Outpatient	100%; 20 visits per year	30 visits/yr. with a $20 copay per visit.	20 visits/yr. with a $20 copay per visit
Alcohol/Drug Abuse			
•Inpatient	10 days at 100% plus 20 days at 50%/yr.	80%; 30 days per calendar year	100% detoxification plus 20 days at 100%/yr.
•Outpatient	100%; 10 visits/yr.	30 visits/yr. with a $20 copay per visit	20 visits/yr. with a $20 copay per visit
Prescription Drugs	$3 copay	$5 copay	$3 copay
Preexisting Condition Clause for New Employees	No	Yes	No
Pre Admission Review	No	Yes	Yes
Managed Second Surgical Opinion	No	Yes	Yes
Midyear Enrollment Allowed	No	Yes, with evidence of insurability	No
Durable Medical Equipment	Not Covered	80%	100%

FIGURE 12–3

An example of services offered employees at the University of Louisville by three different HMOs

ceptance of HMOs is the limited choice of physicians. Some HMOs require that employees and their families choose HMO member physicians. Many people feel more comfortable with physicians they have known for years and are relatively unwilling to change.

Cost is another factor. Many times the monthly HMO premium is more expensive than the cost of a private health insurance plan. While the annual HMO cost of health care to the employee might be less because it provides total health care, some employees

Benefit	Maxicare	Humana Plan 100	Partners
Physical Therapy	100%; 60 days per disability or illness per year	Inpatient—100% Outpatient—80%	Inpatient—100% Outpatient—80%; 2 month limitation per condition
Speech Therapy	100%; 60 days per disability or illness per year	Inpatient—100% Outpatient—80%	Inpatient—100% Outpatient—80% 2 month limitation per condition
Well Child Care	100%	100%	100%
Routine Physical Exams	100%	100%	100%
Emergency Room	Copay 50% not to exceed $25. No charge if admitted.	$25 copay in service area. Out-of-area 80% of first $2500, then 100%.	$25 copay (waived if admitted)
Ambulance	100%	80%	100%
Skilled Nursing Care Facility	100% for 100 days/yr.	100%; 60 days per calendar year	100%; 60 days/calendar year
Home Health Care	100%	100%; 60 days per calendar year	100%; 60 visits per calendar year
Major Medical			
•Deductible—Single Family	No Deductible No Deductible	No Deductible No Deductible	No Deductible No Deductible
•Annual individual out-of- pocket limit	N/A N/A	N/A N/A	N/A N/A
Individual Lifetime Maximum Benefit	Unlimited	Unlimited	Unlimited
Permanent Full Time Employee Cost Single Family	$ 0 $106.74	$ 0 $98.00	$ 0 $99.44

FIGURE 12–3
continued

Compensation and Health

think only of the higher monthly premium and are discouraged.

The lack of HMO facilities has also limited employee enrollment. Since HMOs are a relatively new concept in most cities, there are far fewer HMOs than physicians' offices and hospitals. Therefore, HMOs are less convenient because they may not be located in an employee's neighborhood. However, this situation is quickly changing as more HMOs are formed across the United States.

The Tax Equity and Fiscal Responsibility Act (TEFRA)

Designed to reduce the federal government's involvement in health care, the Tax Equity and Fiscal Responsibility Act (TEFRA) of 1982 provides fixed fees for Medicare and Medicaid patients. Fees for 467 diagnostic-related groups (DRGs) of illnesses were established. Previously, hospitals and physicians could provide unlimited services and the federal government would pay the bill under so-called fee-for-service basis. Under TEFRA, one fee is set for each DRG and the hospital will not be able to add additional fees.[64] The overall effect will be savings of billions of dollars per year to the federal government. But it is expected that most of those savings will be shifted to the private sector. Thus, employers have experienced even greater cost pressures from medical fields. The use of DRGs and other cost-containment measures by business and government have caused hospitals to examine the way in which they do business, as discussed in the feature Marketing Hospitals.

Preadmission Certification

Preadmission certification can be a successful means of reducing employee health-care costs. The process requires prior approval by the insurer or the employer any time an em-

ployee is hospitalized. Thus, if a physician prescribes hospitalization for a nonemergency, a medical review specialist evaluates the admission and the proposed course of treatment. Alternative, less costly methods of treatment may be suggested, such as outpatient care. The patient is given the right to make the final decision, but at least one company, Intracorp, has found that most employees prefer the less-costly outpatient services.[65]

Preferred Provider Organizations (PPOs)

A relatively new health-care cost-control strategy is the preferred provider organization (PPO), which relies on increased competition in the health-care industry. Strongly supported by President Reagan, PPOs involve employers, patients, hospitals and other health-care providers, and insurance carriers. The PPO procedure is simple. A contract is negotiated among the employer, insurance carrier, and various health-care providers, such as hospitals, physicians, and dentists. The contract provides for certain services to be delivered at a discount for a guaranteed increase in patients, with rapid repayment of all bills. Employees are given financial incentives to use those specific health-care providers but are not required to do so. This freedom of choice is critical to the success of the PPO. PPOs have generated a great deal of controversy. In general the advantages of PPOs include:[66]

- The operation is simple, with no claims or premium administration.
- There are no expensive start-up costs.
- Costs are reduced due to increased competition.
- Inducements such as annual physicals and wellness care can increase preventive health care for employees.

- Hospitals benefit from a better cash flow and a broader patient base.
- Physicians benefit from a broader patient base and elimination of claims handling and bad debts.

The disadvantages include:[67]

- One group of providers in an area can freeze out nonparticipating physicians and hospitals, reducing competition.
- Some PPOs may degenerate into marketing schemes to help hospitals fill empty beds and physicians increase their number of patients.
- PPOs do not address the causes of high health care costs; in fact, they encourage more health care usage.
- As PPOs become common, their discounts will become the norm and no real savings will occur.

SAFETY

The U.S. Bureau of Labor Statistics reports that each year one in every eleven workers experiences a job-related injury or illness, which translates into 9.4 injuries or illnesses per 100 full-time workers.[68] Many union leaders and activist groups have criticized the federal government of inaction in the area of employee health and safety. They have been concerned about *safety hazards,* those aspects of the work place that can cause burns, electrical shock, cuts, broken bones, loss of limbs or eyesight, or other impairment of the employee's physical well-being. Of equal concern have been *health hazards,* those aspects of the work place that can impair an employee's general physical, mental, or emotional well-being, usually including toxic chemicals, dust, noise, or other physical or biological agents. Health hazards cause sicknesses or illnesses that may take a long time to appear. Although

states have long had various safety and health laws, the federal government did not establish regulations to protect employees until 1970.

The need for employee safety was first recognized during the Civil War when industries began to manufacture war materials at a fast pace. Rapid industrial expansion forced employers to disregard employee safety in an effort to maintain high output and low cost. In 1869 the first safety law, the Coal Mine Safety Law, was passed. In 1908 the federal government realized the need for workers' compensation for federal employees. The National Safety Council was formed in 1926 to compile injury and accident statistics involving the work place. Industrial and nonagricultural jobs increased rapidly from the 1920s through the 1960s; the U.S. Department of Labor estimated in 1969 that out of every four workers, one would be affected by an injury or illness before retirement.

The U.S. Public Health Service has estimated that 390,000 new cases of occupational disease appear annually. As many as 100,000 deaths occur each year as a direct or indirect result of occupational disease. Heart disease, a leading cause of death, may well be related to hazardous working environments. Cancer is another leading cause of death in the United States; research in the United Kingdom indicates that more than 80 percent of cancer may be environmentally caused, although how much is due to occupational hazards is not known. Occupational illnesses are concentrated in mining, construction, transportation, and heavy manufacturing; most injuries also occur in these industries.[69]

The U.S. Department of Labor, Bureau of Labor Statistics defines *occupational injuries* on OSHA Form 200 as:

> Any injury such as a cut, fracture, sprain, amputation, etc. which results from a work accident or from an exposure involving a single

accident in the work environment. Note: Conditions resulting from animal bites, such as insect or snake bites, or from a one-time exposure to chemicals are considered to be injuries. And *occupational illness* is any abnormal condition or disorder other than one resulting from an occupational injury, caused by an exposure to environmental factors associated with a person's employment. It includes acute and chronic illnesses or diseases which may be caused by inhalation, absorption, congestion, or direct contact.

The following categories of occupational illnesses and disorders are utilized to classify recordable illnesses:

Code

7a. Occupational Skin Diseases or Disorders
Examples: Contact dermatitis, eczema, or rash caused by primary irritants and sensitizers or poisonous plants; oil acne; chrome ulcers; chemical burns or inflammations; etc.

7b. Dust Diseases of the Lungs (Pneumoconioses)
Examples: Silicosis, asbestosis, coal worker's pneumoconiosis, byssinosis, siderosis, and other pneumoconioses.

7c. Respiratory Conditions Due to Toxic Agents
Examples: Pneumonitis, pharyngitis, rhinitis or acute congestion due to chemicals, dusts, gases, or fumes; farmer's lung; etc.

7d. Poisoning (Systemic Effect of Toxic Materials)
Examples: Poisoning by lead, mercury, cadmium, arsenic, or other metals; poisoning by carbon monoxide, hydrogen sulfide, or other gases; poisoning by benzol, carbon tetrachloride, or other organic solvents; poisoning by insecticide sprays such as parathion, lead arsenate; poisoning by other chemicals such as formaldehyde, plastics, and resins; etc.

7e. Disorders Due to Physical Agents (Other than Toxic Materials)
Examples: Heatstroke, sunstroke, heat exhaustion, and other effects of environmental heat; freezing, frostbite, and effects of exposure to low temperatures; caisson disease; effects of ionizing radiation (isotopes, X rays, radium); effects of nonionizing radiation (welding flash, ultraviolet rays, microwaves, sunburn); etc.

7f. Disorders Associated with Repeated Trauma
Examples: Noise-induced hearing loss; synovitis, tenosynovitis, and bursitis; Raynaud's phenomena; and other conditions due to repeated motion, vibration, or pressure.

7g. All Other Occupational Illnesses
Examples: Anthrax, brucellosis, infectious hepatitis, malignant and benign tumors, food poisoning, histoplasmosis, coccidioidomycosis, etc.

Occupational Safety and Health Administration (OSHA)

In 1970 Congress passed the Williams-Steiger Occupational Safety and Health Act (Public Law 91-596). The Williams–Steiger Act was the culmination of years of effort by employee groups, unions, and the National Safety Council to provide safety in the work place. The act established the *Occupational Safety and Health Administration,* commonly referred to as *OSHA,* within the U.S. Department of Labor, and the *National Institute for Occupational Safety and Health (NIOSH)* within the U.S. Department of Health, Education, and Welfare (now Health and Human Services). NIOSH conducts research and gathers data and statistics relating to the occupational safety and health of employees; it helps determine standards for safety within the work place by working closely with OSHA.

The Williams–Steiger Act is somewhat unique because it not only provides federal occupational safety standards through OSHA but also allows states to administer their own occupational safety and health programs. That provision was a compromise between those who believe that employee safety is a national concern and those who believe that the federal government is infringing on states' rights. A state-run OSHA program must receive federal approval and include federal safety requirements. Approximately twenty-four states had occupational safety programs by the early 1980s.

The 1970 act requires employers to furnish working environments free from recognized hazards that may cause injury or illness to employees. Employers are required to comply with safety and health standards created by the act or by states that administer their own programs. Employees are also required to comply with health and safety standards and regulations. Laws are enforced through the U.S. Department of Labor or state labor OSHA agencies or both. Regulations cover the use of toxic chemicals; levels of dust, fumes, and noise; the safe use of equipment and tools; and safe work procedures. A sample of OSHA safety and health regulations is shown in Figure 12–4.

Enforcement is provided by inspectors entering the work place and determining whether employers have violated safety standards. Employers are required to allow the inspectors to enter their work places, answer questions, and provide requested data. If the inspector finds a violation of a safety standard, a written citation is issued; inspectors have the authority to determine whether the employer should be fined or warned and given time to correct the unsafe situation. Employers may be assessed a civil penalty of up to $10,000, a criminal penalty of up to $20,000, or a maximum of one year in prison. In most states, however, inspectors try to work with

FIGURE 12–4

Sample OSHA safety and health regulations (Source: Occupational Safety and Health Standards for the Construction Industry, *Federal Register*, 39, [June 24, 1974], p. 22799)

§1926.300 General requirements

(a) *Condition of tools.* All hand and power tools and similar equipment, whether furnished by the employer or the employee, shall be maintained in a safe condition.

(b) *Guarding.* (1) When power operated tools are designed to accommodate guards, they shall be equipped with such guards when in use.

(2) Belts, gears, shafts, pulleys, sprockets, spindles, drums, fly wheels, chains, or other reciprocating, rotating or moving parts of equipment shall be guarded if such parts are exposed to contact by employees or otherwise create a hazard. Guarding shall meet the requirements as set forth in American National Standards Institute, B15.1-1953 (R1958), Safety Code for Mechanical Power-Transmission Apparatus.

§1926.301 Hand tools.

(a) Employers shall not issue or permit the use of unsafe hand tools.

(b) Wrenches, including adjustable, pipe, end, and socket wrenches shall not be used when jaws are sprung to the point that slippage occurs.

(c) Impact tools, such as drift pins, wedges, and chisels, shall be kept free of mushroomed heads.

(d) The wooden handles of tools shall be kept free of splinters or cracks and shall be kept tight in the tool.

employers to correct the unsafe conditions rather than using penalties. Inspectors may find as many as thirty or forty violations within a work site that has not previously been checked. Thus, the inspector could issue several thousand dollars in fines or instruct the employer to make alterations in order that the standards be met within a reasonable amount of time. Returning to the work site, often without warning, inspectors make sure that those changes have been made. Employers have the right to appeal a citation or fine.

OSHA Requirements   In order to comply with the provisions of the Williams–Steiger Act, employers primarily must meet all state safety and health standards and must prepare and retain certain types of records. Employers should contact the local safety and health office for information regarding applicable safety and health standards and regulations. Almost all private businesses involved in interstate commerce are required to adhere to OSHA regulations. OSHA record keeping requirements include:

Log and summary of occupational injuries and illnesses (OSHA form 200)   Within six working days after learning of the occurrence of each recordable injury or illness, the employer must record it in a log. The log is kept at the place of employment or at another location if updated to within forty-five days. OSHA Form 200 is shown in Figure 12–5. Logs must be maintained and retained for five years following the end of the calendar year to which they apply. Logs must be available for inspection. A copy of the totals and other information for a year must be posted at each establishment in the place or places where notices to employees are customarily posted. This copy must be posted no later than February 1 and must remain in place until March 1.

Supplementary record of occupational injuries and illnesses (OSHA form 101)   The employer must complete this form or an approved substitute state form for each injury or illness within six working days after notification of the incident. OSHA Form 101 is shown in Figure 12–6. The supplementary record is the detailed report of each injury or illness that is recorded on OSHA Form 200. The supplementary record must be maintained by the employer for five years following the year in which it occurs.

Annual occupational injuries and illnesses survey (OSHA form 200-S)   Upon request the employer must provide the U.S. Department of Labor a completed survey of a year's injuries and illnesses. The report is mandatory and must be returned to the Bureau of Labor Statistics. The survey only requests information contained in OSHA Form 200, which the employer keeps. The information is used to compile occupational statistics.

The record-keeping provisions of OSHA have sometimes been criticized by employers as more red tape required by the government. In reality, the record-keeping requirements are rather simple and straightforward.

OSHA Records   To illustrate an example of OSHA record keeping, assume that Elwood College, a hypothetical institution of higher education, experienced five injuries or illnesses during 1988. The OSHA forms that Elwood College is required to use are Form 200 (Figure 12–5) and Form 101 (Figure 12–6). A brief description of each of the injuries or illnesses is logged by the college. The following are the injuries and illnesses Elwood College logged in 1988:

January 7, 1988   Bill Hailey, a maintenance engineer in the security division, suffered a severe back strain while moving desks within the classroom building. An attending physician advised Hailey to stay home for five working days following the accident. After returning to work, Hailey was not allowed to perform many of his normal, routine functions, which required lifting or bending his back or arms. After two weeks, at Hailey's request he was transferred to desk security, which required far less physical effort.

February 8, 1988 Mary Richards, an administrative assistant in the central office, dropped her IBM Selectric typewriter while moving it from one desk to another. The typewriter landed partially on the desk and partially on Richards's left hand, causing multiple fractures. The Metropolitan Emergency Medical Service took her to the hospital to repair her hand. Richards was kept in the hospital for two days for observation and then released but not allowed to use her left hand for typing or other office purposes for almost six weeks following the accident.

June 9, 1988 Ned Oaks, an assistant professor at the college, went to the health clinic with severe dizziness and headaches. Oaks had been exposed to the toxic fluid writers used in place of chalk since new writing surfaces had been installed in the classrooms. After weeks of hospital tests, it was determined that Oaks should be kept in a carefully maintained environment for at least a year to restore his health. Further tests determined that Oaks should live in a southern, dry climate to help speed his recovery. Thus, Oaks secured a teaching position at an Arizona university.

September 1, 1988 When Joan Goldsmith accidentally dropped a lit cigarette into a trash can filled with paper and other flammable materials it instantly caught fire. Goldsmith, a clerk in the central office, received second-degree burns on her right arm and hand while trying to put out the fire. As a result of the injury, she missed four days of work; after returning to her job, she could not use her right hand completely for over three weeks.

November 7, 1988 Sandy Landon, an accountant in the payroll office, experienced a severe skin rash on both arms and hands. Landon developed the rash while changing the copying machine. A clinic physician concluded that the rash was due to a reaction to the cleaning fluid. Landon was able to return to work the next day.

Injury and Illness Rates OSHA statistics help employers determine how safe their work place is in comparison to others of similar size within their industry. By compiling injury and illness rates reported by organizations across the United States, OSHA establishes average incident rates for different industries and various-sized businesses. Some industries have higher average rates of injuries and illnesses than others due to the nature of the work. For employers, employees, and other interested parties to determine the relative safety of employees in a particular work environment, they must be able to compare the organization's incident rate with that of similar organizations. Figure 12–7 illustrates how easily employers can determine an incident rate for their own organizations. The data necessary to determine the rate are compiled on OSHA Form 200.[70]

Assuming 150 employees working fifty forty-hour weeks, the incident rate for hypothetical Elwood College would be computed using the information in Figure 12–4 and the formula in Figure 12–7:

$$5 \times 200,000 \div 300,000 = 3.33$$

After comparing the 3.33 incident rate with that of other colleges of the same size, Elwood College would discover that it has close to the average incident rate.

NOTE:	This form is required by Public Law 91-596 and must be kept in the establishment for *5 years.* Failure to maintain and post can result in the issuance of citations and assessment of penalties. *(See posting requirements on the other side of form.)*	RECORDABLE CASES: You are required to record information about every occupational **death**; every nonfatal occupational **illness**; and those nonfatal occupational **injuries** which involve one or more of the following: loss of consciousness, restriction of work or motion, transfer to another job, or medical treatment (other than first aid). *(See definitions on the other side of form.)*

Case or File Number	Date of Injury or Onset of Illness	Employee's Name	Occupation	Department	Description of Injury or Illness
Enter a nonduplicating number which will facilitate comparisons with supplementary records.	Enter Mo./day.	Enter first name or initial, middle initial, last name.	Enter regular job title, not activity employee was performing when injured or at onset of illness. In the absence of a formal title, enter a brief description of the employee's duties.	Enter department in which the employee is regularly employed or a description of normal workplace to which employee is assigned, even though temporarily working in another department at the time of injury or illness.	Enter a brief description of the injury or illness and indicate the part or parts of body affected. Typical entries for this column might be: Amputation of 1st joint right forefinger; Strain of lower back; Contact dermatitis on both hands; Electrocution—body.
(A)	(B)	(C)	(D)	(E)	(F)
					PREVIOUS PAGE TOTALS ⟶
1	1-7-88	Bill Hailey	Maintenance Engineer	Security	Back strain
2	2-8-88	Mary Richards	Administrative Assistant	Office	Multiple fracture of left hand
3	6-9-88	Ned Oaks	Professor	Faculty	Systemic poisoning
4	9-1-88	Joan Goldsmith	Clerk	Office	Second degree burns on right arm and hand
5	11-7-88	Sandy Landon	Accountant	Payroll	Skin rash on arms and hands
					TOTALS (Instructions on other side of form.) ⟶

OSHA No. 200

FIGURE 12–5
OSHA Form 200, used to log occupational injuries and illnesses

U.S. Department of Labor

Elwood College   For Calendar Year 19 88   Page ___ of ___

Company Name

Establishment Name: Academia City, U. S. A.

Establishment Address

Form Approved
O.M.B. No. 44R 1453

Extent of and Outcome of INJURY						Type, Extent of, and Outcome of ILLNESS												
Fatalities	Nonfatal Injuries					Type of Illness							Fatalities	Nonfatal Illnesses				
Injury Related	Injuries With Lost Workdays				Injuries Without Lost Workdays	CHECK Only One Column for Each Illness (See other side of form for terminations or permanent transfers.)							Illness Related	Illnesses With Lost Workdays				Illnesses Without Lost Workdays
Enter DATE of death. Mo./day/yr.	Enter a CHECK if injury involves days away from work, or days of restricted work activity, or both.	Enter a CHECK if injury involves days away from work.	Enter number of DAYS away from work.	Enter number of DAYS of restricted work activity.	Enter a CHECK if no entry was made in columns 1 or 2 but the injury is recordable as defined above.	Occupational skin diseases or disorders	Dust diseases of the lungs	Respiratory conditions due to toxic agents	Poisoning (systemic effects of toxic materials)	Disorders due to physical agents	Disorders associated with repeated trauma	All other occupational illnesses	Enter DATE of death. Mo./day/yr.	Enter a CHECK if illness involves days away from work, or days of restricted work activity, or both.	Enter a CHECK if illness involves days away from work.	Enter number of DAYS away from work.	Enter number of DAYS of restricted work activity.	Enter a CHECK if no entry was made in columns 8 or 9.
(1)	(2)	(3)	(4)	(5)	(6)	(7a)	(7b)	(7c)	(7d)	(7e)	(7f)	(7g)	(8)	(9)	(10)	(11)	(12)	(13)
	√	√	5	14														
	√	√	2	42														
	√								√					√	√	240	0	
	√	√	4	21														
						√												√
0	4	3	11	77	0	1	0	0	1	0	0	0	0	1	1	240	0	1

INJURIES   ILLNESSES

Certification of Annual Summary Totals By John A. Friend   Title Personnel Director   Date 1-27-88

FOLD

OSHA No. 200   **POST ONLY THIS PORTION OF THE LAST PAGE NO LATER THAN FEBRUARY 1.**

FIGURE 12–6

OSHA Form 101, used for each illness or injury

OSHA No. 101
Case or File No. _____

Form approved
OMB No. 44R 1453

Supplementary Record of Occupational Injuries and Illnesses

EMPLOYER
1. Name _____
2. Mail address _____
   (No. and street)   (City or town)   (State)
3. Location, if different from mail address _____

INJURED OR ILL EMPLOYEE
4. Name _____ Social Security No. _____
   (First name)   (Middle name)   (Last name)
5. Home address _____
   (No. and street)   (City or town)   (State)
6. Age _____   7. Sex: Male _____ Female _____ (Check one)
8. Occupation _____
   (Enter regular job title, *not* the specific activity he was performing at time of injury.)
9. Department _____
   (Enter name of department or division in which the injured person is regularly employed, even
   though he may have been temporarily working in another department at the time of injury.)

THE ACCIDENT OR EXPOSURE TO OCCUPATIONAL ILLNESS
10. Place of accident or exposure _____
    (No. and street)   (City or town)   (State)
    If accident or exposure occurred on employer's premises, give address of plant or establishment in which
    it occurred. Do not indicate department or division within the plant or establishment. If accident oc-
    curred outside employer's premises at an identifiable address, give that address. If it occurred on a pub-
    lic highway or at any other place which cannot be identified by number and street, please provide place
    references locating the place of injury as accurately as possible.
11. Was place of accident or exposure on employer's premises? _____ (Yes or No)
12. What was the employee doing when injured? _____
    (Be specific. If he was using tools or equipment or handling material,
    _____
    name them and tell what he was doing with them.)
    _____
13. How did the accident occur? _____
    (Describe fully the events which resulted in the injury or occupational illness. Tell what
    happened and how it happened. Name any objects or substances involved and tell how they were involved. Give
    full details on all factors which led or contributed to the accident. Use separate sheet for additional space.)

OCCUPATIONAL INJURY OR OCCUPATIONAL ILLNESS
14. Describe the injury or illness in detail and indicate the part of body affected. _____
    (e.g.: amputation of right index finger
    _____
    at second joint; fracture of ribs; lead poisoning; dermatitis of left hand, etc.)
15. Name the object or substance which directly injured the employee. (For example, the machine or thing
    he struck against or which struck him; the vapor or poison he inhaled or swallowed; the chemical or ra-
    diation which irritated his skin; or in cases of strains, hernias, etc., the thing he was lifting, pulling, etc.)
    _____
    _____
16. Date of injury or initial diagnosis of occupational illness _____
    (Date)
17. Did employee die? _____ (Yes or No)

OTHER
18. Name and address of physician _____
19. If hospitalized, name and address of hospital _____
    _____
    Date of report _____ Prepared by _____
    Official position _____

FIGURE 12–7

Computing incident rate (Source: *An OSHA Guide to Evaluating Your Firm's Injury and Illness Experience,* 1974, U.S. Department of Labor, 1976. Report 478, pp. 2 and 3).

To compute an incidence rate:

A = Number of injuries and illnesses occurring during a calendar year (obtained from OSHA Form 100 or OSHA Form 102).

B = Number of hours worked by all employees during the year.

$$\text{Incidence Rate} = \frac{\text{Number of Injuries and Illnesses} \times 200{,}000}{\text{Employee Hours Worked}}$$

$$= \frac{A \times 200{,}000}{B}$$

Incidence Rate = Number of Injuries and Illnesses per 100 employees working 40 hours per week for 50 weeks per year.

OSHA Penalties Employers in various industries know that OSHA means business. As an example, in 1979 Texaco, Inc., agreed to pay an OSHA penalty that was a record at the time. Texaco, OSHA, and the Chemical and Atomic Workers Union agreed on a payment of $169,400 as a penalty for OSHA citations issued at Texaco's Port Arthur, Texas, refinery. OSHA had originally recommended penalties totaling $394,000. The citations included six willful, ninety-nine serious, and seven repeated serious violations. A Texaco official stated that payment of the fine was not admission of negligence or a violation of the law in regard to a fire in which eight workers died.[71]

In some instances OSHA recommends criminal prosecution. OSHA law provides that employers who willfully violate standards can be fined not more than $10,000 or be imprisoned for not more than six months if that violation caused an employee's death. In two cases involving workers' deaths, for example, OSHA recommended criminal prosecution. One case involved an explosion at a chemical plant owned by the Rollins Environmental Services Corporation in Bridgeport, New Jersey. That explosion killed six workers and resulted in serious injuries to others. The second case involved an employee who was crushed by an electrical tractor in the Lake County, Indiana, Number 2 Tin Mill of the Youngstown Sheet and Tube Company. Dr. Eula Bingham, who headed OSHA at the time, noted that she was making the announcement of criminal prosecution in the two cases to demonstrate to employers that OSHA will closely examine employees' deaths to determine if they resulted from employers' willful disregard of job safety and health rules.[72]

OSHA Problems OSHA has received numerous criticisms since its inception in 1970. Employers cite the high expenses of meeting regulations and possible lack of actual benefits to employees. The required paperwork has been criticized as being unnecessary and unwieldy. One of the most severe criticisms came from a two-year congressional study of federal regulatory agencies released in 1979. The study concluded that OSHA "has been, at best, a disappointment" and suggested legislation requiring economic impact statements from OSHA in order to determine if OSHA regulations are desirable when costs are considered. The authors of the report, from the John F. Kennedy School of Government at Harvard University, noted that OSHA's impact on injuries has been minimal. The study's major criticism noted that while human life and health are priceless entities that should not be traded off against dollars, economic comparisons, distasteful as they may be, are inevitable.[73] A thorough study of OSHA citation activities from 1971 to 1976 led to the conclusion that firms with 200 or more employees did have a substantial reduction in days lost due to injury as a result of OSHA.[74]

OSHA has tried to streamline its rules and regulations. In 1978, "nuisance or nitpicking standards" were deleted from the regulations, including 607 general industry standards, 321 special standards, and about 10 percent of the word volume. A "verticalization" project also consolidated rules for construction. For example, the rules for electrical codes shrank from 300,000 to 30,000 words.[75]

Right-to-Know Regulations

OSHA in 1986 began enforcement of a new set of rules formally termed *hazard communication* but popularly known as *right-to-know*. Unlike most OSHA regulations, right-to-know only requires that employers provide employees with information. Specifically, workers are given the right to know what hazardous sub-

Rape Prevention at DuPont

In 1986 after two years of planning and a half million dollars development cost DuPont Company, the U.S. chemical giant, initiated a new employee program: the DuPont Personal Safety/Rape Prevention Program. "The fact that we're bringing more and more women into our workforce, many of them in what have not traditionally been positions for women, prompted us to sit down and ask ourselves, 'Are we really doing what we can to protect these women?'" The answer was, No! DuPont has a long tradition of being safety-conscious in the work place. However, it recognized that now women are being sent out into the field selling agricultural products or working late shifts.

The DuPont program is comprised of four training programs:

- *Rape Prevention Workshop.* A video presentation illustrates five common rape situations which could be avoided. It also teaches self-defense techniques.
- *Manager's Workshop.* Teaches managers their role in assisting rape victims. Confidentiality is stressed.
- *Facilitator Training.* Employee volunteers teaching the trainers all about prevention, aftercare, etc.
- *Personal Safety Meeting.* Open meeting designed to teach employees how to avoid dangerous situations. The meeting uses a video and a handbook, "No, Not Me."

The program also provides a rape crisis hotline, legal assistance for victims, and full disability benefits up to six months.

Source: Adapted from Allan Halcrow, "Are We Really Doing What We Can to Protect These Women?" *Personnel Journal* 65, no. 9 (September 1986): 12–14. Used by permission.

stances they may encounter on the job. Common examples of over 1,000 hazardous substances include asbestos, cyanide, polychlorinated biphenyls (PCBs), gasoline, acetone, and rosin core solder. The regulations do not require employer testing or study of hazardous substances. Nor do they include "mixed articles" such as automobile tires or vinyl upholstery, which contain hazardous substances that are not released in normal use. The regulations generally apply only when hazardous substances are known to be present in the work place and employees can be exposed due to routine operations or a foreseeable emergency. Federal and state hazard communication standards generally require:[76]

- Material safety data sheets (MSDSs) must be maintained for every hazardous substance that employees may be exposed to or handle.

- MSDSs must be kept readily accessible by all affected employees. Many employers keep the MSDSs in three-ring binders and include them in standard operating procedures.
- Labeling must be provided for all types of containers of hazardous substances, including barrels, bags, boxes, cans, cylinders, drums, and tanks.
- A written hazard communication program for employee information and training must be developed. The program should begin with a list of all known hazardous substances in the work place. Employees should receive training in safe procedures, as well as methods of exposure detection such as distinctive odors, gases, and appearances.[77]

Accident Prevention

The number and severity of job-related accidents are not minimized by simply meeting OSHA standards. The National Safety Council advises employers to use the "three E's" to prevent accidents: engineering, education, and enforcement of safety rules.[77] Designing safe working conditions is the task of safety engineers, who, for example, design a work station to include adequate lighting, the right tools or equipment for the job, required safety guards and proper electrical grounding for tools and equipment, adequate ventilation, safe storage and usage of chemicals, paints, and so on, and the wearing of safety shoes, clothing, or goggles when necessary. The proper safety training of new employees or all employees given new tools, chemicals, or equipment is a critical part of accident prevention. An employee who is never shown the safe method of operating a machine or pouring a dangerous liquid cannot be expected to

avoid an accident. Safety programs for employees can effectively reduce accidents. Such programs often offer monetary rewards, prizes, or paid leave for employees or departments who work without an accident for a specified number of days. The enforcement of safety rules is a critical aspect of accident prevention. Yet, unfortunately, supervisors may be hesitant to discipline employees for not wearing safety goggles or for storing chemicals carelessly. Strong top management commitment to and daily emphasis on employee safety can effectively reinforce strong safety discipline.

INTERNATIONAL HRM: HEALTH AND SAFETY

Along with Western Europe, Canada, and Japan, U.S. companies put a tremendous emphasis on the health and welfare of their employees. As noted earlier, it is proving to be good business. Unfortunately, most businesses in underdeveloped countries (as well as some in affluent nations) have not or cannot establish employee benefits and programs that promote health and fitness.

On the other hand, most countries do have laws and regulatory agencies that protect workers from hazardous work environments. U.S. firms planning to build manufacturing facilities abroad must become familiar with the myriad regulations that exist and the cultural expectations of the labor force. Manufacturing facilities in particular, where hazardous work is more common, should be designed and built to meet the expectations of the local work force—not necessarily those of American management. Ignorance of local customs can be disastrous.

Here is one tragic example of what might happen when an overseas plant is built without serious consideration of the local culture. In 1984, a tragic accident occurred at the

Union Carbide pesticide plant in Bhopal, India. A single faulty valve poisoned the air, causing thousands of people to die or suffer serious injury. Union Carbide had built the plant, with an expectation that the managers, supervisors, and employees who worked there would behave like American workers. Consequently, a great deal of money was spent on training the workers about safety procedures. After the disaster that took thousands of lives, it was reported that one on-duty supervisor was informed of the lethal chemical leak during his tea break. He said he would follow it up after he finished his break, which is ''a perfectly reasonable expectation *in India,* where a very high value is placed upon human relations and much less is placed on the workings of machinery.''[78] The lesson U.S. firms must learn is to include the idiosyncrasies of the local culture, as well as the politics and laws, in the design and management of an overseas facility.

CONCLUSIONS AND APPLICATIONS

- Increased foreign competition, rising costs, and the need to increase employee efficiency are major reasons that employers are developing new methods of reducing health-care costs. Approaches to the problem include self-insurance, HMOs, DRGs, PPOs, and preadmission certification. Other approaches, including wellness, physical-fitness, smoking-cessation, and employee-assistance programs, stress

better overall employee health as preventive cost-containment measures.

- Employee assistance programs can help employees overcome serious problems that affect productivity. Employers can retain highly skilled and valuable employees who suffer from alcoholism, drug abuse, depression, family problems, or other common crises. But normal disciplinary procedures should be followed when an EAP is provided. Employee participation may be strongly encouraged, but ultimately the employee must voluntarily seek help.

- Most employers must offer employees the option of joining an HMO if group health insurance is offered. HMOs generally provide the employee with a comprehensive health-care alternative and may reduce employees' total annual health-care costs.

- OSHA regulations require employees to keep records of employee injuries and illnesses. Employers should ensure that relevant OSHA regulations are met. Organizations can benefit from a safe work place through reduced insurance premiums, fewer lost worker hours, and fewer accident claims.

- Policies on smoking in the workplace, drug usage, and AIDS are being developed by many employers as these issues generate greater interest in our society. However, while more employers are adopting a smoking ban and testing employees for illegal drugs, few are adopting an AIDS policy.

CASE STUDY
Family Health Insurance

Laura Gains is a confused employee. Washington Electric Company, her employer, is offering a local HMO as an alternative to the company's health insurance plan. Gains attended the employees' meeting, where an HMO official explained the medical services and costs. The official outlined many services, such as dental checkups and flu shots, which would be provided at little cost. Gains knows she spends over $200 a year in these areas alone. The HMO is located about two miles from Gains' home and is always open—something Gains thinks would add to her use of the services. The company will provide the same dollars for the HMO as it currently does for the employees' health insurance plan. Gains, however, is bothered by the lack of choice of physicians and dentists, though she is not really attached to the ones she is going to now. During this month Gains must decide whether to change to the HMO for at least a year or else wait until next year's sign-up period.

A widow, Gains is the sole support of her three daughters—Shari, age 9; Amber, age 7; and Tracy, age 4. In the past, her annual medical expenses, have often exceeded $3,000. Whereas the company's health insurance plan does not cover most of her medical expenses, the HMO would cover most of her expenses; however, it would cost Gains $60 per month more in premiums. Gains' salary is about $35,000 per year. She prepares her own tax forms and always itemizes deductions.

Questions

1. How should Gains compare the plans? What quantitative criteria should be considered?
2. Exactly what is the purpose of family health-care insurance?
3. What additional information would help Gains?

EXPERIENTIAL EXERCISE
What Do You *Really* Know About AIDS?

Purpose

To determine what you know and don't know about the deadly disease AIDS and to emphasize work place issues.

The Task

Complete the following quiz about AIDS. Following the quiz, your instructor will lead a discussion about your answers and about work place issues concerning AIDS.

1. What does the acronym AIDS stand for?
2. How many people in the United States have AIDS?
3. Can a person carry the AIDS virus and not actually have AIDS?
4. How is AIDS transmitted?
5. Does federal legislation exist to protect employees or applicants with AIDS?
6. Are there any state or local laws that protect employees or applicants with AIDS?
7. Is there a test for AIDS?
8. Most companies have a policy on AIDS. True or false?

9. What rights does the organization have in managing an employee with AIDS? That is, under what conditions could an employer terminate an employee with AIDS without fear of legal problems?
10. Should an organization have a policy on AIDS?

KEY TERMS AND CONCEPTS

AIDS in the workplace

EAP

Health program manager

Health hazards

HMO

Log and summary of occupational injuries and illnesses

Job stress

Kemper, *Management Guide on Alcoholism*

NIOSH

No-smoking policies

Occupational illness

Occupational injury

OSHA

PFP

PPO

Problem drinkers

Right-to-know regulations

Safety hazards

TEFRA

Wellness program

REVIEW QUESTIONS

1. Should an employer have an EAP? How should it be established?
2. How can wellness programs be cost effective?
3. Why must employers be interested in HMOs, PPOs, PFPs, and self-insurance?
4. How can an employer meet right-to-know OSHA regulations?
5. When is the problem drinker cured?
6. What are typical work-related dilemmas that the alcoholic must face?

DISCUSSION QUESTIONS

1. An increasing number of employees are turning to a variety of mood-altering substances to help them through each day. In most instances, union workers can be dismissed for drinking or taking drugs on the job. If your nonunion company has a pleasant, nonstressful environment, would it be justified in dismissing substance abusers rather than spending money on rehabilitation?
2. What is a fair and responsible policy on smoking in the work place?
3. Why are so many employees suffering from occupational illnesses that have been traditional in certain industries for many years?
4. Government officials frequently waver in their enforcement of OSHA. What influences have caused government officials to relax safety rules at times and to create more stringent regulations at others?

5. If supervisors warn their employees about the possible health hazards connected with their jobs and supply safety equipment to the employees, is the company responsible if employees do not use the safety equipment?

6. How can an employer minimize job stress in the work place?

ENDNOTES

1. John Kondrasuk, "Company Physical Fitness Programs: Salvation or Fad?" *Personnel Administrator 25,* no. 11 (November 1980): 47–50.

2. Stephan W. Hartman and Janet Cozzetto, "Wellness in the Workplace," *Personnel Administrator* 29, no. 8 (August 1984): 108–17.

3. *Your Guide to Wellness at the Worksite* (Washington, DC: Health Insurance Association of America, 1983), p. 3.

4. Hartman and Cozzetto, "Wellness in the Workplace," pp. 108–09.

5. Lynn E. Densford, "Wellness Programs Show Healthy Returns," *Employee Benefit News* 1, no. 8 (November–December 1987): 17–19.

6. "Reduced Costs, Increased Worker Production Are Rationale for Tax-favored Corporate Fitness Plans," *Employee Benefit Plan Review* 37 (November 1983): 21.

7. Charles A. Berry, *An Approach to Good Health for Employees and Reduced Health Care Costs for Industry* (Washington, DC: Health Insurance Association of America, 1981), p. 9.

8. Jane Daniel, "An Offer Your Doctor Can't Refuse," *American Health* (November–December 1982): 82.

9. *Your Guide to Wellness,* p. 15.

10. Jack N. Kondrasuk, "Corporate Physical Fitness Programs: The Role of the Personnel Department," *Personnel Administrator* 29, no. 12 (December 1984): 75–80.

11. R. L. Pyle, "Corporate Fitness Programs—How Do They Shape Up?" *Management Review* 68 (December 1979).

12. Kondrasuk, "Corporate Physical Fitness Programs," pp. 78–79.

13. Loren E. Falkenberg, "Employee Fitness Programs: Their Impact on the employee and the Organization," *Academy of Management Review* 12, no. 3 (July 1987): 511–22.

14. A. M. Paolone et al., "Results of Two Years of Exercise Training in Middle-Aged Men," *Physicians and Sports Medicine* 4 (December 1976): 77.

15. M. L. Collis, *Employee Fitness.* (Ottawa, Canada: Minister of Supplies and Services, 1977), p. 81.

16. L. M. Catheart, "A Four-Year Study of Executive Health Risk," *Journal of Occupational Medicine* (May 1977): 357.

17. Sandra E. Edwards and Larry K. Gettmans, "The Effects of Employee Physical Fitness on Job Performance," *Personnel Administrator* 25, no. 11 (November 1980): 41–44, 60–61.

18. William G. Wagner, "Assisting Employees with Personal Problems," *Personnel Administrator* 27, no. 11 (November 1982): 59–64.

19. Virginia K. Tyler, "Growth of EAPs Brings Certification," *Employee Benefit News* 1, no. 4 (May–June 1987): 1.

20. Fred Dickman and William G. Emener, "Employee Assistance Programs: Basic Concepts, Attributes and an Evaluation," *Personnel Administrator* (August 1982): 55–62.

21. Roger K. Good, "What Bechtel Learned Creating an Employee Assistance Program," *Personnel Journal* 63, no. 9 (September 1984): 80–86.

22. Wagner, "Assisting Employees with Personal Problems," pp. 59–64.

23. Donald V. Forrest, "Employee Assistance Programs in the 1980s: Expanding Career Options for Counselors," *Personnel and Guidance Journal* 62 (October 1983): 105–108.

24. Christine A. Filipowicz, "The Troubled Employee: Whose Responsibility?" *Personnel Administrator* 24 (June 1979): 18.

25. Frank E. Kuzmits and Henry E. Hammons, II, "Rehabilitating the Troubled Employee," *Personnel Journal* 58 (April 1979): 239.

26. Ibid.

27. Filipowicz, "The Troubled Employee," pp. 18–19.

28. The Kemper Insurance Companies publish a number of excellent guidebooks on alcoholism and drug abuse. For information on obtaining these guides, write Public Relations, Kemper Insurance Companies, Long Grove, IL 60049.

29. *Summary of 3rd Report on Alcohol and Health,* p. 6.

30. Alander Ross and Thomas Campbell, "An Evaluation Study of an Alcohol and Drug Recovery Program—A Case Study of the Oldsmobile Experience," *Human Resource Management* 14 (Spring 1975): 14–18.

31. Ian A. Miners, Nick Nykodym, and Diane M. Samerdyke-Traband, "Put Drug Detection to the Test," *Personnel Journal* 66, no. 8 (August 1987): 92–97.

32. *New York City Transit Authority* v. *Beager* (U.S. Supreme Court), 1986.

33. David D. Schein, "How to Prepare a Company Policy on Substance Abuse Control," *Personnel Journal* 65, no. 7 (July 1986): 30–38.

34. Miners et al., "Put Drug Detection to the Test," pp. 92–97.

35. Schein, "How to Prepare a Company Policy on Substance Abuse Control," pp. 30–38.

36. Larry Martz et al., "Trying to Say No," *Newsweek* (August 11, 1986): 14–19.

37. Report of the U.S. Surgeon General (Washington, DC: Office of the U.S. Surgeon General, 1986).

38. Philip R. Voluck, "Burning Legal Issues of Smoking in the Workplace," *Personnel Journal* 66, no. 6 (June 1987): 140–43.

39. Alaska, Connecticut, Florida, Maine, Minnesota, Montana, Nebraska, New Jersey, Rhode Island, and Utah.

40. *Vickers* v. *Veterans Administration,* 29 FEP Cases 1197 (1982).

41. "ASPA-BNA Survey No. 51, Smoking in the Workplace: 1987 Update," *Bulletin to Management* (Washington, DC: Bureau of National Affairs, November 26, 1987).

42. Voluck, "Burning Legal Issues of Smoking in the Workplace," p. 140.

43. Alfred Vogel, *Smoking and Productivity in the Workplace* (Washington, DC: The Tobacco Institute, 1985).

44. William L. Weis, "No Smoking," *Personnel Journal* 63, no. 9 (September 1984): 53–58.

45. George Munchus, "An Update on Smoking: Employees' Rights and Employers' Responsibilities," *Personnel* 64 (August 1987): 46–56.

46. R. Craig Scott, "The Smoking Controversy Goes to Court," *Management World* 17, no. 1 (January–February 1988): 14.

47. Frank E. Kuzmits and Lyle Sussman, "Twenty Questions about AIDS in the Workplace," *Business Horizons* 29, no. 4 (July–August 1986): 36–42.

48. William Waldo, "A Practical Guide for Dealing with AIDS at Work," *Personnel Journal* 66, no. 8 (August 1987): 135–38.

49. Ibid.

50. Bureau of National Affairs, *AIDS in the Workplace: Resource Material* (Washington, DC: Bureau of National Affairs, 1986).

51. Phyllis S. Myers and Donald W. Myers, "AIDS: Tackling a Tough Problem Through Policy," *Personnel Administrator* 32 (April 1987): 95–108, 143.

52. Allan Haleron, "AIDS: The Corporate Response," *Personnel Journal* 65, no. 8 (August 1986): 123–27.

53. "AIDS: Employer Rights and Responsibilities," *Human Resource Management*, No. 47 (Chicago: Commerce Clearing House, 1985), pp. 11–24.

54. Lawrence Z. Lorber and J. Robert Kirk, *Fear Itself: A Legal and Personnel Analysis of Drug Testing, AIDS, Secondary Smoke, VDTs* (Washington, DC: ASPA Foundation, 1987), pp. 25–33.

55. M. J. McCarthy, "Stressed Employees Look for Relief in Workers' Compensation Claims," *The Wall Street Journal* (April 7, 1988), p. 27.

56. J. M. Ivancevich and M. T. Matteson, *Stress and Work* (Glenview, Ill.: Scott, Foresman, 1980), pp. 5–9.

57. J. Makower, *Office Hazards* (Washington, DC: Tilden Press, 1983), p. 126.

58. McCarthy, "Stressed Employees Look for Relief in Workers' Compensation Claims."

59. Ivancevich and Matteson, *Stress and Work,* pp. 208–23.

60. K. Per Larson, "Why Health Care Costs Keep Rising," *Personnel Journal* 63, no. 3 (March 1984): 68–74.

61. Larry S. Chapman and Nancy E. Gertz, "A Prescription for Lower Health Care Costs," *Personnel Journal* 64, no. 1 (January 1985): 48–52.

62. Herbert Notkin and Leland Meader, "Health Care Cost Containment," *Personnel Administrator* 24 (March 1979): 58–59.

63. Robert Gumbiner, "Selection of Health Maintenance Organization," *Personnel Journal* 157 (August 1978): 444–45.

64. Daniel C. Stone, Jr., and E. G. Sue Reitz, "Health Care Cost Containment and Its Impact on Employee Relations," *Personnel Administrator 29,* no. 12 (December 1984): 27–33.

65. Donald H. Wilson, "Guarding the Health Care Dollar." *Personnel Administrator* 29, no. 12 (December 1984): 37–41.

66. Martin E. Segal Company, "Are PPOs the Answer to Rising Health Care Costs?" *Personnel Journal* 63, no. 6 (June 1984): 82–86. Reprinted from the Martin E. Segal & Co. Newsletter.

67. Ibid.

68. Berea, OH: American Society for Personnel Administration, *Occupational Safety and Health Review* (March, 1985), p. 3.

69. Nicholas A. Ashford, "The Nature and Dimension of Occupational Health and Safety Problems," *Personnel Administrator* 18 (August 1977): 46–48.

70. *An OSHA Guide to Evaluating Your Firm's Injury and Illness Experience, 1974,* U.S. Department of Labor, Bureau of Labor Statistics report 478. (Washington DC: U.S. Government Printing Office, 1976, pp. 1–8.

71. Berea, OH: American Society for Personnel Administration, *Occupational Safety and Health Review* (March 1979), p. 7.

72. Berea, OH: American Society for Personnel Administration, *Occupational Safety and Health Review* (June 1979), p. 6.

73. Berea, OH: American Society for Personnel Administration, *Occupational Safety and Health Review* (March 1979), p. 4.

74. William N. Cooke, "OSHA, Plant Safety Programs, and Injury Reduction," *Industrial Relations* 20, no. 3 (Fall 1981): 245–57.

75. Berea, OH: American Society for Personnel Administration, *Occupational Safety and Health Review* (December 1978), p. 3.

76. Bruce D. May, "Hazardous Substances: OSHA Mandates the Right to Know," *Personnel Journal* 65, no. 8 (August 1986): 128–30.

77. Lester Bittel, *What Every Supervisor Should Know* (New York: McGraw-Hill, 1974), p. 97.

78. Henry Ferguson, *Tomorrow's Global Executive.* (Homewood, Ill.: Dow Jones-Irwin 1988), p. 65.

Should Pay Increases Be Based on Performance? Is Pay Based on Performance?

Pay incentives are controversial. The public, as well as many personnel directors, are intrigued with the idea of linking pay to performance. But many of the personnel directors responsible for implementing pay-for-performance plans insist that they do not and cannot work. There are several arguments against monetary incentive systems. One articulate personnel director's opinion about linking monetary incentives to performance appraisals is presented.

"The experience that I have had covers a lot of years and a lot of different organizations. Throughout it all, I have seen no single pay-for-performance plan succeed with the hourly worker. There's a half-life that varies as people learn how to beat the appraisal system. I really can't think of a performance appraisal system, regardless of its objectivity, that has proven effective in linking monetary incentives to performance.

"The difficulty lies with the standards that are used and the application of those standards among all the supervisors who have to give the ratings. It's been my experience that it is difficult enough to get supervisors simply to rate performance—if to do nothing else but talk to employees—and when we add other factors in there, such as money, then the task becomes even more difficult. Supervisors start to play political games just so they can get their fair share of the compensation budget.

"Don't misunderstand me. I fully buy into the idea of pay for performance. I think the concept is good—I have tried it a number of times myself—but the practice, in spite of the best training, is so fraught with political infighting, fuzzy standards, and negative attitudes that it is extremely difficult to carry out."

Discussion Questions

1. From your experience, is the overall argument against pay-for-performance valid? Expain.
2. Pay-for-performance plans work on a simple principle: the better the performance, the better the reward. What basic motivational assumption is made in order for this type of plan to work? If pay for performance is possible, is it desirable, or are other methods of achieving employee equity superior?
3. How might reward systems operate to discourage productive workers? Given the productivity lag discussed so frequently in the popular press, can we design compensation systems to spur productivity growth?

The Latest in Corporate Benefits

When Toni Bailey first heard the idea of holding first-grade elementary school classes on her company's premises, she couldn't help but laugh. What began as a brainstorming session for obtaining ideas about better use of the wasted space on Liberty Bank's third floor had suddenly turned into an animated discussion.

Toni supervised nine tellers at Liberty Bank. She had a practice of scheduling the final hour of the working week, Friday afternoon from four until five, as a staff meeting. The nine tellers gathered in the bank's employee lounge for their meetings. Not only were the sessions generally productive, they also gave the employees a chance to unwind from the week's work. In one sense, the last hour was also perceived as a reward. If you survived the previous week, Toni made it a point to recognize specific accomplishments. Mistakes were not mentioned unless they were brought up by the employees. During the meetings, information was exchanged about jobs and new procedures or policies. Morale was excellent in Toni's group; however, turnover was high.

The banking industry has long experienced high turnover among tellers. As a group, tellers are predominantly young. Many have very young children or are pregnant. While some parents prefer employment over staying home, others, by necessity, take jobs separating them from their children during the working days; they need the money. Getting their children to baby-sitters or day-care facilities and to school has always been a problem for many parents, especially when they are several miles from where the parents work.

As Toni began the meeting, she explained that after covering the preliminaries, they were going to take up the topic of space use on the third floor. Recently, Toni had received a memo from the executive vice-president asking department heads for suggestions on how to make better use of the center space. A prize of $500 would be awarded for the best suggestion—the one adopted. When the routine business was completed, the group turned to this subject.

Toni's group made a number of recommendations. They ranged from the usual comments of "more space for employees to retreat to on breaks" to "creating a wellness and fitness center." Then Bonnie said, "I think we ought to convert the space into a day-care center."

"Out of the ten of us here, five have youngsters under seven years of age," Bonnie went on to say. "And two more are expecting. I think a day-care center is in the company's best interests if they really want to keep us happy."

Beth, usually a quiet, almost painfully shy person, in her most assertive voice then said, "If the bank really wants to help us out, they should hire a school teacher, put in a classroom, and start teaching our kids. We need a school that is close and convenient, one where we might be able to observe our kids learning and maybe even help out when we have some time—like on our lunch hour. These are very important years in a child's life, and I, for one, resent missing out. There is plenty of space here. With good soundproofing, there wouldn't be any noise, and it certainly would be a lot more convenient for us. One certified teacher could probably handle at least two grades with help from all of us."

The group quickly agreed that Bonnie and Beth had made excellent suggestions. The group finally agreed to convert the wasted space into a day-care facility, including classrooms for children up to the age of seven, notify the local school board, hire a teacher, and make the facility available only to employees' children. Toni asked the group to continue thinking about the pros and cons of both the day-care center and the school, especially the costs and benefits. In the meantime, she would meet with the personnel manager and discuss the merits of the proposal.

Discussion Questions

1. What are the pros and cons of the bank sponsoring (a) a day-care center and (b) a school?
2. What advantages does the bank derive from increasing employees' job satisfaction and motivation? Why would the bank wish to reduce the turnover of tellers?
3. What steps should the personnel manager take?

Part Four   Employee Relations

Chapter Thirteen

Labor Unions

Chapter Objectives

THERE are many reasons why the study of unions is important for any student of personnel management. The presence of a union has significant implications for the structure of an organization and for the management of human resources. For union employees, personnel procedures and policies are largely shaped by a written agreement between management and the union. A personnel administrator's job in a unionized firm will be markedly different from that same job in a nonunionized firm. And beyond the confines of one organization, the tenor of an area's labor relations, whether they are perceived to be good or bad, can have significant impact on the economic health of that area.

A *union* is an organization of workers formed to further the economic and social interests of its members. There are three kinds of unions: industrial unions, trade unions, and employee associations. An *industrial union* is a union composed primarily of semiskilled blue-collar employees in the "smokestack" industries, such as automobiles, chemicals, and utilities. A *trade union* (sometimes called a *craft union*) generally includes among its membership skilled employees in a single trade, such as electricians, carpenters, and ma-

chinists. An *employee association* is generally composed of white-collar or professional employees, such as teachers, police officers, and clerical, administrative, technical, and health-care employees. *Collective bargaining* is negotiation in good faith between the employer and the union on wages, benefits, hours of work and other terms and conditions of employment. The result is a written contract specifying the agreements they reach.

IMPORTANCE OF UNIONS

Unions are an extraordinary source of power and influence over managerial practices, worker behavior, and the basic conditions of employment. Unionization results in a significant diminution of managerial autonomy in the control of the work place and the employees, particularly for first-level supervisors who interact with employees on a day-to-day basis. Many important personnel decisions must conform to the letter of the labor–management contract. For example, a supervisor desiring to promote a high-performing employee to a more challenging and higher-paying job may find that the contract specifies seniority

PERSONNEL
IN THE NEWS

Saving Jobs at Xerox Corporation

An innovative example of labor–management cooperation has improved productivity and saved jobs at Xerox Corporation. In the early 1980s Xerox determined that some of its products were not internationally competitive due to high labor costs. Subcontracting the work to nonunion firms, however, would provide competitive costs, but would require closing down the U.S. operation.

The Amalgamated Clothing and Textile Workers Union asked the company to form a joint labor–management study team to see if the closing could be avoided. Management was reluctant because it believed only a reduction in wage rates could make the operation competitive.

A study team of six hourly and two management employees was formed and given six months to develop its recommendations. The team had total freedom to investigate any proposal. After informal discussions and visiting other companies, the team identified 40 possible cost reduction suggestions, nine of which were adopted by the executive policy committee. The suggestions included several work flow and job redesign changes, including new equipment and greater employee responsibility. The physical layout was significantly altered to create employee work groups that were self-managing and given direct accountability for quality control and reducing scrap.

After eight months under the new operations, the projected annual savings was $3.7 million—more than enough to be competitive while maintaining current wage levels. Many of the changes could not have been negotiated at the bargaining table. The completely open communication position taken by both sides, however, allowed each to realize the other was serious in its goal—labor to save jobs and management to stay competitive.

Source: John G. Belcher, Jr., "The Role of Unions in Productivity Management," *Personnel* 65, no. 1 (January 1988): 54–58.

as a major criterion in promotion decisions. As a result, a less-effective employee may be promoted.

The contract between management and the union typically covers a two- or three-year period, locking management and labor into many terms and conditions of employment for that period. Provisions usually exist for negotiating changes in certain items while the contract is in force, but the union always strongly resists any attempt by management to "take something away" from the workers.[1] For example, management may think that the existing sick-leave provision causes high absenteeism. The union, however, would surely oppose any attempt to alter the contract and cut back on the number of sick days that workers receive—unless, that is, they received something in return.

Unionization may also result in a hostile labor-management environment. Agitation between labor and management may lead to a working climate that fosters high turnover and absenteeism and low employee morale and productivity. However, cooperative, conflict-free labor–management partnerships do exist in industrial society. Many organizations have enjoyed strike-free, harmonious labor-management relations for decades. But the possibility of labor–management conflict should be of major concern to future managers and personnel administrators, who will bear an important responsibility for creating and maintaining peace between labor and management.

A great deal of time and effort have been devoted to the question "Why do employees choose to join a union?" Studies have failed to find a list of reasons that apply to all organizing efforts. But there is general agreement among labor experts that certain issues are likely to lead to an organizing drive by employees. Among them are the following.[2]

Job Security Employees need to feel secure in their jobs and want to believe that management will not make unfair and arbitrary decisions about their employment. Further, they wish to be protected against layoffs and may look to the union to ensure that jobs are protected against such technological advances as automation and robotics. For example, the union could request that any employee displaced by an industrial robot be retrained and placed in another job. The most important element in job security is seniority, or the

length of an employee's service. It is a common practice for personnel decisions affecting the union employee—such as layoffs, recall, and promotions—to be made according to seniority. Seniority is the primary mechanism for protecting and rewarding the union employee who has shown his or her loyalty through years of service with the employer. Union members think that making personnel decisions by seniority is fair because management is unable to allow bias to affect the decision and because seniority affords a way to reward those employees who have served the company for a long period.

Unions today often consider job security their top priority in contract negotiations. High levels of unemployment, foreign and nonunion competition, and technological advances have forced many unions in affected industries to accept negotiated givebacks of previously achieved wages and benefits. *Givebacks*, or concession bargaining techniques, is a labor relations term that refers to union-negotiated reductions in wages, benefits, or work rules in exchange for management's guarantee of job security, usually in the form of a promise of no layoff or plant closing during the term of the agreement. In addition to concession bargaining, unions can provide job security for their members through a negotiated seniority system that governs decisions on layoff and recall, as well as promotion and training opportunities based on the employee's length of service (see chapter 9). However, unions realize that seniority systems do not provide job security against loss of jobs to nonunion or foreign competition.

Another method of incorporating job security in contracts is the use of provisions limiting management's right to subcontract work to another company if the work can normally be performed by members of the union. Technological change also presents a threat to job security because workers are often replaced with robots or other advanced equipment. In previous years, unions attempted to block such changes in the work place as a means of providing job security to their members. However, too often the result was noncompetitive production, which eventually led to massive plant closings. Therefore, most union leaders today accept technological change as necessary to remain competitive in the global marketplace. Negotiators anticipate such change, and rather than oppose it at the bargaining table, they bargain for advance notice to laid-off workers, retraining rights to provide affected workers with new job skills, and out-placement assistance for permanently terminated workers.

Job insecurity today is a major concern for many workers. While union-negotiated contract provisions such as seniority rights, no layoffs, no subcontracting, retraining rights, and concession bargaining may provide a degree of job security, the only real, long-term security is a highly productive work force that can compete effectively in the international marketplace.

Wages and Benefits Bread-and-butter economic issues have always been an important concern for employees and are always important in unionization. Specifically, employees want to be paid fairly and receive wages on par with those of other workers in the community. Such benefits as hospitalization insurance, life insurance, and paid sick leave, vacations, and holidays are also significant issues in employees' decisions to organize. They may think that the union, with its collective power, will be able to achieve a higher level of wages and benefits than could employees acting individually.

Working Conditions Employees want a healthy and safe working environment. Although federal legislation exists to protect the health and safety in the work place, employ-

ees may feel more secure knowing that a union is directly involved in safety and health issues.

Fair and Just Supervision The day is long gone when supervisors could rule their employees with an iron fist. A significant reason for the general shift in leadership styles from autocratic to people-oriented patterns is the insistence by unions that supervisors treat their employees fairly, justly, and respectfully. Most contracts specify that employees can only be disciplined for "just cause." A union employee who thinks he or she has been mistreated may file a written *grievance* against the employer, initiating a formal procedure through which the complaint will be heard by both union and management representatives. The grievance procedure will be discussed in chapter 14.

Mechanism to be Heard Employees often complain that they have little or no say in matters that affect their work. They often feel powerless to bring about changes that will benefit them. Through unionization, employees have a powerful, collective voice that may be used to communicate to management their dissatisfactions and frustrations. The collective-bargaining and grievance procedures ensure that union employees will have their wants, needs, and concerns brought before management without retaliation.

Need to Belong The need to belong is strong in all human beings in both their personal lives and their work lives. The union provides a mechanism for bringing people together not only to promote common job-related interests but also to provide programs, activities, and social events that create a strong bond among union members.

In general, workers are favorably disposed to unions because of bread-and-butter issues such as job satisfaction. Table 13–1 shows the

TABLE 13–1

Why employees vote for union representation; figures show correlation between a positive response to the question and a vote for union representation (Source: Adapted from Jeanne M. Brett, "Why Employees Want Unions," *Organizational Dynamics,* Spring 1980, p. 51, by AMACOM, a division of the American Management Association)

Issue	Correlation with Vote For Union
Satisfaction with job security	−.42
Satisfaction with wages	−.40
Overall satisfaction with company	−.36
Satisfaction with supervisory treatment	−.34
Satisfaction with fringe benefits	−.31
Satisfaction with supervisory appreciation	−.30
Satisfaction with promotion opportunities	−.30
Satisfaction with the type of work	−.14

results of one study that correlated satisfaction with certain job issues and the propensity to vote for the union. The strongest correlation was with the basic issues of job security and wages; the weakest correlation concerned the type of work being performed.[3] For example, the table shows that dissatisfaction with job security is the strongest predictor of a vote for the union.

The author of the study emphasized that dissatisfaction alone does not automatically lead to efforts by employees to unionize. Rather, the dissatisfied employees must think that as individuals they lack the ability to bring about a positive change in the work place. Further, they must believe that collective action through unionization would bring about improvements that would reduce their sources of dissatisfaction.[4]

UNION HISTORY

The history of the labor movement is rich in tales of gallantry, risk, daring, success, despair, and failure. The movement has been peaceful and violent, law-abiding and lawless, spectac-ular and dull. Many of the memoirs of those who founded and strengthened the organized labor show men and women of ability, courage, power, and sometimes ruthlessness.[5]

Some view U.S. labor history as the history of a few leaders who possessed uncanny skills to motivate and organize great masses of workers. Others see impersonal forces at work, specifically that labor unrest was an inevitable outgrowth of corporate leadership's inability to create fair, safe, and rewarding environments for workers. The growth of organized labor may also be seen as part of wider political movements in U.S. and even world affairs: doomsayers once suggested that sustained union growth would signal an end to the capitalist system. Indeed, eleven unions were expelled from the Congress of Industrial Organization in 1949 and 1950 for following the program of the Communist party.[6] Labor history is a complex and important part of American history. The labor movement resulted from an array of social, political, and economic forces, individual leadership and organization skills, and an unpredictable chain of events.

Early Unions

The labor union is not a new phenomenon on the American scene. One of the first unions, the Federal Society of Journeymen Cordwainers (shoemakers), was organized in Philadelphia in 1794. Boston carpenters organized in 1793 and New York printers in 1794. Early unions were composed of craftsmen—workers who performed a single skill or occupation, such as shoemakers, tailors, and weavers.

The growth and development of the American economy fostered the emergence of craft unions. As new communities sprang up and markets developed, capitalists enlarged their operations and sought competitive edges by, among other tactics, lowering labor costs. In reaction, craftsmen came together as a union and agreed that none would work for less than a specified wage. Many craft unions also sought a *closed shop*, whereby only union members would be hired.

Craft-union successes were closely tied to the ebb and flow of the economy; a recession or depression spelled doom for many labor groups. Much of the gain in union membership during the early 1800s was wiped out during a major depression of 1819. And many—if not most—of the unions formed during the major expansionary period of the mid-1830s disappeared during the panic of 1837.

National Unions In pre–Civil War years, unions were independently organized and managed. Their aims were similar—job security, more pay, improved working conditions—but each operated autonomously. They were not affiliated with a labor federation (a league or association of several unions), such as the AFL-CIO of today.

National Labor Union (NLU) In 1866 the National Labor Union was organized to serve the common interest of laborers in different trades and occupations. Founded by the president of the Iron Molders Union, William Sylvis, the NLU represented the first serious attempt to bring all craft and reform unions into a single national organization. Because the NLU put long-term political goals (women's suffrage and abolition of the convict-labor system) ahead of bread-and-butter issues such as pay and hours worked, the union passed from the scene in 1872.

Knights of Labor A second national union, the Noble and Holy Order of the Knights of Labor, met with greater success. Led by Uriah Stevens, nine Philadelphia garment makers formed the Knights as a secret society in 1869. The Knights emerged as a national federation in 1878. Their broad goal was "to initiate good men of all callings" and organize both craftsmen and unskilled workers. The Knights were not totally void of discrimination in their organizing efforts; they wanted "no drones, no lawyers, no bankers, no doctors, no professional politicians."[7] They also excluded prostitutes and representatives from the alcoholic beverage and tobacco industries!

The Knights enjoyed steady growth amid general economic prosperity and aggressive membership drives. Their meteoric rise reached its apex in 1886 with a membership of some 702,000; their influence thereafter rapidly declined. By 1890 membership had fallen to 220,000; by 1900 the Knights were virtually extinct. There were two reasons for the Knights' demise. First, Chicago's Haymarket Riot (1886), in which several labor demonstrators were killed and scores were injured, resulted in strong national antilabor sentiment. Although the Knights were not directly involved, they suffered greatly from the negative attitudes toward organized labor that resulted from the riot. Second, and perhaps more significant, the federation was poorly led. The Knights' leadership sought utopian social goals—the establishment of consumer cooperatives, temperance, and land reform. The rank and file, however, sought more practical objectives—higher wages, better working conditions, and shorter hours. Such major philosophical differences, in addition to other internal conflicts, brought considerable disarray and, ultimately, extinction.

American Federation of Labor (AFL)

The fall of the Knights of Labor coincided with the rise of a national labor organization that still survives: the American Federation of Labor. The AFL was founded in 1886 as a federation of craft unions composed of skilled workers only. The creation and subsequent success of the AFL were due, in part, to the craft unions' dissatisfaction with the Knights' failure to give proper attention to their special needs. Also, the craft-union members were averse to the Knights' attempt to organize anybody and everybody and to mix skilled and unskilled workers under one roof. The AFL's founder and leader, Samuel Gompers, was the former head of the Cigar Makers Union; he saw to it that the AFL was built around the particular needs, practices, philosophies, and goals of craft unions. The AFL is generally credited with introducing to the labor movement the concept of *business unionism*, that the union is more concerned with bread-and-butter issues (such as wages, benefits, and working conditions) than broad social goals and that it is businesslike in its operations and dealings—much like the unions of today.

The AFL's dramatic growth continued through the early years of the twentieth century. By 1904, the AFL had 120 affiliated unions, about 85 percent of all national unions in the United States. After 1904, mem-bership gains were less dramatic, but the union continued to grow, suffering only temporary setbacks during severe economic declines. At the time of its merger with CIO in 1955, membership totaled 10.9 million.

Congress of Industrial Organizations (CIO)

Beginning with the AFL in 1886, the craft union prevailed as the principal union model for a half century. In 1935, however, the craft union's dominance of organized labor was challenged by the emergence of the Congress of Industrial Organizations.

A colorful, pugnacious event during the 1935 AFL convention marked the beginning of the CIO. When a delegate raised a question about industrial unionism, 6-foot, 220-pound "Big Bill" Hutchinson, president of the Carpenters' Union and staunch supporter of the craft union forces, raised a point of order, stating that the issue of industrial unionism had already been settled. John L. Lewis, president of the United Mine Workers and leader of the proindustrial camp within the AFL, strongly dissented, stating, "This thing of raising points of order all the time is rather small potatoes." To which Hutchinson replied, "I was raised on small potatoes, that's why I'm so small." As Lewis retorted, "Well, then, it's about time you were mashed," he swung at Hutchinson and the two grappled on the floor.[8] In November 1935 Lewis and seven industrial union presidents split from the AFL to form the CIO.

The CIO union model was markedly different from the AFL craft model. Whereas craft unions were organized into skilled occupations, the CIO represented industrial unionism, whereby membership was based upon employment in a particular industry such as automobile, steel, or clothing.

AFL-CIO Merger

After a twenty-year separation, AFL and CIO united in December 1955 into a single federation called the American Federation of Labor and Congress of Industrial Organizations (AFL-CIO). The union claimed a total membership of 16.1 million workers: 10.9 million members from 108 AFL unions and 5.2 million members from 30 CIO unions.

Why did the AFL and the CIO merge? First, the passage of the promanagement Taft–Hartley Act in 1947 signaled the beginning of antilabor sentiments and the potential for further antilabor legislation. Combined forces were believed to be more effective in curtailing such legislation than a divided attack. Second, the merger brought a halt to the problem of raiding, in which one union pirated members from the other. The signing of a no-raiding agreement in 1953 signaled the first step toward a merger. Third, house-cleaning by each union created new mutual respect. The CIO rid itself of Communists from unions in 1949 and 1950 and the AFL expelled the racket-ridden International Longshoremen's Union in 1953.

George Meany became president of the merged federation and reiterated labor's commitment to their traditional goals: greater job security, improved economic rewards, and increased employee benefits through aggressive collective bargaining. In terms of membership, however, the AFL-CIO did not become a more powerful force. Many labor observers believed that the new federation would grow by leaps and bounds, but actually the reverse has taken place. The federation counted 16.1 million members in 1955; by 1985 membership had declined to 13.8 million.

Several factors are responsible for the federation's membership trend. First, 1.5 million workers were lost when the Teamsters Union was expelled in 1957 for failure to oust presi-

dent Jimmy Hoffa. Hoffa and many other union figures were castigated by Senator John McClellans's Select Committee on Improper Activities in the Labor or Management Field. Hoffa was a great embarrassment to the AFL-CIO. Second, the United Auto Workers (UAW), suffering serious conflicts with the AFL-CIO leadership, refused to pay dues in 1968, and the union was expelled. The UAW's departure reduced the AFL-CIO's membership by 1.4 million. (In 1981 the UAW voted to rejoin the AFL-CIO.) Third, the makeup of American industry has changed significantly since the inception of the AFL-CIO. Heavy industry no longer rules the economy. Unskilled and semiskilled workers have been declining as a percentage of the total labor force, whereas significant increases have been recorded by professional, technical, and administrative personnel.

Contemporary Trends

The trend in union membership, as shown in Figure 13–1, spells crisis for many union leaders: a gradual decline in union membership as a percentage of the total labor force. Although the number of organized workers increased from 14.2 million in 1950 to 17 million in 1985, the percentage of union members in the labor force dropped from 22.3 percent in 1950 to about 18 percent in 1985.[9] A variety of reasons caused the decline. First, the country has been shifting from an industrial economy to a service economy since the mid-1950s. Service workers are generally more difficult and costly to organize because they are spread out over a large number of employers, and they often hold promanagement views. Second, automation, particularly in the form of industrial robots, has been displacing an increasing number of blue-collar workers, and the use of robots is expected to continue to increase dramatically in the future. Many large industrial

Employee Relations

Year	Total Membership (thousands)	Percentage of Labor Force	
		Total	Nonagricultural
1935	3,728	6.7	13.2
1940	8,944	15.5	26.9
1945	14,796	21.9	35.5
1950	15,000	22.3	31.5
1955	17,749	24.7	33.2
1960	18,177	23.6	31.4
1965	18,519	22.4	28.4
1970	20,751	22.6	27.3
1975	21,090	20.7	25.5
1980	20,100	18.8	23.0
1985	17,400	17.8	19.1

Sources: U.S. Department of Labor, Bureau of Labor Statistics, Bulletin 2070, *Handbook of Labor Statistics,* (Washington, D.C.: Government Printing Office, 1980), p. 412.

Larry T. Adams, "Changing Employment Patterns of Organized Workers," *Monthly Labor Review* 108, no. 2 (Feb. 1985), pp. 25–31.

FIGURE 13–1

Union membership, 1935–1985

plants built in the 1980s have been planned around industrial robots. Third, foreign competition has slowly undercut the need for blue-collar workers. For example, the growing number of imports (automobiles, electronics, clothing) has reduced the ranks of the industrial employee in this country. Fourth, more and more American manufacturers are building and assembling parts and products in foreign countries such as Mexico, Taiwan, South Korea, and South American countries. Lower labor costs is the reason most often cited for moving a manufacturing operation to a foreign country.

Public Image The decline in union membership in recent years has been coupled with a declining public image. Once viewed as the creators and protectors of the middle class in the United States, unions in recent years have been generally viewed as out of touch with the public and with American economic realities. Union wages and benefits are cited by labor critics as the major cause of the decline of many American industries such as steel, textiles, and rubber. They claim that union strikes, unrealistic work rules, and artificially high wages have caused many American products to suffer from poor quality and high prices, thus strengthening the demand for foreign-made goods. Union leaders respond that unfair trade barriers against American goods and below-poverty-level foreign wages, together with American management's lack of long-range planning, are the real culprits. The media, which publicize only strikes and not peaceful negotiations, are also blamed by union leaders for the poor public image of unions. However, during the 1980s, major strikes by the Air Traffic Controllers (PATCO) in 1981, the National Football League Player's Association in 1982 and 1987, and the AT&T employees in 1983 failed to garner public support, which in each case the union had counted on to pressure management back to the bargaining table.

Union leaders themselves often do not help the cause of organized labor. They are sometimes seen as dishonest and unethical, and as interested only in protectionist legislation in Washington. In reality, many of the old cigar-smoking union bosses have been replaced with younger college-educated professionals who may be more interested in labor–management cooperation than confrontation. However, some of the old-style labor bosses are still in control of national unions, and the public's perception is often slow to change.

Public-Sector Unionism The unionization of public employees is not new, but executive orders and legislative statutes have enabled public-sector unions to enjoy significant gains since 1962.[10] John F. Kennedy's Executive Order 10988, Employee–Management Cooperation in the United States, enacted in 1962, required federal agencies to recognize unions that represented a majority of employees as determined by a vote. Executive Order 10988 was later amended and strengthened by Richard M. Nixon's Executive Order 11491. Nixon's action created a federal labor relations council to administer the order and to improve methods for conducting collective bargaining. Those orders, together with federal and state legislation, helped increase total union membership in federal, state, and local governments from 1.2 million in 1962 to over 7 million today. About 25 percent of all union employees are government workers.[11]

Organized public employees are concentrated in a few unions. These include the American Federation of Government Employees (AFGE), the American Federation of State, County, and Municipal Employees (AFSCME), and the American Federation of Teachers (AFT).[12]

White-collar Unionism Until relatively recent times, the labor movement has been mostly a blue-collar phenomenon. White-collar workers and professionals shunned organized labor, feeling that union membership was beneath their status and dignity. They believed that gains in salaries and other areas of employment could be best achieved through their professional associations and their own individual efforts. That philosophy changed considerably in the 1960s and 1970s as white-collar and professional groups watched their salaries and benefits stagnate while gains were achieved by trade unions. Doctors, professors, engineers, nurses, and professional athletes began taking part in collective bargaining.

One area of white-collar unionization that has met with limited success by unions is in high-technology industries.[13] Most companies making computers and computer parts remain nonunion; and after about 250 largely unsuccessful organizing drives, efforts to organize high-tech employees have slowed.[14] Unions may have done poorly in their attempts to organize high-tech workers for the following reasons.[15]

High Turnover Unions have begun costly organizing drives, only to see targeted employees quit and go to work for another company.

Robotics Robots have replaced workers not only in the smokestacks industries but in high-tech companies as well.

Shift to Overseas Work Trends show that many high-tech companies are beginning to manufacture and assemble their parts and products overseas in order to reduce labor and operating costs.

Boom and Bust Volatility Many one-time high-flying computer companies, such as Osborne and Victor, have now settled down to earth in bankruptcy court. The risk and unpredictability of success in the computer industry have made some unions think twice about mounting costly, long-term organizing campaigns.

Progressive Management The computer industry is generally known for its progressive management styles, including quality circles, participative management, incentive compensation, and extravagant parties for their employees.

For now at least, it appears that unions believe that their efforts are best spent attempting to organize white-collar workers in more stable and appealing industries, such as lower-level office work, health care, government, and teaching.

UNION GOALS

The goals of unions have not changed significantly in almost 200 years. In a broad sense, the primary goal of any union is to promote the interests of its membership. Through collective bargaining and lobbying for labor legislation, union leaders enhance their members' standard of living and improve many conditions that surround their work.

Another goal that has long been an important part of the labor movement is the advancement of social goals. The pursuit of social aims has been a controversial part of the union philosophy, particularly among the rank and file, who generally have preferred that union funds and energies be devoted exclusively to advancing their own welfare. In the modern era, members have increasingly supported such goals, and many unions have been instrumental in effecting critically needed changes in the way society functions. The betterment of society constitutes an important part of organized labor's philosophy.

Union Security

Union security, or the ability to grow and prosper in either good or poor economic times, is organized labor's foremost goal. Labor legislation has created the following security provisions (except the closed shop) that organized labor may collectively bargain for:[16]

Union Shop All new employees in a union shop must join the union within a specified time, usually thirty days. About twenty states have passed *right-to-work* laws, which prohibit compulsory union membership. Most collective bargaining agreements provide for a union shop.

Agency Shop Nonunion employees must pay union dues but are not required to join the union in an agency shop.,

Maintenance-of-membership Shop Employees are not required to join the union. However, employees who do join must remain in the union until the contract expires or until a designated "escape" period occurs.

Closed Shop The new employee must be a union member at the time of hiring. While the closed shop is illegal, it exists in practice, particularly in the construction and printing industries. The practice is promoted by hiring through the union's own placement services, and by management's desire to avoid the trouble that may accompany the hiring of nonunion employees.

Open Shop No employee is required to join or contribute money to a labor organization as a condition for employment.

Job Security

Job security constitutes one of the primary goals of unions. Without jobs, union goals of higher wages and greater benefits are meaningless. Unions provide for job security by restricting the labor supply, controlling output, instituting make-work activities, and resisting productivity-improvement techniques.

Restricting the Labor Supply Aggressive attempts to restrict the labor supply to existing union members is particularly common in the building trades. One strategy involves limiting the enrollment in union-sponsored apprentice training programs. A second is to influence city codes so that only licensed trades workers are permitted to perform certain types of work.

Controlling Output Union leaders have long feared that technological advances and certain management practices would displace unskilled and semiskilled employees. At the turn of the century, union leaders strongly resisted Frederick Taylor's principles of scientific management, in which time and motion studies scientifically determined a fair day's work and replaced haphazard, rule-of-thumb methods of job design. They felt that wide implementation of Taylor's methods would result in widespread unemployment and thus in reduced union membership. Although scientific management eventually fell out of favor, management attempts to make the work more efficient in order to create more output are resisted by unions. In manufacturing situations, union members on job standards committees may apply pressure to create loose job standards; unions may also resist technological advances such as high-speed assembly lines or industrial robots.

Instituting Make-work Activities While it is illegal to require employers to pay for services not rendered (this is termed *featherbed-*

ding), unions may legally negotiate for work rules or conditions that are actually unnecessary to produce a product or service. Examples of make-work activities are the following:[17]

- Electrical workers performing unnecessary rewiring on apparatus purchased from another manufacturer.
- Painters requiring paint brushes to be limited in width and rollers banned unless there is premium pay.
- Compositors performing unnecessary resetting of advertisements run in another paper.
- Plasterers requiring three coats of plaster when the building code requires only two.
- Operating engineers employed merely to push buttons or turn switches.
- More brakemen riding trains in some states (the number written into law) than in others.
- Unnecessary stagehands in theaters.
- Dock workers refusing to use pallets that would increase loading and unloading efficiency.
- Meatcutters refusing to handle precut and prepackaged meats.
- Union electricians required to replace light bulbs.
- Airline employees who can unload baggage, and some who can unload cargo, but not both.
- Thirteen separate crafts required to install bathrooms in a hotel or apartment house.

Resisting Productivity-improvement Techniques In contrast to generations past, labor's resistance to productivity improvement has lessened somewhat, primarily because of the realization that high American productivity (and thus lowered product costs) is one of the strongest defenses against the influx of foreign imports. But labor leaders still oppose—sometimes vociferously—certain techniques that they think may ultimately result in a loss of workers' jobs.

Two contemporary productivity-improvement techniques that certain labor groups have opposed are quality circles and robotics. Some labor leaders think that quality circles may be used to thwart union organizing drives or reduce the union's authority. Perhaps the ultimate fear of the union is that workers will feel that quality circles will solve all their problems, thus making unions unnecessary.[18]

Despite that opposition, many major unions have worked closely with management on the design, implementation, and operation of quality circles. Unions that have become equal partners with management and accepted quality circles include the steelworkers, auto workers, and communications workers.[19]

Industrial robots pose a much greater threat to unions than other techniques, perhaps more than any form of productivity-improvement technique. The result of the implementation of robots—in terms of worker displacement—is profound and easily seen. The robot's imposing mass of steel and cable offers a stark contrast to the humans who once worked the assembly line. The use of robots in plants and factories is rapidly increasing. The number of robots is expected to reach 120,000 by 1990, up from only 1,300 as recently as 1979.[20]

The appeal of industrial robots to management is clear. Even when the initial cost of a robot exceeds $100,000, the robot offers many advantages over the human worker. Representatives of General Motors claim that the robots "don't demand salaries, much less raises, fringes, and holidays. . . . They're more careful, thorough, and speedy than the occasionally imperfect humans who assembly GM cars. . . . They don't breathe paint, nor do they waste it, as humans do."[21] Thus far,

robots have been used primarily in routine jobs that are dirty, dull, and dangerous and in jobs that are relatively easy to program, such as painting, welding, and certain assembly jobs.

The reason for labor's concern over robotics is obvious: these "steel-collar" workers have replaced untold factory workers across the country.[22] Conservative estimates place the number of workers that could be replaced by 1990 at 1 million; and some estimates are as high as 3 million. But realizing that robots are here to stay and will continue to increase in use in the future, unions have by and large accepted robots but are insisting on participating in some of the decisions that pertain to their use. Through the collective bargaining process, unions are seeking guarantees against job losses, advance notice of robot installations, and retraining of displaced workers for jobs at equal or better pay.[23]

It is important to stress that many union officials have no desire to engage in practices that hamper employee productivity; they prefer to cooperate with management on issues of productivity and efficiency. In such cases, union leaders recognize that increased organizational productivity and worker output, in the long run, benefit both the employer and the employee. Many labor leaders have voiced strong support for technological changes designed to improve the nation's standard of living, to help industries deal more effectively with foreign competition, and to strengthen job security. Yet, some local union officials still oppose technological change for fear of worker displacement. It is critical that labor and management work closely to determine how technological change may be implemented with minimal impact on employees.

Improved Economic Conditions

Economic issues have been a central concern to unions since the beginning of the labor movement. Particularly in the industrial sector, demands for higher wages are almost certain to be presented during labor–management contract negotiations. Following World War II, primarily because of government-imposed wage controls, unions struck for and received liberal benefits packages, including insurance, pensions, and paid holidays and vacations.

Working Conditions

Improvements in working conditions have been important union concerns in recent years. Unions have successfully bargained for better safety equipment, shorter workweeks, less mandatory overtime, and longer breaks, lunch periods, and cleanup time.

Fairness and Justice

Underscoring the union philosophy is the fair and equal treatment of all employees. Without the protection of organized labor, union leaders claim, management will show favoritism by providing or withholding privileges and benefits to certain workers. Unions hope to minimize the potential for favoritism and unequal treatment by insisting that major personnel decisions, such as in-grade wage increases, job promotions, transfers, layoffs, and other job actions, be made according to seniority. Although the unions' emphasis on seniority can be criticized because the most productive employee may not receive a promotion or may be the first to be laid off, the use of that criterion does constitute an impartial and objective way to make important personnel decisions and is also used in nonunion firms.

Social Action

Today many unions advocate goals that affect society as a whole. These goals are not achieved through the normal collective bargaining process, but by lobbying for federal and state legislation and government-sponsored programs and policies. As the major voice of labor, the AFL-CIO takes a firm stand on social, political, and economic goals. These goals and the strategies for accomplishing them are shown in Figure 13–2.

LABOR-MANAGEMENT LEGISLATION

Beginning in the early 1930s, labor-management relations have been heavily regulated by federal and state legislation. Prior to this period, lawmakers took a laissez-faire attitude toward unions and management and relied primarily on common law to govern labor-management relations. *Common law,* a heritage of the English legal system, is the body of law based on court decisions, custom, and precedent. In contrast, *statute law* is the body of laws established by legislative acts. When enacting the various statutes, Congress was reacting to public opinion and the special needs of labor and management.[24]

Railway Labor Act (1926)

In 1926 the Railway Labor Act gave railroad workers the right to organize and bargain collectively. It prohibited interference by employers. The act was amended in 1934 to include the airline industry. The provisions of the act foreshadowed those of the Wagner Act of 1935.

Norris–LaGuardia Act (1932)

Throughout organized labor's early history, union power was often undercut by injunctions, which are court orders requiring performance or restraint of a particular act. Management frequently obtained a temporary or permanent injunction prohibiting a strike or picketing. In 1932, the Norris–LaGuardia Act

An Economy That Works . . . By

- increasing employment opportunities
- reducing inflation
- rebuilding the nation's cities
- providing adequate housing
- alleviating hardships caused by unemployment
- achieving energy independence
- encouraging competition
- strengthening the U.S. trade position
- assuring social justice
- strengthening rural areas

Protecting Those Who Work . . . By

- strengthening the unemployment insurance program
- improving workers' compensation
- improving pension protection
- making the workplace safer
- strengthening fair labor standards
- improving labor laws
- protecting worker privacy
- protecting workers from sudden plant closings
- protecting federal workers
- protecting state and local government employees
- improving immigration laws

Civil Rights . . . Through

- strong enforcement of equal employment laws
- ratification of the Equal Rights Amendment
- eliminating discrimination against the handicapped
- strengthening fair housing laws

Making Social Programs Work . . . By

- improving Social Security programs
- improving health programs
- reforming the welfare system
- improving social services
- educating the young and old
- feeding the hungry

A Government That Works . . . By

- making the representative processes more representative
- insuring the proper funding of government
- improving the regulatory process
- protecting consumers
- improving communications and promoting the arts
- improving the state and local governments
- improving the Postal Service

Working For Peace And Freedom . . . Through

- the promotion and protection of human rights
- defense and disarmament
- coordinated defense policies with Western Europe
- trade limits with the USSR
- closer economic ties with Asian countries
- protecting U.S. and allied interests in the Persian Gulf
- closer political and economic ties with Latin American countries
- pressuring for social justice in South Africa
- encouraging a peaceful solution in the Middle East
- playing a more active role in international institutions such as the United Nations
- the use of foreign aid to advance world peace, stability, and humanitarianism

FIGURE 13–2

Social, political, and economic goals of the AFL-CIO (Source: *The AFL-CIO Platform Proposals Presented to the Democratic and Republican National Conventions 1980* [Washington, DC: AFL-CIO, undated].)

expressly forbade the federal courts from issuing injunctions in labor disputes, except to maintain law and order during a union activity. The act also forbade employers from enforcing a *yellow dog contract*, which stipulated as a condition of employment that an employee was not a union member and would not join a union. (Labor believed only a "yellow dog" would accept a job under such terms.)

National Labor Relations Act (1935)

The 1929 stock market crash had plunged the United States into a major depression, the worst in its history. The impact of the Great Depression on workers was devastating. One-third of the country's work force was unemployed. The labor movement made more emphatic efforts to organize and demand recognition and became more politically active. The severity of conditions led to public sympathy for its problems.

For years the United States struggled over the right of workers to organize and to negotiate collectively with employers. Judicial solutions to the struggle were ineffective. Court decisions, by their nature, were confined to particular parties, to narrow situations, and to fixed time frames. Such decisions could not give national guidance. The Great Depression and the selection of Franklin D. Roosevelt as president with strong labor support set the stage for the passage of national legislation. Roosevelt quickly proved his interest in the plight of the worker. The National Industrial Recovery Act (1933) recognized workers' right to select their own representatives. The National Recovery Administration, well intentioned but poorly constructed, had no power to enforce the act, and industry largely ignored it. Within two years the National Industrial Recovery Act was declared unconstitutional.

The unemployment problem continued, and Roosevelt responded with the creation of such New Deal programs as the Civilian Conservation Corps (CCC), unemployment insurance, the Social Security program, and the Works Progress Administration (WPA). But these measures alone were not enough.

Senator Robert Wagner, a champion for labor who had Roosevelt's support, proposed an act that recognized employees' rights to organize and bargain collectively. A quasi-judicial tribunal with the power and authority to enforce its own orders would be created. While the act was purported to protect the public from the disruption of interstate commerce resulting from labor disputes, Senator Wagner stated that it would also give the employee freedom. Labor–management relations generally improved after the passage of this historic act, and union membership rapidly grew to levels previously undreamed of by labor leaders.

The National Labor Relations Act of 1935 is more widely known as the Wagner Act because it was sponsored by New York Senator Robert Wagner. The Wagner Act is often called the Magna Carta of organized labor. In essence, the act protects a worker's right to join a union without the employer's interference. Bringing broad powers and sweeping reform to the labor movement, the act encouraged the movement's spectacular growth between 1935 and the early 1950s. Important provisions of the act include the following:

- The employer may not interfere with, restrain, or coerce employees in the exercise of their right to join unions and bargain collectively through representatives of their own choosing.
- The employer may not dominate or interfere with the formation or administration of labor unions.

- The employer may not discriminate against the employee in any condition of employment for taking part in legal union activities.
- The employer may not fire or discriminate against the employee for charging an unfair labor practice against the company.
- The employer may not refuse to bargain collectively with employee representatives in good faith.

National Labor Relations Board (NLRB) The NLRB was created to administer and enforce the Wagner Act. The National Labor Relations Board is an independent agency of the federal government; members are presidential appointees. The first of the NLRB's two main functions is to investigate charges of *unfair labor practices*. Basically, an unfair labor practice exists when either the employer or the union violates any provision of labor law. For example, a union will likely charge the employer with an unfair labor practice if the employer bribes employees to vote against the union or discriminates against employees who hold prounion sentiments. Examples of activities that may result in a charge of unfair labor practice against a union include instigating violence on a picket line, refusing to bargain in good faith with the employer, charging union employees excessive initiation fees or dues, and featherbedding. If the NLRB finds an employer guilty of a violation and the employer fails to alter certain practices, the board will seek legal action through the U.S. Court of Appeals. Employers may appeal the decisions of the board.

A second function of the board is to conduct certification elections by secret ballot to determine whether employees will be represented by a union. The election process will be discussed later in this chapter.

Labor-Management Relations Act (1947)

While the Wagner Act may be appropriately called prolabor, the Labor-Management Relations Act—more commonly known as the *Taft–Hartley Act*—is decidedly promanagement. Its purpose was to create a balance of power between unions and employers. During the decade following the passage of the Wagner Act in 1935, a feeling developed that unions had grown too big and too influential, that their escalating power had to be brought under control. The act that was sponsored by Senator Robert Taft and Representative Frederick Hartley actually amends the Wagner Act. Important provisions of the Taft–Hartley Act include the following:

- The union may not coerce or restrain employees from exercising their bargaining rights. For example, the union may not make false statements to employees during organizing drives.
- The union may not cause an employer to discriminate against an employee in order to encourage or discourage union membership.
- The union may not refuse to bargain in good faith with the employer.
- The union may not engage in featherbedding. The U.S. Supreme Court has decided that it is lawful to require employers to pay for make-work projects even though they may be inefficient or ineffective.

Section 14b From labor's perspective, a particularly troublesome provision in labor law is Section 14b of the Taft–Hartley Act. This section allows individual states to pass legislation that bars any form of compulsory union membership; such states are known as *right-to-work* *states*. About twenty states, mostly located in the South and Southwest, have passed such legislation.

Section 14B has long been a battleground between organized labor and right-to-work advocates. Labor leaders have for years attempted to repeal it. On the other side, the National Right to Work Committee, whose membership is estimated at 1.25 million, lobbies to advance the right-to-work movement and presses for federal right-to-work legislation.[25]

Labor–Management Reporting and Disclosure Act (1959)

During the 1950s, unionism's reputation was tarnished considerably when a series of exposés uncovered corruption and racketeering in unions, particularly in the Teamsters Union. During 1952 and 1953, the state of New York found widespread racketeering on the New York City waterfront involving the International Longshoremen's Union. The investigation, which uncovered gross mismanagement of the union pension fund, was a principal factor underlying the passage of the Welfare and Pension Plans Disclosure Act of 1958.

The most widely publicized account of union corruption was the investigation held by the McClellan Committee in the U.S. Senate. The committee heard 1,526 witnesses in 270 days of hearings. Over half of the testimony was devoted to racketeering and corruption in the Teamsters Union. The committee hearings ultimately led to the expulsion from the AFL-CIO of the Teamsters Union and the Laundry and Bakery and Confectionery Workers union. The committee hearings influenced the passage of the Labor–Management Reporting and Disclosure Act of 1959, more commonly known as the *Landrum–Griffin Act*.

Important provisions of the act include the following:

- Creation of a "bill of rights" for union members. The act provided equal rights for union members to attend, participate, and vote in meetings; the right to meet and express any views or opinions about union business and candidates; the right to be free of unreasonably high dues, fees, and assessments; the right to testify against and sue the union for violation of their rights; and the right to inspect copies of collective-bargaining agreements.
- Reporting requirements. The act requires unions to submit an annual financial report covering assets, liabilities, income, expenses, and so on to the secretary of labor, who must approve the report.
- Election safeguards. The act set forth the ground rules for proper union conduct during elections. For example, ballots must be secret and every member in good standing must be allowed a vote.
- Restrictions on officers. The act disallows convicted felons from holding union office for five years after conviction. The act also requires union officials to be bonded.

UNION STRUCTURE AND MANAGEMENT

There are approximately 175 national and international unions in America. *National* unions have collective bargaining agreements with different employers in two or more states; *international* unions are headquartered in the United States but have members in Canada. The three largest national unions are those of the teamsters, the auto workers, and the steelworkers.[26]

A union is a private, nonprofit organization whose primary purpose is to advance the interests of its members. In many respects, a union closely resembles the structure and operation of a business firm. Union leaders must plan and organize activities, recruit and hire for union positions, create and manage a budget, influence and motivate other union officials and the rank-and-file membership, see that union goals are met, and be sure that union policies, procedures, and rules are followed. In particular, they must be able to influence and persuade management representatives when a new union contract is being negotiated. A union's function contains basic elements common to all organizations: union goals must be created, jobs must be defined, leaders must be given responsibilities and authority, and departments must be formed. But many real differences exist in the operation and function of a union and a private enterprise. The main differences include:[27]

Power Structure In a business firm, leaders are appointed; authority and power flow from the top to the bottom. Union officials are elected by the rank and file or by convention delegates; power flows (at least theoretically) from the bottom to the top.

Ultimate Authority The ultimate authority in business and government organizations is held by top management. It decides the direction the organization will take and determines how to solve critical problems. The rank and file possess ultimate authority in the union, because collective-bargaining agreements normally must be ratified (approved by a vote) by the membership. Ratification is not always a rubber-stamp procedure. Union members occasionally send their leaders back to the bargaining table to negotiate for better economic rewards and working conditions.

Managerial Selection In industry or government, an individual may become a manager with no managerial experience. For example, a recent college graduate may take a job as a production supervisor or office manager. Many corporate executives find little difficulty in moving from one industry to another. But almost without exception, union leaders work their way up through the ranks. They typically begin as rank-and-file union members. Moving as an official from one union to another is rare.

Salaries Salaries of $100,000 or more a year for top corporate leaders hardly raise an eyebrow. In 1983, the twenty-five highest-paid executives in the United States each received total compensation of over $2 million.[28] But seven-figure salaries—or anything close—are nonexistent for top-level union leaders. Data filed with the U.S. Department of Labor showed that the highest-paid union official in 1984 was the Teamsters' president, who received a salary of $491,000. Lane Kirkland, president of the AFL-CIO, made $117,609, including salary and expenses.[29]

Tenure At the top of the corporate structure, executives rarely remain in the same position for ten or more years. A certain value is placed on fresh leadership and an orderly system for transferring power to new groups of leaders. Historically, top union leaders have enjoyed tenures of considerable length. For example, John L. Lewis was president of the United Mine Workers for thirty-nine years; Dan Tobin led the Teamsters through its early history for forty-five years. There are few roadblocks to long tenure, because length of service tends to perpetuate itself. The power and charisma of a top union leader often prove to be formidable barriers to the up-and-coming union official.

Local Unions

Most local unions are affiliated with national or international unions. Local unions receive their charters from the national union, which may disband or suspend the local. Less than 2 percent of all local unions are completely independent; they generally serve a single employer or small geographical territory.

Local union leaders are elected by their members, usually for a one-year term. While local union leadership varies by size and union, a typical leadership group consists of a president, vice-president, secretary, and treasurer. In very large locals, union officials work full time for the local union. More often, however, the officials have a full-time job and conduct union affairs on their own time and on time allowed by a company during working hours.

Perhaps the local union's most critical function is to negotiate a contract with employers. The contract is most frequently negotiated by either the president of the local or the business agent; sometimes the contract is negotiated by representatives from the national union. A *business agent* is an elected, full-time, salaried official who represents a large union. The agent may also be heavily involved in handling employee grievances or leading union members during a strike.

Another important local union member is the *shop steward*, sometimes referred to as a *committeeman* or *grievance person*. As the last term suggests, the steward acts as the union representative in processing grievances against management. The handling of grievances will be discussed in detail in chapter 14.

National and International Unions

Like a corporate headquarters with plants and offices scattered throughout the United States, national or international unions direct and support local unions. Direction and support are achieved by creating major policies and maintaining important functions and programs. Some of those policies, functions, and programs include:

- Creating uniform contract provisions regarding wages or seniority for local unions in a given area or industry.
- Assisting the local union in contract negotiations.
- Training local union officials in union management and administration.
- Creating and administering strike funds to support local union members on strike.
- Providing data-collection services for cost-of-living data, wage data, and so on.
- Increasing union membership by organizing nonunion employees.

National or international unions often employ elected officials and staff specialists appointed by top union leaders. Economists, lawyers, and public-relations specialists provide valuable services in promoting the union effort.

Independent Unions

The majority of national or international unions are affiliated with the AFL-CIO. The AFL-CIO's share of all union members is about 84 percent.[30] Some unions decided at their inception to remain autonomous and thus never joined the AFL or the CIO. Others, such as the Teamsters in 1957, were expelled from the AFL for corruption; eleven unions were expelled from the CIO. In 1987 the Teamsters rejoined the AFL-CIO, ending one of the deepest rifts in the labor movement.

The AFL-CIO

The AFL-CIO is the heart of American labor. A single federation of autonomous labor unions, the AFL-CIO influences the activities of its member unions and the labor movement as a whole. Eighty-nine of the national and international unions in the United States are AFL-CIO affiliates. The structure of the AFL-CIO is shown in Figure 13–3.

The national and international affiliates operate autonomously, retaining decentralized decision-making authority over their own affairs. AFL-CIO officials are not authorized to call strikes, influence the negotiating process, or control the behavior of affiliate leaders. Why then have most unions joined the AFL-CIO? According to labor expert Martin Esten, the AFL-CIO provides its members with a number of specialized services.[31]

The plain fact is that the AFL-CIO is not directly involved in the fundamental union function of collective bargaining. For all practical purposes that function is reserved for the national unions and, to a lesser extent, for the locals. The primary role of the federation, instead, may be described as broadly political. The AFL-CIO is to organized labor roughly what the United States Chamber of Commerce

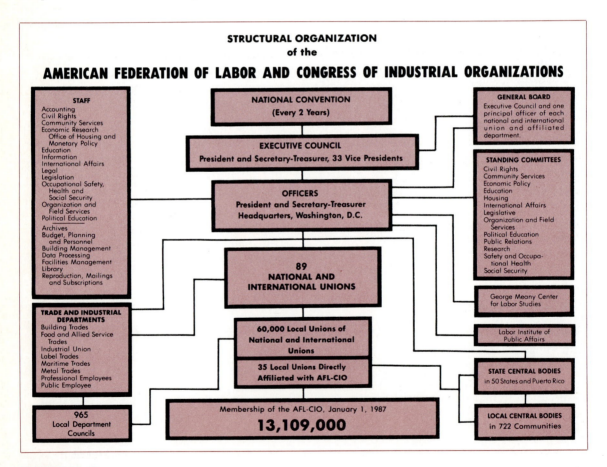

FIGURE 13–3

The structure of the AFL-CIO (Source: *This Is the AFL-CIO,* Publication no. 20 [Washington, DC: AFL-CIO, 1987], by permission of the AFL-CIO.)

is to business; it is engaged in lobbying, public relations, research, and education to present labor's views on countless problems—not only on wages, hours, and working conditions, but also on topics ranging from public housing to foreign policy. In addition, the federation performs various necessary functions within the labor movement. It charters new international unions, tries to minimize friction between affiliated unions and settle the disputes which occasionally break out between them, maintains a staff of organizers, and provides research and legal assistance primarily for unions too small to afford their own research staffs.

Generally, the goals of the AFL-CIO and those of the supporters of management are in stark contrast. On rare occasions, however, the labor federation and management representatives join hands in agreement. In the past, the AFL-CIO and the so-called big three auto makers (General Motors, Ford, and Chrysler) combined forces to oppose the tide of auto imports and successfully lobby for voluntary limits on Japanese imports. In 1985, the AFL-CIO and the U.S. Chamber of Commerce both issued statements opposing congressional plans to tax employee fringe benefits.[32] Labor opposed the plan because it would raise taxes, reduce employee income, and place more demands on government programs. Management fought the proposal because of the additional administrative burdens and the likely pressures from employees to offset higher tax payments with wage and salary increases.[33]

THE ORGANIZING DRIVE

The impetus to organize employees may come from two sources. First, the workers may be dissatisfied with their pay or work conditions and initiate contact with the union. Such is typically the case. Second, workers may be contacted by a *union organizer,* a full-time, sal-aried staff member who generally represents a national union. As the job title suggests, the union organizer increases union membership and strength by organizing groups of workers who are not presently unionized. An organizing drive usually follows the series of events shown in Figure 13–4.

The union's goal is to organize workers and bring them into the union. Labor's strategy is to convince the workers that union membership will bring them benefits they do not presently enjoy. Union organizers may suggest that union representation will result in higher pay, more benefits, better working conditions, and greater fairness in promotions, job transfers, and layoffs. Speaking proudly of the benefits and work improvements they have achieved for other workers, union organizers often cite impressive and convincing statistics about wage gains achieved through collective bargaining. To tell the union side of the story, labor advocates hold formal meetings at the local union hall and encourage supporters to spread the word informally about the benefits a union would bring to the employees' place of work. Prounion handbills and flyers are often passed to workers as they leave work or go to lunch. An example of a handbill is shown in Figure 13–5.

Management's goal is simply to keep the union out of the work place. Their strategy is to convince the workers that unionization will do them more harm than good. Management may attempt to assure workers that their present pay and benefits are competitive and may show data to prove it. Emphasizing a philosophy of fair dealings with all employees, management may discuss the union's involvement in violent or corrupt activities if such has been the case. Management will also enumerate the costs of union membership, which include initiation fees, dues, and other assessments. The workers will be reminded that wages will be lost should a strike occur. Management

FIGURE 13–4
The organizing process

may also talk about the loss of freedom and the potential erosion in labor-management relations that unionization might bring.

Illegal Activities

Throughout the organizing drive, emotions often run high on both sides, and both union and management supporters often make passionate and dramatic arguments to further their causes. To ensure that both labor and management play fair during the organizing drive, labor legislation has spelled out in detail illegal campaign tactics. During the organizing drive, union representatives or prolabor employees cannot:[34]

- Solicit employees where they are working unless employees are normally allowed to converse while they work. Oral solicitation is acceptable during breaks and lunch.

- Distribute union literature in work areas; nonwork areas typically include lunch rooms and break areas.

- Offer an employee free union membership before the election unless free membership is granted to everyone who joins the union up to the time the first contract is negotiated.

- Offer excessive attendance prizes to employees who attend a campaign rally. Payment of a sum of money to each participant is an obvious infraction of the rule.

- Make substantial misrepresentations. While both management and labor are allowed a generous amount of puffing (promises and propaganda), the *Hollywood Ceramics* rule forces the election to be set aside if either side makes a "substantial misrepresentation on a material fact made at a time when the other party has inadequate time to respond and correct the misrepresentation.''

During the organizing drive, representatives of employers cannot:[35]

- Discipline or threaten employees who engage in lawful solicitation or distribution of union material.
- Prohibit existing employees from legal solicitation and distribution activities at work. Management can, if it desires, prohibit outside union organizers from entering the premises. The only exception to this rule is the rare case when employees are normally inaccessible—such as maritime workers on a ship.

FIGURE 13–5
An example of a union handbill

- Engage in antiunion rhetoric before a mass audience twenty-four hours before an election. However, the twenty-four hours rule does not forbid talks to individuals and small groups.
- Speak to employees in ''area of management authority'' such as the bosses' offices or management conference rooms. Such a setting is thought by the NLRB to be overly intimidating.
- Tell employees that absolutely no good will come if the union gets in. Called the *futility doctrine*, this prohibits the employer from making statements suggesting that it is futile for the employees to unionize.
- Appeal to racial prejudice by pitting black or white workers against one another by suggesting that a certain race would benefit from unionization.
- Promise certain benefits if the union loses. Further, a raise in pay or an increase in benefits cannot be given during the drive unless the increase was planned before the election. Similarly, existing benefits or a planned increase in benefits cannot be rescinded because of the union campaign.
- Keep track of employees' union activities or give the impression that prounion employees are under surveillance.

Representation Election

Before an election is called, the union must prove that a sizable number of employees favor union representation by getting at least 30 percent of the employees to sign an *authorization card* or petition. The card, as shown in Figure 13–6, states that the employee designates the union as the bargaining agent. If more than 50 percent of the employees sign authorization cards, the union may formally request the employer to recognize it as the

FIGURE 13–6

A union authorization card

University of Louisville
American Association of University Professors

I, _____, hereby desig-
nate the University of Louisville Chapter of the American Association of
University Professors to represent my professional and economic interests in collective bargaining.

Date:

_____   _____
                                        Signature

                      _____
                                        Department

---

employees' bargaining agent. Even though a majority of the employees may have signed authorization cards, the employer still generally refuses to recognize the union. The union must then formally petition the NLRB to hold an election.[36]

The NLRB oversees the representation election to ensure that at least 30 percent of the employees in the bargaining unit have signed authorization cards and that no illegal campaign activities have taken place. At this time, the NLRB investigator also defines the *bargaining unit*. The bargaining unit is the group of employees the union will represent and bargain for if the election favors the union. Although the NLRB considers several factors in deciding the makeup of the bargaining unit, the most important is the *community of interest principle*; that is, the more employees have in common, the more likely the board is to find that they constitute a valid bargaining unit. Specific factors examined by the board include similarity of work performed, geographical proximity of workers, job integration, similarity of working conditions, prevailing wage rates and benefits, and whether

employees work under a common management group. If the union wins the election, all employees within the bargaining unit—both union and nonunion employees—will be represented by the union. Management cannot treat the union employee any differently than the nonunion employee.

Certification and Decertification

The union becomes the official bargaining agent for the employees if it receives over 50 percent of the votes cast in a secret election. If the union does not receive at least 50 percent of the votes cast, it is not allowed to petition the NLRB for another representation election for at least a year.

Under the provisions of the Taft–Hartley Act, an NLRB certification is valid only for a one-year period. After that time, employees (but not the employer) within the bargaining unit may petition the NLRB for a *decertification election*. In a process similar to the representation election, the NLRB will conduct a vote if at least 30 percent of the employees sign the petition. If labor fails to receive a majority vote, it loses its bargaining rights, and no additional elections within the bargaining unit may be held for one year. The purpose of the decertification election is to allow employees to rid themselves of a union in which they no longer have faith or confidence. As would be expected, employers will campaign strongly for the defeat of a union, and they may use any lawful method to achieve that end.

Since the passage of Taft–Hartley, unions have generally lost a majority of decertification elections. Nonetheless, many labor authorities agree that decertification elections pose little threat to the labor movement. Their reasoning is that the loss of union members through decertification typically falls far short of the total employees gained through successful representation elections. For example, in one year unions lost 73 percent of the 902 decertification elections held, involving 21,249 union members. But in the same year, unions won 45 percent of the representation elections conducted, earning bargaining rights or continuing as representatives for 196,515 employees.

Maintaining Nonunion Status: Dirty Tricks?

Some firms have taken unorthodox and controversial means to ensure a union-free environment. For example, the organizing fight between the DuPont Chemical Company and the United Steelworkers union brought to light a number of questionable techniques that an employer may use to remain non-union. As reported in the *Wall Street Journal*, DuPont engaged in the following activities to keep out the Steelworkers:[37]

- In order to create antiunion sentiment using its employees, DuPont produced a twelve-minute film linking big unions— including the Steelworkers—to the de-

cline of American steel and auto industries.

- The Steelworkers uncovered confidential DuPont documents that showed that union sympathizers were singled out for "neutralization and control." DuPont responded by starting at a DuPont plant in Tennessee a "know your employee" program, which required supervisors to learn as much as possible about each employee's opinions, prejudices, outside interests, and associations.

- Management sent persuasive letters "explaining the issues" in the union campaign to relatives of workers in hopes that they would pass on promanagement sentiments to family members who worked for DuPont.

- A guidebook used by DuPont managers in Delaware included a recommendation that plant officers cooperate with local police to identify owners of unfamiliar cars with out-of-state plates that showed up near the plant.

What was the reasoning behind DuPont's zealous efforts to remain union free? H. Gorden Smith, general manager of employee relations at DuPont, stated that the company was worried that a "remote third party" such as the Steelworkers would cause friction between management and its employees. Smith said, "You would create a more adversarial relationship that would build toward more restrictive work conditions."[38] The company also admitted that it was fearful about the strike threat that the large, powerful Steelworkers could pose.

Other firms strive to maintain nonunion status by coupling a reasonable degree of job satisfaction with a firm message to employees that the employer wishes to remain nonunion. Texas Instruments (TI), one of the country's largest nonunion firms, begins its antiunion indoctrination during a new employee's first hour of orientation. The message in a TI-produced videotape is that unions are detrimental and unnecessary for progress, and an orientation booklet encourages employees to "reject the union attempts to organize should they be approached by union organizers."[39]

A *Wall Street Journal* reporter, disguised as a new employee, also found most TI employees unwilling to even talk about the union for fear that their jobs would somehow be in jeopardy. As one employee told the undercover reporter, "Don't you mess with unions, girl, that's one thing that'll put you out the door faster'n what you come it. If TI finds out you're even bending that way, well, you won't progress at TI. You'll be the first one laid off. They'll put you somewhere you can't make no trouble." TI claims that it has never violated NLRB regulations by discharging anyone for prounion activities or sentiments. According to a top company official, "We don't have to go that far. If we had people who wanted a union we would be very concerned, but we don't. No company can be nonunion if the employees want a union."[40]

Benefits of Unionization

The decision to accept or resist unionization should not be made on ideological or emotional grounds but should be approached rationally and objectively as an important business decision. After considering both sides of the issue, the employer may believe that the union would enhance the effectiveness and profitability of the enterprise. Potential benefits of unionization include:[41]

- Employee recruiting and selection are enhanced by using the union hiring hall. The *hiring hall* is the local building where union activity takes place. The union normally sends the employer only pre-screened, qualified employees.

- Being organized by a union with which the employer has had or is expected to have good working relationships is preferable to being organized by a less acceptable union.

- By organizing all companies in an industry or area, the union forces all companies to pay union scale, which minimizes price competition for employees.

PREVENTIVE LABOR RELATIONS

There are a number of strategies that businesses may implement to maintain nonunion status. These strategies are termed *preventive labor relations*. In the 1970s and 1980s, a number of books, journal articles, seminars, and labor consultants offered an increasing number of techniques for keeping an organization union free. The growth in preventive labor relations is, no doubt, due to the desire to keep labor and operating costs as low as possible. In the 1980s many firms that aggressively pursued union-free status experienced considerable success.

Deterring the Organizing Drive

After weighing the advantages and disadvantages of unionization, if the company decides to remain nonunion, management may attempt to prevent the organizing drive from taking place rather than trying to win the representation election once a drive has gotten under way. First, winning a representation election is expensive. One study of 146 NLRB representation elections found the employer paying between $100 and $125 per hourly employee.[42] Second, research shows that both union and employer campaigns are largely ineffective in changing employees' attitudes, because most will vote as they had planned before the actual campaign got under way. Thus, if management expects to change employees' attitudes toward the union, positive steps must be taken well in advance of the union organization drive.

In general, the most effective way for a firm to practice preventive labor relations is to give the employees the benefit of unionization without the union. Simply put, if an employer provides the kind of work environment that employees want, they will not seek out a union. Administrators who value their human resources and conduct an effective program of personnel management are much less likely to face an organization drive than those who view the employee as simply another factor of production.

Conditions that prevent union drives are generally those that employees have sought since the early stages of the labor movement: a system for resolving employees' complaints, safe working conditions, good wages and benefits, job security, fair and equitable personnel policies, people-oriented supervision, open channels of communication with management, a voice in the decisions that affect their work, and a feeling that management is concerned about their welfare. Inattention to most or all of these job conditions more than likely will bring a union organizer to management's doorstep.

Labor Consultants

A growing number of firms are employing high-priced labor consultants and law firms to help them remain union free. A U.S. House of Representatives labor subcommittee reported that such labor-relations advisors gross more than $500 million a year, a fact that many labor experts claim is in large part responsible for labor's increasing failure to win representation elections. Increasing numbers of workers have also rejected unions in decertification elections.[43]

Labor consultants provide services in one of two general ways. First, they may consult with an employer during an organizing or de-

certification drive, advising management on techniques to keep the union out or to get rid of the union. Second, several consulting firms hold seminars on how to maintain a union-free environment. One popular firm regularly conducts seminars entitled "How to Maintain Nonunion Status" and "The Process of Decertification." A brochure published by the firm lists the following topics for the seminar "How to Maintain Nonunion Status":

- Who are the target industries and target employee groups?
- What makes your organization vulnerable?
- How will the union develop its appeals?
- How will the union attempt to organize?
- How to achieve commitment to your nonunion policy.
- How to conduct a nonunion audit.
- How to react when a union threat is anticipated.
- New strategies available in organizing campaigns.
- How to avoid union campaign pitfalls.

Consultants assert that they use perfectly legal means to help management remain nonunion. Herbert Melnick, chairman of one of the nation's largest labor consulting firms, claims, "We don't use illegal tactics. Our purpose in every campaign is to give employees the right to make an informed choice, and to improve communications."[44] Union organizers disagree, contending that "advisers prevent workers from exercising free choice by teaching managers to harass, intimidate, and threaten their subordinates."[45]

The Future of Unions

The circumstances in many U.S. industries are the same: foreign competition with cheap labor, new labor-saving technology, and companies merging to gain economic strength. The auto industry is the classic example. The

United Auto Workers union estimates that between 1987 and the early 1990s it will lose 30 percent, or 540,000, of the remaining auto manufacturing jobs. For example, in 1987, General Motors made about 70 percent of every car itself, Ford only 50 percent. As GM saw its U.S. market share drop, however, it turned to nonunion and foreign suppliers to cut costs. The underlying problem is productivity to match foreign competition and thus compete in the showroom.[46]

The truth is that unions have been losing ground, in terms of membership, for more than 40 years (see Figure 13–1). The decline in union membership since the 1940s can be traced to several factors. The number of new workers included in organization elections per year has declined significantly, as has the success rate of unions trying to win those new workers in elections. Unions have also lost existing members by losing decertification elections. The 1970s were particularly difficult for unions, as membership declined in highly unionized manufacturing industries hard hit by recession and foreign competition. Even if these industries had not lost employment, union membership would have declined due to unions' poor performance in certification and decertification elections.[47]

What are some of the reasons for the decline? First, the changing economy, from manufacturing to service, is a part of the answer. Even in the traditional union stronghold, production jobs, however, the proportion of union employees also declined, from 73 to 51 percent from 1961 to 1984. This substantial drop in the nation's large cities was not limited to production workers; the membership of nonsupervisory office clerical workers in unions declined from 17 to 12 percent in the same period. Only part of the decline can be attributed to the employment shift toward service industries, because this shift occurred *within* the union core of manufacturing

and related clerical areas. Explanations of the production industry's decline in union membership include the move to less unionized Sun Belt states, the increased number of smaller and harder-to-organize plants, the trend toward building new facilities in rural, less unionized areas, and the dramatic increase in nonunion electronics production facilities such as those found in Silicon Valley near San Jose, California.[48]

Dwindling union membership has caused an increase in the number of mergers of labor organizations. In 1984 alone, five mergers involved over 3.7 million members. Although mergers of labor organizations have always been a part of the labor movement, the five years between 1979 and 1984 saw thirty mergers—35 percent of all mergers since 1955.[49]

Younger workers, women, and minorities in the past generally were not courted by labor and now may find traditional labor unions unresponsive to their needs, although a U.S. Department of Labor survey confirmed that these workers were as willing as white males to join unions if their job conditions warranted unionization.[50]

Union avoidance has become a major task of human resource managers in such traditional nonunion areas as health care, financial planning, and insurance. These white-collar workers are obvious targets of organizational campaigns. Their responsibilities and education cause their expectations of respect and participation in the work place to be higher even than those of assembly-line workers.[51] Clerical employees, the majority of whom are women, may be increasingly attracted to unions, especially when the union organization is geared to their demographics.[52] More employers are developing a company strategy that, hopefully, will keep unions from even starting an organizational effort. In the past, many of these employers would have waited until the union was at their door before beginning any antiunion efforts. Union avoidance strategies appear to be effective; new plants without such strategies are almost six times more likely to be organized than those that have avoidance strategies.[53] A union avoidance strategy generally includes specific personnel policies designed to keep unions out by addressing employees' interests and concerns to reflect changes often sought by unions. Common ways to avoid unions include:[54]

- Instituting valid performance reviews to ensure employees of nonpartial merit raises and promotions to counter the seniority provisions usually contained in union contracts.
- Improving communication with employees so that managers sense discontent before it becomes a major problem.
- Establishing fair grievance procedures.
- Creating a pleasant office environment.
- Promoting potential union leaders to management.
- Pursuing a more people-oriented approach to dealing with employees.

Another reason for the decline in union membership is the past success of unions in achieving changes in laws that have eliminated many workers' problems. Child labor, minimum wage, occupational health and safety, and workers' compensation laws today protect workers from past problems. How long these laws would remain unchanged and enforced without continued union support is an important question. The public's image of unions and their organizing and strike efforts also continues to be a problem that union leaders recognize as significant.

Given the rather bleak statistics and other facts, do unions really have a future in America? Lane Kirkland, president of the AFL-CIO, says "yes" and provides specific reasons for his answer: labor unions were in the same position before. In the early 1930s, it was predicted that trade unions were about to become extinct due to the Great Depression; a large reserve of unemployed workers has always made it difficult for unions to organize and bargain because employers can replace their workers cheaply and easily. But the United States and the unions survived the Depression, just as they will survive the current national adjustment to a service economy and increased foreign competition. For example, while unions have lost millions of industrial workers, they have gained millions in newly organized areas that hold great promise for the future. Union membership is shifting, after a slow start, to reflect the changing composition of the general work force: 42 percent are white-collar and technical workers, 23 percent are craftsmen and supervisors; and only 38 percent are blue-collar workers. Compared to 1955, unions have eleven times as many teachers; ten times as many state, county, and municipal workers; four times as many pilots; three and one-half times as many service employees; three times as many actors and artists; and more than twice as many postal workers, fire fighters, and communication workers.[55]

In 1985 the AFL-CIO's Executive Council noted the findings of the Committee on the Evolution of Work:[56]

- In 1990 the service industry will employ 75 percent of all American workers, only 10 percent of whom will likely be organized.
- The growth of the work force will continue to be in the relatively unorganized Sun Belt states.
- Many workers will continue to find short-term, part-time work instead of the traditional full-time, long-term job opportunities.

- Seventy-five percent of all employers hire consultants to avoid unionization once organizing efforts are started.

- Union workers earn 33 percent more than their counterparts and generally appreciate the benefits of unionization.

In recognition of unions' continuing loss of membership and the findings of the committee, the AFL-CIO in 1985 endorsed sweeping changes and new long-term tactics to rekindle the spirit of unionization among American workers. The new efforts include:[57]

- Corporate campaigns are being directed at large employers with scattered facilities. The corporate strategy generally involves influencing the stockholders, customers, directors, or creditors of the employer. The first successful corporate effort was made by the Amalgamated Clothing and Textile Workers Union, which forced the resignation of several directors of J.P. Stevens and Company, threatened to withdraw $1 billion in union funds from a customer, and even persuaded church groups to boycott Stevens products. Another corporate success is discussed in the "Coors and AFL-CIO End Beer Boycott" feature.

- A new AFL-CIO office of Comprehensive Organizing Strategies and Tactics (COST) was organized, with substantial resources to analyze corporations vulnerable areas and implement organizing campaigns.

- Small businesses, previously largely ignored by unions, will be targeted because they often can be hurt more than large ones by a strike.

- A new esprit de corps is developing among unions. Old jurisdictional disputes will be set aside as unions work together. The Teamsters' move to rejoin the AFL-CIO in 1987 (after being ousted in 1957)

is perhaps most symbolic of this new co-operation. In an organizing effort, eight unions joined together in a nationwide effort to organize 28,000 Blue Cross–Blue Shield employees.

- Associate memberships are being offered to millions of former union members in an effort to regain their support. Almost 28 percent of the nonunion work force enjoy the associate membership benefits: a no-fee Master Card, group life and health insurance, and legal services.

Many union leaders today also realize the need for cooperation between unions and management to survive in some industries. Over 1,000 U.S. employers have labor–management teams that emphasize employee participation and a team approach to doing work and running the company. The team approach is generally credited to Irving Bluestone, vice-president of the United Auto Workers. He negotiated the first contract clause that would allow auto plants to develop a joint problem-solving process involving labor and management.[58] In an automobile assembly plant, for example, rigid job classifications and work rules are eased, and instead of workers performing one specific job, they learn several jobs and can enjoy a greater variety of work, more control over their work, and greater job satisfaction. Job classifications can be substantially reduced in number, work rules loosened, and quality increased. General Electric, Goodyear, and Procter & Gamble have also developed work teams.[59] See chapter 3 for a discussion of work groups, including Volvo's Kalmar auto assembly plant.

Can employees working with a spirit of teamwork develop simultaneous commitments to their unions and their employers? Does the inherent conflict of allegiance in such dual-membership situations force employees to choose one or the other? Studies of these questions have generally reported that employees can develop loyalty and commitment to both their union and their employers when there is a good relationship between the two. However, at times, such as when a union tries to organize new employees, the adversarial relationship between employer and union can cause employees to perceive that they must choose to be loyal to one or the other. They may easily see their vote—for or against union representation—as a forced choice. They cannot envision a long-term positive relationship that would allow them to be loyal to both entities.[60]

New Cooperation?

Can labor and management change from their traditional adversarial relationship to a team approach to problem solving? Today many corporate executives and political leaders are calling for an expansion of cooperative efforts at the work place, such as quality circles, quality of work life (QWL) programs, and continued moderation in wage demands. At the same time, however, the dominant trend among management is to shift investments and jobs to nonunion employment settings.[61] This trend is strengthened by Supreme Court decisions allowing plant relocations, liquidations, and partial closing without union input or consideration of affected workers.[62] It is difficult to see how unions can act cooperatively when management practices often undermine their basic existence. If the trend of the 1980s continues, unions may face a life-and-death struggle, forcing them into confrontation rather than cooperation. American unions will most likely strive to avoid further membership losses by promoting innovations in the work place to maintain organizational competitiveness, increasing their influence on strategic business and governmental decisions that affect membership, and pursuing new organizing strategies.[63]

The U.S. Department of Labor is optimistic that a new era of cooperation is possible. In 1986 it began a comprehensive review of the nation's labor laws and practices.[64] The purpose of this first-ever study is to determine how the federal government can support increased labor-management cooperation and a ''mutual respect for collective bargaining.'' The review will include an analysis of many of the more experimental cooperative efforts such as worker participation plans (AT&T and the Communication Workers of America), worker retraining programs (Ford and the United Auto Workers), and the Fremont, California, joint venture (GM-Toyota and the United Auto Workers). According to Labor Secretary William E. Brock, the framework of our existing labor laws and culture often hinders cooperative efforts such as QWL programs and worker participation. Too often our present values foster confrontation rather than goals that encourage cooperation. The Department of Labor hopes to work with labor and management leaders in the formulation of a legislative strategy to modify existing laws to encourage cooperation and innovation.[65]

Labor Secretary Brock has also strongly suggested that the nation's business schools take the lead in training individuals in labor-management cooperation. Business schools, he noted, can teach the skills necessary for workers and managers to realize their mutual goals. In the past, inadequate preparation in labor–management relations may have aided in developing adversarial positions. Brock has asked the business schools in our universities to modify their curricula and train future labor and management leaders about the totality of the work relationship, with particular empha-

Coors and AFL-CIO End Beer Boycott

As a result of an agreement between Coors and the AFL-CIO signed August 19, 1987, the union says it is now okay to buy the popular beer from Golden, Colorado. And Coors says it is OK to seek union representation—if you are one of its workers and if you really think you have to.

"We have always believed that it's up to the employees," said Coors spokesman John Meadows. "It's their right and freedom of choice. But we've stated in our company philosophy that we happen to believe that third party representation isn't necessary."

In return for some labor concessions by Coors, the AFL-CIO has called off the boycott that recruited not only the general beer drinking public but also blacks, Hispanics, feminists and college students led by Frontlash, the union youth organization. Coors will not impede union efforts to organize. All future building projects will also be managed under a union agreement or a union project agreement that will preestablish the wage rate, the basis on which both union and nonunion companies will bid on each contract.

The union is claiming victory based on the broadsiding of Coors' market by the boycott. "We in the labor movement are immensely proud of the resolution of this boycott and of its guarantee to the Coors workers of a free and fair opportunity to exercise their right to form and join a union," said AFL-CIO President Lane Kirkland. ". . . It is a resounding success—not only for the effort but also for the interest of the workers in the Coors establishment."

Started as a wage and benefit dispute between Coors and Brewery Workers Local 366 in April 1977, the conflict gained national exposure a week after 1,500 workers walked. Coors hired replacements and terminated the union shop rule requiring union membership. The AFL-CIO approved the Coors boycott, appealing to consumers in only the 14 western states that served Coors at that time.

The boycott hurt sales, to be sure. But the company continued to grow, reaching into a total of 47 states by the time the agreement was reached. But over the last decade, the beer company regarded growing competition as a greater threat than a shrinking customer base.

Source: Reprinted from the September 1987 issue of *Resource*, copyright 1987, The American Society for Personnel Administration, Alexandria, VA.

sis on labor-management relations and coop-eration.[66]

ORGANIZING CHALLENGES FOR UNIONS

Health-care Workers

While impressive gains have been scored in adding teachers and government workers to the roles of union employees, other service workers remain largely unorganized. Among those are most of the country's 6 million hospital, nursing-home, and other health-care workers. Today unions represent only 15 percent of these employees. According to one professor of industrial relations, the health-care industry is "one of the key service industries they [unions] need to organize if they're going to adjust to changes in the structure of the economy."[67]

In the past, many health-care employees such as nurses and pharmacists viewed unions as unprofessional and a potential drawback to achieving quality patient care. A number of unprecedented layoffs and wage-and-benefit cutbacks, however, have forced many health-care employees to rethink the union issue. Further, unions such as the Hospital and Health-Care Employees Union, the American Federation of State, County, and Municipal Employees, and the Teamsters have become much more sophisticated in their drives to organize health-care workers: hiring professional pollsters to identify workers' problems, producing videotapes to promote the advantages of unionization, and publicizing problems in patient care as well as the health-care industry.[68]

Because organizing employees hospital by hospital is a slow and often ineffective process, some unions, such as the Service Employees International Union (SEIU), are di-recting their efforts toward large chains of health-care institutions in hopes that successful organizing drives will add hundreds or thousands to their membership. For example, the SEIU, in concert with another union, planned to spend up to $1 million to organize the employees of Beverly Enterprises, Inc., the nation's largest nursing-home chain, employing 60,000 workers. A successful organizing drive at Beverly would likely lead to efforts at other large nonunion hospital and nursing-home chains. Consequently, health-care managers have begun to improve the working conditions of their nonunion employees.

Secretaries and Clerical Workers

According to an official of the SEIU, "With 20 million office workers in the country—ninety percent of them unorganized—there is room for all sorts of organizations providing relief from what are most often low-paying, boring, repetitive, dead-end jobs."[69] As a result, the SEIU created District 925 (as in the popular movie *Nine-to-Five*), whose primary goal is to organize one of the largest and fastest-growing segments of the country's labor force.

But secretaries and clerical workers present a formidable challenge to unions. First, office workers are spread thinly over thousands of employers, making it difficult and time-consuming to organize workers in large numbers. Second, many office employees hold promanagement attitudes and may themselves aspire to management positions.

Of course, a great number of secretarial and clerical workers are women, and efforts to organize lower-level administrative employees must take into account the unique obstacles that women pose. According to one employee, "Labor has got to go where the work force is; it has to appeal to the female who's educated and for equal rights."[70] To attract more female employees to organized labor, unions have focused special attention on the working woman, lobbying, for example, for health and safety laws for employees who use video display terminals. Organized labor is also trying hard to destroy the still-popular image of unions as institutions run for men and by men.

In an attempt to increase the participation of women in the ranks of organized labor, more and more unions are involving women directly in the organizing process. The president of the National Association of Working Women is female, as are the organizing director for the Teamsters and the president of the Association of Flight Attendants.

Although such women may not fit the cigar-smoking, gruff-talking image of the union organizer of generations ago, their philosophies are no different from those of their predecessors. According to the head of the National Association of Working Women, "The key to improving the conditions of working women lies in organizing the private sector."[71]

Japanese Auto Plants in the United States

The United Auto Workers (UAW) has been considered a powerful force in the labor movement since its formative years in the 1930s. Automation and robots have indirectly taken their toll on the UAW through improved plant productivity, but the most publicized and emotional cause of the declining UAW membership has resulted from the tremendous rise in imported automobiles, notably Japanese-made autos from Honda, Toyota, and Nissan.[72] The crisis intensified in the 1980s as Japanese companies began to build auto plants in the United States, almost all of which were nonunion. "Organizing these plants is as important as it was for us to organize Ford and GM in the 1930s and 1940s," said a UAW official.[73]

The Japanese plants in the United States have used a number of methods to remain union free. First, they openly oppose the union and make no secret of the fact during interviews with job applicants. Second, many employees feel they will have a job for life and believe a union may interfere with the Japanese philosophy of lifelong employment. Third, the Japanese approach to human relations has apparently won favor among many U.S. workers. At Honda and Nissan plants, hourly workers meet daily with their managers to discuss production problems in a collaborative, problem-solving environment. At Nissan, employees are referred to as "production technicians"; at Honda, workers are called "associates." The status differential among managers and hourly workers is also deemphasized by having one dining room and one parking lot for all employees, regardless of position.[74]

Efforts to unionize the Japanese-owned plants have generally been unsuccessful. One Honda employee said, "Why do we need a union? We already get good benefits and good pay. Look at all the companies out of business because of unions."[75] Nevertheless, the UAW has continued its effort. Many labor observers believe that the union will ultimately prevail. A top UAW official said, "It may take years, but we'll be in that plant."[76]

Although the UAW has met with little success in organizing Honda and Nissan workers in the United States, organizing efforts were successful at the Toyota–GM joint venture in Fremont, California. Despite being unionized, the new plant incorporated many Japanese management techniques and was run from its beginning much differently than other automobile plants the UAW represents. For example, labor-management cooperation was stressed, along with such productivity-improvement techniques as flexible job classifications, leaner employment levels, and tougher job standards.[77]

Mazda, another Japanese firm, agreed to accept the UAW in a Michigan plant. Mazda's plant will also be much different than the typical "big three" auto plant, incorporating many techniques patterned after its plant in Japan, considered to be one of the most modern auto production operations in the world.[78]

INTERNATIONAL STATE OF THE UNIONS

In Europe, when the recession of the 1970s spilled into the 1980s, unemployment more than doubled (from 6 million in 1980 to 12.3 million in 1987), and union membership tumbled. And in spite of the class solidarity that has traditionally formed such a strong binding agent in Britain, union membership there dipped from 60 percent of the work force in 1980 to 50 percent in 1984. Even in Italy, long accustomed to interunion squabbles, leaders were hit from behind in 1984 when 40,000 Fiat workers who had been called out on strike marched through the streets of Turin and demanded an end to the stoppage. But perhaps the most dramatic example of this change in attitude occurred in Britain in 1984 when the National Union of Mineworkers did battle with the government of Margaret Thatcher.

Twelve years ago, after holding the country ransom to a three-day work week, the mineworkers had brought down the conservative government of Edward Heath. In 1985, after having two strike calls rejected and a third severely hampered by defiant miners crossing picket lines, they eventually suffered a debilitating defeat that caused one union activist to proclaim that labor in Britain was now "weak, divided and increasingly defeatist."

Although this is undoubtedly an exaggeration, it is indicative of the change that has occurred in union thinking. In a similar vein, in the early 1980s the Belgian government imposed a wage restraint in the face of strong union opposition, and in France the strained relationship between the unions and socialist president Francois Mitterrand was weakened even more with that country's move to the economic right.

The impression from these examples is that European unions are generally becoming more cooperative, even though they have traditionally been more cooperative than their American counterparts (partly because, in Europe, union representatives sit on corporate boards).[79]

As in most of Europe, collective bargaining in Germany is done on an industrywide basis. Although only about one-third of the West German work force is unionized, it sets the pay scale for about 90 percent of the country's workers. And since there are virtually no important industries in Europe to which union recognition does not extend, they generally do not encounter the same resistance as their counterparts in North America, where an adversarial relationship has become a tradition.

But it's a tradition that may be slowly ending. For even in Canada, which has the world's highest strike record and which is one of the few Western countries where union membership has increased, the one forceful demands for a reduced work week were tempered with the phrase "in light of the realities of the time."[80]

CONCLUSIONS AND APPLICATIONS

- A union has a major impact on an organization's management. Many personnel decisions must be shared with the union, and the labor contract limits management's flexibility for the length of the agreement. Finally, poor relations between management and labor may result in costly and stressful organizational conflict.

- The labor movement has a history rich in both success and failure. Highlights of the movement include formation of the Knights of Labor, the AFL, and the CIO, enactment of important labor legislation during the 1930s, 1940s, and 1950s, and the AFL-CIO merger.

- The percentage of the labor force that is organized has slowly declined since the 1950s. Reasons for the decline include the shift from an industrial economy to a service economy; automation, including robotics, increasing foreign competition, resulting in unemployment in the United States; and increased manufacturing of goods by the American manufacturers in foreign countries. The AFL-CIO, however, has adopted bold new strategies to increase union membership.

- The goals of the unions have not changed dramatically since their beginning. Important union goals include union security, job security, improved wages and benefits, favorable working conditions, and fair and just treatment for their members. The AFL-CIO supports many broad social and political goals.

- Relations between organized labor and management are strictly governed by federal legislation. Managers and personnel administrators who work in unionized organizations must be intimately familiar with these laws, which include the Wagner Act, the Taft–Hartley Act, and the Landrum–Griffin Act. Knowledge of labor law is also important for managers should an organizing drive take place within the company.

- The heart of the union structure is the local union, though the national union provides important direction and guidance. The local often receives assistance from the national union during the collective-bargaining process. Most national unions are affiliated with the AFL-CIO, which provides many support services for its affiliates.

- During the organizing drive, the union attempts to convince workers that they will be better off by organizing. Management tries to convince them that they are better off without the union. Labor legislation provides a number of ground rules, but a considerable amount of campaign "puffing" takes place on both sides.

- An organization's decision to remain nonunion should be made rationally by viewing the situation from a cost-benefit perspective. If the costs of remaining nonunion exceed the benefits, the union should be accepted. If the firm decides to stay nonunion, it should practice preventive labor relations by providing workers with good wages and benefits, fair and equitable working conditions, a secure job, supervisors who practice good human relations, and other conditions that represent sound personnel practices and procedures.

CASE STUDY
Dr. Allen's Request for Promotion

"What should I do?" the president of the Argay Company thought as he looked out of his window. Dr. Albert B. James had assumed the presidency of the company less than a year ago. He had already successfully negotiated labor agreements with several of the unions in his company, but two more had to be negotiated within the next twelve months. One of the unions with a contract expiring soon represented Dr. Allen, the employee in question.

Dr. Ivan R. Allen had joined the Chemical Research Division of Argay four years ago as an assistant research chemist. Prior to that, he had spent three years at the University of Illinois, earning a Ph.D. in chemistry. Before doing his doctoral work, Dr. Allen had received a B.Sc. as well as an M.Sc. in chemistry and had been a very successful salesman for a major chemical company. He had left his career in chemical sales after nine years because his goal of working in the sales training area had not been achieved. His manager had intended to place Ivan in the next sales training slot that opened up (a lateral move), but Ivan left the company to pursue his doctoral studies before an opening was available.

Since joining the Chemical Research Division of Argay, Dr. Allen had greatly impressed his associates as well as his managers. He was responsible for research in the synthetic fibers department, and the manager of his department, Dr. George G. Brandt, had remarked in his annual evaluation that Dr. Allen was the best at this job that he had ever seen. As a researcher, Dr. Allen was also expected to present papers at chemical research conferences and publish papers. He performed at only an acceptable level in the presentation/publishing aspect of his job.

The Synthetic Fibers Division was unionized, as were the other research departments. Although he was not required to be, Dr. Allen was a member of the union, but had not been very active. The union had a rule that promotion from assistant to associate research chemist normally took place in five years, but Dr. Allen had requested that he be promoted one year early. If a research chemist was doing a good job, promotion was almost automatic after five years. The promotion would result in Dr. Allen's receiving a salary increase of slightly less than $70 per month. That was in addition to the annual raise of approximately 6 percent. Dr. Allen earned $48,000 last year. His earnings while in sales had been significantly higher, but Dr. Allen appeared to love research.

The promotion request had received a positive endorsement from Dr. Allen's Departmental Review Committee. The committee was composed of three research chemists from the Synthetic Fibers Division. Dr. Allen's request had also received very strong support from his department head, as well as from the manager of the Chemical Research Division. A committee composed of one researcher from each of the three departments within the Chemical Research Division had also given its blessing to the promotion request.

The promotion had to clear three additional hurdles before becoming effective. The Research Review Committee, which consisted of one researcher from each of the nine research divisions, had to okay the request, as did the president, Dr. James. The final step was the vote of the Board of Directors. The board usually endorsed the promotion recommendations of the management team.

The problem occurred at Research Review Committee. That body had voted against Dr. Allen's request for promotion and had so informed him. Dr. Allen appealed the decision to the president. The president could overrule the vote of the committee, but this was an unusual situation. Ordinarily, potential conflict arose when the Research Review Committee (the researchers on this committee were all union members) wanted a union member to receive a promotion or wage increase and a department head, division manager, or the president did not feel that the promotion or wage increase was justified.

Dr. James had met Dr. Allen several times but did not really know him. Dr. Allen had developed several products that had received praise from Argay's cus-

tomers. Dr. Allen felt that his nine years in sales made him better able to understand the customer's needs than would one more year of research in the laboratory. In fact, it was based upon his sales experience that Dr. Allen had requested
promotion at the end of his fourth year at Argay.

The president wanted to promote people who genuinely deserved it, but
there was the consideration of the Research Review Committee. If Dr. James
overruled the committee's recommendation, he was obligated to explain his reasons. Then too, there were the upcoming negotiations with the researcher's
union. Most people agreed that if Dr. Allen did not receive the promotion this
year, he would surely receive it next year.

Questions

1. What should Dr. James do? Why?
2. What should Dr. Allen do? Explain your reasoning.

Source: This case was written by Irvin A. Zaenglein, Ph.D., School of Business and Management,
Northern Michigan University. Used by permission.

**EXPERIENTIAL
EXERCISE
Attitudes
Toward Union
Scale**

Purpose

To examine your attitudes toward unions and to recognize the underlying reasons for them.

The Task

Complete the following survey. Score it by summing the scores for all items.
Following the completion of the survey, your instructor will lead the class in a
discussion of attitudes toward unions and labor-management relations.

Directions The statements in this survey are listed in pairs. Put an "X" next
to the statement that you agree with more firmly. If you *strongly* agree with the
statement, put *two* "X's" next to it. You may not entirely agree with either of
them, but be sure to mark one of the statements. *Do not omit any item.*

1. a. Unions are an important, positive force in our society.
   b. The country would be much better off without unions.
2. a. Without unions, the state of personnel management would be set back
      100 years.
   b. Management is largely responsible for introducing humanistic programs
      and practices in organizations today.
3. a. Unions help organizations become more productive.
   b. Unions make it difficult for management to produce a product or service
      efficiently.
4. a. Today's standard of living is largely due to the efforts of the labor move-
      ment.

    b. The wealth that people are able to enjoy today is largely the result of creativity, ingenuity, and risk taking by management decision makers.

5. a. Most unions are moral and ethical institutions.

    b. Most unions are as corrupt as the Mafia.

6. a. Unions afford the worker protection against arbitrary and unjust management practices.

    b. Managers will treat their employees fairly regardless of whether a union exists.

7. a. Unions want their members to be hard-working, productive employees.

    b. Unions promote job security rather than worker productivity.

8. a. Unions promote liberty and freedom for the individual employee.

    b. With the union, employees lose their individual freedoms.

9. a. Section 14b of the Taft–Hartley Act (which allows individual states to pass right-to-work laws) should be repealed.

    b. Congress should pass federal right-to-work legislation.

10. a. Unions are instrumental in implementing new, efficient work methods and techniques.

    b. Unions resist management efforts to adopt new, labor-saving technology.

11. a. Without unions, employees would not have a voice with management.

    b. Labor-management communication is strengthened with the absence of a union.

12. a. Unions make sure that decisions about pay increases and promotions are fair.

    b. Union politics often play a role in deciding which union employee gets a raise or gets promoted.

13. a. The monetary benefits that unions bargain for are far greater than the dues the member must pay to the union.

    b. Union dues are usually too high for what the members get through collective bargaining.

14. a. Employee discipline is administered fairly if the organization is unionized.

    b. Union procedures generally make the disciplinary process slow, cumbersome, and costly.

15. a. Without the union, the employee would have no one with whom to discuss work-related problems.

    b. The best and most accessible person for the employee to discuss personal problems with is the immediate supervisor.

16. a. Union officers at all levels carry out their jobs in a competent and professional manner.

    b. Union officers are basically political figures who are primarily interested in their own welfare.

17. a. Most unions seek change through peaceful means.

    b. Most unions are prone to use violence to get what they want.

18. a. Unions are truly democratic institutions with full participation of the rank and file.

    b. Unions are controlled by the top leadership rather than by the rank and file.

19. a. Union members do the real work in our society and form the backbone of our country.
    b. Union employees are basically manual laborers who would flounder without management's direction and guidance.
20. a. Unions are necessary to balance the power and authority of management.
    b. The power and authority of management, guaranteed by the Constitution and the right to own private property, are severely eroded by the union.

KEY TERMS AND CONCEPTS

AFL-CIO
Authorization card
Bargaining unit
Business unionism
Certification
Closed shop
Decertification
Employee association
Featherbedding
Givebacks
Independent union
Industrial union
Job security
Knights of Labor
Landrum-Griffin Act

Local union
Maintenance-of-membership shop
Make-work activities
National Labor Relations Board
National union
Norris-LaGuardia Act
Open shop
Preventive labor relations
Railway Labor Act
Representation election
Section 14b
Trade union
Union avoidance
Union shop
Wagner Act

REVIEW QUESTIONS

1. How do unions affect management decisions?
2. What are the major events of labor history?
3. How has union membership changed since the 1940s?
4. What are the goals of the unions?
5. What are the major labor laws, and what are their key provisions?
6. What are the functions and duties of the national and local unions? What is the AFL-CIO, and what are its functions?
7. What are the primary events in a union organizing drive?
8. How may a firm remain nonunion if it chooses to do so?
9. What are the challenges that lie ahead for the union movement?

DISCUSSION QUESTIONS

1. Assume that you are a recent graduate applying for a job as foreman trainee. During a series of interviews, the plant manager says, ''Tell me your philosophy toward unions. We are nonunion, and I would specifically like

to know how you would feel about this company becoming unionized." How would you respond?

2. Would you prefer to manage union or nonunion workers? Why?

3. Why has organized labor failed to increase its membership significantly in the past two decades? What do you believe must be done to increase union membership?

4. Comment on the following statement: "We live in an age of professional management. The average worker has a safe job, fair wages, good benefits, and competent supervision. Therefore, unions have outlived their purpose."

5. Many organizing campaigns are taking place at colleges and universities to bring their faculties into a union. Do you think that professors should organize? Why or why not?

6. One of the most controversial parts of the Taft-Hartley Act is Section 14b, which enables individual states to ban union and agency shops. Since the passage of the act, labor has lobbied long and hard to repeal Section 14b. On the other hand, many employers feel that a federal right-to-work law should be passed banning union and agency shops throughout the country. Do you believe society would benefit most from the repeal of Section 14b or the passage of a federal right-to-work law? Discuss.

7. How will the composition of the labor force change in the next twenty years? Do you believe labor will be a stronger or a weaker force in 2000 than it is today?

ENDNOTES

1. See D. R. Sease and R. L. Simison, "UAW Switch on Revising Contracts Reflects Growing Concern For Jobs, *The Wall Street Journal* (December 21, 1981), p. 16.

2. See D. H. Rosenbloom and Jay M. Shafritz, *Essentials of Labor Relations* (Reston, VA: Reston, 1985); P. L. Martin, *Contemporary Labor Relations* (Belmont, CA: Wadsworth, 1979); and J. M. Brett, "Why Employees Want Unions," *Organizational Dynamics* (Spring 1980).

3. Brett, "Why Employees Want Unions."

4. Ibid.

5. For a detailed account of the history of the union movement see A. Sloan and F. Whitney, *Labor Relations* (Englewood Cliffs, NJ: Prentice-Hall, 1981), chapter 2; J. G. Rayback, *A History of American Labor* (New York: Free Press, 1966); S. Lens, *The Labor Wars: From the Molly Maguires to the Sitdowns* (Garden City, NY: Doubleday, 1974).

6. M. Esten, *The Unions* (New York: Harcourt, Brace, and World, 1967), p. 28.

7. A. Sloan and F. Whitney, *Labor Relations,* p. 63.

8. Esten, *The Unions,* p. 28.

9. Larry T. Adams, "Changing Employment Patterns of Organized Workers," *Monthly Labor Review* 108, no. 2 (February 1985): 25–31.

10. For details of the legislative acts that protect government workers, see B. S. Feldacker, *Labor Guide to Labor Law* (Reston, VA: Reston, 1980).

11. Rosenbloom and Shafritz, *Essentials of Labor Relations,* p. 42.

12. Ibid.

13. Ibid., p. 45.

14. M. W. Miller, "Unions Curtail Organizing in High Tech," *The Wall Street Journal* (November 13, 1984): 39.

15. Ibid.

16. Rosenbloom and Shafritz, *Essentials of Labor Relations*, p. 76. See also N. W. Chamberlain, D. E. Cullen, and D. Lewis, *The Labor Sector* (New York: McGraw-Hill, 1980), p. 281.

17. Wendell L. French, *The Personnel Management Process* (Boston: Houghton Mifflin, 1978), p. 478.

18. R. S. Greenberger, "Quality Circles Grow, Stirring Union Worries," *The Wall Street Journal* (September 22, 1981): 34.

19. Ibid.

20. J. S. Lubin, "As Robot Age Arrives, Labor Seeks Protection Against Loss of Work," *The Wall Street Journal* (October 26, 1981): 1.

21. C. W. Stevens, "Neat, Fast, but Lacking Humanity, Painters Join GM's Assembly Line," *The Wall Street Journal* (February 10, 1981): 25.

22. J. S. Lubin, "As Robot Age Arrives," p. 1.

23. Ibid.

24. For a detailed treatment of labor legislation, see Bruce Feldacker, *Labor Guide to Labor Law* (Reston, VA: Reston, 1984); B. J. Taylor and F. Whitney, *Labor Relations Law* (Englewood Cliffs, NJ: Prentice-Hall, 1979).

25. Sloan and Whitney, *Labor Relations*, p. 378.

26. *This Is the AFL-CIO*, Publication No. 20 (Washington, DC: AFL-CIO, 1987).

27. Esten, *The Unions*, p. 46.

28. "Executive Pay: The Top Earners," *Business Week* (May 7, 1984): 88.

29. "Most Union Honchos Escaped the Squeeze that Pinched the Rank and File," *Business Week* (June 25, 1984): 109.

30. *This Is the AFL-CIO*.

31. Esten, *The Unions*, p. 36.

32. *The Wall Street Journal* (January 15, 1985): 1.

33. See H. Bacas, "Passing the Buck on Benefits," *Nations Business* (February 1985), p. 18.

34. Feldacker, *Labor Guide to Labor Law*, chapters 3 and 4.

35. Ibid.

36. Sloan and Whitney, *Labor Relations*, p. 108.

37. D. Alsop, "DuPont, Steelworkers Step Up the Intensity of Unionization Battle," *The Wall Street Journal* (July 28, 1981): 1.

38. Ibid.

39. B. Nussan, "At Texas Instruments, If You're Pro-Union, Firm May Be Anti-You," *The Wall Street Journal* (July 28, 1978): 1.

40. Ibid., p. 27.

41. J. G. Kilgour, "Before the Union Knocks," *Personnel Journal* (April 1978): 186.

42. Ibid., p. 187.

43. J. S. Lubin, "Labor Strikes Back at Consultants That Help Firms Keep Unions Out," *The Wall Street Journal* (April 2, 1981): 28.

44. Ibid.

45. Ibid.

46. Wendy Zellner and Aaron Bernstein, "The UAW Faces a Plant-by-Plant Struggle," *Business Week* (August 10, 1987): 25.

47. William T. Dickens and Jonathan S. Leonard, "Accounting for the Decline in Union Membership, 1950–1980," *Industrial and Labor Relations Review* 38, no. 3 (April 1985): 323–34.

48. Philip M. Doyle, "Area Wage Surveys Shed Light on Declines in Unionization," *Monthly Labor Review* 108, no. 9 (September 1985): 13–20.

49. Larry T. Adams, "Labor Organization Mergers 1979–84: Adapting to Change," *Monthly Labor Review* 107, no. 9 (September 1984): 21–27.

50. Joseph R. Antos, Mark Chandler, and Wesley Mellow, "Sex Differences in Union Membership," *Industrial and Labor Relations Review* 33, no. 2 (January 1980): 162–69.

51. Daniel C. Stove, Jr., "Can Unions Pick Up the Pieces?" *Personnel Journal* 65, no. 2 (February 1986): 37–40.

52. Amos N. Okafor, "White-Collar Unionization," *Personnel* 62, no. 8 (August 1985): 17–21.

53. John Chalykoff and Peter Cappelli, "Union Avoidance: Management's New Industrial Relations Strategy," *Monthly Labor Review* 39, no. 3 (April 1986): 45–46.

54. John P. Bucalo, Jr., "Successful Employee Relations," *Personnel Administrator* 31, no. 4 (April 1986): 63–84.

55. Lane Kirkland, "Labor Unions Look Ahead," *The Futurist* (May–June 1986): 48–49.

56. *The Changing Situation of Workers and Their Unions* (Washington, DC: AFL-CIO, 1985).

57. Kirkland Ropp, "State of the Unions," *Personnel Administrator* 32, no. 7 (July 1987): 36–40.

58. Beverly Geber, "Teaming Up with Unions," *Training* 24 (August 1987): 24–30.

59. Aaron Bernstein and Wendy Zellner, "Detroit vs. the UAW: At Odds Over Teamwork," *Business Week* (August 24, 1987): 54–55.

60. Harold L. Angle and James L. Perry, "Dual Commitment and Labor-Management Relationship Climates," *Academy of Management Journal* 29, no. 1 (March 1986): 31–50.

61. T. A. Kochan, R. B. McKersie, and H. C. Katz, "U.S. Industrial Relations in Transition," *Monthly Labor Review* 108, no. 5 (May 1985): 28–29.

62. *First National Maintenance Corporation* v. *NLRB,* 452 U.S. 666 (1981); *Otis Elevator Company,* 269 NLRB 891 (1984).

63. Kochan et al., "U.S. Industrial Relations," pp. 28–29.

64. Stephen J. Schlossberg and Steven M. Fetter, Department of Labor, Office of Labor-Management Relations and Cooperative Programs press release (Washington, D.C: U.S. Department of Labor, 1986).

65. "Labor Month in Review," *Monthly Labor Review* 109, no. 7 (July 1986): 2.

66. William E. Brock, speech at the fortieth anniversary of the New York School of Industrial and Labor Relations, Cornell University, May 2, 1986.

67. J. S. Lubin, "Health Care Workers Are Target of Big Union Organizing Drive," *The Wall Street Journal* (February 24, 1984): 26.

68. Ibid.

69. P. Pagans, "Labor, Women Get Together for 925," *Louisville Courier-Journal* (March 4, 1981): 36.

70. C. Trost, "The Labor Activists Lead a Growing Drive to Sign Up Women," *The Wall Street Journal* (January 29, 1985): 1.

71. Ibid.

72. D. D. Buss, "Japanese Owned Auto Plants in the U.S. Present a Tough Challenge for the UAW," *The Wall Street Journal* (March 24, 1983): 1.

73. Ibid.

74. M. Kanabayashi, "How a Japanese Firm Is Faring in Its Dealings with Workers in U.S.," *The Wall Street Journal* (October 2, 1981): 1.

75. D. D. Buss, "Japanese Owned Auto Plants."

76. Ibid.

77. Ibid.

78. A. Nag, "Mazda Will Begin Making Cars in U.S. in Fall '87, Employing UAW Workers," *The Wall Street Journal* (December 3, 1984): 6; see also W. J. Hampton," Mazda's Bold Embrace of the United Auto Workers," *Business Week* (December 17, 1984): 40.

79. Keith Atkinson, "State of the Unions," *Personnel Administrator* 31, no. 9 (September 1986): 55–57.

80. Ibid.

Chapter Fourteen

Collective Bargaining

Chapter Objectives

1. To identify the stages in the collective bargaining process and to recognize the various negotiating strategies that labor and management may employ.
2. To cite the subject areas that are included in most labor–management contracts.
3. To describe the tactics used by both labor and management to end a strike on favorable terms.
4. To understand how public sector collective bargaining differs from bargaining in private industry.
5. To cite the elements in the grievance handling process and to discuss how management may keep the level of grievances at a minimum.
6. To compare and contrast the role of mediators and arbitrators in the labor-management relationship.
7. To cite the importance of labor–management cooperation and to illustrate how improved relations between unions and their employers benefit both parties.

Work Rules at Issue in Six GE Strikes

General Electric's (GE) Vice President, Tom Dunham, claims management is "delivering a message that we're not competitive" due to increasing competition and flat sales. The GE Appliance Park in Louisville, Kentucky, which produces refrigerators, washers, dryers, and ranges, has witnessed a reduction of 12,000 employees in twenty years. The company, according to Dunham, is "out to change the culture," which is characterized by inefficient use of workers. He acknowledged that management helped build the culture. Management made several work rule changes based on an article in the national agreement:

> Article 29
> The Union and Locals recognize that the Company retains the exclusive right to manage its business, including (but not limited to) the right to determine methods and means by which its operations are to be carried on, to direct the work force, and to conduct its operations in a safe and effective manner.

Kenneth M. Cassidy, President of the Electrical Workers Union Local 761, called six strikes in 1988 to protest the work rules changes. Cassidy claims the company violated the terms of the agreement because of the language which precedes the above section of Article 29: "Subject only to any limitations stated in this agreement, or in any other agreement between the company and the Union or a Local."

Some of the work rules at issue include:

- *Work Assignment.* Management proposed job rotation of employees for ergonomic reasons—to minimize the risk of injury. For example, several employees will rotate through a job that requires lifting a washer tub—so no one does it long enough to get hurt. The union proposed that the company provide a hoist to lift the tub so that no one risks injury.
- *Attendance.* Management warned workers that it would begin strict enforcement of a contract provision that limits to five days the vacation that can be taken on a daily basis. The rest must be taken in increments of at least a week. The purpose was to reduce absenteeism on Fridays, which often equaled 1,000 workers. The union claimed that management's past practice was to allow up to three weeks to be taken for sick or personal leave.
- *Overtime.* Management began strict enforcement of a new policy within the limits of the agreement which stated, "paying for work

not performed will be reduced and eliminated.'' For example, an employee by seniority is entitled to work overtime, but the supervisor decides that the work is not needed and does not notify the employee. The union complained that the company in such cases has erred and thus should be penalized by paying for the work not performed.

Shortly after the sixth strike GE went to court, declaring the strikes to be an illegal breech of the contract. A U.S. District Court judge agreed that the strike activity was illegal because management's actions were within the provisions of Article 29. The union was following a past practice of ''showing strength'' before new contract talks began.

Source: Adapted from Joe Ward, ''Work Rule Revision at Heart of GE–Union Strife,'' *The Louisville Courier-Journal* (February 14, 1988): E1, E2. Copyright © 1988. Reprinted with permission.

ONE of the union's main functions is to bargain collectively with management in negotiations for a labor contract. The terms and conditions specified in the agreement they reach define the economic rewards and the work environment for each union member. The stakes are high for each side because a bad contract could adversely affect morale, productivity, and, ultimately, a company's profitability. To most union members, a union's effectiveness is tied directly to its success in achieving work-related wants and needs. The methods and techniques of collective bargaining have changed little throughout labor's history; they remain the cornerstone of union activity. Collective bargaining is the *sine qua non* of organized labor.

Through collective bargaining, workers participate in the decisions that affect their work. Thus, collective bargaining may be viewed as a form of participative management whereby the employees, through their union representatives and the authority to approve or reject a union contract, have a major say about their working life. Collective bargaining was the result of one of the earliest infusions of democratic principles into the industrial world.

Collective bargaining comprises two broad and highly related processes: contract negotiations and grievance handling. The first process involves activities associated with the creation of the labor–management contract. In essence, the contract spells out the rules of the game: seniority rights, wages and benefits, work rules (see the chapter-opening article), disciplinary procedures, and so on. But rules need interpretation and enforcement; therefore, the collective bargaining process includes a judicial mechanism for handling what are believed to be violations of the labor agreement. These steps, referred to as *grievance handling*, are an important part of most modern labor–management contracts. The first part of this chapter discusses the steps involved and the issues related to contract negotiations; the second part examines grievance handling, with attention devoted to how grievances may be kept at a minimum.

CONTRACT NEGOTIATIONS

Unions and employers may conduct contract negotiations within two basic structures: single-employer bargaining and multiple-employer bargaining. Most labor agreements involve a single employer and a single union. Should a single employer have several plants in various parts of the country, the union usually represents employees at all plants with one master agreement. Certain issues (normally a small number) are left to local negotiation. For example, a basic agreement between the United Auto Workers (UAW) and General Motors covers employees at all GM plants, and each plant negotiates a supplemental agreement with the local union.

A large single employer with diverse activities and manufacturing processes will generally negotiate contracts with more than one union. For example, in Louisville, Kentucky, publishers of the *Courier-Journal* and the *Times* have contracts with six unions: the Electrical Workers, Graphic Arts, Mailers, Machinists, Printing and Graphic Communications, and Typographical workers. The structures involved in *single-employer bargaining* are shown in Figure 14–1.

In *multiple-employer bargaining*, two or more employers join together to bargain with one or more unions. Two types of multiple-employer bargaining are common today. One involves contract negotiations between an association of two or more employers and a union council representing a group of craft or industrial unions. This bargaining arrangement is common in the construction industry, in which all unionized contractors in a given area will bargain with a variety of craft unions through their building trades council. A second type involves industrywide bargaining, whereby several companies in a given industry bargain with a union through an employers' association. For example, the International Woodworkers of America bargains with the Western States Wood Products Employers' Association, which represents the Crown Zellerbach Corporation, the Georgia-Pacific Corporation, and the Weyerhaeuser Company, among others. The structures involved in mul-

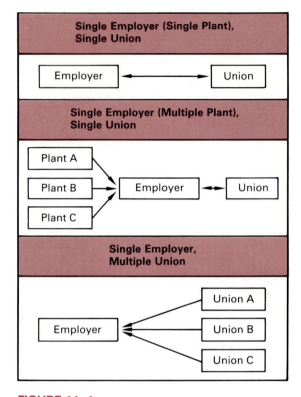

FIGURE 14–1
The structures involved in single-employer bargaining

tiple-employer bargaining are shown in Figure 14–2.

Both the union and the employer cite advantages to multiple-employer bargaining. Bargaining with an employers' association is less costly for unions than bargaining individually with several employers. Further, the union favors the creation of uniform wages and work conditions (such as grievance procedures) among unionized firms within a particular industry.

A common wage and benefits package is also advantageous to employers because it eliminates intercompany wage competition and the threat of employees' leaving to work for competitors for higher wages or benefits. Multiple-employer bargaining has also en-

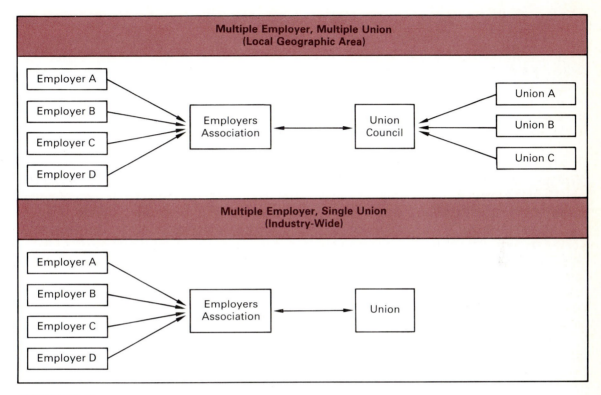

FIGURE 14–2
The structures involved in multiple-employer bargaining

abled employers to increase bargaining strength and has, perhaps, enabled them to achieve agreements more attractive than those that would be negotiated individually.

On the negative side, multiple-employer bargaining may have drawbacks for the individual employer. First, by negotiating through an association, the employer will lose a certain degree of control over internal operations and affairs. Second, the weaker employers in the association will most likely lose power and prestige to the stronger members.[1]

Prenegotiation

According to the Wagner Act, an employer must recognize and bargain with a union that has been certified by the National Labor Re-

lations Board (NLRB) following a representation election. An employer is also required to bargain with an existing union for a new or modified agreement in order to replace a labor contract about to expire. Both parties are required, by law, to bargain in good faith, but neither party is compelled to agree or to conclude the negotiation with a contract. In the case of either a newly certified union or an existing union, the collective-bargaining process follows three distinct phases: prenegotiation, negotiation, and administering the labor-management agreement.

Labor and management representatives are involved in a great deal of preparation long before they actually sit down at the bargaining table. Local union officials meet with the rank and file to learn what they consider to be major contract issues and problem areas. A questionnaire such as the one shown in Figure 14–3 may be used to help collect information on employee needs. Union officials study the gains made by other unions and familiarize themselves with trends in new benefits packages, shorter workweeks, cost-of-living adjustments, and so on. If possible, they should know the employer's financial status and have an inkling of which concessions the company can and cannot afford. In large national and international unions, full-time staff researchers often assist in these preparations.[2]

The employer also prepares for the bargaining sessions. Responsibility for doing pre-negotiation homework often falls upon the personnel or industrial-relations director and staff. They scrutinize the existing contract, looking for vague contract language or for problem areas that need to be modified. Plant managers and supervisors pinpoint areas of the contract that are difficult to administer. Studying their financial position, the personnel staff examines prevailing wage rates and benefits packages to determine what wage or benefits increases can be afforded, if any at all. A union may be forced to concede certain economic gains if the employer is in serious financial trouble. For example, the UAW had little choice but to accept an unfavorable agreement with the Chrysler Corporation in late 1979. The federal government forced the UAW to agree to certain economic concessions as one condition for guaranteeing a multi-million-dollar loan package for the financially troubled automaker.

Negotiation

To begin the actual negotiation process, both management and labor send a team of representatives to bargain at a neutral site—usually a hotel suite. Labor representatives may include the local union president, the business

agent, local officers, or perhaps an official from the national union. The employer is typically represented by one or two top manufacturing executives, the personnel or industrial-relations director, and, perhaps, the company's labor attorney. A company's chief executive will rarely participate in labor negotiations, except when a small firm is involved.

More and more, both labor and management are using computers during contract negotiations to determine the costs of various proposals. Almost instantly, the cost of a proposed pay plan or benefits package may be computed to aid in the negotiation process.[3]

Good Faith   Both sides are legally bound to bargain in good faith, which simply means that labor and management must negotiate with each other and make every reasonable effort to enter into an agreement. Good faith does not mean that either labor or the employer must agree to the contract terms or that either must make concessions. The stronger party may use its power to obtain a favorable agreement, as long as its representatives show an intent to reach an agreement.

Over the years, the concept of good faith has created a great deal of controversy. Often, when the parties fail to reach an agreement, one side (or both) may claim that the other side is violating the good-faith principle and is acting in bad faith. Labor law enables either labor or management to take their complaints concerning bad-faith bargaining to a labor relations board for adjudication.

One controversial bargaining strategy related to this issue was known as *boulwarism*, after Lemuel R. Boulware, a General Electric Company vice-president during the 1950s. Using boulwarism, GE canvassed first-line supervisors to determine employee needs, and integrated those needs and managerial considerations into a so-called package. The package was publicly announced and backed with a

FIGURE 14–3

A sample membership questionnaire used by union officials to collect information on employee needs (Source: K. Gagala, *Union Organizing and Staying Organized* [Reston, VA: Reston, 1983], pp. 257–258.)

Union Survey

This survey is being distributed to all members of the bargaining unit during lunch periods. Your union would like to know your views on how well it is representing your interests and what it can do to improve. Please take a few minutes to answer the questions. Do *not* sign the survey. Place the completed survey in the envelope provided to you, seal the envelope, and place it in the collection box maintained by your union representative. All responses are *confidential*.

1. Would you trust management to give you a fair deal on grievances, if there was no union?
   Yes _____   No _____

2. While the union does not always win, do you believe that it tries hard to represent you and your interests on grievances?
   Yes _____   No _____

3. Would you trust management to make fair decisions regarding promotions and layoffs without the seniority clause in the union contract?
   Yes _____   No _____

4. Do you believe that the union has been able to raise your wages and fringe benefits to a higher level than they would be without the union?
   Yes _____   No _____

5. Do you believe that you can express your views on union matters?
   Yes _____   No _____

6. Do you believe that you have the opportunity to run for union office?
   Yes _____   No _____

7. Do you believe that the union is run democratically, meaning that union members control the union?
   Yes _____   No _____

8. If a majority of union members voted to strike, would you join the strike?
   Yes _____   No _____

9. Union meetings are currently held at 8 p.m. on the first Tuesday of every month. Would you be more interested in attending union meetings if they were held immediately after work?
   Yes _____   No _____

10. How much of the union newsletter do you read?
    Almost all _____   Some _____   Very little _____

11. What are your major gripes about the union?

12. What can the union do to improve?

13. Please indicate your years of seniority:
    _____ 1 month to 2 years
    _____ 3 to 10 years
    _____ Over 10 years

14. Please indicate your job classification:
    _____ Production   _____ Maintenance

public-relations campaign. When collective bargaining was to begin, GE announced that the package was its first and last offer. The union fiercely protested this practice as a gesture of bad faith, and in 1969 boulwarism was found to be in violation of the Wagner Act by a New York Circuit Court. In essence, the practice was found to constitute bad faith because management circumvented the union by communicating directly with the workers.[4]

Negotiating skills are important to all managers, not only those managers in contract discussions. In fact, as much as 20 percent of a manager's time may be spent dealing with conflict resolution, primarily through the process of negotiation.[5] What are some simple guidelines for effective, ethical negotiating?[6]

- Never Ask for Something You Don't Want or Can't Justify
  Example: Don't ask for a two-week delivery date causing a supplier unnecessary expense, only to discover that you had two more weeks. The next time you really need it, will you get it?
- Separate the Issue of Trust
  Example: Negotiations have nothing to do with trust. A job applicant became offended when asked to produce her college transcript. The issue is not trust, replied the personnel manager. Not everyone tells the truth; thus, we must ask everyone for documentation.
- View Negotiating as a Problem-Solving Process, Not a Contest of Wills
  Example: A supervisor decided to give an employee with an absenteeism problem a lower pay increase than other employees. The employee objected, citing her high work output rate. The supervisor agreed to raise her pay to the plant average after six months if her absence record improved.

Bargaining Strategies

The actual bargaining process and the events that take place during negotiation depend to a great degree upon the relationship between management and the union. Depending on the strength of the employer and the union and on the degree of cooperation that characterizes their relationship, a number of different bargaining strategies may be employed. They include distributive bargaining, integrative bargaining, productivity bargaining, and concessionary bargaining.

Distributive Bargaining Distributive bargaining, perhaps the most common form of bargaining, takes place when labor and management are in disagreement over the issues in the proposed contract, such as wages, benefits, work rules, and so on. This form of bargaining is sometimes referred to as *win-lose* bargaining, because the gains of one side are achieved at the expense of the other (e.g., a wage increase won by labor may be considered a loss suffered by management). The mechanics of this process are shown in Figure 14–4.

The union's *initial offer* on an issue (such as a wage rate) is generally higher than they expect to receive; the *resistance point* is the minimally acceptable level; the *target point* is realistic and achievable. For the employer, these points are basically reversed. Management's resistance point is a ceiling, or upper limit, on a particular issue; its initial point is the low end of an issue to be used to begin negotiations; its target point is in the general area that management would like to achieve. The *settlement range* lies somewhere between the resistance points of labor and management. If both sides are unable to come to terms on a particular issue or issues, a *bargaining impasse* results. The consequences and possible actions taken by both sides during an impasse will be discussed later in this chapter.

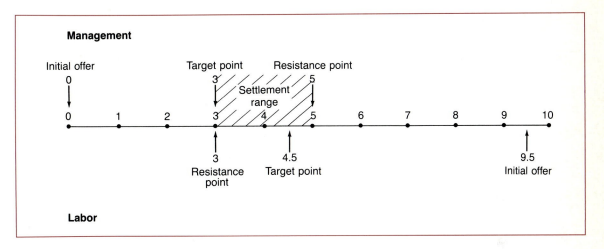

FIGURE 14–4

The mechanics of distributive bargaining [increase in base wage rate percent, first year of new contract] (Source: Michael R. Carrell and Christina Heavrin, *Collective Bargaining and Labor Relations,* 2nd ed. [Columbus, OH: Merrill, 1988], p. 130. Used by permission.)

Integrative Bargaining   The purpose of integrative bargaining is to create a cooperative negotiating relationship that benefits both parties. In this situation, both labor and management win rather than face a win-lose situation. Although integrative bargaining is not nearly as common as the distributive process, signs seem to indicate a steadily growing trend toward this cooperative form of bargaining.

One popular form of integrative bargaining is a jointly-sponsored, labor-management quality of working life (QWL) program. A recent example is the Ford Motor Company–UAW program called *Employee Involvement (EI),* a QWL program designed to strengthen plant productivity and quality through enhanced job satisfaction and cooperative labor-management relationships. At the heart of the EI program are quality circles. By using quality circles, Ford scored a number of impressive improvements in quality and productivity. Some examples of improvements made through EI at the Dearborn plant are shown

in Figure 14–5. The improvements in Ford's productivity, partly as a result of the program's effort, has strengthened their competitive position in the national and international automobile and truck markets. The benefits to the UAW membership at Ford are stable employment, job security, and a more satisfying work environment.[7]

Some labor and employer groups are extending integrative bargaining to a formal organization in which both sides may jointly examine industry issues and find solutions to common problems. For example, the Bricklayers Union and the Mason Contractors of America have formed an organization entitled the International Masonry Institute. The institute will focus on four areas: labor-management relations, research and development in masonry, apprenticeship and training, and market development. Officials from both labor and management claim that the joint effort is necessary to ensure the long-term health and growth of the masonry industry.[8]

FIGURE 14–5
The EI program was a
joint effort between
Ford's Dearborn Engine
Plant and UAW Local
600 (Source:
"Employee
Involvement . . . It
Works!" UAW–Ford
Committee on Employ-
ee Involvement, April
1981)

The Dearborn Engine Plant's joint steering committee was formed in March and employee volunteers were chosen by lottery. Problem-solving training started in May and the first employee problem-solving group presentation to the joint steering committee was made in June. Following are some examples of the problems addressed—and the fixes implemented—at this location:

Problem: *Excessive scrap and tool breakage on cylinder head milling machines caused by broken timing belts.*

Solution: Install limit switch to automatically stop the head feed when timing belts break.

Payoff: Reduced scrap and tool breakage . . . improved quality and reduced tool cost.

Problem: *Lack of information about EI activities for employees not participating in problem-solving groups.*

Solution: Install bulletin boards in the plant for posting of EI information. Devote part of the plant newspaper to EI news.

Payoff: Better communication . . . better informed employees.

Problem: *Coolant dripping from parts hung on an overhead conveyor.*

Solution: Install drip pans.

Payoff: Better housekeeping . . . improved work environment.

Problem: *Quality problems and excessive tool breakage on cylinder head transfer machine.*

Solution: Redesign fixture to include set screws to secure locating pins and bushings.

Payoff: Reduced tool breakage and downtime . . . better product quality.

Problem: *Inefficient dust collection on a cutter grinder.*

Solution: Replace fixed exhaust duct with flexible duct to permit operator to adjust duct to most effective position.

Payoff: Improved working conditions . . . better observation of the work in process.

Productivity Bargaining One of the primary purposes of productivity bargaining is to improve the effectiveness of the organization by eliminating work rules and inefficient work methods that inhibit productivity. Getting labor's agreement to eliminate old, ineffective work habits is not easy. Some unions fear that this form of bargaining will eventually lead to unemployment and a weakening of the union's power base. Despite the reluctance of various unions, many changes have been made to improve productivity, signifying a

shift from distributive to productivity bargaining.[9] A primary reason for a union's acceptance of new, improved work methods is a feeling that jobs will become more secure as the employer's productivity strengthens. Some examples of recent changes in work rules in various industries are summarized in Table 14–1.

An excellent example of labor–management cooperation on the elimination of restrictive work rules in exchange for job security involves GE's "factory of the future" in

TABLE 14–1
Productivity bargaining has brought a number of changes in work rules in various industries

Area	Changes in Work Rules	Industry
Job assignments	Cutting size of crews, enlarging jobs by adding duties; eliminating unnecessary jobs	Steel, autos, railroads, meatpacking, airlines
Skilled maintenance and construction	Combining craft jobs such as millwright, welder, rigger, and boilermaker; allowing journeymen to perform helpers' duties; permitting equipment operators to run more than one machine	Autos, rubber, steel, petroleum, construction
Hours of work	Giving up relief and wash-up periods; allowing management more flexibility in scheduling daily and weekly hours; working more hours for the same pay	Autos, rubber, steel, meatpacking, trucking, airlines (pilots), textile
Seniority	Restricting use of seniority in filling job vacancies, 'bumping' during layoffs, and picking shifts	Autos, rubber, meatpacking, steel
Wages	Restricting pay to hours worked rather than miles traveled	Railroads, trucking
Incentive pay	Reducing incentives to reflect changing job conditions	Rubber, steel
Team work	Allowing team members to rotate jobs; permitting pay for knowledge instead of function; allowing management to change crew structure to cope with new technology	Autos, auto suppliers, steel, rubber

Source: Reprinted from the May 16, 1983, issue of *Business Week* by special permission, © 1983 by McGraw-Hill, Inc.

Lynn, Massachusetts. The factory, which employs only about half as many workers as a conventional factory, builds aircraft engine parts and uses robot carts to move engine parts between computer-controlled work centers. GE promised the Electrical Workers that it would maintain a minimum level of jobs for a specified time. GE also promised to spend $450 million to add plant capacity over a period of several years. In return, the Electrical Workers Union agreed to the following work rules:[10]

- To enable the factory to operate twenty-four hours a day, the union agreed that employees will work seven twelve-hour shifts every fourteen days, with four hours' overtime pay for each shift.
- The number of job classifications shrank from twelve to three to enable the plant to operate with only 100 employees, who perform a variety of tasks.
- For the first time, the union agreed to let GE set production goals.

The agreement was not without controversy. Although 60 percent of the rank and file approved the agreement, it was opposed by a majority of the stewards' council. Opponents argued that production goals would make it easier to fire employees and that by broadening job classifications skilled workers would be forced to perform unskilled labor.[11]

Another type of productivity bargaining ties worker productivity to a system of incentive pay. Such systems are certainly not new (Frederick Taylor's piece-rate plans were popular at the turn of the century), but contemporary productivity plans often involve the use of plantwide committees in which labor and management seek ways to lower operating costs and increase efficiency and productivity. One of the most popular plans is the Scanlon plan. The plan involves the creation of departmental labor-management committees that evaluate suggestions from employ-

ees. Suggestions determined to be of value are implemented, and when labor costs decrease in relation to productivity a part of the savings are shared by the employees.[12]

Concessionary Bargaining The recession in the 1980s saw many companies facing plant closings, mass layoffs, and, in the worst of cases, bankruptcy. To solve their problems, many employers sought agreements from their unions to freeze and in some cases reduce economic rewards such as wages, benefits, and paid vacations, holidays, and sick leave. Unions reluctantly agreed. Concessionary, or giveback, bargaining has been common in both manufacturing and services industries, but most prevalent in those industries with the greatest financial difficulties, such as auto and steel.[13]

Union members grant such concessions because they feel they have little choice. For example, the employees of the ARCO Metals Company, who were members of the Aluminum, Brick, and Glass Workers unions, agreed to give up $1.40 an hour in pay as well as double-time pay for Sundays. The workers also agreed to begin to contribute $13.50 per worker per month for health benefits. The president of the local union said that he was "not tickled with the contract, but it is the best we could get at this time. It's one of those unfortunate situations where the economy was down and they [management] took hold of that and beat us."[14]

The historic General Motors–UAW pact signed in 1984 has the characteristics of concessionary bargaining but also of productivity bargaining. The UAW accepted moderate wage increases in return for several innovative job security measures. With the new agreement, GM agreed not to lay off any worker with at least one year's seniority who was displaced by new technology, plant consolidation, productivity improvement, or the transfer of work to another facility. Instead, these workers were to be placed into a "job opportunity bank" where they would perform a variety of jobs. The plan also included a bonus program for good attendance and profit-sharing payments estimated to be $1,000 per worker per year.[15]

One result of concessionary bargaining aimed at reducing labor costs is known as *two-tier wages* (see chapter 10). Under such a wage structure, current workers may receive a pay increase (or perhaps have their wages frozen), but newly hired employees doing the same or similar jobs receive lower wages. Firms using this approach include Boeing, GM, Greyhound, and American Airlines. For example, American Airlines' agreement with mechanics pays current mechanics $16 an hour but new mechanics $8 an hour.[16]

Most rank-and-file employees favor the system because their own pay isn't cut. But according to some labor officials, a two-tier system could reduce both employee morale and productivity, as well as further weaken the power of organized labor. Nonetheless, many firms feel that the system is the only way they can remain competitive. According to the chairman of Greyhound, "We need this two-tier structure to survive in the business.[17]

An analysis of successfully concluded concession negotiations showed that in more than half, the union agreed to wage and benefit reductions. In the remaining contracts, unions consented to a wage and benefit freeze. The most common concession, found in 40 percent of the contracts, was an agreement to give up paid holidays. The second most common concession involved a work rule or production change (see the chapter-opening example). In exchange, employers generally agreed to future wage and benefit improvements and greater job security.[18]

Union concessions generally involve wage, benefit, or work rule changes, with reduced benefits generally more acceptable to employees than wage concessions, although future wage increases may be renegotiated. Often work rule changes are easier to sell to employees and have a more lasting effect. Employers, however, must expect to pay the price for these concessions through one or more of five areas of negotiation:[19]

- *Increased job security* The union will most likely try to extract a promise not to close plants or not to subcontract with non-union producers. The Ford Motor Company's example of a guaranteed income stream will be pursued by many unions. Such restrictions can be very expensive and limiting to employers.
- *Increased financial disclosure* The employer will have to make a claim of inability to pay or financial hardship. While the company's financial information normally need not be disclosed in collective bargaining, when the employer puts profitability or financial conditions in contention, the financial data must be provided to substantiate the position.
- *Profit-sharing plans* Union members generally feel that sharing in austerity now should mean sharing profits in the future. For example, in 1983, Chrysler Corporation's employees demanded a share of the record profits, only three years after the UAW made major concessions to guarantee the federal loan to Chrysler. In 1984, over 158,000 union and nonunion employees of the Ford Motor Company received an average of $440 as their part of the new Ford–UAW profitsharing plan.[20]
- *Equality of sacrifice* Employers must demand the same sacrifices from management and nonunion employees as union employees. For instance, GM tried to increase its executive bonus program just after the UAW made major concessions in 1982. The UAW and its members demanded, and got, the increases rescinded.

PERSONNEL IN THE NEWS

Concession Bargaining: Reality of the 1980s

Management threatens massive layoffs or even a plant shutdown. Union officials believe them and agree to "give back" wage, benefit, and work rule gains of past negotiations. Why? Stiff foreign and non-union competition combined with an aging industrial plant. The scene was the same all across America in the 1980s—the decade of union concession bargaining, the first such decade in modern labor history.

Arvin Industries, Inc., of Columbus, Ohio, an automotive components manufacturer negotiated a typical concession package with the International Association of Machinists and Aerospace Workers District 90 in their 1988–1991 contract. The negotiated concessions included:*

- Wage cuts as high as $1.45/hour for some workers
- Cost-of-living adjustments (COLAs) eliminated
- Incentive pay eliminated
- Employees will pay an additional 15 percent of their medical insurance
- Employees will be required to take drug-abuse tests if asked by management

What did the union receive in return? Union officials asked for a nonbinding pledge that the plant would not close, but they did not get it.

*Source: Adapted from "Arvin Workers Vote to Accept Pay Concessions," *The Louisville Courier-Journal* (February 23, 1988): B1.

- *Participation in decision making* Unions may seek greater participation in various management decisions, including plant closings and the use of new technological methods. If properly used, this concession can help develop greater understanding and improve employee relations.[21]

The essence of successful and continued concession bargaining is the development of mutual trust and respect by both parties. The union must be willing to give up some gains made through the years, especially in terms of nonproductive paid time off and other expensive benefits. The employer, in somewhat of a role reversal, must convince the union of the need to negotiate concessions to guarantee the survival of the business. The obvious and ultimate proof is that the company is losing money, which usually must be verified by an objective third party such as an outside auditor.

Generally, the reduction of pay for time not worked is more acceptable to employees than outright wage reductions. Reduction of pay for time not worked also enables employers to increase productivity. Contract provisions that are particularly vulnerable to concession bargaining include the following:*

1. *Vacation pay* Lengthening service or work time requirements and shortening length of time off are usually acceptable.

2. *Holiday pay* Elimination of paid personal holidays or lowering the number of general days granted generates savings and more production time with fewer employees.

3. *Break periods* Eliminate or shorten rest periods and wash-up time to produce relief but not in direct ratio to minutes saved. Productive output is more often merely spread over the extra time. Breaks are very necessary in some operations, so approach proposals in this area cautiously.

4. *Nonproductive downtime and classification inflexibility* Propose work be done for all time paid, so a productive effort is given even when the standard job is not operating because of irregularities. This can eliminate indirect labor costs in custodial or quality control areas.

5. *Pension benefits* This is a complex area. There are real cash flow benefits to be realized from changing assumptions and delaying or postponing contributions. Changing from a defined benefit plan to defined contributions or, even better, a profit-sharing plan, will shift the costs to more profitable times and not hold corporate assets hostage.

6. *Insurance program* Benefit amount, timing, and deductibles can be changed to save considerable costs in this area. Pay particular attention to health, medical, sickness, and accident coverages, which are most costly. Pay for extended coverage on layoff, leave of absence, and retirement can be eliminated or paid by employees. Preserve flexibility to change carriers to obtain premium reductions.

7. *Seniority provisions* Streamline bidding and bumping procedures to eliminate excessive turmoil and retraining. Ensure assignment of qualified, experienced personnel to jobs to maintain peak efficiency.

8. *Overtime assignment* Provide for only qualified people to work and eliminate unnecessary make-work assignments.

9. *Bonus payments* Eliminate or reduce extra payments.

10. *Wages* Consider eliminating or suspending future increases and cost-of-living allowances. If this doesn't achieve your economic objective, propose a wage reduction. Reductions of over $1 per hour have been approved in many companies.

Bargaining Categories

The NLRB identifies three broad categories of bargaining subjects: mandatory, permissive, and unlawful.[22] The parties must negotiate mandatory items if either party requests to do so. Typical mandatory subjects include provisions concerning wages, benefits, and layoffs. A list of mandatory bargaining subjects is shown in Table 14–2.

Permissive or voluntary subjects include those not directly related to wages, benefits, or conditions of work. If one party desires to bargain a permissive subject, the other party may agree or refuse to do so. For example, the union may wish to bargain for an increase in the size of the bargaining unit, but the employer could refuse to negotiate this permissive subject if it so desires. Neither side can refuse to sign a contract because the other refuses to discuss a permissive subject.

---

*Source: John W. Falahee, "Concession Bargaining: The Time Is Now!" *Personnel Administrator* 28, no. 1 (January 1983): 27–28. Reprinted from the January 1983 issue of *Personnel Administrator*, copyright 1983, The American Society for Personnel Administration, 606 North Washington St., Alexandria, VA 22314.

TABLE 14–2
A list of mandatory bargaining subjects

Wages	Severance pay
Hours	Nondiscriminatory hiring hall
Discharge	Plant rules
Arbitration	Safety
Holidays—paid	Prohibition against supervisor's doing unit work
Vacations—paid	Superseniority for union stewards
Duration of agreement	Checkoff
Grievance procedure	Partial plant closing
Layoff plan	Hunting on employer forest reserve where previously granted
Reinstatement of economic strikers	
Change of payment from hourly base to salary base	Plant closedown and relocation
Union security and checkoff	Change in operations resulting in reclassifying workers from incentive to straight time, or cut work force, or installation of cost-saving machine
Work rules	
Merit wage increase	
Work schedule	Plant closing
Lunch periods	Job-posting procedures
Rest periods	Plant reopening
Pension plan	Employee physical examination
Retirement age	Union security
Bonus payments	Bargaining over "Bar List"
Price of meals provided by company	Truck rentals—minimum rental to be paid by carriers to employee-owned vehicles
Group insurance—health, accident, life	
Promotions	Musician price list
Seniority	Arrangement for negotiation
Layoffs	Change in insurance carrier and benefits
Transfers	Profit-sharing plan
Work assignments and transfers	Motor-carrier—union agreement providing that carriers use own equipment before leasing outside equipment
No-strike clause	
Piece rates	
Stock-purchase plan	Overtime pay
Work loads	Agency shop
Change of employee status to independent contractors	Sick leave
	Employer's insistence on clause giving arbitrator right to enforce award
Management-rights clause	
Cancellation of seniority upon relocation of plant	Company houses
Discounts on company products	Subcontracting
Shift differentials	Discriminatory racial policies
Contract clause providing for supervisors' keeping seniority in unit	Production ceiling imposed by union
	Most-favored-nation clause
Procedures for income tax withholding	

Source: Reed Richardson, *Collective Bargaining by Objectives* (Englewood Cliffs, NJ; Prentice-Hall, Inc., 1977), pp. 113–15.

The inclusion of illegal subjects renders an agreement invalid and unenforceable. An example of an illegal item would be a provision that permits discrimination on the basis of religion, sex, or national origin or a provision that establishes a closed shop. Any subject that violates any federal, state, or local law is an unlawful bargaining item.

Contract Agreement

After both sides have arrived at an informal agreement, the agreement is taken back to their representatives for final and formal approval. For the employer, top management—often the board of directors—must approve the contract; for labor, the rank and file normally must ratify the contract by a majority vote. Under labor law, union representatives may be given the authority to enter into a contract without ratification. Most unions, however, choose to allow their members to vote on the agreement. Failure to ratify the contract sends union representatives back to the bargaining table to negotiate a revised agreement. Most contracts, however, are ratified on the first vote.

The agreement becomes official once approved, ratified, and signed by labor and management representatives. Once signed, labor and management meet with their respective members to go over the details of the contract. Union members and members of management all receive copies of the agreement. Supervisors and union stewards who have the day-to-day responsibility for administering the contract should be intimately familiar with the agreement so that they may avoid any activity or decision that violates it.

Contract Format

Labor contracts may vary considerably in length and content. Some agreements contain ten or fifteen pages; others, hundreds of pages. The more mandatory and permissive subjects that are negotiated, the lengthier the contract. The order of topics may also vary somewhat, but the following list is fairly representative of most agreements:

Union Recognition and Scope of the Bargaining Unit This section reflects the employer's recognition of the union as the sole bargaining agency for its employees and defines specifically which employees are included within the bargaining unit.

Management Rights This section reflects the union's recognition of the employer's sole and exclusive right to determine the way in which the business shall be managed. Management rights include determining production methods, which products and services to produce, and how products and services should be marketed.

Union Security This section defines the type of union security (union shop, maintenance-of-membership shop, etc.).

Strikes and Lockouts This section outlines the approach each side will take toward strikes and lockouts (a lockout is management's refusal to allow employees to work). Typically, this section includes a statement such as "there will be no strikes or lockouts during the term of this agreement" (although a strike may be permitted over certain specific items detailed in the agreement).

Job Rights and Seniority This section defines how transfers, promotions, layoffs, and recalls are to be made. Generally, the contract will stipulate that these decisions are to be made on the basis of seniority.

Wages This section outlines the wage structures and related provisions such as wage adjustments, wage incentives, shift differentials, and bonuses.

Benefits and Time Off This section lists the employee benefits such as hospitalization, pensions, holidays, vacations, sick leave, and rest periods.

Safety and Health This section normally includes statements that underscore both the union's and the employer's desire to maintain safe and healthy working conditions. Many contracts include provisions for the creation of a labor-management safety committee and the administration of a health-and-safety program.

Discipline, Suspension, and Discharge This section outlines the procedures an employer must follow to discipline, suspend, or discharge an employee. Many contracts include provisions for progressive disciplinary systems, whereby additional infractions of a work policy, standards, rules, or regulations result in increasingly serious disciplinary action leading to discharge. Some contracts include a very detailed list of violations and resulting penalties. For example, taking drugs on the job results in immediate dismissal, horseplay results in a verbal warning, and so on.

Grievance Handling and Arbitration This section normally details (1) the steps an employee follows to lodge a formal grievance against the employer and (2) the procedure for bringing in an outside arbitrator if the union and employer are unable to settle the grievance.

BARGAINING IMPASSE

Historically, collective bargaining has proven to be an effective method for settling differences between labor and management. Most negotiations (about 98 percent) end in a signed contract that is agreeable—although not necessarily favorable—to both sides. Management and labor generally recognize that continuous, dispute-free operations are important to preserve harmonious labor relations and maximize the goals of the employee and employer alike.

Serious conflicts do sometimes occur, however, during the course of negotiations. Labor and management may simply be unable to reach accord over certain issues dealing with wages or other contract provisions. When negotiations break down, or when the existing contract expires and the union and employer have been unable to reach an agreement, a *bargaining impasse* results. Should this occur, there are three options. One, the parties may ask for assistance in settling the dispute from an impartial third party called a *mediator*. Two, the union may exert a show of force so that their demands will be accepted. Three, the employer may also show force through one of several pressure techniques. Let us first explore common union strategies for ending the bargaining impasse on their terms.

Union Power Tactics

A union's primary power tactics include calling a strike, waging a corporate campaign, setting up a picket line, or imposing a boycott.

Strike Officially termed a *work stoppage*, the strike is the refusal of union members to work and is recognized as a basic union right. Strike tactics and procedures, however, are subject to considerable regulation by a variety of labor statutes. Various types of strikes are the following:

Economic Strike A strike over an economic issue such as wages, benefits, or working conditions. The employer is free to maintain operations and hire permanent replacements for economic strikers. An employee who is not replaced is entitled to reemployment if the labor dispute is settled.

Unfair-Labor-Practice Strike A strike over an unfair labor practice by the employer, for example, discrimination against union members because of union activity. A worker who strikes because of an unfair labor practice cannot be permanently replaced.

Sympathy Strike A strike in which other unions agree to a work stoppage, not because of actions by their own employer, but to support other union members striking other firms. A common example of the sympathy strike is the refusal of truck drivers to cross a picket line and make deliveries to an employer whose employees are on strike. Legally, the sympathy striker is in violation of a no-strike clause in the agreement unless the contract specifically permits this form of strike activity.

Wildcat Strike An unauthorized work stoppage. The wildcat strike is an unlawful activity if the contract contains a no-strike clause; therefore, wildcat strikers are not sanctioned by union leadership. If a wildcat strike does occur, the union must disavow it or risk being charged with violation of the contract and federal law. The employer may generally take disciplinary action, including suspension and discharge, against wildcat strikers.

Other forms of union pressure include a *sit-down strike*, in which employees strike but remain at their jobs and refuse to work; a *sick out*, in which employees call in sick en masse; and a *slowdown*, in which workers remain at work but cut back their output significantly. Unions, however, usually disapprove of individual worker pressures and support a work stoppage only if it has been formally approved by union leadership. For example, the national union must usually approve a strike by a local affiliate, even after a majority of the local members have approved it.

An extended strike may deal a serious blow to a single company, union, or small geographical area. Yet the time lost to strikes actually constitutes a relatively small percentage of the total working time for the United States as a whole. Less than 1 percent of total working time is lost to work stoppages. Unions strike for a variety of reasons, but the majority of work stoppages are caused by disputes about general wages and plant administration (discipline, output standards, rules and regulations, and health and safety). Major work stoppage issues are shown in Table 14–3.

If a strike takes place, both sides should attempt to contain and resolve it. Both parties will usually benefit if the strike is of short duration. A protracted strike may have disasterous effects on both the employees' and the employer's economic viability. For example, the UAW's long strike against International Harvester in the early 1980s almost ruined the company and caused a permanent loss of jobs for many UAW members. Some considerations for coping with and resolving the strike include:[23]

- Keep communication channels open. Notations should continue during the strike, and regular meetings should be scheduled.
- Both the union and the company should set up ''rumor control centers.'' Rumors that may harm the prospects of settling the strike must be minimized.
- Both parties should refrain from unfair labor practices during the strike.
- Public statements (in newspapers, etc.) should be factual and should avoid threats, speculation, and misleading information.
- Pickets should be orderly and law-abiding.
- Avoid miscalculating the resolve of the other side. In the example just cited, In-

1990s NFL Corporate Campaigns?

The 1987 National Football League (NFL) players' strike failed miserably. Over 10% of the players crossed picket lines, and the owners hired nonunion players to play the scheduled games with "replacement teams" until the union players returned. In the future the players' union may put on a corporate campaign to strengthen their position. The union could, according to M. J. Daberstein, Director of Research, form their own league, rent college football stadiums, and put on games to compete with any future replacement teams. The union could also try to "persuade" major television advertisers to withdraw their sponsorship of any replacement team games and sponsor player-team games instead. The players might also try to present their case to the public, which did not support their 1987 strike. Finally, if they cannot organize their own games, the players could organize a traditional work slowdown, which would allow them to collect their paychecks but embarrass the owners.

Source: Adapted from Alex Kotlowitz, "Broken Play: Labor Experts Fault Football Players' Strike Strategy," *The Wall Street Journal* (October 14, 1987): 1. Reprinted by permission of The Wall Street Journal, © Dow Jones & Company, Inc. 1987. All Rights Reserved.

---

ternational Harvester never believed the UAW would strike for so long. Nor in 1981 did striking air traffic controllers believe the federal government would actually fire strikers and hire replacement employees, thus resulting in the death of the Professional Air Traffic Controllers Union (PATCO).

Corporate Campaign The feeling among many labor leaders is that the strike has lost its effectiveness as a technique for achieving its goals. According to a labor economist, "Unions very seldom win a strike today. That is why they're turning to other means."[24] One of these means is the corporate campaign, which, as discussed in chapter 13, is also a tactic to organize new union members.

A corporate campaign may take several forms, including proxy fights at shareholders'

meetings to publicly pressure the company's major creditors.[25] A proxy fight occurs when a group tries to gather enough shareholders' votes to change corporate policy. The most highly publicized corporate campaign involved the attempt by the Amalgamated Clothing and Textile Workers Union (ACTWU) to organize workers at the J. P. Stevens Company, a large textile firm with several plants located primarily in the eastern coastal states.

J. P. Stevens had a history of being fiercely antiunion and had successfully resisted unionism in spite of union victories in representation elections, numerous unfair labor practice rulings against the company, and an ACTWU-backed national boycott of Stevens products. Stevens finally lost the battle when an agreement with the union was signed covering ten Southern plants in which

TABLE 14–3
Work stoppages by major issue

Major Issue	Stoppages		Workers		Days Idle	
	Number	Percent	Number*	Percent	Number*	Percent
All stoppages	**5,506**	**100.0**	**2,040.1**	**100.0**	**34,821.8**	**100.0**
General wage changes	3,135	56.9	899.5	44.1	21,694.8	60.6
Supplementary benefits	78	1.4	22.8	1.1	453.5	1.3
Wage adjustments	141	2.6	65.3	3.2	1,625.3	4.5
Hours of work	15	.3	2.8	.1	84.8	.2
Other contractual matters	276	5.0	71.4	3.5	1,350.7	3.8
Union organization and security	252	4.6	41.2	2.0	955.0	2.7
Job security	211	3.8	99.8	4.9	1,708.9	4.8
Plant administration	1,002	18.2	696.8	34.2	7,249.2	20.2
Other working conditions	137	2.5	62.7	3.1	338.8	.9
Interunion or interunion matters	246	4.5	77.1	3.8	335.4	.9
Not reported	13	.2	.5	−0.05	25.4	.1

*Thousands

Source: Adapted from U.S. Department of Labor, *Analysis of Work Stoppages,* Bureau of Labor Statistics, Bulletin, 2032, 1979, p. 18.

the union had previously won representation elections. The ACTWU's unorthodox strategy involved bringing pressure to bear on the Metropolitan Life Insurance Company, a major Stevens lender. Metropolitan held $97 million of Stevens' $226 million in long-term debt. The union threatened to run two dissidents (a black woman minister and a Metropolitan insurance salesman) to oppose Metropolitan's nominees to the board of directors and set the wheels in motion to wage a proxy battle. The chairman of Metropolitan intervened, claiming that the proxy battle would not only cost the firm millions of dollars but would also cause a great deal of embarrassment to the company. Because of Metropolitan's intervention, an agreement was signed between Stevens and the ACTWU, and the union called off the proxy fight.[26]

Picket The picket, a line of strikers who patrol the employer's place of business, can be a powerful union pressure tactic. Picketing can help keep a plant or building site closed during a strike. Applicants who cross the picket line to apply for the jobs of striking workers must often confront the jeers and taunts of the picketers. Such strikebreakers, often disparagingly labeled *scabs* because they "close the wound," are held in great contempt by union members and union sympathizers. The courts allow picketing at the primary employer's place of business, or *primary situs picketing*, as long as laws are observed. The picketers must avoid violence, must not mass in large numbers, and must not create physical barriers to the employer's entrance. But the Supreme Court has ruled that *common situs picketing* is illegal. At a common site, employees of several employers work side by side. At a construction site, for example, plumbers, carpenters, masons, electricians, and other skilled workers are represented by different unions and work for different subcontractors. Therefore, one striking union generally cannot picket the entire project; the courts have ruled that each employer at a common situs is a separate employer. If there is only one gate to a construction project, the union may picket there; if there is a special gate reserved for each contractor, the union picket must be confined to that gate.[27]

Boycott A boycott is the refusal to purchase an employer's goods or services. An important distinction must be made between primary and secondary boycotts. A *primary boycott* involves only those parties directly involved in a dispute, such as a large appliance manufacturer and the electrical workers' union. In a primary boycott, the union pressures members (and often the public) to avoid patronizing an employer, even going as far as to levy fines against members that do. Primary boycotts are generally legal. A *secondary boycott* involves a third party not directly involved in a dispute, such as an electrician's union persuading retailers not to buy the manufacturer's products. A secondary boycott is an attempt to increase the power and strength of the union so that the employer is more likely to give in to union demands. Under the Taft–Hartley Act, secondary boycotts are illegal, except in the construction and clothing industries.

The purpose of boycott efforts by picket lines at grocery stores is to urge consumers to avoid buying a particular product, such as grapes or lettuce. This is often referred to as *product picketing*. This is not an illegal secondary boycott, because the Supreme Court has ruled that the use of pickets to discourage the purchase of a specific product is not a secondary boycott.

Handbills, or leaflets urging consumers not to purchase a specific product or deal with a company involved in a labor dispute, are legal as long as they are truthful. An example of a handbill is shown in Figure 14–6.

Employer Power Tactics

Employers use a number of methods designed to end a bargaining impasse on terms favorable to management. These include the lockout of employees, hiring nonunion employees during a strike, hiring replacement employees, contracting out work, and filing for bankruptcy.[28]

Lockout The first tactic, a lockout, is the refusal to allow employees to work until an agreement is signed. Because an employer must normally halt operations with this tactic, the lockout sees only limited use. In addition, most contracts contain a no-lockout clause prohibiting a lockout while a contract is in force.

Nonunion Workers Should a union strike, the employer may still attempt to maintain operations. One way is for supervisors and other nonunion employees to perform the duties of striking employees. This strategy may be successful where operations are highly automated or routine and where little training is required to perform the strikers' jobs. During a 1983 strike between American Telephone and Telegraph and the Communications Workers of America Union, for example, supervisors and administrators were able to keep phone lines open and force strikers back to work with no pay increase.[29]

Another method of obtaining nonunion workers during a strike is through the resignation of the striking union employees. In a landmark 1985 decision, the U.S. Supreme Court decided that union members have the

FIGURE 14–6
An example of a
boycott handbill

UNITED FOOD AND COMMERCIAL WORKERS

AFL—CIO—CLC

District Union Local 227

"TO THE PUBLIC

We are picketing at this Valu Supermarket to advise the general public that the owners of this store determined to close their Union store at 7100 Preston Highway and to operate in its place a non-union grocery store located at this address and another non-union store located on Whittington Parkway.

If you are a friend of organized labor or if you are in sympathy with the principles they espouse, we know you do not approve of such highhanded and uncaring conduct.

If you desire to buy your groceries from stores operated under the terms and conditions of a union contract whose workers are enjoying union wages and union fringe benefits and do not know where such stores are located, we will be more than happy to inform you of the locations of such union stores. You can receive this information by calling the Union Office, telephone number 778-4453, or you may ask our member who is presently picketing this non-union store and he or she will be more than happy to assist you.

District Union 227, U.F.C.W."

right to resign from the union during a strike and cross the picket line to return to work.[30] The Court noted that Section 7 of the National Labor Relations Act gives every employee the right to "bargain collectively . . . and . . . the right to refrain from any or all such activities." The decision, however, does not affect union security clauses (union shops), which provide that employees continue to pay dues and fees until they resign under the contractual procedures. The union may suspend or expel an employee who has violated a union rule by resigning. This may become important should the strike end and the union workers return. Employers may inform their employees of their rights under the court decision.[31]

Replacement Employees   A second anti-strike tactic is to hire replacement employees for strikers. According to labor law, an employer may hire permanent replacements for economic strikers but only temporary replacements for unfair-labor-practice strikers. This strategy is not without problems. First, many workers will be extremely hesitant to cross picket lines to be ridiculed by picketers and union sympathizers as scabs. Second, in the case of an unfair-labor-practice dispute, workers may hesitate to accept what is likely to be only short-term employment. Third, this practice is almost sure to seriously damage labor-management relations and lower worker morale if a settlement is reached.

Contract Out   Another technique for maintaining business is to contract out, or arrange for another company to handle the employer's business during a strike. This may be a useful strategy for firms in very competitive fields or those that fear that a strike would damage customer relations. For example, a janitorial service that cleans office buildings may contract out their work until the strike is over. If the subcontractor is unionized, however, its employees may legally refuse to perform work for the struck firm. Courts have ruled that this action does not constitute an illegal secondary boycott.

Bankruptcy   In the past, an organization was bound to the terms of the labor agreement, including the level of wages and benefits, until the agreement expired. A 1984 Supreme Court decision has changed that interpretation of the law, enabling organizations to use Chapter 11 of the bankruptcy laws to cancel a union contract, cut wages, and lay off workers. In addition, an organization may do this without having to prove that the labor pact would cause the company to go completely broke. The company must only show that "the labor contract burdens its prospects for recovery and that it has made reasonable attempts to bargain with the Union for deferred or smaller wage increases or other money saving measures."[32]

In the 1980s, two major corporations, Wilson Foods and Continental Airlines, chose bankruptcy to void labor contracts and slash wages and benefits. In the case of Wilson Foods, top management decided to file Chapter 11 because of massive losses from sliding revenues and what it claimed was an excessively costly labor contract. Wilson's estimated net worth was $67 million, but the company estimated its losses at $1 million a week. Shortly after filing for bankruptcy, the company terminated its labor contract and cut almost in half the wages for its 6,000 union employees. Nonunion employees also faced similar pay cuts. At Continental Airlines, many workers were laid off and pilots' and other staff members' pay was cut by as much as 50 percent after the airline filed Chapter 11.[33]

Labor leaders were distraught over the Supreme Court's decision. The head of the International Association of Machinists called the ruling "outrageous."[34] The president of the UAW forecasted more strikes and less conciliation. On the other hand, employers generally applauded the ruling. The executive of a large airline stated that "the ruling helps us all because it makes it clear to unions that management has other options." The legal counsel for a nationwide building-supply firm was more blunt: "Unions will know and the company will know that the company has an additional weapon."[35]

Successorship   Management can decide to "sell out" to a new owner as a means of ending a labor dispute or ending an existing contract. When there is a change in the ownership of the organization or the union, the courts refer to the collective bargaining situation as a matter of successorship. Corporate mergers and acquisitions have occurred much more frequently in recent years and have posed a new threat to the effectiveness of labor unions.

In a recent decision, the U.S. Supreme Court reaffirmed that when a genuine change of employer occurs, the new employer is required to recognize (and negotiate with) the union as the representative bargaining unit of the employees. However, the new employer is not bound by the conditions of any existing labor agreement (even if unexpired).[36] Thus, the new employer may be free to negotiate an entirely new contract with the existing labor unions unless a contract clause binds it to the old contract. If, however, a new owner substantially changes the nature of the business, the successor employer may not be required to recognize the union as the collective bargaining representative of the unit.

Breaking the Impasse

When a bargaining impasse occurs and negotiations stall, labor and management may implement certain techniques to ward off an impending strike or lockout. These techniques, which keep both parties communicating, negotiating, and examining each other's positions, may lead to an eventual resolution of their differences. Each of these methods—mediation, fact finding, and interest arbitration—requires the involvement of a third party.

Mediation The mediation process, in which a neutral third party attempts to bring the union and employer into agreement, follows no particular format. Mediation may, in fact, take place before an impasse occurs. In such cases, labor and management practice *preventive mediation,* requesting that a mediator participate in the negotiations during the early stages. The presence of a mediator during collective bargaining is often instrumental in keeping both parties working toward an agreement and thus avoiding an impasse. In other cases, an impasse may have been reached and a mediator may be called in after negotiations have completely broken off.

The primary role of a mediator is to lead the parties to an agreement by acting as a go-between for the union and the employer. The mediator does not have the authority to impose a decision. After feeling out the parties, the mediator determines which demands are actually firm and which may still be negotiated. The mediator must have the confidence of both sides and be perceived as truly unbiased and impartial.

After an initial joint session with all three parties, labor and management teams are often assembled in separate meeting rooms. The mediator then presents proposals and counterproposals to each side. Although the mediator avoids injecting public opinion or personal feelings into the proceedings, it may become necessary to criticize an extreme demand or unworkable solution presented by either side. Fundamentals that underscore the mediation process and illustrate effective mediator behavior are the following.[37]

- Conveying understanding and appreciation of the problems confronting both parties.
- Conveying to the parties a feeling that the mediator understands their problems.
- Getting the parties to realize that all of their positions are not valid.
- Suggesting alternative approaches that may facilitate agreement.
- Maintaining neutrality.
- Maintaining confidentiality of information disclosed by the parties.

Mediators are often full-time employees of the Federal Mediation and Conciliation

Service (FMCS), which was created by the Taft–Hartley Act to help solve labor disputes. Before becoming mediators, most have had experience in labor relations. After formal training in Washington, D.C., mediators are assigned to a regional office to work with experienced mediators.

Fact-finding Compared to the mediation process, fact-finding is rarely used in the private sector. This public-sector process is commonly used to settle disputes involving police officers, teachers, and public-health employees. The fact-finding board, composed of three nonpartisan individuals, holds a hearing in which each side presents its views regarding the disputed issues. After studying each party's position and arguments, the board publicly announces a recommended settlement, putting pressure on both sides to accept the pact.

Fact-finding appears to be successful in resolving an impasse. It is estimated that 90 percent of the disputes going to fact-finding are resolved and that the fact-finder's reports are responsible for the resolution in 60 to 70 percent of the cases.[38]

Interest Arbitration This process occurs when an arbitrator (or panel) is called to solve a possible dispute involving issues in a future contract. Interest arbitration has seen relatively greater use in the private sector. But unlike mediation and fact-finding, the arbitrator not only studies the dispute but also determines the terms of agreement, which is final and binding on both parties.

Interest arbitration received considerable publicity in labor circles when the United Steelworkers and an employers' association of ten steel companies agreed to submit unresolved issues to an interest arbitration panel in order to avoid a strike or lockout. Although differences were resolved and the panel was not called, the inclusion of the interest-arbitration provision in the negotiation agreement (formally termed an *Experimental Negotiating Agreement*) may have helped the parties reach agreement.

Final-offer Arbitration This method requires both parties to submit their final offer to the three-member panel that has the authority to select one of the proposals. Final-offer arbitration gives the parties the motivation to make their final offers reasonable. Both parties realize that an unreasonable offer will have a lower chance of selection. Therefore, they strive to make their offer appear as fair and reasonable as possible. In 1987 Detroit Tiger Jack Morris won a $1.85 million contract dispute through final-offer arbitration. The baseball players' union and major league owners had agreed to begin using the impasse resolution technique in 1974 to settle salary disputes. When the Tigers and their star pitcher could not reach a salary agreement they each presented their final offer to an arbitrator who could only choose one of the two offers and could not choose a compromise. The Tigers' last offer was $1.35 million—$500,000 larger than the previous largest final-offer arbitration award. Morris proposed $1.85 million based on his 123–81 record (most wins in the major in the 1980s) and performance in the 1984 World Series.[39]

Mediation-Arbitration Using this combination method, both parties agree to bring in a mediator with authority to arbitrate *any* unresolved issues. Since the parties must agree to abide by the mediator-arbitrator's decision, they will likely agree on the substantive issues as well.

COLLECTIVE BARGAINING IN THE PUBLIC SECTOR

By and large, collective bargaining for public-sector employees at federal and local government levels is very similar to collective bargaining for private-sector employees. The processes are similar primarily because unionization of government employees did not become widespread until the 1960s, well after the establishment of collective-bargaining procedures in the private sector. Some important distinctions regarding bargaining in the public sector are worthy of mention.

Right to Organize

The Wagner Act provides the basic right to organize for private-sector employees. Federal employees were granted the right to engage in collective bargaining by President John F. Kennedy's Executive Order 10988. Later, President Richard M. Nixon's Executive Order 11491, which superseded Executive Order 10988, listed public-sector unfair labor practices similar to those enumerated in the Taft–Hartley Act.

In 1978, the Civil Service Reform Act (CSRA) was passed, enacting into law the provisions of Executive Orders 10988 and 11491. The act safeguards the right of federal employees to organize and eliminates the threat of discharge as a result of a change in political party at the leadership level. The act also abolished the U.S. Civil Service System and created the Office of Personnel Management (OPM) and the Merit Systems Protections Board. One of the responsibilities of the OPM is to create job-related performance standards. The OPM then must use appraisal results in making such personnel decisions as compensation, promotions, training and development, transfers, and discharge.[40] Specific measures of the Civil Service Reform Act that pertain to labor-management relations include:

- Establishment of the Federal Labor Relations Authority (FLRA), an independent, bipartisan agency to investigate and remedy unfair labor practices within the federal government. The FLRA serves in a capacity similar to that of the NLRB, which functions in the private sector.
- Requirement of formal grievance procedures and binding arbitration in all labor agreements.
- Outlawing of strikes by federal employees.
- Establishment of the Office of General Counsel to investigate charges of unfair labor practices.

State laws regarding collective bargaining for public employees vary widely. Virtually all of the states have enacted legislation that provides collective bargaining for state employees. Some states allow all public employees to organize; other prohibit certain classes of employees from organizing.[41]

Members of management, including the first-level supervisor, are not protected by labor law in the private sector. But some lower-level government administrators may join a union and bargain collectively with their employers. For example, U.S. postal supervisors have their own union, the National Association of Postal Supervisors.

Ban on Strikes

With rare exception, employees in the public sector are forbidden to strike; the Taft–Hartley Act prohibits strikes against any U.S. government agency. State statutes may prohibit strikes, but some states allow a limited number of exceptions. Ten states allow public workers to strike, either directly by law or indirectly by not prohibiting it.[42]

Nonetheless, employees at all levels of government have struck in spite of no-strike legislation. A nationwide strike by over 200,000 postal workers in 1970 over wage issues remains one of the country's greatest public strikes; it was the first major strike against the federal government. Most strikes in the public sector, however, take place at local and state levels, typically involving teachers, firefighters, police officers, and sanitation workers.

Perhaps the most publicized strike by government employees involved PATCO in a work stoppage against the federal government in 1981. Working conditions rather than money caused the action; rather than accept an average annual salary of $38,000, PATCO members voted to strike. They wanted twice-a-year cost-of-living increases; a four-day, thirty-two-hour workweek; and retirement after twenty years at 75 percent of base salary. The union's mistake lay in their perception that they could not be replaced. They also greatly underestimated President Ronald Reagan's resolution and greatly overestimated support from other unions. The government cut back scheduled flights, brought in as replacement employees retired controllers and supervisory personnel, and began a massive recruiting campaign for new controllers. President Reagan reminded the nation that federal employees are forbidden to strike and that each controller was under oath to that effect. Some 11,000 controllers who stayed on strike permanently lost their jobs, and PATCO filed for bankruptcy. The end of PATCO marked the first time the Federal Labor Relations Authority had ever decertified a union of government employees.[43]

A greater use of fact-finding and interest arbitration is found in the public sector compared to the private sector. Because public employees are generally denied the right to strike, these mechanisms act as substitutes for the strike and enable the union to maintain a balance of power should an impasse result. Impasse procedures vary widely from state to state and differ for various bargaining units. Frequently, binding arbitration is applied to groups responsible for public safety, such as police officers and firefighters.

GRIEVANCE HANDLING

The discussion thus far has focused on the creation of a labor-management agreement and the methods for breaking impasses that may result. Many agreements are created without any serious stalemate. Even though problems may occur during the bargaining stage, an agreement will be signed at some point, except the rare situations in which a strike forces a company out of business or an employer destroys a union. The signing of the contract spells a new relationship between management and labor, because the agreement often reflects significant changes in wages, benefits, work regulations, and other conditions of employment. In effect, the agreement constitutes a new set of game rules, and both management and labor are bound to abide by the new rules. Implementation and enforcement of the agreement, referred to as *contract administration*, represents a critical responsibility for the personnel or industrial-relations director.

Exactly what is a grievance? A *grievance* is a formal complaint by an employee concerning a possible violation of the labor contract, an employer's past practice, or a local, state, or federal law. A grievance is not a *gripe*, which is generally defined as a complaint by an employee concerning an action by management that does not violate the contract, past practice, or law. As an example, an employee may only have a gripe if his supervisor speaks to him in a harsh tone, but when the supervisor assigns him work outside of his job classification, he may have a grievance.

Regardless of how clearly and objectively a contract is written, disputes will generally arise during its enforcement. Only rarely does any agreement run its term completely void of any dispute. For this reason, most contracts contain a quasi-judicial process to solve conflicts internally. If management finds that an employee has violated work rules or some aspect of the contract, it will discipline the employee. An employee may be disciplined for any one of many causes: excessive absenteeism, fighting, drinking on the job, verbal abuse, deliberate work slow-down, or disregard for the safety of others. Most disciplinary systems are progressive and contain several separate disciplinary steps, beginning with an oral warning and ending in discharge.

The Grievance Procedure

Many labor–management disputes arise because the union thinks the employer has violated some term or provision of the agreement. For example, employees may think they were unfairly disciplined. If employees and union representatives agree that the violation is serious enough, they will file a grievance against the employer. This sets in motion a formal procedure designed to settle the differences between the two parties, known as *grievance handling*.[44] The procedure for handling grievances varies from agreement to agreement, but most involve four steps.

Step One   In the initial step, the employee generally discusses the grievance with the shop steward. Experienced in grievance matters and familiar with contract terms and provisions, the steward probably has a good idea of how the contract language should be interpreted. In effect, the shop steward screens complaints and often persuades employees to drop those that are insignificant or invalid, but the steward will encourage an employee to pursue a legitimate grievance.

The steward normally investigates the grievance to provide documented facts on the case. The pertinent facts are written on a grievance form such as the one in Figure 14–7. A good rule for remembering the crucial facts in a grievance is the "5 W's":

- What happened?
- When did the event take place?
- Who was involved? (witnesses?)
- Where did it happen?
- Why is the complaint a grievance?

The written grievance is delivered to the supervisor, and a meeting of the three parties is held (the shop steward is occasionally accompanied by a personnel or industrial-relations representative). In discussing the grievance, all of the parties make an attempt to settle the matter at that point. Research shows that most grievances are settled at the first step. If the grievance cannot be resolved there, the employee and union may appeal the decision to step two of the process. Figure 14–7 shows that the disposition resulted in management's rejecting the employee's grievance and that the union has decided to refer the grievance to step two.

Step Two   The format for step two is basically the same as for step one: both sides meet to discuss the grievance, with labor representing the employee. Higher-level union and management officials are involved at this step. The union representative may be the steward or business agent; the management representative is often the plant superintendent or plant manager. If the employee and union representatives are not satisfied with management's decision, they may appeal to the next step.

Step Three   At this step, the employee is often represented by a plantwide union grievance committee. The plant manager and the

---

GRIEVANCE NUMBER _82-003_   DATE FILED _4/23/82_   UNION _Local 1233_

NAME OF GRIEVANT(S) _Flacko, George_   CLOCK # _0379_

DATE CAUSE OF GRIEVANCE OCCURRED _4/20/82_

CONTRACTUAL PROVISIONS CITED _Articles III, VII, and others_

STATEMENT OF THE GRIEVANCE:

   On April 20, Foreman Pat Zajac asked George Flacko to go temporarily to the Rolling Mill for the rest of the turn. Flacko said he preferred not to, and that he was more senior to others who were available. The foreman never ordered Flacko to take the temporary assignment. He only requested that Flacko do so.
   Flacko was improperly charged with insubordination and suspended for three days. The foreman did not have just cause for the discipline.

RELIEF SOUGHT:

   Reinstatement with full back pay and seniority.

GRIEVANT'S SIGNATURE _George Flacko_ _____ DATE _4/22/82_
STEWARD'S SIGNATURE _Paul Smith_ _____ DATE _4/23/82_

<u>STEP 1</u>

DISPOSITION:

   Foreman Zajac gave Flacko clear instructions to report temporarily to the Rolling Mill for the remainder of the shift. Flacko refused to do so and was warned that it could result in discipline. When he again refused the foreman's directive, he was disciplined.
   The discipline was for just cause. The grievance is rejected.

SIGNATURE OF EMPLOYER REPRESENTATIVE _J. K. Ellis_ _____ DATE _4/26/82_

_____ Grievance Withdrawn   or   _✓_ Referred to Step 2

SIGNATURE OF UNION REPRESENTATIVE _Paul Smith_ _____ DATE _4/28/82_

FIGURE 14–7

A standard grievance record form, step 1 (Source: Donald S. McPherson, _Resolving Grievances: A Practical Approach,_ © 1983, p. 55. Reprinted by permission of Prentice-Hall, Inc., Englewood Cliffs, N.J.)

industrial-relations director often represent management. Again, management hears the union's case and arguments and then issues its ruling on the matter. If the employee and union are still unsatisfied with the results, they may appeal to a fourth and final step: arbitration.[45]

Step Four *Arbitration* is a quasi-judicial process in which the parties agree to submit an unresolved dispute to a neutral third party for binding settlement.[46] During the arbitration process, the arbitrator studies the evidence, listens to the arguments on both sides, and renders a decision. The arbitrator's decision, an *award* to one of the sides, is *binding* in that it must be accepted by both sides and cannot be appealed further. Just how does arbitration work? Some common questions about arbitration are the following:

Is Arbitration Included in Most Agreements? Almost all contracts provide for binding arbitration if the parties are unable to settle the grievance internally. Either side may request arbitration as a final step to resolving a grievance. Despite the inclusion of arbitration in most contracts, the labor–management agreement for one of the nation's largest employers does not include arbitration as a final step in the grievance handling process. GE's contract with the Electrical Workers' Union does not include arbitration, and the union may legally strike over a grievance that remains unresolved. GE managers think that arbitrators' rulings may adversely influence corporate policy.

How Are Arbitrators Selected? Labor and management may agree on the selection of an impartial arbitrator. But if they cannot agree, the contract often stipulates that they request a panel or list of seven arbitrators from the FMCS. Arbitrators are also supplied by the

American Arbitration Association (AAA), which like the FMCS acts as a clearinghouse between arbitrators and disputing parties. The AAA also sends a panel of names, normally five or seven. Each side, in turn, eliminates a name on the list until one arbitrator is agreed upon by both sides.

Who Are Arbitrators? Arbitrators are private consultants, not employees of the FMCS or AAA. There are no special qualifications necessary to be an arbitrator; some are full-time arbitrators (such as labor attorneys). Others are part-time arbitrators; they are often full-time college professors of law, management, personnel, or economics. Lawyers and law professors make up about 60 percent of all arbitrators.[47]

How Much Are Arbitrators Paid? As privately employed professionals, arbitrators set their own fees. The better-known, more experienced arbitrators command higher fees than those just breaking into the business. The average per diem for an FMCS arbitrator is $354.[48] The arbitrator's fee is usually jointly paid by the union and employer.

What Are the Major Issues That Go to Arbitration? A great variety of contract issues are arbitrated every year, but most focus upon a few general areas. Of the issues heard by FMCS arbitrators, most deal with discharge and disciplinary issues, economic issues (wages and other forms of pay), and with general issues (e.g., seniority, working conditions, and work assignments).[49]

What Role Does the Arbitrator Play? The arbitrator is often thought of as a judge hearing a case between two disputing parties. His or her primary responsibility is to make a fair, impartial, and just decision based on the labor agreement. The arbitrator is free to study the awards of other arbitrators but is not bound to the decisions handed down by other arbitrators. Generally, the arbitrator cannot modify the agreement in any way, even when certain language is unclear or the terms of the contract conflict with federal or state legislation.

Each arbitration case is unique, and arbitrators generally vary somewhat in their approach to researching and investigating a particular case. But the following issues provide a research format that is followed by arbitrators in many cases:[50]

Express Language of the Contract   The arbitrator will usually begin by carefully examining the contract language and its provisions.

Prior Arbitration between the Parties   A prior decision regarding a particular contract clause will affect subsequent arbitration decisions. For example, if one arbitrator interpreted a contract provision in a certain way and the provision remains unchanged in subsequent agreements, another arbitrator will likely conclude that the interpretation had become part of the agreement.

Past Practices of the Parties   Some contracts contain ambiguous terms and provisions and are silent on various issues. Should this be the case, the arbitrator will examine the past practices of both parties to help in deciding an issue.

Prior Arbitration within the Same Industry   Arbitrators are not bound to follow precedent. But the arbitrator may follow industry precedent in the rare situation where the agreement is silent or ambiguous, past practice is not an issue, and the parties are confronting an issue for the first time.

Other Arbitration Decisions   Arbitrators' decisions outside the industry seldom enter into the investigative process. There may be times, however, when a prior decision outside the industry is directly to the point, was written by a competent and well-known arbitrator, and adds validity to an arbitrator's decision.

Grievance Handling in Nonunion Organizations

Most formal grievance-handling procedures are found in unionized companies. Relatively few nonunion companies provide mechanisms for processing grievances on par with unionized firms. A survey of 1,958 readers of the *Harvard Business Review* showed that only 14 percent worked in companies that had a management grievance committee.[51] Another study found that twenty-two of thirty-four nonunion companies had some type of formal grievance procedure.[52] These results are somewhat surprising, because an organizational climate of fairness and justice is dependent, in part, upon a formal channel for handling employee dissatisfaction.

Nonunion organizations that have formal grievance procedures generally pattern them after labor-management contract provisions. An example of a grievance procedure for two affiliated large nonunion hospitals is shown in Figure 14–8.

Reducing Employee Grievances

The best interests of both management and labor demand that frivolous grievances be kept as few as possible while serious attention is given to legitimate labor–management problems. Management should regularly monitor the volume of grievances and take positive steps to reduce them should they reach excessive levels. Although some grievances may be written for trivial reasons or simply to display union power, the grievance may be a true representation of some area of mismanagement or poor supervisory practice. Excessive grievances may result, for example, from inadequate employee training, faulty promotion procedures, discriminatory practices, or overbearing or antagonistic supervision. Thus, excessive grievances often indicate a need to improve some aspect of the labor contract. The union—concerned about the satisfaction, wel-

In order to protect the individual rights of the employee, the hospitals have established and maintain a grievance procedure, whereby an employee may present what he/she considers to be a personal injustice regarding his/her employment relationship. Such a grievance must be filed by the employee within five days from the time the situation occurred that may have caused the grievance. Also the following steps should be taken in pursuing the grievance:

(1) The aggrieved employee should first let his/her supervisor know of the complaint. If the employee does not receive a satisfactory reply within two working days, he/she should proceed to Step 2.

(2) At this step, the department head is notified of the complaint in writing by the employee. If the employee wishes assistance in writing the grievance, he/she may request assistance from the personnel department. If a satisfactory reply to the grievance is not received in three working days, then the employee should proceed to Step 3.

(3) At this stage, the director of personnel services or his/her designate is informed of the grievance by the employee. After a review of the facts, the personnel director or his/her designate and the employee may reach a satisfactory solution to the grievance. However, if this does not occur, then the fourth step should be taken.

(4) A peer review committee composed of three impartial employees will be established to review the grievance and establish the facts of the complaint. The members of this committee are subject to the approval of the aggrieved employee. The director of personnel services or his/her designate will serve as a resource person for the committee. However, the peer review committee, alone, makes the recommendation of how the complaint is to be resolved. Within five working days of the hearing, the employee will receive the committee's written recommendation.

(5) Finally, if the employee and/or the department head is not satisfied with the committee's recommendations, then the last step in the appeal process is administration where the final determination is made.

In no way, either directly or indirectly, is the employee to consider his/her job in jeopardy as a result of participating in this procedure.

FIGURE 14–8
A formal grievance procedure in a nonunion organization (Source: *Norton-Children's Hospitals Employee Handbook* [Louisville, KY: Norton-Children's Hospitals, Inc., Undated], pp. 17–18.)

fare, and morale of its membership—should also take excessive grievances seriously and work with management to keep grievances at a minimum.

A second reason to keep grievances at the lowest level possible is that they take a great deal of time and money to handle. The meetings and conferences of the grievance procedure take the employee and management representatives away from their jobs, decreasing productivity. Cases that end up in arbitration require that professional fees be paid to arbitrators, and some of the largest industrial firms and labor groups spend thousands of dollars a year on arbitration fees and expenses.

As in many areas of personnel management, maintaining minimum levels of grievances is a responsibility of line managers and staff administrators. The personnel or industrial-relations staff should devise programs and procedures to keep employee discontent and grievances at low levels. While there is no one sure-fire program or technique that will guarantee a grievance-free operation, several methods and practices have been recognized as valuable ways to keep grievances at minimum levels.

Healthy Climate An organization that strives to create and maintain a healthy working climate is much more likely to enjoy a low grievance rate than one that shows little concern for the working conditions of the employee. Very important in this concern is a clearly written, easily understood labor contract, one that has been thoroughly studied by the first-level supervisors who are primarily responsible for its day-to-day administration. Management and labor will get off on the right foot toward peaceful coexistence by creating an agreement that does not contain ambiguous or vague terms and provisions.[53] Also important in creating a healthy climate are fair and just dealings with all employees. Fairness in promotions, transfers, layoffs, merit increases, disciplinary action, and other work conditions is critical to keep labor-management conflict at low levels.

Lastly, management and the union should cooperate in achieving peaceful and harmonious labor relations. Unavoidable problems are sure to occur throughout the lifetime of a contract, but a spirit of problem solving—rather than an "I win, you lose" atmosphere—will enhance the effectiveness of the union and the employer. Such cooperation can extend to joint labor-management training that may result in significantly fewer grievances.

People-oriented Supervisors The attitudes and behavior patterns of supervisors may have a pronounced effect on the griev-

ances written. By controlling many of the day-to-day work activities of the employee, the supervisor may become a powerful source of job satisfaction or dissatisfaction.

In a classic study at the International Harvester Company, researchers found a strong relationship between supervisory behavior and the number of grievances filed.[54] Supervisors who were characterized as considerate (those who exhibited trust, respect, and warmth toward employees) had significantly fewer grievances filed by their employees than did supervisors who were rated high in structure (those who showed a great concern for production).

Research indicates that management training programs should develop employee-oriented behaviors in addition to such traditional management skills as planning, organizing, and controlling. Further, people-oriented skills and aptitudes should be considered when selecting new supervisors. The assessment-center concept discussed in a previous chapter is a valuable technique for determining the extent to which a management candidate may possess human-relations skills in addition to technical and conceptual skills.

LABOR–MANAGEMENT COOPERATION

As the United States struggles to meet greater international competition and domestic needs, the process of collective bargaining will need to undergo substantial changes. From the early 1800s on, management fought labor as combinations in restraint of trade and used other techniques to combat its very existence. The passage of the National Labor Relations Act in the 1930s and the subsequent Taft–Hartley amendments legitimized the rules of collective bargaining. But the general adversarial relationship has remained the same.[55]

Can the labor–management relationship change from an adversarial to a problem-solving one? Such a change should, of course, benefit both management and employees. The collective bargaining process is adversarial by design and is usually perceived as a win–lose proposition. In order to win on one issue, a negotiator is willing to lose on another. Management has traditionally considered the organizational problem-solving process as strictly a management prerogative. Examples include product decisions, production design and techniques, financial matters, and so on.[56]

While these two separate processes have worked well for many years, both union and management leaders in many companies have recently concluded that they are inadequate in times of rapid change and increased foreign competition in a global economy. Thus, in recent years, many leaders have realized that a new process based on labor–management cooperation is needed to develop a collaborative, problem-solving process. The impetus for such a radical change in philosophy is usually nothing short of survival. The goals are usually cost reduction, improved productivity, expanded markets, and so on. By 1988 the U.S. Department of Labor had reported over 200 successful labor-management collaborations, including the following examples:[57]

- The Fiber Products Division of the Diamond International Corporation and the United Paperworkers Union, through a cooperative project, reported a 16 percent productivity increase, a 40 percent reduction in quality problems, and a 55 percent reduction in grievances.
- For Bethlehem Steel and the United Steelworkers, companywide worker participation teams significantly reduced production costs, equipment downtime, and waste.

- Rohm and Haas of Tennessee, Inc., and the Aluminum, Brick, and Glass Workers Union increased productivity by 50 percent through job redesign.
- Uniroyal, Inc., and the United Rubber Workers saved $5 million in production costs through work rules changes alone.

Today many corporate executives and political leaders are calling for an expansion of cooperative efforts at the work place, including quality circles, QWL programs, and continued moderation in wage demands. At the same time, however, the dominant trend among management is to shift investments and jobs to nonunion employment settings.[58] This trend is furthered by Supreme Court decisions allowing plant relocations, liquidations, and partial closings without union input by declaring such practices to be permissive items and not mandatory.[59] It is difficult to see how unions can act cooperatively when management practices in some organizations undermine their basic existence.

American unions have generally chosen to avoid further membership losses by promoting innovation in the work place to maintain organizational competitiveness, increasing their influence on strategic business and governmental decisions that affect membership, and pursuing new organizing strategies.[60]

Business Schools

U.S. Labor Secretary William E. Brock has strongly suggested that the nation's business schools take the lead in training individuals in labor–management cooperation. Business schools, he noted, can teach the skills necessary for workers and managers to realize their mutual goals. In the past, inadequate preparation in labor–management relations may have aided the development of adversarial positions. Brock asked the business schools in our universities to modify their curricula and train future labor and management leaders in the totality of the work relationship, with particular emphasis on labor-management relations and cooperation.[61]

INTERNATIONAL HRM: NEGOTIATION AND CULTURE

In *The Master of Go*, a Nobel Prize winner's novel about the Japanese board game, the Japanese protagonist plays Go with an American. As the Japanese contemplates his moves, he silently observes, "[the American] had taken lessons . . . [and] . . . lined his forces up after patterns he had been taught, and his opening plays were excellent; but . . . [t]he spirit of Go was missing. I thought it all very strange, and I was conscious of being confronted by his utter foreignness." Foreign behavior of one sort or another has also struck culturally sensitive observers of negotiation. As a result, like the American who took lessons in Go, we have been presented with negotiating "plays" or actions typical of certain cultures. Japanese negotiators who say "yes" to a proposal, for example, rarely mean they consent. Chinese rely on connections and mutual commitments—obligations—of reciprocation (*guanxi*) to get things done. Arabs are offended by negotiators who expose the soles of their shoes.[62]

With respect to bargaining in particular, Japanese hold firm to their initial positions rather than systematically making concessions. Chinese negotiators concentrate on establishing general principles. Arabs engage counterparts in prolonged social discourse. Observations of this kind do not take us very far, however. Keeping one's sole to the ground may prevent a slip in Saudi Arabia, but it is not one of the more significant actions for a negotiation researcher to study or for a

practitioner to heed. Single conventions or tactics like that usually do not educate us about the "spirit" of the interaction, the interconnected rules and procedures, or even the defining features of the interaction. Negotiators' discourse in some cultures appears so nonspecific or oblique to naive Americans and Europeans that they often fail even to recognize it as negotiation.

Further, there may be major differences between intracultural and intercultural behavior in negotiations. Negotiators' attitudes and actions toward foreigners may not be captured in observations based solely on studies of domestic negotiation behavior. Finally, few of these contemporary writings, which are descriptive studies, directly provide recommendations for negotiating effectively in cross-cultural settings.[63]

At this point, it seems we have a long way indeed to go.

CONCLUSIONS AND APPLICATIONS

- Both single-employer and multiple-employer bargaining structures are common today. Multiple-employer structures are generally less costly for both parties, and both the union and the employer enjoy certain advantages from a uniform, industrywide wage structure.

- Both labor and management do a great deal of prenegotiation homework before actual negotiations begin. The union becomes aware of the needs of its members and of general trends in collective bargaining. Management must pay close attention to how an increase in labor costs will affect its profitability and then determine the kinds of terms and provisions it can and cannot afford.

- There are a variety of different bargaining strategies. The most common form involves distributive bargaining, or win–lose bargaining, though this strategy seems to be giving way to more cooperative forms such as integrative bargaining and productivity bargaining. Concessionary bargaining, or giveback bargaining, has increased as a result of nonunion and foreign competition.

- The actual negotiation process typically involves a great deal of give and take on both sides before an agreement is reached. But a bargaining impasse may result in a strike by the union or in a lockout by the employer. During a strike or lockout, the employer may attempt to maintain operations by using nonunion staff and strikebreakers or by contracting out.

- A variety of mediation and arbitration techniques are being increasingly used to reach a negotiation settlement without losing production.

- Collective bargaining in the public sector generally parallels the process in the private sector. But though federal employees have been given the right to organize by presidential executive order, state laws regarding unionization vary widely.

- Grievance handling is a critical part of the day-to-day administration of the labor agreement. Handling most grievances involves a multi-step procedure that includes arbitration as a final step. The arbitrator has authority to decide the outcome of the case, and his or her decision must be accepted by both parties.

- A high grievance rate should receive management's full attention. The grievances may represent a real problem area within the organization, such as poor supervision or a vague or subjective contract provision. In addition, the grievance procedure is time-consuming and may result in a considerable outlay for arbitrator's fees. In general, grievances may be kept at minimal levels with a healthy working climate, fair dealings with employees, people-oriented supervisors, and good two-way communication systems between labor and management.

- Labor–management cooperation appears to be on the increase in the United States. However, both sides recall their adversarial past and have been slow to change.

CASE STUDY
Making Coffee on Company Premises

On February 10, 1981, the Sheridan Machine Company posted the following notice on all bulletin boards in the plant:

"Over the years the matter of making coffee, etc., has expanded to the point where the lost time involved has become very costly. We have installed brewed coffee machines for the convenience of office and engineering employees. Those employees who do not wish to bring their own beverages in thermos bottles will find the quality of the coffee in these machines quite good. Also, the proceeds from these machines will go into the employees' fund as do proceeds from the other vending machines.

"In the interest of good management and the efficient operation of the plant, the making of coffee is to be discontinued. Effective Monday, February 13, 1981, all coffee pots, urns, and hot plates are to be removed from the premises. No food preparations will be permitted after this date."

Sheridan Machine Company management enforced the provisions of the February 10 notice. The International Union of Electrical, Radio and Machine Workers filed a grievance to protest the company notice and its enforcement. Since the union and company were unable to agree about the employees' practice of brewing coffee and preparing other food on the premises of the company, the grievance was submitted for settlement to an arbitrator.

Both parties to the grievance agreed to the following facts: coffee making by the employees had been permitted for almost fourteen years, as union representatives estimated. Representatives for the company estimated that this activity had continued during the negotiations of the three previous contracts. However, the question was not raised during negotiation of the last three contracts. Both parties agreed that the right of an employee to drink coffee was not at issue, this right being granted freely by the management.

The union contended that the issuing of the notice was illegal, since it was prohibited by the past-practice clause of the 1980 contract. Page 3 of the 1980 contract would indicate that the unilateral abolition of the right of employees to make their own coffee is a direct violation: "Practices and policies now in effect and not covered by this agreement shall continue in effect for the duration of this agreement unless changed by mutual consent between the Company and the Union."

To support its position, the union offered the following evidence: (1) Many employees were dissatisfied with the quality of coffee furnished by the machines installed by the company. (2) Expenditures for coffee by employees would be raised by as much as $3 per week. (3) The expense of bringing coffee from home would be increased because of periodic thermos bottle breakage. (4) The time involved in making coffee is minimal; the activity does not interfere with plant efficiency. (5) Plant efficiency is increased because of higher morale, with morale being boosted by the making of coffee to the individual taste. (6) Some supervisors in recent years had joined workers' coffee pools. (7) The issue was raised previously in a meeting attended by management in which a tool-room foreman's order to his employees to cease making coffee was overruled by management, when the union offered the past-practices argument to support its protest. Management thus had acknowledged the validity of the union's position. (8) In negotiations of the 1977 and 1980 agreements, management had an opportunity to raise this issue, but it failed to do so.

Management contended that only the right to have coffee available constituted a past practice. The method of making coffee was not a past practice but was within management discretion. Management contended that the question had not been raised seriously until recently for three reasons: (1) the participation by workers in making coffee had substantially increased and had been extended recently to include the preparation of short order dishes during working time before mealtime; (2) the introduction of a wide variety of utensils such as hot plates, sandwich grills, and frying and cooking pans constituted a fire hazard; (3) a wide enough variety of coffee to suit an adequate number of tastes was now available in the new machines installed by management.

Management further contended that these abuses interfered with plant efficiency, thus violating a management right stated in paragraphs 3(a) and 3(b) under Article II, Section 1 of the contract as follows: "It is the responsibility of the Management of the Company to maintain discipline and efficiency in its plant."

In this regard, management contended that the practice of coffee making took substantial time away from work, which detracted from plant efficiency and, therefore, must be curtailed. Management's notice was both reasonable and within its rights to manage the plant in an efficient, profitable fashion.

Questions

1. Should this grievance be considered a trivial dispute? Why is this the type of grievance that can be of serious consequence to both union and management interests?

2. Was management justified in posting its notice of February 10? Does management in this case have the right to prohibit the use of various utensils on its plant premises?

3. Which clause of the contract must be considered as being overriding in this case: the practices clause or the management rights clause? Are these clauses in basic conflict with each other?

4. What is the fundamental issue at stake for the management of the plant in this case?

Source: Taken from S. H. Schoen and R. L. Hilgert, *Cases in Collective Bargaining and Industrial Relations* (Homewood, IL: Richard R. Irwin, Inc., 1969). All names have been disguised and dates have been revised.

EXPERIENTIAL EXERCISE
Negotiation Issues

Purpose

To help you become familiar with current labor relations issues and the general union and management positions on each issue.

The Task

Through news articles and other sources, identify ten current collective bargaining issues and summarize each side's general position. Your instructor may divide the class into union and management and require you to negotiate an agreement on these issues.

Example:

Two-tier wage system	Management will propose to keep long-run wage rates competitive.	The union will accept only if given job security and wage guarantees for current members.

	Issue	Management	Union
1.			
2.			
3.			
4.			
5.			
6.			
7.			
8.			
9.			
10.			

KEY TERMS AND CONCEPTS

Arbitration

Bargaining categories

Bargaining impasse

Boulwarism

Collective bargaining

Common situs picketing

Concessionary bargaining

Distributive bargaining

Economic strike

Fact-finding

Final-offer arbitration

Good-faith bargaining

Grievance/gripe

Grievance handling

Integrative bargaining

Interest arbitration

Lockout

Mediation

Multiple-employer bargaining

Picket

Primary boycott

Primary situs picketing

Productivity bargaining

Secondary boycott

Single-employer bargaining

Successorship

Sympathy strike

Unfair-labor-practice strike

Wildcat strike

REVIEW QUESTIONS

1. What are the various forms of bargaining structures?
2. What activities take place during the prenegotiation and negotiation phases of collective bargaining?
3. What are the various kinds of bargaining strategies?
4. What pressure tactics may the union and the employer use during a bargaining impasse? What techniques may be used to bring an end to a bargaining impasse?

5. How does the grievance procedure work, and what is the role of arbitration in resolving grievances?
6. What strategies are available to management to keep grievances at a minimum level?

DISCUSSION QUESTIONS

1. The ABC Manufacturing Company has twelve work units on the factory floor. The grievances filed by employees of three work units are over four times higher than those of the other nine departments. Why might this be so? What should management do?
2. The strike has long been a controversial part of the collective bargaining process. Proponents claim that the threat of a strike provides a critical balance of power between the union and employer. Critics say that the strike is a crude, outmoded practice in modern times. What are your opinions about the right to strike?
3. What are the principal differences between the role of the mediator and the arbitrator?
4. How does the collective bargaining process differ in public and private organizations?
5. Do you feel that public employees such as police officers and fire fighters should have the right to join a union, bargain collectively, and strike? Why or why not?
6. As the president of a small nonunion baking company of 100 employees, you would like to introduce a grievance procedure for your employees. Develop a procedure that you feel would enable employees to resolve their formal complaints.
7. How important do you feel the supervisor is in avoiding strike situations? Discuss.

ENDNOTES

1. Recently, the steel industry has seen a disintegration of its bargaining power as members have attempted to gain more control over internal affairs and seek ways to be more competitive with nonunion companies. See T. F. O'Boyle and C. Hymouritz, ''Steel Industry's Bargaining Group Appears to Be on Verge of Collapse,'' *The Wall Street Journal* (August 8, 1984): 14.
2. See G. Daniels and K. Gagala, *Labor Guide to Negotiating Wages and Benefits* (Reston, VA: Reston, 1985), pp. 4–10.
3. Ibid., pp. 256–60.
4. D. H. Rosenbloom and J. M. Shafritz, *Essentials of Labor Relations* (Reston, VA: Reston, 1985), pp. 140–41. For a detailed account of boulwarism from the perspective of its creator, see L. R. Boulware, *The Truth About Boulwarism* (Washington, DC: Bureau of National Affairs, 1969).
5. Dennis King, ''Three Cheers for Conflict,'' *Personnel* (January–February 1987): 21.
6. Joseph F. Byrnes, ''Negotiating: Master the Ethics,'' *Personnel Journal* 66, no. 6 (June 1987): 97–101.

7. Similar benefits were achieved by the Jones & Laughlin Steel Corporation and the United Steel Workers. See "Steel Listens to Workers and Likes What It Hears," *Business Week* (December 19, 1983): 92–95.

8. P. Shakecoff, "Bricklayers and Contractors Form Group to Improve Masonry Industry," *The Louisville Courier-Journal* (October 7, 1983): 33.

9. See E. Weinberg, "Labor-Management Cooperation: A Report on Recent Initiatives," *Monthly Labor Review* (April 1976): 13–21; R. E. Winter, "Firms' Recent Productivity Drives May Yield Unusually Strong Gains," *The Wall Street Journal* (June 14, 1983): 39; R. Guenther, "Plan for Construction Productivity Stirs Industry, Takes Aim at Unions," *The Wall Street Journal* (April 21, 1983): 33; "R. S. Greenberger, "Work Rule Changes Quietly Spread as Firms Try to Raise Productivity," *The Wall Street Journal* (January 25, 1983); and M. H. Schuster, *Union-Management Cooperation* (Kalamazoo, MI: Upjohn Institute, 1984).

10. "Swapping Work Rules for Jobs at GE's "Factory of the Future,'" *Business Week* (September 10, 1984): 43.

11. Ibid.

12. See B. E. Moore and T. L. Ross, *The Scanlon Way to Improve Productivity: A Practical Guide* (New York: Wiley, 1978). For a discussion of an unsuccessful experience with the Scanlon plan, see T. Q. Gilson and M. J. Lefcowitz, "A Plant-Wide Productivity Bonus in a Small Factory: Study of an Unsuccessful Case," *Industrial and Labor Relations Review*, (January 1957).

13. See M. H. Dodosh, "Companies Increasingly Ask Labor to Give Back Past Contract Gains," *The Wall Street Journal* (November 27, 1981): 21; and M. Brody, "Union Blues," *Barrons* (January 23, 1984): 22. For a discussion of union resistance to concessions, see R. S. Greenberger, "Resisting a Trend, Machinists Union Continues to Oppose Concessions," *The Wall Street Journal* (September 2, 1983): 13.

14. J. Peters, "Workers Accept ARCO Contract," *The Louisville Courier-Journal* (November 22, 1983): B-5.

15. "The GM Settlement Is a Milestone for Both Sides," *Business Week* (October 8, 1984): 160–62.

16, R. J. Harris, Jr., "More Firms Set Two-Tier Pay Pacts with Unions, Hurting Future Hire," *The Wall Street Journal* (December 15, 1983): 34.

17. Ibid.

18. Bureau of National Affairs, *Collective Bargaining and Labor Relations Database* (Washington, DC: Bureau of National Affairs, 1984), p. 21.

19. Michael R. Carrell and Christina Heavrin, Collective Bargaining and Labor Relations, 2nd ed. (Columbus, OH: Merrill, 1988), p. 410.

20. "Ford Employees Average $440 as Part of Profit-Sharing Plan," *Resource*, pamphlet (Alexandria, VA: American Society for Personnel Administration, April 1984), p. 12.

21. Scott A. Kruse, "Giveback Bargaining: One Answer to Current Labor Problems?" *Personnel Journal* 62 (April 1983): 286–89.

22. Carrell and Heavrin, *Collective Bargaining and Labor Relations*, chapter 5.

23. Rosenbloom and Shafritz, *Essentials of Labor Relations*, pp. 178–79.

24, C. W. English, "When Unions Turn Tables on the Bosses," *U.S. News and World Report* (February 4, 1985): 69–70.

25. Ibid.

26. G. Bronson and J. H. Birnbaum, ''How the Textile Union Finally Wins Contracts at J. P. Stevens Plants,'' *The Wall Street Journal* (October 20, 1980): 1.

27. Rosenbloom and Shafritz, *Essentials of Labor Relations,* 108.

28. See R. S. Greenberger, ''More Firms Get Tough and Keep Operating in Spite of Walkouts,'' *The Wall Street Journal* (October 11, 1983): 1.

29. R. S. Greenberger, ''AT&T's Managers Weather Strike Despite Long Hours, Tedious Work,'' *The Wall Street Journal* (August 17, 1983): 26.

30. *Pattern Makers League* v. *NLRB,* 53 U.S.L.W., 4928 (1985).

31. John J. Coleman, ''Can Union Members Resign During a Strike?'' *Personnel Journal* 65, no. 5 (May 1986): 99–102.

32. ''Bankruptcy as an Escape Hatch,'' *Time* (March 5, 1984): 14.

33. J. S. Lublin, ''Conservative Pilots' Union Turns Militant in Response to Fight at Continental Airlines,'' *The Wall Street Journal* (November 22, 1983): 35.

34. ''Bankruptcy as an Escape Hatch.''

35. ''Unionists are Alarmed by High Court Ruling in a Bankruptcy Filing,'' *The Wall Street Journal* (February 24, 1984): 1.

36. *Fall River Dyeing and Finishing Corp.* v. *NLRB,* No. 85–1208 (1987).

37. Walter A. Maggiolo, *Techniques of Mediation in Labor Disputes* (Dobbs Ferry, NY: Oceana, 1971), p. 12.

38. Rosenbloom and Shafritz, *Essentials of Labor Relations,* p. 163.

39. Carrell and Heavrin, *Collective Bargaining and Labor Relations,* p. 142.

40. *Manager's Handbook: A Handbook for Federal Managers* (Washington, DC: U.S. Office of Personnel Management, Office of Public Affairs, 1979).

41. A. S. Sloane and F. Whitney, *Labor Relations* (Englewood Cliffs, NJ: Prentice-Hall, 1981), p. 39.

42. Bernard F. Ashe, ''Current Trends in Public Employment,'' *The Labor Lawyer* 2, no. 2 (Spring 1986): 277–98.

43. Rosenbloom and Shafritz, *Essentials of Labor Relations,* pp. 154–56.

44. Details of the grievance handling process are discussed in D. S. McPherson, *Resolving Grievances* (Reston, VA: Reston, 1983).

45. Not all grievance-handling procedures include arbitration as the final step, as both parties may liken the arbitration process to a form of Russian roulette where the outcome of a case is unknown. See D. Beeler and H. Kurshenbaum, *Roles of the Labor Leader* (Chicago: Union Representative, 1969).

46. Sloane and Whitney, *Labor Relations,* pp. 244–56.

47. Ibid., p. 259.

48. Ibid., p. 263.

49. U.S. Mediation and Conciliation Service, *Thirty-Second Annual Report* (Washington, DC: U.S. Government Printing Office, 1980).

50. McPherson, *Resolving Grievances,* pp. 88–91.

51. D. W. Ewing, ''What Business Thinks About Employee Rights,'' *Harvard Business Review* (September–October 1977): 81–84.

52. M. S. Trotta, *Arbitration of Labor-Management Disputes* (New York: American Management Association, 1974), p. 218.

53. S. C. Walker, ''The Dynamics of Clear Contract Language,'' *Personnel Journal* (January, 1981): 39–41.

54. E. A. Fleishman and E. F. Harris, "Patterns of Leadership Behavior Related to Employee Grievances and Turnover," *Personnel Psychology* (Spring 1962): 47–48.

55. Robert R. Blake and Jane S. Morton, "Developing a Positive Union-Management Relationship," *Personnel Administrator* 28, no. 6 (June 1983): 23–31.

56. John G. Belcher, Jr., "The Role of Unions in Productivity Management," *Personnel* 65, no. 1 (January 1988): 54–58.

57. Ibid.

58. T. A. Kochan, R. B. McKersie, and H. C. Katz, "U.S. Industrial Relations in Transition," *Monthly Labor Review* 108, no. 5 (May 1985): 28–29.

59. *First National Maintenance Corporation* v. *NLRB*, 452 U.S. 666 (1981); *Otis Elevator Company*, 269 NLRB 891 (1984).

60. Kochan, "U.S. Industrial Relations," pp. 28–29.

61. William E. Brock, speech at the fortieth anniversary of the New York School of Industrial and Labor Relations, Cornell University, May 2, 1986.

62. Stephen E. Weiss, "Negotiation and Culture: Some Thoughts on Models, Ghosts, and Options," *Dispute Resolution Forum* (Washington, DC: National Institute for Dispute Resolution, 1987), p.3

63. Ibid.

Chapter Fifteen

Discipline and Counseling

Chapter Outline

POOR PERFORMANCE
    Performance Analysis
DISCIPLINE
    Incorrect Discipline
    Preventive Discipline
    Positive Discipline
    Supervisory Resistance to Discipline
    The Hot-Stove Rule
DISCIPLINARY DISCHARGE
    Don't Let a Firing Backfire
    Discharging the Manager or Professional
    Administering the Discharge Decision
    Employee Rights in Discharge Decisions
    Termination at Will
    Office Romances
INTERNATIONAL HRM: STRONG EMPLOYMENT RIGHTS
CONCLUSIONS AND APPLICATIONS

Chapter Objectives

1. To recognize the various sources of poor performance through the illustration and discussion of an unsatisfactory performance model.
2. To explain both good and poor ways to discipline employees, with emphasis on effective disciplinary techniques.
3. To discuss how organizations can manage employees in such a way as to keep disciplinary problems at a minimum.
4. To illustrate a model of positive discipline and describe the procedures for ensuring that discipline achieves its goals.
5. To identify the procedures for carrying out the discharge decision humanely and tactfully.
6. To recognize the increasing rights of employees in discharge decisions and to understand how the erosion of the termination-at-will concept affects the personnel/human resource function.

The Sadistic Boss

We doubt that anyone would publicly label himself or herself a sadistic manager. But if you have any doubts about your leadership style, the following quiz may help set the record straight. (If you're sure about yourself, complete the quiz using your boss.) Do you (or does your boss):

- Verbally assault workers in public?
- Reshape the past—manipulate facts, events and relationships—to further your own best interests?
- Take hostile, vindictive action against employees who rock the boat or fail to toe the line?
- Severely and excessively criticize employees over petty and insignificant issues?
- Set vague job standards so that employees never are sure what you expect?
- Demand complete obedience and complete submissiveness from your employees and threaten dissenters with loss of job or promotional opportunities?
- Shape company policy, rules, and regulations to further your own personal gain?
- Exhibit an overwhelming self-interest and a total lack of concern or loyalty to productive subordinates?
- Demonstrate wide swings in styles and moods—from the gentle to the unpredictable, irrational, devious, and brutal?

If you answered "yes" to five or more questions, you may well be a sadistic manager—or have the misfortune of working for one.

The quiz items were developed from a fascinating article by Norma K. Clarke, "The Sadistic Manager," published in *Personnel.* The author, director of personnel for Mitre Corporation, interviewed employees from several companies to learn more about managerial sadism and the effect a sadistic boss has on employees.

What impact does the sadistic manager have on the behavior of subordinates? Without exception, this style of managing creates a highly stressful and threatening situation, one most employees find extremely traumatic.

According to Clarke, few employees chose to fight with their sadistic bosses, and those who did were usually driven out of the organization. Most workers chose either to transfer out of the work unit or leave the organization altogether.

The small number of employees who decided to stick it out with their sadistic leaders suffered fear, helplessness, paranoia, and a lack of self-confidence. They eventually became hostile toward the organization and produced only at a level necessary to keep their jobs.

Sadistic bosses keep their jobs through "the old boy network" and by scapegoating subordinates when things go wrong. The sadistic manager can be identified by upper management in several ways:

- Tap the informal communications network to determine how particular managers treat their employees.
- Analyze turnover patterns and conduct exit interviews to find out why people are leaving their work units.
- Analyze grievance and complaint patterns with attention to those managers who accumulate high incidents of grievance and complaints.

Source: Adapted from N. K. Clarke, "The Sadistic Manger," *Personnel* (February 1985): 34–38.

EVEN in the most sophisticated organizations—those blessed with high-quality personnel programs and competent supervisors—a small percentage of employees will be unwilling or unable to achieve a satisfactory level of performance. The percentage of an organization's human-resource group that may be considered unsatisfactory will vary considerably from firm to firm. No level of the organization—from highest to lowest—can be considered immune to problems of incompetence. Managers who view the employee as a resource rather than simply a factor of production will take positive steps to maintain high levels of job satisfaction and productivity. But those who view the worker as a necessary evil will, more than likely, show little attention to employee needs and suffer "people problems" and performance shortfalls. Thus, management may choose to minimize performance problems or to accept them. In the end, unsatisfactory performance is a management problem.

Some managers place the responsibility for performance problems on the shoulders of employees or the union. But such an attitude reflects an inability or unwillingness to assume an important managerial responsibility: the creation and maintenance of an effective, productive work group. Although employees must bear the responsibility for meeting job standards, management must ensure that standards are defined, communicated, understood, and achieved. The buck stops at management's doorstep.

POOR PERFORMANCE

Consider the case of John Bradley, a hypothetical press operator for a large printing company. Both his output and quality level are consistently below standard. His absenteeism rate is about double the plant average. John is an unsatisfactory performer. But *why* is John an unsatisfactory performer? Is he lazy and shiftless? Is his boss giving him a hard time for no apparent reason? Does he have a substance-abuse problem? Was he assigned to a machine that frequently malfunctions? Is he really not sure what the job standards are?

Determining why an employee is performing at an unsatisfactory level is of critical importance, because a problem cannot be corrected unless its causes are known. Effective managers not only stay alert for employee performance problems but also recognize that productivity problems stem from a variety of causes. Rather than relying on a gut feeling or hunch, the prudent manager strives to uncover the true causes of performance problems and seeks solutions to eliminate or minimize them.

Performance Analysis

The proper analysis of a performance problem is a critical managerial skill. The model in Figure 15–1 shows the major causes of unsatisfactory performance and the solutions available for solving them. Examination of the components of the model is helpful in understanding how managers should treat problems of poor performance.

Communication Some managers assume that the employee knows what good performance is and think it unnecessary to state management's expectations. For the new employee or for the experienced employee who receives a promotion or new job assignment, the manager may describe performance standards in vague or subjective terms, leaving the employee to decipher the job standards on his or her own, or perhaps by learning them from other employees. The problem is that an employee's perception of good performance may differ markedly from that of the manager. A well-intentioned, achievement-oriented employee may quickly fall from the manager's grace simply because the employee misunderstood what was expected.

One of the manager's major responsibilities is to define clearly and precisely what good performance means. Managers who neglect this important task are likely to have more than their share of performance problems.

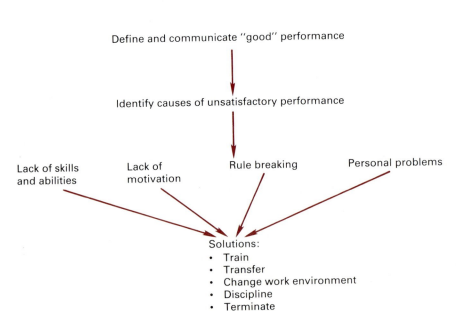

FIGURE 15–1
A model for analyzing unsatisfactory performance (Source: Adapted from F. Kuzmits, R. Herden, and L. Sussman, *Managing the Unsatisfactory Employee* [Homewood, IL: Dow Jones–Irwin, 1984], p. 8.)

Identifying Causes Recognizing that a gap exists between ideal and actual employee performance brings the supervisor to another issue: What is the cause of the performance shortfall? Without proper analysis of the problem, any solution implemented will probably be ineffective, and thus unsatisfactory performance will likely continue. Effective management of unsatisfactory performance greatly depends upon selecting the correct solution or solutions to the problem.

Lack of Skills On too many occasions, organizations place an employee in a job for which he or she is unsuited. This difficult problem for management (and for the employee) can normally be remedied in only one of three basic ways: (1) train the employee and remove the skill deficiency; (2) transfer the employee to a job that utilizes the skills the employee does possess; or (3) terminate the employee.

Lack of Motivation Scores of books and articles have been written on what can be done to motivate employees. A multitude of theories and approaches to employee motivation exists, but most motivational strategies boil down to one seemingly simple axiom: *determine what the employee wants and offer it as a reward for good performance.* Yet as most students of management know, determining the needs of an employee and creating an environment in which those needs are satisfied is one of the manager's most challenging tasks. In addressing that challenge, decision makers must know the common techniques for motivating the unmotivated:

Create Meaningful Goals and Objectives Goals should be challenging, attainable, and important to the employees who are expected to achieve them. In addition, goals should be clearly communicated to employees, and su-

pervisors should ensure that employees understand their goals and agree with them. Finally, managers should involve the employees in the goal-setting process by soliciting their feelings and suggestions when creating goals.

Invite Employee Participation Employees often have meaningful ideas and suggestions for making their work more productive, satisfying, and interesting. Managers should earnestly solicit these ideas, give serious consideration to them, and implement them whenever possible.

Let Employees Know Where They Stand Employees do not like to be left in the dark; they want to know how their performance and behavior stack up against the supervisor's expectations. Managers should tell employees how well they are doing and discuss any problems they might be having. By being approachable and receptive to discussions about performance problems, supervisors can nip many minor problems in the bud—before they become major crises.

Reward Good Work Good work should never go unnoticed. Employees often complain, "When I do something wrong, I'm sure to catch hell. When I do something right, my boss never says a word." Praise for a job well done, given sincerely, is a powerful motivator. Always recognize good work and be generous with praise.

Treat Employees Fairly Equity theory provides evidence that fair and equitable treatment of employees is a strong determinant of employee behavior and a significant factor influencing employee motivation. In turn, unfair and unequitable treatment can lead to negative consequences such as employee grievances, absenteeism, and turnover. Employers want to work for supervisors who are fair and just and who give people their due. Playing favorites and giving breaks to friends (such as easy assignments or a promotion) is a sure way to bring about dissatisfaction and low motivation.

Let Employees Know What Is Happening and Why Most employees have a genuine concern about their jobs, the company, and what the future holds for them. Employees do not like surprises, particularly when the surprise has a direct effect upon their jobs. Management decisions that affect employees and their future with the organization should be communicated to each employee through the manager, along with the rationale behind the decision.

Be a Good Listener Employees generally have something on their minds and expect their supervisors to show a genuine interest in what they have to say. The ability to listen enhances the supervisor's ability to communicate and solve problems. The desire to listen also demonstrates that the supervisor is interested in the welfare and well-being of the employee.

Make Work as Interesting as Possible Many jobs are boring and routine. Jobs are often designed with efficiency in mind, not the needs of the employees who perform them. Managers should do whatever they can to make the work as interesting as possible for employees who seek greater levels of satisfaction from performing their jobs. Although many jobs cannot be altered, some jobs can—particularly those outside the assembly or manufacturing environment. Strategies for job redesign, discussed in a previous chapter, include job enlargement, in which the number of tasks the employee performs is increased; job rotation, in which the employee swaps jobs with another employee for a period of time; and job enrichment, in which the employee is given more authority to plan and control the work he or she performs.

Enable Employees to Grow and Develop Many employees are not content with "just a job." They want careers with opportunities for growth and promotion. They want to learn new skills and abilities and expect the company to make these opportunities available. The manager plays a role by providing on-the-job training and by setting up off-the-job developmental activities such as seminars and short courses. In addition, the manager should urge employees to develop themselves by attending night school, joining professional organizations, and regularly reading professional journals and books. These opportunities not only motivate employees by helping to satisfy their personal needs but also strengthen the organization's human resources through a more competent, motivated work force.

Rule Breaking A third type of unsatisfactory performance is associated with rule breaking. An example of the rule breaker is the employee who is occasionally absent or late to work, who violates the dress or safety code, who swears at the manager, or who drinks excessively during the lunch period. This employee has the necessary skills and normally does a fair day's work but nevertheless disregards the policies, rules, and regulations of the work place.

Although the situation of each rule breaker is different, the most effective approach for dealing with this form of unsatisfactory performance is to apply positive discipline, a technique discussed in detail later in this chapter. Positive discipline avoids the use of harassment, intimidation, and threats, and instead focuses on counseling and self-improvement. Not all rule breakers respond favorably to positive discipline (for a small number, only the "get tough" approach works), but this technique has a better likelihood of achieving results than other disciplinary methods.

Personal Problems   A final type of unsatisfactory performance is associated with the *troubled employee*. A troubled employee is one whose personal problems are so significant that they prevent the employee from performing satisfactorily at work. Although the troubled employee may suffer from a variety of problems—such as emotional illness, financial crises, drug dependency, chronic physical problems, and family problems—by far the most common ailment of the troubled employee is the abuse of alcohol. Because of the significance and severity of this problem in business and industry today (alcoholism is estimated to cost billions of dollars a year in lost productivity and other expenses), many organizations have created employee assistance programs, a topic discussed in chapter 12.

DISCIPLINE

The primary objective of discipline is to motivate an employee to comply with the company's performance standards. An employee receives discipline after failing to meet some obligation of the job. The failure to perform as expected could be directly related to the tasks performed by the employee or to the rules and regulations that define proper conduct at work.

A second objective of discipline is to create or maintain mutual respect and trust between the supervisor and employee. Improperly administered, discipline can create such problems as low morale, resentment, and ill will between the supervisor and the employee. In such cases, any improvement in the employee's behavior will be relatively short-lived, and the supervisor will need to discipline the employee again in the near future. The proper administration of discipline will not only improve employee behavior but will also minimize future disciplinary problems

through a positive supervisor–subordinate relationship.

In effect, discipline is management's last resort to improve the performance of employees. Generally, discipline for poor task performance should not be applied while employees are being trained and are learning the job. Nor should employees be disciplined for problems beyond their control, for example, failure to meet output standards caused by a lack of raw materials.[2] Discipline should be applied only when it has been determined that the employee is the cause of unsatisfactory performance.

When someone breaks the rules, many approaches may be used to correct the problem. Most of us have observed the full range of alternatives to discipline in the supermarket as parents discipline rambunctious children in various ways. Many children do not need to be disciplined; they understand proper behavior in the supermarket and behave accordingly. They stick close to their parents, do not push the shopping carts into other patrons, and do not beg incessantly for candy bars or soda pop. Disciplined children gracefully take no for an answer. But other children treat the supermarket like a giant playground, running up and down the aisles, sampling fruit and candy, screaming and hollering, and creating trouble for everyone concerned. Faced with such behavior, some parents react thoughtlessly and angrily, subjecting the child to public verbal and physical abuse. Shaking their fingers and fists, these parents sternly warn the sobbing child that repeated rowdiness will result in further punishment. The child has been struck with the fear of God, at least for the time being.

Other parents take a different approach to such inappropriate behavior. Calmly taking the child aside, the parents clearly explain what is expected and why the misconduct creates problems for the store management and other customers. They speak to the child without charged emotions, threats, or abuse, and treat the child with respect and maturity. Parents and their children walk away with a mutual understanding about what is right and what is wrong.

Incorrect Discipline

Just as incorrect disciplinary techniques are applied by parents in supermarkets and shopping centers, they are also applied by managers in organizations. Some of the mistakes associated with the disciplinary process in the work setting include:[3]

Punitive Discipline Punitive discipline, sometimes referred to as *negative discipline,* is discipline through fear. Punitive discipline often involves threats, harassment, intimidation, and browbeating. Widespread in the industries of the early twentieth century, punitive discipline is little used today, largely because of union protection and greater acceptance of human-relations techniques. Punitive discipline still exists in some firms, however, particularly among supervisors who prefer to do things the "old way."

Negative Feedback Some supervisors give employees feedback only when unsatisfactory performance occurs and fail to provide positive reinforcement when performance improves or when a job is done well. Feedback should be both positive and negative, depending upon the employee's level of performance.

Late Intervention Perhaps best labeled *procrastination discipline,* this form of discipline takes place when supervisors allow a problem to drag on until it reaches a serious level. The problem may begin as a minor one, but the supervisor's inattention to the situation allows the unsatisfactory performance to become habitual and thus difficult to change.

Inadequate Definition During counseling to rectify a performance problem, a supervisor may tell an employee that he or she is "uncooperative," "disloyal," or not a "team player." Couching a performance problem in such vague and ambiguous terms only serves to confuse and frustrate the employee.

Labeling Employees, Not Behavior Unsatisfactory performance may result in an employee's being labeled "lazy," "shiftless," or "goof-off" by the supervisor. Such labeling has two major problems. First, the employee may carry the label over to other jobs and work units, and the label may serve as a self-fulfilling prophecy. Second, such descriptions focus on the employee and not on the act of unsatisfactory performance—which is what must be addressed.

Misplaced Responsibility Supervisors often have to realize that they themselves sometimes contribute to the performance problems of their employees. When the entire responsibility for changing behavior falls on the employee and improvement does not occur, the supervisor applies further disciplinary action. But without a change in supervisory behavior, a change in employee behavior is unlikely.

Preventive Discipline

Of all the approaches to discipline, preventive discipline is the most desirable. Through preventive discipline, people are managed in a way that prevents behaviors that need to be disciplined.[4] Much like the person who eats nutritious food and exercises regularly to avoid health problems, managers and supervisors who practice preventive discipline create an organizational climate conducive to high levels of job satisfaction and employee productivity. In such cases, the need to discipline will be minimal. To create a working environment that supports a preventive-discipline approach, managers must:

- Match the employee with the job through effective selection, testing, and placement procedures.
- Properly orient the employee to the job and provide any necessary training.
- Clarify proper employee behavior.
- Provide frequent and constructive feedback to employees on their performance.
- Enable employees to address their problems to management through techniques such as an open-door policy and management–employee group meetings.

Positive Discipline

Positive discipline corrects unsatisfactory employee behavior through support, respect, and people-oriented leadership. The purpose of positive discipline is to help rather than harass the employee. Positive discipline is not an attempt to soft-pedal or sidestep an employee problem. Rather, it is a management philosophy that assumes that improved employee behavior is most likely to be long-lived when discipline is administered without revenge, abuse, or vindictiveness. Positive discipline assumes that most employees are willing to accept personal responsibility for their work problems and, with management's confidence and support, will reverse their unsatisfactory performance. While positive discipline is not a panacea, this process offers a number of advantages over the punitive approach.

Positive discipline is much more than the simple act of a supervisor discussing performance problems with an employee. Rather, it is a process that comprises a series of policies and procedures. Important steps in that process are shown in Figure 15–2.

Clarify Responsibility The question of who should administer discipline is subject to some debate. In theory, the responsibility for discipline should fall on the shoulders of an

FIGURE 15–2
Steps in the process of positive discipline

employee's immediate supervisor. Because the immediate supervisor is responsible for the employee's output, that supervisor should possess the authority to correct the employee's performance problems. Some managers, however, think that decentralizing the responsibility for discipline will result in the inconsistent application of discipline throughout the organization. An equitable and uniformly administered disciplinary system can take priority over other considerations, and such uniformity may be achieved only by allowing personnel department employees to apply the discipline. But this approach also has its drawbacks: the personnel staff must spend inordinate amounts of time on disciplinary matters, and the supervisor will lose some control over subordinates.

To overcome the problem of where to place the responsibility for discipline, many organizations give the supervisor authority to administer less severe forms of discipline, such

Employee Relations

as a verbal warning or a written notice. For situations involving suspension or discharge, the supervisor is often required to consult with a personnel representative; in some cases the decision is made by an upper-level line manager or personnel executive. With this type of approach, consistency in the applica-

tion of discipline can be achieved while the supervisor retains authority and control over employee behavior. A study by the Bureau of National Affairs (BNA) showed that this approach was generally followed by most companies that took part in the research. Results of the BNA study are shown in Table 15–1.

TABLE 15–1

Managers who must approve disciplinary actions

	All Companies	Percent of Companies				
		By Industry			By Size	
		Mfg.	Nonmfg.	Nonbus.	Large	Small
Oral Warnings	(206)	(91)	(58)	(57)	(96)	(110)
Department head	45%	44%	36%	56%	43%	47%
Personnel/employee relations manager	15	24	7	9	10	19
Top line manager	7	5	12	4	4	9
Other offical	3	4	5	—	3	4
No approval required	49	46	55	46	52	45
Written Warnings	(213)	(95)	(60)	(58)	(101)	(112)
Department head	70	75	57	76	69	71
Personnel/employee relations manager	47	59	42	34	37	57
Top line manager	28	21	42	24	24	31
Other official	7	6	8	5	9	4
No approval required	14	9	18	17	17	12
Suspensions	(185)	(85)	(45)	(55)	(95)	(90)
Personnel/employee relations manager	86	88	76	93	83	90
Department head	71	74	47	85	75	67
Top line manager	54	48	62	55	53	54
Other official	14	14	16	13	14	14
No approval required	2	—	7	—	1	2
Discharges	(219)	(97)	(62)	(60)	(103)	(116)
Personnel/employee relations manager	93	93	90	97	94	92
Department head	74	76	63	82	72	76
Top line manager	65	69	65	58	64	66
Other official	27	25	26	32	25	28
No approval required	1	—	3	—	1	1

Note: Percentages are based on the number of companies responding for each disciplinary action, as shown in parentheses.

Reprinted by special permission from Personnel Policies Forum, Survey no. 139, 1985, by the Bureau of National Affairs, Inc., Washington, D.C.

Define Performance Expectations A central part of every disciplinary process is the definition of behavior that management expects from its employees. Disciplining an employee for unsatisfactory performance is imprudent unless management has clearly defined good performance. Management must ensure that employee standards are consistent with the organization's objectives and that standards are revised as new organizational goals are developed.

Communicate Disciplinary Policies, Procedures, and Rules Good communication is of the utmost importance in maintaining satisfactory levels of employee performance. Management is responsible for telling employees precisely what is expected of them and for ensuring that all standards, rules, and regulations are clearly communicated. These expectations may be communicated by the following methods:

- Employee handbooks.
- Orientation programs.
- Union contract.
- Rules and regulations distributed in writing to employees.
- Rules and regulations posted on bulletin boards.
- Supervisor–subordinate discussions of job standards and company policies and procedures.

Some administrators avoid publishing rules and regulations, feeling that such a list is demeaning and condescending to employees. As one executive put it, "We have resisted publishing the whole painful list on the theory that it is more insulting than useful, and that there is going to be some rule overlooked, and if everything is spelled out, then you have no recourse and are in trouble. I speak particularly of the nonunion situation, as evidently unionized companies feel that the contract must be all-inclusive in the matter of behavior."[5] Most firms do formalize their rules for employee conduct. A BNA survey of 218 companies found that 79 percent put their rules and regulations in writing for nonunion workers. The figure increased to 85 percent for 97 companies sampled.[6] Table 15–2 shows the percentages of companies with rules for various types of discipline problems.

Collect Performance Data Before an employee is disciplined, there must be indisputable proof that some standard, rule, or regulation was violated. Discipline should not be a gut reaction by a supervisor. There must be no doubt that unsatisfactory performance has taken place, and the collection of information clearly indicating an employee's wrongdoing makes discipline more effective and easier to administer.[7]

Some performance data are easy to collect; others are difficult. For example, an employee's absenteeism is routinely recorded and rarely subject to misinterpretation. Many companies with computerized absenteeism records furnish their supervisors with weekly or biweekly printouts so that employees requiring discipline for unsatisfactory attendance can be pinpointed. Production and quality statistics are routinely collected—often daily—in many manufacturing companies. Other measures of performance, however, are somewhat subjective and difficult to record. For example, as Table 15–2 indicates, many firms have specific rules against "horseplay," "carelessness," "insubordination," and "abusive or threatening language to supervisors." Inexperienced supervisors may ask: What does "carelessness" mean? How do I know when an employee is "insubordinate"? When is an employee guilty of "horseplay"? Although describing all possible occasions of un-

TABLE 15–2
Disciplinary progression used for specific problems

	Percent of Companies (Total respondents: 222)				
	No Policy/ No Answer	1 Step Discharge	2 Steps Suspension Discharge	3 Steps Written Warning Suspension Discharge	4 Steps Oral Warning Written Warning Suspension Discharge
Attendance Problems					
Unexcused/excessive tardiness	4%	*%	–%	14%	82%
Excessive absences	3	1	1	18	77
Unexcused absence	5	3	2	18	73
Leaving work without permission	5	9	16	37	33
Performance/Production Problems					
Failure to maintain quality/quantity standards	5	1	5	25	64
Refusal to work overtime	30	3	13	28	26
Failure to follow safety precautions	11	5	11	35	38
Discourtesy to customers	14	9	9	32	36
Unauthorized work slowdown	31	17	26	17	10
Refusal to obey order or accept assignment	4	29	29	27	10
Unauthorized work stoppage	30	31	22	11	6
Honesty/Loyalty Issues					
Failure to report injuries/accidents	23	3	13	28	32
Outside work/moonlighting	82	3	*	5	10
Wage garnishment	60	5	4	12	18
Using company time/resources for personal gain	14	25	16	29	16
Indictment/conviction for outside criminal actions	49	32	14	3	2
Working for competitor	45	40	5	9	2
Punching another employee's time card	20	49	18	11	3
Computer fraud/security violations	18	68	12	1	1

satisfactory performance is impossible, upper-line management should work closely with the training staff to ensure that supervisors are trained to recognize and record unsatisfactory performance in difficult areas.

Concrete, indisputable records of unsatisfactory performance are important for three reasons. First, the burden of proof lies with the employer. This practice is derived from common law, which holds that a person is in-

TABLE 15–2
continued

	Percent of Companies (Total respondents: 222)				
	No Policy/ No Answer	1 Step Discharge	2 Steps Suspension Discharge	3 Steps Written Warning Suspension Discharge	4 Steps Oral Warning Written Warning Suspension Discharge
Falsification of work records	5	69	17	7	2
Divulging trade secrets or proprietary information	18	71	9	1	*
Willful damage to employer property	4	76	17	3	*
Falsification/omission on employment application	8	78	10	4	*
Theft of employer property	2	84	11	3	—
Workplace Behavior Problems					
Violation of dress/grooming code	41%	*%	1%	11%	46%
Horseplay	11	4	12	33	40
Smoking where/when prohibited	24	5	10	20	40
Unauthorized soliciting	14	6	9	31	40
Sleeping on the job	5	18	30	27	20
Gambling	20	18	26	24	11
Sexual harassment	10	24	25	32	9
Abusive/threatening language to supervisor	4	25	38	23	10
Reporting to work under the influence of drugs or alcohol	3	29	43	18	8
Fighting (physical assault)	6	50	33	9	2
Possession of alcoholic beverages	7	50	30	10	3
Possession of a weapon	13	62	18	7	*
Possession of illegal drugs	4	65	23	6	2

Note: Only one answer was accepted for each disciplinary problem. Percentages may not add to 100 across the row because of rounding.
*Figure is less than 0.5 percent.

Reprinted by special permission from Personnel Policies Forum, Survey no. 139, 1985, by the Bureau of National Affairs, Inc., Washington, D.C.

nocent until proven guilty. Second, an employee is more likely to improve his or her behavior if presented with facts about poor performance. Conflicting, disputable data will not motivate an employee to change. Third, if

the unionized employee files a grievance indicating that discipline was unjustly administered and the grievance then reaches arbitration, the arbitrator will look very closely at the data management has collected. If performance data are questionable or carelessly or sloppily recorded, the award will most likely go to the employee. The employer is required to document that there is just cause for suspending or discharging an employee.

Administer Progressive Discipline   Most companies follow a procedure of progressive discipline. Two important characteristics of progressive discipline are (1) a penalty commensurate with the offense and (2) a series of increasingly serious penalties for continued unsatisfactory performance. For nonunion firms, progressive discipline is often discussed in the employee handbook; unionized firms normally include a procedure for progressive discipline in the labor–management agreement. The progressive disciplinary procedure for various kinds of unsatisfactory performance is shown in Table 15–2. A progressive disciplinary procedure included in a labor–management contract is shown in Figure 15–3.

Administer Corrective Counseling   The final step in the process of positive discipline is corrective counseling. The purpose of positive discipline is to solve an employee's problems rather than simply to administer penalties and punishment. For corrective counseling to be effective, a supervisor must be genuinely interested in helping an employee overcome problems and must offer support, encouragement, and assistance. Each counseling session will differ somewhat, but there are a number of steps common to every corrective-counseling interview.[8] Figure 15–4 lists the steps and gives examples of how a supervisor might handle an employee being disciplined about excessive absenteeism.

One important way that corrective counseling differs from traditional techniques is that a supervisor avoids telling employees how to solve problems. Supervisors tend to tell employees the "right thing to do." With corrective counseling, however, a supervisor

helps employees find solutions. Thus, employees are responsible for determining the most effective way to overcome the problem. With greater problem-solving participation by the employee, the chances for a long-lasting improvement in behavior are greatly increased.[9]

Successful Process   General Electric implemented positive discipline in one of its plants with the goal of creating an adult-to-adult problem-solving method that focused on supervisory coaching and individual responsibility. The program included supervisory training, discussions with employees to recognize good performance, and nondisciplinary counseling sessions to bring attention to a problem situation and prevent the need to administer formal discipline. Company representatives claim that the program resulted in improved employee morale, greater supervisory confidence, consistency in the administration of discipline, and fewer disciplinary sessions and terminations. For example, 3,565 informal counseling sessions were held by supervisors to discuss performance-improvement needs during the first year of the program. The success of the counseling sessions was indicated by the need to administer the first level of formal discipline in only 90 cases—a success rate of 97.5 percent. The success rate rose to over 98 percent during the second year of the program.[10]

Supervisory Resistance to Discipline

Many managers and supervisors find disciplining an employee difficult and painful. Some supervisors will even put off discipline, preferring to trade short-range relief for future performance problems.

Discipline is often a dreaded task for a number of reasons. First, supervisors may find it distasteful to discipline an employee who is also a friend. Over the years, many supervisors build strong personal relationships with

Unless otherwise noted, any proven infractions of the following rules will initiate one of the following disciplinary actions, on an impartial and fair basis. The level of discipline varies with the severity of the rule infraction.

☐ Foreman will give verbal warning to employee, and written account to employee for record.
☐ Oral reprimand form for file.
☐ Written reprimand form for file, union, company, employee, union hall.
☐ Three days suspension without pay.
☐ Discharge.

General Plant Rules—Employees shall not:

☐ Bring intoxicants or narcotics into, or consume intoxicants or narcotics in the plant or on the plant premises, excluding prescribed medicine.
☐ Report for duty under the influence of liquor or narcotics.
☐ Smoke in prohibited areas.
☐ Deliberately or through continued carelessness destroy, deface, or wrongfully remove the company's or another employee's property.
☐ Alter time punched in or out on time card.
☐ Intentionally punch another employee's time card.
☐ Be guilty of unsanitary practices.
☐ Be guilty of carelessness or recklessness, horseplay, or other disregard for the safety and comfort of fellow workers.
☐ Roam about the plant, interfere with, or keep others from the performance of their duties.
☐ Initiate an act of physical violence in the plant or on the plant premises, or directly threaten a supervisor, any salaried personnel, or any union employee with physical violence.
☐ Participate in any gambling or other game of chance on company premises at any time.
☐ Bring firearms or other lethal weapons into the plant or on company premises at any time without permission.
☐ Refuse to obey the work orders of or refuse to perform work assigned by their supervisor.
☐ Fail to wear safety glasses or other designated safety protection (clip-ons, goggles, coverall goggles, face shields, etc.).
☐ Receive more than two (2) sustained garnishments on separate indebtedness during a contract year.
☐ Knowingly provide false information with regard to production, product control, equipment, equipment control, process, process control, doctors' excuses, or any phase of the company's operations.
☐ Leave the company premises without permission, for any reason, without clocking "in" and "out."

FIGURE 15–3

A union–management procedure for progressive discipline (Source: Agreement between Multi-Metals and the International Association of Machinists and Aerospace Workers, AFL-CIO, 1977–1980, pp. 61–63. Used with permission.)

Get the Facts before Counseling

☐ Make sure you understand the attendance policy.

☐ Closely review the employee's attendance behavior.

☐ Have a copy of absenteeism policies at hand, the employee's attendance record, and any other forms or documents that may be necessary.

Discuss in Private

☐ Get away from the work area.

☐ Keep phone calls and interruptions at a minimum.

☐ Hold the discussion as soon as possible but at a time convenient to both of you.

Put the Employee at Ease, but Get to the Point

☐ Offer the employee a comfortable seat.

☐ Keep cool. Don't show anger or resentment.

Describe the Problem, Using Facts

☐ Emphasize the act, not the employee.

☐ State the problems caused by employee absence.

"Good attendance is really important for us to do a good job and produce a quality product. When people don't come to work, all kinds of problems can occur."

☐ Be specific—talk numbers and dates.

"About two weeks ago, we couldn't start the line in binding on the night shift because of absenteeism. It took us over an hour to get people shifted around and get the line going. A lot of employees really got upset because of all the moving around."

"When I have to replace you, that employee just can't do the job as well as you can. Sometimes I have to spend a half hour or so making sure the replacement employee can do the job, and usually I have to check back every couple hours or so to make sure everything is going OK. I don't have to do that with you."

"When everybody comes in, it makes my job and everybody else's so much easier."

"Our absenteeism policies contain progressive disciplinary actions that relate to the number of absences an employee accumulates. The first step of the system requires that I discuss attendance with an employee who accumulates three occurrences within a twelve-month period."

☐ Go over attendance form(s) with the employee.

"Mary, you were absent on Friday, May 25; Monday, July 29; and Wednesday, August 22. Therefore, I must apply the first disciplinary step."

FIGURE 15–4

Steps in a corrective-counseling interview, using an example concerning excessive absenteeism

□ State the consequences of continued unsatisfactory performance.

"If an employee accumulates five occurrences within a twelve-month period, he or she is placed on written probation—step 2. Seven and nine occurrences within a consecutive twelve-month period will result in suspension and discharge, respectively."

Get Agreement on the Problem

□ Make sure the employee understands policies and disciplinary system.

□ Make sure the employee agrees with the facts (even though he or she may not like the facts).

"Do you have any questions concerning the new policies and disciplinary system?"

"Do my records agree with attendance records that you may be keeping?" (If employees do not keep their own attendance records, suggest that they do.)

Involve the Employee in Problem Solving

□ Get ready to listen.

□ Get the employee to talk about the problem—particularly work problems.

"What can we do to avoid another absence occurrence?"

"Is there any aspect of your work situation that relates to your absenteeism?"

"What can you do to make sure you are at work on time?"

□ Avoid offering suggestions unless absolutely necessary.

□ Discuss the problem until you feel the employee reaches a satisfactory solution.

Have Employee Sum Up Problem and Solution

"OK, Marvin, now I would like for you to sum up the problem and tell me how you're going to make sure we don't have to go to the next disciplinary step."

State Goal, End in Positive Note

"Mary, as you know, a calendar month of perfect attendance will remove one occurrence. Will you shoot for this?"

"Barry, when you're here, you do a great job. You get along with the other employees, and we value and appreciate your efforts here. But as I mentioned earlier, good attendance is critical, and we need you here every workday. And please keep in mind I'm here to do whatever I can to make your job as satisfying as possible and one which you want to come to every day. If there's a work problem, let's talk about it.

"OK, Pat, unless you have any questions, I'll let you get back to the press."

FIGURE 15–4
continued

their employees. They may find disciplining employees they share lunch with or socialize with extremely stressful and uncomfortable. The supervisor may not want to jeopardize this relationship because of a disciplinary action. Second, some supervisors feel that the application of discipline forces them to "play God." They are uncomfortable in the role of judge and jury, and they think that the complexities of organizational life make it difficult, if not impossible, to define precisely what is right and what is wrong. Third, a supervisor who lacks the ability to discipline may rationalize, "If I try to discipline the employee, I'll probably make matters worse. So I'll just sidestep the issue."

The potential for supervisory resistance to discipline underscores the need to ensure that all supervisors are trained in the purpose, techniques, and application of discipline. Specifically, training should focus upon:

- The objectives of discipline and why proper discipline is important.
- Various kinds of discipline, with emphasis on the preventive and positive approaches.
- The need to conduct discipline fairly and impartially.
- Corrective counseling methods.

Role play is particularly valuable in training supervisors in discipline and counseling. Role play enables supervisors to practice effective techniques and receive feedback from the instructor and other participants in the training. Videotaping of role plays allows trainees to observe and critique their own performance.

The Hot-Stove Rule

One effective way to approach the disciplinary process is to follow what is popularly known as the hot-stove rule, which suggests that ap-

plying discipline is much like touching a hot stove:[11]

- The burn is *immediate;* the cause is clear-cut.
- The person had a *warning;* knowing that the stove was hot, the person should have known what would happen if it was touched.
- The burn is *consistent;* all who touch the stove are burned every time it is touched.
- The burn is *impersonal;* the stove will burn anyone, regardless of who he or she is.

Like touching a hot stove, the application of discipline should also be immediate, with warning, consistent, and impersonal. These guidelines are consistent with the positive approach to discipline. Supervisors who follow these guidelines should experience less tension and anxiety when applying discipline and should learn to view discipline as a supervisory responsibility rather than as a personal dilemma.

Immediate Discipline Some supervisors find it easy to procrastinate about discipline: "I'm busy today. I'll get to it tomorrow." But putting off discipline until a later date often reduces the impact. The greater the time between the offense and the application of discipline, the less likely it is that the employee will see a direct cause-and-effect relationship between the unsatisfactory performance and the discipline.

Discipline should be administered as soon as it has been determined that unsatisfactory behavior has taken place. Of course, the supervisor must fully investigate any issue that is not clear-cut. For example, a supervisor may issue an oral warning to an employee for a slowdown of production. A complete investigation of the problem, however, may have shown that a machine malfunction was, in fact, responsible for substandard output. In unionized firms, misapplication of discipline may result in the filing of a formal employee grievance. At best, relations between the supervisor and the employee will be cooled. Gathering the facts as soon as possible—and before disciplining—is a good rule of thumb.

Warn Employees An employee who receives unexpected discipline will more than likely raise cries of unfairness and favoritism. Discipline is more likely to be accepted without resentment if the employee has prior knowledge that certain behavior will result in disciplinary action. Thus, the personnel staff and supervisory team are responsible for ensuring that all employees realize that unsatisfactory behavior will result in discipline.

Even though a disciplinary system is detailed in an employee handbook or labor-management contract, good face-to-face communication between the supervisor and the work group is necessary if all employees are to understand the system and how it works. Too frequently, written communications such as an employee handbook are so quickly glossed over that the message may not be fully understood. Through the spoken word, management can make sure that employees know what is expected of them and are aware of the consequences of unsatisfactory behavior.

Consistent Discipline Employees want to be treated fairly and impartially. Feelings of unfairness may result in low morale, absenteeism, turnover, and grievances.[12] To minimize these problems, management must administer discipline consistently, without bias or favoritism. Consistent discipline means that:

- Every employee who requires discipline receives it.
- Employees who commit the same offense receive the same discipline.

- Discipline is administered in the same way to all employees. That is, the application of positive discipline to one employee and negative discipline to another is avoided.

Consistent application of discipline is not an easy task because personality issues often interfere. Supervisors are human, and thus they may occasionally overlook the unsatisfactory behavior of likable employees and come down hard on those they dislike. Consistency may also require that discipline be administered at an inconvenient time. Assume, for example, that a supervisor who leads a large assembly line with sixty employees has four employees requiring immediate discipline. The supervisor may reason, "I'll discipline José and Harry this afternoon but I can't get to Greta and Frank until next week. If I spend all afternoon in disciplinary sessions, we won't meet our production quota this week." Such inconsistency will generate more problems than it avoids. A consistent, uniform disciplinary system may be difficult to achieve at times, but it will help the supervisor avoid personnel problems and earn the respect and confidence of the entire work group.

Impersonal Discipline One significant drawback of punitive discipline is that an employee often takes personally the harsh, condescending methods that this technique involves. A supervisor barks at an employee, "This is your third warning, Blanche. If you show up for work stinking like a distillery one more time, it's pink-slip city. This isn't skid row, you know." With this approach, even though she may be guilty of the offense, Blanche is likely to suffer great personal indignity and to harbor resentment and anger. Perhaps worse, the punitive approach does not find ways to overcome the employee's problems.

Are English-Only Rules Enforceable?

Can an employer require employees to speak only English for business reasons? In a historic 1987 case the U.S. Ninth Circuit Court approved an employer's discharge of an employee who refused to comply with the English-only rule. The employee, a California radio announcer of Mexican-American descent, ignored repeated warnings of the management at radio station KIIS. The court in its decision stated, "An employer can properly enforce a limited, reasonable and business related English-only rule against an employee."

Source: *Jurado* v. *Eleven-Fifty Corporation*, et al., No. 86-5606 (April 1987), U.S. Ninth Circuit.

When discipline is applied impersonally, the supervisor focuses on the act of unsatisfactory behavior, not the employee as a bad person. The most effective way to achieve this goal is to employ corrective counseling. Using this method, the supervisor places less stress on why unsatisfactory performance took place than on how the problem can be solved. With tact and maturity, the supervisor applies discipline in a supportive environment, emphasizing the improvement of performance rather than the infliction of punishment.

An important part of corrective discipline is salvaging the unsatisfactory employee.[13] The primary emphasis is on solving the problem rather than getting rid of the employee. Consistent with good personnel management, this approach documents an organization's social responsibility to its human resource group. Nonetheless, administrators will occasionally find necessary the ultimate disciplinary action—discharge.

DISCIPLINARY DISCHARGE

A great deal of colorful jargon describes the act of discharge. Employees talk about getting canned, sacked, booted, axed, pink slipped, and so on. Perhaps the most common lament of the discharged employee is "I got fired."

An employee may be *laid off* because a company has severe financial problems or a plant closes. A *disciplinary discharge* occurs, however, when an employee has committed a serious offense, has repeatedly violated rules and regulations, or has shown a consistent inability to meet performance expectations. For example, in many disciplinary systems, the first offense of intoxication at work, insubordination, theft, willful damage to company property, or falsifying work records will result in discharge.

A discharge has consequences for both the employee and the employer. Loss of income is usually the most serious setback, because an employee discharged for disciplinary reasons generally cannot collect company-provided supplemental benefits or state unemployment insurance. For many employees, dismissal is a personal crisis that can possibly lead to serious family problems, alcoholism, or emotional trauma. To the upper-level executive, dismissal is a particularly tragic event, and some companies attempt to ease the financial and emotional trauma of dismissal through outplacement assistance programs. Discharge is also costly to the company because of the loss of the investment in orientation, training, and development, not to mention the costs involved in hiring and training a replacement employee.

Discharge is a relatively infrequent personnel action. Most employees leave an employer voluntarily. The majority of employees perform their jobs satisfactorily; only a small percentage may be labeled unsatisfactory performers. Effective administration of corrective discipline successfully prevents many employees from continually performing at unsatisfactory levels. Other factors also keep the disciplinary discharges at a relatively low level. Powerful unions are often instrumental in pressuring the employer not to lay off a problem employee; in government organizations, a strong civil-service program may also hold down discharges. Public officials sometimes say, "It's impossible to fire an incompetent employee. There's nothing I can do." Although a public manager, according to personnel rules and regulations, can dismiss an unsatisfactory employee, the paperwork and the case that must be built on an unproductive employee—in addition to the large number of hearings required—often make discharge extremely difficult and time-consuming. Succumbing to the administrative burdens of discharge, a government official may say, "It's easier to live with the problem employee than to get the employee discharged."

Any discharge should be carried out fairly and legally. At worst, a botched discharge can lead to a highly publicized, costly lawsuit and significant damage to the firm's reputation. At best, the disgruntled employee will probably bring disrepute to the company whenever the opportunity arises. A great deal has been written about the consequences of poor discharge procedures and what organizations should do to ensure that their discharges are carried out properly.

Don't Let a Firing Backfire

What can be done to protect yourself against lengthy internal grievance procedures and potentially costly lawsuits? Your risk can be reduced by paying close attention to ten items:[14]

1. Prior to hiring, review all documents—application blanks, personnel handbooks and manuals, and so on—to be sure that they say what you want them to say. For example, many companies have deleted statements from their personnel handbooks that suggest that employees cannot be fired as long as they are performing satisfactorily.

2. Don't make promises (about job security, etc.) that you cannot or do not intend to keep.

3. Make sure that new employees receive written work rules and realize that violations can lead to discipline and discharge.

4. When disciplining, deal with the worst offenders first.

5. Use progressive disciplinary procedures. This gives employees the opportunity to reverse the unsatisfactory behavior.

6. When a dispute arises, get the employee's side of the story with witnesses present. Before acting, check out the employee's reasons for his or her behavior.

7. Apply discipline consistently; make sure that similar infractions receive similar discipline.

8. Apply discipline fairly. Consider the extent to which the background of the employee—seniority, productivity, attitude—should influence the discipline.

9. Consider buying out a potential problem discharge with additional severance pay. Additional compensation can be exchanged for a release from any discharge-related claim.

10. Don't become an obstacle to the discharged employee's future employment. Bad references may lead to a costly law-

suit, and good references will be seen as an admission that the discharge was without cause.

Discharging the Manager or Professional

Thus far, the discharge process has been described as the final step in a procedure of progressive discipline that spells out what kinds and how many occasions of unsatisfactory performance must occur before an employee will be discharged. But such is not the case with managerial or professional employees. First, the upper-level employee is generally not a union employee subject to the work conditions, requirements, and protection that are included in the labor–management contract. Second, a detailed written procedure of progressive discipline is rarely administered for managers and administrators. In fact, formal disciplinary systems refer almost exclusively to the operative and clerical levels. This is not to suggest, however, that upper-level employees are immune to discharge. Few companies will guarantee any employee a life-long job; in some firms, job security is greater for the production workers than for the middle or top manager. Many managers testify, "In my company, it's up or out. There's no deadwood here. But there are an awful lot of ulcers and short fingernails. And it's a smart practice to keep your resumé current."

Because the executive's or administrator's job is often difficult to evaluate, determining if and when an upper-level employee should be discharged is difficult. Many poor managers are able to "muddle along" because their jobs and expectations have been poorly defined. Ill-defined jobs and performance standards also enable politics to affect significantly the promotion or discharge of an employee. This situation may be rectified with a management-by-objectives (MBO) approach to work planning, evaluation, and control. With writ-

ten, measurable objectives, there is less ambiguity about managerial performance. Many MBO programs have resulted not only in greater sales and profits but also in more effective personnel decisions about which employees to reward, promote, or discharge.

After deciding to remove a manager or administrator from the job, many superiors seek alternatives to firing. Some may "kick the employee upstairs" in a move that appears to be a promotion, complete with a prestigious title and greater salary. Other employees are strongly advised to take early retirement. Others are demoted to less responsible jobs. The final alternative to firing is to *dehire* the employee. A dehired employee is encouraged to quit before being fired. For example, at the end of a performance-appraisal session, the employee may be told: "The job isn't right for you. . . . Have you considered other employment? I think it would be in your best interests to find employment more suited to your particular skills and abilities. . . . I like you personally, Fred, but the job isn't working out. You might want to use some of your lunch hours to check into other job opportunities around town."

Why dehire rather than fire an employee? Perhaps the primary advantage of dehiring is that the employee saves face by leaving the company before being fired. Avoiding the disgrace and embarrassment of being discharged, the employee does not have to explain a firing to family members, friends, or prospective employers. The superior may even allow the dehired employee to seek other employment on company time.

The employer also benefits from the dehiring process. From a public-relations point of view, dehiring indicates that the company has a moral obligation to its employees and that it has a heart. Also, most executives would much rather dehire a subordinate than face the stress and anguish that often accompany the act of firing.

Administering the Discharge Decision

Companies approach the problem of unsatisfactory performance in different ways. Many firms do everything they possibly can to avoid firing employees. Other employers have few or no qualms or regrets about firing employees who have toiled for many years with the company or who are middle or top managers. Some administrators think that the best interests of the company and the employee necessitate a direct approach in discharging an employee who has a minimal or nonexistent chance to perform satisfactorily.

The discharge decision should be taken seriously and carried out in a professional manner. There are few real instances when an employee reporting to work has found the office door locked, the lock replaced, and personal belongings piled in the hallway, but on many occasions firings are badly bungled. Managers and professionals receive terse notes from their superiors, stating without any explanation whatsoever that "your services are no longer required as of two weeks from this date." Other employees have been fired after being treated to drinks and lunch at the finest restaurant in town—presumably to soften them up for the blow.

Carrying out the discharge decision should involve tact, maturity, and careful planning. The discharge should be administered so that ill feelings between the employee and the company are minimized. As with the administration of any step in a disciplinary procedure, the discharge should be conducted unemotionally and without vindictiveness, revenge, or malice.[15]

Employee Rights in Discharge Decisions

Employees are afforded a considerable amount of protection from unjust, arbitrary discipline and discharge decisions. Primarily, this protection is derived from federal legislation and court decisions that safeguard employees' rights, including the right to due process. Federal legislation enacted to protect employees from unfair discipline and termination decisions includes:[16]

Civil Rights Act of 1964, Title VII Title VII makes it unlawful to discriminate against an employee with respect to any term or condition of employment, including discharge, because of race, color, religion, sex or national origin. Further, an employee may not be disciplined or discharged for making a charge, testifying, or participating in an investigation or hearing under Title VII.

Wagner Act The Wagner Act provides two broad areas of protection for union employees in regard to discharges. First, the act prohibits the discipline or discharge of an employee who takes part in lawful organizing activities (such as holding prolabor views or attending organizing drive meetings). Second, labor–management contracts generally stipulate that a union employee can only be discharged for just cause. Many labor contracts spell out in great detail the types of unsatisfactory performance that will lead to discipline or discharge (e.g., striking a supervisor or fellow employee or theft). A union employee who feels that he or she was unjustly disciplined or discharged may, with the support of the union, file a grievance and force a formal hearing regarding the issue.

Age Discrimination in Employment Act (ADEA) The ADEA forbids the discipline and discharge of employees because of their age. The 1986 amendment to the act makes it illegal to require retirement at any age and prohibits employers from using age as even one (of possibly several) factor in making discharge decisions. The act covers employees over age forty.

Any personnel action covered by ADEA— termination, demotion, transfer or suspension—may be questioned as to whether age was a factor in the decision. Clearly, employers must develop objective, job-related performance appraisal systems to support any actions taken against employees of age forty or older.[17]

Occupational Safety and Health Act of 1970 The act prohibits discipline or discharge in relation to two issues. First, it is unlawful to discipline or discharge an employee who contacts OSHA regarding an alleged violation of OSHA regulations. Second, the act protects workers who refuse to work in areas they consider unsafe and hazardous.

Termination at Will

Historically, employers have enjoyed the legal right to discharge an employee for any reason, barring a specific statutory restriction (e.g., Civil Rights Act, ADEA), contractual agreement, or just-cause protection afforded the union employee. Over 100 years ago, a Tennessee court held that an employee could be fired for "good reason, bad reason, or no reason at all," thus giving rise to the doctrine known as termination at will.

In recent years, however, this doctrine has been eroding at an accelerated pace, primarily because of the actions of several state courts.[18] Generally, the courts have decided that a discharge is wrongful when (1) the discharge is contrary to public policy, (2) the discharge lacks good faith and fair dealing, or (3) the discharge violates an implied contract. These recent court decisions have led to a weakening of the termination-at-will doctrine:

- International Business Machines (IBM) was ordered to pay $300,000 to a sales manager who was dismissed for dating a former IBM salesman who had gone to work for a competing firm.

- Courts in Indiana and Kentucky have determined that it is against public policy to fire an employee for filing a workmen's compensation claim.
- A California court decided that an employer's discharge of an employee for refusing to comply with his employer's order to commit perjury before a state legislative committee was wrongful and contrary to public policy.
- Courts in several jurisdictions have ruled in favor of employees who were discharged for disclosing an employer's violations of state or federal laws. In these cases, public policy was said to have been violated by the employers.
- The supreme court of Michigan, in a case involving an employee of Blue Cross–Blue Shield of Michigan, held that the employer's personnel-manual clause stating that employees would be discharged only for "cause" created an *implied contractual agreement* between the employer and the employee.

Court rulings concerning termination at will have forced employers to scrutinize their personnel practices and eliminate those that may result in potentially costly court battles with disgruntled employees. For many employers, the result has led to significant changes in the way employees are hired, evaluated, disciplined and discharged. Some of the personnel practices that have been affected include:

Recruiting Employers are advised to avoid any suggestion that the job applicant will have a job for life. Terms such as *permanent employee* are being purged from job information, help-wanted advertisements, and employee handbooks.

Interviewing Company representatives have become very cautious about promises made during employment interviews and much more specific about job duties and responsibilities.

"At-will" Statements Employers may require applicants to sign at-will statements on the application blank. These statements generally read: "In consideration of my employment, I agree to conform to the rules and regulations of the company, and my employment and compensation can be terminated, with or without cause, at any time, and with or without notice at the option of either the company or myself." While employers who require such statements may believe that they are a necessary and effective means of limiting their legal liability, some authorities disagree. They believe that signed at-will statements are simply an overreaction to legal concerns. Their legal defense value certainly is questionable, since applicants are forced to sign them or lose a job opportunity. An equally effective method would be to include an at-will statement in an employee manual or personnel policy. Perhaps most important, employees would be less resentful than they would if required to sign an at-will statement.[19]

Performance Appraisal The concepts of fairness and validity are becoming critical in regard to the issue of performance evaluations. Supervisors and managers are strongly encouraged to give fair and honest appraisals and to use a progressive disciplinary procedure when unsatisfactory performance results.

Discharges Prior to dismissing an employee, employers are ensuring that he or she has been warned and notified and that detailed written documentation is included in the employee's personnel file.

Grievance Procedure Historically, union employees have been able to voice grievances with management through a formal grievance procedure. Increasingly, however, organizations are creating and implementing formal internal grievance procedures for nonunion employees so that their complaints may be heard efficiently and fairly. One of the goals of the formal grievance procedure—for both union and nonunion employees—is to solve employee problems before termination is considered.

Office Romances

An office romance is a relationship that occurs between a man and woman working together and that is known to others in the work place. At present, few employers have adopted discipline policies regarding office romances. Many managers simply choose to ignore the situation. Policies that have been adopted include a continuum of responses: (1) management counseling of employees with regard to possible problems that may arise if the relationship continues or ends, (2) oral reprimands and an order to cease, (3) written warnings, and (4) transfer and termination.

Management usually enacts the above responses only when the relationship is not only known to other employees but impairs the performance of the individuals involved or of their work group. If no negative impact occurs, usually no action is necessary. The last step in the policy continuum, termination, is seldom taken. It is usually considered too high a price to pay by the individual and the organization. Instead, the transfer of one individual, particularly one in a supervisory capacity, is usually the action taken. The key criterion for management's choice of action in these cases should be the individual's work record and the degree of negative impact on productivity.[20] Once problems arise, however, management must neither ignore them nor overreact, but should follow the stated policy. If no specific policy exists (again, usually the case), routine disciplinary procedures should be followed.

INTERNATIONAL HRM: STRONG EMPLOYMENT RIGHTS

In many foreign countries, the courts have established over a long period the rights of individual employees to be protected from wrongful or unfair dismissal. Huge termination indemnities are required, not only for situations where an individual discharge is disputed, but even where the terminations are based on economic considerations. Indeed, many multinational companies have been unpleasantly surprised to find out just how expensive it is to shut down an operation in Europe.[21]

Foreign workers are protected by strong labor laws and union rules, and the employer who is unaware of them will risk costly lawsuits and penalties. Ignorance of the law is no excuse. A Mexican labor law, for example, gives workers complete protection. After a thirty-day trial period, they are regarded as virtually permanent employees.

In Indonesia employees can't be fired without a long process involving government red tape. An employer must give three written warnings over a year, specifying the bad work, with written copies distributed to certain officials. A manager must meet with the employee to suggest changes in performance, and must do it diplomatically. One old hand advises, "Offer him a transfer somewhere else in the company, and over three years you can move him from job to job until he can be eased down to the kitchen and out the back door."

In the Soviet Union, workers are guaranteed jobs—the government boasts that there is no unemployment—and only serious infractions justify dismissal. Employers in Russia must hire Soviets through the UPDK (Agency to Provide Assistance to the Diplomatic Corps), the agency that supplies all personnel. One can fire an employee, but the UPDK is not likely to make a replacement for a long time.

Even where laws do not tie the employee to the employer, firing is not without consequences. In Taiwan and other paternalistic cultures, dismissal is considered a mark against the superior, who has failed to shift unsatisfactory workers to "uncles" in other departments.[22]

CONCLUSIONS AND APPLICATIONS

- Many reasons may cause an employee to perform unsatisfactorily. Some of these reasons may be directly attributable to management's shortcomings or to some other problem of the organization. When attempting to determine the cause of poor employee performance, managers should recognize that the employee may not be responsible for the unsatisfactory behavior.

- Discipline should be applied only when it has been determined that the employee is the cause of the unsatisfactory performance. There are different approaches to the disciplinary process; the most effective technique involves administration of *preventive* discipline. If discipline must be administered, the *positive* approach should be used.

- Positive discipline is administered with maturity and respect and without threats or abuse. The focus of positive discipline is on solving the employee's problem rather than simply handing out punishment.

- Corrective counseling is a particularly important part of the positive–discipline process. It helps build respect and trust between the supervisor and subordinate and encourages the employee to find his or her own solutions to problems. The more the employee participates in the problem-solving process, the greater the chances for a permanent improvement in employee behavior.

- Much of the supervisory resistance to change can be reduced by training supervisors to follow the so-called hot-stove rule. With this technique, discipline is administered immediately, with warning, consistently, and impersonally. Personnel managers must ensure that supervisory training programs provide instruction in applying each of the hot-stove rules.

- Discharge can be traumatic and costly for both the dismissed employee and the organization. The discharge should be thoroughly planned and carried out in a professional manner. It is particularly important that the employee be given complete details regarding the discharge, including why it is taking place and how the discharge is to be carried out.

- The doctrine of termination at will has eroded considerably in recent years because court decisions have supported employee claims of unfair and unjust treatment. Personnel rules, policies, and procedures must be closely examined to ensure that they comply with federal laws.

- International managers struggle with the problem of finding good personnel, but a tougher problem is getting rid of employees who don't work out. From Switzerland to Mexico to Indonesia, the unsentimental American "hire and fire" habit seems unnaturally brutal to foreign employees. Foreign personnel are usually more firmly attached to their company and are used to being protected during their working lives. Firing is never abrupt or taken lightly.

CASE STUDY
Midwestern Chemicals

Bruce Helm slid from his seat in the forklift and sat on the edge of the loading dock. It was 10 o'clock in the morning—break time. He lit a cigarette, took a long pull, and blew about a half dozen smoke rings that quickly disappeared in the cool morning breeze. This was only his second day at Midwestern Chemicals—a small manufacturer of cleaning chemicals and solvents. The warehouse job seemed okay so far, Helm thought. The pay was not bad and benefits were pretty good. And he liked the fellow workers he had met so far.

All of a sudden, Helm's supervisor, John Huber, came running out of nowhere, shouting:

"Put that cigarette out! Put it out, you damn fool! Are you crazy? You want to blow us all to smithereens?" Huber grabbed the cigarette from Helm's hand and stomped it with his steel-tipped, thick-soled safety shoes.

Helm was startled. Silence befell nearby workers who had been enjoying their break.

"What's the problem?" Helm seriously asked. Huber replied, "This is a no-smoking area. Look around you. There are fifty-gallon drums of inflammable solvents practically within an arm's length of you. And you're puffing on a cigarette. How dumb can you get?"

Apologetically, Helm explained, "But I didn't know this was a no-smoking area. Nobody told me. You didn't mention it yesterday when you showed me around the warehouse. Besides, I still don't see any no-smoking signs."

Huber responded: "Well, the no-smoking sign is covered up by the stack of drums over there. But it should be obvious to everyone that you shouldn't smoke around these chemicals. Anyway, you've been warned. Any more problems and we'll have to let you go." Huber turned and strolled back to his office.

Helm cursed under his breath and went for a walk around the plant. He tried to get the incident out of his mind.

About a week later, Helm and three fellow employees were walking to their cars after work. Helm walked up to his van and said to his friends, "Come over here. I want to show you guys something." Opening the back of his van, Helm proudly displayed his new 12-gauge automatic shotgun. He said, "Those quail are in real serious trouble when the season opens next weekend. How do you like this beauty?" As Helm's pals were admiring the new shotgun, Huber drove by, saw the shotgun, and brought his pickup to a screeching halt. Huber jumped out and howled, "Possessing firearms on company property is cause for immediate dismissal, Helm. It's in the union contract plain as day. You're fired. You other guys are witnesses." Huber jumped back in his pickup and sped away.

Questions

1. Was the discharge justified? Why or why not?
2. What should have been done differently?
3. What employee actions warrant immediate discharge?

EXPERIENTIAL EXERCISE
Counseling the Troubled Employee

Purpose

To show the importance of using correct counseling techniques with troubled employees.

Introduction

Disciplining and counseling the troubled employee—the employee who suffers from a personal problem such as alcoholism to the extent that he or she is unable to perform effectively—presents a special challenge to supervisors.

For example, it's not appropriate for the supervisor to discuss drinking or a suspicion of drinking because diagnosis is the job of trained professionals. What is the job of the supervisor?

The supervisor's job is to focus on *job performance* during counseling. The supervisor should confront the employee with specific performance problems in an attempt to motivate the employee to seek treatment and rehabilitation. The supervisor will only aggravate the problem by accusing the employee of having a personal problem such as alcoholism, drug abuse, or emotional instability. In addition, it is the supervisor's job to make it clear to the employee what will happen if the unsatisfactory performance continues. Usually, that means discipline, including the possibility of discharge.

The theory behind this method is simple: if the employee's job is on the line, he or she will likely seek treatment rather than face being fired.

The Task

Listed below are several statements that a supervisor made to an employee suspected of excessive drinking. These are actual statements that have been collected anonymously from employees through surveys. Your job is to evaluate the supervisor's statements and, if necessary, to write what the supervisor should have said. After you have completed the exercise, your instructor will lead a discussion on discipline and the troubled employee.

Effective counseling depends very much on saying the right thing to the employee who is suspected of being troubled. Saying the wrong thing will do little to motivate the employee to overcome the problem and could well make matters worse.

Kim, the supervisor of a large group of computer personnel, suspects that Skip, a computer operator, is suffering from alcoholism. At one time, Skip was an excellent employee, but he has recently begun to perform erratically and demonstrates behavioral problems. For example, Skip has made many errors in operating the computer and has experienced several interpersonal problems with Kim and other co-workers. Kim has just begun to talk to Skip in her office. All of Kim's statements are poor and represent the use of improper counseling techniques. Your job is to decide what Kim should have said.

What Kim said:	**What Kim should have said:**
1. "Skip, I've really been troubled by your performance lately. You've made a lot of computer errors and you haven't gotten along well with the other employees."	_____ _____ _____
2. "Skip, I strongly suspect that problems stem from excessive drinking. It's no secret that you've had drinking problems for some time."	_____ _____ _____
3. "If your performance does not improve, you'll be digging your own grave."	_____ _____ _____

What Kim said:	**What Kim should have said:**

4. (With a heated voice) "Don't disagree with me, Skip, I can back up everything I say. Like it or not, these are the facts."

5. "I have decided that the best thing for you to do is attend AA meetings once a week until your problem clears up."

6. "The company has special programs available for alcoholic employees."

7. "I heard you were drinking in the men's room this morning. Is that true?"

8. "Look, don't disagree with me. You've got a drinking problem and you know it. All the facts point to it."

9. "You have a real attendance problem and I think I know why. You're on some kind of drug, aren't you? Aren't those needle marks on your arms?"

10. "I know what your problem is, but don't worry, we're not going to fire you if you attend the special program the personnel department has for alcoholics."

Source: Adapted from F. Kuzmits, R. Herden, and L. Sussman, *Managing the Unsatisfactory Employee* (Homewood, IL: Dow Jones-Irwin, 1984), pp. 82–83.

KEY TERMS AND CONCEPTS

Corrective counseling

Foreign employment rights

Hot-stove rule

Model for analyzing unsatisfactory performance

Positive discipline

Preventive discipline

Progressive discipline

Punitive discipline

Termination at will

REVIEW QUESTIONS

1. What are the four general causes of unsatisfactory employee performance?
2. Compare and contrast punitive, preventive, and positive discipline.
3. What are the steps involved in the process of positive discipline?
4. How may supervisory resistance to discipline be overcome?
5. What are some important considerations to keep in mind when discharging the managerial or professional employee?
6. What laws exist to protect employees from unfair discipline and discharge?
7. What is termination at will, and how can organizations avoid legal problems involving this doctrine?

DISCUSSION QUESTIONS

1. In the past, supervisors often used punitive discipline against their employees. What reasons might account for this?
2. With corrective counseling, the supervisor encourages the employee to find solutions to his or her problems. Why might this method be more effective than having the supervisor tell employees how to solve their problems?
3. Why do many supervisors resist applying discipline to an employee? How can this resistance be reduced?
4. Assume that you were recently appointed to the job of personnel director for a small bank. How would you communicate the company's rules and regulations to employees?
5. If an employee shows up at work intoxicated, what action should the supervisor take? Should the supervisor counsel the employee about the evils of drinking? (Review the material on the alcoholic employee in chapter 12.)
6. In what ways does the discharge of a lower-level operative employee differ from the discharge of a manager or professional? Do you feel that these differences reflect an unfair and unjust dismissal system?

ENDNOTES

1. Abstracted from F. Kuzmits, R. Herden, and L. Sussman, *Managing the Unsatisfactory Employee* (Homewood, IL: Dow Jones-Irwin, 1984). For a description of other modes of unsatisfactory performance, see D. Laird, *Approaches to Training and Development* (Reading, MA: Addison-Wesley, 1978); R. Mager and P. Pipe, *Analyzing Performance Problems* (Belmont, CA: Pitman Learning, 1970); and L. Steinmetz, *Managing the Marginal and Unsatisfactory Performer* (Reading, MA: Addison-Wesley, 1969).
2. See D. Cameron, "The When, Why, and How of Discipline," *Personnel Journal* 63 (July 1984): 37–39.
3. I. Asherman, "The Corrective Discipline Process," *Personnel Journal* 61 (July 1982): 528–31.
4. Cameron, "The When, Why, and How of Discipline," p. 38. See also J. Belohlav, *The Art of Disciplining Your Employees: A Manager's Guide* (Englewood Cliffs, NJ: Prentice-Hall, 1985).
5. *Employee Conduct and Discipline* (Washington, DC: Bureau of National Affairs, 1973), p. 4.

6. *Employee Discipline and Discharge* (Washington, DC: Bureau of National Affairs, 1985), p. 4.

7. See I. Asherman and S. Vance, "Documentation: A Tool for Effective Management," *Personnel Journal* 60 (August 1981): 641–43.

8. See H. Le Van, N. Mathys, and D. Drehmer, "A Look at Counseling Practices of Major U.S. Corporations," *Personnel Administrator* 27 (June 1982): 143–46; and P. C. Cairo, "Counseling in Industry: A Selected Review of the Literature," *Personnel Psychology* 36 (1983): 1–18.

9. Steinmetz, *Managing the Marginal and Unsatisfactory Performer,* p. 83.

10. A. Bryant, "Replacing Punitive Discipline with a Positive Approach," *Personnel Administrator* 10 (February 1984): 79–87.

11. The originator of the popular hot-stove role remains a mystery, though many ascribe this simple but meaningful axiom to Douglas McGregor, author of the classic management book, *Human Side of Enterprise.*

12. J. E. Dittrich and M. R. Carrell, "Organizational Equity Perceptions, Employee Job Satisfaction, and Departmental Absence and Turnover Rates," *Organizational Behavior and Human Performance* 24 (1979): 29–40.

13. See Steinmetz, *Managing the Marginal and Unsatisfactory Performer,* chapter 5.

14. P. M. Panken, "How to Keep a Firing from Backfiring," *Nation's Business* (June 1983): 74–75.

15. R. F. Westcott, "How to Fire an Executive," *Business Horizons* (April 1976): 34–36.

16. For a review of employee rights, see the March 1988 issue of *Personnel Administrator* 33, no. 3.

17. Michael R. Carrell and Frank E. Kuzmits, "Amended ADEA's Effects on HR Strategies Remain Dubious," *Personnel Journal* 66, no. 5 (May 1987): 111–20.

18. See K. B. Stickler, "Limitations on an Employer's Right to Discipline and Discharge Employees," *Employer Relations Law Journal* (Summer 1983): 70–80; Panken, "How to Keep a Firing from Backfiring"; M. Leonard, "Challenges to the Termination-at-Will Doctrine," *Personnel Administrator* 28 (February 1983): 49–56; and P. Lansing and R. Pegnetter, "Fair Dismissal Procedures for Non-Union Employees," *American Business Law Journal* (Spring 1982): 75–91.

19. Raymond L. Hilgert, "How At-Will Statements Hurt Employers," *Personnel Journal* 67, no. 2 (February 1988): 75–76.

20. Lisa A. Mainiero, "A Review and Analysis of Power Dynamics in Organizational Romances," *Academy of Management Review* 11, no. 4 (October 1986): 750–62.

21. Daniel W. Kendall, "Rights Across the Waters," *Personnel Administrator* 33, no. 3 (March 1988): 58–61.

22. Lennie Copeland and Lewis Griggs, *Going International* (New York: Random House, 1985), pp. 136–37.

Farmer in the Dell

Part 1

At 10:30 A.M. on Thursday, May 12, Tom Burke, the shift supervisor at the Dell County Water Treatment Plant, received a phone call from Jenny Miller stating that her husband, Tony Miller, would not be able to report for his regular shift at 3 P.M. She told Burke that Miller had hurt his back that morning lifting sacks of hog feed from his pickup and that he did not feel he could perform his regular duties as water treatment operator.

Mrs. Miller stated that her husband thought that he would also miss the next day, but that after resting Thursday, Friday, and over the weekend (his regular two days off), he would be in Monday afternoon for his 3 P.M. shift. Tom asked to speak to Tony, but Mrs. Miller said that he had gone into town to get some medication or to see a doctor, but she didn't know which.

Burke knew that Miller dabbled in farming and raised a few hogs. Burke had been on Miller's shift as a bargaining unit employee before becoming a supervisor, and Burke remembered having to work extra shifts for several years in the spring and fall when Miller was off "with a sore back," "with headaches," or "for personal reasons."

Burke filled the vacancy with another employee who was normally off that day, but it did involve a sixth day's overtime shift to cover Thursday. Looking ahead, it appeared that the same approach would have to be taken to cover Miller's Friday shift with overtime.

At 3 P.M. Burke met with Norb Maier, Miller's immediate supervisor. The two discussed the situation, and Burke told Maier about his own experience when he had worked in the union with Miller. Maier was upset, but he realized that in the past Miller had been given more or less free rein to do his farming every spring and fall. Maier decided to talk the matter over with Alan Jacoby, the plant personnel manager.*

---

*There are four other "farmers" on the jobs throughout the plant, including one shift supervisor who has an excellent attendance record but who takes two weeks' vacation every October. Also, rumor has it that last year one of the supervisors took it upon himself to check on Miller after one of his "illness report-offs" and saw a man on a tractor working Miller's back forty, but he didn't stop to determine if indeed it was Miller. Miller was given a written reprimand at that time, but it had been changed to a verbal warning during the grievance procedure when the supervisor admitted that he could not positively identify the man on the tractor as Miller.

Discussion Questions

1. You are Alan Jacoby. What action will you recommend to Norb Maier?
2. Will you take any action at all, or just continue the practice of the past years?

Part 2

It was decided that on Friday morning Tom Burke would call Miller's home at 8 A.M. to talk to him about his sore back. When Burke did this, Mrs. Miller said Tony was out and was not expected until about noon, and that his back was still sore. She thought he was in town.

Allan Jacoby, the personnel manager, called Miller's supervisor, Norb Maier, and the two of them rode out past Miller's farm, where off in the distance they saw a tractor working in the field. With the use of binoculars they quickly identified the driver as Miller, and they went back to the plant.

Jacoby then made arrangements to cover Miller's Friday shift. At about 10:30 A.M. Mrs. Miller called the plant and told Tom Burke that Tony would be in to work at 3 P.M. Burke explained that Tony had been suspended without pay until further notice and that his future with the Dell County Water Treatment Plant was in serious jeopardy, based on her previous day's call and on the basis of his discussion with her that morning.

Within a half hour, Miller called the plant and spoke to Burke. He was irate and threatened to file a grievance. Burke recommended that Miller report to the Personnel Office before the start of the 3 P.M. shift that day.

Discussion Questions

1. You are Alan Jacoby. What action will you take?
2. Will you allow Tony Miller to report to work?
3. Will you discipline or fire Miller?

Part Five   Special Issues

Chapter Sixteen

HRM for the Small Business

Chapter Objectives

1. To emphasize the growing need for human resource skills in the small business.
2. To trace the transition of the personnel function from employer to HRM specialist.
3. To describe personnel practices in the small firm.
4. To specify the steps in setting up the personnel function.
5. To define personnel policies, procedures, and rules.
6. To describe staffing strategies that are most appropriate for the small firm.

Why Small Is Large

Of the 17.3 million businesses in the United States today, approximately 16.95 million, or 98 percent, can be considered small. Their contributions to the economy are as numerous as the businesses themselves. For example, small companies employ one-half of the nation's private sector work force, even though they possess less than one-fourth of the total business assets. And, because they are primarily labor intensive, small businesses actually create more jobs than do big businesses. Small businesses also produce 38 percent of the country's Gross National Product (GNP) and account for 42 percent of business sales. Overall, small firms provide directly or indirectly the livelihoods of over 100 million Americans. Research conducted for the National Science Foundation concluded that small firms create four times more innovations per research and development (R&D) dollar than medium-sized firms and 24 times as many as large companies.

Source: Norman M. Scarborough and Thomas W. Zimmerer, *Effective Small Business Management,* 2nd ed. (Columbus, OH: Merrill, 1988), p. 15.

AS noted in the preceding news article, the vast majority of firms in the United States are small businesses. About 99.3 percent have ninety-nine or fewer employees. The majority employ fewer than twenty people. They provide 67 percent of initial job opportunities and on-the-job training. Most small businesses are in the wholesale, service, and construction industries.[1]

Small businesses have a failure rate significantly higher than that of larger established companies. A small business's first years focus on survival. In their first year, 50 percent of all new businesses fail, and by the tenth year, between 80 and 90 percent have failed. Fifteen small businesses are launched for every ten that fail.[2]

Limited resources is a perplexing and constant problem of the small business. Because the small business can rarely afford to hire specialists, employees are expected to perform multiple jobs. Priorities are based on short-term needs and not on long-term planning. The owners manage their businesses reactively rather than proactively. Full-time personnel managers are rarely found in the very small firm.

Bad Management

Of course, there are many reasons why a small business fails, but one constant theme is the inexperience or incompetence of the owner-manager. Surveys investigating the reasons for these failures have often placed human resource problems at or near the top of the list.[3] Large firms, for the most part, rely on a formal, well-organized HRM department, whereas small businesses depend upon unsophisticated and informal personnel practices, many of which are unprofessional.

The success of a small business, relative to a big business, is more dependent on the productive and creative power of its employees. With only a few employees, it is critical that the owner-manager of a small business be surrounded with the proper combination of people.[4] While large companies have a greater margin of error in absorbing bad hiring decisions, small companies do not. Because they do not have hundreds of people contributing ideas, skills, and energy to solve a specific problem and complementing one another, most owner-managers cannot afford even a single staffing mistake. Indeed, a Roper Organization poll revealed that the most difficult problem for small businesses was attracting good people and motivating them to perform.[5]

Small businesses should seek to create a work environment that encourages productivity because *each* employee has a significant impact on the bottom line. To the owner-manager, hiring, retaining, and motivating employees should be as important as sales, marketing, finance, and production. The reality, however, is just the opposite.

Small businesses generally treat the human resource function with benign neglect. Employees are not mistreated as much as they are ignored. For the typical owner, the only essential personnel functions are keeping payroll records and providing a few statistical reports to comply with federal and state discrimination laws. During the early stages of a business, the owner's priorities are obvious—to survive by making as much money as possible. Personnel problems, meanwhile, are seldom anticipated and only reactively confronted.

The Evolution of the Personnel Function

During the initial phases of the business, the owner is typically the one who, however reluctantly, handles the basic personnel func-

tions. In more than half of the small firms studied in the state of Louisiana, for example, the owner-manager assumed responsibility for establishing wage and salary levels, screening and interviewing applicants, counseling and discipline, and performance evaluation.[6]

Later, as a firm approaches fifty employees in size, basic personnel functions may be assigned to the bookkeeper or payroll clerk. Alternatively, they may be spread out among several employees who are expected to assume dual (or multiple) responsibilities in both personnel management and production work. Perhaps one or two more functions are added, such as maintaining a simple benefit plan.

As firms grow, the number and types of personnel functions that must be performed become more sophisticated, thus requiring the time and talent of a knowledgeable and skilled staff. This stage in the personnel evolution becomes painfully apparent if a small business receives a visit from a government agency representative because a disgruntled employee filed a discrimination or unsafe work complaint. The owner, to his or her astonishment, cannot understand the record-keeping system because the employee's personnel records were disorganized and lacked uniformity. Furthermore, the owner never bothered to formalize, in writing, personnel policies of any kind. Now he or she is left scurrying around, with no realistic hope of convincing the investigator of the firm's innocence. After paying a hefty fine and the prospect of facing even more visits, the owner decides that it's time to put his personnel house in order.

Personnel Practices in the Small Firm

Small businesses with fewer than fifty employees are less likely to employ a full-time person whose duties are personnel related. In these businesses, the owner-manager will shoulder the responsibility for writing a few key personnel policies and job descriptions. Wage and salary levels are often determined arbitrarily. Recruitment and selection strategies generally consist of nothing more elaborate than newspaper advertisements, application blanks, and an interview. A scientific validation of selection techniques is rarely done.[7]

Furthermore, a small business is usually not in a strong financial position to support various long-term personnel programs. Formal training and development, human resource planning, employee assistance, and tuition benefits are often not available to employees of the small business.

A surprising contrast to the dismal picture just painted is the pervasiveness of performance appraisal systems. One study estimated that 75 percent of small businesses have formal performance appraisals.[8] For the smaller firm, the most frequently cited technique of performance evaluation is the use of objective measures of productivity. Larger firms often rely on conventional trait rating scales, probably because so few jobs have a measurable output directly under the influence of the employee. Smaller firms provide more opportunities to see the impact and contributions that employees make.

Employee motivation is another matter. While small businesses tend to rely on recognition and praise, merit pay and bonuses, and job security as primary motivators, their owners pay little attention to intrinsic rewards.[9] Strategies that use challenging work—a prime intrinsic reward—offer substantial motivational opportunities at low cost. There is no good reason why small firms cannot take advantage of whatever flexibility they have to design and enrich jobs, especially since the capital investment per worker is low and guidance is readily available from the owner.[10]

One final difference between large and small businesses is the degree of legal and economic pressure they experience. Small firms are not bombarded with federal and state laws and regulations, as are larger firms. It is true that reporting and other requirements have been extended to smaller and smaller firms, particularly through state and local agencies. But it is also true that, due to their limited staffs, government agencies have not given the same scrutiny to small companies as to large ones.

STARTING FROM SCRATCH: SETTING UP THE PERSONNEL FUNCTION

Separate personnel departments with professional staffs are usually reserved for the bigger companies. But even an IBM, for example, had to start its personnel function from scratch when it was a small business. Eventually any growing business reaches a point where the owner-manager has to hire at least one personnel generalist or manager.

Hiring a Personnel Specialist

When should a personnel manager be recruited? The exact point in a firm's life cycle when it makes the most economic sense will vary, depending on the following conditions:

- When the company reaches a critical size, usually when it consists of around 100 employees, but perhaps as few as 70.
- When the owner-manager is unable to keep up with all of the federal, state and local laws, reports, and regulations.
- When employee morale is having a significant negative impact on productivity and turnover.
- When employee recruitment and selection mistakes can no longer be tolerated.

- When the cost of recruiting increases dramatically.
- When the work force threatens to unionize.

One approach to getting started is to hire a permanent part-time personnel manager. This gives the business the specialized knowledge it needs without investing huge sums of money. Another approach is to retain the services of professional consultants who specialize in small business operations. The major drawback to using consultants, however, is the absence of continuity and accountability for the results of personnel programs that are initiated.

Staffing

Once a person is brought into the firm to establish the personnel function, one of the first tasks is to design a plan for staffing the growing business. This is also an appropriate time to develop and formalize important personnel policies, assuming this has not already been done.

Staffing is the process of ensuring that the firm has qualified workers available and determining when they will be needed, where they can be found, and how much they cost. Figure 16–1 depicts the different functions that comprise staffing. It is only one of several key personnel functions (others are training and development, compensation and benefits, safety and health, employee and labor relations, and personnel research), but it is the one that needs to be addressed fairly early by the personnel administrator.

Staffing should not be planned in a vacuum. Recruiting competent and productive people, for example, is difficult when the company's salary scales are not competitive. Also, the experience level of new employees can influence the need for costly training and development programs. Because small busi-

nesses are *small,* staffing decisions have to complement other functional areas more quickly and directly than they do in larger firms. The success of the business, for example, may depend on how well the company is able to recruit, select, and train outside sales people.

In a broad sense, staffing functions also include job analysis, job evaluation, recruitment, selection, and orientation. Since each of these subjects has been discussed in preceding chapters, additional comments will only address how the functions differ between large and small businesses.

DEVELOPING PERSONNEL POLICIES

At some point in the growth of a small business, the owner (or manager) will usually come to the conclusion that the unwritten policies about how specific situations ought to be handled are not working. Problems may occur over issues of time off from work, overtime pay, work rules, insurance benefits, or any number of matters. The owner may hear criticisms about unfair employment practices, discrimination, or inconsistencies in the way the work force is managed. The owner may also receive unwanted visitors from federal, state, or local civil rights agencies.

Quasi-personnel policies work as long as one person runs the show. When problematic situations occur, the typical small business owner relies on "good" judgment to make the right decisions. Sometimes the decision made is taken as policy setting and will influence similar decisions in the future. Employees may think they understand the quasi-policy; thus a modest degree of consistency is achieved. Sometimes the precedent set is a bad one. The owner, for example, refuses to pay employees on their break, only to learn later (after being charged with pay discrimi-

FIGURE 16–1
Setting up the HRM functions

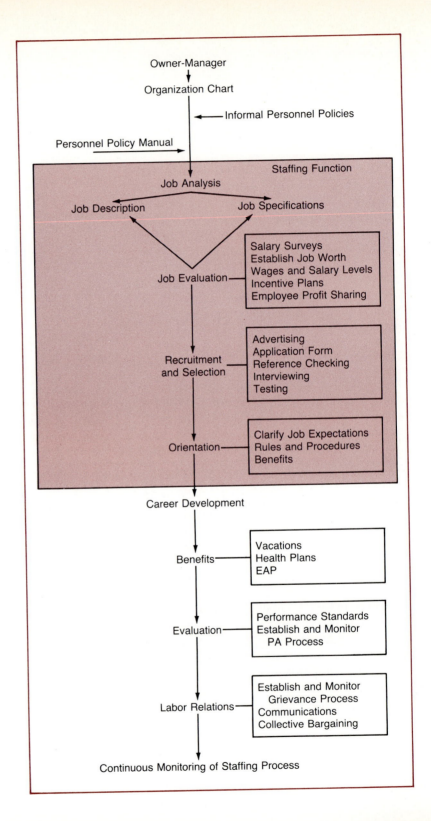

nation) that this practice violated state wage and hour regulations.

Small businesses with fewer than twenty employees can sometimes manage with unwritten policies because employees have a pretty good idea of where the company stands on certain basic issues. But with growth, new supervisors, and more employees, those initial understandings become blurred and vague. Written personnel policies are essential because there must be a single, current, consistent source of guidance and information to which employees can turn.

What Is a Policy?

Subsequently, written policies, rules, procedures, and objectives are created for exercising control over company activities and functions.[11] A policy is a general guide to action under a given set of circumstances. It does not tell an employee what to do; rather, it identifies directions. A policy manual may state: ''Promotions are based on merit.'' In most cases, a specific policy provides guidelines for dealing with an important aspect of a recurring problem. Perhaps the problem is a constant stream of complaints from employees about the owner's arbitrary promotion criteria. A policy, such as the one above usually leaves the owner enough discretion for deciding what constitutes merit, and adds some measure of consistency and fairness.

Policies can provide explicit guidance. But when a policy dictates specific actions to take or what decision to make, it ceases to be policy and, instead, becomes a *rule*. For example, rules may specify the number of vacation days employees receive based on the number of years worked. A rule may be just one part of the company's policy.

When a detailed sequence of steps is prescribed for carrying out a policy, the company has developed a *procedure*. The vacation pol-

icy, for example, may entail a procedure for computing the number of months worked that assures consistency for both full-and part-time employees. *Objectives* represent goals that the company has set for itself—for example, to hold turnover to less than 10 percent.

Policies are sometimes treated with disregard or even disrespect. Supervisors who are expected to enforce a specific policy may ignore it when it is regarded as a challenge to their own authority. A policy on promotion, for example, may be resented by supervisors who once had the discretion to pick and choose successors as they saw fit. On the other hand, employees may disregard that same policy because they believe that the old rules are still in effect.

Advantages of a Policy Manual

Personnel policies, as the heart of any HRM program, achieve several important objectives:

- Equitable and consistent treatment for all employees.
- Optimum level of cost effectiveness in personnel decisions.
- Serve as guidelines to decision making in difficult situations.
- Create confidence in the company, minimizing the potential for union organizing.
- Ensure that the company complies with federal, state, and local civil rights regulations.[12]

For managers, a thorough, current, and official policy manual will point the way to the right course of action or back up a justifiable decision. Moreover, it will enable managers to manage decisively, fairly, and consistently. Although the personnel policy manual is used principally by managers and supervisors, employees may also benefit by gaining a better understanding of their rights, as well as the rules under which they work.

Personnel Policy Coverage

There are probably as many opinions as there are small businesses of what is appropriate subject matter for personnel policies. In general, topics defined as worthy of personnel policies include:

- Salary programs and benefits involving direct payment to the employee or direct cost to the organization (policies of salary grades and ranges, shift premium pay, vacation leave, benefits, retirement, and life insurance).
- Nonmonetary benefits and employee services, including those whose cost to the organization is not obvious (employee credit unions, discounts with local businesses and health clubs, preretirement counseling).
- Employee relations practices, including organizationwide work rules and employee rights (grievance and disciplinary procedures, meal and rest/break provisions, attendance and absenteeism policies).
- Employee review and development programs, including performance appraisal, salary review, training and development, and counseling services.
- Management policies and procedures, including hiring, probationary period, employment of relatives, employee status, and job analysis.
- Statements of support and compliance with laws and regulations, including Equal Employment Opportunity, Occupational Safety and Health, and the Employee Retirement Income Security Act disclosure provisions.

The actual choice of topics to include depends on the targeted audience. It may be ap-propriate to prepare two manuals—one for managers and supervisors and a separate handbook for employees. If the manual is for the former group, a sample of the questions that need to be addressed include the following: Are exempt employees to be treated differently than nonexempt employees? How is the manual to be used? For example, is it to be considered a training and orientation resource, or a single authoritative source of guidance and information when the supervisor needs direction? Is the policy expected to be unpopular, and will it be necessary to give a brief explanation of why the policy is needed? Lastly, what topics do not belong in the manual (e.g., confidential information, proposals in the planning stage, policies that change too frequently)?[13]

Local and State Laws

For the most part, small business owners concentrate on federal laws, such as Title VII of the Civil Rights Act and the Fair Labor Standards Act, without considering whether local or state laws apply as well. It is not unusual for state (and some local) laws to extend coverage beyond a specific federal law. An illustration of how ignorance of state laws can cause personnel problems occurred when a company was charged with employment discrimination because it failed to hire a qualified applicant who happened to be handicapped. The company claimed that according to Title VII they weren't obligated to hire him. Although that was true, the company was in violation of a state law protecting the handicapped.

Local laws can be even more stringent. In one county, for example, a commission was established to protect the civil rights of employees working in businesses with as few as two employees.[14] Legal or expert advice may be needed to make the small business owner aware of applicable state and local laws.

Policy Consistency

Small businesses often grow into large ones. Policies, procedures, and rules that were created in the early days can become woefully out-of-date. Performance reviews, for example, may involve a different set of forms and procedures (e.g., management by objectives) that do not say the same thing as the policy manual. Benefit coverage may have been added. Policies that once applied to nonunion employees, such as grievance procedures, have to be changed if the business has been unionized. Even procedures within a single document may not be internally consistent.

A policy on employment at will, for example, must not be contradicted by other statements in the manual that could cast doubt on the validity of the at-will statement.[15] Any statement that suggests that employment will be terminated "for cause" or that continued employment will be granted following a probationary period, makes the at-will statement shaky.

A wise owner will seek help and advice from attorneys and experts (e.g., benefits consultant) before issuing a policy manual (or handbook) to employees.[16] These experts can offer good advice on how to comply with existing laws. Once a policy statement is made public, the courts will treat it as a legally binding contract in the event of a dispute or an unfair employment practice claim.

Once issued, the policy manual should occasionally be reviewed to determine if changes in the work force or organization require updating of the manual. The appendix to this chapter outlines the major items that should be included in a personnel policy manual, along with the problems to avoid when it is being drafted.

STAFFING STRATEGIES THAT WORK FOR A SMALL BUSINESS

The challenge to anyone thinking about starting a business goes beyond having a good idea for a product or service and the capital to finance it. It includes persuading employees to join in an effort to achieve that goal. And this means finding competent workers and motivating them to perform.

Aggressive Recruiting

A major problem confronting the small business is the need for trained people. The initial step in acquiring competent people is recruitment. Often the successful small business will take an aggressive recruiting posture. It will capitalize on the advantages of being small and may go as far as attractively packaging and promoting its uniqueness in ways that appeal to the types of applicants desired.

How can small firms compete with their larger counterparts in recruiting and retaining competent people? Actually, small firms have a number of advantages, including greater opportunities for:

- Close, meaningful friendships (social needs).
- Exposure to a wider variety of critical business functions—a plus for someone who plans some day to start his or her own business (achievement needs).
- Making significant contributions to the firm's bottom line (experiencing meaningfulness).
- Being recognized and rewarded for good work (recognition needs).
- Personal visibility, not falling through the cracks and being forgotten by top management (self-esteem needs).
- Advancement into management (power needs).

PERSONNEL IN THE NEWS

The Joy of Working: How Employee Satisfaction Gives Small Companies the Competitive Edge

The small business magazine *Inc.* identified 500 of the fastest-growing small and midsize private companies in America. Almost every manager dreams of starting one someday. And every venture capitalist dreams of backing one. But what is it really like to work for one? Remarkably satisfying, as it turns out.

That is the conclusion of a six-month study completed in November 1987 by *Inc.* in collaboration with the nationally known management consultants, the Hay Group. Twenty-eight hundred workers were surveyed from more than 100 *Inc.* 500 companies around the country. What they found were employees who were more satisfied with their jobs, and had more respect for their companies, than the employees of Corporate America.

What one notices about these *Inc.* 500 employees is not simply that they are more satisfied, but the ways in which they are more satisfied. In terms of pay and benefits, they lag well behind the employees of large publicly held corporations. But what they miss in hard currency is more than compensated for in the soft currencies of satisfying work. Small business employees find themselves in jobs that offer challenges and a sense of accomplishment. They experience a company culture that values initiative and ideas. And they are confident that they work for companies that put out quality products, treat their employees with respect, and compete effectively in the marketplace. In terms of almost all the important indices of employee relations, these are companies with plenty of momentum.

Source: "The Joy of Working." Reprinted with permission, *Inc.* magazine, November, 1987. Copyright © 1987 by *Inc.* Publishing Company, 38 Commercial Wharf, Boston, MA 02110.

- Profit sharing and, perhaps, ownership (economic needs).[17]

On the one hand, small firms have to take an aggressive recruiting posture and do whatever they can to attract desirable applicants. On the other hand, they must resist the temptation to misrepresent what they can offer.

The Where and How of Recruiting

Knowing what to promote is only half the battle. The other half is knowing where and how to obtain qualified applicants. There are numerous recruitment sources, which were discussed in chapter 4. In general, small businesses restrict their recruiting efforts to the local area. The most common techniques include word-of-mouth referrals, walk-in applications, employment agencies and union hiring halls, and newspaper advertising.

The smaller firm needs to be cautious about recruiting methods that discriminate against protected classes. Word-of-mouth job advertising, for example, can lead to perpetuating the effects of past discriminatory practices. Also, the persistent use of employee referrals for filling vacancies may result in discrimination against protected classes. Even the use of an employment agency can bring legal problems to an unsuspecting small company if the agency's methods are biased. Lastly, fictitious educational requirements, arrest records, or age limits are "red flags" that may result in complaints of discrimination.

SELECTION

Effective recruiting provides qualified applicants and sets the stage for the selection process. However, for 90 percent of the small businesses in one study, the selection process simply amounts to filling out an application blank and sitting through an interview.[18] Since the purpose of selection is to make predictions about the future job performance of applicants, there is obviously plenty of room for improvement in many small businesses.

The logical place to begin making improvements is on the application blank. Given how easy it is for applicants to distort their responses, it is surprising to learn that verifiable application blank information compares quite favorably with other job success predictors such as interviews.[19] Even so, too much depends on the quality of the information collected not to verify pertinent facts, dates, previous training, job experience, and references.

Background Checks

The typical small business may not have the talent or resources to run a thorough background check on applicants.[20] But at the very least, an owner-manager can and should take certain precautions to verify the employment history contained on the application. If the applicant authorized the owner to run a background check, it should be done. Every effort should be made to talk with the applicant's former supervisor and co-workers.

Unfortunately, there are cases in which unsuccessful applicants have sued their former employers for giving unflattering references.[21] In order to protect themselves against these legal maneuvers, many companies have instituted a policy that prohibits anyone but the personnel department from saying anything about current or past employees. It is virtually impossible, and unrealistic, for the personnel department to impose and enforce a "gag order" on everyone in the company. This policy is often futile because co-workers and supervisors are usually willing to volunteer their opinions, especially if they feel strongly about the applicant's abilities.

To protect themselves from lawsuits, such as for defamation of character, some companies are asking applicants, as part of the application form, to sign a waiver (see Table 16–1) releasing former employers from liability for discussing their performance. This strategy will not always prevent lawsuits, but it is still a sound policy. A better strategy is to ensure that anything and everything said about the applicant is kept confidential, especially remarks that could be construed as derogatory, harmful, or damaging to a person's reputation.

In addition to checking with applicants' previous employers, it is sometimes worthwhile to contact personal references. Al-

TABLE 16–1

Illustration of an applicant authorization to do a background check

I authorize an inquiry to be made on the information contained in this application. Upon written request, the nature and scope of this inquiry will be made available to me.

Former employers named herein are authorized to give information regarding me. They are hereby released from all liability for giving such information.

_____

Applicant's signature

_____

Date

though references listed on application forms are expected to give favorable comments (perhaps too favorable), an owner who asks the right questions may gain real insight into the applicant's potential.[22] Be prepared to ask:

1. If this employee hadn't left, would you have retained him or her? Why?
2. How far would this employee have gone in your company in five years?
3. What are the most productive and creative things he or she did for you?
4. On a scale of one to ten, how would you rate the employee's job performance?
5. How could the employee's job performance have been improved?

Again, as noted in an earlier chapter, rather than writing a formal letter of inquiry to references and employers, a phone call or visit is suggested. People are more inclined to speak candidly about former employees face-to-face than they are to put critical remarks in writing.

Interviews and Work Samples

Small businesses rely extensively on interviews in making selection decisions. But research on interviews reveals that they are typically flawed (see Table 16–2). The interview's usefulness and accuracy improve, however, when the interview questions reflect actual job content. When possible, the interview should include having the applicant perform a sample of the work.[23]

In a small business, the ability to gather critical information is limited by the cost and the staff. The time it takes to contact references is time taken away from other business functions. Rather than collect every piece of information on the applicant, an appropriate goal for the personnel specialist in the small firm is to collect only the most relevant information.[24]

For example, instead of evaluating applicants for a job as accounts receivable manager on the basis of academic degrees and previous job titles, it would be wiser to look for specific characteristics of applicants that are important

TABLE 16–2
Flaws in the interview process

Interviewers weigh the same information on different applicants differently

"Contrast effects" occur: following a "bad" applicant can make an applicant look "less bad"

Interviewers do not cover the same material consistently

The way a question is presented affects the answer given, e.g., "You don't smoke, do you?"

Interviewer attitude affects interpretation of response

Interviewers are influenced more by unfavorable than by favorable information

Interviewers make decisions early in the interview; the first four minutes are critical

Early interviewer impressions are hard to overcome

Interviewers have inaccurate stereotypes of successful job applicants

Attitudinal, racial, and sexual factors affect interviewer evaluations

Source: Adapted from Robert J. Solomon, "Using the Interview in Small Business," *Journal of Small Business Management* (October 1984): 17–23.

to job performance. In the example cited, perhaps the only critical knowledge needed is double-entry bookkeeping.

Developing a selection program that works is a three-step procedure. The first step is conducting a job analysis. The second step is identifying worker characteristics necessary to perform the job tasks. The last step is developing selection devices that measure these characteristics.[25] Each step has been discussed in preceding chapters. If implemented correctly, this three-step procedure is considered to be *content valid.*[26]

COMPENSATION AND BENEFITS

If big companies have any advantages over smaller firms, it is in the areas of compensation and benefits. Larger companies pay better—as much as double for technical people

with computer skills. Benefit packages are also stronger in most cases. Furthermore, the perception, at least, is that the jobs are more secure. And yet, the job satisfaction of employees in large firms is less than that of their counterparts at small companies. Research supports the claim that employee morale declines as companies grow.[27]

Nevertheless, an effective compensation and benefit program often does more to attract and retain competent and productive people than any other action a relatively small firm can take. Employee incentive plans, for example, may be more effective in small firms than in large ones, because the effects of an employee's actions on profitability are more immediately apparent.[28] Yet, reward systems tied to the fortunes of the small firm, like profit sharing and stock options, are still a rarity.[29] The owner-manager of a typical small

"If I Were a *Fortune* 500 CEO, I'd Be Worried!"

So says Michael Cooper, president of the Hay Group's Research for Management, after surveying over twenty-eight hundred employees from over one hundred *Inc.* 500 firms. "The positive attitudes of their employees give small companies a great competitive advantage." Cooper has found that all new employees bring enthusiasm to jobs, no matter what size the company. "Smaller companies are able to sustain this enthusiasm by empowering workers and giving them a sense of common purpose. To get similar results, large companies have to pay cash—higher wages and benefits—and that makes their cost structure just that much less competitive."

Of course, not all small companies have workers as motivated and satisfied as those of the *Inc.* 500. In fact, the circumstantial evidence is that employee motivation is a major force behind the extraordinary growth of these companies, rather than simply the result of it. "These companies are not successful simply because they have a good product or a brilliant founder," says Cooper. "They are also successful because they have managed their people in ways that keep their involvement and sense of partnership high."

Yet for all their positive feelings, these employees express only slightly more pride in, or loyalty to, their small and growing companies than do the employees of the giant corporations. Part of it is that they have not been locked in by generous salaries and pension benefits. Another part of it it that these are people who seem more energized by the type of work they do than by the company they do it for. But there also run unmistakable undercurrents of dissatisfaction within these growing companies—concerns that favorites are being played, that company plans are too closely guarded, and that employees' interests and suggestions are ignored. And although these are successful companies, they are not companies that have gone out of their way to share their success with their employees.

"These are early warning signals that shouldn't just be dismissed as predictable grousing," says Harold Glass, who directs the Hay Group's strategic management practice. "They are extremely accurate predictors of future problems—not just in terms of employee relations, but in terms of product quality and operating costs, and company profits and growth."

Source: "The Joy of Working." Reprinted with permission, *Inc.* magazine, November, 1987. Copyright © 1987 by *Inc.* Publishing Company, 38 Commercial Wharf, Boston, MA 02110.

business is not inclined to share hard-earned profits after taking all the risks.

The benefit packages of smaller firms are generally weak because of the high cost of benefits. Benefits add substantially to the direct wage costs, which may account for more than 50 percent of the small firm's labor payroll.[30] Yet, benefits are an expense that must be assumed if attracting and retaining employees are serious problems. While the firm may not be able to offer the variety of benefits of larger firms, it may still achieve the greatest impact by carefully pinpointing what benefits employees want.

Many small companies are banding together and forming cooperative associations to cut down on the cost of benefits. For example, although it is impractical for small businesses to form their own employee assistance programs (EAP) to help troubled employees, small firms throughout the nation are establishing consortiums to purchase EAP services from providers at reasonable rates.

Small businesses tend to do a poorer job of informing their employees about what benefits they have and what those benefits cost. Few firms do little more than post memos about new benefits or give brochures to employees. Whether in small or large firms, employees tend to take such benefits for granted unless they are reminded periodically about them.[31]

STRATEGIES FOR MANAGING

How does the owner-manager of a small business keep morale and productivity at a high level? Unlike many large firms, small businesses generally have more opportunities to make the company a better place to work. They can do this by molding challenge into the work, adopting the employees' ideas, recognizing good work, and treating employees

with respect. Growing companies may also provide more opportunities for advancement.

Small businesses must also guard against failure to reward employees. If they cannot pay their people competitive salaries and wages, they should at least bolster their benefits programs. Only 13 percent of the *INC.* 500 employees cited profit sharing and stock options as a reason for staying at their firms, putting it last on a list of company attractions.[32] More attention should be given to certain benefits, such as pension plans and health care. Instead of perceiving these programs strictly as costs, it would be better to think of them as long-term investments that have measurable returns in lower employee turnover, greater commitment, and productivity improvement.[33]

CONCLUSIONS AND APPLICATIONS

- Over 98 percent of businesses in the United States are small. Most are labor intensive and are in service, wholesale, and construction industries. In fact, small businesses employ approximately one-half of the nation's private-sector work force. But the failure rate of small businesses is high, with only half surviving their first year. Only about one out of ten will exist in ten years.

- The most common reason for the high dropout rate of small business is poor management. An owner-manager's inexperience or incompetence, especially in terms of poor hiring decisions, and very limited resources to work with, are often cited as major problems. Although big companies have their share of incompetent managers too, they have a better chance of overcoming this problem. Having only a few employees, small businesses cannot afford too many selection mistakes. Unfortunately, the human resource function is usually a low priority.

- The right time to hire a personnel specialist depends on size (usually around seventy employees), morale problems, selection mistakes, scarcity of labor, and the presence or threat of unions. Any one or more of these conditions may require a part-time personnel specialist to set up a HRM function.

- One of the first HRM tasks is to develop personnel policies. Policies are needed to provide explicit guidance when certain situations occur. Managers and supervisors are the primary beneficiaries because policies enable them to manage more decisively, consistently, and fairly. It is often appropriate to prepare two policy manuals—one for supervisors and one for employees (i.e., an employee handbook).

- One of the most difficult problems small businesses face is attracting competent and productive people. Because a small business cannot offer salaries and other perks that a larger firm can, it is necessary to take an aggressive recruiting posture. There are numerous advantages of working in a small business, and applicants should be told that a small business can be a very appealing place to work.

- Selecting the right person is another critical personnel function given scant attention in most small firms. Typically, the application blank and interview are relied on when making selection decisions. Much more could be done to improve the selection process, including more thorough background checks and job analyses.

- Management strategies that build employee commitment and improve productivity are not only possible but promising. Small businesses offer many opportunities for job enrichment, growth, recognition, and achievement. While the potential exists, it remains to be seen whether owner-managers will capitalize on it.

CASE STUDY
"Where Do I Begin?"

Terry Van Eyck was hired to set up the HR function in a small, privately owned manufacturing concern. Just six years old, the firm had grown in this period from two brothers producing computer parts in their garage during their spare time to six production lines and more than 80 full-time employees. If the business continued to expand at its present rate, it would need more than 500 employees in the next six years.

Before Van Eyck was hired, the sales manager (one of the brothers who owned the firm) had handled some of the organization's personnel activities. In general, though, the personnel activities of the organization were decentralized and highly idiosyncratic: the six foremen of the production lines individually handled employees' recruitment, selection, hiring, orientation, training, wages, promotions, discipline and terminations. They consulted the elder of the two brothers, who served as the firm's general operating manager, before making decisions on particularly important matters—especially those related to pay increases or terminations. The employees were not unionized.

During the first few weeks of his new job, Van Eyck devoted most of his time to examining current personnel practices in the organization, speaking with employees and foremen and looking through the personnel records. To his astonishment, he discovered that the employee personnel records were disorganized and lacked uniformity, that the organization had no formal personnel policies, and that the firm's managers had only a vague idea of personnel costs or manpower needs. There were no formal job descriptions, no job specifications, no performance appraisal system, and no records on turnover or absenteeism. There was a formal pay plan, but many employees received wages well above prevailing rates as specified in the plan.

In discussions with employees, Van Eyck found that they were quite bitter about what they perceived as the capricious and inconsistent practices of the foremen. Yet the foremen were pleased with the present arrangement, which they felt allowed them sufficient flexibility and power to reward or punish workers as they saw fit. They made it clear that they did not want a centralized personnel function, nor did they need staff advice about how to manage their lines. The owner-manager recognized the need for an HR function that the firm could grow into; however, at the same time he wished to avoid, as he put it, "stirring up trouble or interfering with the present work or duties of the foremen I hired and promoted."

As a first-year budget, Van Eyck was provided $5,000 (excluding his salary). He has an office, a desk, a telephone, two filing cabinets, a wastebasket, and a part-time secretary who worked only two mornings per week.

Questions

1. Where should Van Eyck begin?
2. Can he successfully design and implement an HR function under these conditions? How?
3. What must Van Eyck do in order to get the backing of the foremen?

Source: Adapted from William J. Rothwell, "Setting Up the Human Resource Function in a Small Organization," *Personnel Administrator* (April 1981): 23–24. Copyright 1981, The American Society for Personnel Administration, Alexandria, VA.

EXPERIENTIAL EXERCISE
Dos and Don'ts in Job Interviews and on Application Forms

(Circle)

1. Do   Don't   ask about marital status or the names and ages of dependents.
2. Do   Don't   ask a woman's maiden name or her father's surname.
3. Do   Don't   ask if the applicant has previously worked for a company under a different name.
4. Do   Don't   ask about the lineage, ancestry, or national origin of the applicant.
5. Do   Don't   ask if the applicant is pregnant or if she plans to have children.

6. Do   Don't   ask about the applicant's race or any other information directly or indirectly indicating race or color.

7. Do   Don't   ask the applicant's native tongue.

8. Do   Don't   ask whether the applicant is a minor or not.

9. Do   Don't   ask about the racial, national, or religious affiliation of a school that the applicant attended.

10. Do   Don't   ask about the birthplace of the applicant or his or her parents.

11. Do   Don't   ask about the names and relationships of people with whom the applicant lives.

12. Do   Don't   ask whether the applicant rents or owns his or her own home.

13. Do   Don't   ask about the hours the applicant would be available for work.

14. Do   Don't   ask what color the applicant's hair or eyes are.

15. Do   Don't   ask if the applicant's wages ever have been garnisheed.

KEY TERMS AND CONCEPTS

Background checks

Benefits

Compensation

Critical mass

Defamation

Employee handbook

Failure rate

Interviews

Objectives

Personnel Practices

Policy

Policy consistency

Policy coverage

Procedures

Recruiting

Rules

Selection

Staffing

Work samples

REVIEW QUESTIONS

1. What types of personnel/human resource functions are practiced by the small business? Which functions are critical to its survival?

2. At what point and under what circumstances should an owner-manager begin thinking about using a specialist in designing and managing a personnel system?

3. How would a new personnel specialist, starting from scratch, begin setting up a personnel system?

4. Why do small businesses need formal personnel policies? Should they be in writing, and why?

5. Assume that you have a small market research business and are in need of a data-entry clerk. How would you proceed? Assume that you are recruiting a statistician. How would you proceed?

6. When conducting a background check on an applicant, what should you be looking for and how should you be going about it?

7. What advantages do small businesses have over larger companies from the perspective of job satisfaction?

DISCUSSION QUESTIONS

1. What are the four most critical job behaviors for the following two jobs:
   a. Data-entry clerk in a market research firm.
   b. Statistician in a market research firm.

2. Based on your answer to question 1, write a job description and specifications for each job.

3. What might an owner-manager do to make the job of data-entry clerk more challenging and interesting? What conditions need to be present before the change is made?

4. How feasible is profit sharing from an implementation perspective? What types of difficulties can be expected?

5. What types of items should be included in the personnel policy manual of a market research firm that employs 50 percent professionals and 50 percent clerical employees?

ENDNOTES

1. Ralph M. Gaedeke and Dennis H. Tootelian, *Small Business Management* (Glenview, IL: McGraw-Hill, 1985), p. 382.

2. *The Dun and Bradstreet Business Failure Record* (New York: Dun and Bradstreet, 1986), pp. 12–13. Also see "Opinion Survey of Businessmen's Problems," *President's Task Force on Improving the Prospects of Small Business* (Washington, DC: U.S. Government Printing Office, March 1970); and President of the United States and the U.S. Small Business Administration, *The State of Small Business* (Washington, DC: U.S. Government Printing Office, March 1983).

3. Glen M. McEvoy, "Small Business Personnel Practices," *Journal of Small Business Management* (October 1984): 1–8.

4. For a more detailed treatment of small business problems, see Norman M. Scarborough and Thomas W. Zimmerer, *Effective Small Business Management*, 2nd ed. (Columbus, OH: Merrill, 1988), p. 431.

5. *The Wall Street Journal* (March 20, 1980): 1.

6. Beverly L. Little, "The Performance of Personnel Duties in Small Louisiana Firms: A Research Note," *Journal of Small Business Management* (October 1986): 66–69.

7. McEvoy, "Small Business Personnel Practices," p. 4.

8. Ibid., p. 4.

9. Ibid., p. 5.

10. See George W. Rimler and Neil J. Humphreys, "The New Employee and the Small Firm: Some Insights into Modern Personnel Management," *Journal of Small Business Management* (July 1976): 22–27.

11. See Terry W. Smith, "Developing a Policy Manual," *Personnel Journal* 61 (June 1982): 446–49.

12. Ibid., p. 447.

13. Ibid., p. 448.

14. See *Gonzalez* v. *Prestress Engineering Corporation,* 55 U.S.L.W. 2350 (Ill. Dec. 19, 1986). Also see *Anderson* v. *Ford Motor Company,* 55 U.S.L.W. 2241 (8th Cir., Oct. 23, 1986).

15. See *Dell* v. *Montgomery Ward & Co., Inc.,* 811 F.2d 970 (6th Cir. 1987).

16. Robert C. Wood, "When You Need Experts to Help with Your Staff," *INC.* (February 1983): 112–18.

17. For more information, see G. W. Rimler and N. J. Humphreys, "The New Employee and the Small Firm: Some Insights into Modern Personnel Management," *Journal of Small Business Management* (July 1976): 22–27. See also M. D. Ames and N. L. Wellsfy, *Small Business Management* (St. Paul, MN: West, 1983) pp. 368–69.

18. McEvoy, "Small Business Personnel Problems," p. 3.

19. See W. F. Cascio, "Accuracy of Verifiable Biographical Information Blank Responses," *Journal of Applied Psychology* 60 (1975): 767–70.

20. A more thorough treatment of background checks is found in chapter 5.

21. See *Bailey* v. *USX Corporation,* 658 F. Supp. 279 (N.D. Ala., 1987).

22. Source: Adapted from Theodore Cohn and Roy Lindberg, *Survival and Growth: Management Strategies for the Small Firm* (New York: AMACOM, a division of the American Management Association, 1974), p. 133.

23. For additional information, see Robert J. Solomon, "Using the Interview in Small Business," *Journal of Small Business Management* (October 1984): 17–23. Also see R. D. Arvey and J. E. Campion, "The Employment Interview: A Summary and Review of Recent Research," *Personnel Psychology* (1982): 35, 281, 322.

24. Robert D. Gatewood and Hubert S. Field, "Personnel Selection Program for Small Business," *Journal of Small Business Management* (October 1987): 17.

25. Ibid.

26. Although content validity is a nonstatistical approach to validation, the courts have increasingly acknowledged that it is an acceptable strategy. The key to content validity is that the skills, knowledge, and behaviors needed to perform the job are measured; no attempt is made to measure abstract and/or qualitative abilities. For more discussion on this issue, see F. L. Schmidt and J. E. Hunter, "The Future of Criterion-Related Validity," *Personnel Psychology* (Spring 1980): 41–60; also S. D. Maurer and C. H. Fay, "Legally Fair Hiring Practices for Small Business," *Journal of Small Business Management* (January 1986): 47–54.

27. This is particularly true for managers, professionals, and salespeople. Reasons cited include challenging and interesting work, a chance to have ideas adopted, a sense of accomplishment, and dignity and respect. For more information, see "The Joy of Working," *INC.* (November 1987): 62–67.

28. Robert D. Swanson, "Compensation Options for Small Business Management," *Journal of Small Business Management* (October 1984): 31–38. See also Vance Jacobson, cited by Thomas Richman, "Show Employees What They Earn," *INC.* (August 1980): 55.

29. "The Joy of Working", p. 63.

30. Justin G. Longenecker and Carlos W. Moore, *Small Business Management*, 7th ed. (Cincinnati: South-Western, 1987), p. 443.

31. Earnest H. Schnell, "Take the Wraps Off Your Employee Benefits Package," *INC.* (August 1980): 72.

32. "The Joy of Working," p. 63.

33. Ibid.

CHAPTER APPENDIX
How to Write a Personnel Manual

Some executives prefer to make policy decisions on the basis of personal hunches, likes and dislikes, or just plain delight in running the show. They don't want to delegate authority in hiring and firing, or rewarding and punishing employees.

But that's a risky and time-consuming way of managing personnel. Eventually every executive finds that his life would be a lot easier—and his employees a lot happier—if the policies he is constantly being called on to make were written down.

Any company with more than 20 employees, and some with as few as half a dozen, should issue a policy handbook. It should answer some of the most important questions employees ask—questions about salary review, holidays, benefit programs, leaves of absence, and other critical policies that often affect morale and whose absence can create legal problems. The handbook should have two

goals: It should keep all employees informed about company regulations and changing policies, and it should give supervisors the support they need when they have to enforce those regulations and policies.

Your lawyer, or a legal expert in the field of labor relations, is the best person to consult before you issue a policy statement to employees. (Remember, a policy handbook may be considered legally binding in the event of a dispute or an unfair employment practice claim.) On the following pages we've outlined some of the major items that should be included in a personnel policy handbook along with some dos and don'ts to consider when you're drafting or revising yours.

Edgar S. Ellman is a personnel administration consultant in Chicago.

Policy Item	What it should say	Problems to avoid
Equal opportunity statement	State that an employee's religion, age, sex, national origin, race, or color will have nothing to do with hiring, promotion, pay, or benefits.	Don't include the Affirmative Action Plan, if you're required to have one, in this section. Refer instead to a separate handbook.
Physical examinations	Establish your right to conduct both pre- and post-employment physical exams, at company expense.	Be sure your decisions to conduct a physical are nondiscriminatory—i.e., don't just examine older people or minorities.
Probationary period	Define the period (usually 30, 60, or 90 days) during which a new employee can be dismissed without a hearing on the cause; also indicate when benefits start to accrue.	Avoid a great discrepancy between the probationary period and the period before an employee qualifies for group insurance.
Hiring of relatives	State whether you will allow a married couple or close relatives to work together in the same department.	Too strict policies—e.g., requiring two employees who get married to choose which will remain with the company—are bad for morale.
Work hours	Define the workweek and time allotted for lunch and breaks. Indicate the cut-off time for each pay period.	Provide yourself with the option of rescheduling individual hours of work in any given week at the discretion of the supervisor.
Employee status	Define the nature of each type of employee—full time, part time, temporary, and "exempt" and "nonexempt." Make clear what benefits each is eligible for.	Be specific to avoid any chance of misconception.
Overtime pay	Establish clearly whether overtime is paid for work over 40 hours a week or over 8 hours in a given day, and how much is paid for work on a holiday. Make it clear that pay for overtime must be approved by a supervisor.	Don't say that you are bound to assign overtime on the basis of seniority.

Source: Edgar S. Ellman, *How to Write a Personnel Manual.* Reprinted with permission, *INC.* magazine (October 1981): 69–72. Copyright 1981 by INC. Publishing Co., 38 Commercial Wharf, Boston, MA 02110.

PERSONNEL HANDBOOK

Policy Item	What it should say	Problems to avoid
Pay reduction for lateness	The usual policy is to go by the clock, i.e., to dock an employee's pay in units of six minutes or tenths of an hour.	Using too large a unit, such as a quarter of an hour, may cause problems. It may be illegal to dock an employee's pay by that much if he or she is only a few minutes late.
Severance pay	Determine this on the basis of seniority, e.g., a week's pay for less than three years tenure, two weeks for up to six years, etc. Exclude employees who are released for "cause." You may also exclude those who leave voluntarily.	Unless state law requires it, you don't have to pay for accrued vacation time.
Performance review and merit increases	Review wages either on the anniversary of employment or during a set annual or semiannual period.	This policy is essential—some employees would rather quit than ask for a raise. Don't commit yourself to cost-of-living increases unless required by a union contract. Make all raises based on merit.
Time clock or sign-in systems	Rules should prohibit employees from recording another's time, causing another employee to record for him or her, or failing to record his or her time. They should also forbid signing in too soon or out too late without authorization.	You must keep some sort of record of hours worked by "nonexempt" employees. Early sign-ins or late sign-outs will make you liable for overtime pay in case of a conflict or dispute.
Emergency shut-downs	Consider whether you will pay some minimum "call-in" wage in case you have to close down because of bad weather, a power failure, or some other unforeseen problem. What advance notice will you provide, if possible, in the event of such a shutdown?	Don't lock yourself in too tightly, but be sure you treat everyone the same. If you pay the regular wage to those who don't show up, those who do come in should be paid more.
Group insurance benefits	State coverage generally and briefly, indicating what portion of premium costs the company pays for, how long a new employee has to wait for coverage, and mentioning the conversion privilege.	Don't be too specific, but simply refer to the separate booklet the insurance company provides.
Holidays	List all holidays, and state how long an employee has to work to qualify for a paid holiday. Also indicate that employees have the right to take religious holidays without pay. What happens if the holiday occurs during an employee's vacation? What pay is given for work on a holiday?	Leave some room to reschedule a holiday depending on business conditions. You don't have to pay overtime in a week with a holiday unless more than 40 hours are worked.
Vacations	Policies should conform with local practices (consult Bureau of Labor Statistics surveys and other published information). How does a new employee qualify for vacation? May a person choose to work instead of taking a vacation? May one take off more than two weeks at a time? As little as a day at a time? Are permanent part-timers given any vacation? Will accrued vacation pay be given at severance? Will a person on leave of absence accrue vacation time?	Don't let vacation scheduling supersede the needs of any individual department. Check state laws regarding payment of accrued vacation time at severance.
Personal time / sick leave	Six to ten days per year is the typical number allowed. Give employees the option of accumulating a reasonable number of days (20 or 30) for the future, or create a payback system for those who don't abuse the privilege.	The advantage of calling it "personal time" rather than "sick leave" is that employees will take sick leave without giving advance notice. Require "proof of illness" if you pay for time off only in the case of illness. Don't let personal time accrue during an extended leave of absence.
Disability leave of absence	Federal law requires leave time for disability due to pregnancy to be equal to that allowed for disabilities that affect only males. You must set some reasonable time limit during which you will guarantee job protection for a disabled worker. A 60 to 90 day period is typical. You may require pregnant women to sign statements of intent to return to work provided you require male workers disabled for other reasons to do the same. You may also reserve the right to require a physical examination by a company-appointed doctor if required of both males and females.	You do not have to have a leave policy at all if you don't want it, but some states have laws requiring a minimum leave time for pregnant women.
Military leave of absence	Required under federal law for National Guard or Reserve service.	Employees may not be compelled to use up vacation or personal time during military leave, and the job must be held open for the employee. He or she must not be discriminated against in pay, promotion, or job assignment.

Policy item	What it should say	Problems to avoid
Personal leave of absence	If you decide to grant such leaves, you may want to specify that they may not exceed 30 (or 60) days, and that they may not be taken to look for or perform another job, or to start another business.	Smaller firms may want to omit this item, and play it by ear. If you plan to grant only discretionary leaves, omit the item.
Jury service	Required by law, and some local statutes also require you to pay all or a portion of wages. Depending on local laws, you may want to set limits on how many days of jury duty you will pay for, and set a qualifying period of employment before you will pay for jury leave.	Don't require that employees sign over to the company the checks they receive from the court for serving on a jury. This may cause tax problems. Just pay them the difference between the amount of the check and the pay they would have received.
Bereavement pay	Employees expect the company to be very lenient in this matter. Typical policy allows three to five workdays off with pay in the event of a death in the immediate family.	Absence of a policy of some sort is bad for morale, but it's important to be consistent in granting this benefit.
Pension or profit-sharing plans	Mention that you have a plan, when and how the employee becomes qualified for it, whether an employee contribution is permitted or required, and when an employee becomes vested.	Don't go into great detail; refer instead to a separate description of the plan.
Suggestion system	State that the company encourages employees to submit ideas and suggestions to improve operations and reduce costs, and that an employee who submits ideas is considered to be a highly conscientious one. Suggestions should be addressed in writing to a member of top management, not the immediate supervisor.	Small firms should avoid a formal system. Committing yourself to a specific system of reward for ideas is also unwise.
Tuition assistance	Set a length of tenure requirement before the assistance is available. Require proof of course completion and consider awarding a larger percentage of costs for a high grade.	A good policy because it substantiates your desire to provide equal advancement opportunities, but don't commit yourself to paying all costs or fees.
Bulletin boards	State that this is an official means of communication with employees, and that only authorized people may put up, take down, or alter items on the board.	Though you may think this item unimportant, the bulletin board is looked upon legally as an official "business practice" for keeping employees informed. Don't let items on the board get outdated; otherwise people will stop reading the announcements.
Confidentiality	Make employees aware that they are not to divulge company or customer information to outsiders, including the media and government representatives, without approval from management.	Certain government representatives (OSHA, EEOC) are privileged to speak privately with employees, with advance notice to employers.
Causes for discipline	Some industries, most often those employing unskilled or semiskilled workers, believe that a list of shop rules is essential. These must be as comprehensive as possible.	Legally, a list is deemed to be complete, and once it's published, anything not on the list would not be considered legally limiting on the employee. So don't commit yourself to publishing a list unless you feel you must, and don't make any violation of a rule an absolute cause for dismissal—or you may have to fire a good employee for a one-time infringement of the rules. Be sure rules are nondiscriminatory.
Discussing complaints and grievances	There should be some basis for appeal in the event an employee feels a supervisor's policies are unjust. All union contracts cover this procedure.	Don't have an "open door" policy allowing employees to bypass supervisors. Encourage them to talk things over with supervisors first.
Solicitation or distribution of literature	If you don't want employees selling merchandise or circulating petitions during working hours, specify that you will not allow the distribution of any literature, petitions, or surveys or the sale of any merchandise, raffle tickets, etc.	Don't impose this rule after a union has won the right to an election.

Additional items for your employee handbook			
Reporting absence	Hiring of ex-felons, handi-capped	Athletic activities	Change of address, phone, etc.
Annual bonus	Wages during a transfer	Retirement	Bonding of employees
Purchase of company mer-chandise	Fines and penalties	First aid	Role of the personnel dept.
	Accepting gifts	Preemployment credit investi-gation	Polygraph examinations
Dress code	Annual party or outing		Attending seminars/meetings
Safety rules	Use of company equipment	Confidentiality agreement	Conflict of interest
Aptitude and ability tests	Good housekeeping	Repayment of loans	Access to personnel file
Service awards	Rehiring former employees	Expense reimbursement	Proof of citizenship
Relocation expense	Use of telephones	Referring applicants	Security checks
Outside employment	How pay is computed	Coffee breaks	Overtime pay for supervisors
Exit interviews	Employee gift fund	Parking lot rules	Bond purchases
Noncompetition agreement		Fire drills	Check cashing

Chapter Seventeen

Computers and the Human Resource Department

Chapter Objectives

1. To trace the evolution of computers in personnel from payroll to human resources information systems (HRIS).
2. To describe the components of a computerized HRIS.
3. To describe the value of an HRIS.
4. To define what the human resource staff should know about computers.
5. To discuss the important issues in selecting and implementing an HRIS.
6. To identify the categories of computer applications in the human resource department.

A Software Link between Performance Appraisals and Merit Increases

The Montek Division of E-Systems, Inc., in Salt Lake City recently examined its procedure for distributing merit funds. Mathew B. Chalker, personnel manager of the division, discussed some of the issues that management considered and the relatively simple computer program that was devised to quickly calculate the amount of merit increase available to each employee.

"We recognized that performance must be solidly and consistently linked to rewards in order for pay for performance to be a viable concept," said Chalker. "The lack of a consistent correlation between the appraisal rating and the merit increase will severely debilitate even the most accurate performance appraisal—largely nullifying many of the benefits of the merit concept."

To strengthen its pay-for-performance program, the company developed a computer-aided merit increase distribution system (CAMIDS). The system bases merit distributions on each individual performance appraisal rating in relationship to all other ratings, the wage rate of each employee, and the total amount of money available for raises.

Once performance appraisals have been completed for all employees, compensation personnel load the ratings into the CAMIDS program. (The database already contains the base rate of pay for each employee.) The overall merit budget is then entered into the program along with several parameters (assumptions) intended to manipulate the calculation in order to yield a large increase for outstanding performers and, likewise, an appropriate increase for poorer performers. On the basis of the options selected, a merit increase schedule is instantly produced showing the available merit increase (see Figure 17–1).

By "experimenting with the optional parameters, various scenarios can be quickly produced until an optimum balance is reached providing a substantial raise for outstanding performers while allowing all other performance levels appropriate raises based on the available budget and distribution of performance," Chalker explained. "These scenarios are analyzed by the human resource department, and a proposal is then reviewed by management for approval. One immediate benefit of this program is that merit budget expenditures can finally be controlled and manipulated with enough precision to delight any controller."

At Montek, CAMIDS is tied to a mainframe and interfaced with the personnel/payroll systems. This setup simplifies the quantity of data entry and greatly extends the possible range of features. "Once the performance ratings are loaded," said Chalker, "a unique and very useful

Name	Appraisal Rating	Current Rate	Increase Amount	Increase Percentage	New Rate
Employee 1	3.2	$ 7.30	$ .34	4.6%	$ 7.64
Employee 2	1.8	5.80	.00	.0%	5.80
Employee 3	4.5	13.50	1.01	7.5%	14.51
Employee 4	3.0	10.70	.46	4.3%	11.16
Employee 5	2.9	8.90	.34	3.8%	9.24
Employee 6	3.6	12.20	.66	5.4%	12.86

CAMIDS Summary Schedule

(Appraisal Rating = Merit Increase Percentage)

5.0=8.9%,	4.9=8.6%,	4.8=8.4%,	4.7=8.1%,	4.6=7.8%,	4.5=7.5%,	4.4=7.3%,
4.3=7.0%,	4.2=6.7%,	4.1=6.5%,	4.0=6.2%,	3.9=6.0%,	3.8=5.8%,	3.7=5.6%,
3.6=5.4%,	3.5=5.2%,	3.4=5.0%,	3.3=4.8%,	3.2=4.6%,	3.1=4.5%,	3.0=4.3%,
2.9=3.8%,	2.8=3.4%,	2.7=3.0%,	2.6=2.6%,	2.5=2.1%,	2.4=1.7%,	2.3=1.3%,
2.2=0.9%,	2.1=0.4%,	2.0=0.0%,	1.9=0.0%,	1.8=0.0%,	1.7=0.0%,	1.6=0.0%,
1.5=0.0%,	1.4=0.0%,	1.3=0.0%,	1.2=0.0%,	1.1=0.0%,	1.0=0.0%,	

FIGURE 17–1

Computer-aided merit increase distribution system (CAMIDS) wage-rate circulation and summary schedule

database is born that can be tapped for a broad range of statistical analysis."

In summing up the benefits of CAMIDS, Chalker commented: "CAMIDS was designed to provide a solid and consistent link between performance appraisal and merit increases while controlling merit budget expenditures. It did that and more. Along the way, CAMIDS literally opened a new dimension of compensation planning and analysis."

Source: Adapted from William H. Wagel, "A Software Link between Performance Appraisal and Merit Increases," *Personnel* 65 (March 1988): 10–14. © 1988 American Management Association, New York. All rights reserved.

THIS chapter describes various uses for a computer in the human resource management setting. Because computers represent a major change in most departments—in terms of both people and job content—it is important that all ramifications be understood before the department leaps into action. While the power of a computer can be harnessed and produce amazing results (see the chapter opening story regarding CAMIDS), it is only one more management tool. Companies should be cautious and should look to a computer system only to help them do the job—not to do the job for them.

FROM PAYROLL TO HRIS

Usually one of the last areas automated, personnel has lagged behind applications in other functions such as accounting, manufacturing, and financial planning. The uneven progress of computers in personnel has resulted from the rapid change in technology and the changing role of the personnel department.[1]

The typical personnel computer system of the 1960s developed as an outgrowth of the company payroll system. Payroll was one of the first functions to be automated, and since the payroll file contained mostly information about employees that was already computerized it seemed logical to use these files for personnel as well.[2]

It was payroll that gave birth to the first personnel data base and, ultimately, to human resource information systems (HRISs). But it was a long, roundabout process. Basic payroll information such as name, salary, date of birth, sex, and department code were available to the personnel department for analysis. Business computer languages, COBOL in particular, made possible new accounting application programs that analyzed employee records.

Perhaps the first nonpayroll personnel system appeared in the defense industry. In this system, inventories of skills were compiled—on tapes and cards—and used for bidding on government contracts. Despite the potential benefits, however, the use of computers in personnel continued to be the exception rather than the rule. There were too many drawbacks, cost being the most serious.

The high cost of computers, facilities (e.g., air conditioning was a requirement for mainframes), and programming staff deterred most companies from entering the computer age. Only the bigger companies could afford the luxury of a mainframe computer, along with the frequent downtime for computer maintenance and repairs. Computer technology was so unreliable during the early days that many companies maintained dual systems—manual and automated.

Packaged software was almost nonexistent, which meant that programs had to be written inhouse using sometimes inflexible early computer languages that were difficult to learn and even more difficult to apply.

Programmers were often recruited with backgrounds in engineering and research science. Their interests reflected their backgrounds and their nickname—*number crunchers.* The organization's human resource needs, if not ignored, were treated with benign neglect.

While payroll information was helpful to personnel managers, it was limited. There is only so much that can be gleaned from a payroll master file designed for fixed reporting requirements. It soon became apparent that the personnel department needed to take control of and responsibility for its own data rather than depend on jerry-rigging payroll systems.

What seemed like a sensible idea at the time—tying all the management systems together and cutting down on redundancy—seldom moved beyond the planning stage. The idea of the management information system (MIS) as a single, completely integrated supersystem, was popular during the late 1960s and early 1970s. But it was an idea whose time had not yet come. It was simply too complicated, given the existing technology, to design one system that could satisfy the variety of organizational needs. Mainframes, for example, could not handle the thousands of job grades and steps, the exceptions, and the constant updating that gave the system validity.

This situation began to change when, in the 1970s, governmental regulatory acts, such as EEO, OSHA, ERISA, and, more recently, COBRA, required almost every company—

large and small, profit and nonprofit—to compile hundreds of statistics on employees and to submit elaborate quarterly and annual reports. For big companies in particular, these regulatory reports were simply not feasible without automation.

The microcomputer's introduction moved control of information systems from data processing to any department that could afford the cost (less than $5,000). User-friendly software has made the micro easy to master. One personnel computer application soon led to another. Combined with new technology, abundant and affordable software, and lower costs, the microcomputer heralded the coming of the human resource information system.[3]

WHAT IS HRIS?

Personnel managers, as a group, are only beginning to use the computer as a management decision tool. The computer was once used only to maintain personnel files. But times are changing.

A lot of attention is now being given to the human resource information system (HRIS). This is defined as a computer-based method for collecting, storing, maintaining, retrieving, and validating human resource data.[4] More than just a system for preparing standard reports, a HRIS is typically designed and structured to permit the retrieval of user-defined ad hoc reports, comparative analyses, and employee (or applicant) data items.

In addition to employee and applicant information, the HRIS data base contains organizational and job-related data. The creation of the data base may be the most important step in implementing the system.[5] If essential data items are not identified during the planning phase, chances are that they cannot be added later once the system is in place. Figure 17–2 shows the components of a comprehen-

sive HRIS data base and the organizational concerns it can be used to address.

One obvious benefit of having a comprehensive data base is the capacity to answer questions like "what," "how much," and "when." Typically, HRIS accomplishes this function by drawing on standard reports, for instance, salary reviews due next month, EEO-1 reports, work force analysis, or "tickler" memos.

But the real benefit of a HRIS is that it is a system that goes beyond the "what" questions and uses the computer to answer the "whys" and "what ifs." The technology is available. In addition, user-friendly software is improving. Sophisticated HRIS systems often include integrated word processor, spreadsheet, and data manipulation packages enabling the user to design custom reports or perform "what if" analyses. At least a few companies have HRISs that have evolved to the point where they can provide the human resource manager with a variety of answers to "what if" questions.

WHAT THE HUMAN RESOURCE STAFF SHOULD KNOW ABOUT COMPUTERS

What is often called a *computer* is actually a computer system that includes hardware, software, a central processing unit (CPU), peripheral devices (printer, diskettes, hard-disk drives, etc.), and people.[6] The CPU is the brain and is designed to control the interpretation and execution of instructions. It causes data to be read, stored, written, or otherwise processed.[7] Basic computer terminology is provided in Table 17–1.

The arrangement and speed of the various pieces of equipment that make up the CPU can be grouped into three categories. The largest, fastest, and most expensive computer con-

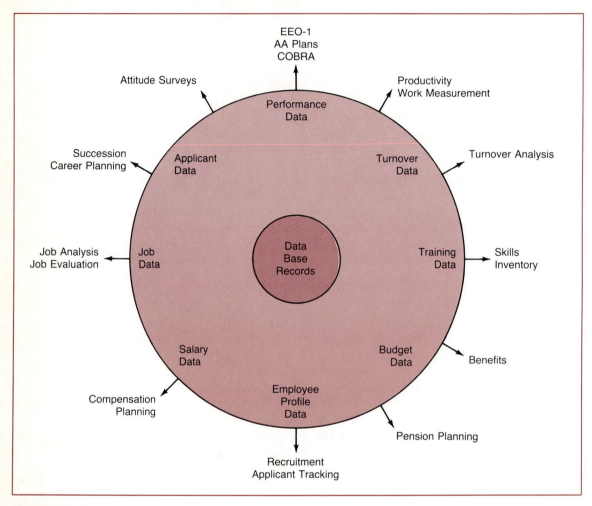

FIGURE 17–2
HRIS data base illustration

figuration is called a *mainframe.* Originally, this term referred to the elaborate array of large rack and panel cabinets that held thousands of vacuum tubes in the early computers.[8] A mainframe will typically serve as the hub of a big company's information systems. The second category of computers is called a *minicomputer.* Not quite as fast as a mainframe but still able to handle simultaneous users (and at a much lower cost), the mini continues to be a popular system.

The *microcomputer* is the smallest and least expensive category of computer. It uses a microprocessor as its CPU (i.e., basic arithmetic, logic, and control elements contained on one integrated circuit chip).[9] Microcomputers are also called *personal computers (PCs), desktop computers,* or *home computers.* The latest release

TABLE 17–1

Defining some computer terminology

The probabilities of encountering one or more of the following technical terms are extremely high for the personnel manager involved in a computer project.

Backup: A duplicate copy of a file of information on a diskette, magnetic tape, or other kind of storage medium created to protect against loss of the original information.

Backup site: An off-site location where a computer is available to run systems when the on-site computer is inoperative.

BASIC (Beginners All-purpose Symbolic Instruction Code): A simple programming language widely used with microcomputers.

COBOL (Common Business-Oriented Language): An English-like, high-level programming language predominantly used in business applications, for which it is better suited than BASIC.

CRT (cathode ray tube): Used for the video display of information being communicated to or from a computer. Also called a *VDT (video display terminal), VDU (video display unit), monitor, screen,* or *tube.*

Data base: A large collection of related information stored inside the computer memory and indexed in such a way as to minimize the time and effort involved in access and retrieval. Typically it serves as a central information source to multiple users.

Download: To transmit information from a central computer to a smaller computer for localized processing.

Hardware: The physical components of computer systems, e.g., CPUs, printers, disk drives.

HRIS (human resource information system): Vendors of prepackaged personnel systems commonly refer to their products by this acronym. These kinds of systems are designed to meet the needs of all key areas of human resource management from affirmative action analysis to manpower planning. Can also refer to an internally developed personnel management information system.

Microprocessor: A basic arithmetic, logic, and control function contained on one integrated circuit chip.

Migration path: The ladder of potential increased computing power plateaus that can be achieved without acquiring completely new systems. Can be accomplished via add-on memory and peripherals.

Software: The programs that tell a computer exactly how processing is to proceed in sequential fashion. It includes both the operating system, user programs, and those acquired externally in packages.

Upload: Transferring data from a user's system to a remote computer system.

Source: Adapted from Gary Meyer, "What Every Personnel Manager Should Know About Computers," *Personnel Journal* 65 (August 1984): 60–61.

of top-of-the-line 16-to 20-MHz 80386 micro-processors combined with high-capacity fixed disk drives and the new OS/2 operating systems give microcomputers the power and flexibility of minicomputers. In effect, microcomputers have brought computing to the smallest department.

The term *management information systems (MIS)* is commonly used in reference to computers. It is a system for collecting, storing, retrieving, and synthesizing information that can be used in management decision making. MIS is a more encompassing function than HRIS.[10] A MIS starts with any information-related problem and works backward to get the relevant data to solve it. Many organizations have MIS departments that generate, process and distribute pertinent information throughout the company. The MIS department may also play an invaluable advisory role in selecting and implementing a human resource computer system.

During the 1970s, a new approach emerged for providing decision-making information to managers. Called *decision support systems (DSS),* the approach helps managers to solve unstructured decision problems.[11] For example, a human resource manager might ask: if a new flexible benefits program is added, how will it affect labor overhead and profits? Because so many variables in different combinations are involved in the calculation, the DSS staff would probably build a computer model that best fits the situation. The model would then be simulated on the computer, giving the human resource manager some idea how the company's bottom line might be affected.

Micros versus Mainframes

It is no exaggeration to say that for some companies micros are as much an office staple as the telephone. Ironically, while micros appear to be a major factor behind the increased interest in HRIS, most human resource computer applications still reside on mainframes. For example, recent surveys report that micros, despite their prevalence, are used less often than their bigger cousins—the mainframes.[12]

Computer mainframes are extensively used for payroll, various government regulatory requirements (e.g., ERISA, EEO-1), management of benefits and pensions, employee profiles, and historical analyses.[13] Micros, on the other hand, are only occasionally used for these activities.

In regard to ensuring security and privacy, there are limitations with both types of computers. Nevertheless, mainframes appear to have more overall security than micros. If records are stored on a mainframe, access is limited. Furthermore, conditions are more stable and consistent; for example, big computers are usually housed in their own dust- and smoke-free rooms, the temperature is controlled, and power surges are unlikely. By comparison, the diskettes used in a micro are subject to breakage, heat, and other hazards. Finally, one could never hear of someone walking off with a mainframe.

Perhaps the greatest threat to ensuring privacy with micros is the ease of accessing information on a diskette. If the micro and data files are on someone's desk, it is accessible to anyone who takes the time to use it. But this problem is diminishing thanks to new file protection software that controls access to files.

Without the microcomputer, however, the benefits of automating would be less obvious to many managers. Where computers were once the domain of the relatively few departments that had the budget to support them, the microcomputer has made computing affordable for literally every personnel department.

But perhaps the biggest breakthrough for human resource automation is the increased top-level management support for the personnel department to procure and maintain its own mainframe (or minicomputer) system. In one survey, 60 percent of the human resource departments reported that they receive strong top-level management support for acquiring a mainframe computer.[14] Greater support usually means higher status and more organizational clout.

For companies that depend on mainframes, the micro tends to be used on downloaded portions of a centralized data base. This was once a time-consuming and complicated process, but the technology and more sophisticated software are getting better.[15] Two questions remain: Given the popularity and availability of micros, is state-of-the-art technology sufficient to support a microcomputer-based HRIS? And can the HRIS feasibly and affordably reside on a micro?

Micro-based HRIS

Although micros offer a company more flexibility at less cost than mainframes, there are limitations. Specifically, the following technological barriers remain: (1) microcomputers' slow processing speed; (2) inadequate networking and remote communications over long distances; and (3) human resources software that is unsophisticated and unfriendly, with weak enhancement capability.[16]

In large companies, a great deal of personnel computer time is spent producing reports. Mainframes can rapidly process great amounts of data. The micro's processing speed is slow in comparison. For example, some mainframes can produce an alpha listing for a 5,000-employee organization in seconds. An IBM XT micro takes thirty minutes. Only recently has processing speed improved on a few micros. The same 5,000-employee alphabetized listing takes only four minutes with a Compaq 386. The difference is the 80386 microchip.[17] But technological breakthroughs are becoming commonplace in the computer chip industry. The human resource manager can expect to see new technologies that will make even the 80386 chip obsolete in just a few years.

But even processing speed won't help unless microcomputers have the ability to communicate and share data with one another, as well as update and inquire on a single common data base. By 1984 the first microcomputer networks had appeared. Although they were slow by today's standards and very hard to install, they became an overnight success. What makes the system possible is that each networked micro "thinks" it has its own hard disk; in reality all of the micros are linked to a single disk called a *file server*. While micros can accommodate local area networks, where several stations are electronically networked within the same building, technology has not developed to the point where it is cost effective to link permanently micros separated by great distances.[18]

The remaining question is whether micro-based software meets the demands placed on a HRIS. Unfortunately, at the present time, the answer is maybe.[19]

If HRIS needs are straightforward and simple, a micro-based system that can produce standard reports may suffice (see Table 17–2 for an illustration). If, on the other hand, there are occasional requests to prepare user-defined ad hoc reports, the flexibility may not be available. Management may ask for a complicated report, for example, they may request immediate information on turnover by job class for the entire organization. Once the report is delivered, personnel may never receive that particular request again.

TABLE 17–2
Action due report

JAN 07 1986			SALARY REVIEWS OVERDUE				
SCHEDULED SALARY REVIEW	LAST NAME	FIRST NAME	LAST SALARY CHANGE DATE	ANNUAL SALARY	LAST INCREASE PERCENT	LAST PERFORMANCE RATING	JOB TITLE
DEPARTMENT: Accounts Payable							
DEC 12 1986	Klinger	Debra	DEC 12 1985	117600.00	9.1	Outstanding	Controller
1 Base Records Printed : Accounts Payable							
DEPARTMENT: Billing							
NOV 17 1985	Summers	Kathleen	NOV 17 1984	20020.00			Billing Clerk
JAN 12 1986	Alexander	Jane	JAN 12 1985	23660.00	7.1	Outstanding	Billing Clerk
FEB 15 1986	Reardon	Virginia	FEB 12 1985	20800.00	6.7	Adequate	Billing Clerk
APR 05 1986	Hoffman	Gilbert	APR 05 1985	17680.00			Billing Clerk
MAY 14 1986	Carson	Mary Faith	DEC 14 1985	18070.00			Billing Clerk
5 Base Records Printed : Billing							
DEPARTMENT: Eastern Sales							
FEB 12 1986	Allen	Ruth	FEB 12 1985	30720.00	8.9	Commendable	Sales Representative
NOV 30 1986	Day	Thomas	JUL 07 1986	36000.00	42.9	Outstanding	Senior Sales Rep.
2 Base Records Printed : Eastern Sales							
DEPARTMENT: Executive							
DEC 13 1985	Simpson	Ana	DEC 13 1984	96000.00	45.5	Outstanding	Director Personnel
DEC 15 1986	Howard	Lillian	DEC 15 1985	18200.00	16.7	Outstanding	Executive Secretary
DEC 15 1986	Smith	Frank	DEC 01 1985	120000.00	25.0	Outstanding	President
DEC 30 1986	Johnson	Emily	DEC 15 1985	96000.00	60.0	Outstanding	V.P. of Marketing
4 Base Records Printed : Executive							
DEPARTMENT: Labor Relations							
FEB 05 1986	Todd	Benjamin	FEB 05 1985	34800.00			Personnel Analyst
DEC 15 1986	Dundee	Shirely	DEC 15 1985	51480.00	32.0	Outstanding	Personnel Assistant
2 Base Records Printed : Labor Relations							
DEPARTMENT: Maintenance							
DEC 12 1985	Houden	Harrison	DEC 12 1984	18200.00	4.5	Marginal	Electrician
MAR 30 1986	O'Connell	Brian	MAR 30 1983	35100.00	14.9	Outstanding	Maint. Supervisor
MAY 03 1986	Kish	Donna	DEC 03 1985	23400.00		Superior	Electrician
DEC 30 1986	Suarez	Joseph	DEC 30 1985	21008.00			Electrician
4 Base Records Printed : Maintenance							

Furthermore, most companies will not always want their data to be reported in the same format. While some software packages can be enhanced by a technologically sophisticated user, it is rare to have such a specialized person on the human resource staff. And if that person happens to quit, a real problem develops in finding someone who can decipher the enhancement.

The day is not far off when micro-based networking and software will be available and affordable. But until then, even in a mainframe-based HRIS company, chances are that there will be a micro next to the phone.

SELECTING AND IMPLEMENTING A SYSTEM

Converting the human resource department's manual system to a computerized system should not be left to chance. Careful and meticulous planning is required. Great care should be taken to make the system accessible and easy to learn. Unlike the data processing/MIS system, the new system will probably be used by more nontechnical workers than any other information system.

Technical assistance in selecting and implementing the system is mandatory. While assistance may come from outside consultants or from human resource technical staff, the group most logically sought is data processing/MIS. Occasionally encountered, however, is an adversarial relationship between the human resource and data processing staffs.

Managing Conflict and Politics

To paraphrase one human resource department head, "the management of a human resource information system is too important to leave in the hands of data systems professionals."[20] Statements such as this often reflect deep-seated mistrust of data processors. Misperceptions of data processors can be better understood when viewed in the context of intergroup relations.

Opposing groups commonly develop unrealistically positive perceptions of themselves and unrealistically negative perceptions of each other.[21] Data processors and human resource staffers are no different. Over the past few decades, data processors have grown in power, prestige, and number. This fact has led to their becoming, in some circles, the in-group. Such selective perception by the in-group of out-groups leads to ethnocentrism that, in turn, fosters a distorted reality that can appear as professionalism.[22]

In a few isolated instances, data processors have been guilty of "empire building," using their technical knowledge of the computer system's capabilities. Other departments, too, have done this. For example, purchasing people are frequently accused of building their own little materials management empires. Nevertheless, without data processors—systems analysts, programmers, and operations personnel—there would be no automated management information systems and no HRIS.

The automation of human resource operations has traditionally been accomplished in conjunction with data processors. This trend should continue for several reasons, but one in particular: the typical human resource department couldn't do it without them. The standard arrangement is for data processing/MIS to commit a systems analyst and one or more programmers to a designated project and charge back the cost of their time to the human resource department's budget.[23]

Clarifying Roles, Responsibilities, and Needs

The pivotal person for automating the human resource department is usually not a member of the human resource staff; rather, it is the "on-loan" systems analyst. That person must know how to frame questions in an effort to combine two different languages and two different perspectives, establish rapport with nontechnical personnel, and translate the client's needs into the unique language of program specifications.[24] Data processing professionals are making strong efforts to be more client oriented.

The systems analyst should not shoulder the burden of computerization entirely. He or she must be met at least halfway. The human resource manager is the ideal person to interface with data processing professionals. Who else better understands the big picture—the politics, department accountability, expectations, and paybacks? Who else better knows the computer needs and requirements of the department? Chances are, however, that each person will be looking for different rewards from the same project. For example, while the human resource manager is looking for a clear report that plainly answers a question, the computer professional is enjoying the beauty and efficiency of the new program itself.[25]

Over the long term, larger human resource departments should consider adding at least one skilled data processor to their staff. The advantages are learning how to work with the technical person, learning a little about what the data processor does (e.g., programming), and having a computer person who will adopt the interests and culture of the human resource department.

It should be clear that a lot of planning is needed before venturing into automation. Rather than approach it haphazardly, a systematic plan is recommended. One approach is described in Table 17–3. The many computer horror stories do not often point to technical failures as the cause, but rather to planning failures.

TABLE 17–3

Steps to human resource department computerization

1. The human resource department accepts responsibility to computerize and agrees to establish an automation plan.
2. Secure technical assistance from data processing/MIS department or retain an outside systems consultant.
3. Make specific staff assignments to develop a working knowledge about computers and potential applications for the department.
4. Conduct departmental needs analyses to identify and prioritize needs and problems that a computer system can remedy.
5. Make a first attempt to develop a computerization strategy (several attempts will be necessary); decide among (a) purchasing a system, (b) leasing from a service bureau, or (c) utilizing the in-house data processing/MIS department.
6. Submit a written proposal, including a budget, outlining a feasible master plan.
7. Wait for top management to approve the proposal or request additional information.
8. Define detailed system requirements, describing the user's end product requirements, reports, and specifications.
9. Select and implement the system; for example:
    a. If purchasing a computer:
        (1) Determine new work flow and perform job analyses.
        (2) Anticipate resistance and prepare a strategy to overcome it.
        (3) Rearrange facilities for housing and storing the computer, peripherals, and files.
        (4) Solicit detailed descriptions of systems, using the request for proposal (RFP) from vendors that addresses user and technical requirements.
        (5) Build in adequate time for testing every phase of the new system.
    Other system strategies might include:
    b. Contracting with a service bureau.
    c. Using the data processing/MIS department.
    d. Contracting with a systems consultant.
10. Document each application module (e.g., benefits management) so that others will understand its purpose, input, operating instructions, and outputs.

Evaluating Hardware and Software

It is rare for human resource departments to install computer systems completely on their own. The exception might be the purchase of a microcomputer. Occasionally members of the human resource staff will work with a consultant or data processing professional to identify suitable mainframe hardware and software. Since there are thousands of products available—software, hardware, and peripherals—the task is a formidable one and assistance is often necessary.

Despite all the marketing promoting various computer hardware, the experts believe that software deserves more attention and study.[26] The reason is that software defines what can be done with the computer. Processing speed and networking capability—hardware attributes—are important, but the differences among these products are too insignificant at this time.

Software dictates not only the outputs and service that can be obtained from a given computer, but also how much training and expertise will be required to master the system. It usually takes far more time to learn to use the software than it does to continue using the old manual system that it is designed to replace.

Software is often purchased (or leased) from vendors rather than produced in-house.[27] Although some larger companies may create programs to meet specific needs, such as computer-based instruction, purchasing is the most realistic solution, especially for small and medium-sized companies. Vendors now offer simple, user-friendly, single-system packages that support a broad range of human resource applications. For companies with limited resources and few (if any) in-house computer specialists, packaged software is the only choice.

Software vendors have been known to promise more than they deliver, so it is wise to go through a thorough selection process before making a final choice. Also, it is wise to remember that if the user's requirements are unfocused, the vendor may mirror this fuzziness with obscure claims. Precise answers from vendors can be expected only if precise questions are asked that clearly define the user's needs, the scope of the proposed system, and its functional and technical requirements.[28]

COMPUTER APPLICATIONS

Top management has long recognized the value of computers in solving financial, production, and accounting problems. It is only within the past few years, however, that it has begun to manage human resources as effectively as it manages these other functions. Considering that employees are almost always the largest corporate expense, the advantages of a computerized human resource department are enormous. Computer applications in human resource departments range from benefits management to administration and boundary-spanning uses (see Table 17–4).

Computer applications in the human resource department can be categorized into three areas—data management, data manipulation, and decision making.[29]

Data Management and Manipulation

The first category, data management, is the oldest and most frequently used application. It is a record-keeping function. Every large company is required by law to maintain employee files that contain information on date of employment, sex, race, work history, and salary level. Usually other types of employee infor-

TABLE 17–4
Computer applications in human resource departments

Benefits management
   Cost accounting and containment
   Actuarial analysis
   Benefits statements

Compensation
   Maintenance of an equitable pay plan
   Payroll administration
   Report and word processing capabilities

Employee and labor relations
   Rapid response capability at negotiation time
   Safety programs
   Cost monitoring
   Termination analysis
   Union membership reports
   Layoff/bumping lists

Recruitment
   Applicant reporting, retrieval, and communication
   Test administration
   Applicant tracking
   Job posting
   Specialized mailings

Affirmative action/equal employment opportunity reporting
   EEO-1 reports on compliance, monitoring, and use
   Affirmative action goals, timetables, and progress

Employee profiles
   Employee history
   Performance appraisals
   Bio-demographic analyses

Training and development
   Career pathing
   Tailoring, monitoring, and support of training programs
   Computer-based training

Administration and boundary-spanning uses
   Manpower planning and forecasting
   Ad hoc reporting using spreadsheet and data base analyses
   Human resource activity monitoring
   Skills inventory
   Absenteeism/turnover analyses
   Electronic mail
   Attitude survey analysis
   Tuition reimbursement analyses
   Graphics
   Telecommunications
   Expert systems to answer "what if" questions

mation are added, such as education, job skills, and benefits. Having employee data on computer files reduces the paperwork necessary to carry out day-to-day functions by speeding up the preparation and increasing the accuracy of management reports.

The availability of human resource software makes data manipulation of employee files a popular computer application. Depending on the sophistication of the software and the completeness of the employee data base, many different analyses may be performed. Reports on turnover ratios by position, department, or division, applicant tracking and flow, and salary survey analyses are only a few of the many types of reports that can be generated on even the most basic computer systems.

Decision-support Systems

Decision-making software is the newest application for computers in personnel. Discussed earlier, decision-support (DSS) programs help managers make better decisions. The various packages now available all have in common the ability to take masses of information and rearrange, compile, present and, to some degree, analyze it. A software package called PRIMUS, for example, is designed to assist decision making with regard to career and succession planning by helping the human resource user understand how effective recruiting has been, where to target retention and turnover efforts, whether affirmative action programs are effective, and so on.[30] Programs like PRIMUS offer good potential for improving human resource managers' effectiveness by removing irrelevant or unimportant details and allowing them to concentrate more fully on the most important matters at hand.

The real benefits of computer applications in human resource departments are still to be realized. If anything, the computer potential

in personnel is largely untapped. Hindsight, of course, is always perfect, but it seems clear now that the early promoters of the computer in personnel set their sights too low, focusing only on the record-keeping needs. The computer is capable of providing far more. One of the most promising applications is training.

Computer-based Training

Experts have estimated that two out of three U.S. employees are involved in some kind of formal training. Due to technological advances, such as robotics and office computers, workers need continuous and effective training. In order to meet this challenge, the persons responsible for the training function—often human resource managers—are seeking instructional methods that are more responsive and adaptive than traditional teacher instruction. Ironically, one promising technique can be found amid the new technologies that created the problem.[31]

Computer-based training (CBT) refers to the delivery of instruction through a computer terminal.[32] It can meet a variety of training needs; from robotics maintenance and customer relations to supervisory techniques. CBT is also useful for transferring skills that involve memorization of step-by-step procedures of formulas, such as those found in programming system languages. Even the strongholds of soft training—sales, management, and customer service—are beginning to incorporate extensive CBT applications.

Accessibility is a plus because CBT courses may be run on mainframe, mini-, or microcomputers, enabling trainees to receive instruction when and where they choose. Of course, its effectiveness and efficiency are partially determined by the number and location of terminals available to trainees (see the accompanying news story).

Custom Courses Test Employees' Skill Levels

In order to keep up in the fast-paced securities brokerage business, Charles Schwab offers its employees in-house computer-based training (CBT).

Because nearly 1,550 of Schwab's employees use desktop computer terminals nationwide in various branch offices, CBT has become a key ingredient.

The training department is responsible for teaching employees brokerage operations, new accounts processing, and cashiering procedures. It is capable of training many people in far-flung locations quickly and efficiently.

An employee must use a special identification code to access a course, complete and master it before he/she will be registered and activated for the next one.

But even before employees can begin specialized job training, they must complete two other in-house-authored prerequisite courses: Beta, which teaches the use of the in-house computer system, and Leads, which helps branch employees learn how to input information from prospective customers.

In Beta, students learn how to sign onto the computer and use basic computer functions and files. All employees who use the computer for their job are required to complete this five-hour training.

The second three-hour Leads course teaches employees not only how to set up new account information on the computer, but how to access the screen to provide account information to current customers.

As many as 50 Charles Schwab employees access on-line training through the remote network each day. A maximum of three people in any one office can be registered to take a course.

"We want training to be taken during office hours, and not on an employee's personal time," said one training specialist, "so we set a limit to make sure our smaller branch offices are not inadequately staffed during employee training."

But CBT is not without its critics. Promoted as a training cure-all, CBT can be a monotonous learning environment and a headache for training specialists—unless system authors entertain their students and occasionally subject their courses to a process of quality control. The training specialists at Charles Schwab, for example, must possess a sense of humor.

"I use a very conversational style," another CBT author said, "And, I think it is important to give students a glimpse of the person behind a course; not only does it make them more receptive, but this type of personalization seems to make authoring easier.''

Indeed, the key to making CBT effective depends on the author's ability to keep the student's interest. The author who provides feedback that is light but not frivolous, and who is a bit adventurous in trying new methods, is indispensable to building a worthwhile CBT system.

Source: Adapted from ''CBT Plays a Key Role in HRMS,'' *Software News* (January 1986): 46.

The advantages of CBT are worth noting.[33] Trainees who are geographically dispersed, even worldwide, can still receive CBT as long as they have access to a microcomputer. This creates a number of economic advantages, especially as travel costs, instructor costs, and other training costs continue to escalate. Because it is self-paced, CBT allows trainees to move as slowly (or quickly) as they wish, thus eliminating the need to tailor courses to the learning speed of the weakest students. Further, the quality of instruction is guaranteed to be the same from class to class.[34]

CBT is totally interactive, which means that the trainee must respond before the course continues. A trainee who fails a unit test may be ''branched'' to a remedial module. Usually the trainee must demonstrate mastery of a topic before advancing to the next unit.

Adults are slower learners than children, in part because of established beliefs, attitudes, values, and habits acquired over the years.[35] When the first steps to learning are relatively easy and nonthreatening, the adult learner will gain confidence. CBT permits the trainee to increase the learning at a gradual rate, rather than overwhelming the learner with complex details. ''Practice makes perfect'' is also appropriate when describing CBT.[36] Practice is a basic principle of learning. Numerous studies consistently demonstrate that when

people are encouraged to practice what they have learned as soon as they have learned it, their retention rate is higher.[37] CBT provides as many opportunities to practice as trainees need or want. But practice alone is meaningless. Following through on the Vince Lombardi philosophy that only perfect practice makes perfect, trainees need help in practicing perfectly—that is, they need accurate and timely feedback that lets them know when they have mastered the skill.[38] CBT offers an excellent way to teach through technology.

Although CBT users often develop their own courses, this is an expensive undertaking. It is not unusual to take 100 hours to develop 1 hour of CBT.[39] However, users are turning to vendors of off-the-shelf or generic software. There are new CBT products every year, ranging in price from less then $100 for simple courses to thousands of dollars for sophisticated CBT applications.[40]

Expert Systems

At the end of 1985, only a handful of businesses were using expert systems.[41] As the ''Personnel in the News'' story illustrates, expert systems have really exploded in popularity (see ''Putting Knowledge to Work''). They have become the most common commercially available form of artificial intelligence (AI).[42]

Putting Knowledge to Work

Although supercomputers are dazzling in their power and engineering virtuosity, hardware alone will only partly achieve the eventual goal of computer scientists: the creation of systems that can mimic the decision-making powers of human beings. This goal is called AI, for artificial intelligence, and it has eluded computer programmers for decades. Now, however, even as supercomputers open up new worlds of possibility, researchers are taking major strides toward making their machines both smarter and more versatile.

Their work has spawned a new phase of the great computer revolution that has been going on for the past 40 years or so. Whereas the early use of computers revolutionized information handling, late developments promise to better manage raw computer power and the increasing complexity of modern information technology. For the first time in history, these systems allow computers to deal with ambiguity and questions of judgment that are too subtle for conventional data processing, however powerful. After years of false starts and overblown promises, the new systems, called expert or knowledge-processing systems, have exploded onto the commercial scene in the U.S., Western Europe and Japan, which is also trying to develop AI technologies.

Source: Eugene Linden, "Putting Knowledge to Work," *Time* (March 28, 1988): 60. Copyright 1988 Time Inc. All rights reserved. Reprinted by permission from TIME.

An expert system incorporates the knowledge, skill, and reasoning that underline human expertise. Computer programs, using logic-based programming languages such as PROLOG (PROgramming in LOGic), model relationships, following the same rules of thumb that experts employ.

There are several promising human resource applications for expert systems. Although training is probably the most popular, others are waiting in the wings (see Table 17–5). In general, they can be used as job performance aids, intelligent assistants, and benefits advisors.

OPPORTUNITIES FOR HRIS CAREERS

An emerging field will usually offer many career opportunities. The HRIS field is no different. Over the past few years, recruiters have not looked for human resource professionals to program computers; instead, they have hired aspiring professionals with the ability and training to design and implement human resource applications—manually.

More recently, however, recruiters have begun looking for people who can use the computer, especially the microcomputer. But

TABLE 17–5
Emerging expert system applications

1. The retention of expert knowledge when skilled employees leave the company.
2. The reproduction of human expertise so that it can be used consistently throughout an organization.
3. Advising inexperienced employees.
4. The training of new or temporary employees.
5. Facilitating greater accomplishment from fewer employees.
6. Improving the reliability of decision making and problem solving.
7. Facilitating the use of less expensive employees.

Source: Valdis Krebs, ''Can Expert Systems Make HR Decisions?'' *Computers in Personnel* (Winter 1988): 4.
Auerbach Publishers, a division of Warren, Gorham & Lamont, Inc., New York.

rather than computer science skills, recruiters want people who, at the very least, have the capability to master the standard business software packages already available in most organizations. At the most, recruiters want employees who use the micro as an everyday human resource tool.

CONCLUSIONS AND APPLICATIONS

- Automation came late to the human resource department. And when it did, the system put in place resembled payroll more than personnel. Data base files reflected the needs and requirements of accounting and fixed reports. The high cost of computers discouraged all but the biggest companies from converting to automated systems. When conversion did occur, the emphasis was on automating accounting, finance, and production. Personnel was not a priority.

- During the 1970s, federal and state regulatory agencies required most companies to compile statistics and submit reports on work force composition and wage and hour payments. The benefits of automating personnel applications became more and more obvious to top management. Report preparation soon gave birth to the computer as a human resource management tool. It wasn't long before the personnel department became a major user of a company's computer system.

- The microcomputer's appearance, perhaps more than any other single event, shifted control of automation away from the data processing/MIS department. The micro's relatively low cost—compared to that of mainframes—and the availability of user-friendly software are largely responsible for this shift in computer residency. In addition, human resource staffs have become acquainted and comfortable with the computer and its possibilities.

- The computer is becoming an integral part of the personnel department. As a tool, it has moved beyond producing simple reports to helping human resource managers make complex decisions. Human resource information systems (HRISs) are making this possible. As a whole, HRIS creates more opportunities for the human resource profession to influence the company.

- The categories of computers are many and varied. Large companies prefer to run standard applications on a large mainframe computer, usually one with all the "bells and whistles." Such computers may cost millions, but they are state-of-the-art in terms of processing speed, and networking capabilities.

- At the other end of the spectrum are the micros. While they may not be the preferred tool for preparing large reports and doing complicated analyses, such as benefits management, they do serve a useful purpose. The advantages of a micro are flexibility and cost. Departments can balance budget priorities with data base needs on micros. Companies can also automate their data in half the time it would take to get a mainframe up and running.

- The choice between a micro and a mainframe depends on several factors, including staff size, number and location of users, security, enhancements and support needed, time and cost allowed for implementation, and obsolescence. While large firms still prefer the mainframe to house the HRIS, the micro is catching on in smaller companies.

- New computer applications are being discovered every day. Most of these applications fall into one of three categories: data management, data manipulation, and decision-support systems (DSSs). The first application concentrates on report preparation. The second category involves data base retrieval and analyses. The third approach is the newest and offers the most potential. It takes the computer to a new level as a management modeling tool by permitting the human resource department to answer "what if" questions.

- A decision support application that is most promising is computer-based training (CBT). It is a totally interactive system between the trainee and the computer. The trainee must demonstrate adequate progress during each step of the learning module; if this does not occur, the trainee will be branched to a remedial module. Human resource computer applications such as CBT depend on competent and creative software authors and programmers. Currently, the field of human resource automation is faced with a critical shortage of skilled technical people who can write DSS software. Consequently, the opportunities for making a career in HRIS are promising and should remain so in the years ahead.

CASE STUDY
Ward
Industries, Inc.

Ward Industries, Inc., wishes the computer had never been invented. One year ago, top management decided to scrap the traditional point method of job evaluation that had been in place for over twenty years. The old method divided jobs into specific factors determined to be critical to the organization.

Under the old method, a job evaluation committee, composed of employees from the affected areas, determined the value (i.e., salary) of new jobs and reevaluated existing jobs. However, as the company grew, new product lines were added that created new job families and occupations. The committees were not only losing control and making inconsistent decisions, they were incorrectly pricing the value of too many new job families.

There were other reasons for changing as well. Managers began complaining that the old job evaluation system was not meeting their needs. With (and without) permission, they began using their own systems. Prior to implementation of the new system, multiple and divergent systems were embedded throughout the company. One division, for example, was simply ranking and pricing jobs in terms of market supply (i.e., how hard it was to recruit).

Perhaps the most serious problem was the backlog of requests for job reclassifications (some requests were over four months old). Another often cited complaint was the bickering between human resource and division personnel. The perception among employees was that organizational politics predetermined the outcome.

About one year ago, the human resource department purchased an off-the-shelf computerized job analysis/evaluation system. It was believed to be the best way to lessen human error and minimize alleged charges of favoritism and politics. Indeed, the system offered a number of advantages, namely, objectivity, speed in evaluating jobs, consistency of application, and use of identical compensable factors company wide.

Top management and the human resource staff selected about seventy-five jobs that they believed were currently assigned to an appropriate salary grade. These benchmark jobs became the foundation of the computerized system. All incumbents in the benchmark jobs were asked to complete a structured job-analysis questionnaire that could be entered directly into the computer. Multiple regression analysis was used to analyze the data, identify those factors that correlated most closely with current salary grade midpoints, and weight the factors appropriately. The end result was similar to a computer-generated point factor plan.

Ward Industries purchased the packaged program because it was easy to implement and could be applied companywide. Employees simply had to complete a structured questionnaire, and the computer provided the answers. It seemed—and was—simple.

But somewhere along the line this simple system proved to create more problems than it solved. Specifically:

1. The system did not differentiate adequately between technical career steps. The differences between Engineer I and II, for example, were not readily distinguishable using either quantitative or qualitative data.
2. The system was too sensitive to job titles and organizational changes. Simply changing a job title, and nothing else, could boost an individual into a higher salary grade.
3. The system was insensitive to market changes; for example, the internal rankings produced by the computer for certain high-demand jobs in one year often did not correspond to market realities for the same job two years later.

At this time there are more complaints than ever. Each division is dead set against the computerized system. There are rumors that managers are circumventing the system with such tactics as fictitious job titles, irrelevant compensable factors, and compensable factors that don't exist.

Questions

1. Why did the good idea of computerizing the job evaluation system go wrong?
2. What are the advantages of computerizing the system? Disadvantages?
3. What steps should Ward Industries have taken to ensure successful implementation of its computerized job evaluation process?
4. Should Ward Industries change back to the old system? Explain.

EXPERIENTIAL EXERCISE
Micro-based HR Applications

Divide the class into small groups and have each group identify several local human resource/personnel departments in which a microcomputer is used. A member of the group should contact one or more departments and ask them for permission to visit and learn how the micro and its software are used as a management tool. The group should then arrange a visit to see demonstrations of human resource applications being performed on the micro.

Particular attention should be paid to identifying the types of applications—data management, data manipulation, and DSS. Also, does the department use packaged software, or does it create its own application software using spreadsheet analysis, data-based analysis, graphics, word processing, electronic mail, or data retrieval? Does the department link into a mainframe computer? If so, ask how they download data from the mainframe into the micro. Ask how they determined the process and the costs associated with acquiring a microcomputer and related software. Finally, has the introduction of the microcomputer into the human resource department saved the company money?

Each group should present to the class its observations and conclusions about the micro's current and potential role in a typical human resource department.

KEY TERMS AND CONCEPTS

Artificial intelligence (AI)
CBT
COBOL
Computers
CPU
Data base
Data management
Data manipulation
Data processor
DSS
Download
Expert systems
File server

Hardware
HRIS
Interactive
Mainframe
Microprocessor
Minicomputer
MIS
Peripheral
PROLOG
RFP
Software
Vendor

REVIEW QUESTIONS

1. How did the microcomputer change the course and growth of MIS?
2. What is the difference between human resource computer applications and the HRIS?
3. Why do most human resource computer applications still reside on mainframe systems?
4. What are the biggest disadvantages of a micro-based HRIS?
5. Why is it too important to leave human resource automation totally in the hands of data systems professionals?
6. When planning a HRIS, why is it more important to spend more time choosing software than hardware?

DISCUSSION QUESTIONS

1. Assume that new human resource systems cannot be justified. The benefits are essentially intangible; they can't be expressed in hard dollars. Start-up costs are overwhelming. Add to that the problem of payback; human resource systems cost a lot, and there's no payback at all. To make matters worse, because of top management's distance from the HRIS function, there is no commitment to costly human resource projects. Management has heard plenty about failures with expensive human resource systems, but not much about successes.
It is your assignment to dispute each of these statements.
2. The microcomputer brings a number of benefits to the human resource department; one of the most significant applications is the provision of high-quality training when it is needed. Discuss the different ways in which the micro might become responsive to training and development needs.
3. It would be difficult to design and implement a HRIS without the advice and technical know-how of a professional data processor. Discuss how the human resource manager might approach the data processing department with a request for HRIS assistance.
4. Discuss the pros and cons of security on mainframes and microcomputers.
5. One emerging trend resulting from the increased use of computers in human resources is the creation of new HRIS jobs. The human resource data administrator (HRDA) has been called the newest job in personnel. What might the job description of the HRDA contain, including skills, responsibilities, and educational qualifications?

ENDNOTES

1. Alfred J. Walker, ''Arriving Soon: The Paperless Personnel Office,'' *Personnel Journal* 61, (July 1980): 559.
2. Alfred J. Walker, ''A Brief History of the Computer in Personnel,'' *Personnel Journal* 61, (July 1980): 555.
3. Ed Bride, ''HRMS Moves to HRIS,'' *Software News* (January 1986): 47.
4. Alfred J. Walker, *HRIS Development: A Project Team Guide to Building an Effective Personnel Information System* (New York: Van Nostrand Reinhold, 1982), p. 16.

5. Ibid., p. 17.

6. Gary Meyer, "What Every Personnel Manager Should Know About Computers," *Personnel Journal* 65 (August 1984): 58.

7. Nicholas Beutell, "Computers and the Management of Human Resources," *Readings in Human Resource Management*, 3rd ed., ed. R. S. Schuler, S. A. Youngblood, and V. L. Huber (St. Paul, MN: West, 1988), p. 86.

8. Donald Spencer, *The Illustrated Computer Dictionary*, 3rd ed. (Columbus, OH: Merrill, 1986), p. 181.

9. Ibid., pp. 188–90.

10. R. McLeod, Jr., *Management Information Systems* (Chicago: Science Research Associates, 1983), pp. 16–17.

11. B. C. Romann, "Decision Support Systems: Strategic Management Tools for the Eighties," *Business Horizons* 28 (September–October 1985): 71.

12. In a survey published by the Association of Human Resource Systems Professionals, 83 percent of the respondents reported that their systems were mainframe based. PC-based systems were used by only 9 percent. This small percentage does not reflect the fact that many mainframe-based systems tie into PCs at individual work stations.

13. For more details about the survey, see Allen S. Lee, "Despite Microcomputer Proliferation, Mainframes Are Still Preferred," *Computers in Personnel* (Winter 1988): 45–50. Lee's survey combined mainframes and minicomputers in one category.

14. Ibid., p. 49.

15. Stephen G. Perry, "The PC-based HRIS," *Personnel Administrator* 33 (February 1988): 60–63.

16. Ibid., p. 61.

17. Ibid., p. 62.

18. Ibid., p. 63.

19. Ibid.

20. Joe Pasqualetto, "Computers: No More Us vs. Them," *Personnel Journal* 66 (December 1987): 61–67.

21. A number of studies examine this topic. See M. Sherif, "Superordinate Goals in the Reduction of Intergroup conflict," *The American Journal of Sociology* 53 (January 1958): 349–56; R. R. Blake, H. A. Shepard, and P. R. Mouton, *Managing Intergroup Conflict in Industry* (Ann Arbor, MI: Foundation for Research on Human Behavior 1964); and E. Schien, *Organizational Psychology*, 3rd ed. (Englewood Cliffs, NJ: Prentice-Hall, 1980).

22. For a complete discussion, see R. Levine and D. Campbell, *Ethnocentrism* (New York: John Wiley & Sons, 1972), and C. P. Alderfer, "Group and Intergroup Relations," In *Improving Life at Work*, ed. J. R. Hackman and J. L. Suttle (Santa Monica, CA: Goodyear Publishing, 1977).

23. Gary J. Meyer, *Automating Personnel Operations: The Human Resource Manager's Guide to Computerization* (Madison, CT: Bureau of Law and Business, 1984), pp. 109–10.

24. Ibid.

25. "How to Get Along with Your Data Processing Professionals," *Resource* (November 1987): 10.

26. Meyer, *Automating Personnel Operations*, pp. 78–79.

27. One study reported that approximately half of the software used in human resource applications was purchased. See Margaret Magnus and Mort Grossman, "Computers and the Personnel Department," *Personnel Journal* 64 (April 1985): 42–48.

28. Randy A. Velez, "The Hidden Dangers of Vendor Selection," *Computers in Personnel* (Winter 1987): 4–7.

29. "Computers in the Executive Suite," *Small Business Report* (November 1984): 74.

30. For a more complete listing of micro-based HRIS software, see Richard B. Frantzreb, "The Microcomputer-Based HRIS: A Directory," *Personnel Administrator* 31 (September 1986): 71–100.

31. Vandra L. Huber and Geri Gay, "Channeling New Technology to Improve Training," *Personnel Administrator* 30 (February 1985): 49.

32. Jeff N. Gee, "Training Program Haute Couture," *Personnel Administrator* 32 (May 1987): 69–72.

33. For a more thorough discussion on the pros and cons of CBT, we recommend: William C. Heck, "Computer-based Training—the Choice Is Yours," *Personnel Administrator* (February 1985): 39–46. Also see Stephen Schwade, "Is It Time to Consider Computer-based Training?," *Personnel Administrator* 30 (February 1985): 25–35.

34. Schwade, "Is It Time," pp. 31–32.

35. Ron Zemke and Susan Zemke, "30 Things We Know for Sure About Adult Learning," *Training/HRD Journal* 18 (June 1981): 45–52.

36. Schwade, "Is It Time," p. 31.

37. A complete review of learning theory is found in Craig Schneier, "Training and Development Programs: What Learning Theory and Research Have to Offer," *Personnel Journal* 53 (April 1974): 288–93.

38. Norbert F. Elbert and Richard Discenza, *Contemporary Supervision* (New York: Random House, 1985), pp. 325–49.

39. Heck, "Computer-based Training," p. 39.

40. The *ICP Software Directory*, Microcomputer Series (Autumn 1987), lists CBT courses, ranging from "Conducting Successful Meetings" at $99 to a course called SIMPLER for training course authors at $30,000.

41. Some writers draw a distinction between expert systems and knowledge systems. The more general term *knowledge systems* is applied to systems that employ the same underlying programming technologies as expert systems but are based on broader "composite" sources of knowledge. In our discussion, we use the term *expert* to include knowledge-based systems. See John P. Gallagher, *Knowledge Systems for Business: Integrating Expert Systems and MIS* (Englewood Cliffs, NJ: Prentice-Hall, 1988), p. 4.

42. Valdis Krebs, "Can Expert Systems Make HR Decisions?" *Computers in Personnel* (Winter 1988): 4–8.

Chapter Eighteen

Personnel Research and Problem Solving

Chapter Objectives

1. To recognize the importance of the personnel research function and to cite the individuals and institutions that conduct personnel research.
2. To cite the academic and practitioner journals in which personnel and human resource research is published.
3. To provide an overview of the major personnel research methods.
4. To describe in detail the employee survey process—by far the most common form of personnel research.
5. To recognize the importance of conducting—whenever possible—a cost-benefit analysis of personnel activities and to provide an example using employee absenteeism.
6. To cite some of the major personnel/human resource problems—absenteeism, turnover, job dissatisfaction, and perceptions of unfairness.

How Lufkin Industries "Stamped Out" Absenteeism

Lufkin Industries, Inc., a Texas manufacturing facility, produces oilfield machinery. From 1980 to 1985 the firm grew by over 300% to $215 million in sales. Unfortunately, absenteeism also grew to about 14%. The attendance policy allowed eight excused absences for the usual reasons. Unexcused absences were detailed on a form and entered into the employee's record. Penalties included a written warning after two unexcused absences, a five-day layoff after five absences, and termination after six absences. The punitive system was not working; 255 production days were lost due to unexcused absences in 1985.

Lufkin decided to change its approach to the problem by offering positive incentives for good attendance. Known as the Attendance Incentive Program (AIP), the new program appended the current policy. Each month employees without an unexcused absence were given a book of trading stamps. After the sixth month of perfect attendance employees received six books of stamps for months seven through twelve. However, with even one unexcused absence, they started over. A bonus of 25 books for a year of perfect attendance made it possible for each employee to earn as many as 67 books in a year.

Was it successful? At the end of the first year absenteeism dropped 25% or 191 days. The total cost of the program was $64,818; total savings, $804,864. While Lufkin may need to offer different rewards over the years, they believe positive reinforcement can work.

Source: Johnny Long and Joseph Ormsby, "Stamp Out Absenteeism," *Personnel Journal* 67 (November 1987): 94–97. Used by permission.

FOR many managers and administrators, people problems rank high among causes of frustration and stress. High levels of absenteeism and turnover, a steady stream of employee grievances, low morale, poor work attitudes, and resistance to change all serve to diminish employee productivity and push up operating costs. But the damage caused by extraordinary human problems often extends beyond the firm's current profit picture. An ineffectual and recalcitrant human resource group—together with the absence of sound personnel problem-solving techniques—may result in a gradual erosion of an organization's ability to remain competitive in a complex and uncertain business environment. In serious cases of personnel mismanagement, an organization's survival may well be at stake.

The ability to conduct personnel research and solve personnel problems is critically important to personnel administrators and managers. In contrast to years past, the personnel staff in many organizations is being called upon to play more of a role in the diagnosis of human problems and the creation of policies and programs to solve them. The creation, implementation, and evaluation of many of the personnel programs discussed in this book—such as job enrichment, management development, flextime, and career development—usually involve some form of personnel research. Because personnel management and personnel research are closely intertwined, the ability to perform research is rapidly becoming a basic requirement for personnel administrators in organizations of all kinds.

The first part of this chapter examines many aspects of personnel research: kinds of research, who does it, where the results of research are published, and commonly used research techniques. The second part of the chapter points out five troublesome problems that personnel managers commonly face: absenteeism, turnover, job dissatisfaction, perceptions of unfairness, and sexual harassment.

PERSONNEL RESEARCH

Personnel research is the collection and investigation of facts related to human resource problems in order to eliminate or reduce those problems. Through personnel research, managers and administrators are able to substitute facts about human behavior for armchair theorizing, hunches, guesswork, and gut reactions. In the end, research helps the administrator manage more productively. Personnel research is not a luxury of the personnel department or something that should be done only if the budget permits. Personnel research is a critical part of all ongoing human resource programs. Specific uses of personnel research include:[1]

- The measurement and evaluation of present conditions.

- The prediction of conditions, events, behavioral patterns.
- The evaluation of current policies, programs, and activities.
- The discovery of rational bases for revising current policies, programs, and activities.
- The appraisal of proposed policies, programs, and activities.

Types of Research

Most research can be classified as basic or applied. *Basic research,* sometimes referred to as *pure research,* is undertaken simply to advance knowledge in a particular field or to gather information about a given subject. It is knowledge for the sake of knowledge. The knowledge gained from pure research does not have an immediate application or particular use. Although most basic research takes place within the confines of the scientist's laboratory, a great deal of basic research is also performed in human resource management. Most basic research in the personnel area is conducted by faculty members of colleges and universities and by private, nonprofit institutions.

Applied research is conducted to solve a particular problem; its results may be put to immediate use. The majority of personnel research in business firms and government agencies is of this type. Perhaps the earliest example of systematic, comprehensive applied research is the famous Hawthorne studies, which took place at the Western Electric Company's Hawthorne Works during the late 1920s.[2] The Hawthorne studies involved thousands of employees and focused on employee productivity, morale and job satisfaction, group dynamics, and leadership styles. Modern applied personnel research is concerned not only with these areas but also with equal employment opportunity, job design, organization development, human resource planning, recruitment and selection, and labor-management relationships.

The Researchers

Personnel research is conducted by individuals and a variety of public and private organizations. One study in the 1960s showed that $25 to $55 million was spent on personnel research annually, with 39 percent of the research conducted by private research organizations, 34 percent by academic institutions, 22 percent by agencies of the federal government, and 5 percent by business firms.[3]

A study in the late 1970s by the Bureau of National Affairs, a private research organization, reported that only about half of the ninety-one organizations surveyed conducted personnel research, with the most commonly researched areas being effectiveness of training, recruiting sources, performance evaluation, and validation of employee selection systems.[4]

Federal Government Many federal government agencies conduct both basic and applied research. In the personnel field, agencies within the Department of Labor, primarily the Bureau of Labor Statistics (BLS), conduct and report research. The Department of Labor's *Monthly Labor Review* contains the results of studies of a wide range of human resource topics.

Private Research Organizations Many private organizations have been formed with the sole purpose of conducting pure and applied research in the personnel area. Some of these organizations include the National Industrial Conference Board (NICB), the Bureau of National Affairs (BNA), and the Brookings Institution.

Personnel Associations Large national and international personnel associations periodically conduct research concerned with the practices and activities of their members' organizations. Some of these associations include the International Personnel Management Association (IPMA), the American Society for Personnel Administration (ASPA), and the American Society for Training and Development (ASTD). The results of these studies are often reported in the association's journals, such as ASPA's *Personnel Administrator* and ASTD's *Training and Development Journal.*

Colleges and Universities Institutions of higher learning not only disseminate information but bear an important responsibility for discovering and analyzing information as well. The colleges and universities as a whole represent one of the greatest sources of basic and applied research in the personnel field. Many faculty members conduct research as a normal part of their employment responsibilities. In addition, many learning institutions, such as Ohio State University, the University of California, and the Carnegie Institute of Technology, also operate research centers to conduct both basic and applied research in conjunction with the business community. One of the best-known university research centers is the University of Michigan's Survey Research Center. That center's long standing work on employee job-satisfaction trends remains one of the most sophisticated studies of workers' attitudes to date.

Business Firms Many business firms conduct applied personnel research to solve a particular problem or evaluate a present or proposed program or project. Several larger firms, such as General Electric, International Business Machines (IBM), and AT&T, operate full-scale departments of behavioral research. Most firms do not have personnel research specialists but require personnel administrators to perform research as a normal part of their jobs. Common examples of ongoing research responsibilities of the personnel staff may include:

- Evaluating training and development programs.
- Conducting periodic wage and salary surveys.
- Predicting future human resource requirements.
- Conducting surveys of employee attitudes.
- Conducting studies of employee productivity.
- Validating selection and testing instruments.

Personnel administrators frequently receive requests from line managers to conduct special ad hoc studies of personnel problems. These studies are often requested because of some personnel problem the manager is facing. Special studies of this type are an important part of the personnel department's service responsibility. Examples of research requests from other departments may include:

- Investigation of extraordinarily high employee grievances in a particular manufacturing department.
- A program to reduce absenteeism among clerical personnel.
- Evaluation of changes in a labor–management agreement that may affect employee productivity.
- Development of a strategy to enable the employer to win a union certification election.
- Development of a special performance-appraisal method for sales personnel.

Although line managers may occasionally oversee a personnel research project themselves, it is normal for the personnel staff to create and implement the project. For any research study to be successful, the personnel administrator generally needs the cooperation and assistance of the line manager. Examples of the ways in which line managers can lend support include assisting with the design of the study, providing performance data, allowing employees to be interviewed or to complete survey forms, and reviewing research results. Personnel administrators can gain the support of line managers by explaining why research is necessary and showing how research results may help them perform their jobs more effectively.

Personnel Research Publications

The results of personnel research may be found in a wide variety of printed media. Reading all of the research literature in the field is impractical—and physically impossible—for any manager or administrator. But the prudent manager and staff member should keep up-to-date on major research results and use the findings to promote managerial effectiveness, employee productivity, and job satisfaction. A knowledge of important research is one way to keep abreast of the newly developed policies, programs, and techniques that show promise for making organizations function more efficiently.

Scores of bulletins, research reports, working papers, and monographs containing personnel research are regularly published by numerous public and private organizations. But perhaps the most practical and expedient way for a personnel administrator to keep on top of the research is by regularly reading a selected group of personnel journals and magazines. Table 18–1 contains a list of journals,

TABLE 18–1
Journals, indexes, and abstracts useful to a personnel administrator

Primarily for the Academician
Academy of Management Journal
Administrative Science Quarterly
Industrial and Labor Relations Review
Journal of Applied Behavioral Science
Journal of Applied Psychology
Personnel Psychology

Primarily for the Manager or Administrator
Academy of Management Executive
Advanced Management Journal
Business Horizons
California Management Review
Harvard Business Review
Human Resource Management
Labor Law Journal
Management Review
Monthly Labor Review
Organizational Dynamics
Personnel
Personnel Administrator
Personnel Journal
Public Personnel Management
Supervisory Management
Training

Useful Indexes andd Abstracts
Business Periodicals Index
Employee Relations Index
Management Abstracts
Personnel Management Abstracts
Psychological Abstracts

written primarily for managers and professionals focus on the application of research and are often written in a "how to" format.

RESEARCH TECHNIQUES

Many different research techniques exist, and the choice of a particular one depends on the purpose of the research and the type of problem under study. Familiarity with various research techniques is important for two reasons. First, practitioners encounter a variety of human problems in the work place, and the appropriate research technique must be applied to the particular problem in question. The selection of an inappropriate research technique may seriously affect the study's overall validity and usefulness. Second, a broad knowledge of research techniques is necessary in order to read and understand the studies reported by other employers and researchers. Managers must be able to evaluate the research of others, differentiate between good and poor research, and develop research-oriented skills in subordinates. The research techniques most often used to conduct studies in personnel include the survey, interview, historical study, and controlled experiment.

Surveys

The employee survey is the most widely used research technique among personnel administrators. The most common surveys include the wage survey and the job-satisfaction survey. The job-satisfaction survey is often referred to as an *attitude* or *morale survey*.

Job-satisfaction Survey Since the beginning of the human-relations movement some fifty years ago, managers have sought their employees' opinions and attitudes concerning a wide range of topics and issues. Because

indexes, and abstracts that frequently report research results in a variety of personnel areas. Journals written primarily for the academician are heavy on technical discussions of research techniques and normally report the results of a research undertaking. Journals

morale and job satisfaction have been important determinants of employee productivity, absenteeism, and turnover, managers have systematically collected and analyzed data concerning employee attitudes in order to make jobs more satisfying and ultimately more productive.[5]

Many factors contribute to employee job satisfaction. However, the following are the four elements that most surveyed employees reported they like best about their jobs:

- *The job itself:* Top among job satisfaction factors is the kind of work employees perform (especially when it is challenging or interesting) and the freedom that they have to determine how the work is done.
- *Co-worker relations:* The quality of relationships within the work group is very important to employees, especially the extent to which the individual is accepted as part of the work unit and the friendliness and support of his or her fellow employees.[6]
- *Good supervision:* Job satisfaction is considerably improved when supervisors are perceived to be fair, helpful, competent, and effective. This includes the supervisor's skill as a problem solver, coach, trainer, listener, and as the timely, authoritative source of key job-related information for employees.
- *Opportunity to grow:* Employees derive a great deal of job satisfaction from learning new things and from the chance to develop new skills. Advancement opportunity is also very important to them.

On the other hand, the most frequently reported factors that detract from job satisfaction are:[7]

- *Poor supervision:* Insensitive, incompetent, and uncaring supervisors seem to have the most negative effect on employee job

satisfaction. This includes unfair, biased treatment by supervisors, failure of supervisors to listen and respond to employees' problems or concerns, and problems with management communication credibility. The most frequent negative ratings occur among those survey issues that are directly affected by supervisory practices. These include failure of supervisors to recognize employees for good work performance; failure of supervisors to take appropriate action to correct nonperformance by employees; lack of fairness, uniformity, and consistency by supervisors in administering company policy; and the existence of favoritism.

- *Interpersonal conflicts:* Interpersonal conflicts, lack of teamwork, unfriendliness among co-workers, and unproductive rivalries among managers and supervisors are reported to have a major negative effect on employee job satisfaction.
- *Poor work environment:* Dirty, noisy, unsafe, and unhealthy work conditions, including heat and poor ventilation, also are leading detractors from job satisfaction.
- *Poor pay:* Possibly symptomatic of other problems, low, uncompetitive pay is nonetheless often reported as one of the things that detracted from overall job satisfaction.

One of the most widely used job satisfaction surveys is the *Job Descriptive Index (JDI)*. Sample questions on the JDI are shown in Figure 18–1.

Specific-use Questionnaire Aside from collecting data about job satisfaction, personnel researchers often find it useful to gather employees' opinions about specific job-related issues. For example, employees may be asked to evaluate the organization's training and development function, orientation program, or a

FIGURE 18–1

Sample questions from the JDI (Copyright, 1975, Bowling Green State University, Bowling Green, OH.)

Supervision

Think of the kind of supervision that you get on your job. How well does each of the following words describe this supervision? In the blank beside each word below, put:

    _y_   if it describes the supervision you get on your job

    _n_   if it does NOT describe it

    _?_   if you cannot decide

Supervision on Present Job

    Asks my advice   _____

    Hard to please   _____

    Influential   _____

    Quick tempered   _____

    Tells me where I stand   _____

    Stubborn   _____

Promotion

Think of the opportunities for promotion that you have now. How well does each of the following words describe these? In the blank beside each word, put:

    _y_   for "Yes" if it describes your opportunities for promotion

    _n_   for "No" if it does NOT describe them

    _?_   if you cannot decide

Opportunities for Promotion

Good opportunities for promotion   _____

Opportunity somewhat limited   _____

Promotion on ability   _____

Dead-end job   _____

Regular promotions   _____

Work

Think of your present work. What is it like most of the time? In the blank beside each word given below; write:

    _y_   for "Yes" if it describes your work

    _n_   for "No" if it does NOT describe it

    _?_   if you cannot decide

Work on Present Job

    _____ Fascinating

    _____ Boring

    _____ Respected

    _____ Challenging

    _____ Frustrating

proposed flextime or job-enrichment program. Because these questionnaires focus on an organization's particular problems or issues, they are generally custom-made by members of the personnel staff or an outside consultant.

A questionnaire concerned with employee absenteeism is shown in Figure 18–2.

Survey Administration The total process of planning, implementing, and analyzing em-

---

1. At present, to what extent is employee absenteeism a productivity problem in your work unit?

   Not a problem at all ————————————————————————————————————— A very significant problem
       1   2   3   4   5

2. As a supervisor, about how many hours per week do you feel you spend on problems related to absenteeism (talking with employees who call in to report an absence; calling absent employees; securing, training, and checking the work of replacement employees; counseling chronic absentees, etc.).

   0–1 hours ____   2–3 hours ____   4–5 hours ____   6–7 hours ____   8 or more hours ____

3. Overall, I am satisfied with the present absenteeism control system.

Strongly Agree	Agree	Neither Agree nor Disagree	Disagree	Strongly Disagree
1	2	3	4	5

4. The present system allows employees to be absent and tardy too often.

Strongly Agree	Agree	Neither Agree nor Disagree	Disagree	Strongly Disagree
1	2	3	4	5

5. The present system has no rewards for employees who come to work regularly.

Strongly Agree	Agree	Neither Agree nor Disagree	Disagree	Strongly Disagree
1	2	3	4	5

6. The present system is difficult for employees to understand.

Strongly Agree	Agree	Neither Agree nor Disagree	Disagree	Strongly Disagree
1	2	3	4	5

7. Supervisors in my work area interpret the present system differently.

Strongly Agree	Agree	Neither Agree nor Disagree	Disagree	Strongly Disagree
1	2	3	4	5

8. The present system allows supervisors to treat employees differently.

Strongly Agree	Agree	Neither Agree nor Disagree	Disagree	Strongly Disagree
1	2	3	4	5

9. The present system puts supervisors in a difficult position of having to decide when an absence is "acceptable" or "unacceptable."

Strongly Agree	Agree	Neither Agree nor Disagree	Disagree	Strongly Disagree
1	2	3	4	5

10. What do you consider to be the strong and weak points of the present absenteeism control system?

    _____

    _____

FIGURE 18–2

A questionnaire concerning absenteeism (Source: Frank E. Kuzmits, University of Louisville. With permission.)

ployee surveys and questionnaires includes a number of important elements. Regardless of the type of survey implemented, the following steps must be considered:[8]

Objectives   As an initial step, management must identify the objectives of the survey. Common objectives of surveys include the identification of communication problems, excessive turnover, concerns about pay and benefits, training and development needs, predict unionization efforts, and problems dealing with advancement opportunities and discipline.

Top-management Commitment   The support of top management is critical if the survey is to be of benefit to the organization. In particular, management must be willing to act upon the survey results and communicate the outcome of the survey to the employees.

Survey Development   Surveys may either be developed internally or prepared by an outside consulting firm. While management may be inclined to prepare the survey themselves, research indicates several advantages to outside development. The outside consultant brings proven competence, experience, and objectivity, and employees are apt to have more faith in the process when they see the company pay an outside firm to develop and administer the survey. Regardless of who develops the survey, the statements and questions must reflect the problems faced by the organization. In addition, the effectiveness of the survey will be enhanced by allowing the entire management and supervisory team to participate in drafting the survey.

Announcing the Survey   A few weeks before implementing the survey, a member of top management should send a letter to all employees explaining the purpose of the survey,

when it will be given, and when the results will be communicated. The letter should also stress that honesty in completing the survey is essential and that individual employee responses cannot be identified. Survey anonymity will enhance the validity of the employee responses.

Implementation   Some important considerations for administering the survey are as follows: (1) allow employees sufficient time to complete the survey, (2) administer the survey (if possible) to all employees at the same time, and (3) administer the survey on company premises (research shows that only about one-third of the employees who take a survey home will complete and return it).

Analysis   Survey results should reflect total organizational results in comparison to individual employee groups (e.g., older vs. younger, male vs. female, long length of service vs. short length of service, etc.; such groups are identified from the information requested on the cover letter attached to the survey). Based on the results, problem areas are identified, and recommendations to overcome these problems are developed. If an outside firm is not employed, the personnel department normally assumes the responsibility.

Feedback   Survey results should be communicated to the employees soon after they have been tabulated and reviewed by top management. Face-to-face meetings between supervisors and employees are usually most effective for providing survey feedback, and the use of overhead transparencies, slides, and illustrations enhances the effectiveness of the presentation. The supervisor making the presentation should encourage comments and suggestions, and should pass this information on to higher management (without identifying individual employees).

Follow-up Survey follow-up is important to ensure that good relations are maintained between employees and management and that action is undertaken and completed.

Exit Interviews

Organizations often conduct exit interviews with employees who have voluntarily decided to leave. These employees can provide valuable information about the work environment that might not be available through any other source. The employer is often able to pinpoint sources of unwanted turnover such as unfair treatment (e.g., sexual harassment), perceived low pay or benefits, or poor supervisors.

The success of the exit interview depends largely on the employees' belief that their responses will be held in strict confidence and will not affect the employer's response to future reference requests. Personnel interviewers generally agree that to obtain the employee's cooperation, the interviewer should be someone from the personnel department and definitely not the immediate supervisor. The questions are generally open-ended and may require probing follow-up questions to uncover the employee's sentiments. Critical to obtaining candid responses is the guarantee that no retaliatory action will be taken. This verbal guarantee can be enhanced by providing the employee with a written copy of the only authorized reference letter that will be given to future employers. The interview should be conducted before the last day of work, which is usually hectic, and in a relaxed area away from the employee's work site. The subject matter usually includes the reason for leaving, perceptions of the supervisor, salary, benefits, training, and opportunities for advancement. Questions about the content of the job may help uncover job design or scheduling problems. The employee may provide

more candid responses if the interviewer's interest in improving conditions for his or her co-workers is emphasized. Many employees have strong personal friendships with co-workers and are sincerely interested in helping correct any minor or major work environment problems.[9]

Historical Studies

Personnel researchers often find that tracking certain data over time helps them gain greater insight into human behavior. By isolating a small number of variables, a historical study analyzes patterns over weeks, months, or in some cases, years. For example, many organizations analyze absenteeism and turnover data to assess whether these problems are increasing, decreasing, or remaining unchanged. One example of a long-standing historical study is a project mentioned earlier—the University of Michigan's Survey Research Center Job Satisfaction Survey. Since 1958, the center has tracked a large sample of employee attitudes concerning overall satisfaction with work. The research indicates that most employees are satisfied with their jobs and that workers' attitudes have changed little since the study began.

Controlled Experiments

Compared to surveys and interviews, controlled experiments are seldom used in actual personnel practice. Unlike the scientist's laboratory or a professor's classroom, where variables are created and controlled with relative ease, the personnel researcher in an organization has no such control. Manipulating human or technological factors simply for the sake of experimentation is very difficult and often impractical. But there are some occasions when this technique is feasible and may help a research effort.[10] To illustrate the steps

Reach Out and Touch Someone—But Please, Not So Often

Most of us agree that Alexander Graham Bell's invention is one of the most significant technological marvels of all time. The telephone has done more to revolutionize the process of personal communication than any creation of man to date. Without the telephone, life would be frustrating at best, and unbearable for many—particularly for teenagers who live on the phone roughly from 7 to 10 P.M. and often beyond.

But the wireless wonder is not all good, even though Mr. Bell's intentions were no doubt nothing but benign. It seems that many employees abuse the phone, according to one estimate, to the point where personal use makes up as much as 40 percent of a company's phone bill. Personal use includes local and long-distance calls to friends, relatives, and recordings that feature jokes, messages (such as time and weather)—and even pornography. Indeed, an audit revealed that employee calls to a pornographic recording in New York were running about 10,000 calls a month—for a cost of about $25,000.

Such abuses have motivated many firms to install computerized call-accounting systems that record the time, length, source, and destination of a phone call. Naturally, the use of such systems is controversial because of the privacy issue, but employers feel they have a right to know how their phones are being used, primarily because telephones are company property.

Call tracking systems can reveal even the most [intimate] secrets of employees. The system of one firm showed a large number of long-distance calls from one executive to the home of another executive. It seems that the executive whose calls were being monitored was having an affair with the wife of the other executive. Needless to say, the executive was terminated.*

*C. Rucce, "Personal Use of Company Phones Is Target of Cost-Cutting Efforts," *The Wall Street Journal* (April 11, 1984): 31.

---

involved, a job enrichment pilot study in a large manufacturing plant will be used.

Define the Problem For example: poor productivity, excessive rejects.

Evaluate Alternatives and Select an Alternative For example: possible alternatives may be to

implement incentive pay system, introduce new technology, tighten up through closer supervision, and job enrichment. Select job enrichment.

State the Hypothesis For example: six months after the implementation of job enrichment, average employee productivity will have increased by 20 percent and the average rejects per employee will have decreased by 25 percent.

Select Experimental and Control Groups For example: implement job enrichment in one area; select a similar area to serve as a control group.

Measure Experimental and Control Groups Prior to the Experiment For example: Collect productivity and quality data for both groups before the experiment begins.

Conduct the Experiment For example: implement job enrichment (experimental group only).

Measure Experimental and Control Groups After the Experiment For example: collect productivity and quality data for six months after the implementation of job enrichment.

Analyze Data, Draw Conclusions, Report Results For example: compare before and after data, determine the impact of the program, report conclusions to top management.

Personnel Information System

High-quality research takes a good deal of planning and organizing by a competent researcher. The researcher must possess a thorough knowledge of the research process in order to select the appropriate research design and techniques. Working closely and cooperatively with line managers and staff administrators, the researcher communicates and discusses research results, their implications, and any changes or further research that is indicated.

Extremely important in carrying out high-quality personnel research is timely, accurate, and relevant personnel information. Without information, any form of decision making is impossible. Personnel administrators are often frustrated in their attempts to carry out meaningful research because they lack sound personnel data. A sophisticated study of absenteeism, for example, is impossible without relevant absenteeism data broken down by employee, supervisor, department and, perhaps, by other important categories such as age, sex, and job title. A comprehensive survey of training needs cannot be undertaken unless the researcher can gather accurate information about an employee's previous training and experience, current level of performance, and anticipated job changes. Accurate and complete information is important not only for undertaking research, but also for managers and administrators to make effective day-to-day decisions. Because of the importance of collecting meaningful information quickly and inexpensively, more and more personnel managers have developed and implemented a formal personnel information system. This information system is usually computer based and designed to store and retrieve personnel data for applications in record keeping, personnel decision making, and personnel research.[11]

Personnel managers and administrators have always had information systems to assist them in performing their jobs. Before the advent of electronic data processing, the personnel administrator's information system usually consisted of rows of filing cabinets packed with manila folders. This rather inelegant technology was satisfactory for storing data but totally inappropriate for meaningful personnel decision making and research, particularly in a large organization. In a firm with several thousand employees, the cost of manually collecting data from employees' folders could conceivably outweigh the potential benefits of using the data to solve a personnel problem or conduct personnel research.

Computer technology has enabled significant advances in the management of information in all areas. In personnel, computerized information systems enable administrators to store vast amounts of personnel data that may be easily and quickly retrieved. In addition to providing storage and retrieval, the computer may be programmed to carry out practically any form of mathematical operation quickly and with almost no chance for error. Reports and analyses that are too time-consuming and laborious with manual systems may be processed in a fraction of the time with a computer system. One example of how mechanical devices can aid in reducing one of management's most common and irritating problems—abuse of the office telephone—is described in the feature "Reach Out and Touch Someone—But Please, Not So Often."

Cost-Benefit Analysis

Human resource activities such as recruiting, selection, training, and labor relations are increasingly being measured and evaluated in economic terms. By attaching dollars-and-cents criteria to personnel programs and problems, personnel administrators are able to generate support and confidence from top management, who ultimately decide upon the size of the personnel budget and approve personnel programs and projects. By analyzing human resource activities and problems by cost, personnel administrators and researchers can not only evaluate proposed programs but also identify costly personnel problems that require immediate attention. Examples of activities that may be so analyzed include:[12]

Turnover Costs associated with turnover that may be estimated include separation costs, replacement costs, and training costs.

Absenteeism Costs associated with employee absenteeism include lost salaries (paid sick leave only), benefits payments, supervisors' time spent on absenteeism problems (wages and benefits), and incidental absenteeism costs (e.g., premium for temporary help, overtime premium, quality and productivity problems,

etc.). An example of how absenteeism costs may be estimated is shown in Figure 18–3.

Smoking Not surprisingly, cigarette smoking has been linked with a number of employee problems in several research efforts. Researchers are now going a step further and are attaching cost estimates to the problems associated with smoking. Performance problems for which cost estimates may be made include absenteeism, medical care, insurance, property damage and depreciation, on-the-job time lost (the informal breaks due to lighting and puffing), and involuntary smoking (the problems suffered by nonsmokers who work around smokers).

Employee Attitudes Dissatisfaction with the job may result in a number of performance problems. While the strength of the link between job attitudes and performance remains a hotly debated topic among behavioral scientists, there is a significant amount of research to suggest that improved job satisfaction will generally improve employee performance, probably in the areas of absenteeism, turnover, tardiness, and grievances. To estimate the costs of employee attitudes in a particular organization, researchers must first determine what dimensions of job performance are related to job satisfaction and then attach cost estimates to those dimensions (e.g., absenteeism).

Labor Contracts In many organizations, labor costs are by far the largest costs incurred. Thus, in a collective bargaining situation, it is important for management to know how a proposed labor contract will affect the company's financial condition. Many organizations have developed sophisticated techniques (often computerized) for analyzing the cost of a proposed labor contract. Costs may be estimated for average compensation for the bargaining unit, cost of increases in compensation over the term of the contract, overtime,

Item	Acme International	Your Organization
1. Total manhours lost to employee absenteeism for the period	78,336	_____
2. Weighted average wage/salary per hour per employee	$4.32	_____
3. Cost of employee benefits per hour per employee	$1.90	_____
4. Total compensation lost per hour per absent employee		
A. If absent workers are paid (wage/salary plus benefits)	$6.22	_____
B. If absent workers are not paid (benefits only)	_____	_____
5. Total compensation lost to absent employees (total man-hours lost × 4.A or 4.B, whichever applicable)	$487,250	_____
6. Total supervisory hours lost on employee absenteeism	3,840	_____
7. Average hourly supervisory wage, including benefits	$9.15	_____
8. Total supervisory salaries lost to managing problems of absenteeism (hours lost × average hourly supervisory wage—item 6 × item 7)	$35,136	_____
9. All other costs incidental to absenteeism not included in the above items	$38,500	_____
10. Total estimated cost of absenteeism—summation of items 5, 8, and 9	$560,887	_____
11. Total estimated cost of absenteeism per employee		

$$\frac{\text{(Total Estimated Costs)}}{\text{(Total Number of Employees)}} \quad \frac{\$560,886}{1200} = \underline{\quad\quad} =$$

$487.41
per employee

FIGURE 18–3

An example of how absenteeism can be estimated by an organization (Source: Frank E. Kuzmits, "How Much Is Absenteeism Costing *Your* Organization?" p. 31. Reprinted with permission from the June 1979 issue of the *Personnel Administrator*, copyright 1979, the American Society for Personnel Administration, 30 Park Drive, Berea, OH 44017.)

longevity pay, shift differential, vacations, holidays, hospitalization, clothing allowance, and pensions.[13]

PROBLEM SOLVING

People problems are some of the toughest and most burdensome problems managers face. One sometimes hears a manager claim, "If it weren't for people, my job would be a breeze." Of course, the mechanical side of organizational life can present problems, too. But with proper preventive maintenance procedures, a machine or assembly line will generally hold up its end of the job. In addition, a machine is highly predictable; it never gets sick, never is late for work, never leaves early, and when switched on will do the same thing time after time after time. Not only is a machine reliable, it works without complaints, gripes, grumbles, or squawks—legitimate or otherwise. The machine fares well under verbal abuse and can even withstand physical abuse—at least the sturdy ones. And a machine does all this without financial reward. Wages or benefits are not necessary to keep the machine hard at work; it would never dream of asking for a raise, merit increase, or cost-of-living adjustment. A little oil here and there, maybe fuel of some sort, and periodic doses of tender loving care by its operator are about all it ever wants or needs.

But people—with all their problems and promises—will always be the most important resource for any organization, regardless of how sophisticated and advanced technologies become. Good managers waste little time wishing for impossible utopias; instead they recognize the inevitability of human problems, create structures that minimize people problems, and deal with such problems when they occur.

One important responsibility of the personnel manager is to identify and resolve those human resource problems that claim the lion's share of management's time and effort. In many organizations, particularly large manufacturing firms and service organizations, a small number of hard-core personnel problems require the special attention of line management and personnel staff. Solving these problems often requires a researcher to learn more about the problem, followed by the implementation of one or more strategies to reduce or eliminate the factors causing the problem. The most pressing personnel problems include absenteeism, turnover, job dissatisfaction, perceived unfairness, and sexual harassment.

Absenteeism

The failure to show up for work creates problems of widely varying degrees for managers and administrators. The Monday morning absence of a personnel secretary or administrative assistant may not present significant hardships for the boss, because the employee's work can often be put off until he or she returns to work. But when 10 to 15 percent of the midnight-to-seven shift of a large manufacturer stays away from work on Friday night, havoc may result. Gaps in the assembly line may force supervisors to transfer employees from noncritical areas to jobs where a worker must be present before the line can begin to move. Replacement employees must be quickly trained to perform unfamiliar jobs; and even if the task is routine and easy to learn, their unfamiliarity with the job often creates quality and productivity problems. The supervisor must check the work of replacement employees closely, and this takes time that should be spent on other supervisory duties. In short, excessive employee absenteeism can significantly drain productivity and profits, creating innumerable problems for supervisors and the employees who work regularly.

Nationwide, the cost of absenteeism in the United States is more than $30 billion annually. Managers consider absenteeism their most serious discipline problem.[14] Absenteeism is not unique to any industry or geographic area. It continues to be a major problem for every organization.[15] The cost of absenteeism to the organization depends on the size of the work force. In large manufacturing firms employing several thousand workers, the annual cost of employee absenteeism could easily amount to a six-digit figure. Decision makers should periodically compute the cost of absenteeism to their organizations. Figure 18–3 illustrates a procedure for making these computations. The resulting data will indicate the severity of the problem and the impact of absenteeism upon profits; a historical study will indicate whether the total absence-related costs are increasing or decreasing.[16]

Causes of Absenteeism Although absenteeism is one of today's most complex employee problems, it is possible to isolate the variables that influence employee decisions to attend work. A model illustrating the interaction of these variables is shown in Figure 18–4. As the model suggests, personal characteristics affect both the employee's motivation and the ability to attend. Put another way, absenteeism results when an employee cannot work (ill, missed the bus, sick child to care for) or does not want to work (job too boring, job too stressful, dislikes co-workers or supervisor, receives no rewards for attendance). These two variables often interact. For example, an employee may not feel good on a Monday morning following a long, boisterous week-end. An employee may be tired but physically able to go to work. Yet because the job is boring, the boss is hostile, the co-workers are unfriendly, or the union contract includes a liberal provision regarding sick leave, the employee may decide to call in sick. Be-

cause each employee faces a unique personal and work situation, no two employees will be absent for the same reasons. Largely for this reason, employee absenteeism represents one of the organization's toughest personnel problems.

Measuring Absenteeism Administrators will generally find it useful to compute and analyze these absenteeism measures:

Total Time Lost Total time lost, one of the most popular measures, is used by the BNA to study absenteeism in firms throughout the nation. The computation gives a percentage of total scheduled worktime that is lost to absenteeism. The formula for the measure is:

$$\text{Total Time Lost} = \frac{\text{Days Lost to Absenteeism for a Period}}{\text{Average Number of Employees} \times \text{Total Days in Period}} \times 100$$

FIGURE 18–4
Variables in employee absenteeism (Source: R. M. Steers and S. R. Rhodes, "Major Influences on Employee Attendance: A Process Model," *Journal of Applied Psychology*, 1978, 63, 393. Copyright 1978 by the American Psychological Association. Reprinted by permission.)

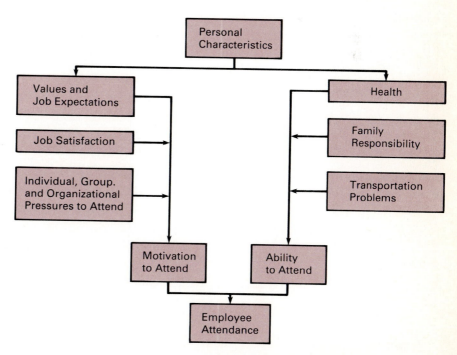

Figure 18–5 illustrates BNA absenteeism survey results for one year.

Absence Occurrences An absence occurrence is an absence of any length. For example, an employee absent on Monday collects one absence occurrence. An employee absent Monday, Tuesday, and Wednesday also collects one absence occurrence. A manager must decide which employee would create more problems at work: an employee who is absent twenty times a year for a total of twenty days or an employee who is absent once for twenty days straight. Employees who collect numerous one-day absence occurrences generally present a much greater problem than the employee who may have one or two short-term illnesses. Measuring absence occurrences is valuable in identifying the chronic absentee, who creates real headaches for the first-line supervisor.

Tardiness Tardiness is a form of absenteeism that can create work problems, particularly in manufacturing environments where machines and assembly lines are scheduled to start at a specific time. Excessive tardiness disrupts normal working operations, making it difficult for first-level supervisors to synchronize the beginning of a shift operation.

Researching Absenteeism Historical studies are often useful in identifying absence problems. For example, a one-year study of absences may be analyzed by employee, work group, shift, department, and plant to determine which individuals and groups may be major contributors to the problem. In areas of high absence, the results of attitude surveys and exit interviews should be analyzed to locate sources of dissatisfaction that may be partially responsible for the problem. Costs should be computed for high absenteeism

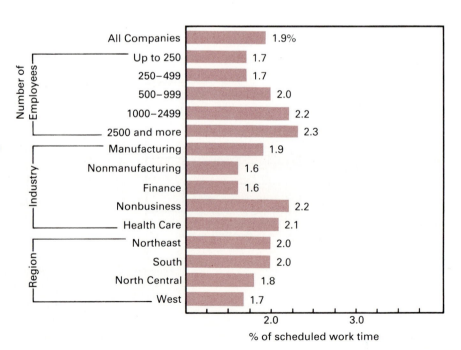

FIGURE 18–5

Data collected by the BNA on absenteeism for firms. The study included 274 employers. (Source: Reprinted by special permission from *BNA's Quarterly Report on Job Absence and Turnover* [Washington, DC: Bureau of National Affairs, Inc.]: 1985).

areas, and interorganizational comparisons of absence data made by examining BNA survey data. An audit can assess the overall effectiveness of a firm's absenteeism control system.[17] The audit procedures would involve examining the variables that affect employees' decisions to attend work, including absenteeism policies and goals, discipline and rewards, employee alcoholism, employee selection practices, and supervisory practices. The personnel information system would be quite helpful in such cases.

Reducing Absenteeism Because decisions to attend work result from a mix of variables, no single approach will solve the problem. Control of absenteeism in large, complex organizations will normally involve multiple strategies that address both the motivation and ability of the employee to attend work. Specific strategies for enhancing motivation include a proper match between employee and job, job enrichment, rewards for good attendance, people-oriented supervision, and clear attendance standards.[18] Strategies for enhancing the ability to attend work include creating a safe and healthy work environment, providing day-care facilities at the work place, creating programs to assist troubled employees, providing programs for reducing job stress, and providing recreational and exercise facilities.

A research study involving 987 organizations examined a number of methods for controlling absenteeism and management's perception of their effectiveness.[19] Table 18–2 illustrates the ten methods that received the highest ratings from users. The table also shows the percentage of respondents who use each method.

The problem of absenteeism still remains significant for many employers who use an absence control method. Reasons for the continuance of the problem despite an absence control method include (1) no written absenteeism policy despite a disciplinary method,

TABLE 18–2

Ten methods rated best in controlling absenteeism. The rating for each method is an average of ratings by all firms using that method.

Control Method	Effectiveness (on a scale of 4.0)	Percent of Firms Using
A consistently applied attendance policy	3.47	79%
Termination based on excessive absenteeism	3.47	96%
Progressive discipline for excessive absenteeism	3.43	91%
Identification and discipline of employees abusing attendance policies	3.39	88%
At least monthly analysis of daily attendance information	3.38	57%
Daily attendance records maintained by personnel department	3.36	48%
Employee call-in to give notice of absence	3.35	99%
A clearly-written attendance policy	3.33	76%
Daily attendance records maintained by supervisors	3.31	68%
Allow employees to build a paid "absence bank" to be cashed in at a percentage at a later date, or added to next year's vacation time	3.28	10%

Source: Adapted from D. Scott and S. Markhaus, "Absenteeism Control Methods: A Survey of Practices and Results," *Personnel Administrator* (June 1982): 76.

(2) inconsistent enforcement by supervisors, and (3) lack of absence documentation or grievance cases that lead to arbitration losses. Effective employer discipline for absenteeism should include:[20]

- A written policy statement.
- Distinguishing between absenteeism and other examples of employee misconduct as a reason for discipline.
- Using progressive discipline on the absence record, separate from other misconduct issues.
- Explicit absenteeism standards and a definition of excessive absenteeism.
- Allowing employees to improve their records through good attendance.
- Consistent application of the policy. Lax enforcement by supervisors should result in their discipline.

A relatively recent innovation in the control of absenteeism involves a concept known as *no-fault absenteeism*.[21] Under this approach, there is no distinction between excused and unexcused absenteeism, nor is there a provision for paid sick leave. The no-fault policy incorporates a point system for various forms of absenteeism and defines the types of absenteeism that are nonchargeable (i.e., without penalty). An example of a no-fault policy is shown in Figure 18–6. By adopting a no-fault policy, a cabinet manufacturer reduced absenteeism by 13 percent, and absenteeism-related grievances fell from an average of fifteen per year to four during the first year with no-fault.[22]

Turnover

As noted in a previous chapter, most personnel movement takes place through employee promotions, demotions, and transfers. Another form of employee movement involves turnover: the movement of employees out of the organization. Turnover results from resignations, transfers out of organizational units, discharges, retirement, and death.

A certain amount of turnover is expected, unavoidable, and considered beneficial to the organization. New employees may inject fresh blood into the firm by introducing new ideas and methods and innovative, more effective ways of doing things. In addition, turnover may help rectify poor hiring and placement decisions. Thus, some turnover renews a stagnating organization. But excessive turnover creates an unstable work force and increases personnel costs and organizational ineffectiveness. Examples include:

- Increased recruitment, selection, and placement costs.
- Increased training and development costs, including more on-the-job orientation and coaching required by supervisors.
- Lower productivity and more accidents, scrappage, and quality problems as new employees learn their jobs.
- Disruption in programs and projects as managers and administrators leave in excessive numbers.

The cost of turnover to American industry is estimated to be several billion dollars a year. Total annual costs for an individual firm will vary according to the size of the firm and the kinds of employees leaving. Because upper-level managers and administrators require a great deal more training and development time and are much more difficult to replace, significant turnover among these employees will be quite costly to the firm.

Over 1,500 scholarly studies of turnover have appeared in this century. The effect that a change in top management can have on an organization has been of great interest to managers. What is the effect? The results are mixed. For small firms, changes in top man-

FIGURE 18–6

A policy of no-fault absenteeism

As a result of excessive absenteeism and/or tardies, disciplinary action may be required and will be based on frequency of occurrences in accordance with the following:

Absenteeism is defined as being absent from work on any scheduled work day, even though the employee has reported off.

Each period of consecutive absence will be recorded as "one occurrence" regardless of the number of days duration.

Tardiness will be considered reporting to work within ten (10) minutes of the scheduled starting time. One occasion of tardiness will be charged as one quarter (1/4) occurrence of absenteeism.

Employees who report to work late, as provided for in the reporting regulations, or who leave before the end of the shift (with management's permission) will be charged with one-half (1/2) of an absence occurrence for either of these occurrences.

Employees who are absent without call-in will be charged with two occurrences of absence for that occasion.

Absence due to Funeral Leave, Military Obligation, Jury Duty, or Union Business, (each as defined by the Contract), and further including hospital confinement and work incurred injury will not be recorded as an occurrence of absence for purposes of disciplinary action.

For each calendar month of perfect attendance, an employee with an absentee record, will have one occurrence deducted from his absentee record.

Absence records will be maintained for a consecutive twelve month period, starting with the employee's first occurrence of absence. All absence records and warning slips which are one year old, or older, shall not be considered for purposes of disciplinary action under this policy.

Corrective discipline will be administered according to the following:

Three occurrences or "points," within a twelve month period—verbal warning

Five occurrences, or "points," within a twelve month period—written warning

Seven occurrences, or "points," within a twelve month period—second written warning

Twelve occurrences, or "points," within a twelve month period—discharge

The above policy is in addition to action which may be taken: when cumulative time lost from work for any reason substantially reduces the employee's services to the company; or as may be related to provisions of the contract.

agement can substantially threaten profits. By contrast, a study of changes in the top management of 167 large corporations over twenty years found little effect on sales, earnings, or profit margins. The same lack of effect was found in a study of twenty-two National Basketball Association (NBA) teams. However, changes in NBA coaches were found to have a significant effect on subsequent team performance. A similar study of the influence of city mayors found that a change of mayors did not affect budget expenditures or income. Finally, the death of known key executives, when a sudden and unanticipated event, does tend to cause a negative reaction in the securities market.[23]

Causes of Turnover The causes of turnover are a complex mix of factors both internal and external to the organization. Figure 18–7 shows the various factors that have been determined to affect the turnover rate. General economic conditions have an important bearing on the overall availability of jobs. Thus, turnover closely follows economic swings; turnover is generally high during periods of growth or prosperity (when jobs are plentiful) and low during recessions and low points in the business cycle. Another factor that affects turnover is the local labor market, which is determined by both the local economic conditions and the supply-demand ratio for specific kinds of occupations and

professions in that labor market. Thus, the outlook for a particular field could be good or poor regardless of general economic conditions. Personal mobility, or the extent to which one is bound to a particular area because of family or other social ties, is also a factor in deciding whether to leave a particular job. Employees who perceive a low degree of job security in their present jobs may be motivated to seek employment in organizations where they believe a greater degree of security exists. This perception is influenced to some extent by the involuntary transfers and terminations that occur. Finally, several demographic factors have been linked to the high turnover. Employees with a propensity to quit are young employees with little seniority who are dissatisfied with their jobs. A large percentage of voluntary turnover occurs in the first few months of employment. Employees with relatively large families and important family responsibilities tend to remain on the job.[24]

Job performance is also related to turnover. Studies of over 7,000 employees found that turnover was significantly lower among good performers than among poor ones. Why? There are two possible reasons: (1) receiving a low or below-average performance rating is a stressful event for most employees, causing them to seek other employment; (2) employees with high performance levels are generally more satisfied with their job, receive

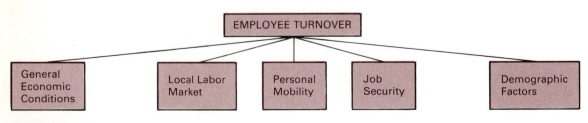

FIGURE 18–7
Factors that affect turnover

greater organizational rewards, and thus are less likely to leave. In general, performance and turnover are negatively related.[25]

Measuring Turnover Like absenteeism, turnover may be viewed as a multifaceted form of employee behavior. Each form of turnover can be computed for a given period of time. Formulas for three measures of turnover are:

$$\begin{array}{l} \text{Total} \\ \text{Separation} \\ \text{Rate} \end{array} = \frac{\text{Separations}}{\begin{array}{c}\text{Average Number}\\ \text{of Employees}\end{array}} \times 100$$

$$\begin{array}{l} \text{Resignation} \\ \text{Rate} \end{array} = \frac{\text{Resignations}}{\begin{array}{c}\text{Average Number}\\ \text{of Employees}\end{array}} \times 100$$

$$\begin{array}{l} \text{Avoidable} \\ \text{Turnover} \\ \text{Rate} \end{array} = \frac{\begin{array}{cc}\text{Total} & \text{Unavoidable}\\ \text{Separations} - \text{Separations}\end{array}}{\begin{array}{c}\text{Average Number}\\ \text{of Employees}\end{array}} \times 100$$

While all three formulas may provide important data for decision makers, most organizations measure the total separation rate when computing their own turnover statistics. Recommended by the U.S. Department of Labor, the total separation rate is used by most companies that take part in BNA surveys.[26] When making comparisons across firms, it is important that the same formula be used throughout to avoid mixing apples and oranges. BNA turnover data for firms are shown in Figure 18–8.

Researching Turnover Like absenteeism, turnover may stem from a variety of causes. Therefore, it is generally prudent to research the problem by using a variety of research methods. When researching turnover, management is usually concerned only with learning more about voluntary turnover—the reasons why good employees quit. Those who retire or are terminated for unsatisfactory per-

FIGURE 18–8

BNA turnover data for firms (Source: Reprinted by special permission from *BNA's Quarterly Report on Job Absence and Turnover* [Washington, DC: Bureau of National Affairs, Inc.]: 1985)

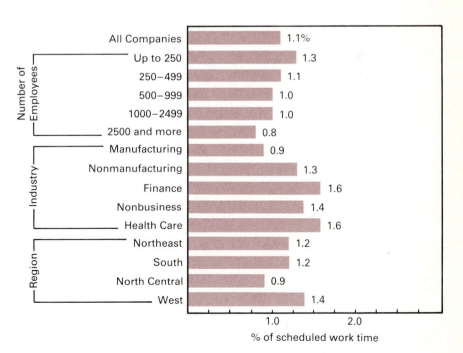

% of scheduled work time

All Companies	1.1%	
Number of Employees		
Up to 250	1.3	
250–499	1.1	
500–999	1.0	
1000–2499	1.0	
2500 and more	0.8	
Industry		
Manufacturing	0.9	
Nonmanufacturing	1.3	
Finance	1.6	
Nonbusiness	1.4	
Health Care	1.6	
Region		
Northeast	1.2	
South	1.2	
North Central	0.9	
West	1.4	

formance are generally not the focus of research.

Because job dissatisfaction is a significant cause of turnover, researchers often pinpoint specific areas of work that are causing high levels of dissatisfaction. Attitude surveys and interviews can be most useful for this purpose. Exit interviews are particularly valuable in discovering the causes of turnover. In fact, one of the prime reasons for conducting the exit interview is to determine why the employee is quitting.

One interesting way to research turnover is to determine why people stay. In studying this question, researchers have found that a variety of work and nonwork factors keep employees from leaving. Financial rewards have been found to be important, as were geographical location, social ties, and the local school system. Researchers have developed four profiles to describe most employees.[27]

Turnovers Highly dissatisfied at work, free of external pressures to stay, and will quit at the first chance.

Turn-offs Dislike the job but stay because of pay, benefits, or some other extrinsic job reward.

Turn-ons Highly satisfied and motivated at work, but may leave if external pressure becomes significant.

Turn-ons Plus Highly motivated at work and satisfied with the local environment; likely to remain and continue to be productive.

Reducing Turnover An organization's success in reducing turnover is closely tied to its success in identifying the real reasons why employees choose to leave or stay. Assuming that researchers have collected valid data on the causes of turnover, the next task is to implement policies, procedures, or programs to correct the deficiencies that exist. A program to control turnover that works for one company may not work for another, because the underlying causes may vary significantly from firm to firm. Companies that report success in reducing turnover usually begin by researching the causes of the problem. Programs, policies, and changes that have reduced turnover include:[28]

- Programs designed to enhance job satisfaction may reduce turnover because of the link between job dissatisfaction and turnover. Such programs include fair and equitable wage and salary structures, competitive benefits packages, training, opportunities for advancement, and employee grievance procedures.
- Selection procedures that place the right person in the right job.
- Proper orientation procedures.
- Close contact between the supervisor and the new employee, so that the supervisor may iron out early job problems and support the employee.
- Supervisory training and open lines of communication between the supervisor and the employee.
- Explaining benefits to employees and showing how their total wage and benefits package compares favorably to that of other firms in the area.
- Exit interviews and employee surveys to identify areas of discontent.

Job Dissatisfaction

When some or even a few employees become dissatisfied, costly problems can result. Excessive absenteeism, turnover, and grievances often result when workers experience high levels of job dissatisfaction. While it is difficult to put a monetary value on job dissatisfaction, estimates can be made of the economic cost of the results of job dissatisfaction, such as absenteeism, turnover, and employee grievances. As part of their social responsibility, many managers strive to create rewarding and satisfying work environments for their employees. Therefore, managers have many reasons to recognize the significance of job satisfaction and understand the potential results of both satisfying and dissatisfying work environments.

Causes of Job Dissatisfaction An employee's satisfaction is the "difference between the amount of some valued outcome a person receives and the amount of that outcome" the person thinks he or she should receive.[29] Thus, an employee becomes dissatisfied when things are not the way they should be. Job satisfaction or dissatisfaction generally depends on pay and benefits, supervision, co-workers, work, and the organization in general.

Measuring Job Satisfaction Survey techniques are by far the most common and valid method of collecting data on job satisfaction. Some managers may attempt to get an insight into their employees' job satisfaction or dissatisfaction through observation or informal discussions. While these methods are, no doubt, informative, such perceptions cannot be used to compare job satisfaction among work units, departments, or organizations. Further, not many employees can openly and honestly discuss sensitive issues with immediate bosses, particularly if the employee feels that the boss is part of the problem.

Nonattitudinal organizational data, such as on absenteeism and turnover, are sometimes used as surrogate measures of job satisfaction. But measuring job satisfaction through such indirect means has two pronounced shortcomings. First, job dissatisfaction may not be the sole cause of an employ-

ee's decision to be absent or to quit. For example, a child's illness, transportation problems, marital discord, drug addiction, or alcoholism may influence an employee's absence. Second, measuring job dissatisfaction by analyzing results provides no information about causes. One of the greatest benefits of a well-constructed survey on job satisfaction is that it will cover all significant job dimensions that affect job satisfaction. A valid and reliable paper-and-pencil survey is usually the least costly and most valid way to measure employees' satisfaction with their jobs and the conditions that surround their work.

Reducing Job Dissatisfaction Survey results only identify the type and degree of job dissatisfaction. The most difficult challenge for management is to implement the policies and programs that will transform dissatisfying work experiences into satisfying ones. Ways to improve satisfaction include:[30]

- Increase pay and benefits to make them more competitive with those of other organizations.
- Institute incentive pay programs.
- Enrich the jobs by giving employees more decision-making and control over the work, teamwork through small work groups, and greater variety of tasks.
- Train and develop employees to increase their skills and abilities.
- Improve working conditions (e.g., temperature, lighting, safety).
- Train and develop supervisors to clarify job responsibilities, let employees know where they stand, supervise fairly and justly, help people with work problems, solicit workers' opinions on decisions that affect their work, and support workers before upper management.
- Increase teamwork and cooperation by clarifying group goals, decreasing work-

group size to increase group cohesiveness, and involving groups in decision making for important decisions.

- Create group incentive pay and bonus systems.
- Enforce policies and standards for all group members fairly.
- Create greater opportunities for advancement, and base promotions on performance.
- Aggressively pursue affirmative action goals.
- Promote from within.
- Maintain open lines of communication throughout the organization.

Perceptions of Fairness

Most employees expect to be treated fairly and justly in all aspects of their work. Those who think the organization has treated them unfairly may react in one of many ways. Senior employees will often decide that they have invested too many years to risk creating a disturbance. Instead, they may perform marginally until retirement. Young employees may feel less inclined to stay with the organization and may quit for better opportunities elsewhere. The union employee may file a grievance and set in motion a time-consuming and potentially costly mechanism to formally address the perceived unfairness.

The costs of unfair employee treatment are difficult to compute. Research has determined that employees' perceptions of inequitable treatment are very strong predictors of job absence and turnover, two costly employee behaviors. The results of unfair treatment of employees include lower production quantity, lower production quality, greater absenteeism, greater turnover, less initiative, lower morale, lack of cooperation, spread of dissatisfaction to co-workers, fewer sugges-

tions, and less self-confidence. Each result has a cost, whether direct or indirect.[31]

Measuring Perceptions of Fairness Measuring employee feelings about fair treatment is a complex process. Because the probability of receiving honest answers through interviews and group discussions is low, the only practical alternative is to use anonymous survey techniques. One advantage of using written questionnaires is that the possible sources of perceived inequity can often be identified. Identification can be accomplished by comparing the results of a fairness survey among departments, jobs, and supervisors. Sample statements from one such instrument, the Organization Fairness Questionnaire, are shown in Figure 18–9.

Researching Fairness Companies should routinely measure employee perceptions of fairness. If the organization waits until a crisis occurs, employees may feel that they are being patronized and suspect that the organization does not really care how they feel. An advantage of conducting a fairness study on an annual basis is that organizations can analyze changes in employee perceptions and possibly identify reactions to organizational changes.

Reducing Unfairness After reviewing the results of a survey of employee perceptions of fairness, management may consider introducing certain changes in the organization. Changes that may reduce perceptions of unfairness include the following:

- Reclassify jobs that appear to be inequitably paid (establish internal pay equity).
- Base promotions on objective measures of performance.
- Train supervisors to distribute the work load more fairly.

FIGURE 18–9
The scheme of the
Organization Fairness
Questionnaire (Source:
Organization Fairness
Questionnaire, © by
John E. Dittrich,
Ph.D., University of
Colorado, 1977. Used
by permission.)

PAY RULES (nine questions). Perceptions of the fairness of one's pay relative to one's co-workers and the fairness of the rules for granting pay
increases and promotions. Sample Statement: "The rules for giving pay
raises are not fair to some employees."

PAY ADMINISTRATION (five questions). Perceptions of the fairness of the
supervisor in administering the rules for pay raises and promotions.
Sample Statement: "My supervisor rates people unfairly in considering
people for promotion."

WORK PACE (eight questions). Perceptions of the fairness of the supervisor in maintaining a fair pace of work activity. Sample Statement: "My
supervisor sees to it that all of us meet work standards."

PAY LEVEL (five questions). Perceptions of the fairness of one's pay relative to others' pay outside of the employing organization. Sample Statement: "Other companies in this area pay people doing my kind of job
less than I am getting paid."

RULE ADMINISTRATION (four questions). Perceptions of the fairness of
supervisors in maintaining acceptable forms of general behavior in the
work place. Sample Statement: "My supervisor allows workers to tease
other employees, be late to their work stations, and to act improperly
in other ways."

DISTRIBUTION OF JOBS (six questions). Perceptions of the fairness of
supervisors in distributing tasks to subordinates. Sample Statement:
"My supervisor sees that everybody in my department does a share of
the more unpleasant jobs."

LATITUDE (six questions). Perceptions of the fairness of supervisors in
permitting subordinates latitude for planning and personal decision making on the job. Sample Statement: "In working with me, my supervisor
is fair in letting me decide how to do my work."

- Conduct wage surveys of the local labor market to determine compatibility with local firms (establish external pay equity).
- Allow employees more latitude in planning and controlling their work.
- Ensure that policies, procedures, rules, and regulations are uniformly adminis-tered and enforced.

INTERNATIONAL HRM: THE INTERNATIONAL CHALLENGE TO MANAGEMENT RESEARCH

In 1986 the U.S. trade deficit reached $166 billion. The United States is now the world's largest debtor nation, far surpassing Brazil, Mexico, and Argentina. Each year, the United States owns less and less of its own economy.

As American firms decline, companies in other nations often prosper. Consider, for example, some comparisons with Japan:[32]

- Toyota and Nissan are now the third and fourth largest auto companies in the world after General Motors and Ford.
- Nippon Steel is now larger than U.S. Steel, or what is now USX. In fact, consider the American Steel Institute, located outside of Cleveland. This campus-like institute stands as a monument of U.S. achievement in the steel industry. At the center of the building complex is a huge section of pipe used in making the Alaska pipeline—a major U.S. technological achievement. However, inside the huge piece of pipe, it reads "Nippon Steel." The Alaska pipeline was made possible by Japanese production superiority.
- If you open your Apple Macintosh computer, you will note that most of its technical components are made by Samsung in Korea. The popular and economical Leading Edge microcomputer is made by Daewoo.
- The car with the most successful sales record ever for a new entry in both Canada and the United States is made by the Korean-based Hyundai Corporation.

In addition to these macro issues, there are several micro-level reasons why a better understanding of the international dimensions of management is required. Mr. Fujisawa, the co-founder of the Honda Motor Corporation, once observed that "Japanese and American management is 95 percent the same, and differs in all important aspects." We need a better or more accurate understanding of managerial and organizational differences if we are to compete successfully in a global environment. For example, assuming that Japanese business executives negotiate in the same way as Americans almost guarantees failure. So,

too, do we guarantee failure if we send an American-trained plant manager to South America or the Middle East without extensive cross-cultural training. In short, we need to ensure that we have managers who understand the cultural context as a major factor in the business environment.

In addition, cultural differences often define what constitutes "legitimate" research. For example, several years ago a U.S. manager gave a talk on employee absenteeism to a group of professors in Denmark. After listening patiently to his speech, a senior professor raised his hand and said: "I don't understand why you are studying absenteeism. It is none of your business why people are not at work. That is a personal matter. I assume you are doing this research to further exploit workers and squeeze more productivity out of them." At the same time, in Italy, the government was forming a national commission to study the problem of absence from work. (Unfortunately, the first commission meeting had to be canceled because no one showed up.) In any event, these examples point out how cultural realities serve to encourage or constrain our research on various topics. They often define how we do research and how we disseminate the results.[33]

CONCLUSIONS AND APPLICATIONS

- Sound personnel research can significantly strengthen an organization's human resource program. Some specific uses of research include measurement and evaluation of current personnel policies, programs, and activities and appraisal of proposed polices, programs, and activities.
- Research is generally classified as basic or applied. Most personnel administrators' research is applied research to solve a

particular problem or evaluate a proposed personnel program or activity.

- Personnel research is conducted by a variety of individuals and public and private organizations, including government agencies, private research organizations, personnel associations, colleges and universities, and individual business firms. In a business firm, personnel research is usually conducted by a member of the personnel staff. Results of personnel research are available in a number of journals and other publications.

- Techniques that are frequently used in personnel research include surveys, specific-use questionnaires, interviews, and historical studies. The controlled experiment has only limited use because of the difficulties in applying this technique in an organizational setting. The primary uses of surveys, questionnaires, and interviews are to gather employee feelings and perceptions about areas of job satisfaction and dissatisfaction and to evaluate present and proposed personnel programs and policies.

- An important requirement for personnel research is a valid personnel information system. Without relevant information, it will not only be difficult to carry out meaningful research but will also limit the personnel administrator's day-to-day effectiveness.

- Whenever possible, personnel professionals should analyze personnel problems and evaluate their programs, using a cost-benefit analysis. Some personnel problems and activities that lend themselves to this form of analysis are turnover, absenteeism, attitudes, and employee grievances.

- Although personnel administrators and line managers must confront a wide array of people problems, a small, hardcore group of problems seem to permeate many organizations and consume an inordinate amount of the time of line and staff decision makers. These problems typically include absenteeism, turnover, job dissatisfaction, and unfairness. For problems such as these, decision makers must, through the use of personnel research, systematically analyze the extent of the problem in their organizations, determine where the problems exist, and develop strategies to overcome them.

CASE STUDY
Absenteeism at Digitronics, Inc.

Samuel Dominquez, personnel manager for Digitronics, Inc., quickly glanced over his quarterly personnel report. He was due to go over the report with Plant Manager Jane Newberry in about five minutes. The report contained information on a wide range of personnel areas, including direct and indirect labor costs; cost of employee benefits; new hires, transfers, resignations, and discharges; and data on the firm's absenteeism rate.

Digitronics is a medium-sized maker of computer components located in Los Angeles, California. Digitronics sells its parts to large computer manufacturers such as IBM and Honeywell, Inc. The firm has enjoyed relatively peaceful labor relations and is not unionized.

Sam walked a few doors down to Jane's office and took a seat beside her desk. After exchanging a few pleasantries, they turned their attention to the report.

Newberry: "Sam, all the data look pretty good. Our labor costs are in pretty good shape, and our turnover is a little below the industry average. But there seems to be one problem—absenteeism. I see our overall absenteeism rate is 8.5 percent. That's pretty high, I believe. And the quarterly trends are slightly increasing. How do our absenteeism rates compare with industry averages?"

Dominquez: "Uh, Jane, I'm not sure. It's pretty hard to find comparable absenteeism data. I guess most firms don't want to air their dirty laundry. But I'll check around and see what I can find."

Newberry: "Okay. Incidentally, just what does that 8.5 percent absenteeism rate represent? How is it figured? Do you have departmental breakdowns so we can see where the problem is the greatest?"

Dominquez: "Well, the 8.5 percent figure is for the whole company—all twelve hundred employees. I'm pretty sure it represents the total time lost to all kinds of absenteeism. My assistant prepares the data, and I'm not positive just how the statistic is computed. I'll check when I get back to the office. I don't have any breakdown on that figure, but it shouldn't be too hard to get."

Newberry: "I think we'll need some more details on that 8.5 percent figure. We need to compare departments, shifts, and maybe even look at male and female rates. But Sam, the real question is, how can we get that rate down to about 3 or 4 percent?"

Dominquez: "Well Jane, I'm not sure. You know, absenteeism is a real tough problem, but I don't think there's a whole lot that can be done about it. Maybe we should hire a consultant to look into the problem."

Questions

1. Could an effective research process help Digitronics reduce its absenteeism? How?
2. Where might Digitronics look for absenteeism data for similar industries?
3. Would you recommend that Digitronics revise its absenteeism information system? If so, now?

EXPERIENTIAL EXERCISE
Figuring the Cost of Employee Absenteeism

Purpose

To recognize the various cost elements of employee absenteeism and to determine the cost of absenteeism in a hypothetical organization.

The Task

Tables 1, 2, and 3 include cost data for the hypothetical XYZ Corporation. Using the model provided in Figure 1, determine the cost of absenteeism for 1988. Once you have completed Figure 1, your instructor will lead a discussion regarding the purpose of computing absenteeism costs.

Midwest Tube and Tire Company

The Midwest Tube and Tire Company is a medium-sized tube and tire manufacturer located near Indianapolis. The firm employs about 450 operative employees and about 85 managerial, professional, clerical, and administrative personnel. The forty-two-year-old company manufactures primarily tires and tire tubes for large lawnmowers, tractors, and other farm implements. Products are marketed nationwide through a large network of independent dealers.

While Midwest Tube and Tire enjoys considerable success with an excellent product line, it experiences more than its share of personnel problems. Poor labor-management relations (the firm is unionized with the United Auto Workers) have plagued the firm almost from the start. In addition to high levels of grievances and turnover, the firm has suffered excessive absenteeism for several years. Janice Dillon, newly appointed personnel manager for the company, has

TABLE 1
Total Time Lost Absenteeism Rates, and Wage/Salary Data per Occupational Group for 1988[1]

	Blue-Collar	Clerical	Management and Professional
Total employees	450	46	39
Total days absent	7,988	564	215
Absenteeism rate	7.1%	4.9%	2.2%
Average hourly wage/salary	$7.47	$6.20	$13.85

[1] Assume employees received their direct hourly wages/salaries for *all* days absent.

TABLE 2
Total Benefits Cost for 1988 (Employer's Costs Only)[1]

Legally required payments (old age and survivors insurance, worker's compensation, unemployment compensation)	$ 763,980
Private pensions (employer's share)	163,324
Insurance (life, accident, hospitalization)	955,296
Paid vacations, sick leave, holidays, rest and lunch periods, wash-up, etc.	1,160,620
Subsidized costs regarding recreation, cafeteria, education, safety, equipment and clothing	225,984
Other: annual physicals, shift differential, employee discounts	126,345
	$3,395,549

[1] Per-employee differences among job classes (e.g., blue-collar vs. clerical vs. managerial) are minor. Assume employees work 2,080 hours per year.

TABLE 3
Supervisory Data Related to Absenteeism (1988)

Average number of supervisors for the period: 21

Average supervisory salary per hour: $10.05

Total estimated hours lost per supervisor per week to absenteeism: 4

FIGURE 1
Total Estimated Cost of Employee Absenteeism:

1. Total worker-hours lost to employee absenteeism for the period   _____

2. Weighted average wage/salary per hour per employee   _____

3. Cost of employee benefits per hour per employee   _____

4. Total compensation lost per hour per absent employee
   a. If absent workers are paid (wage/salary plus benefits)   _____
   b. If absent workers are not paid (benefits only)   _____

5. Total compensation lost to absent employees (total worker-hours lost × 4(a) or 4(b), whichever is applicable)   _____

6. Total supervisory hours lost on employee absenteeism   _____

7. Average hourly supervisory wage, including benefits   _____

8. Total supervisory salaries lost to managing problems of absenteeism (hours lost × average hourly supervisory wage—item 6 × item 7)   _____

9. All other costs incidental to absenteeism not included in the preceding items   _____

10. Total estimated cost of absenteeism— summation of items 5, 8, and 9   _____

11. Total estimated cost of absenteeism per employee:

$$\frac{\text{(Total Estimated Costs)}}{\text{(Total Number of Employees)}}$$ _____

= $ _____
per employee

been asked by the plant manager, Wayne Boulton, to determine how much absenteeism cost the firm in 1988. Boulton wanted to use the data to persuade the union of the need for a more conservative absenteeism provision in the upcoming labor contract.

Over the next few weeks, Dillon collected the information shown in Tables 1–3.

Finally, in discussing the problem with plant personnel, it was estimated that annual costs for 1988 due to overtime, production delays, and quality problems related to absenteeism totaled $93,750.

Using Figure 1, determine the total cost of absenteeism for 1988, in addition to the cost of absenteeism per employee.

KEY TERMS AND CONCEPTS

Absenteeism	Job dissatisfaction
Applied research	Job-satisfaction survey
Basic research	Personnel information system
Controlled experiment	Specific-use questionnaire
Cost-benefit analysis	Structured interview
Equity	Turnover
Historical study	Unfairness
Job Descriptive Index (JDI)	Unstructured interview

REVIEW QUESTIONS

1. Describe the primary uses of personnel research.
2. Discuss the areas in which a business firm may find it beneficial to conduct applied research.
3. What are the steps involved in conducting a controlled experiment?
4. What causes employee absenteeism? How may absenteeism be reduced?
5. Is turnover good or bad for the organization? What problems may result from excessive turnover?
6. What is the most effective way to measure job dissatisfaction? In what different ways may job attitudinal data be analyzed?
7. Why may an employee feel that he or she is being treated unfairly? What personnel programs may be implemented to reduce feelings of employee unfairness?
8. What is the EEOC definition of sexual harassment? How can an organization determine the extent of the problem? What can be done to reduce sexual harassment?

DISCUSSION QUESTIONS

1. Assume you are a personnel manager in a large insurance company. At a luncheon meeting, a sales representative for MUSICO, a firm that sells piped-in music in office buildings, claims, "If you install MUSICO, your clerical employees will be happier and more productive." Could you set up

a controlled experiment to determine the effects of MUSICO on employee morale and productivity? Should your company buy the MUSICO system?

2. In analyzing turnover records, you find that over half of your MBA management trainees leave your large urban bank within one year of being hired. How would you conduct research on this problem? Speculate on some reasons for the turnover problem and offer some alternative solutions to eliminate or reduce these causes.

3. Whose responsibility is it to control employee absenteeism—the line manager's or the personnel manager's? Explain how responsibility for controlling this problem might be divided.

4. Many companies enjoy outside consultants to research an organizational problem and recommend a solution. What are the advantages and disadvantages of using consultants rather than having internal personnel staff research a problem?

5. Research shows that the greatest percentage of absenteeism occurs among blue-collar and clerical workers, and that managers and staff professionals are absent from their jobs very infrequently. What reasons account for this pattern?

6. The Schwartz Company does an attitude survey once a year. The personnel manager has found that job satisfaction increased overall among Schwartz employees from 1979 to 1980; the organization has done nothing specifically to improve job satisfaction. What could account for these results?

7. Why is relatively little basic research conducted within the organization by personnel researchers?

8. Assume that your company has a significant turnover problem and you want to read about the subject. At the library, (1) find out what organizations regularly publish turnover data, (2) determine how these turnover figures are computed, and (3) gather some recent turnover data and report them to the class.

ENDNOTES

1. Michael J. Jucius, *Personnel Management* (New York: Irwin, 1971), pp. 534–35.

2. See F. J. Roethlisberger and W. J. Dickson, *Management and the Worker* (Cambridge, MA: Harvard University Press, 1939).

3. William C. Byham, *The Uses of Personnel Research,* Research Study 91 (New York: American Management Association, 1968), p.8

4. Bureau of National Affairs, Inc., ASPA-BNA survey no. 37, Personnel Policies: Research and Evaluation, Bulletin no. 1516 (March 22, 1979), p. 2.

5. Although job dissatisfaction has been linked with absenteeism and turnover in many studies, the relationship between job satisfaction and productivity remains controversial. See Arthur H. Brayfield and Walter H. Crockett, "Employee Attitudes and Employee Performance," *Psychological Bulletin 52,* no. 5 (September 1955): 396–424; and Charles N. Green, "The Satisfaction-Performance Controversy: New Developments and Their Implications," *Business Horizons* 15 (October 1972): 31–41.

6. Louis E. Tagliaferri, "Taking Note of Employee Attitudes," *Personnel Administrator* 33, no. 4 (April 1988): 96–102.

7. Ibid.

8. W. Martin, "What Management Can Expect from an Employee Attitude Survey," *Personnel Administrator* 24 (July 1981). See also W. J. Rothwell, "Conducting an Employee Attitude Survey," *Personnel Journal* 62 (April 1983).

9. Donald A. Drost, Fabius P. O'Brien, and Steve Marsh, "Exit Interviews: Master the Possibilities," *Personnel Administrator* 32, no. 2 (February 1987): 104–10.

10. For details of the various forms of experimental design, see D. T. Campbell and J. C. Stanley, *Experimental and Quasi-Experimental Designs for Research* (Chicago, IL: Rand-McNally, 1963) and T. S. Bateman and G. R. Ferris, *Method and Analysis in Organizational Research* (Reston, VA: Reston, 1984).

11. See E. P. Bloom, "Creating an Employee Information System," *Personnel Administrator* 27 (November 1982): 67–74.

12. W. F. Cascio, *Costing Human Resources* (Boston: Kent, 1982).

13. Michael R. Carrell and Lynn Hampton, "Computer Enhanced Labor Negotiations," *Labor Law Journal* 36, no. 10 (October 1985): 795–800.

14. K. Dow Scott, Steven E. Markham, and G. Stephen Taylor, "Employee Attendance: Good Policy Makes Good Sense," *Personnel Administrator* 32, no. 12 (December 1987): 98.

15. Johnny Long and Joseph Ormsby, "Stamp Out Absenteeism," *Personnel Journal* 66 (November 1987): 94–97.

16. F. E. Kuzmits, "How Much Is Absenteeism Costing Your Organization?," *Personnel Administrator* 24 (June 1979): 29–33.

17. F. E. Kuzmits, "How Good Is Your Absenteeism Control System?," *Advanced Management Journal* 12 (Winter 1980): 4–15.

18. Journal articles on the analysis and control of absenteeism problems abound. See *Personnel Administrator, Personnel Journal, Personnel, Business Horizons,* and *Supervisory Management.*

19. D. Scott and S. Markham, "Absenteeism Control Methods: A Survey of Practices and Results," 27 *Personnel Administrator* (June 1982): 73–84.

20. Scott et al., "Employee Attendance," pp. 98–106.

21. See F. E. Kuzmits, "Is Your Organization Ready for No-Fault Absenteeism?", *Personnel Administrator* 29 (December 1984): 119–27.

22. Ibid.

23. Dan L. Worrell, Wallace N. Davidson III, P. R. Chandy, and Sharon L. Garrison, "Management Turnover Through Deaths of Key Executives: Effects on Investor Wealth," *Academy of Mangement Journal* 29, no. 4 (December 1986): 674–94.

24. L. W. Porter and R. M. Steers, "Organizational, Work and Personal Factors in Employee Turnover and Absenteeism, *Psychological Bulletin* 80 (1973): 151–76.

25. Glenn M. McEvoy, "Do Good or Poor Performers Leave? A Meta-Analysis of the Relationship Between Performance and Turnover," *Academy of Management Journal* 30, no. 4 (December 1987): 744–62.

26. *Employee Absenteeism and Turnover* (Washington, DC: Bureau of National Affairs, 1974).

27. V. S. Flowers and C. L. Hughes, "Why Employees Stay," *Harvard Business Review* 51 (July–August 1973): 49–60.

28. Personnel and management journals periodically treat issues related to turnover. See the journals listed in endnote 18; also R. T. Mowday, C. S. Koberg, and A. W. McArthur, "The Psychology of the Withdrawal Process," *Academy of Management Journal* 27 (March 1984): 79–94.

29. M. J. Gannon, *Organizational Behavior* (Boston, MA: Little, Brown, 1979), p. 186.

30. See E. A. Locke, "The Nature and Causes of Job Satisfaction," in *Handbook of Industrial and Organizational Psychology*, ed. M. D. Dunnette (Chicago: Rand McNally, 1976).

31. R. C. Huseman, J. D. Hatfield and E. W. Miles, "A New Perspective on Equity Theory: The Equity Sensitivity Construct," *Academy of Management Review* 12, no. 2 (June 1987): 222–34.

32. Richard M. Steers, "The International Challenge to Management Education," *The Academy of Management Newsletter* 17. no 4 (October 1987): 2–3.

33. Ibid.

Employees' Rights After Hours

Mike Wright was nervous. In a few moments he would have to confront Laura Hester, one of his field sales representatives. This was one of the most sensitive issues Mike had ever had to address. Rumors had been running rampant that Laura had been seen dating Bob Moore, a former field sales representative. The grapevine reported that they had become more than just an item; they were involved in a serious relationship.

The fact that Laura was involved with someone didn't bother Wright. It was who she was involved with that created the problem. Wright was seriously concerned that his company's secrets would fall into the wrong hands—his competitor's.

Wright felt that he had to present the problem to Laura, but he didn't have the foggiest notion of what he was going to say. After all, the computer firm they worked for dealt in high-technology equipment, and company secrets were kept very strictly. As everyone knows, the competition in the computer industry is fierce and, as the saying goes, "loose lips sink ships." Or computer firms.

"Mike, you wanted to see me?" Laura was standing in the doorway, waiting for him to acknowledge the beginning of a delicate meeting.

"Why, yes," Mike responded in the most positive tone he could muster.

And with that, Laura Hester, one of the company's best sales representatives, walked in and sat down. Ever since she received the message from Mike to stop by, she had sensed that this wasn't going to be a pleasant experience. She even wondered if perhaps this meeting would be about her relationship with Bob Moore. They had been seeing each other quite a bit lately, and she had to admit that a long-term relationship was very likely. But this issue was none of the company's business. After all, she had been a loyal and productive employee for too many years, and certainly Mike wouldn't suspect her of betraying the company's confidence—even if Bob did work for a competitor.

But the next few minutes proved that Laura's intuition was correct after all. As Mike started to talk, it became increasingly clear that he was issuing an ultimatum—either break off with Bob Moore or accept a transfer to a less sensitive position (which really meant a demotion).

After many heated words from both parties, Laura finally said as she stormed out of his office, "You can forget that transfer nonsense. The way I see it, you're just trying to get rid of me. Well, I'm going to call my lawyer right now!"

Discussion Questions

1. What mistakes did Mike Wright make? What should he have done?
2. What role could the personnel department play in preventing situations such as this from occurring?
3. How far does the employer's responsibility go in regulating the social life of the employees?

Experiential Exercise/ Textbook Cross Index

Each exercise in *Experiential Exercises in Personnel/Human Resource Management,* 2nd ed., by Frank E. Kuzmits, corresponds with a chapter or chapters in this third edition of *Personnel.* Some of these exercises are included in this text. The following list correlates the Experiential Exercises in the Kuzmits book with the relevant chapters in this text.

1. Personnel Information: Where to Find It (Chapters 1 and 16)
2. Are These Effective Job Descriptions? (Chapter 2)
3. Job Analysis (Chapter 2)
4. Can This Job Be Enriched? (Chapter 3)
5. Alternate Work Schedules (Chapter 3)
6. Recruiting Sources: Where to Get the People You Want (Chapters 4 and 16)
7. Ads That Work (Chapters 4 and 14)
8. Recruitment and Selection at Bronzebaby Lotion Company (Chapters 4 and 5)
9. Measuring Employee Potential: The Assessment-Center Technique (Chapters 5 and 8)
10. Which Employment Test is Most Valid? (Chapter 5)
11. The Inference-Observation Problem, or, Is What You See What You Really Get? (Chapter 5)
12. The Structured Employment Interview (Chapter 5)
13. The Candid Interview: A Look at the RJP (Chapter 5)
14. Oldies-but-not-so-goodies: A Look Back at 1960s Help-Wanted Ads (Chapters 4 and 5)
15. Help Wanted, Male; Help Wanted, Female: A Look at the Bona Fide Occupational Qualification (BFOQ) (Chapters 4 and 5)
16. Are These Application Blanks Lawful? (Chapter 5)
17. I Shouldn't Have Asked: Acceptable and Unacceptable Queries During the Employment Interview (Chapters 4 and 5)
18. Sexual Harassment (Chapters 5 and 15)
19. Is Your Chauvinism Showing? (Chapter 8)
20. Women and Work: A Quiz (Chapters 5 and 8)
21. Designing a Behaviorally Anchored Rating Scale (BARS) (Chapter 6)

Glossary

Absenteeism. The failure of employees to report for regularly scheduled work.

Achievement test. A test designed to measure the degree to which a person has learned in a specific subject or area.

Acquired immune deficiency syndrome (AIDS). A disease caused by a virus that, in active cases, kills specialized T-4 blood cells that serve as the master control for the body's immune response system. The immune system eventually fails, leaving the victim susceptible to many diseases. AIDS in the work place is considered a physical handicap under the 1973 Rehabilitation Act. Many experts believe that AIDS is not transmitted through normal work place contact.

Adverse impact. Occurs as a result of any employment process in which a minority applicant is given unequal consideration for employment and discrimination against that applicant is charged.

Affirmative action. A hiring policy that requires employers to analyze their work force for underuse of protected-class individuals and to develop a plan of action to correct that problem.

Age Discrimination in Employment Act (ADEA). Passed by Congress in 1967, amended in 1978 and 1986. The ADEA makes it illegal for employers, government agencies, and labor unions to discriminate against individuals over age forty. Any mandatory retirement age is prohibited. Employers are also required to provide the same health benefits to workers of all ages.

American Federation of Labor and Congress of Industrial Organizations. (AFL-CIO). The organization formed in 1955 from the merger of the AFL and the CIO. Although not a union in itself, it is a federation composed of over 100 unions and serves to coordinate and represent its membership.

Application blank. A formal record of an individual's application for employment, providing essential information about the individual and his or her job qualifications.

Applied research. Research or study conducted to find a solution to a particular problem.

Apprentice training. A combination of on-the-job training and required classroom instruction.

Aptitude tests. A set of tests designed to measure a person's ability to achieve in a particular area.

Arbitration. An official process in which the negotiating parties agree to submit the unresolved dispute to a neutral third party whose decision is final and binding.

Assessment center. A process in which employees are evaluated through a series of exercises to determine their promotability.

Audiovisual. Refers to the use of sight and sound techniques to assist a trainer.

Authorization card. A card that states that the employee is willing to be represented by a labor organization in collective bargaining with the employer.

Bargaining impasse. The breakdown of negotiations when the union and employer are unable to reach an agreement.

Bargaining unit. A group of employees who share common employment interests and working conditions. The individuals are treated as a distinct group for the purposes of collective bargaining.

Basic research. A study undertaken to gain knowledge in a particular field or gather information about a given subject.

Behaviorally anchored rating scale (BARS). A performance appraisal method that combines the use of critical incidents and a rating scale.

Benchmark job. A job consisting of standardized characteristics easily identified with similar jobs in other organizations.

Blind ads. Job advertisements that briefly describe a job at an unnamed organization, giving only a box number to which the applicant responds.

Bona fide occupational qualification (BFOQ). A term derived from Latin that refers to a legitimate or honest job qualification, such as an age requirement necessary for the safe operation of equipment.

Boulwarism. A collection bargaining approach in which management deals directly with the workers concerning their needs, develops an offer from these needs to present to the union, and then declares it to be the company's first and last offer.

Bumping. A process whereby one employee identified for layoff displaces another employee with less seniority.

Business unionism. The concept that a union is more concerned with basic issues, such as wages and benefits, than with social goals, and that it conducts its operations in a businesslike manner.

Career development. The long-term process that spans an employee's entire working career.

Career management. The process of designing and implementing goals, plans, and strategies that enable administrators to satisfy work force needs and allow individuals to achieve their career objectives.

Career stages. The progressive stages an employee goes through while advancing in his or her career development.

Case study. A written description of an organizational problem.

Central processing unit (CPU). The area of the computer in which problem instructions are executed.

Central tendency. A general tendency, when evaluating employees, to rate them about the same, such as average.

Certification. The determination by an administrative agency such as the National Labor Relations Board that a union will become the official bargaining agent for a group of employees (the bargaining unit).

Child-care programs. An employer service that often includes either on-site child-care facilities for the children of employees or reimbursement for the use of outside child-care centers.

Civil Rights Act of 1964. A federal law designed to eliminate racial and sexual discrimination, making it unlawful for an organization to discriminate against an individual because of race, color, religion, sex or national origin.

Classification method. The grouping of jobs according to written descriptions into broad classes or grades.

Closed promotion system. A promotional system in which the responsibility for identifying promotable employees lies with the supervisor of the job to be filled.

Closed shop. A form of union security requiring new employees to be union members at the time of hiring.

Coaching. A management process that provides assistance, guidance, and feedback to employees.

Collective bargaining. The negotiation of written terms of agreement by a union and the employer.

Committee assignments. The tasks or problems assigned to specific committee members.

Common situs picketing. A common situs is a work site that employs workers represented by several unions; therefore, a striking union may picket only part of the site, rather than the entire work site.

Comparable worth. The concept that women should receive pay equal to that of men in jobs that may not be strictly defined as equal but are comparable, that is, requiring similar skills, effort, responsibilities, and working conditions.

Compensable factors. Basic or fundamental job elements including responsibilities, effort, skills, and working conditions.

Compensation. A general term referring to all rewards, payments, and benefits given by an organization.

Compensatory selection. A hiring or selection procedure in which all parts of the screening process are summarized and the applicant is considered on total performance.

Compressed workweek. Any workweek in which the scheduled working days are fewer than the traditional five workdays per week.

Computer. Mechanism designed for solving problems or manipulating data by accepting data, performing prescribed operations on the data, and supplying the results.

Computerization in personnel. Increasing the use of computers in the personnel department beyond payroll tasks and record keeping to include such items as job status, work history, and skills inventory, greatly expanding the depth and capabilities of the department.

Conceptual skills. The ability to view an organization as a whole and to coordinate its functions, activities, goals, and purposes.

Concession bargaining. A form of collective bargaining in which economic rewards, such as wages, may be frozen or reduced (givebacks) to prevent layoffs or plant closings.

Conference/discussion. Two-way oral communication between a trainer and a trainee.

Controlled experiment. An experiment in which all factors are held constant while one factor is varied to determine its significance.

Coordination of benefits (COB) program. Programs established to prevent paying duplicate claims when more than one medical policy covers a claimant.

Core cafeteria plan. A flexible employee benefit plan that provides employees with minimum coverage in several areas and then allows the employees to choose either additional benefits or cash.

Corrective counseling. The final stage of positive discipline in which employers help employees find solutions to their problems during counseling sessions.

Cost-benefit analysis. The process of evaluating company objectives in terms of cost versus effectiveness.

Cost-of-living adjustment (COLA). The compensation increase given an employee based on the percentage by which the cost of living has risen, usually measured by a change in the consumer price index (CPI).

Critical incidents. A performance ranking based on a listing of specific examples of outstanding or poor employee job performances.

Data base. A set of organized data under the control of a data base management system. Most often, a data base consists of one or more files of related information.

Davis–Bacon Act. An act passed in 1931 requiring employers holding federal government construction contracts for $2,000 or more to pay the prevailing wage rate to employees working on the project.

Decertification. The determination by an administrative agency such as the National Labor Relations Board that a union will no longer be the official bargaining agent for a group of employees.

Decision-support system (DSS). An easily accessible microcomputer-based information system that aids managers in planning and decision making.

Defined benefit retirement plan. A retirement plant that provides the beneficiary a specific monthly benefit determined by a formula. The formula usually is similar to: $ monthly benefit = years service $\times$ base pay $\times$ ___%.

Defined contribution retirement plan. A retirement plan that establishes the basis upon which the employer contributes to the pension fund.

Degrees of factors. The breaking down of a compensable factor into degrees signifying the extent to which that factor exists in a particular job.

Demotion. The reassignment of an employee to a lower job.

Dictionary of Occupational Titles (DOT). The U.S. Employment Services' dictionary, which classifies jobs by field of work, tasks performed, and the relationship of the job to data, people, and things.

Discretionary workweek. A varied-schedule workweek designed to offer employees greater freedom in regulating their lives.

Discrimination. A general term referring to the situation in which an individual who has an equal probability of being successful in a job does not have an equal probability of getting the job.

Dismissal pay. Compensation, also referred to as *severance pay,* awarded to employees permanently removed from their jobs through no fault of their own.

Distributive bargaining. A form of bargaining in which labor and management cannot agree on issues in the work contract, such as wages.

Dual-career couple. A marriage in which both the husband and the wife are employed.

Economic Recovery Tax Act of 1981. A law that provides for a reduced maximum tax rate, favorable treatment for stock options, a maximum capital gains rate, and dramatic changes in the taxation of inherited wealth.

Economic strike. An employee strike over an economic issue such as wages, benefits, or working conditions.

Elastic clause. A clause sometimes included in a job description to allow a supervisor to add to or change an employee's duties without changing the job description.

Employee assistance program (EAP). Any one of numerous programs that an organization may provide to enhance employee well-being. Examples range from alcohol rehabilitation programs to professional counseling in outside agencies.

Employee association. A union composed primarily of white-collar or professional employees such as teachers, police officers, and health-care employees.

Employee orientation. The initial contact or training period a new employee has with an organization. Usually included in this introduction are such items as company tours, introductions to staff, and meetings with management to discuss salary, benefits, vacations, and so on.

Employee relocation. The movement of an employee from one city to another for internal promotion within an organization.

Employee Retirement Income Security Act of 1975 (ERISA). A federal law passed to protect employee pensions. Additionally, it places strict regulations on private pension plans, protects the vested rights of employees, and protects the rights of employees' beneficiaries.

Employee stock ownership plan (ESOP). Employee benefit plan in which the employer contributes shares of stock to a trust for the purpose of stock purchases by employees.

Equal Employment Opportunity Commission (EEOC). A commission given authority by the Civil Rights Act of 1964 to investigate employee complaints of job discrimination and to act as their attorney.

Equal Pay Act of 1963. An act that requires organizations of all sizes to pay equal wages to men and women who perform substantially equal work, thus eliminating sexual discrimination.

Equity (theory). A theory of employee motivation that states that employees compare their perceived ratio of organizational inputs and outputs with that of their co-workers. Perceptions of inequity occur when an employee perceives an imbalance in the ratios.

Ergonomics. The engineering of work stations to include the human factor. Involves designing the job to fit the person by considering such factors as lighting, noise, tools, and so on.

Essay method. A performance appraisal consisting of a written essay from the supervisor specifying specific employee strengths and weaknesses.

Executive compensation. The total benefits an organization pays to its executive and upper-level employees.

Executive Order 11246. An executive order created by President Lyndon Johnson that requires all government agencies, contractors, and subcontractors to develop programs of affirmative action.

Executive succession chart. A management planning tool that indicates likely successors for each position in the management hierarchy.

Exempt. A term referring to positions that are not covered by the overtime provision of the Fair Labor Standards Act.

Expert system (ES). An advanced computer program that emulates the problem-solving abilities of human experts through the use of artificial intelligence.

External environment. Forces outside of an organization, such as society, law, and labor unions, over which personnel administrators have little or no control.

Extrinsic rewards. The tangible compensatory items given to an employee, such as salary and benefits.

Fact-finding. The introduction of a neutral party who listens to both sides of a dispute and then publicly recommends a reasonable solution, but has no binding authority.

Factor-comparison method. An evaluation method developed by Eugene Benge that combines the ranking method and the point system. In it, each job is divided into specific factors, each factor is ranked, and the rankings are totaled to give an overall numerical rating.

Fair Labor Standards Act of 1938. A federal law designed to regulate employment practices by establishing such items as minimum wage levels, overtime compensation, child labor standards, and maximum working hours. The act has been amended several times since its origination.

False negative. An incorrect decision by management, such as rejecting an applicant (marking him or her negative) who would have been successful.

False positive. An incorrect decision by management, such as accepting an applicant (marking him or her positive) who turned out to be unsuccessful.

Featherbedding. A labor practice in which workers are paid for work not performed or more workers are paid than a job requires.

Final-offer arbitration. When labor and management have reached an impasse in negotiations, both submit their final offer to an arbitrator (or panel). One of the two final offers, without any change, is chosen as the settlement.

Flexible benefit plans. Also called *cafeteria plans,* these programs allow employees some choice of benefits (or level of benefits) to be included in their total compensation package.

Flextime. An alternative work schedule that allows employees to determine their starting and stopping times, provided that they work a set number of hours per day or week.

401(K) retirement plans. Company-sponsored, IRS-qualified retirement plans, such as employee payroll deduction plans, provided for under section 401(K) of the Internal Revenue Code.

Forced choice. A method of performance appraisal that requires the rater to choose from a group of performance descriptions one (or more) that describes an employee.

Forced distribution. A method of performance appraisal that requires the rater to place each employee into one of several performance categories, which are given a maximum percentage of the total number of employees.

Foreign employment rights. In many foreign countries, individuals are protected from wrongful or unfair dismissal.

Four-day workweek. An example of a compressed workweek, where the number of working days is reduced to four by lengthening the number of hours worked per day.

Four-fifths (80 percent) rule. A quantitative selection rate outlined in the 1978 Uniform Guidelines on Employee Selection Procedures that determines if an organization demonstrates evidence of adverse impact.

Functional job analysis (FJA). A method of job analysis that expands the Department of Labor's method to include such specific requirements as worker instructions, educational development, reasoning development, mathematical development, and language development.

Gainsharing. A general method of management that uses small groups of employees to manage and perform organizational work. In addition, employees equally share in the profits realized above a targeted level. A gainsharing system is generally a combination profit sharing and an employee involvement program.

Garnishment. The legal procedure of withholding a portion of an employee's earnings for payment of a debt.

Gate hires. A term referring to applicants who apply in person to an employer, usually not in response to a recruitment ad; these applicants are also referred to as *walk-ins*.

Givebacks. Collectively bargained reductions in previously negotiated wages, benefits, or work rules in exchange for management-guaranteed employment levels during the term of the contract.

Global appraisal. The generality created by ranking a job in its entirety rather than by its various factors.

Goal setting. The assigning of specific goals to an employee to increase job production and to provide a more accurate evaluation method.

Good faith bargaining. A term referring to the reasonable efforts that both management and labor demonstrate during labor negotiations; it does not require either side to concede or agree, but rather to show reasonable intent.

Graphic rating scales. Performance scales composed of a list of employee traits and a scale of performance achieved. The employee is rated by marking the score that best describes his or her performance level for each trait.

Graphology. A handwriting test administered and examined by a trained graphologist to determine a person's personality traits.

Grievance. A complaint by an employee concerning a possible violation of the labor contract, law, or past practice of the employer.

Grievance handling. The formal process followed when a grievance has been filed to determine if the contract has been violated.

Gripe. A complaint by an employee concerning an action by management that does not violate a labor contract, law, or past practice of the employer.

Guaranteed income stream (GIS). An alternative to supplemental unemployment plans. A GIS plan usually gives benefits to employees until they retire, thus providing a guaranteed lifetime wage. Laid-off workers receive benefits that are only partially offset by outside earnings, thus creating an incentive to seek other employment.

Halo effect. A bias occurring when one particular aspect of an employee's performance, whether positive or negative, tends to influence the evaluation of his or her total performance.

Health hazards. Those aspects of the work place that have the capability of impairing an employee's general physical, mental, or emotional well-being, such as chemicals, dust, and noise.

Health maintenance organization (HMO). An organization of physicians and other health-care professionals that provides a wide range of health services for a fixed fee on a prepaid basis.

Hierarchy of needs. A five-level classification of human needs developed by the psychologist Abraham Maslow. The needs, in order of importance, are (1) physiological, (2) security, (3) social, (4) self-esteem, and (5) self-actualization.

Historical study. The gathering of data over a period of time on specific variables to analyze developing patterns.

Hit rate. The percentage of correct predictions an organization makes about the future performance of employees.

Hot-stove rule. A rule of discipline that compares the touching a hot stove to the application of discipline in that a warning is given, the response is immediate, enforcement is consistent, and is applied impersonally to all.

Human relations. Applying behavioral sciences to the working environment to enhance both employee satisfaction and production by focusing on individual employee needs and on the informal group.

Human relations skills. The skills required to deal effectively with people; included are the ability to communicate, to establish interpersonal relations, and to establish effective work-group relationships.

Human resource information system (HRIS). A system, frequently computerized, for collecting, storing, maintaining, retrieving, and validating data concerning an organization's personnel.

Human resource planning. Also referred to as *manpower planning*, it is the ability to project the future needs and skills required of employees.

Human resource management (HRM). Includes all functions and activities of traditional personnel management, with the expanded goal of maximizing an organization's use of its human resources to achieve personal and organizational objectives.

Human resources. Generally, a term used to identify all employees or workers in an organization.

Immigration Reform and Control Act (IRCA) of 1986. A federal law that requires employers to verify the identity and work eligibility of each new employee. In addition, the act makes it illegal for an employer to hire, recruit, refer, or continue to employ an illegal alien. The act also makes it illegal for employers to discriminate against ''foreign-looking'' applicants.

In-basket exercises. A set of hypothetical problems given to lower-level managers to develop their problem-solving skills.

Incentive stock option (ISO). An executive stock option whereby taxation is delayed until the stock is sold and the company receives no tax benefit.

Incidence rate of occupational injuries and illnesses. The rate of occurrence of injury or illness in various businesses and industries, as determined by the Occupational Safety and Health Administration after compiling the injuries and accidents reported by organizations across the United States.

Independent union. Unions that remain autonomous and are not affiliated with any national union or the AFL-CIO.

Individual career planning. The process whereby each employee, together with a personnel specialist, plans career goals.

Individual retirement account (IRA). Investment account that allows individuals to contribute up to a specific amount annually for the purpose of providing a retirement fund.

Industrial union. A labor union whose membership is composed primarily of semiskilled or unskilled blue-collar workers working in the same industry, such as the automotive industry.

Initial applicant screening. The initial interview to determine if an applicant possesses critical job specifications, thus eliminating unqualified applicants.

Integrative bargaining. A form of collective bargaining that creates a cooperative negotiating relationship whereby both labor and management benefit.

Intelligence test. A standardized test used to measure a person's mental abilities and skills; these tests are often used to predict a person's success in a school setting.

Interest arbitration. The process of using an arbitrator to solve a possible dispute in a future contract.

Interest test. A test designed to measure an individual's activity preferences; the results are often used to correlate an individual's interests with occupational choices.

Internal staffing. The shifting or reassigning of personnel positions within an organization, such as by promotions, demotions, transfers, and layoffs.

Intrinsic rewards. The intangible compensatory items given to an employee, such as recognition and promotional opportunities.

Job analysis. A systematic investigation into the tasks, duties, and responsibilities of a job.

Job classification. The grouping or categorizing of jobs on some specified basis, such as by the nature of the work performed or by the level of pay; classification is often used as a simplified method of job analysis.

Job description. Written summaries of the tasks, duties, and responsibilities of specific jobs.

Job descriptive index (JDI). A widely used job satisfaction survey.

Job design. The manipulation of the content, functions, and relationships of jobs in order to satisfy both organizational purposes and the personal needs of individual job holders.

Job dissatisfaction. The displeasure or negative attitude of an employee toward his or her job.

Job enlargement. Increasing the scope of a job or the number of tasks performed in order to increase employee satisfaction.

Job enrichment. A program designed to increase the satisfaction derived from the work accomplished by changing the nature of the work and including the worker in decision making.

Job evaluation. The determination of the worth of a job to an organization; usually a combination of a comparison of internal job levels and an analysis of the external job market.

Job instruction training (JIT). A series of steps for supervisors to follow when training their employees.

Job posting. A method of filling open positions by inviting employees in an organization to apply for the jobs.

Job rotation. Periodically assigning employees to different jobs for periods of time ranging from a few hours to several weeks to enhance employee motivation, reduce repetition, and provide cross-training.

Job satisfaction survey. An instrument designed to compile employee work-related attitudes and opinions.

Job scope and depth. Two dimensions of a job that determine its degree of specialization: scope—how long it takes a worker to complete the task; depth—the degree to which the worker is involved in the planning, decision making, and control of the job.

Job security. The guarantee of work. In collective bargaining agreements, it may be provided through a seniority system, retraining rights, a no-layoff clause, or some other mechanism.

Job sharing. Generally refers to dividing the hours worked in a full-time job into two part-time positions; in personnel work, it often refers to the holding of a position by two employees who are friends or relatives.

Job splitting. A method of scheduling part-time work in which the tasks of a single job are divided into two separate part-time jobs, each having separate duties.

Job specifications. The minimum skills, education, and experience necessary for an individual to perform a job.

Job stress. The physical or psychological response by an individual caused by an external action, situation, or event in the work place.

Kemper *Management Guide on Alcoholism.* A pamphlet designed by the Kemper Insurance Companies that outlines its employee rehabilitation assistance program for alcoholism.

Knights of Labor. A labor union formed as a secret society in 1869, led by a group of garment workers. Their goal was to organize both craftsmen and unskilled workers to achieve social and economic reform by political action.

Labor force participation rate. The rate by which any specific group is represented in the work force; the rate can be calculated on a national, regional, or local level.

Labor reserve. A term that refers generally to persons who are capable of being employed but who choose not to work currently.

Landrum–Griffin Act. Also known as the *Labor–Management Reporting and Disclosure Act of 1959*, it was passed as a result of union corruption. It provides a ''bill of rights'' for union members, reporting requirements, election safeguards, and restrictions on officers.

Lateral promotions. Job rotation assignments given to upper-level management, usually lasting for one or more years.

Law of effect. A learning theory that states that behavior pleasantly rewarded tends to be repeated, whereas behavior unpleasantly rewarded tends not to be repeated.

Layoff. A term referring to the temporary non-employment of an employee due to lack of work, with the intent to recall the employee when work is available.

Learner-controlled instruction (LCI). An effective form of on-the-job training, LCI is a results-oriented program composed of five basic training elements: The actual working environment, competency-based learning, individualized instruction, results-oriented feedback, and learning contracts.

Leasing (employees). Employers choose to lease personnel from an outside company as a means of increasing the work force without hiring permanent employees, paying overtime, or using temporary services.

Lecture. A speech delivered to an audience on a particular subject for informational or instructional purposes.

Leniency. The tendency of a supervisor to give high evaluations to all employees regardless of their actual performance.

Levels of training evaluation. A training program evaluation process designed by D. L. Kirkpatrick, including four levels of review: participants' reaction, participants' learning, change in participants' behavior, and impact of the program on organizational effectiveness.

Local union. The small union that represents a specific employer unit or geographic area and is affiliated with a national union. One main function of the local union is to negotiate and administer contracts with employers.

Lockout. An employer's refusal to allow employees to return to work until an agreement is signed.

Log and summary of occupational injuries and illnesses. An Occupational Safety and Health Administration regulation, Form 200, requiring an employee to log an injury or illness within six working days after learning of its occurrence.

Mainframe. A general term applying to large computers. There is no clear distinction between mainframes and minicomputers.

Maintenance-of-membership shop. A union security provision that employees are not required to join the union, but that those employees who do join must remain until the contract expires.

Make-work activities. Work activities that are unnecessary to produce a product or that tend to limit the amount of work accomplished.

Management by objectives (MBO). A performance appraisal method in which specific goals are set jointly by the supervisor and the employee, who then jointly review them periodically.

Management development. A systematic process by which persons acquire the skills, knowledge, and abilities to lead and manage organizations successfully.

Management games. The simulation of conditions faced by real organizations, used primarily for educational purposes.

Management information system (MIS). A formal, usually computerized, structure for providing management with information, often through an MIS department.

Management succession planning (MSP). The process of identifying projected vacancies in upper-level management and choosing qualified replacement candidates, eliminating simple promotions; included in the process is the identification of development and training needs to assure future availability of qualified personnel.

Managerial obsolescence. The result of an organization's not keeping pace with new methods and procedures that enable employees to remain effective.

Mandatory bargaining category. Those items that must be negotiated if either party so requests, such as wages and benefits.

Maternity and paternity leave. An unpaid leave of absence granted to a parent upon the birth or adoption of a child, usually providing continued benefits and a guarantee of the same job when the employee returns to work.

Mediation. The introduction of a neutral third party into collective bargaining when the union and management are unable to reach an agreement.

Mentoring. When a senior, experienced manager develops a relationship with a younger employee and facilitates his or her career development. Mentorships may be formally established by an organization, or they may develop informally between employees.

Merit pay increases. The compensation given employees based on performance appraisal of their work.

Microcomputer. Smallest and least expensive class of computers. They use microprocessors in their central processing unit.

Microprocessor. Basic arithmetic, logic, and control elements required for processing, generally contained on one integrated circuit chip.

Minicomputer. Distinguished from a microcomputer by higher performance, more powerful instruction sets, a higher price, and a wider selection of programming languages and operating systems.

Model for analyzing unsatisfactory performance. A model used to analyze employees' poor performance; the components of the model identify both the causes of unsatisfactory behavior and the solutions available.

Motivation-intensive job. A job designed for motivated and challenged workers, providing more employee involvement and greater job satisfaction.

Multiple-employer bargaining. Two or more employers joining together to negotiate a contract with one or more unions.

Multiple hurdles selection. A hiring or selection process in which an applicant must pass each step of the process (such as the initial screening) in order to proceed to the next step.

National Council on Alcoholism (NCA). An organization concerned with all aspects of alcoholism, from gathering data to distributing public information.

National Institute for Occupational Safety and Health (NIOSH). A division of the Department of Health and Human Services. Working closely with the Occupational Safety and Health Administration, it gathers data related to the health and safety of employees, conducts research, and helps determine safety standards within the workplace.

National Labor Relations Board (NLRB). An independent agency of the federal government with two main functions: (1) to investigate charges of unfair labor practices and (2) to conduct certification elections by secret ballot to determine whether employees will be represented by a union.

National union. A union that has collective bargaining agreements with different employers in two or more states.

Negligent hiring. In general, an employer's inadequate investigation into an applicant's background when the person is hired for a job that might include the risk of injury or harm to customers or co-workers.

Nepotism. The showing of favoritism or patronage to relatives in hiring or promotional processes.

Networking. The process of making informal professional contacts that can be used as a source to recruit applicants, give career assistance, and so on.

Noncontributory retirement plan. A retirement plan financed entirely by the employer; the employees contribute nothing.

Nonexempt. A term referring to employees who are entitled to overtime pay as provided by the Fair Labor Standards Act of 1938.

Nongraphic rating scale. A performance scale composed of a list of employee traits with a description of each and a performance scale, each division of which is clarified.

Norris–LaGuardia Act. An act passed in 1932 that restricts the federal courts from issuing injunctions in labor disputes except to maintain law and order. The act also made yellow dog contracts illegal.

Objectives. The targeted goals of an organization to which resources and efforts are channeled.

Occupational illness. Any disorder, not including occupational injury, acquired as a direct result of exposure to occupational environmental factors.

Occupational injury. Any injury that results from a work accident.

Occupational Safety and Health Administration (OSHA). A division of the Department of Labor established to develop and regulate occupational health and safety standards.

Off-the-job training Any form of training performed away from an employee's work area.

On-call pay. A fixed amount of money paid to employees when they must be available to work if called by the employer.

On-the job training. Job instruction normally given by an employee's supervisor or by an experienced employee.

Open-plan systems. An office design system using panels to create modular work stations or spaces, clearly defining an employee's work area without the use of visible walls.

Open promotion system. A promotional system that publicizes job vacancies through internal communication systems and encourages all interested employees to apply.

Open shop. A form of union security whereby the workers decide whether or not to join a union and those who do not are not forced to pay any dues or fees.

Organization chart. A diagram of an organization's structure, showing the functions, departments, reporting relationships, and positions of the organization and how they are related.

Organizational career planning. The process whereby management plans career goals for employees.

Out-placement assistance. A service offered to terminated employees, providing them with skills assessment, counseling, and job-search advice.

Paid time off work. Specified times during which employees are not working but continue to be paid their standard rate, such as holidays, vacations, sick leave, military duty, and civic duty.

Paired comparisons. A performance appraisal method that requires the rater to compare two employees and indicate which one is better.

Pay equity . The equality established in a standardized pay system.

Pay grades and steps. The divisions of a compensation system in which each level or grade is assigned a standard pay rate.

Pension Benefit Guaranty Corporation (PBGC). An organization designed to encourage employers to continue voluntary pension plans and the payment of pension benefits to former employees.

Performance appraisal. A method of evaluating employee behavior in the workplace; it may include both quantitative and qualitative analyses.

Performance-based system. A compensation system based at least partially on employee performance and production (individually or in groups).

Permanent part-time work. The hiring of employees for positions requiring less than forty hours per week; often includes the advantages (to the employer) of lower pay, fewer benefits, and better morale.

Permissive bargaining categories. Those items not related to wages, benefits, or working conditions that can be negotiated in collective bargaining but may be rejected by either party without affecting the final contract signing.

Personnel administration/industrial relations (PAIR). An undergraduate degree in personnel administration/industrial relations, concentrating in areas related to personnel function.

Personnel information system. The system, usually computer based, that an organization uses to compile complete and accurate data on all of its personnel.

Personnel management. A set of programs, functions, and activities designed to maximize both personal and organizational goals.

Personnel roles. Five critical roles performed by personnel administrators: create and implement policies, design communication methods, offer advice, provide services, and control personnel programs and procedures.

Peter principle. A theory by Laurence F. Peter that employees tend to be promoted beyond their level of competence.

Physical fitness program (PFP). Organizational health programs designed to improve employee health, endurance, and general well-being.

Picket. A line of striking union employees who patrol an employer's place of business to advertise their dispute with the employer and discourage other people from entering.

Pirating. The active recruitment of an employee of one organization by another organization offering a higher salary, better working conditions, or other benefits.

Plateauing. A career stage in which the likelihood of additional hierarchical promotion is very low.

Point method. A method of job evaluation that divides a job into specific factors and identifies the degree to which each factor has been accomplished.

Policy. A standing plan that establishes general guidelines for decision making.

Polygraph. A device used to measure an emotional response by recording the person's physiological responses (blood pressure, pulse, and respiration rates) as questions are answered.

Portability. The right of an employee to transfer pension benefits accrued from one employer to a new employer.

Position Analysis Questionnaire (PAQ). A standardized quantitative questionnaire used to describe a job's elements.

Positive discipline. Discipline that affects unsatisfactory behavior through help and support and focuses on the correction of the behavior.

Preferred provider organization (PPO). A contracted health care service that offers discounts on specific services due to an increase in the number of employees who use the services.

Premium pay. Special compensation given to employees for working under undesirable circumstances, such as weekends.

Preventive discipline. Discipline obtained by managing people in such a manner that negative behavior is minimal.

Preventive labor relations. Refers to a number of strategies that an organization may implement to maintain a nonunion status.

Primary boycott. A boycott involving only those parties directly involved in the dispute.

Primary situs picketing. Picketing demonstrated at the primary employer's place of business.

Probable cause. A general term referring to the reasonable possibility that a certain condition exists, such as employer wrongdoing in a discrimination case.

Problem drinkers. People who feel socially pressured to drink, use alcohol for relaxation, and have difficulty dealing with depression and anxiety.

Procedures. A standing plan of detailed guidelines for handling organizational actions that occur regularly .

Productivity bargaining. A form of collective bargaining in which there is a general exchange of increased production for concessions on issues such as wages.

Professional organizations. Societies or groups of professional people that meet periodically to discuss a common field of interest.

Professionalism in personnel. The development of specific educational programs for personnel practitioners, designed to prepare them for the complexity of today's personnel department.

Profit-sharing plan. A pay incentive system in which employees receive a share of the employer's profits. The profit share is paid in addition to the employee's regular wages.

Programmed instruction. A self-instruction program presented in text form to be completed without the presence of a trainer.

Progressive discipline. Discipline that equates the penalty with the offense and provides progressively increasing penalties for continued unsatisfactory performance.

Promotion. The reassignment of an employee to a higher-level job within an organization.

Punitive discipline. Discipline based on fear, relying on threats, harassment, and intimidation.

Quality circles. The voluntary meeting of groups of workers with common work interests to identify, analyze, and develop solutions to work problems.

Quality of working life (QWL). The extent to which an employee's personal needs are met through work.

Railway Labor Act. Legislation that gave railroad workers the right to organize and bargain collectively without the employer's interference.

Ranking. A performance appraisal method that compares employees to each other (best-worst) rather than rating them according to a standard.

Ranking method of job evaluation. Method that requires the job evaluation committee to rank all jobs in an organization according to their relative worth in comparison to each other.

Recency. The tendency of a supervisor to base an employee's appraisal on recent performance rather than their performance during the entire evaluation period.

Red circle job. A job whose current pay exceeds the maximum for that pay grade.

Reference check. A confidential investigation to verify information given by a job applicant.

Reporting pay. The minimum pay guaranteed employees who report for work even though work is not available.

Representation election. A poll taken by the National Labor Relations Board to determine if a group of employees will be represented by a union for the purpose of collective bargaining.

Reverse discrimination. Generally, a nonlegal term referring to giving preference to minorities over white males beyond affirmative action requirements.

Robotics. The operation of programmable robots to perform routine assembly operations.

Right-to-know regulations. Occupational Safety and Health Administration rules and state laws formally termed *hazard communication.* Workers are given the right to know what hazardous substances they may encounter on the job. The rules also require the labeling of containers, employee training, and the maintenance of material safety data sheets (MSDSs).

Role play. The acting out of expected individual behaviors created by assigning certain roles to those involved in organizational problems.

Rules. Standing plans that detail specific actions to be taken in a given situation.

Safety hazards. Those aspects of the work place that have the capability of impairing an employee physically, such as electrical shocks, burns, cuts, or loss of limbs.

Scientific management. A systematic investigation and approach to management designed to find the most efficient means of production and employee productivity.

Secondary boycott. A boycott in which third parties, such as suppliers, customers, or the public, are encouraged to assist the striking union by not conducting business with the employer.

Section 14b. A division of the Taft-Hartley Act that allows individual states to pass legislation that bars any form of compulsory union membership.

Selection. The process of choosing qualified individuals who are available to fill positions in an organization.

Seniority system. A set of rules governing the allocation of economic benefits and job opportunities on the basis of service to the employer.

Sensitivity training. A method designed to increase behavioral awareness through the use of open and honest discussion groups.

Separation agreements. An employer–employee contract under which the employee voluntarily accepts early retirement during a *retirement window* (usually a 30-day period). The employee chooses to accept and sign an agreement that provides enhanced retirement benefits in exchange for voluntary early retirement.

Severance pay. A lump-sum payment to employees who are permanently laid off.

Sexual harassment. Unwelcome sexual advances, requests for sexual favors, and other verbal or physical conduct having the purpose or effect of unreasonably interfering with an individual's work performance or creating an intimidating, hostile, or offensive working environment.

Sick-leave bank. A pool or accumulation of unused employee sick leave days from which employees with long-term illnesses may draw extended sick leave.

Single-employer bargaining. When a single employer bargains alone with one or more unions.

SKAs. The minimum qualifications that job applicants must possess to be considered for a job; these are often grouped into three categories: skills, knowledge, and abilities.

Smoking policies. Employer policies on smoking in the work place include a total ban on smoking anywhere in the work place, a ban at the work stations (not in restrooms, cafeteria, etc.), a ban in dangerous work areas (e.g., near combustible materials), giving reasonable accommodation to nonsmokers by separating them from smokers, and encouraging employees not to smoke.

Social Security system. A government system established in 1935 to provide supplemental income to retired workers.

Source trust. An understanding established with a private employment agency concerning the qualifications of applicants so that unqualified applicants are not sent for interviews.

Specialization-intensive job. A job designed for high productivity by unskilled workers, requiring little training, and allowing greater management control.

Specific-use questionnaire. A questionnaire designed to gather employees' opinions concerning specific job-related issues.

Staggered start. An example of the discretionary workweek system in which the employee chooses one of several different starting times and works a normal workday.

Stock option. The right of an executive to purchase an organization's stock at an option price, usually the market value.

Straight piecework. An incentive wage program in which an employee is paid according to an established rate per unit of production.

Strictness. The tendency of a supervisor to give low evaluations to all employees as a result of unreasonable performance expectations.

Structured interview. An interview in which all respondents are asked substantially the same questions.

Substantially equal. The basis on which jobs can be compared, evaluating effort, skill, working conditions, and responsibility, concluding that two jobs, though not identical, may be considered equal and require equal pay.

Successorship. The question of the collective bargaining situation between an employer and the union when a change in the ownership of the union or the organization occurs.

Supervisory bias. The conscious or unconscious tendency of a supervisor to show a preference for certain employees.

Supplemental retirement plan. A plan that gives retirees a fixed number of retirement dollars, to be provided by Social Security and a private pension.

Supplemental unemployment benefits (SUBs). Company-provided benefits paid to laid-off employees in addition to unemployment compensation.

Supplementary record of occupational injuries and illnesses. An Occupational Safety and Health Administration regulation, Form 101, requiring an employer to complete a detailed report of each injury or illness recorded on Form 200 within six working days after notification of the incident.

Sympathy strike. A strike in which unions agree to a work stoppage unrelated to actions of their employer but designed to support other striking union members.

Systems analyst. One who studies the activities, methods, procedures, and techniques of organizational systems to determine what actions need to be taken and how these actions can best be achieved.

Technical skills. Managerial skills that include knowledge of equipment, work methods, and work technology often required for on-the-job training of employees.

Telecommuting. Work scheduling that allows employees to do some or all of their work at home, usually with the use of computers.

Termination at will. The termination or discharge of an employee by an employer for any or no reason.

Time-based system. A compensation system in which the employee is paid by the hour worked or by a division of an annual rate of pay, such as weekly or monthly.

Title VII. A section of the Civil Rights Act of 1964 that allows the Equal Employment Opportunity Commission to investigate an employee's complaints and act as his or her attorney.

Trade union. A labor union whose membership is generally composed of skilled employees in a single trade, such as plumbers or electricians.

Training evaluation. A review of the training program used to determine if the desired knowledge of the program was acquired by the trainees.

Training feedback. Information given to the trainee on how he or she is progressing in the training program.

Training needs assessment. The process followed by the personnel department to determine the training needs of the organization.

Training objectives. The objectives that a new employee should be able to achieve on the completion of training.

Training systems model. An orientation checklist for personnel representatives that includes the items to be covered during orientation.

Transfer. The reassignment of an employee to a job with pay, status, and responsibilities similar to those of a former job.

Transfer of learning. The inability of a trainee to transfer his or her off-the-job training to the job area or organization.

Transportation programs. The methods employers use to aid employees in getting to work, such as ride sharing and van pools.

Turnover. The movement of employees out of an organization resulting from resignations, transfers, retirements, discharges, and deaths.

Two-tier wage system. A wage system that pays employees hired after a certain date less than current employees performing the same job.

Types of validity. Verifications that determine if a test accurately measures what it is intended to measure.

Underemployed. Workers who remain in jobs unrelated to their interests and training due to a shortage of better-paying positions; while not actively looking for another job, they can be recruited to a job for which they are better qualified.

Underuse of minorities. Having fewer minorities or women in a particular job category than would be found in the relevant labor market.

Unemployment insurance. A program established to provide compensation to workers who are currently unemployed through no fault of their own and are actively seeking employment.

Unemployment rate. The ratio of the number of unemployed individuals in the labor force divided by the number of employed plus unemployed individuals.

Unfair-labor-practice strike. A strike over an unfair labor practice by an employer such as employee discrimination because of union activity.

Unfairness. The partiality or prejudice that an employee perceives in an organization.

Union avoidance. The practice of adopting personnel policies that are designed to keep unions out. Such policies are often begun before any organizing attempt by a union.

Union shop. A union security provision that all new employees must join the union and pay dues within a specified time.

Unlawful bargaining categories. Those items that cannot legally enter into negotiations, such as a discriminatory provision.

Unstructured interview. An interview that collects a respondent's opinions concerning work-related issues.

Variable hours. A method of employment in which the employee contracts to work for a specified time each day, week, and so on, with the option of varying the schedule daily if both parties agree.

Vendor. A company that sells computers, peripheral devices, time-sharing services, or software.

Vestibule. A training area created to resemble an actual work area.

Vesting. The employees' right to receive retirement benefits paid into a plan by an employer.

Vietnam Era Veterans Readjustment Act of 1974. An act passed to help Vietnam War veterans secure jobs, requiring all organizations holding government contracts of $10,000 or more to hire and promote these veterans.

Vocational Rehabilitation Act of 1973. A federal law that requires any employer with federal contracts of $2,500 or more to establish an affirmative action program for the handicapped; this program must include recruitment efforts, advancement, and environmental changes within the organization.

Volvo work groups. The concept of assembly teams that were given total autonomy over their work at the Kalmar, Sweden, Volvo assembly plant. The assembly line common in U.S. auto plants was replaced with moving carriers, allowing workers to set the pace needed for each vehicle.

Wage survey. An appraisal used to determine the average salary for specified positions in the job market.

Wagner Act. Also known as the National Labor Relations Act of 1935, this act gave most private sector employees the right to bargain collectively through representatives of their own choosing; established the National Labor Relations Board; determined unfair labor practices by empoyers; and specified the secret-ballot union certification process.

Walsh–Healey Act. An act passed in 1936 requiring employers holding federal contracts of $10,000 or more to pay overtime for hours worked over the eight per day at a rate of one and one-half times the normal hourly rate.

Wellness programs. Programs designed by an organization to focus on an employee's well-being such as physical fitness programs, drug and alcohol rehabilitation programs, stress management, and cancer detection programs.

Wildcat strike. Any work stoppage not authorized by the union.

Work force analysis. An organization's written review to determine the degree to which it complies with its affirmative action program.

Work groups. Groups within larger organizations that manage themselves; control, planning, and goal achievement are accomplished independently.

Work samples. A test in which an applicant performs part of the job for which he or she is applying.

Work sharing. A method of reducing the number of employees to be laid off by asking all employees to work fewer hours.

Work standards. The norm set for employee production or performance; comparison to the norm may be used for employee evaluations.

Worker's compensation. A program designed to provide employees with assured payment for medical expenses or lost income due to injury on the job.

Index

WE VALUE YOUR OPINION—PLEASE SHARE IT WITH US

Merrill Publishing and our authors are most interested in your reactions to this textbook. Did it serve you well in the course? If it did, what aspects of the text were most helpful? If not, what didn't you like about it? Your comments will help us to write and develop better textbooks. We value your opinions and thank you for your help.

Text Title _____ Edition _____

Author(s) _____

Your Name (optional) _____

Address _____

City _____ State _____ Zip _____

School _____

Course Title _____

Instructor's Name _____

Your Major _____

Your Class Rank _____ Freshman _____ Sophomore _____ Junior _____ Senior

_____ Graduate Student

Were you required to take this course? _____ Required _____ Elective

Length of Course? _____ Quarter _____ Semester

1. Overall, how does this text compare to other texts you've used?

   _____ Superior _____ Better Than Most _____ Average _____ Poor

2. Please rate the text in the following areas:

	Superior	Better Than Most	Average	Poor
Author's Writing Style	_____	_____	_____	_____
Readability	_____	_____	_____	_____
Organization	_____	_____	_____	_____
Accuracy	_____	_____	_____	_____
Layout and Design	_____	_____	_____	_____
Illustrations/Photos/Tables	_____	_____	_____	_____
Examples	_____	_____	_____	_____
Problems/Exercises	_____	_____	_____	_____
Topic Selection	_____	_____	_____	_____
Currentness of Coverage	_____	_____	_____	_____
Explanation of Difficult Concepts	_____	_____	_____	_____
Match-up with Course Coverage	_____	_____	_____	_____
Applications to Real Life	_____	_____	_____	_____

3. Circle those chapters you especially liked:
   1   2   3   4   5   6   7   8   9   10   11   12   13   14   15   16   17   18
   What was your favorite chapter? _____
   Comments:

4. Circle those chapters you liked least:
   1   2   3   4   5   6   7   8   9   10   11   12   13   14   15   16   17   18
   What was your least favorite chapter? _____
   Comments:

5. List any chapters your instructor did not assign. _____

6. What topics did your instructor discuss that were not covered in the text?_____

   _____

7. Were you required to buy this book? _____ Yes   _____ No

   Did you buy this book new or used? _____ New   _____ Used

   If used, how much did you pay? _____

   Do you plan to keep or sell this book? _____ Keep   _____ Sell

   If you plan to sell the book, how much do you expect to receive? _____

   Should the instructor continue to assign this book? _____ Yes   _____ No

8. Please list any other learning materials you purchased to help you in this course (e.g., study guide, lab manual).

   _____

9. What did you like most about this text? _____

   _____

10. What did you like least about this text? _____

   _____

11. General comments:

    May we quote you in our advertising? _____ Yes   _____ No

    Please mail to: Boyd Lane
                      College Division, Research Department
                      Box 508
                      1300 Alum Creek Drive
                      Columbus, Ohio 43216

    Thank you!